Advanced French Grammar

This reference grammar, written for advanced students of French, their teachers, and others who want to improve their understanding of the French language, combines the best of modern and traditional approaches. Its objective is not only practical mastery of the language, but familiarity with its structure. Taking into account modern linguistic research, the *Grammar* approaches the French language primarily through the study of syntactic structures, but without excessive emphasis on formalism. It provides a generous number of examples, based on the author's own experience of teaching French to foreigners, to help the student to understand the different meanings of apparently similar syntactic alternatives. The norms of 'correct expression' are given, together with current usage and deviations, and appendixes provide information on the 1990 spelling reforms and on numbers. A substantial index of French and English words and of topics provides easy access to the text itself.

Monique L'Huillier is a Senior Lecturer in French at Royal Holloway, University of London. After studying theoretical linguistics in Paris, she obtained an MSc in computer science in England, with a dissertation on machine translation, and went on to teach at Bradford and Brunel universities. She has published extensive computer-assisted language learning software for the study of French grammar and articles in French linguistics and grammar.

Advanced French Grammar

MONIQUE L'HUILLIER

CAMBRIDGE
UNIVERSITY PRESS

CAMBRIDGE UNIVERSITY PRESS
Cambridge, New York, Melbourne, Madrid, Cape Town, Singapore, São Paulo,
Delhi, Dubai, Tokyo, Mexico City

Cambridge University Press
The Edinburgh Building, Cambridge, CB2 8RU, UK

Published in the United States of America by Cambridge University Press, New York

www.cambridge.org
Information on this title: www.cambridge.org/9780521484251

First published 1999
8th printing 2011

Printed in the United Kingdom at the University Press, Cambridge

A catalogue record for this publication is available from the British Library

Library of Congress cataloguing in publication data
L'Huillier, Monique.
    Advanced French grammar / Monique L'Huillier.
        p.   cm.
    Includes bibliographical references and index.
    ISBN 0 521 48228 3 (hb). – ISBN 0 521 48425 1 (pb)
    1. French language – Grammar.   2. French language – Textbooks for
foreign speakers – English.   I. Title.
    PC2112.L485   1999
    448.2′421—dc21   98–22110
                                                                                    CIP

ISBN   978-0-521-48228-8 Hardback
ISBN   978-0-521-48425-1 Paperback

To Dizzy, Lizzy and G-M

Contents

Acknowledgements

I wish to thank all the friends and colleagues who have given me their support while writing this book, in particular Juliet Laxton, who read the manuscript with the fresh outlook of an enthusiastic student and contributed to the explanations given, Peter Flake, who read the manuscript with a non–linguist's eye and kept the jargon under control, and Dominique Lagorgette, who reminded me that there is more to the pronunciation of French than a Parisian accent.

Most of all I would like to thank Mary-Annick Morel, for her patience and dedication in answering my innumerable questions over the years of the preparation of the book, and Marina Yaguello, whose linguistics seminars at the Institute of Romance Studies in London were an endless source of inspiration.

I would like to thank the following for giving permission to quote:

Le Monde, Libération, The Economist and *Radio Times* (various extracts); M. Alain Reynaud-Fourton for quoting from his play *Monsieur Amédée*, Editions Gallimard for quoting from Albert Camus, *L'étranger* and *L'exil et le royaume*, Michel Tournier, *Le roi des Aulnes*, Jean Cocteau, *Les parents terribles*, Proust, *Du côté de Guermantes*, Charles Baudelaire, *Petits poèmes en prose, Tableaux parisiens* and *L'invitation au voyage*; Librairie Plon for Raymond Devos, *Ouï-dire*; Editions Christian Bourgois for Georges Perec, *Tentatives d'épuisement d'un lieu parisien*; Chatto and Windus for Richard Hughes, *In Hazard* and Iris Murdoch, *Nuns and Soldiers*, Editions Albin Michel for Paul Guth, *Le naïf amoureux*; Editions Tallandier for Christian Melchior-Bonnet, *Grand livre de l'histoire de France*; Faber and Faber Ltd for George Steiner, *Language and Silence*.

In addition, permission was obtained from The Society of Authors as the literary representative of the estate of L. P. Hartley to quote from L. P. Hartley, *The Hireling*; from the Estate of Georges Simenon to quote from Georges Simenon, *Maigret et la jeune morte*.

Extracts from *Keep the Aspidistra Flying* (Copyright © 1936 by George Orwell) and *Animal Farm* (Copyright © 1945 by George Orwell) are reproduced by kind permission of Mark Hamilton as the Literary Executor of the Estate of the Late Sonia Brownell Orwell and Martin Secker & Warburg Ltd.

Every possible effort has been made to trace and acknowledge ownership of copyright; I apologise for any omissions and would welcome these being brought to my attention.

Introduction

The aim of this book is to be as comprehensive as possible in its coverage of all the points of French grammar normally encountered by undergraduate students in French. It can serve as a textbook but its main purpose is to be a reference book. As it covers all levels from basic to very advanced, it should fill the gaps which may be present in even an advanced student's knowledge.

Many of the examples given to illustrate various points of grammar were inspired by students' essays and proses. The explanations reflect the author's experience of teaching French to English-speakers, and an awareness of their particular problems.

Constant references are made in the book to the terms and concepts explained in the framework chapters, i.e. chapter 1 Parts of Speech, chapter 2 Syntax and Grammatical Functions, chapter 3 Pronunciation, Spelling, Registers, Punctuation, and chapter 4 Introduction to Verbs. Although these chapters provide a useful overview for the advanced student, the beginner should refer to them only when further explanation of a grammatical term is needed.

Whenever possible, equivalent French terminology is given so as to facilitate reference to French grammar books.

The book indicates the 'correct' grammar that an undergraduate is expected to use in written and oral examinations, but also mentions deviations that are used by French writers for literary effect. It is not unusual for a turn of phrase which is deemed 'incorrect' at one time to become the norm later. Hence turns of phrase for which usage is currently shifting (e.g. *c'est* vs *il est*; *après que* + subjunctive vs indicative) are discussed. In the meantime, deviations are identified which have not yet become current usage and which should be avoided by the undergraduate.

The term 'informal French' refers broadly to most spoken French and relaxed writing (e.g. most personal correspondence). The term 'formal French' refers to oratory, careful style in broadcasting, essay or other literary writing, and formal correspondence. Students are normally expected to emulate formal French in their written and oral examinations.

The terms 'speaker', 'interlocutor' and 'discourse' are used throughout the book.
– The discourse is the set of utterances constituting speech or text. Hence a word is used 'in discourse' as opposed to appearing as an entry in a dictionary.
– The speaker is the narrator, whoever says *je* in writing or speaking.
– The interlocutor is whoever is *tu* and reads or listens to the speaker.

Whenever relevant, pronunciation is given using the International Phonetic Alphabet (IPA).

The symbols used in the book are:
– a slash / to indicate an alternative
– square brackets [ ] to indicate an optional part of an utterance, or IPA transcriptions
– an asterisk ⋆ to indicate an ungrammatical or otherwise unacceptable utterance in the given context
– a question mark ? at the beginning of an utterance to indicate that it is not immediately acceptable or interpretable, or that the register is not appropriate
– round brackets ( ) to indicate an explanation
– a single underscore _ to indicate ellipsis of a word or a missing letter (e.g. for comparison purposes between the two languages)
– an arrow → to indicate a possible transformation or an implication

The common abbreviations used are:
– sb somebody
– sth something
– *qn quelqu'un*
– *qch quelque chose*

1 Framework

1 Parts of speech

1 Introduction

It is generally considered by most grammarians that there are eight grammatical classes of words or 'parts of speech', or nine if one includes interjections.
They are:
- nouns
- verbs
- determiners
- qualifying adjectives
- adverbs
- pronouns
- prepositions
- conjunctions
- interjections

However, in order to define the part of speech which a word belongs to, three criteria should be considered: semantic, morphological and syntactic. Hence the part of speech depends not only on the word selected but the way in which it is used (see 11 below).

2 Nouns

See also chapters 23 Articles and 27 Nouns.

2.1 Definition

(i) Traditionally, the noun is described as representing what is called a **substance**, hence its other name: substantive (*substantif*), i.e. 'what is'. However, nouns do represent all sorts of other things, for instance abstract notions (*l'amour*) or actions (*la natation*). They are an open or non-finite class of words, i.e. new ones can be invented or borrowed from other languages.

    Ex: *l'intégrisme (religieux), la gouvernance; le zapping*

(ii) They have a gender and a number.
- gender: masculine   **un** *homme*
  - feminine   **une** *femme*
- number: singular   **un** *chat*
  - plural   **des** *chats*

NB: Some nouns are only used in the plural, e.g. *les fiançailles*.

(iii) They can be simple (*un chou, une fleur*) or compound (*un chou-fleur, un gratte-ciel*).

2.2 Properties

Nouns can be organized in sub-classes with different semantic and syntactic characteristics called lexical features (*traits lexicaux*). They can:

(i) **be common or proper**

    – common:
        Ex: *un homme; un chat; une table*

    – proper:
        Ex: *Marie, Médor; la France, la Seine, la rue de Rivoli, Paris; le Conseil d'Etat*

NB(1): The first letter of a proper noun is a capital.

NB(2): Common nouns are generally preceded by an article (*le chat*) whilst proper nouns referring to animates (*Paul*) are generally used by themselves, but see exceptions in chapter 23 Articles.

(ii) **represent animates or inanimates**

    – animates (human or non-human):
        Ex: *un homme, une femme; un chat*

    – inanimates, including concrete or abstract (see below):
        Ex: *une table, la natation, la philosophie*

This distinction is important in several contexts, e.g. relative, interrogative and personal object pronouns, or the use of *c'est/il est* (see relevant chapters).

(iii) **be concrete or abstract**

    – concrete (can be seen, felt or heard):
        Ex: *la table, du vin, le vent*

    – abstract:
        Ex: *la force, l'amitié, la psychologie*

(iv) **be countable or uncountable**

    – countable (can be counted):
        Ex: ***un** pain complet* (**a** wholewheat **loaf**)

    – uncountable (refer to quantities):
        Ex: ***du** pain complet* (wholewheat **bread**)

(v) **be collective or individual**

    – collective (refer to groups of the same category):
        Ex: *la famille, la vaisselle*

    – individual:
        Ex: *un père, une assiette*

3 Verbs

According to the traditional definition, verbs express actions (e.g. *marcher*) or states (e.g. *être*). The set of forms that a verb can take is called its conjugation. An introduction to verbs is given in chapter 4.

4 Determiners

The determiner introduces the noun, with which it agrees in gender and number. Determiners constitute a closed or finite class, i.e. new ones cannot be invented or borrowed.

There are seven classes of determiners:
- articles
- demonstrative adjectives
- possessive adjectives
- interrogative and exclamative adjectives
- relative adjectives
- numeral adjectives
- indefinite adjectives

A specific determiner (*déterminant spécifique*) cannot be combined with another. The specific determiners are:
- articles: *le chat*, **un** *chat*, **du** *lait*
- demonstrative adjectives: **ce** *chat*
- possessive adjectives: **mon** *chat*

Other determiners (*déterminants complémentaires*) can be combined with another, and with specific determiners according to precise rules (see relevant chapters). For instance:
- numeral adjectives: *les* **trois** *chats*
- indefinite adjectives: **tous mes** *chats*

The article is the most common determiner of the noun.

Note that the above 'adjectives' are also called 'non-qualifying adjectives' or 'determiners' to distinguish them from 'qualifying adjectives' (see 5 below).

4.1 Articles

An article marks the gender and the number of the noun it determines. There are three kinds of articles:

(i) definite (*le, la, l', les*)

The use of the definite articles implies that the interlocutor can **identify** that referent, i.e. the 'object of the world' the word refers to.

> Ex: *Passez-moi* **le** *livre qui est sur* **la** *table.*
> Pass me the book that is on the table.

(ii)   indefinite (*un*, *une*, *des*)

Indefinite articles imply the **existence** of a set of referents. They extract one or several elements from that set, without identifying them.

> Ex: *J'ai acheté **des** oranges.*
> I've bought [some] oranges.

(iii)   partitive (*du*, *de la*, *de l'*)

The partitive article is used with uncountable nouns.

> Ex: *Voulez-vous **du** fromage?*
> Would you like [some] cheese?

The choice of articles depends on whether the noun is concrete or abstract, countable or non-countable, considered in its generic sense, etc. See chapter 23 Articles.

4.2   Demonstrative adjectives

(i)   The **simple** demonstrative adjectives are: *ce* (*cet*), *cette*, *ces*. These can be translated as 'this' or 'that', 'these' or 'those', depending on the context.

> Ex: *ce livre*; *cet hôtel*; *cette robe*; *ces gens*

(ii)   The **compound** adjectives add *-ci* or *-là* after the noun, to indicate distance from or proximity to the speaker.

− distance from the speaker in time:

> Ex: *Ce jour-**là**, je ne me sentais pas très bien.*
> That day, I wasn't feeling very well.

− proximity to the speaker in space:

> Ex: *Ces fleurs-**ci** me plaisent.*
> I like these flowers.

See chapter 25 Demonstrative Adjectives.

4.3   Possessive adjectives

The possessive adjectives are:

mon, *ma*, ***mes***	my
ton, *ta*, ***tes***	your
son, *sa*, ***ses***	his/her
notre, ***nos***	our
votre, ***vos***	your
leur, ***leurs***	their

They agree in gender and number with the element possessed **and** in person with the possessor.

> Ex: *les livres de **Marie: ses** livres*
> **Marie**'s books: **her** books
>
> *la maison de **Paul et Marie: leur** maison*
> **Paul and Marie**'s house: **their** house

> *la cravate de **Paul**: **sa** cravate*
> **Paul**'s tie: **his** tie

For details regarding possessive adjectives, and their use with parts of the body, see chapter 24 Possessive Adjectives.

4.4 Interrogative and exclamative adjectives

(i) Interrogative adjectives: ***quel, quelle, quels, quelles***

Interrogative adjectives enable one to ask a question about the noun.
> Ex: ***Quelle*** *personne demandez-vous?*
> **Which** person are you asking for?

(ii) Exclamative adjectives: ***quel, quelle, quels, quelles***

Exclamative adjectives are used to express surprise, indignation, joy, fear, etc. Their forms are the same as those of the interrogative adjective.
> Ex: *Il ne vous a pas prévenu?* ***Quel*** *sans-gêne!*
> Didn't he warn you? **What** a nerve!

See chapter 39 Interrogative and Exclamative Structures.

4.5 Relative adjectives

Relative adjectives are constructed with *quel*, preceded by the definite article (→ ***lequel, laquelle, lesquels, lesquelles***).

They are used as relative determiners, particularly in literary and administrative styles. The group 'relative adjective + noun' is the equivalent of a relative pronoun (see 7.4 below).
> Ex: *Je lui ai envoyé un dossier,* ***lequel dossier*** *ne lui est jamais parvenu.*
> (= *Je lui ai envoyé un dossier,* ***qui*** *ne lui est jamais parvenu.*)

4.6 Numeral adjectives

(i) Also part of the 'quantifiers' (see 4.7 Indefinite Adjectives below), they are used before nouns which refer to elements that can be counted (see countable nouns above), to specify the number or quantity of elements.
> Ex: *Il y avait* ***cent dix*** *personnes à cette conférence.*

(ii) Combinations:

They can be preceded by a specific determiner.
> Ex: ***mes deux*** *chats;* ***les trois*** *mousquetaires;* ***ces six*** *roses rouges*

4.7 Indefinite adjectives

(i) As determiners, they generally imply a certain quantity of elements, which may be countable or uncountable (they are also called 'quantifiers').

Ex: ***Quelques*** *personnes viennent d'arriver.*
A few people have just arrived.

*J'ai encore **pas mal de** travail à faire.*
I've still got **a fair amount of** work to do.

NB(1): Some indefinite adjectives can be combined with another determiner:
Ex: ***tous les*** *chats noirs*; **les *quelques*** *chats noirs*
NB(2): Others cannot:
Ex: **les plusieurs chats noirs*
For further details, see chapter 36 Indefinite Words.

(ii) Some indefinite adjectives are **not** determiners. They express, for instance:
 – imprecision:
 Ex: *Il lisait une revue **quelconque**.*
 – identity:
 Ex: *J'ai la **même** robe que toi.*
 – difference/contrast:
 Ex: *J'ai un **autre** parapluie, si celui-ci ne te plaît pas.*

For further details, see chapter 36 Indefinite Words.

4.8 No determiner

The 'zero article' refers to cases where there is no specific determiner before nouns in French.
Ex: *Elle est **journaliste**.*
 Entrée *interdite.*
See chapter 23 Articles, section 6.

5 Qualifying adjectives

(i) A qualifying adjective expresses a **quality** of the referent of the noun.

(ii) It agrees with the noun in gender and number.
Ex: – masculine or feminine:
 *un livre **intéressant**; une **belle** robe*
  masculine   feminine
 – singular or plural:
 *une **grande** maison; des gens **importants***
  singular   plural

Qualifying adjectives form an open class of words, i.e. new adjectives can be created; a recent example: *anabolisant*.

For details on the gender and number of adjectives and of the position of the adjective in relation to the noun, see chapter 28 Qualifying Adjectives.

6 Adverbs

(i) Adverbs provide extra information about the meaning of a verb, adjective, other adverb or whole clause.

> Ex: *Tu marches* **lentement**.
> *Vous êtes* **trop** *gentil*.
> *Il conduit* **si** *vite!*
> **Hier**, *je suis allée au cinéma*.

(ii) Adverbs are normally invariable (but see exceptions in chapters 28 Qualifying Adjectives, 29 Adverbs and 36 Indefinite Words).

(iii) Adverbs can be simple (e.g. *bien, mal, vite*) or compound (e.g. *avant-hier, tout à fait*). They constitute an extremely varied class from the point of view of their morphology, but the largest category is that of adverbs in *-ment*.

(iv) Adverbs which modify a clause are optional elements of that clause. They can be moved around according to certain rules (see chapters 2 Syntax, section 2.13 and 29 Adverbs, section 5).

Adverbs of negation (e.g. *Elle* **ne** *parle* **pas**) are treated in chapter 38 Negative Structures. Interrogative and exclamative adverbs (e.g. **Combien** *coûte ce fauteuil?* **Comme** *c'est beau!*) are treated in chapter 39 Interrogative and Exclamative Structures. Indefinite adverbs (e.g. *Il est* **tout** *content*) are treated in chapter 36 Indefinite Words.

7 Pronouns

In principle, the purpose of a pronoun is to **replace** another element in a text. To this end, they form an essential part of text cohesion. However, they do not all replace something, hence the traditional distinction between 'nominal' and 'representative' pronouns.

– **Nominal** pronouns:
  – Some refer **directly** to their **respective referents** (i.e. not through a noun or anything else). It is the case for the first and second persons of the discourse. Indeed, *je* and *tu* do not refer to anybody else but the speaker and his/her interlocutor.
  – Others do not replace any expressed words either but refer **directly** to an **undetermined referent** (e.g. *quelqu'un*).

– **Representative** pronouns refer to an element already present in the context, called its **antecedent**.
  – This antecedent can be a noun (hence the term 'pro-noun').
  – But it can also be a lengthy noun phrase (see chapter 2 Syntax), another pronoun, an adjective, a verb in the infinitive, a clause or even a whole sentence (which is why some grammarians prefer to call them '**proforms**').

– The antecedent is normally placed **before** the representative pronoun: we
have an **anaphor**.

Ex: <u>Un homme</u> est arrivé. **Il** est entré dans le café.

– It can sometimes be placed **after** the pronoun, generally for stylistic effect:
we have a **cataphor**. However, what is represented by the pronoun is still its
'antecedent'.

Ex: **Elle** est vraiment sale, <u>ta voiture</u>.

'*Elle*' refers cataphorically to '*ta voiture*'.

– The antecedent and its pronoun generally have the same referent, i.e. they
refer to the same 'object of the world' (*un homme* and *il*, *elle* and *ta voiture*):
there is **co-reference** between the antecedent and its pronoun (but see
relevant chapters for cases when there is anaphora without co-reference).

There are seven classes of pronouns:

– personal and impersonal
– demonstrative
– possessive
– relative
– interrogative and exclamative
– indefinite
– numeral

In most cases, these can be either nominal or representative, but see relevant
chapters for details. Agreement and syntax of pronouns are also treated in the
relevant chapters.

7.1 Personal and impersonal pronouns

(i) Personal pronouns refer to the persons of the discourse.

– 1st person = the speaker: *je, moi (me); nous*
– 2nd person = the interlocutor: *tu, toi (te); vous*
– 3rd person = the one, or what, the speaker and/or interlocutors are talking
about: *il, ils, lui, eux, elle, elles, le, la, les*

(ii) The pronouns of the 1st and 2nd persons refer to or 'name' themselves.

Ex: **Je** pars en vacances la semaine prochaine. Et **toi?**

(iii) In contrast, the pronouns of the 3rd person most of the time refer to or
'represent' another element with the same referent, expressed previously in the
context (this is an example of anaphor).

Ex: J'ai vu <u>Pierre</u> ce matin. **Il** était très content.

'*Il*' refers to '*Pierre*' in the preceding sentence.

The forms of the personal pronoun (clitic, e.g. *je* or tonic, e.g. *moi*) and its
functions (e.g. subject, object) are treated in chapter 31 Personal Pronouns.

(iv) The impersonal pronoun *il* is treated in detail in chapter 19 Impersonal
Verbs.

7.2 Demonstrative pronouns

There are two types of demonstrative pronouns, simple and compound.

7.2.1 *Simple demonstrative pronouns*

celui, *celle*, *ceux*, *celles* (+ the neutral pronoun *ce, c'*)

(i) These are mostly representative but not 'complete' in the sense that, in most cases, they must be accompanied by a complement (e.g. prepositional phrase, relative clause) which identifies the referent.
   – identification with a prepositional phrase:
> Ex: *Vous cherchez <u>un dictionnaire</u>? Prenez **celui de Marie**.*

   – identification with a relative clause:
> Ex: *Vous voulez <u>un dictionnaire</u>? Prenez **celui qui est sur l'étagère à droite**.*

(ii) They can also be nominal. They are used by themselves as **animate** introducers to a relative clause with no antecedent.
> Ex: *Malheur à **celui** qui n'aime pas les chats!*
> ***Ceux** qui ont fini peuvent partir.*

7.2.2 *Compound demonstrative pronouns*

celui-ci, *celui-là*, *celle-ci*, *celle-là*, *ceux-ci*, *ceux-là*, *celles-ci*, *celles-là* (+ the neutral pronouns *ceci, cela, ça*)

For details on the opposition *-ci/-là*, and the neutral forms *ce, ceci, cela, ça*, see chapter 34 Demonstrative Pronouns.

7.3 Possessive pronouns

Possessive pronouns are the nominalized forms of the now obsolete stressed possessive adjectives. The nominalization is made explicit by the presence of the definite article.
> *le mien, la mienne, les miens, les miennes*
> *le tien, la tienne, les tiens, les tiennes*
> *le sien, la sienne, les siens, les siennes*
> *le nôtre, la nôtre, les nôtres*
> *le vôtre, la vôtre, les vôtres*
> *le leur, la leur, les leurs*

Possessive pronouns agree in gender and number with the element possessed, and in person and number with the possessor.

7.4 Relative pronouns

(i) The relative pronoun has simple and compound forms:

   – The simple relative pronouns are: *qui, que, quoi, dont, où*.
   – The compound relative pronouns are: *lequel, laquelle, lesquels, lesquelles*, which form the basis for further compounds with prepositions, e.g. *à laquelle, sur lequel*, etc.

See chapter 32 Relative Pronouns.

(ii)   A relative pronoun links two clauses, a main clause and a subordinate relative clause (see chapter 2 Syntax, section 3.2.2).

> Ex: *J'ai retrouvé <u>le livre</u> **qui** me manquait.*
>
> '*qui*' represents '*livre*', which is its **antecedent**; '*livre*' is the object of '*ai retrouvé*' in the main clause, and the subject of '*manquait*' in the subordinate clause.

7.5   Interrogative and exclamative pronouns

The forms of the interrogative pronouns are based on those of the relative pronouns (see also interrogative adjectives and adverbs in chapter 39 Interrogative and Exclamative Structures). Interrogative pronouns can be nominal or representative.

(i)   Nominal interrogative pronouns are used to ask questions about the identity or the quality of elements: **qui? que? quoi? qui est-ce qui? qui est-ce que? qu'est-ce qui? qu'est-ce que?**

> Ex: **Qui** *est là?* **Qu'est-ce que** *vous voulez?*
>
> Who's there? What do you want?

(ii)   Representative interrogative pronouns are used to ask questions about elements already mentioned in the context: **lequel, laquelle, lesquels, lesquelles.**

> Ex: *De ces deux <u>voitures</u>,* **laquelle** *préférez-vous?*
>
> Of these two cars, which one do you prefer?

Note that the latter are also used as exclamative pronouns.

> Ex: *Je n'ai qu'un chat mais* **lequel**!
>
> I've only got one cat, but what a cat!

7.6   Indefinite pronouns

Indefinite pronouns are a motley collection! For details, see chapter 36 Indefinite Words. Most indefinite pronouns imply:

(i)   either the imprecision of the element

> Ex: *Vous avez entendu* **quelque chose**?
>
> Have you heard anything?

(ii)   or a certain quantity of elements

> Ex: **Tous** *sont arrivés à l'heure.*
>
> Everybody arrived on time.

7.7   Numeral pronouns

(i)   Cardinal numbers are normally used as determiners. However, they can also be used as pronouns.

> Ex: *Marie avait invité* **quarante** *personnes.* **Dix** *sont venues.*
>
> determiner · pronoun
>
> Marie had invited forty people. Ten came.

(ii) Ordinal numbers are used as adjectives or pronouns.

Ex: *C'est la **troisième** maison à droite.*
adjective

It's the third house on the right.

La troisième! *Vous êtes sûr?*
pronoun

The third one! Are you sure?

See chapter 37 Numbers, section 2.

8 Prepositions

Prepositions are subordinating words. They introduce a new element and place that new element in relation to an element already present in a phrase, clause or sentence. They are invariable. Prepositions can be simple (e.g. *sur, sous*) or compound (e.g. *à côté de*).

(i) They can be part of a verb and form a prepositional phrase introducing an indirect object:

Ex: *Nous parlons souvent **de** Paul. (parler de qn)*
*Nous pensons souvent **à** vous. (penser à qn)*

(ii) They can be part of a noun phrase and form a prepositional phrase introducing:
- another noun   *une bague **en** or*
- a pronoun   *les besoins **de** chacun*
- a verb in the infinitive   *une machine **à** laver*
- an adverb   *la vaisselle **d'**hier*

(iii) They can be part of an adjectival phrase introducing:
- a noun   *couvert **de** neige*
- a pronoun   *satisfait **de** rien*
- a verb in the infinitive   *facile **à** faire*

(iv) They can introduce a prepositional phrase which modifies a sentence (adverb phrase).

Ex: *J'ai posé les livres **sur** le bureau.*
*Je ne sais pas encore où je vais **pour** les vacances.*

The function of the prepositional phrase depends on its position in the sentence (see chapters 2 Syntax and 26 Prepositions).

9 Conjunctions

Conjunctions are invariable. There are two types of conjunctions.

9.1 Conjunctions of coordination

(i) Coordination establishes a non-hierarchical relation (addition, opposition, etc.) between the elements which it links together. Conjunctions of coordination in frequent use include: ***mais, ou, et, donc, pourtant, cependant, ainsi***.

(ii)   They link terms with the same function (e.g. subjects, objects, whole clauses or sentences).

> Ex: *Il a mangé une pomme **et** une poire.*
> ('*et*' links two noun objects)
>
> *Mon chat **et** mon chien s'aiment beaucoup.*
> ('*et*' links two noun subjects)
>
> *J'ai acheté le journal **mais** je n'ai pas trouvé votre magazine.*
> ('*mais*' links two sentences).

(iii)   Some grammarians make a distinction between conjunctions of coordination and disjunctive conjunctions. The latter express an alternative (e.g. *ou, tantôt . . . tantôt*). For details, see chapter 40 Coordination and Juxtaposition.

9.2   Conjunctions of subordination

(i)   Conjunctions of subordination introduce a **subordinate clause**.

(ii)   Conjunctions of subordination can be:

– simple (e.g. *que, quand, comme, si*)

– compound with *que* (e.g. *avant que, après que, pour que*, etc., and also *lorsque, puisque, quoique*).

(iii)   The conjunction *que* introduces *que*-clauses (*propositions complétives*).

(iv)   Other conjunctions introduce an adverbial clause (*circonstancielle*) of time, place, aim, consequence, condition, etc.

> Ex: ***Lorsqu****'il fait mauvais temps, personne ne sort.*

See also chapter 2 Syntax, section 3.2.3.

When using a conjunction of subordination, it is important to know which **mood** should be used in the subordinate clause: indicative or subjunctive. This is treated in chapter 12 Subjunctive, section 4.

10   Interjections

Interjections are fixed words or phrases which express a comment made by the speaker.

> Ex: *Attention! Au secours!*

See chapter 2 Syntax, section 2.14.1.

11 Synonyms, homonyms, derivation and word class shifts

11.1 Synonyms and homonyms

11.1.1 *Definitions*

- **synonyms** are different words with similar or identical meanings.
  Ex: *redouter, craindre, avoir peur de*

- **homonyms** can be subdivided into:
  - **homophones**, i.e. words which share the same sound (but not the same spelling), and have different meanings (they are unrelated).
    Ex: *saint, sein, seing, sain* [sɛ̃]
    vin, vain [vɛ̃]
    Troie, Troyes, trois [trwa]
    au, eau [o]
    mer, mère, maire [mɛr]

  - **homographs**, i.e. words with the same spelling but different meanings (they are unrelated).
    Ex: *(un boulet de) canon, un canon (de beauté)*

11.1.2 *Examples of homographs in parts of speech*

(i) *que*

- relative pronoun object; introduces a relative clause; has an antecedent:
  Ex: *Je vais vous montrer <u>les photos</u> **que** j'ai prises l'année dernière.*

- conjunction of subordination; introduces a *que*-clause (*complétive*):
  Ex: *Il est essentiel **que** vous soyez à l'heure demain.*
  *Je pense **que** les Dupont viendront.*

(ii) *leur*

- personal object pronoun (indirect):
  Ex: *Elle parle <u>à ses chats</u> → Elle **leur** parle.*

- possessive adjective; the possessor is plural, the thing possessed is singular:
  Ex: *C'est **leur** chat.*
NB: If the thing possessed is plural, *leurs* is used.
  Ex: *Ce sont **leurs** chats.*

Hence *leur* can appear as two different parts of speech in the same sentence.
  Ex: *On **leur** a rendu **leur** chat/**leurs** chats.*

(iii) *en*

- preposition:
  - before a noun:
    Ex: *C'est une montre **en** or.*

  - before a present participle (gerund):
    Ex: ***En** allant au marché, j'ai rencontré . . .*

- personal object pronoun:
  - direct:
    Ex: *J'ai acheté des cerises* → *J'**en** ai acheté.*
  - indirect:
    Ex: *J'ai besoin de la voiture* → *J'**en** ai besoin.*

- adverbial pronoun:
  Ex: *Je reviens juste de Paris* → *J'**en** reviens.*

Hence *en* can appear as two different parts of speech in the same sentence.
   Ex: *Ne prenez que quatre comprimés: **en en** prenant plus, vous risqueriez des ennuis.*

(iv) ***y***

- personal object pronoun (indirect):
  Ex: *Mes prochaines vacances? J'**y** pense souvent.*

- adverbial pronoun:
  Ex: *Je vais à Paris demain* → *J'**y** vais demain.*

(v) ***le, la, les, l'***

- definite articles:
  Ex: ***le** chat, **la** chèvre, **les** animaux, **l'**asticot*

- personal object pronouns (direct):
  Ex: *Mon chat? Je **le** fais garder quand je pars en vacances.*
  *Tu as les mains sales. Va te **les** laver.*

(vi) ***du, des***

- partitive article (*du*), indefinite article (*des*):
  Ex: *J'ai acheté **du** chocolat et **des** bonbons.*

- contraction of preposition *de* + definite article *le*; contraction of preposition *de* + definite article *les*:
  Ex: *Le bureau **du** (= de + le) directeur est à votre gauche.*
  *C'est le chat **des** (= de + les) voisins.*

11.2   Derivation and word class shifts

One part of speech may derive from another, by proper or improper derivation.

(i) Proper derivation
   Ex: noun: *courage* → adjective: *courageux*

   verb: *conserver* → noun: *conservateur*
   adjective: *conservateur*

   verb: *aimer* → adjective: *aimable*

adjective: *beau* → verb: *embellir*

adjective: *jaune* → verb: *jaunir*

In the above cases, the suffixes help to distinguish a verb from a noun or adjective, for example.

(ii) Improper derivation

Ex: verb: *effrayer*   → adjective: *effrayant* (from present participle)

verb: *passer*   → noun: *un passant* (from present participle)

verb: *percevoir*   → adjective: *perçu* (from past participle)

verb: *mourir*   → noun: *un mort* (from past participle)

verb: *devoir*   → noun: *un devoir* (from infinitive)

adjective: *rouge* → noun: *le rouge*

In the above cases, a given word may be one part of speech or another, depending on the syntactic context.

Ex: *Elle porte un pantalon **bleu**.*
<u>adjective</u>
She's wearing blue trousers.

*Je n'aime pas le **bleu**.*
<u>noun</u>
I don't like (the colour) blue.

NB: In contemporary French and particularly in the world of advertising, there is a tendency to use nouns as predicative or attributive adjectives.

Ex: *des sous-vêtements classe*
un manteau confort
une femme enfant
un cocktail évasion
Elle fait un peu zone.
Ce travail, c'est galère.

See also adjectives used as adverbs or even prepositions in chapter 28 Qualifying Adjectives, section 5.2.

2 Syntax and grammatical functions

1 Introduction

A sentence is a sequence of words linked together in a particular way (**syntax**) in order to produce a meaning (**semantics**). A text consists of one or more sentences.

A simple sentence is an independent clause (*proposition indépendante*), made up of phrases (*syntagmes*), which are themselves made up of words.

A complex sentence is made up of two or more clauses, which are linked either in a non-hierarchical relationship (coordination) or a hierarchical relationship (subordination).

2 The simple sentence

Traditionally, a simple sentence is said to be composed of:
subject + verb + complement(s) [+ adverbs]

Ex: *Le chat boit son lait.*
<small>subject   verb complement</small>

However, a subject can take many forms (it can even be a whole clause). Some complements are compulsory, others are not. There are also incomplete sentences.

A sentence can be analysed according to the following basic structure:
– a **noun phrase** (*syntagme nominal*) or equivalent, which represents all the forms which the subject can take: NP/E

plus

– a **verb phrase** (*syntagme verbal*), which represents all the forms which a verb can take (VP), from the verb on its own to the verb followed by several complements. These complements are basically noun phrases (or equivalent) and may be very similar to the noun phrase subject.

plus

– sentence **adverbs** or adverb phrases (*compléments circonstanciels*).

Hence there are three basic constituents in the simple sentence (S):
S = NP/E + VP + [sentence adverbs].

Note:
– the NP/E and VP are usually present
– sentence adverbs are optional
– the order 'NP/E + VP + sentence adverbs' is the norm, but there are numerous exceptions.

There are four **modalities** of the sentence:
- declarative
- interrogative
- exclamative
- imperative

In turn, all these are either positive (affirmative) or negative. Negation is treated in chapter 38 Negative Structures. The syntax of the other modalities is studied in the relevant chapters.

For this study of the simple sentence, we shall concentrate on the **functions** of words in **declarative** sentences. Thus, in this chapter we are going to examine the possible forms that a subject and an object can take, the relations between the subject and the verb, and between the verb and its objects. Then we shall look at sentence adverbs (which modify the whole sentence) and also 'incomplete sentences'. Finally we shall look at ways of expressing emphasis.

2.1   The noun phrase (NP)

The NP (or equivalent) is the first compulsory constituent of the simple sentence. It can be simple or extended.

2.1.1   The simple NP

> Ex: – determiner + noun
> *le chat, cette philosophie*
>
> – [determiner] + proper noun
> *Paul, la France*

2.1.2   The extended NP

Optional constituents or expansions are:

(i)   Qualifying adjectives

They agree in gender and number with the noun and can appear in an attached or a detached position:
> Ex: *C'est une voiture **puissante**.*
> ***Satisfait**, Paul ferma son livre.*

Qualifying adjectives can themselves be extended:
- with an adverb: *très jolie*
- with a noun complement in direct construction: *bleu azur, jaune paille*
- with a noun or pronoun complement in indirect construction: *pâle de colère, rouge de honte, satisfait de rien.*

These **adjectival phrases** (*syntagme adjectival*) behave like single qualifying adjectives towards the noun they qualify.
> Ex: *Dizzy est **beau** comme un ange.*

See also chapter 28 Qualifying Adjectives, section 2.3.1.

(ii)   Noun complements

    (a) in direct construction, i.e. without a preposition.
        Ex: *l'Avenue* **Georges-V**; *un crayon* **feutre**; *un sac* **poubelle**

    (b) in indirect construction, i.e. with a preposition:
        Ex: *le chat* **de la voisine**
        'de la voisine' is a **prepositional phrase** (*syntagme prépositionnel*) and
        is itself included in the noun phrase that it completes: **le chat de la**
        voisine

(iii)   Appositions

    (a) Without a determiner, they have a descriptive value, giving a definition to the
        noun.
        Ex: *M. Sagouin,* **charcutier**, *vend de l'excellent boudin.*

    (b) With a determiner
      – the indefinite article gives extra information, a property to the noun:
        Ex: *Eric,* **un ami**, *était venu me voir.*
      – the definite article identifies the noun:
        Ex: *Je vous présente M. Dupont,* **le pâtissier** *de St-Firmin.*
    Note that appositions are not strictly part of the noun phrase, since they are
    detached from it.

(iv)   Relative clauses

    The relative clause qualifies the noun which is its antecedent. Hence it is
    sometimes called *complément de l'antécédent.*
        Ex: – attached
           Les conseils **que vous nous avez donnés** *étaient excellents.*
        – detached
           M. Sagouin, **qui est le charcutier du quartier**, *vend de l'excellent boudin.*

    Note that all the adjectives and all the nouns in apposition to a noun can be
    replaced by detached relative clauses, with the same values and the same roles. See
    also 3 below, The Complex Sentence.

2.1.3   *The NP with several expansions*

  (i)   The only limits on the number of *optional* constituents of an NP are set by
    comprehensibility and style.
        Ex: *?Le chat de la voisine du troisième étage d'en face qui a déjà deux chiens et*
           trois perroquets dont je ne connais pas les noms bien que la dite voisine me
           les ait souvent dits n'arrête pas de pourchasser les miens.

  (ii)   Since the adjective, the noun complement and the relative clause are syntactically
    equivalent in the NP, they can be coordinated.
        Ex: *Un chat extraordinaire, voleur de bifteck et qui n'avait encore jamais attrapé*
           de souris, débarqua un beau matin.
    Again, questions of style should be taken into consideration. See also chapter 40
    Coordination and Juxtaposition.

22

2.2 Other types of subject

Other words or even clauses can be syntactically equivalent to a noun phrase subject.

(i) Personal pronouns
>   Ex: *je mange*; **elle** *est tombée*

(ii) Impersonal pronouns
>   (See also chapter 4 Introduction to Verbs, sections 7.1(iv) and 7.3.)
>   – with impersonal verbs:
>>   Ex: **il** *pleut,* **il** *neige*
>>   **Il** *s'agit d'un rapport.*
>   – with the impersonal voice:
>>   Ex: **Il** *est arrivé deux personnes.*

Here, the impersonal '*il*' is the apparent or grammatical subject (*sujet apparent or grammatical*); '*personnes*' is the real or semantic subject (*sujet réel or sémantique*). The verb agrees with '*il*'.

(iii) Indefinite, possessive and demonstrative pronouns
>   Ex: **Quelqu'un** *vous a demandé.*
>   **Rien** *n'est prêt.*
>   **Le tien** *n'est pas encore arrivé.*
>   **Celle-ci** *vous conviendrait mieux.*

(iv) Nominal infinitives
>   Ex: **Nager** *est relaxant.*

(v) Relative clauses (see 3 below, The Complex Sentence) without antecedent
>   Ex: **Qui dort** *dîne.*
>   **Ce que vous dites** *n'est pas exact.*

(vi) *que*-clauses (see 3 below, The Complex Sentence)
>   Ex: **Qu'il soit d'accord** *me surprend.*

2.3 Relation of subject and verb

The subject can be defined as the performer of the action, or the entity about which something is asserted or which undergoes the action.
>   Ex: **Le chat** *boit son lait.*
>   The subject is indispensable → **boit son lait.*

As a general rule, if there is one subject, the verb agrees with the subject:
– in person:
>   Ex: *je marche*; **tu** *marches*
– in number:
>   Ex: *il marche*; **ils** *marchent*
– in the case of compound tenses with *être*, in person with the auxiliary, and in gender and number with the past participle:
>   Ex: **Catherine est venue** *nous voir.*
>   3rd person, feminine, singular

If the subjects are different grammatical persons:
- the 2nd person overrides the 3rd:
> Ex: *Toi/Vous et Catherine*, **vous** *viendrez me voir demain.*
- the 1st person overrides all the others:
> Ex: *Toi/Vous et moi*, **nous** *allons faire les courses.*
> *Paul, Catherine et moi*, **nous** *allons faire les courses.*

As a general rule, if the verb has several subjects, the verb is in the plural.

2.4 Order of subject and verb in a declarative sentence

The normal order is subject–verb.
> Ex: *Le chat miaule.*
> _{subject}   _{verb}

The order is reversed in the following cases:

(i) Impersonal constructions (see below)
> Ex: *Il est arrivé un accident.*
> (= *Un accident est arrivé.*)

(ii) Reporting clauses (*propositions incises*)

In reporting clauses (to report direct speech), the subject comes after the verb in a **simple** inversion. See chapter 41 Reported Speech, section 2.
> Ex: *Il est parti à 5 heures,* **a annoncé Marie.**
> *Je vais essayer,* **dit–il,** *d'arranger ça.*

NB: For comment clauses (*propositions de jugement ou de commentaire*), where the speaker intervenes in his own discourse, or with reporting clauses appearing **before** the reported speech, the order is subject–verb.
> Ex: *Ce n'est pas,* **je pense,** *ce qui manque le plus.*
> **Marie a annoncé**: *'Il est parti à 5 heures.'*

(iii) Presence of an adverb of affirmation, doubt or opinion

If the sentence begins with *au moins, du moins, aussi, tout au plus, peut-être, sans doute*, the order may be reversed in the following cases, depending on the register.

- Formal register: the subject comes after the verb in a **complex** inversion. The order is: adverb + complex inversion.
> Ex: *Au moins vous* **a–t–il écouté.**
> *Peut-être* **Nicolas viendra–t–il** *demain.*

Note that if there is another adverb in the sentence, *sans doute* or *peut-être* should come first, if only for stylistic reasons.
> Ex: *Sans doute ont-ils finalement compris ce que vous vouliez dire.*
> sounds better than:
> *Ils ont sans doute finalement compris . . .*

– Informal register: there is no inversion.

(a) with *au moins, du moins, aussi, tout au plus*
The order is: adverb + comma + subject + verb.
> Ex: *Au moins, il vous a écouté.*

(b) with *peut-être, sans doute*
The order is: adverb + *que* + subject + verb.
> Ex: *Peut-être que Nicolas viendra demain.*

If the sentence begins with *à peine . . . que* (formal French), the complex inversion is used.
> Ex: ***A peine Robert avait-il*** *terminé ce travail* ***qu'****on lui en a donné un autre.*
> Robert had hardly finished that job when he was given another one.

Informal French would be:
> *Robert avait à peine terminé ce travail qu'on lui en a donné un autre.*

(iv) Stylistic choice

It is possible to invert subject and verb (simple inversion), for instance:
– in a relative clause object (see 3.2.2.2 below)
> Ex: *La nouvelle maison qu'****ont achetée les Dupont*** *fait l'envie de tous leurs amis!*

– in a comparative clause (see chapter 30 Comparatives, section 2.1)
> Ex: *M. Dupont est plus riche que ne le* ***pensent les gens****.*

– with verbs of movement conjugated with *être*, or a passive with no agent. This device is often used in declarative emphatic sentences (administrative style) with noun or noun phrase subject only (not pronouns).
> Ex: *Sont arrivés en premier Messieurs les délégués.*
> *Sont convoqués pour dix heures Mlle Martin, M. Dupont . . .*

This structure is even more commonly used when preceded by an adverb phrase (or *y/en*, implying a link with the previous context) and can then be extended to all intransitive verbs.
> Ex: *Sur un fauteuil dormaient deux chats.*
> *Dans ce laboratoire sont préparées toutes sortes de potions. 'Passe un*
> *96 . . . ; en descend Geneviève Serreau . . .'*

> Georges Pérec, *Tentatives d'épuisement d'un lieu parisien*

2.5 The verb phrase (VP)

The VP is the second compulsory constituent of the simple sentence and corresponds to the traditional concept of 'predicate'.

The conjugated verb is the essential constituent of the VP. Verbs may be followed by zero, one or two complements. Hence the constituents of the VP can be:
– V
– V + NP/E
– V + PP (prepositional phrase)
– V + NP/E + PP
– V + PP + PP
– V + subject complement
– V + object complement

NB: Unlike in English, the sequence 'verb + NP + NP' is only possible in French when the two NPs are co-referential (i.e. refer to the same object of the world). Compare:

> He gave Paul a book.
> *Il a donné **un livre à Paul**.*
> (See section 2.6.6.)
>   and:
> Robert was elected chairman of the Committee.
> *On a élu **Robert président du Comité**.*
> (See section 2.12.)

2.6 Transitivity

Verbs can be transitive or intransitive, as explained below. This feature can be checked in a dictionary.

2.6.1 Intransitive verbs *(verbes intransitifs)*

They **cannot take an object**: VP = V.

> Ex: *Le chat **miaule**.*
> *Nous **partons**.*

but they can be followed by an adverb or adverb phrase.

> Ex: *Nous **partons** tout de suite.*
> *Le chat **miaule** de toutes ses forces.*

2.6.2 Transitive direct verbs *(verbes transitifs directs)*

They **can take an object**, in direct construction (the direct object is an NP): VP = V + NP/E.

> Ex: *Les manifestants bloquent la circulation.*
>   subject   verb   direct object

Characteristics:

(i) They can be made passive.

> Ex: *La circulation a été bloquée [par les manifestants].*

(ii) Most transitive direct verbs **can** also be used without an object (= *verbes à prédication complète*). This is referred to as the 'absolute' use of transitive verbs.
    – without any change of meaning:

> Ex: *Je mange une pomme.*
> *Je mange.*

    – with a change of meaning:

> Ex: *Il boit de la bière* → He's drinking beer.
> *Il boit* → either: He is drinking (sth).
>   or: He has a drink problem.

> *Elle écrit un roman* → She's writing a novel.
> *Elle écrit* → either: She is writing (sth).
>   or: She writes (as a job).

(iii) Some transitive direct verbs **cannot** be used without an object (= *verbes à prédication incomplète*).

> Ex: **Je quitte* → *Je quitte mon bureau.*

2.6.3 Transitive indirect verbs (verbes transitifs indirects)

They **can take an object** in indirect construction, i.e. with a preposition (the indirect object is a prepositional phrase): VP =V + PP

> Ex: *Catherine a parlé à Paul.*
> subject   verb   indirect object

(i) Unlike in English, they cannot be made passive.

> Ex: **Paul a été donné un livre [par Catherine].*

Exceptions: *obéir, désobéir, pardonner* (see chapter 18 Active and Passive Voices, section 6).

(ii) Some transitive indirect verbs **can** be used without an object.

> Ex: *Je pense à Nicole.*
> *Je pense.*

(iii) Some transitive indirect verbs **cannot** be used without an object.

> Ex: *Marie ressemble à sa sœur.*
> **Marie ressemble.*

2.6.4 Transitive or intransitive?

The same basic verb can be intransitive, transitive direct or indirect, with different meanings. Compare:

> *J'ai tenu **bon**!* (intransitive + adverb)
> I stayed the course!

> *Il tenait **son chapeau** à la main.* (transitive direct)
> He had his hat in his hand.

> *Je tenais tant **à ce vieux meuble**.* (transitive indirect)
> I was so fond of that old piece of furniture.

> *Je tiens **de ma grand-mère**.* (transitive indirect)
> I take after my grandmother.

> *Je **te** tiendrai **l'échelle**.* (bitransitive, see 2.6.6 below)
> I'll hold the ladder for you.

2.6.5 Transitive direct or indirect?

Compare:

> *Quelqu'un demande **Anne** au téléphone.*
> *(demander qn)*
> Someone on the telephone is asking for Anne.
>   and:
> *Quelqu'un demande **à Anne** si elle est libre.*
> *(demander qch à qn)*
> Someone is asking Anne if she's free.

This distinction can also depend on the nature of the object, e.g. NP, *que*-clause or infinitive (see also section 2.8 below, Other Types of Object).

> Ex: *Il doute **de ma bonne foi**.*
> <small>indirect object</small>
>
> *Il doute **que je sois de bonne foi**.*
> <small>direct object</small>
>
> *Il apprend **le français**.*
> <small>direct object</small>
>
> *Il apprend **à jouer au tennis**.*
> <small>indirect object</small>

Unlike the examples quoted in section 2.6.4 above, the above examples show that even with the same meaning, a verb is not limited to one particular construction.

2.6.6 *Bitransitive verbs (verbes bitransitifs)*

The verb can be followed by a direct object + indirect object, or two indirect objects (the second one is also called *complément d'attribution* or *complément d'objet second*).

Hence: VP = V + NP/E + PP   or   V + PP + PP

(i) V + NP + PP

– The PP can be introduced by **de**. For instance:

*équiper qn **de** qch*	*recevoir qch **de** qn*
*charger qn **de** qch*	*penser qch **de** qn*
*couvrir qn/qch **de** qch*	*dire qch **de** qn*
*menacer qn **de** qch*	*éloigner qn/qch **de** qn/qch*
*remplir qch **de** qch*	*entourer qn/qch **de** qch*

> Ex: *Nous allons entourer <u>le jardin</u> **de haies**.*
> <small>direct object   indirect object</small>
>
> We're going to surround the garden with hedges.
>
> *<u>Que</u> pensez-vous **de lui**?*
> <small>direct object   indirect object</small>
>
> What do you think of him?
>
> *J'ai reçu <u>une lettre</u> **de Sylvain**.*
> <small>direct object   indirect object</small>
>
> I've received a letter from Sylvain.
>
> *Vous devriez éloigner <u>les enfants</u> **du feu**.*
> <small>direct object   indirect object</small>
>
> You should keep the childen away from the fire.

– The PP can be introduced by **à**. Note that most imply a transference, in a literal or figurative sense, of something to or from someone. For instance:

> *donner/laisser/accorder/envoyer qch **à** qn*
> *annoncer/communiquer/dire/promettre/avouer qch **à** qn*
> *prêter/emprunter/voler qch **à** qn*
> *prendre/rendre/vendre/acheter/louer qch **à** qn*

Note: *recevoir qch **de** qn.*

They all are about 'giving' or 'saying' something to someone.

Ex: *Michel a vendu <u>sa vieille voiture</u> **à son frère**.*

direct object   indirect object

*J'ai donné <u>un bonbon</u> **au petit garçon**.*

direct object   indirect object

NB: The passive voice:

− is always possible with the NP

Ex: *Nicolas a donné un livre à Pierre.*

→ *Un livre a été donné à Pierre [par Nicolas].*

− is not possible with the PP

→ *★Pierre a été donné un livre [par Nicolas].*

(but see exceptions in 2.6.3(i) above).

(ii)   V + PP + PP

Ex: *J'ai parlé <u>de toi</u> <u>à ton frère</u>.*

2.7   Expansions of the NP object

The NP object can be extended in the same way as the NP subject (see 2.1.2 above).

2.8   Other types of object

Syntactic alternatives to an NP or PP object:

(i)   Clitic (joint/unstressed) personal pronoun, placed before the verb

Ex: *Catherine? Je **la** vois souvent.*

*Paul? Je **lui** ai parlé hier.*

*Des cerises? Je n'**en** mange jamais.*

*Mes vacances? J'**y** pense encore.*

(ii)   Tonic (disjoint/stressed) personal pronoun, placed after the verb

Ex: *Pierre et Paul? Marie pense souvent à **eux**.*

(iii)   Indefinite, possessive and demonstrative pronouns

Ex: *Je n'ai **rien** pris.*

*Je n'ai vu **personne**.*

*Tu penses à **quelqu'un**?*

*Je ne trouve pas **le mien**.*

*Tu aimes **celui-ci**?*

(iv)   Infinitive

Ex: *Il espère **acheter une nouvelle voiture bientôt**.*

*Il faut que je pense **à fermer la porte à clé ce soir**.*

*Il a arrêté **de fumer**.*

(v)   *que*-clause

Ex: *Je pense **que vous avez raison**.*

*Je m'attends **à ce que vous ne soyez pas d'accord**.*

(vi)   Relative clause without antecedent
             Ex: *J'ai acheté **ce qu'il y avait**.*

(vii)   Indirect interrogative clause
             Ex: *Je ne sais pas **si j'aurai le temps**.*
                  *Il veut savoir **à quel parti vous appartenez**.*
                  *Je ne sais pas **de qui il parle**.*

Note that the last three are complex sentences.

2.9   Position of objects in a declarative sentence

(i)   One object: V + NP; V + PP
             Ex: *J'ai mangé **deux gâteaux**.*
                  *J'ai téléphoné **à Pierre**.*

(ii)   Two objects: V + NP + PP
             Ex: *J'ai offert **un cadeau** <u>à Frédéric</u>.*

NB: The reverse order is possible for stylistic reasons (e.g. the direct object is longer than the indirect object):
             Ex: *Nicolas a donné <u>à Pierre</u> **toute sa collection de timbres rares**.*

(iii)   Two objects: V + PP + PP
The order is optional, but there may be risks of ambiguity.
             Ex: *J'ai parlé <u>de mon collègue</u> **au directeur**.*
                  I spoke about my colleague to the manager.

             *J'ai parlé **au directeur** <u>de mon collègue</u>.*
                       is likely to be understood as:
                  I spoke to my colleague's manager.

NB: The position of object **pronouns** is treated in chapter 31 Personal Pronouns, section 2.2.3.

2.10   Other verb complements ('measure' verbs)

They express measure, weight, cost, etc. and describe a property of the subject (see 2.11 Subject Complements below). They are in direct construction (no preposition).
             Ex: *Ce vin coûte 50F.*
                  Ces draps sentent la lavande.
                  Mon chat pèse 10kg.
                  La cuisine mesure 3 mètres sur 5.

NB: These complements are not objects but adverb phrases. Compare:
             *Cette valise pèse **20 kg*** and *Cette valise pèse **lourd***
             *Ce vin coûte **200F*** and *Ce vin coûte **cher***
             *J'ai dormi **douze heures*** and *J'ai dormi **longtemps***

(see chapter 29 Adverbs). Because there is no object, the sentences cannot be made passive (*10kg sont pesés par mon chat*), except when the measurement, etc. has been carried out by an agent (*Le vétérinaire pèse le chat* → *Le chat est pesé par le vétérinaire*).

2.11 Subject (or predicative) complements (*attributs du sujet*)

Copulas (*copules ou verbes attributifs*) such as *être, paraître, sembler, demeurer, devenir, rester, vivre, avoir l'air* and *faire semblant* can take subject complements.

(i) Meaning

- The subject complement generally expresses a quality, a way of being or a property which is attributed to the referent of the subject. The meaning of the subject complement is closely associated with that of the verb. For instance:
  - *devenir* = to go into a state
  - *être, rester, demeurer* = a continuity in the state
  - *paraître, sembler, avoir l'air* = an opinion of a state

- The subject complement can also express a place, in particular with *être, rester, demeurer*.

- Note that some 'ordinary' transitive or intransitive verbs can also be used as copulas. Compare:
  >> *Eric est tombé **malade**.*
  >>> subject complement
  >> Eric fell ill.
  >> and:
  >> *Eric est tombé **en courant/en descendant les escaliers**.*
  >>> adverb phrases
  >> Eric fell while running/going downstairs.

(ii) Grammatical type

Subject complements can be:

- adjective:
  >> Ex: *Ce village est très **pittoresque**; Paul est devenu **fou**.*

- adverb:
  >> Ex: *Le chat est **là**.*

- PP:
  - with a qualifying value:
    >> Ex: *Cette table est **en chêne massif**.*
  - expressing location:
    >> Ex: *Il est resté **à l'hôtel** pendant une semaine.*

- NP:
  - without article (qualifying value):
    >> Ex: *Françoise est **professeur**.*

       – with indefinite article (giving extra information/expressing a property):
           Ex: *Paul est **un** bon **docteur**.*
               *Le persil est **une herbe** à haute teneur en fer.*
       – with definite article (identifying value):
           Ex: *Paul est **le** meilleur **docteur** du quartier.*

   – pronoun (with or without article):
           Ex: *Elle est **étudiante**.*
               *Il est **l'auteur** de nombreux articles.*
See chapter 35 *C'est/Il est*, section 6.

   – nominal infinitive (with or without *de*):
           Ex: *Consentir n'est pas **approuver**.*
               *L'important est **de savoir**.*

   – subordinate clause:
     – *que*-clause:
           Ex: *Le fait est **qu'il a eu raison de partir**.*
     – relative clause with pronoun antecedent:
           Ex: *Cette maison est **celle qui me plaît le plus**.*

Note that the last two examples belong to the complex sentence.

(iii)   Agreement

   – Adjectives, and nouns without a determiner (i.e. with a qualifying value), agree with the subject.
           Ex: ***Marie** est **grande**.*
              ***Ils** sont **ingénieurs**.*

   – Otherwise, the subject complement is 'independent'.
           Ex: ***Son départ** a été **une grande joie**.*

(iv)   Word order

The normal order is: subject + copula + subject complement.
           Ex: *Cette route est longue/un désastre.*

Exceptions:
– with the indefinite pronoun *tel*:
           Ex: ***Telles** furent ses dernières paroles.*
– in emphatic declarative sentences, where the order is:
           subject complement (adjective or adverb)
           + copula
           + subject (NP, not pronoun).
           Ex: ***Nombreux** sont les problèmes.*
               ***Là** est la question.*
NB: Only those adjectives which can appear **before** the noun may be placed before the verb (see chapter 28 Qualifying Adjectives, section 2.3.4).

2.12 Object complements (*attributs du complément*)

With the following verbs:

– *estimer, considérer comme, tenir pour, juger, croire, traiter de, rendre, trouver* + adjective

Ex: *On l'a estimé <u>bon pour le service</u>.*
*Je trouve **ce livre** <u>passionnant</u>.*
*Catherine a traité **Paul** <u>d'égoïste</u>.*
*Marie a rendu **Robert** <u>malheureux</u>.*

– *avoir pour, avoir comme, élire, nommer, appeler, prendre pour, proclamer* + NP

Ex: *Nous l'avons proclamé <u>gagnant du concours</u>.*
*Moi, j'appelle **un chat** <u>un chat</u>!*
*Et dire que je **le** prenais pour <u>un ami</u>!*

– *considérer comme, déclarer* + adjective or NP

Ex: *On l'a considéré comme <u>bon pour le service</u>.*
*On a déclaré **Nicolas** <u>grand gagnant du concours</u>.*

2.13 Sentence adverbs (*compléments circonstanciels*)

Adverbs can modify a verb (*je vais **régulièrement** à Paris*; *il marche **vite***; *je ne me sens pas **bien***), an adjective (***souvent** gai*), another adverb (***extrêmement** lentement*) or a whole sentence.

Two types of adverbs modify the whole sentence: sentence adverbs and sentence connectors (see chapter 29 Adverbs, section 5.3).

Sentence adverbs or adverb phrases can be described as follows:

(i) Characteristics

– optionality:

Ex: *Marie a cueilli les cerises [ce matin].*
J'ai offert un cadeau à Paul [pour son anniversaire].

– mobility:
The 'unmarked' adverb phrase comes at the end of the sentence.

Ex: *Marie a cueilli les cerises **ce matin**.*

Any other place corresponds to a stylistic choice or one of emphasis. The adverb phrase is then in a detached position.

Ex: ***Ce matin**, Marie a cueilli les cerises.*

NB: There can be more than one adverbial structure in a sentence.

Ex: *Frédéric arrive **demain** <u>par le train de 10 heures</u>.*

(ii) Meaning

Sentence adverbs express the 'circumstances' of the action, state, or transformation expressed by the verb. The most common ones express time, place, manner, means, cause, aim, opposition or concession.

33

(iii) Grammatical type

A sentence adverb phrase can be:

− a noun phrase:
> Ex: *Je suis allée en Grèce **l'année dernière**.*

− a prepositional phrase:
> Ex: ***Depuis ce matin**, je ne me sens pas très bien.*

− an adverb:
> Ex: *Je voudrais bien vous voir **demain**.*
> ***Lentement**, il s'est approché.*

− a preposition + infinitive:
> Ex: *J'irai vous rendre visite **avant de partir**.*

− a participial clause:
> Ex: ***La pluie cessant**, ils purent repartir.*
> ***Tout le monde assis**, le spectacle put commencer.*

− a gerundive clause:
> Ex: *Paul s'est coupé **en aiguisant les couteaux**.*

− an adverbial subordinate clause (*proposition subordonnée circonstancielle*):
> Ex: *Je terminerai cet article **quand j'en aurai le temps**.*

(iv) Ambiguities

Prepositional phrases can be a great source of ambiguity; it may be difficult to distinguish whether they are noun complements, verb complements or sentence adverbs. This is particularly the case with prepositions *à* and *de* which present one of the great stumbling blocks in automatic translation. In a discourse situation, ambiguities are resolved by the context in which they are found or by the knowledge of certain logical or universal 'truths' (also called 'knowledge of the world') which we bring to our interpretation of sentences.

> Ex: *On peut voir les fleurs du balcon.*
> either:
> → '*les fleurs du balcon*' is the direct object of '*peut voir*' and '*du balcon*' is the noun complement of '*les fleurs*'.
> You can see the balcony's flowers (i.e. those which are on the balcony).
> or:
> → '*les fleurs*' is the direct object of '*peut voir*' and '*du balcon*' is an adverb phrase of place.
> You can see the flowers **from** the balcony.

2.14 Incomplete sentences

2.14.1 *No verb*

These are sometimes called nominal sentences (*phrases nominales*) even though they are not exclusively made up of nouns.

(i) Interjections and other fixed expressions

They express a comment made by the speaker. In spoken French, the interpretation is conveyed by the intonation.

– only one word:
> Ex: *Hein? Déjà?* (question)
> *Hein! Déjà!* (surprise)
> *Aïe!* (pain)
> *Bof!* (indifference)
> *Heu . . .* (hesitation)
> *Pouah! Berk!* (disgust)
> *Zut! Merde!* (annoyance)
> *Attention!* (warning)
> *Dommage! Hélas!* (regret)

– more than one word:
> Ex: *A demain!*
> *Au secours!*
> *Grands Dieux!*
> *Nom d'un chien!*
> *Nom d'une pipe!*

(ii) Labels, book titles, advertisements, newspaper headlines, etc.
> Ex: '*huile d'olive extra vierge pressée à froid*'
> '*Vittel, la vitalité à l'état pur*'
> '*la notion de signe*'
> '*Départs en vacances: embouteillages dès ce soir.*'

(iii) Semantic ellipsis

Semantic ellipsis is a way of making an utterance shorter, but still understandable to the interlocutor. Ellipsis of the verb or even subject + verb is used in conversation as a matter of course.
> Ex: *Tout droit!* (= *Il faut aller tout droit!*)
> *Autre chose?* (= *Vous désirez autre chose?*)
> (*Qui en reveut?*) – *Moi!* (= *Moi, j'en reveux.*)
> *Extra, ce gigot!* (= *Ce gigot est extra.*)
> *Intéressant, tout cela.* (= *Tout cela est intéressant.*)
> *Très heureux.* (= *Je suis très heureux de faire votre connaissance.*)

NB: Grammatical ellipsis is found in coordination and comparatives, where the rules of syntax allow them (see chapters 30 Comparatives, section 2.1, and 40 Coordination and Juxtaposition, section 5.1).
> Ex: *Lizzy attrape des souris et Dizzy [attrape] des oiseaux.*
> Lizzy catches mice and Dizzy [catches] birds.
>
> *Robert est plus gentil que [qu'il ne l'était] l'année dernière.*
> Robert is nicer than [he was] last year.

35

2.14.2 No subject

(i) Imperative

In the imperative mood, the sentence appears without an explicit subject. The subject is shown by the **form of the verb** and the sentence ends in an exclamation mark. Hence a sentence could be made up of one word only.

Ex: *Partons!* (1st person plural)

Buvez votre café! (2nd person plural)

Prête ta voiture à ton frère! (2nd person singular)

(ii) Infinitive

– orders, instructions:

Ex: *Ne pas faire de bruit.*

– questions, exclamations:

Ex: *Que faire?*

Comment acheter sans se tromper?

Voir Venise et mourir!

– narrative:

Ex: '*Et grenouilles de se plaindre.*'

La Fontaine, *Les grenouilles qui demandent un Roi*

2.15 Emphasis (*emphase syntaxique*)

Emphasis is a way of drawing attention to a particular constituent of the sentence.

2.15.1 Focalization (thème et focus)

Consider the following example:

Un homme *marchait le long de la rue.* **Il** *est entré dans un café.*

– '*Il*' in the second sentence is the theme. It appears at the beginning of the sentence, and represents what is already known (*information ancienne*).

– '*est entré dans un café*' is the focus, and represents new information (*information nouvelle*).

Focalization, i.e. emphasis on the focus, can be achieved in various ways (see below).

2.15.2 Detachment

An adverb modifying the whole sentence can be placed in a detached position, at the beginning or in the middle of the sentence. See 2.13 above.

2.15.3 Presentative forms (présentatifs)

Presentative forms are words or expressions which are used to 'show' someone or something in a particular situation. They are: *il y a, il est, c'est, voici, voilà*.

Ex: **Voici** *mon père.*

C'est *le chat de la voisine!*

Regarde, **il y a** *un homme bizarre dans la rue.*

Note that:
- *voici* and *voilà* are invariable
- *il y a* can be conjugated in other tenses, but is **always singular**
- *il est* can only be conjugated in the present or the imperfect
- *c'est* can be conjugated in other tenses, and can also vary in number in formal French (*C'étaient d'honnêtes gens.*).

c'est is the most commonly used presentative form. It is also the weakest (it presupposes that what we are talking about is already known), hence it can follow e.g. *il y a* or *voici* but not precede them.

> Ex: **Voilà** M. Durand qui arrive. **C'est** notre professeur de français.
>
> **Il y a** dix kilos d'abricots à la cave. **C'est** pour faire ma confiture.

When they are associated with *qui* and *que*, these presentative forms can also be used to perform a focalization with a cleft construction (see below).

2.15.4 Cleft constructions (constructions clivées)

Presentative forms are used to focus on particular NP constituents of the sentence. Whatever its function, the NP is detached and normally placed at the beginning of that sentence. It is introduced by the forms *c'est, voilà, il y a* and then repeated by the relative pronouns *qui* or *que* (or, less frequently, *dont*). The sentence is called a cleft sentence. Thus presentative forms can be used to focus on:
- the subject:

> Ex: *L'argent fait tourner le monde.*
>
> → **C'est** l'argent **qui** fait tourner le monde.

- an object, direct or indirect:

> Ex: *Paul a vendu sa voiture à Marie.*
>
> → **C'est** sa voiture **que** Paul a vendue à Marie.
>
> → **C'est** à Marie **que** Paul a vendu sa voiture.

- an adverb phrase:

> Ex: *J'ai oublié mon sac dans le train.*
>
> → **C'est** dans le train **que** j'ai oublié mon sac.

The focalized element can also be placed at the end of the sentence, in which case it is introduced by a pronoun.

> Ex: **Celui qui** me plaît le plus, **c'est** Alain.
>
> **Ce qui** m'ennuie, **c'est** que vous soyez toujours en retard.

2.15.5 Dislocated constructions (constructions disloquées)

In a dislocated sentence, one of the constituents is moved to either the left or right for emphasis. The constituent that has been moved is repeated by the corresponding personal pronoun, in the normal position. Dislocated structures apply to all four modalities of sentences but are normally only used in **informal** French.

(i)   **Declarative**

> Ex: *Je veux parler à Juliette.*
> → **Juliette**, *je veux **lui** parler.*
> → *Je veux **lui** parler, à **Juliette**.*
>
> *Paul a vendu sa voiture à Catherine.*
> → **Sa voiture**, *Paul **l'**a vendue à Catherine.*
> → **Catherine**, *Paul **lui** a vendu sa voiture.*

Several constituents can be displaced in this way, which create constructions which some consider as being on the verge of acceptability.

> Ex: *On a crevé les pneus de la voiture de mon père.*
> → *?Mon père, sa voiture, les pneus, on lui a crevé.*

(ii) **Exclamative**

> Ex: *Qu'est-ce que Marie est bête alors!*
> → **Marie**, *qu'est-ce qu'**elle** est bête alors!*

(iii) **Interrogative**

> Ex: *Tu as vu sa voiture?*
> → **Sa voiture**, *tu **l'**as vue?*

NB: In interrogative constructions of the type *Paul est-il venu?*, a tonic pronoun can be added for emphasis.

> Ex: **Paul** *est-il venu, **lui**?*

(iv) **Imperative**

> Ex: *Va chercher mon manteau!*
> → **Mon manteau**, *va **le** chercher!*

NB: In *Toi, va chercher mon manteau!*, there is no emphasis but an address (*apostrophe*) to the interlocutor.

3   The complex sentence

A complex sentence is a sentence made up of two or more clauses. Whether simple or extended, these clauses (*propositions*) can be linked by coordination, juxtaposition or subordination.

3.1   Coordination and juxtaposition

(i)   Coordination:
      − the clauses have the same status
      − they are linked by a conjunction of coordination
      − the conjunction of coordination indicates the type of relation.

> Ex: *Il fait beau **et** les oiseaux chantent.* (addition)
> *Il fait beau **mais** il fait froid.* (opposition)

(ii) Juxtaposition:
– the clauses have the same status
– they are separated by a comma or a semi-colon:
Ex: *Il est venu, il a vu, il a vaincu.*
The type of relation is implicit and understood from the context.

(iii) Each of the clauses linked by coordination or juxtaposition is autonomous and can therefore become an independent clause.
Ex: *Il fait beau.*
Les oiseaux chantent.
Il est venu.

(iv) The figure of asyndeton (*asyndète*) is the systematic suppression of coordinating words, which creates a juxtaposition.
Ex: *Je te demande, prie, supplie de le faire à ma place.*
Conversely, the figure of polysyndeton (*polysyndète*) is the multiplication of coordinating words.
Ex: *Elle est jeune et belle et intelligente.*

Coordination and juxtaposition apply to various parts of speech, as well as clauses and sentences. For details, see chapter 40 Coordination and Juxtaposition.

3.2 Subordination

(i) Subordination creates a **hierarchical relation** between two clauses, namely a subordinate clause which is dependent on the main clause.
Ex: *Je voudrais bien* | *que vous m'aidiez.*
main clause   subordinate clause

(ii) A subordinate clause can be subordinated to another:
Ex: *Je voudrais bien* | *que vous m'aidiez* | *si vous en avez le temps!*
1. main clause   2. subordinated to 1   3. subordinated to 2

(iii) A subordinate clause can be:

– explicit; the subordinating word can be:
– a conjunction of subordination:
Ex: *Je sais **que** vous êtes malade.*
***Bien qu'**il pleuve, je sors.*
– an interrogative adverb or pronoun:
Ex: *Elle ne sait vraiment pas **où** elle a bien pu laisser son sac.*
*Elle se demande **à qui** tu as écrit.*
– a relative pronoun:
Ex: *J'ai lu le livre **que** tu m'avais recommandé.*

– implicit
The two clauses are **syntactically** juxtaposed, but unlike genuine juxtaposed clauses (see above), they are not autonomous: they are **semantically** subordinated. Hence the subordination is called implicit or semantic (informal French only).

Ex: *Il me le donnerait, je n'en voudrais pas.*
(= *S'il me le donnait . . .*)

Faut-il donner un coup de main, Paul est toujours prêt.
(= *S'il faut/Quand il faut . . .*)

(iv)   There are three main types of subordinate clauses:

– *que*-clause (*complétive* or *conjonctive*)
– relative clause
– adverbial clause (*circonstancielle*)

Other types include:
– indirect interrogative clauses and *que*-clauses belonging to indirect reported speech, treated in chapter 41 Reported Speech, section 3
– infinitive clauses, treated in chapters 15 Infinitive and 12 Subjunctive, section 4.4
– participial clauses, treated in chapters 16 Present Participle, section 4, and 17 Past Participle, section 5
– comparative clauses, treated in chapter 30 Comparatives, section 2

(v)   Functions

A subordinate clause can be:

– a modifier of an NP:
Ex: *J'aime les enfants **qui sont sages**.*
The relative '*qui sont sages*' modifies the NP '*les enfants*'.

– an object of the verb:
Ex: *J'espère **que vous allez bien**.*
The *que*-clause '*que vous allez bien*' is the object of '*espère*'.

– a subject of the verb:
Ex: ***Qu'il soit d'accord** me surprend.*
The *que*-clause '*Qu'il soit d'accord*' is the subject of '*surprend*'.

– an adverbial clause:
Ex: ***Lorsqu'il fait mauvais temps**, personne ne sort.*
'*Lorsqu'il fait mauvais temps*' is an adverbial clause which modifies the main clause '*personne ne sort*'.

(vi)   Subject–verb agreements

Care must be taken with subject–verb agreements in complex sentences with more than one subordinate clause. Consider the following example:
***Les pouvoirs** dont **le président** <u>dispose</u> et qui lui <u>permettent</u> de maîtriser le jeu politique <u>sont</u> les suivants.*
The powers that the president has at his disposal and which enable him to control the political game are the following.
'*le président*' is subject of '*dispose*' but '*les pouvoirs*' is subject of '*permettent*' and '*sont*'.

3.2.1 que-*clauses* (complétives)

These are introduced by the conjunction of subordination **que**, not to be confused with the relative pronoun *que* (see 3.2.2 below), which normally has an NP (its antecedent) just before it.

(i) The *que*-clause as an object

This is the most frequent case.
>   Ex: *Je préfère **que vous veniez la semaine prochaine**.*

The mood of the subordinate clause (indicative or subjunctive) depends on the verb of the main clause.
>   Ex: *Je pense **qu'il viendra** demain.*
>   *J'aimerais **qu'il vienne** demain.*

See chapter 12 Subjunctive, section 4.1.

When the verb in the main clause expresses a declaration with verbs such as *dire, affirmer, prétendre, soutenir, nier,* etc., or an opinion with verbs such as *penser, croire, juger, comprendre,* etc., the *que*-clause constitutes the indirect reported speech.
>   Ex: *Il a dit **qu'il serait là demain**.*

See chapter 41 Reported Speech, section 3.

When the verb in the main clause expresses a question, it introduces an indirect interrogative clause (see chapter 41 Reported Speech, section 3.5).
>   Ex: *Il m'a demandé **ce que je voulais**.*

(ii) The *que*-clause after an impersonal verb

The subordinate clause is always in the subjunctive.
>   Ex: *Il faut **que** tu **sois** là à six heures.*
>   *Maintenant, il s'agit **que** vous **fassiez** très attention.*

(iii) The *que*-clause as a subject complement

The mood depends on the meaning of the subject.
>   Ex: *Mon avis est **que** vous **pouvez** mieux faire.*
>   *Mon souhait est **que** vous **puissiez** réussir.*

(iv) The *que*-clause as an adjective or a noun complement

The mood depends on the meaning of the adjective or noun.
>   Ex: *Je suis sûr **que** vous **réussirez**.*
>   *Je suis heureux **que** vous **ayez réussi**.*
>   *Il est essentiel **que** vous **réussissiez**.*
>   *L'idée **qu'il peut/puisse** encore nous nuire m'effraie.*

See chapter 12 Subjunctive, section 4.1.

(v) The *que*-clause as a subject

This is always at the beginning of the sentence and always in the subjunctive.
>   Ex: **Que** Nicolas **soit** de bonne foi n'est pas certain.*
>   'Que Nicolas soit de bonne foi' is the subject of '*est*'.

3.2.2   *Relative clauses*

These clauses are introduced by a relative pronoun. When the relative pronoun has an antecedent – which is the most common case – it represents this antecedent.

> Ex: *J'ai acheté le livre* **que** *Paul m'a recommandé.*

For details of the nature and functions of relative pronouns, see chapter 32 Relative Pronouns. For details of the use of the subjunctive in relative clauses, see chapter 12 Subjunctive, section 4.3.

3.2.2.1   THE RELATIVE PRONOUN AND ITS ANTECEDENT

(i)   Whenever possible, relative pronouns should come immediately after their antecedents to avoid ambiguity or clumsiness. This rule is not followed as strictly in English.

> Ex: *Nous avons aussi un certain nombre de problèmes avec le personnel.*
> *Ces problèmes ne sont pas faciles à résoudre.*
> → *Nous avons aussi avec le personnel un certain nombre de* **problèmes**
> **qui** *ne sont pas faciles à résoudre.*
> We also have a certain number of problems with the personnel which are not easy to solve.
> > is better than:
> *?Nous avons aussi un certain nombre de problèmes avec le* **personnel qui**
> *ne sont pas faciles à résoudre.*

Note that this example is clumsy rather than grammatically ambiguous.

(ii)   However, the relative pronoun can be separated from its antecedent in order to produce a stylistic effect.

> Ex: **Ces gens** *ne savaient toujours rien,* **qui** *retournaient maintenant chez eux.*

3.2.2.2   WORD ORDER

(i)   If the relative pronoun is the subject of the relative clause, the order is:
subject + verb + [complement]
> Ex: *Paul a acheté une voiture* **qui** + **tombe** *toujours en panne.*

(ii)   If the relative pronoun is a direct object and there is no other complement, there is a choice between:

– direct object + verb + subject
> Ex: *La voiture* **qu'** + **a achetée** + **Paul** *tombe toujours en panne.*

– direct object + subject + verb
> Ex: *La voiture* **que** + **Paul** + **a achetée** *tombe toujours en panne.*

Note that only the second construction is possible if the subject is a pronoun:
> → *La voiture* **qu'il a achetée** *...*

(iii)   If the relative pronoun is a direct object, and there is also an indirect object, the order is:

        direct object + subject + verb + indirect object

            Ex: *la voiture **que** + **Paul** + **a achetée** + **à son ami***

(iv)   If the relative pronoun is an indirect object itself and there is no other complement, there is a choice between:

    – indirect object + verb + subject

        Ex: *La personne **avec qui** + **discute** + **Paul** est un ami.*

    – indirect object + subject + verb

        Ex: *La personne **avec qui** + **Paul** + **discute** est un ami.*

The following example shows how the flexibility of this rule can be put to good use.

        Ex: *On nous a donné la liste de tous les avantages **dont jouissent** les employés rattachés au Service de la Documentation.*

            rather than:

        ⋆*. . . **dont** les employés rattachés . . .*

The long subject and the verb should be reversed here so that the sentence does not end abruptly on the verb.

(v)   If the relative pronoun is an indirect object and there is another indirect object, the order is:

        indirect object (rel. pron.) + subject + verb + indirect object

            Ex: *La personne **avec qui** + **Paul** + **parle** + **de voitures** est un ami.*

3.2.2.3   THE RELATIVE CLAUSE WITHOUT ANTECEDENT

When the relative pronoun has no antecedent, it refers to an undetermined referent. Constructions with *qui* refer to an animate referent, constructions with other relative pronouns refer to an inanimate referent.

(i)   The relative clause with no antecedent can be introduced by:

    – a simple relative pronoun:

        Ex: ***Qui** m'aime me suive.*

    – an indefinite relative pronoun:

        Ex: *J'en ferai part à **quiconque** s'y intéresse.*

    – a demonstrative + relative pronoun:

        Ex: ***Ceux qui** pensent cela ne sont pas mes amis.*

            ***Ce que** vous pensez ne me concerne pas.*

    – the indefinite pronoun *tel* + relative pronoun:

        Ex: ***Tel qui** rit vendredi dimanche pleurera* (proverb)

(ii)   Functions of the relative clause with no antecedent

    – subject:

        Ex: ***Ceux qui** pensent cela ne sont pas mes amis.*

            'ceux qui pensent cela' is the subject of 'sont'.

— complement of the subject:

> Ex: *Ces roses rouges sont **celles que je préfère**.*
> '*celles que je préfère*' is the complement of the subject '*Ces roses rouges*'.

— object:

> Ex: *Donnez **ce que vous pouvez**.*
> '*ce que vous pouvez*' is the object of the verb '*Donnez*'.

Note that the infinitive relative clause is always an object.

> Ex: *Je ne sais pas **quoi faire/à qui m'adresser**.*

— adverbial clause:

> Ex: ***Depuis ce que vous avez fait**, tout le monde a peur.*
> ***Sans ce que Pierre lui donne**, Marie n'y arriverait pas.*

3.2.2.4 FUNCTIONS OF RELATIVE CLAUSES WITH ANTECEDENT

(i) Attributive (*épithète*)

— attached:

> Ex: *Elle répète **toutes les histoires** | qu'on lui raconte.*
> antecedent of '*que*' — attribute of '*histoires*'
> — object of '*répète*'

— detached:

> Ex: *Lizzy, qui mange trop de souris, n'arrête pas d'être malade.*
> *Jean-Charles, que je connais depuis longtemps, s'est marié récemment.*

(ii) Object complement

This is normally found after verbs of perception (*voir, entendre*). (See section 2.12.)

> Ex: *Je vois **Paul** qui parle au jardinier.*
> '*qui parle au jardinier*' is the complement of the object '*Paul*'.
>
> *Je **le** vois qui parle au jardinier.*
> '*qui parle au jardinier*' is the complement of the object '*le*'.

(iii) Connective relative clause (*relative de liaison*)

This is always separated from its antecedent by a pause, hence it appears next to the main clause as if in juxtaposition.

> Ex: *Elle nous présenta son chat, qui ronronnait très fort.*
> → *Elle nous présenta son chat, il ronronnait très fort.*

3.2.3 Adverbial clauses (circonstancielles)

— There are seven main types of adverbial clauses, which are classified according to their meanings: time, cause, consequence, aim, hypothesis and condition, concession and opposition, comparison.
— They are introduced by conjunctions other than *que*.

– The mood in the subordinate (indicative or subjunctive) depends on the conjunction used.

        Ex: ***Quand** tu **rentreras**, je serai sortie.*

            ***Bien qu'**il **pleuve**, je sors quand même.*

NB: The subordination can be implicit (see section 3.2(iii) above).

        Ex: *Vous me le diriez, je ne vous croirais pas.*

            (= Si vous me le disiez . . .)

3 Pronunciation, spelling, registers, punctuation

1 Introduction

A phoneme is an abstract unit of sound ('the smallest distinctive unit of the language') which can be heard with a variety of pronunciations but which can be understood despite these variations. There are 36 phonemes in French (46 in standard English), represented by the signs of the International Phonetic Alphabet (IPA). A good dictionary will give the pronunciation of words using this alphabet, which is to be found in square brackets after the word concerned (e.g. *phonème* [fɔnɛm]).

There are three types of sound in French: vowels (*voyelles*), consonants (*consonnes*) and glides, also called semi-consonants (*semi-consonnes*) or semi-vowels (*semi-voyelles*).

Phonetic transcriptions are conventionally written in square brackets. In the tables below, the sounds to be learnt are on the left, followed by illustrative examples and their full transcriptions in the IPA.

2 Vowels

There are 16 vowels, divided into two categories: oral and nasal.

2.1 Oral vowels

[i] *petit* [pəti]; *maïs* [mais]
[y] *voulu* [vuly]; *(il a) eu* [y]
[u] *vous* [vu]; *goût* [gu]
[e] *été* [ete]; *chez* [ʃe]; *les* [le]
[ɛ] *lait* [lɛ], *belle* [bɛl]; *mais* [mɛ]
[ø] *peu* [pø]; *gazeux* [gazø]; *neutre* [nøtr]; *bœufs* [bø]; *jeûne* [ʒøn]
[œ] *beurre* [bœr], *peur* [pœr]; *bœuf* [bœf]; *jeune* [ʒœn]
[ə] *demi* [dəmi]; *je* [ʒə]
[o] *eau* [o]; *rose* [roz]; *mot* [mo]; *saule* [sol]; *(le) nôtre* [notr]
[ɔ] *pomme* [pɔm]; *bord* [bɔr]; *vogue* [vɔg]; *sol* [sɔl]; *notre* [nɔtr]
[a] *la* [la]; *là* [la]; *patte* [pat]; *chat* [ʃa]; *voie* [vwa]
[ɑ] *âtre* [ɑtr], *pâte* [pɑt], *phrase* [frɑz], *bas* [bɑ]

NB: The so-called '**mute e**' ('e' *muet*) is never stressed, except for emphasis. The way it is pronounced − [ə] − or its absence (see 7 below) is one of the characteristics of the French language.

2.2 Nasal vowels

(i) There are four nasal vowels in French:

[ɛ̃] *vin* [vɛ̃]; *main* [mɛ̃]
[ã] *blanc* [blã]; *dans* [dã]; *en* [ã]
[ɔ̃] *bon* [bɔ̃]; *pont* [pɔ̃]; *long* [lɔ̃]; *plomb* [plɔ̃]
[œ̃] *un* [œ̃]; *brun* [brœ̃]; *parfum* [parfœ̃]

Practise saying: '*un bon vin blanc*'! [œ̃bɔ̃vɛ̃blã]

NB: The distinction between [ɛ̃] and [œ̃] (e.g. *vin* and *brun*) is ignored by a lot of French speakers today, who tend to say [ɛ̃] for both sounds.

(ii) When the vowel is followed in writing by double '*n*' or double '*m*', it is not usually nasal.

Ex: *bon* [bɔ̃] but *bonne* [bɔn], *un pan* [pã] but *une panne* [pan]
ennemi [ɛnmi]; *emmenthal* [ɛmãtal]
immoral [imɔral]; *immobile* [imɔbil]

(See also cases when [ɔ̃] and [ã] are denazalised before a vowel or mute '*h*' in 5.1 below.)

However, there are exceptions.

Ex: *ennui* [ãnɥi]; *enneigement* [ãnɛʒmã]; *ennoblir* [ãnɔbliʀ]
emmagasiner [ãmagazine]; *emmêler* [ãmɛle]
emménager [ãmenaʒe]; *emmener* [ãmne]
immanquablement [ɛ̃mãkabləmã]

3 Consonants

3.1 16 or 19 consonants?

[p] *Paul* [pɔl]; *appel* [apɛl]
[b] *beau* [bo]; *abbé* [abe]
[t] *tenir* [tənir]; *théâtre* [teɑtr]; *attacher* [ataʃe]
[d] *danse* [dãs]; *addition* [adisjɔ̃]
[k] *coca* [kɔka]; *chaos* [kao]; *kilo* [kilo]; *quel* [kɛl]
[g] *gant* [gã], *Gustave* [gystav], *guérir* [gerir]; *aggraver* [agrave]
[f] *femme* [fam]; *physique* [fizik]
[v] *voir* [vwɑr]; *wagon* [vagɔ̃]
[s] *sous* [su], *assis* [asi], *ceci* [səsi]; *attention* [atãsjɔ̃]; *garçon* [garsɔ̃]
[z] *oiseau* [wazo] *zéro* [zero]; *deuxième* [døzjɛm]
[ʃ] *chat* [ʃa]; *acheter* [aʃte]
[ʒ] *je* [ʒə], *gèle* [ʒɛl], *girafe* [ʒiraf]; *Georges* [ʒɔrʒ]
[m] *pomme* [pɔm]; *Marie* [mari]
[n] *nez* [ne], *Nadine* [nadin]; *sonne* [sɔn]; *damné* [dane]
[l] *la* [la]; *ville* [vil]
[r] *rue* [ry]; *arrivé* [arive]

[ɲ]   *agneau* [aɲo]; *gagner* [gaɲe]; *campagne* [kɑ̃paɲ]
[ŋ]   *camping* [kɑ̃piŋ]

NB(1): French has in fact three 'r' sounds: [r], [ʀ] and [ʁ], which correspond to variant pronunciations of 'r' in French. For convenience, only [r] is used here. Hence, although French has 36 'phonemes', it may have more 'sounds'.

NB(2): – [ɲ] is often pronounced [nj]
          – the English [ŋ] is used for words borrowed from English.
          Ex: *le parking, le camping, le ring.*

3.2   'c' and 'g'

(i)   *c+i* or *c+e* is pronounced [s], whereas *c+a, c+o* or *c+u* is pronounced [k], hence *cicatrice* [sikatris].

(ii) *g+e* or *g+i* is pronounced [ʒ], whereas *g+a, g+o* or *g+u* is pronounced [g], hence *garage* [garaʒ].

See also 8.4 below on cedillas.

3.3   'h'

In French, 'h' is never pronounced in the way it can be pronounced in English.

– The so-called 'aspirated h' ('h' *aspiré*) is also called 'disjunctive h', since 'h' is no longer aspirated in modern French. This means that neither liaison nor elision can take place (see sections 5.2 and 6 below). A disjunctive 'h' is shown in phonetic transcriptions by an apostrophe.
    Ex: *la haine* [la'ɛn]; *hâtive* ['ativ].

– With a 'mute h', on the other hand, there can be a liaison or an elision. Compare:
    l'homme [lɔm]; *les hommes* [lezɔm]
    l'hôtel [lotɛl]; *les hôtels* [lezotɛl]
              and:
    le hibou [lə'iby]; *les hiboux* [le'iby]
    la hache [la'aʃ]; *les haches* [le'aʃ]

3.4   Glides

Glides are sounds which are near vowels, but they cannot be pronounced on their own, hence they are also called semi-vowels or even semi-consonants, and there are three of them in French:

[ɥ]   which is near [y], as in *puis* [pɥi], *nuit* [nɥi], *huit* [ɥit]
[w]   which is near [u], as in *oui* [wi], *loi* [lwa], *noix* [nwa]
[j]   which is near [i], as in *yoyo* [jojo], *rouiller* [ruje], *hier* [jer], *pied* [pje], *fille* [fij], *abeille* [abɛj]

4 The syllable

A syllable can be made up of only a vowel but it is generally the result of the association of a vowel with one or more consonants. It is therefore always the **vowel** which plays the central role in a syllable.

NB(1): The **oral** syllable does not always reproduce the **graphic** syllable, depending on the register (see 10 below) used by the speaker and/or the number of 'mute *e*' (see 7 below) pronounced. The graphic syllable is used for hyphenation and the oral syllable for poetry, song lyrics, etc.

NB(2): Orthographical apostrophes do not mark the end of a syllable: they are part of a syllable.
> Ex: *au/jour/d'hui; d'a/bord*

5 Linking (*enchainement*) and elision

5.1 Linking

Linking is the connecting of a **pronounced** final consonant to the initial vowel of the following word. It is an **oral** phenomenon.
> Ex: *cette île; sept îles* [sɛtil]
> *cinq ans* [sɛ̃kã]
> *notre arrivée* [nɔtrarive]
> *leur entrée* [lœrãtre]
> *un bel habit* [œ̃bɛlabi]
> *la grande armée* [lagrãdarme]

Linking is compulsory in French and, unlike liaison (see 6 below), does not entail any modification in the consonants pronounced.

Exception: the '*f*' of *neuf* is pronounced [v] in *neuf heures* [nœvœr] and *neuf ans* [nœvã] (both linking and liaison).

Note the linking with endings in *-rs*, *-rt* and *-rd*.
> Ex: *Ton chien **mord encore?*** [mɔrãkɔr]
> *Je **pars en** train.* [parã]
> *Elle l'a **toujours aimé.*** [tuʒurɛme]
> *Nous sommes **fort heureux.*** [fɔrørø]

Exception: personal pronouns after the verb, where there is a liaison.
> Ex: ***part-il?*** [partil]

5.2 Elision

The suppression of the final **written** vowel of grammatical words (e.g. determiners, pronouns, the conjunction *si*) before another word beginning with a vowel, semi-vowel or mute '*h*' is an elision. It is expressed in writing by an **apostrophe**, which is the **orthographical** mark of this elision. For instance:

(i)   Elision of the '*e*':

        *l'hôtel; l'ouest; je l'ai fait; **qu'**on me parle! **j'**aime, je **m'**habille,*
        *tu **t'**assieds, elle **s'**en va, **c'**est bien, il parle **d'**argent, je **n'**ai pas le temps,*
        *les cadeaux **qu'**ils nous ont offerts; jus**qu'**à demain, ce **qu'**on dit*

(ii)   Elision of the '*a*':

        l'orange; l'habileté; je l'ai faite; l'eau; l'oie

(iii) Note that there is no elision of *le, la, je, ce* after a verb.

        Ex: *Puis-je aller à la Mairie avec vous?*
        *Est-ce **un** accident?*
        Prends-le avec toi!

(iv)   If the word that follows begins with a consonant or a disjunctive '*h*', there is no elision.

        Ex: *le hibou, je me hâte, de la houille, ce que je veux,* etc.

(v)   Elision and the mute '*e*':

The rules above concern **orthographical** elision only. The rules for the non-pronunciation of the mute '*e*' still apply (see 7 below).

        Ex: *ce que je veux* [səkəʒəvø] or [skəʒəvø] or [səkəʒvø] or [skəʒvø]

(vi)   Elision of the '*i*':

The '*i*' of *si* is elided only before *il* or *ils*, but not before *elle* or *elles*.

        Ex: *s'il vient, s'ils viennent, s'il vous plaît*
        but: *si elle vient, si elles viennent*

(vii) Generally, there is no elision before:

– *un* and *onze*: *le (chiffre) un, le onze, la onzième heure*
– *le oui* (following the model of *le non*)
– names of letters: *le a, le o, le u, le h, le y,* etc.
– certain words beginning with '*y*'

        Ex: *le yacht, le yoga, la Yougoslavie, le Yémen*
        but: *l'Yonne, le duc d'York*

6 Liaison

A liaison means the pronunciation of a syllable made up of the final **mute** consonant of a word and the initial vowel of the following word. Compare:

        les [le] and *les orages* [lezɔraʒ]
        sont [sɔ̃] and *sont-ils* [sɔ̃til]

6.1 Phonetic modifications

Unlike with linking, a consonant can change its nature in a liaison:

- the letters '*s*' and '*x*' are pronounced [z]
  > Ex: *six œufs* [sizø]; *dix hommes* [dizɔm]
  > *les œufs* [lezø]; *les hommes* [lezɔm]

- '*d*' is pronounced [t]
  > Ex: *un grand arbre* [grɑ̃tarbr]
  > *Prend-il du sucre?* [prɑ̃til]

- '*f*' is pronounced [v]
  > Ex: *neuf heures* [nœvœr]; *neuf ans* [nœvɑ̃]

- the nasal vowel [ɛ̃] loses its nasality. Thus adjectives in *-ain*, *-ein* or *-en* are pronounced as if they were feminine.
  > Ex: *lointain* [lwɛ̃tɛ̃]   but *un lointain ami* [lwɛ̃tɛnami]
  > *plein* [plɛ̃]   but *un plein arrosoir* [plɛnarɔzwɑr]
  > *moyen* [mwajɛ̃]   but *le Moyen Age* [mwajɛnaʒ]

However, [ɔ̃] tends to keep its nasality.
  > Ex: *ton* [tɔ̃] and *ton ami* [tɔ̃nami] rather than [tɔnami]
  > *bon* [bɔ̃] and *un bon hôtel* [bɔ̃notɛl] rather than [bɔnotɛl]
  > *on* [ɔ̃] and *on y va* [ɔ̃niva] rather than [ɔniva]

Exceptions: *le bonheur* [bɔnœr]; *un bonhomme* [bɔnɔm]

The following words also keep their nasality: *un, aucun; en; rien, bien, combien.*
  > Ex: *un orage* [œ̃nɔraʒ], *en avance* [ɑ̃navɑ̃s], *bien audacieux* [bjɛ̃nodasjø]

6.2 Liaison and usage

(i) Current usage

Current usage employs a liaison:

- between the determiner and the noun:
  > Ex: *mes amis* [mezami]
  > *les animaux* [lezanimo]

- between the subject pronoun and the verb, and the verb and pronoun in the case of an inversion:
  > Ex: *Ils ont réussi* [ilzɔ̃]; *Ont-ils réussi?* [ɔ̃til]
  > *Ils étaient en retard* [ilzetɛ]; *Etaient-ils en retard?* [etɛtil]

- between the verb *être* and the subject complement (or the auxiliary *être* and past participle):
  > Ex: *Il est enseignant* [ɛtɑ̃sɛɲɑ̃].
  > *Mes amis sont arrivés* [sɔ̃tarive].

- between the adjective and the noun:
  > Ex: *un petit homme* [pətitɔm]
  > *un savant Italien* [savɑ̃titaljɛ̃] (a learned Italian)

However, there is no liaison between noun + adjective. Hence:
  > *un savant Italien* [savɑ̃italjɛ̃] (an Italian scholar)

(ii)   Liaison and registers

Liaison is optional in all other cases. However:

— the more formal the register (see 10 below), the more frequent the liaisons.
Hence:

> *Pouvez-vous y aller?*
> [puvevuziale]   or: [puvevuiale]

— inappropriate liaisons can be a source of humour:
> Ex: *Allons au zoo!* [alɔ̃zozo] (*Allons, Zozo!*)

— there is no liaison after the conjunction of coordination *et*, even if it implies a
hiatus (see 6.3 below):
> Ex: *Elle est triste et aigrie.* [ɛlɛtristeegri]

6.3   Hiatus

— A hiatus is the juxtaposition of two vowel sounds, the first one at the end of a
syllable, the second at the beginning of the next.
> Ex: *Ils ont mangé et bu.*
> *Il va à Paris.*
> *Elle a à apprendre.*

— Hiatuses are avoided as much as possible in French because they sound
awkward. Hence a consonant is sometimes added (see individual chapters for
details).
> Ex: *Ira-t-elle?*
> *Mange-t-il?*
> *Vas-y!*

7   The 'mute *e*'

At the end or in the middle of a word, '*e*' without an accent is called 'mute *e*'
('*e*' *muet, instable* or *caduc*). It is not normally pronounced (except in the South
of France) unlike the preceding consonant which is. The round brackets used
below show that [ə] may or may not be heard.
> Ex: *je pense* [pãs]; *une porte* [pɔrt]; *lentement* [lãt(ə)mã]
> Compare with: *un port* [pɔr]

NB: *-es* is also mute in verbs and plural of nouns, adjectives, etc.
> Ex: *tu penses* [pãs]; *des portes* [pɔrt]
> Compare with: *des ports* [pɔr]

-ent is mute when it is the plural ending of a conjugated verb.
> Ex: *ils pensent* [pãs]

But: *souvent* [suvã]; *vraiment* [vrɛmã]; *un agent* [aʒã]

Think of: *Les poules du couvent couvent.* [lepuldykuvãkuv]
> The hens at the convent are brooding.

(i) **Current usages**

– The mute '*e*' inside a word is pronounced when it is preceded by two consonants and followed by one.

> Ex: *aimablement* [ɛmabləmɑ̃]
> *mercredi* [mɛrkrədi]
> *probablement* [prɔbabləmɑ̃]; *vendredi* [vɑ̃drədi]; *prenez* [prəne]

– In other configurations, the internal mute '*e*' is not normally pronounced (but see also (ii) below).

> Ex: *le petit chat* [ləpətiʃa] or [ləptiʃa] or [lpətiʃa]
> *normalement* [nɔrmal(ə)mɑ̃]
> *samedi* [sam(ə)di]

– Hence the number of **graphic syllables** does not always correspond to the number of **oral syllables**.

> Ex: *acheter sans se tromper* (*a/che/ter/sans/se/trom/per*)
> [aʃ-te-sɑ̃s-trɔ̃pe]

This phrase has seven graphic syllables and only five oral syllables as the mute '*e*', at least in standard French, is not pronounced in *acheter* and *se* in this particular configuration.

(ii) **Regional accents; formal registers**

– In the south of France, the mute '*e*' is generally pronounced.

> Ex: *Qu'est-ce que vous voulez faire?* [kɛsəkəvuvulefɛr]

– In formal registers (e.g. formal speeches, reading aloud, classical theatre, poetry), the pronunciation of mute '*e*' is frequent, which entails liaisons which do not occur in current usage.

> Ex: *Ils rampent, flagellés par les bises͜ iniques,*
> *Frémissant͜ au fracas roulant des omnibus,*
> *Et serrant sur leur flanc, ainsi que des reliques,*
> *Un petit sac brodé de fleurs͜ ou de rébus . . .*

> Charles Baudelaire, *Tableaux parisiens*

8 Accented letters, cedillas and diaereses

In written French, accents, cedillas and diaereses either give an indication of pronunciation or they are a distinguishing mark. Hence the temptation to add them at random in a prose or essay – on the grounds that they make the piece look more French – should be strongly resisted! It is better to check their presence or absence in a dictionary and it is best to learn every word with (or without) its accent(s) as an integral part of the spelling.

> Ex: *la religion* [rəliʒjɔ̃] but *représenter* [rəprezɛte]

Note that accents are frequently omitted over capital letters.

> Ex: *en Egypte*
> *A ce soir!*

Regardless of spelling, the phonetic distinctions between [e] and [ɛ], [o] and [ɔ], [a] and [ɑ] may be blurred by native speakers, depending on regional accents and/or registers. What follows is the pronunciation of standard French.

8.1 Acute accent: the sound [e]

An acute accent over an '*e*' indicates that '*é*' is pronounced [e].
> Ex: *évident*; *le passé composé*; *une clé*, *une poignée*, *etc.*

Exception: the '*é*' of *crémerie* is pronounced [ɛ].

8.2 Grave accent: the sound [ɛ]

(i) A grave accent over '*e*' indicates that '*è*' is pronounced [ɛ]. Note that there is no consonant after the '*è*' in the same graphic syllable.
> Ex: *pè/re*, *mè/re*, *frè/re*, *Sè/te*, *mè/tre*, *j'a/chè/te*, *en/lè/ve/ment*

(ii) In the following types of word, '*e*' without an accent is also pronounced [ɛ]:

– when the '*e*' is followed by an '*x*':
> Ex: *exemple*, *lexique*, *flexible*, *exorcisme*, *réflexion*, *exclusif*, *exception*, *exécrable*

– when the '*e*' is followed by a double consonant (it forms a graphic syllable with the first one):
> Ex: *un ef/fort*, *de l'es/sence*, *la ter/re*, *je jet/te*

NB: It could be argued that *effort* and *essence* begin with the sound [e], not [ɛ]. However, there is still no accent.

– when the '*e*' is followed by a consonant and forms a syllable with it (compare with (i) above):
> Ex: *per/mis*, *ber/ceau*, *es/pé/rer*, *per/cep/tion*, *es/prit*, *ec/zé/ma*

(iii) A grave accent over '*a*' or '*u*' is a distinguishing mark and does not affect the pronunciation.
> Ex: the preposition *à* and the auxiliary *a*
> the adverb *là* and the definite article *la*
> the adverb *où* and the conjunction *ou*
> the adverb *çà* and the demonstrative pronoun *ça*

8.3 Circumflex accent

(i) A circumflex accent on '*e*' indicates that '*ê*' is pronounced [ɛ].
> Ex: *une bête*; *la tête*; *la forêt*; *la fenêtre*

Exceptions: *le poêle* [pwɑl] (stove); *la poêle* [pwɑl] (frying-pan)

(ii) A circumflex accent on '*o*' generally indicates that '*ô*' is pronounced [o].
> Ex: *un pôle* [pol]; *un hôte* [ot]; *une côte* [kot]; *tôt* [to]

Exceptions: *un hôtel* [ɔ(o)tɛl]; *un hôpital* [ɔpital]

With no circumflex accent, '*o*' is generally pronounced [ɔ].
> Ex: *une pomme* [pɔm]; *une hotte* [ɔt]

Exceptions: *une zone* [zon], *un clone* [klon], *un atome* [atom]

(iii) A circumflex accent on 'a' generally indicates that 'â' is pronounced [ɑ].

>   Ex: *de la pâte* [pɑt]; *un âne* [ɑn], *à la hâte* ['ɑt], *bâtir* [bɑtir], *une tâche* [tɑʃ];
>   *le hâle* ['ɑl]

Exceptions: *de la pâtisserie* [patisri], *un château* [ʃato]

With no circumflex accent, 'a' is generally pronounced [a], though not always.

>   Ex: *une patte* [pat], *une tache* [taʃ]; *une halle* [al]; *une panne* [pan]; *une rame*
>   [ram]; *une lame* [lam]; *une bague* [bag]; *une marmite* [marmit]
>   but: *un tas* [tɑ], *las* [lɑ], *bas* [bɑ]; *rase* [rɑz], *gaz* [gɑz], *phrase* [frɑz]

(iv) A circumflex accent can be found on any other vowel, including the 'i' of 'ai', 'ei' or 'oi', and the 'u' of 'eu' or 'ou'.

>   Ex: *une île; un abîme*
>   *une flûte*
>   *un maître; il paraît*
>   *une boîte; un goître*
>   *qu'il eût*
>   *le goût; la moûture*

In those cases, the circumflex accent does not affect pronunciation. It can either indicate a contraction from an earlier spelling (e.g. *goût* from the Latin *gustus*), or it is used as a distinguishing mark in the spelling of words (as in 8.2(iii) above), or to distinguish between tenses. Compare:

>   **crû** (past participle of *croître*) and
>   **cru** (past participle of *croire*)
>
>   **dû** (past participle of *devoir*) and
>   **du** (partitive article)
>
>   **eût** (imperfect subjunctive of *avoir*) and
>   **eut** (past historic of *avoir*)

8.4 Cedillas

A cedilla (*cédille*) is placed under a 'c' and before 'a', 'o' and 'u' in order to obtain the sound [s].

>   Ex: *il lança, une leçon, ça et là, un reçu*

Hence none is needed before 'e' or 'i'.

>   Ex: **ceci; merci; cette; macérer; France**

Compare with:

>   **connaître, Carcassonne, le vécu**

where 'c' is pronounced [k].

The cedilla plays the same role as 'e' placed after 'g' to obtain the sound [ʒ].

>   Ex: *nous mangeons* [mãʒɔ̃], *une gageure* [gaʒyr], **Georges** [ʒɔrʒ]

Hence no 'e' is needed before 'e' or 'i' to obtain [ʒ]

>   Ex: **gérer, une girafe**

Compare with:

>   *une **ga**rgotte* [gargɔt], *une **gou**tte* [gut], **Gustave** [gystav]

If a [g] sound is needed before 'e' or 'i', a 'u' must be inserted between the 'g' and the 'e' or 'i'.

> Ex: *narguer; une guitare; St-Guénolé*

Note the pronunciation of *linguiste* [lɛ̃gɥist]
See appendix 1 about latest proposals for changes.

8.5   Diaereses

(i)   A diaeresis (*tréma*) over an 'e' or an 'i' indicates that the vowel is pronounced separately from the preceding vowel: i.e. the two vowels are pronounced in two syllables.

> Ex: *ha/ïr* ['aiʀ]; *No/ël* [nɔɛl]; *Mo/ïse* [mɔiz]; *une héro/ïne* [eʀɔin]; *ambigu/ïté* [ãbigɥite]
>
> But: *je hais* [ɛ]; *de la moelle* [mwal]; *un moine* [mwan]; *Guignol* [giɲɔl]

(ii)   If there are three vowels, the diaeresis is placed on the last vowel.

> Ex: *ouïr* [wir] : *j'ai ouï dire* [ʒewidir]

(iii) Adjectives in *-gu* add a diaeresis on the final 'e' of the feminine so that the 'u' is pronounced [y].

> Ex: *une pièce exiguë* [ɛgzigy]; *une note aiguë* [ɛgy]; *la ciguë* [sigy]; *contiguë* [kõtigy]

8.6   Sound-based stylistic devices

The following figures of literary style are of interest in that they demonstrate the use of oral phenomena in the written text. It is therefore necessary to recite the texts in order to produce the desired effect.

8.6.1   Assonance

Assonance (derived from the Latin *sonare* – 'to sound') is the euphonic effect obtained when several identical or similar vowel sounds appear in the same phrase or clause.

> Ex: *métro, boulot, dodo*
> *les longs sanglots des violons*

Assonance can be used as a source of humour.

> Ex: *Ce que nous oyons, l'oie l'oit-elle?*
> [. . .]
> *Et qu'a ouï l'ouïe de l'oie de Louis?*
> *Elle a ouï ce que toute oie oit . . .*

> Raymond Devos, *Ouï-dire, a plus d'un titre*

8.6.2   Alliteration

Alliteration (derived from the Latin *littera* – 'letter') is the effect obtained when several identical or similar consonants appear in the same phrase or clause.

Ex: *Pour qui sont ces serpents qui sifflent sur vos têtes . . .*

Jean Racine, *Andromaque*

' "*La mort est au bout. Je revois sa griffe grise, sur le visage de Georges Pompidou . . ." Il répétait "griffe grise" en savourant l'allitération.*'

Bertrand Poirot-Delpech, *Le Monde*, 1996

9 Word and sentence stress

9.1 Word stress

In French, the stress falls on the final syllable of an isolated word regardless of how many syllables it may contain.

Ex: (stressed syllables are shown in bold)
*gar**çon***
*portu**gais***
*indivi**duel***
*anticonstitutionelle**ment***

However, if the final syllable of a word ends in a mute 'e', the stress then falls on the penultimate syllable.

Ex: *li**vre***
*pe**ti**te*
*magni**fi**que*

In a short phrase, the stress falls on the final syllable of the final word.

Ex: *man**teau*** → *un manteau **gris***

In English, however, word stress can fall on different syllables. This sometimes indicates a different meaning. Compare:

record (noun) and re**cord** (verb)
contrast (noun) and con**trast** (verb)

9.2 Sentence stress

Sentence stress (or 'syntactic stress') is placed on a whole word or words within a sentence. In the case of a single-word exclamation or interjection, it can be placed on any syllable. The speaker can use it:
– to place emphasis on a desired word or words
– to contrast or oppose two or more words ('contrastive stress')
– to distinguish between semantic differences
The various uses of sentence stress contribute to a more refined production and interpretation of an utterance.

Ex: *Ma**gni**fique!*
*Cet exercice est **infaisable**, vous savez.*
*Je n'ai pas dit **tentacule**, j'ai dit **denticule**!*

Compare:

> **Mon** *frère revient du Brésil.* (i.e. – not **your** brother)
> *Mon* **frère** *revient du Brésil.* (i.e. – not my **sister**)
> *Mon frère* **revient** *du Brésil.* (i.e. – not **going** there)
> *Mon frère revient du* **Brésil.** (i.e. – not from **Ecuador**)

10 Registers

The distinction between formal and informal registers is not an easy one to define. Indeed, a term may be tagged as 'familiar' in one dictionary and 'popular' in another or have one asterisk in one and three in another. Register varies according to many factors, including how comfortable people feel in the presence of one another. Register may shift as a conversation progresses. Finally, the higher the linguistic awareness, the more likely we are to encounter 'mixed' registers. For instance, many linguists love to manipulate perfect syntax and 'gutter' vocabulary. In other words, nobody ever 'speaks informally' all the time, or uses systematically all the features that come under the label 'informal'. We can also witness this mixing of levels in the media and the world of advertising, where dislocated constructions join hands with subjunctive imperfects. As Françoise Gadet (author of *Le français ordinaire* and *Le français populaire*) often points out, '*On pardonnera plus facilement à un étranger de ne pas connaître une expression familière que de faire une gaffe.*' Students are therefore advised to keep to **formal** French, in their written and oral examinations, as well as in any professional contacts they may have in French-speaking countries.

11 Different types of spoken French

11.1 Authentic language

'Authentic' spoken French is that of spontaneous conversation between Francophones. Genuine spoken French has its own specific syntax: repetitions and discontinuities are characteristics of this.

However, authentic spoken French is governed by specific rules and constraints which concern all elements of language, namely:
- phonetic considerations: linking and liaisons, accents and relaxed pronunciation, etc.
- morphosyntactical considerations: the use of moods and tenses, the modalities of the sentence (statement, question, command, exclamation), comment clauses, interjections, incomplete sentences, presentative forms, repetition, ellipsis, etc.
- lexical considerations: all the various registers, specific vocabulary, etc.

11.2 Oratorical language

'Oratorical' French is non-spontaneous or prepared speech. It is used in speeches and public readings. This type of spoken French presents several aspects which depend on the degree of spontaneity.

– With a fair amount of spontaneity: this is the speech of lecturers from notes which they develop, radio or TV interviewees, or participants in a public debate. (This is the type of spoken language which **students should emulate for the purposes of oral examinations**.)

– With less spontaneity: this is the speech of actors who deliver memorized lines, the journalists or presenters who read a paper or autocue in front of a microphone or camera, or public speakers who read from a script while trying not to make it sound as if it were literally 'read'.

– With no spontaneity at all: this is the written rhetorical speech which is 'performed' with all the nuances of oratorical art (e.g. Malraux's speeches).

All these forms of spoken French owe far more to the written form of the language than to the 'authentic' spoken form. We could say that this is the 'oralization' of the written form.

11.3 Fictional dialogue

Fictional dialogue is the speech which is attributed to characters in a novel (which entails all the variations of reported speech – see chapter 41 Reported Speech) or in a dramatic work, or the speech of the narrator in a first-person narrative work.

12 Punctuation

Punctuation is the system of signs used in writing to clarify the structure of text. Note that many writers (particularly poets) manipulate the rules of punctuation to artistic ends. Note also that French punctuation is **not always** the same as in English and that it is the use of the colon in French which differs most from English usage – closely followed by commas.

The main punctuation marks are:

. the full stop (*le point*)

This marks an important pause at the end of a declarative sentence (including incomplete sentences). See also question mark and exclamation mark.

> Ex: *Paul s'éloigna. Soudain, il fit demi-tour. Bizarre.*

, the comma (*la virgule*)

It marks a short pause:
– to separate items in a list (see chapter 40 Coordination and Juxtaposition).

> Ex: *Le chat, la belette et le petit lapin sont arrivés ensemble.*
> *Adieu veau, vache, cochon, couvée.*

– exceptionally before *et*, when *et* coordinates two unrelated items in the sentence or two unrelated sentences or parts of sentences.

> Ex: *Les femmes sont les premières victimes de licenciements, et peu d'efforts sont faits pour leur remise au travail.*

– to detach a word or group of words, including an adverb phrase (particularly at the beginning or in the middle of the sentence), a noun/noun group, an adjective or relative clause in apposition or a reporting clause (see chapter 2 Syntax).

> Ex: *Pour aborder le problème wallon, j'ai donc choisi un Wallon qui nous a fait part de ses opinions et de ses états d'âme en la matière.*
> *'J'ai gagné!', a crié Sylvain.*

NB: Items such as indirect objects, subject complements or adverb phrases which appear in first position in the sentence followed by a **subject–verb inversion for stylistic purposes**, should not be confused with adverb phrases in apposition: the former are **not** isolated by commas.

> Ex: *Au travail professionnel s'ajoute le travail ménager.*
> *Par la porte entr'ouverte entraient des senteurs d'herbe fraîchement coupée . . .*

: the colon (*les deux points*)

The colon establishes a semantic relation between what precedes and what follows. This relation can be:

– the introduction of a list of examples:

> Ex: *Tout le monde était là: Paul, Catherine, Anne-Marie et Françoise.*

– a relation of cause or consequence:

> Ex: *Mets un manteau: le temps s'est refroidi.*

– the introduction of direct reported speech:

> Ex: *Il a dit: 'Ce sera prêt ce soir.'*

– an explanation or development:

> Ex: *En 1972, la première journée nationale de la femme à Bruxelles récolte un succès inattendu: on dénombre dix à douze mille participantes, parmi lesquelles . . .*

; the semi-colon (*le point-virgule*)

This is a medium pause, a briefer pause than a full stop but longer than a comma. Unlike the full stop, it is internal to the sentence.

> Ex: *'A midi, Charles rentrait; ensuite il sortait; puis elle prenait un bouillon . . .'*

> Gustave Flaubert, *Madame Bovary*

? the question mark (*le point d'interrogation*)

This marks an important pause at the end of an interrogative sentence, including incomplete sentences.

> Ex: *Quand venez-vous?*
> *Lui ici?*

! the exclamation mark (*le point d'exclamation*)

This marks an important pause at the end of an exclamative sentence (including incomplete sentences) and also often the end of an imperative sentence.

> Ex: *Que vous êtes beau et que vous sentez bon!*
> *Paul!*
> *Allez-y!*

. . . suspension marks (*les points de suspension*)

- They indicate that the sentence is unfinished or has been interrupted.
  > Ex: *Mais qu'est-ce qu'il me . . .*
- Between parentheses or square brackets, they indicate that part of a quotation has been omitted.
  > Ex: *'Il a dit qu'il prendrait le train à 9 heures (. . .) et qu'il serait là à 10 heures.'*
- Finally, they can mark the emphatic prolongation of a complete sentence or clause.
  > Ex: *'Et je trouve une dame qui se confesse, mon rêve qui s'écroule, une horreur sans nom . . .'*

> Jean Cocteau, *Les parents terribles*

NB: Suspension marks should not be added after 'etc.', which already indicates a continuation (*et cetera* = 'and other things').

( ) brackets (*les parenthèses*)

They enclose a portion of a sentence which is not indispensable for its structure, such as comment clauses. Thus they imitate speech.

> Ex: *Ce repas (et vous serez bien d'accord) n'était pas très bon.*

Their use is similar to that of dashes.

– the dash (*le tiret de séparation*)

- dashes can be used in the same way as brackets, to introduce a comment clause:
  > Ex: *Mon chat – celui que vous avez vu hier – a encore attrapé une souris.*
- they can indicate the interlocutors in direct speech:
  > Ex: *– Que désirez-vous?*
  > *– Je voudrais . . .*

' ' quotation marks (*les guillemets*)

- They enclose the words of direct reported speech.
  > Ex: *Paul a dit: 'Ce sera prêt pour ce soir.'*
  > *La première chambre civile du tribunal de Nanterre avait jugé que 'le syndicat professionnel FN-RATP privilégie l'action politique'.*

> *Le Monde*, 29 June 1996

- They identify a phrase which has the value of a proper noun, when capitals are insufficient or inappropriate.
  > Ex: *Cette grève donne lieu à la création du comité 'A travail égal, salaire égal', qui s'occupera de l'égalité professionnelle.*

– They indicate that the writer wants to dissociate him/herself from what is being reported.

>   Ex: *A Tours, la polémique porte sur des 'subventions' qu'auraient accordées le conseil général d'Indre-et-Loire et le conseil municipal de Tours.*

>   *Le Monde*, 29 June 1996

See also chapter 41 Reported Speech, section 2.

- the **hyphen** (*le trait d'union*)

It is used:

– in the interrogative form (verb–subject pronoun inversion) and in injunctions (imperative).

>   Ex: *Irez-vous chez les Dupont ce soir?*
>   *Que se passe-t-il?*
>   *Dépêchez-vous!*
>   *Donnez-moi ça!*

See chapters 14 Imperative and 39 Interrogative Structures.

– in compound demonstrative adjectives and pronouns.

>   Ex: *cette pièce-ci; celle-là*

See chapters 25 Demonstrative Adjectives and 34 Demonstrative Pronouns.

– to link a stressed pronoun and the indefinite adjective *même*.

>   Ex: *moi-même, toi-même, eux-mêmes*, etc.

See chapter 31 Personal Pronouns, section 3.2.1.

– in compound numerals (see chapter 37 Numbers).

>   Ex: *quarante-deux*

– in a number of other compound words.

>   Ex: noun: *la Nouvelle-Zélande, un wagon-lit*
>   pronoun: *quelques-uns*
>   adverb: *peut-être, là-bas*

2 Verbs

4 Introduction to verbs

Le passé n'est jamais simple,
le présent seulement indicatif
et le futur toujours conditionnel

1 Definition

According to the traditional definition, verbs express actions (e.g. *marcher*), states (e.g. *être*) or transformations (e.g. *jaunir*). That which is expressed or referred to by a verb when it is used in discourse, is called a **process**.

2 Lexical meaning and actualization

2.1 Lexical meaning

A verb has a lexical meaning, i.e. the meaning that can be found in a dictionary. This meaning is its **virtual referent**. The **actual referent** of the verb is given when it is used in discourse. This is called the **actualization** of the verb and affects all parts of speech to various degrees.

2.2 Actualization

(i) The processes expressed for instance by the actualizations of the verb *marcher* include information about the time (e.g. present, past), as well as other information (e.g. who or what is carrying out the process).

> Ex: *je marche; nous avons marché; marchez!*
> I am walking; we have been walking; walk!

(ii) The actualization of the verb is made possible thanks to the various forms of the conjugation.
Consider for instance the verb *marcher*:
– lexical meaning: *se déplacer avec ses jambes ou ses pattes*
– possible actualizations:

> – *Je marche tous les dimanches.*
> I walk/go walking every Sunday.
> – *Elle a marché toute la journée.*
> She has been walking all day.
> – *Il faudrait que nous marchions plus vite.*
> We should walk faster.

showing who carries out the process, when, whether it is over or still in progress, etc.

3 Semantic constraints

For instance, the verb *chanter* demands an **animate subject** noun (human or non-human).

> Ex: *Catherine chante à la chorale de la paroisse.*
> *Le rossignol chante la nuit.*

Ignoring this constraint leads to:
– metaphorical uses of the verb:

> Ex: *Le vent chantait dans les branchages.*

– nonsense (or poetic licence):

> Ex: ?*La table chante dans la cuisine.*

The constraint can equally apply to the object of the verb. For instance, *avaler* demands an **animate subject** and an **edible object**. Compare:

> *Catherine a avalé son café.*
> *Michel a dû avaler ses mots.*
> ?*L'herbe a avalé l'oiseau.*
> ?*Le chat a avalé la planche à pain.*

Knowledge of these constraints can be important when translating from one language to the other.

> Consider the following examples of the use of the English verb 'to agree', and its translations into French:
>
> > On this point I **agree with** Paul, not with you.
> > *Sur ce point je **suis d'accord avec** Paul, pas avec vous.*
> >
> > The adjective **agrees** in gender and number **with** the noun.
> > *L'adjectif **s'accorde** en genre et en nombre **avec** le nom.*

être d'accord avec demands animate subjects and objects. Hence:

> ★*L'adjectif est d'accord avec le nom.*

has the effect of personifying both the adjective and the noun. It could suggest for instance that there has been an argument and the adjective has come to an agreement with the noun!

4 Categories of conjugation

The set of forms that a verb can take is called its conjugation.

4.1 Person

The subject dictates the **person marker** of the verb. In French, there are three persons singular and three persons plural, as shown in the following list of person subjects:

	singular	plural
1st person	*je* I	*nous* we
2nd person	*tu* you/thou	*vous* you
3rd person	*il/elle* he/she/it	*ils/elles* they

Note that there are two forms of saying 'you' in French, where no such distinction operates in modern English. See chapter 31 Personal Pronouns, section 2.1.2(iii).

The verb normally agrees in number with the person subject and, in the case of compound tenses, the past participle may also agree in gender. See chapter 9 Perfect, section 3.

The person expresses the corresponding relation between the speaker and what is being said. However, there are two main exceptions:
– in the imperative mood, it is the **form of the verb** which indicates the person(s) addressed by the speaker, namely 1st person plural and 2nd person singular and plural only. See chapter 14 Imperative.

– impersonal verbs and verbs in non-personal moods (see below) are not affected by the category of the person, except for pronominal verbs.

4.2   Mood

Modalization is the process by which speakers convey their attitudes towards what they say to their interlocutors. There are six moods in French, which convey different shades of meaning.

– four personal or 'finite' moods:
  – indicative   (*indicatif*)
  – subjunctive   (*subjonctif*)
  – conditional   (*conditionnel*)
  – imperative   (*impératif*)

– two non-personal or 'non-finite' moods:
  – infinitive, or nominal form of the verb (*infinitif*)
  – participle, or adjectival form of the verb:
    – present participle (*participe présent*) and gerund (*gérondif*)
    – past participle (*participe passé*)

NB: The conditional mood is also considered as a **tense of the indicative**. See chapter 13 Conditional, section 3.

(i)   **Personal moods** (*modes personnels*): all or part of the six persons of the conjugation can be used, namely six persons with the indicative, subjunctive and the conditional, and three persons with the imperative.

(ii) **Non-personal moods** (*modes non personnels*): there is no distinction between the various persons of the conjugation (except for pronominal verbs). They are the infinitive and the participles (present participle and gerund, and past participle).

(iii) Actualization: certain moods contribute to the actualization of the verb insofar as they can give an indication of the temporal and aspectual, as well as the modal values of the verb.

– In the indicative mood, the degree of actualization is highest. It shows:
  – tense:
    Ex: *Je mange.* (present)
      I am eating.
  – aspect:
    Ex: *Il a éteint la lumière.* (accomplished)
      He has switched off the light.
  – modal values:
    Ex: *Et s'il ne venait pas?* (supposition)
      What if he wasn't coming?

– In the subjunctive and imperative moods, the degree of actualization depends on several constraints (see chapters 12 Subjunctive and 14 Imperative).
    Ex: *Viens dimanche!* (order/invitation)
      Come on Sunday!

    Je voudrais qu'il vienne dimanche. (wish)
      I would like him to come on Sunday.

– In the infinitive mood, there is no actualization. For instance, the infinitives *chanter*, *manger* and *marcher* give no indication of the tense, aspect or modal values.
See also chapter 21 Modals.

4.3 Tense

Each mood can be expressed in various tenses. Thus we have grammatical tenses of the conjugation such as the 'present indicative', the 'imperfect subjunctive', etc.

4.3.1 French system

The following refer to the French tense system, as referred to in this book.

(i) The indicative has a full range of tenses:
– simple:
  – present   (*présent*)
  – future   (*futur*)
  – imperfect   (*imparfait*)
  – past historic   (*passé simple*)
– compound:
  – future perfect   (*futur antérieur*)
  – perfect   (*passé composé*, or *indéfini*)
  – pluperfect   (*plus-que-parfait*)
  – past anterior   (*passé antérieur*)
  – double compound past   (*passé surcomposé*)

(ii)   Subjunctive
  - present
  - imperfect
  - perfect
  - pluperfect

(iii)   Conditional
  - present
  - perfect   (*passé 1e forme*)
  - pluperfect   (*passé 2e forme*)

(iv)   Imperative
  - present
  - perfect (rare)

(v)   Infinitive
  - present
  - past

(vi)   Participles
  - present and perfect
  - past participle

However:
- Tenses do not express solely temporal values, but also aspectual and modal ones.

- The meaning of a tense can vary. For instance, the 'present tense' can express a 'future'.
    Ex: *Je pars demain.*

- The expression of time is not confined exclusively to verbs. For instance, an adjective or a prefix can also situate the referent of the noun in relation to the moment of speaking.
    Ex: *un **ancien** président*
        *l'**ex**-PDG de chez Renault*
        *l'**actuel** premier ministre*
        *le **futur** pape*

4.3.2   English system

As a reminder, here is a summary of the English tense system as referred to in this book:

present	I do
present continuous	I am doing
past simple	I did
past continuous	I was doing
present perfect	I have done
present perfect continuous	I have been doing

past perfect	I had done
past perfect continuous	I had been doing
future simple	I will/shall do
future continuous	I will/shall be doing
future perfect	I will have done
future perfect continuous	I will have been doing

4.4 Defective verbs (*verbes défectifs*)

These are verbs which are not used with all the persons, all the tenses or all the moods. For instance:

– *faillir* (to fail) and *faillir faire qch* (to almost do sth) can only be used in the past historic and compound tenses

>   Ex: *Il **faillit** manquer son train.*
>   He nearly missed his train.
>
>   *J'ai **failli** à ma tâche.*
>   I failed in my task.

– *promouvoir* (to promote) is mainly used in the passive or the infinitive (with *falloir, vouloir*, etc.)

>   Ex: *Elle **a été promue** chef de section.*
>   She has been/was promoted to Head of Department.
>
>   *Il **faut promouvoir** ce produit.*
>   We must promote this product.

– weather verbs: normally used with impersonal *il* only

>   Ex: *Il pleut; il neige.*
>   It is raining; it is snowing.

5 Aspect

Aspect expresses the way a process is realized. In French, it is not a category which is clearly defined by characteristic markers. In numerous cases, it results from an interpretation of what the speaker says.

The aspects which are most likely to affect the process can be divided into **lexical** and **grammatical** considerations, as follows:

(i) **Lexical aspect**

>   – stative
>   – dynamic (events: perfective)
>   – dynamic (processes: imperfective)

The opposition between these three aspects rests on the **meaning of the verbs** used.

– stative (*d'état*)

Stative verbs express no beginning, 'middle' or end, i.e. they are concerned with situations which are stable over time and do not involve any 'activity': *être*, *avoir*, *sembler*, *paraître*, *savoir*, *connaître*, *croire*, etc.

– dynamic

– perfective/conclusive (*événementiels, ponctuels* or *instantanés*)

These verbs express an end, a result, i.e. a process that can only be envisaged to its completion. When the process stops, a new state starts. The limits of the process are thus integrated into the meaning of the verb.

> Ex: *arriver, atteindre, entrer, sortir, accourir, naître, mourir, tomber, casser, éclater, couper, fermer, trouver, abattre, aboutir*, etc.

– imperfective/inconclusive (*de processus* or *duratifs*)

These verbs express continuity or duration of the action, i.e. the process is taking place over a period of time whose limits are thus not part of the meaning of the verb.

> Ex: *aimer, admirer, haïr, craindre, redouter, chanter, manger, dormir, ressembler, marcher, courir, nager, voyager, parler, méditer, rire, travailler, exister, vivre, durer, habiter, régner*, etc.

NB: Verbs can shift between perfective and imperfective, and between stative and dynamic, according to the context in which they are used. Compare:

> *J'ai acheté 'Le Nouvel Economiste'.* (perfective)
> I bought/have bought [a copy of] Le Nouvel Economiste.
> and:
> *J'achète 'Le Nouvel Economiste' depuis un mois.* (imperfective)
> I have been buying Le Nouvel Economiste for a month.

In the second example, the presence of the adverb phrase of time '*depuis un mois*' means that '*acheter*' no longer refers to the punctual event normally associated with the meaning of that verb, but to a repetition of events over a period.

This distinction is essential to determine, for instance, which tense to use with *depuis*: see chapter 6 *depuis* and Other Tense Markers.

(ii) **Grammatical aspect**

– accomplished
– non-accomplished

This opposition rests on the **forms of the conjugation**, i.e. the 'couples' simple/compound tenses. Each couple presents the two aspects, hence the perfect is the accomplished form of the present, the pluperfect is the accomplished form of the imperfect, etc.

– non-accomplished (*inaccompli*)

The non-accomplished aspect is expressed by simple tenses, since the process has not been completed yet.

> Ex: – present   *je chante*
>   – imperfect   *elle chantait*
>   – future   *tu chanteras*

– **accomplished** (*accompli*)

The accomplished aspect is expressed by the corresponding compound tenses, plus the past historic, since the process has been completed.

Ex:		
–	perfect	*vous avez chanté*
–	pluperfect	*nous avions chanté*
–	future anterior	*il aura chanté*
–	past historic	*ils chantèrent*
–	past anterior	*elle eut chanté*

NB(1): It should be noted that the compound forms are also used with the temporal value of anteriority, i.e. they occur before another event in the discourse. This explains the development of the double compound forms in French, which serve to express anteriority to the compound forms (e.g. perfect and double compound past). See chapter 11 Other Past Tenses.

NB(2): The distinction between accomplished and non-accomplished (verb forms) must not be equated with that of perfective and imperfective (lexis). For instance, *j'ai accouru* is perfective and accomplished; *j'accours* is perfective and non-accomplished; *j'ai couru* is imperfective and accomplished and *je cours* is imperfective and non-accomplished.

(iii) **Syntactical aspect**

French also uses a number of aspectual semi-auxiliaries (*verbes de suppléance aspectuelle*) whose role is to fill in the remaining gaps. The main ones express:

– The phase before the process begins, with *aller, être sur le point de* + infinitive.
> Ex: *Nous **sommes sur le point de** partir.*
> We're about to leave.

– The phase of accomplishment of the process, with *commencer à, se mettre à, être en train de* + infinitive.
> Ex: *Elle **a commencé à** écrire sa thèse.*
> She's started writing her thesis.

– The phase after the process has been accomplished, with *venir de, finir de, cesser de* + infinitive.
> Ex: *Il **a cessé de** pleuvoir.*
> It has stopped raining.

Finally, the continuation of the process can be expressed with *ne cesser de* or *ne faire que* + infinitive (see also section 2.2.2(vii) in chapter 38 Negative Structures).
> Ex: *Il **n'a cessé de** pleuvoir toute la journée.*
> It hasn't stopped raining all day.

6 Morphology

6.1 Radical and ending

(i) A verbal form is made up of:

  – a **radical**, i.e. the element which carries the lexical meaning of the verb.
  Ex: *donn-, pens-, chant-*

  – an **ending**, which carries grammatical markers.
  Ex: *-e, -erons, -eraient*

(ii) The ending carries several pieces of information. For instance in *donnerons*, the ending *-erons* carries the following information:
  – 1st person
  – plural
  – future of the indicative

(iii) Verbs are traditionally divided into three (or four) groups according to the ending of their infinitive, ER, IR, (OIR) or RE. This classification has been criticized because the verbs do not form a homogeneous set within each group. An alternative system is to group verbs according to their number of radicals (from one to nine). However, this classification is not particularly satisfactory in terms of helping students with the acquisition of verb forms. Hence the traditional division has been retained in this book. For each verb, the basic radical is the infinitive minus the ending (e.g. the radical of *chantER* – for all conjugations – is *chant-*). Verbs are thus called 'regular' or 'irregular' according to the extent of the changes undergone by the basic radical for each conjugation. Certain verbs in OIR or RE are in that sense particularly 'irregular'.

6.2 Simple and compound tenses

(i) Forms

  – **Simple tenses**: the verbal form is made up of the radical and the ending.
  Ex: *donn-e, donn-erions, donn-ait,* etc.

  – **Compound tenses**: the verbal form is made up of the auxiliary *être* or *avoir* and the past participle of the conjugated verb. The auxiliary carries the endings of the conjugation.
  Ex: *ai mangé, avons dormi*
  In certain cases, the past participle carries the markers of the gender and number.
  Ex: *sont venu(e)s, est parti(e)*
  See chapter 9 Perfect, section 3.

(ii) **Auxiliaries**

  – *être* is used:
    – to construct the compound tenses of pronominal verbs:
    Ex: *Il s'**est** levé; nous nous **sommes** promené(e)s.*

     – to construct the compound tenses of some intransitive verbs with a
        perfective meaning, namely: *aller, venir*, etc. (see chapter 9 Perfect, section 3.1).

           Ex: *Elle **est** revenue.*

     – to construct the passive:

           Ex: *La souris **est** pourchassée par le chat.*

See also chapter 18 Active and Passive Voices, section 3(iv) for other auxiliaries.

     – *avoir* is used to construct the compound tenses of all the other verbs, including
        être and *avoir*.

           Ex: *j'**ai** été, j'**avais** eu, tu **auras** vendu, il **eut** pris*

NB(1): *aller* is also called an auxiliary when it is used to construct the immediate
future (*futur immédiat ou périphrastique*). See chapters 5 Present, section 3.6, 7
Future, section 5, and 8 Imperfect, section 3.3(i).

           Ex: *Je **vais** prendre un bain.*

NB(2): Other phrasal verbs are considered as **semi-auxiliaries**:

– of tense: *venir de, être sur le point de, devoir* + infinitive (see chapter 5 Present,
  section 3.5)

– of aspect: *être en train de, commencer à, finir de*, etc.

– of mood: *pouvoir, devoir, vouloir, savoir* + infinitive (see chapters 21 Modals and
  22 *Savoir* and *Connaître*)

– of voice: *(se) faire, (se) laisser; se voir, s'entendre* + infinitive (see chapters 18 Active
  and Passive Voices, section 7.2 and 20 Pronominal Verbs,
  section 3.1.1(iv)).

6.3   The double compound tenses

(i)   These are constructed by adding the auxiliary *avoir* in a compound tense to the
pre-existing compound tense (see chapter 11 Other Past Tenses).

(ii)   The double compound past (*passé surcomposé*) is the only one still in common use.

           Ex: *Quand j'**ai eu fini** de ranger, je suis sortie.*

(iii) The double compound past is not used with pronominal verbs.

7 Voices and forms

The following are treated in detail in the relevant chapters:

7.1   The voice (*la voix* or *la diathèse*)

(i)   Active

           Ex: *Le chat **mange** la souris.*
              The cat is eating the mouse.
              ('*le chat*' is the agent of the process)

              *On **a annoncé** la bonne nouvelle.*
              The good news was announced.

(ii)   Passive

Ex: *La souris **est mangée** par le chat.*
The mouse is being eaten by the cat.
('*la souris*' is the patient of the process;
'*le chat*' is the agentive complement)

*La bonne nouvelle **a été annoncée**.*
The good news was announced.

(iii)   Middle (with pronominal verbs)

Ex: *De nouvelles maisons **se construisent**.*
New houses are being built.
(the subject is normally inanimate)

*Ces livres **se vendent** bien.*
These books sell well.

See chapter 18 Active and Passive Voices, section 5.3.

(iv)   Impersonal

Ex: ***Il passe** un bus toutes les deux heures.*
(= *Un bus passe toutes les deux heures.*)
There's a bus every two hours.

***Il a été retrouvé** deux portefeuilles.*
(= *Deux portefeuilles ont été retrouvés.*)
Two wallets were found.

See chapter 19 Impersonal Verbs and the Impersonal Voice, section 7.

(v)   Factitive

Ex: *La pluie **fait pousser** l'herbe.*
(→ *L'herbe pousse.*)
Rain makes grass grow.
(Here, '*l'herbe*' is the real agent of the process)

*Je **laisse** les enfants **jouer** dans le jardin.*
(→ *Les enfants jouent.*)
I let the children play in the garden.

See chapter 15 Infinitive, sections 3.1.3.1(iii) and (iv).

7.2   Pronominal verbs and the pronominal form

Ex: *Ils **s'aiment**.*
They love each other.

*Nous **nous écrivons** tous les jours.*
We write to each other every day.

*Je **me souviens** de ce que vous avez dit.*
I remember what you said.

See chapter 20 Pronominal Verbs.

7.3 Impersonal verbs

Ex: ***Il pleut***.
It is raining.

Il s'agit *du rapport que j'ai envoyé hier.*
It is about the report I sent yesterday.

Il arrive *que nous soyons en retard.*
Sometimes we are late.

See chapter 19 Impersonal Verbs and the Impersonal Voice.

5 Present indicative

1 Introduction

The present indicative basically expresses the non–accomplished aspect: it does not specify the limits of the length of the process.

The present is not so much a tense as as kind of 'threshold' between what has been (the past) and what is not yet (the future). As this threshold can be envisaged in several ways, the present is not attached solely to the present moment. Thus it has a variety of uses, e.g. it can express the present moment, a variable length of time, or even a past or a future.

The present tense is also used:
- with *depuis/depuis que* and equivalent expressions, when English uses a past tense: see chapter 6 *depuis* and Other Tense Markers.
- after *si*: see chapter 13 Conditional and the Expression of Hypothesis, section 3.2.3.
- to express the recent past: see 3.5 below.
- to express the immediate future: see 3.6 below and chapter 7 Future, section 5.

2 Formation

The present of the indicative is not particularly easy to conjugate as both regular and irregular verbs in all categories (ER, IR, OIR and RE) can have several radicals (see chapter 4 Introduction to Verbs, section 6.1). Furthermore, the endings can also differ. This chapter examines each verb category in turn and looks at their conjugation peculiarities.

2.1 Verbs in ER

The radical is the infinitive minus the ending ER. The endings are:

–e	*–ons*
–es	*–ez*
–e	*–ent*

- **aimer** is a regular verb:

j'aime	*nous aimons*
tu aimes	*vous aimez*
il/elle/on aime	*ils/elles aiment*

– *aller* is irregular:

je vais	*nous allons*
tu vas	*vous allez*
il/elle/on va	*ils/elles vont*

(i) Verbs in *-cer* or *-ger*

In order to keep the sound [s] of '*c*', a cedilla must be added to the '*c*' before '*a*', '*o*', '*u*': this rule affects the first person plural, *nous*.

　　　　　Ex: ***placer****: je place*　but:　*nous plaçons*

In order to keep the sound [ʒ] of '*g*', an '*e*' must be added after the '*g*' before '*a*', '*o*', '*u*': this rule affects the lst person plural, *nous*.

　　　　　Ex: ***manger****: je mange*　but:　*nous mangeons*

(ii) Verbs in *-guer*

These verbs do **not** drop their '*u*' before '*a*' or '*o*', even though it is not needed.

　　　　　Ex: *j'élague*　　*nous élaguons*

Note that ***arguer*** is pronounced [argɥe], whereas ***narguer*** is [narge].

(iii) Penultimate mute '*e*'

The '*e*' becomes '*è*' except for *nous* and *vous*.

Ex: ***peser****: je pèse*	*nous pesons*
tu pèses	*vous pesez*
il/elle/on pèse	*ils/elles pèsent*

(iv) Penultimate '*é*'

The '*é*' becomes '*è*' except for *nous* and *vous*.

Ex: ***céder****: je cède*	*nous cédons*
tu cèdes	*vous cédez*
il/elle/on cède	*ils/elles cèdent*

Note that for verbs in *-iéger*, an '*e*' is added between '*g*' and '*o*' with *nous* to keep the sound [ʒ], the same as for *manger* (see above).

Ex: ***siéger****: je siège*	*nous siégeons*
tu sièges	*vous siégez*
il/elle/on siège	*ils/elles siègent*

(v) Verbs in *-eler* or *-eter*

– The majority double the '*l*' or '*t*' before the mute '*e*', hence not with *nous* and *vous*.

Ex: ***jeter****: je jette*	*nous jetons*
tu jettes	*vous jetez*
il/elle/on jette	*ils/elles jettent*

Also: *feuilleter*.

Ex: ***appeler****: j'appelle*	*nous appelons*
tu appelles	*vous appelez*
il/elle/on appelle	*ils/elles appellent*

Also: *rappeler, épeler* (but not *peler*, see below).

– The exceptions add a grave accent to the mute '*e*' before '*l*' or '*t*'.

Ex: **acheter**: *j'achète*   *nous achetons*
      tu achètes   *vous achetez*
      il/elle/on achète   *ils/elles achètent*

Also: *racheter, haleter.*

Ex: **geler**: *je gèle*   *nous gelons*
      tu gèles   *vous gelez*
      il/elle/on gèle   *ils/elles gèlent*

Also: *dégeler, congeler, surgeler, modeler, peler, déceler, démanteler.*

(vi)   **créer, procréer**

Note the two consecutive '*e*'s and the fact that the '*é*' is kept throughout the conjugation.

    je crée   *nous créons*
    tu crées   *vous créez*
    il/elle/on crée   *ils/elles créent*

(vii)   Verbs in *–oyer* and *–uyer*

They change their '*y*' into '*i*' before a mute '*e*', hence not with *nous* and *vous*.

Ex: **essuyer**: *j'essuie*   *nous essuyons*
      tu essuies   *vous essuyez*
      il/elle/on essuie   *ils/elles essuient*

(viii)   With verbs in *–ayer*, two conjugations are possible.

Ex: **payer**: *je paie / je paye*   *nous payons*
      tu paies / tu payes   *vous payez*
      il/elle/on paie / paye   *ils/elles paient / payent*

(ix)   Verbs in *–ier* or *–uer*

It is a common error to forget to write (and to pronounce!) the '*i*' or the '*u*' of the radical.

Ex: **étudier**: *j'étudie*   *nous étudions*
      tu étudies   *vous étudiez*
      il/elle/on étudie   *ils/elles étudient*

Ex: **continuer**: *je continue*   *nous continuons*
      tu continues   *vous continuez*
      il/elle/on continue   *ils/elles continuent*

2.2 Verbs in IR

Regular verbs have their present participles in *–issant* (e.g. *finir* → *finissant*) whilst irregular verbs have their present participle in *–ant* (e.g. *partir* → *partant*).

NB: It is a common error to forget the '*iss*' in the plural forms, particularly when the verb in the infinitive looks like its English equivalent.

Ex: *Les conditions qui* **définissent** *notre vie . . .*
      and not: **qui définent . . .*
      The conditions which define our lives . . .

2.2.1 Regular verbs in IR

(i) Radical and endings

   – The radical is the infinitive minus IR.
   – The endings are:

-is	*-issons*
-is	*-issez*
-it	*-issent*

Ex: ***finir****: je finis*   *nous finissons*
            tu finis   *vous finissez*
          il/elle/on finit   *ils/elles finissent*

NB: The diaeresis of ***haïr*** is kept only in the plural.

je hais	*nous haïssons*
tu hais	*vous haïssez*
il/elle/on hait	*ils/elles haïssent*

(ii) Verbs based on adjectives

This category contains a lot of verbs based on adjectives.

Ex: adjective	verb	present participle
beau	*embellir*	*embellissant*
laid	*enlaidir*	*enlaidissant*
sale	*salir*	*salissant*
jeune	*rajeunir*	*rajeunissant*
vieux	*vieillir*	*vieillissant*, etc.

and particularly adjectives of colour:

Ex: adjective	verb	present participle
rouge	*rougir*	*rougissant*
jaune	*jaunir*	*jaunissant*
pâle	*pâlir*	*pâlissant*, etc.

But note the following exceptions:

foncé	*foncer*	*fonçant*
bronzé	*bronzer*	*bronzant*

(iii) Verbs indicating a transformation

All these verbs indicate a transformation.

   – With the meaning of 'to become' when the action of the verb applies to the subject of the verb (the verb is intransitive):
      Ex: *Il a beaucoup maigri depuis sa maladie.*
            He's lost a lot of weight since his illness.

– With the meaning of 'to make something' + adjective, when the action of the verb applies to the object of the verb (the verb is transitive):

Ex: *Le soleil brunit la peau.*
Sun makes the skin brown.

Compare:

Les fleurs embellissent votre jardin.
Flowers make your garden look more attractive.

Marie embellit de jour en jour: ce doit être l'amour!
Marie is becoming more beautiful every day: it must be love!

and note the difference between *grandir* and *agrandir*:

Les enfants grandissent si vite!
Children grow so fast!

J'ai agrandi la salle de séjour en abattant la cloison avec la salle à manger.
I've made the sitting room larger by knocking down the partition with the dining room.

2.2.2 Irregular verbs in IR

(i) For most irregular verbs in IR, the last consonant of the radical of the infinitive is dropped in the singular but kept in the plural. The endings are:

–s	–ons
–s	–ez
–t	–ent

Ex: **sentir**:

je sens	nous sentons
tu sens	vous sentez
il/elle/on sent	ils/elles sentent

Similarly:

servir:	je sers	nous servons
dormir:	je dors	nous dormons
courir:	je cours	nous courons
bouillir:	je bous	nous bouillons

(ii) **fuir**: the 'i' becomes 'y' with *nous* and *vous*:

je fuis	nous fuyons
tu fuis	vous fuyez
il/elle/on fuit	ils/elles fuient

(iii) **mourir** has two radicals:

je meurs	nous mourons
tu meurs	vous mourez
il/elle/on meurt	ils/elles meurent

(iv) **tenir, venir** and their derivatives (e.g. *appartenir, revenir*) have three radicals:

je tiens	nous tenons
tu tiens	vous tenez
il/elle/on tient	ils/elles tiennent

je viens   *nous venons*

tu viens   *vous venez*

il/elle/on vient   *ils/elles viennent*

(v)   The endings of the five following verbs are exceptionally those of regular verbs in ER: *ouvrir* (*entrouvrir*), *couvrir* (*découvrir*), *cueillir* (*accueillir, recueillir*), *offrir, souffrir*.

Ex: **couvrir**: *je couvre*   *nous couvr**ons***

*tu couvr**es***   *vous couvr**ez***

il/elle/on couvre   *ils/elles couvr**ent***

2.3   Verbs in OIR

(i)   Verbs in *-voir* (apart from **avoir**, see 2.5 below): the '*i*' becomes '*y*' with *nous* and *vous* (two radicals).

Ex: **voir**: *je vois*   *nous vo**y**ons*

tu vois   *vous vo**y**ez*

il/elle/on voit   *ils/elles voient*

Also: *revoir, entrevoir, prévoir, pourvoir*

(ii)   Verbs in *-cevoir*: note the '*ç*' before the '*o*', and note the difference between them and verbs in *-voir* (three radicals).

Ex: **recevoir**: *je reçois*   *nous recevons*

tu reçois   *vous recevez*

il/elle/on reçoit   *ils/elles reçoivent*

Also: *apercevoir, concevoir, décevoir, percevoir*

(iii)   **savoir** and **valoir** have two radicals: one for the singular and one for the plural.

je sais   *nous savons*   *je vaux*   *nous valons*

tu sais   *vous savez*   *tu vaux*   *vous valez*

il sait   *ils savent*   *il vaut*   *ils valent*

(iv)   **devoir**, **pouvoir** and **vouloir** have three radicals.

je dois   *nous devons*   *je peux/je puis*   *nous pouvons*

tu dois   *vous devez*   *tu peux*   *vous pouvez*

il doit   *ils doivent*   *il peut*   *ils peuvent*

je veux   *nous voulons*

tu veux   *vous voulez*

il veut   *ils veulent*

NB: *puis* must be used in verb–*je* inversions (see chapter 39 Interrogative and Exclamative Structures, section 2.1.5.1).

(v)   **(s')asseoir** has two conjugations:

je m'assieds   *nous nous asseyons*   *je m'assois*   *nous nous assoyons*

tu t'assieds   *vous vous asseyez*   *tu t'assois*   *vous vous assoyez*

il s'assied   *ils s'asseyent*   *il s'assoit*   *ils s'assoient*

(vi)   **falloir** and **pleuvoir** are normally used only with impersonal *il* (see chapters 4 Introduction to Verbs, section 7.3, and 19 Impersonal Verbs).

   il faut   il pleut

2.4   Verbs in RE

2.4.1   One radical

The following verbs are 'regular' in the sense that they only have one radical, the radical of the infinitive minus RE. The endings are:

   –s   –ons
   –s   –ez
   –   –ent

(i)   Verbs in *–endre* (except **prendre** and its derivatives, see 2.4.2 (x) below), *–ondre*, *–ordre*, *–erdre* and *–andre*.

   Ex: **rendre**: *je rends   nous rendons*
               tu rends   vous rendez
               il/elle/on rend   ils/elles rendent

(ii)   Verbs in *–ompre* are also regular except that a '*t*' is added to the 3rd person singular.

   Ex: **rompre**: *je romps   nous rompons*
               tu romps   vous rompez
               il/elle/on rompt   ils/elles rompent

(iii)   **battre, mettre** and their derivatives have only one '*t*' in the singular.

   je bats   nous battons   je mets   nous mettons
   tu bats   vous battez   tu mets   vous mettez
   il bat   ils battent   il met   ils mettent

(iv)   **conclure**, *inclure*; **rire**, *sourire*: a '*t*' is added to the 3rd person singular; note the juxtaposition of vowels in the plural.

   je conclus   nous concluons   je ris   nous rions
   tu conclus   vous concluez   tu ris   vous riez
   il conclut   ils concluent   il rit   ils rient

2.4.2   More than one radical

The endings are:

   –s   –ons
   –s   –ez
   –t   –ent

(i)   **croire**: the '*i*' changes into '*y*' with *nous* and *vous* (two radicals).

   je crois   nous croyons
   tu crois   vous croyez
   il/elle/on croit   ils/elles croient

(ii)   Verbs in *-ivre* have two radicals: singular and plural.

Ex: **suivre**: *je suis*   *nous suivons*

tu suis   *vous suivez*

il/elle/on suit   *ils/elles suivent*

(iii) **lire**: an '*s*' is added to the radical plural.

je lis   *nous lisons*

tu lis   *vous lisez*

il/elle/on lit   *ils/elles lisent*

Also: *relire, élire, suffire*

(iv)   **écrire**: a '*v*' is added to the radical plural.

j'écris   *nous écrivons*

tu écris   *vous écrivez*

il/elle/on écrit   *ils/elles écrivent*

Also: *décrire, inscrire, souscrire, transcrire, prescrire*

(v)   Verbs in *-uire*: an '*s*' is added to the radical plural.

Ex: **conduire**: *je conduis*   *nous conduisons*

tu conduis   *vous conduisez*

il/elle/on conduit   *ils/elles conduisent*

(vi)   (**se**) **plaire**: an '*s*' is added to the radical of the plural, and the 3rd person singular has an '*î*'.

je plais   *nous plaisons*

tu plais   *vous plaisez*

il/elle/on plaît   *ils/elles plaisent*

NB: (*se*) *taire* is conjugated in the same way except that there is no circumflex on the '*i*' in the 3rd person singular.

(vii) Verbs in *-aître*: the '*t*' is dropped and replaced by '*ss*' in the radical of the plural, and the '*î*' is kept only for the 3rd person singular.

Ex: **connaître**: *je connais*   *nous connaissons*

tu connais   *vous connaissez*

il/elle/on connaît   *ils/elles connaissent*

(viii) Verbs in *-aindre*, *-eindre* or *-oindre* have two radicals: singular and plural.

Ex: **craindre**: *je crains*   *nous craignons*

tu crains   *vous craignez*

il/elle/on craint   *ils/elles craignent*

(ix)   **vaincre** and **convaincre**: the '*c*' is dropped and replaced by '*qu*' in the radical of the plural.

Ex: *convaincre: je convaincs*   *nous convainquons*

tu convaincs   *vous convainquez*

il/elle convainc   *ils/elles convainquent*

(x) **boire** and **prendre** (and its derivatives) have three radicals:

je bois	*nous buvons*	*je prends*	*nous prenons*
tu bois	*vous buvez*	*tu prends*	*vous prenez*
il boit	*ils boivent*	*il prend*	*ils prennent*

(xi) **résoudre**, **dissoudre** and **absoudre** are conjugated in the same way: note the radical of the plural and the fact there is no '*d*' in the radical singular:

Ex: *résoudre: je résous*	*nous résolvons*	
tu résous	*vous résolvez*	
il/elle/on résout	*ils/elles résolvent*	

(Compare with *coudre* and *moudre*.)

(xii) **coudre** and **moudre**: note the respective radicals for the plural.

je couds	*nous cousons*	*je mouds*	*nous moulons*
tu couds	*vous cousez*	*tu mouds*	*vous moulez*
il coud	*ils cousent*	*il moud*	*ils moulent*

(xiii) **faire** and **dire** are particularly irregular:

je fais	*nous faisons*	*je dis*	*nous disons*
tu fais	**vous faites**	*tu dis*	**vous dites**
il fait	**ils font**	*il dit*	*ils disent*

Also: *défaire, satisfaire; redire*

NB: With *médire, contredire, interdire, prédire, vous* is regular:

Ex: **vous médisez**, *vous contredisez*, etc.

2.5 *être* and *avoir*

(i) **être**:

je suis	*nous sommes*
tu es	*vous êtes*
il/elle/on est	*ils/elles sont*

(ii) **avoir**:

j'ai	*nous avons*
tu as	*vous avez*
il/elle/on a	*ils/elles ont*

2.6 Negative and interrogative forms

(i) Interrogative form with verb–subject pronoun inversion: a '*t*' between hyphens is added in the 3rd person singular of verbs in ER to avoid a hiatus.

Ex: *Mange-**t**-elle assez?*
*Aime-**t**-il la soupe?*

(ii) Negative form: *ne* and *pas* are placed before and after the verb respectively.

Ex: *Elle **ne** mange **pas** assez.*
*Il **n'**aime **pas** la soupe.*

(iii)   Negative interrogative form.
>   Ex: *Ne mange–t–elle pas assez?*
>   *N'aime–t–il pas la soupe?*

3 Use

Whilst English distinguishes between the simple present ('I walk') and the present continuous ('I am walking'), there is no such distinction in French (*je marche*), although French does have its own 'continuous present'. Hence:

>   **I am working.** → *Je travaille.*
>   and not **Je suis travailler.*
>   or even **Je suis travaille.*

but see also 3.3 below.

French also has its own emphatic form. There are a few cases where French uses a present tense but not English. There are also cases where English uses a present but French uses a future, and these are described in chapter 7 Future.

3.1 French present indicative used as in English

As in English, the French present indicative is used in the following cases:

(i)   Events (finite actions) happening at the precise moment of speaking.
>   Ex: *J'allume ma cigarette.*
>   I'm lighting my cigarette.

(ii)   Actions (or states) taking place at or around the time of speaking.
>   Ex: *La nuit tombe; il neige; il fait froid; les parents dorment; les enfants s'amusent.*
>   Night is falling; it is snowing; it is cold; the parents are sleeping; the children are having a good time.

(iii)   General facts about somebody or something.
>   Ex: *Les Dupont sont riches; Robert et Marie s'aiment.*
>   The Duponts are rich; Robert and Marie love each other.

(iv)   Actions which happen all the time (as a matter of course), or which are habitual or repeated.
>   Ex: *En France, les vendanges se font en octobre.*
>   In France, the grape harvest takes place in October.
>
>   *Quand il fait beau, Paul va au bureau à pied.*
>   When the weather is fine, Paul walks to the office.
>
>   *Les Anglais parlent toujours du mauvais temps.*
>   The English always talk about the bad weather.

NB: In all these examples, it is the time complements ('*en octobre*', '*quand il fait beau*', '*toujours*') which indicate the habitual or iterative nature of the process, not the present tense itself. Hence, outside any context, some utterances may be ambiguous.

> Ex: *Philippe **chasse** le sanglier.*

could mean either 'He is hunting boars right now, at the time of speaking' (see (ii) above), or 'It is his habitual activity' (see (iv) above).

(v) 'Eternal'/scientific truths, definitions (generic present).

> Ex: *L'eau **bout** à 100°.*
> Water boils at 100°.

See also chapter 21 Modals, section 5.7(iii).

> *Deux et deux **font** quatre.*
> Two and two make four.

> *Le chat **est** un mammifère.*
> The cat is a mammal/Cats are mammals.

Note that here, the noun phrase '*le chat*' is considered as a class, not an individual (see chapter 23 Articles, section 2.2).

The generic present is widely used in proverbs, and also in scientific, philosophical or legal documents.

> Ex: *Pierre qui **roule** n'**amasse** pas mousse.*
> A rolling stone gathers no moss.

> *Les hommes **naissent** libres et égaux en droits.*
> Men are born free and equal in rights.

(vi) Expression of a future.

The present can also be used to express a future, either very near or considered as inevitable, otherwise expressed by *aller* + infinitive (see chapter 7 Future, section 5), or even a distant future, but with the indispensable presence of adverbs or adverb phrases of time. This use of the present is particularly frequent in spoken French.

> Ex: *Je **retourne** à Paris la semaine prochaine.*
> (= *Je vais retourner à Paris la semaine prochaine.*)
> I'm going back to Paris next week.

> *Que **faites**-vous demain?*
> (= *Qu'allez-vous faire demain?*)
> What are you doing tomorrow?

But see also below, in section 3.2(ii), cases when a French present **must** be an English expression of the future.

3.2 French present indicative not used as in English

These are mainly cases of a stylistic use of the present tense in French.

(i) Expression of the immediate past

The present in French can express the immediate past, otherwise expressed by *venir de* + infinitive (see section 3.5 below), particularly with verbs such as *arriver, sortir, rentrer* or *revenir.* The process has been achieved but is still considered as present in its consequences. In English, the recent past is kept ('to have just done something').

> Ex: *J'**arrive** de Londres.*
> (= *Je viens d'arriver de Londres.*)
> I've just arrived from London.
>
> *Yves? Il **sort** de la bibliothèque.*
> (= *Il vient de sortir de la bibliothèque.*)
> Yves? He's just come out of the library.

The context should determine whether the immediate past or a present tense are expressed.

(ii) Sequence of actions in the future

To express a sequence of actions in the future, the present in French can be used throughout whilst English must use an expression of the future.

> Ex: *Je **fais** ma valise et dans deux minutes, je **suis** prête.*
> I'm packing my case and in two minutes I'**ll be** ready.
>
> ***Fais**-moi ça tout de suite ou je te **tue**!*
> Do this at once or I'**ll kill** you!
>
> *Si je n'**ai** pas de nouvelles de Paul d'ici ce soir, je te **rappelle**.*
> If I haven't heard from Paul by tonight, I'**ll call** you **back**.

(iii) Literary and historic present

– The present in French can be used as a 'literary present' to express narrative and description. This can be used instead of a past tense – usually the perfect or past historic – to make the action seem more immediate or dramatic. However, this practice has become so commonplace nowadays that the 'dramatic' claim may be somewhat lost.

> Ex: *'Après un bref temps d'observation, des CRS **tentent** une charge. Ils **sont** repoussés. **Surviennent** une cinquantaine de policiers en tenue anti-émeute qui ne **réussissent** pas à faire évacuer la place maintenant noire de monde. Ce **sont** plus de quatre cents personnes qui **sont** rassemblées . . .'*
>
> Le Monde, October 1990

English can also use the narrative present, but normally only in spoken narrative.

> Ex: *Hier, je **rentre** de bonne heure et qu'est-ce que je **trouve**? La maison en chantier et le dîner pas prêt!*
> Yesterday, I come home early and what do I find? The house a mess and no dinner ready!

– The present in French can also be used for historical texts, with dates.

> Ex: *'Mais la vie de la duchesse à la cour n'**est** bientôt plus qu'un calvaire. Le roi **se détache** d'elle et Mme de Montespan **devient** maîtresse en titre. Les courtisans **accablent** Louise de vexations. En 1671, elle **s'enfuit** à nouveau au couvent Sainte-Marie de Chaillot, mais Louis XIV l'en **fait** sortir encore, cette fois par Colbert.'*
>
> Christian Melchior-Bonnet, Le grand livre de l'histoire de France

In English, the past would normally be kept, although the 'vivid present' is sometimes still used.

> Ex: 'Occupation.'
> 'The Netherlands **live** under Nazi rule for four years. At first most people **find** it easy enough to carry on their normal lives but when persecution of the Jews **begins**, the Dutch **organise** a unique public services strike in their defence. In consequence the Germans **cease** to be conciliatory and the occupation **grows** harsh forcing people to decide where their loyalties **lie**.'
>
> *Radio Times*, 7–13 January 1995

– Both past and present (and even future!) can appear in the same text in French, particularly in newspaper articles.

> Ex: '*Né avec le siècle, Marcel Légaut **a été**, dans l'Eglise de France, un témoin privilégié de l'évolution spirituelle de son temps. Comme le père Teilhard de Chardin et Jacques Maritain, il **fut** d'abord reconnu dans les milieux universitaires catholiques, puis dans un cercle beaucoup plus large. A l'âge de la première maturité, alors qu'il **est** professeur agrégé de mathématiques à la faculté de Rennes, Marcel Légaut **décide** d'explorer ce qui **sera** l'intuition de sa recherche et de ses voix . . .*'
>
> *Le Monde*, November 1990

3.3 Continuous present

(i) In some cases, the expression *être en train de* + infinitive can be used to insist on the fact that an action is in progress. However, it is important to note that it is more emphatic than the widely used present continuous tense in English. It corresponds approximately to 'to be in the process of doing sth'.

> Ex: *Qu'on ne me dérange pas; je **suis en train de** travailler.*
> I do not want to be disturbed; I am working.

(ii) *en train de faire quelque chose* can be useful when translating an English progressive form with ellipsis of 'to be' (rather than using a present participle).

> Ex: 'How should she present herself to him? [. . .] Or as the lady of leisure, **reading** a book?'
>
> L. P. Hartley, *The Hireling*

> → '. . . ***en train de lire*** *un livre?*'
> rather than:
> '. . . *lisant un livre?*'

(iii) Where appropriate, *être en train de* + infinitive can also be used in the imperfect and in the future.

> Ex: *J'**étais en train de** lire le dernier roman de Marguerite Duras quand quelqu'un a sonné à la porte.*
> I was reading the latest novel by Marguerite Duras when the doorbell rang.

*Catherine vient de partir pour la Grèce: demain à la même heure, elle **sera en train de** se faire bronzer sur la plage!*
Catherine's just gone to Greece: tomorrow at the same time, she'll be sunning herself on the beach!

3.4 The emphatic form

The emphatic form, generally expressed in English by 'do' followed by the verb, can be rendered in French in a variety of ways, according to context and register.

Ex: *Je veux **vraiment** partir avant cinq heures, vous savez!*
I **do** want to leave before five, you know!

The emphatic form of course exists in other tenses.

Ex: *Je lui ai **bien** dit de faire attention avant de traverser la rue.*
I **did** tell him to be careful before crossing the street.

3.5 Present tense to express the immediate past

The immediate past is expressed with ***venir de*** + infinitive. It exists mainly in the present and imperfect tenses.

(i)   The present is used to indicate that an action has just taken place.

Ex: *Je **viens de passer** trois mois à Paris.*
I have just spent three months in Paris.

*Elle **vient de voir** son ami Paul.*
She has just seen her friend Paul.

(ii)   The imperfect is used to indicate that an action had just taken place in the past before another one (in the perfect or past historic).

Ex: *Elle **venait** juste **d'écrire** à Paul quand il l'appela.*
She had just written to Paul when he called her.

*Je **venais d'ouvrir** la porte quand le téléphone a sonné.*
I had just opened the door when the telephone rang.

(iii)   The future can be applied to *venir de* + infinitive, but is fairly rare.

Ex: *Vous prendrez les médicaments que vous **viendrez d'acheter**.*
You will take the medicine you have just bought.

(iv)   This also applies to the conditional.

Ex: *Un coup d'état **viendrait de se produire** en Afghanistan.*
Apparently, a *coup d'état* has just occurred in Afghanistan.

See also chapter 8 Imperfect, section 3.3(ii).

3.6   Expression of the immediate future

(i)   with *aller* + infinitive.
Note that *aller* operates here as an auxiliary (see chapter 4 Introduction to Verbs, section 6.2(ii)).

> Ex: *Je **vais** faire du café.*
> I am going to make some coffee.

(ii)   with *être sur le point de* + infinitive.

> Ex: *Je **suis sur le point** de partir.*
> I am about to leave.

See also chapter 7 Future, section 5.

6 *depuis* and other tense markers

1 Introduction

Expressions with *depuis, depuis que, il y a . . . que*, etc. pose a particular problem for the English student because:
- English and French may use different tenses with these types of tense markers;
- French tense markers such as *depuis, il y a . . . que* cannot be translated systematically into English by tense markers such as **for, since, ago**, etc.

2 *depuis* and *depuis que*

With *depuis* or *depuis que*, the **present** is used to express the fact that an action or a state, begun in the past, **still continues in the present**.

(i) *depuis* is a preposition; *depuis* + **noun**/noun phrase has two uses:

- to introduce a **period of time (for)**:
> Ex: *Paul vit dans le Midi **depuis** plusieurs années.*
> Paul has been living in the South of France **for** several years.

- to refer to the **beginning** of an action or state (**since**), usually followed by an indication of date:
> Ex: *Paul vit dans le Midi **depuis** le 3 juillet 1988.*
> Paul has been living in the South of France **since** July 3rd 1988.

(ii) *depuis que* is a conjunction; *depuis que* + subordinate **clause** is used to refer to the **beginning** of an action or state (**since**).
> Ex: *Paul vit dans le Midi **depuis qu'**il est à la retraite.*
> Paul has been living in the South of France **since** he retired.

2.1 Period of time ('for')

depuis refers to a period of time between the beginning of the action (or state) and the present.

depuis + present = English present perfect continuous + **for**
('to have been –ing for . . .'). It may be prompted by the question:
'*Depuis combien de temps* + present . . . ?'

Ex: *Depuis combien de temps habitez-vous à Londres?*
(*Vous y habitez encore.*)
How long have you been living in London?
(You're still living there.)

*Je vis à Londres **depuis** cinq ans.*
(*J'y vis encore.*)
I've been living in London **for** five years.
(I'm still living there.)

2.2 Beginning of action or state ('since')

depuis and *depuis que* refer to the time at which an action (or state) began:
depuis/depuis que + present = English present perfect continuous + **since**
('to have been –ing since . . .'). It may be prompted by the question:
'*Depuis quand* + present . . . ?'

Ex: *Depuis quand étudiez-vous le russe?*
Since when have you been studying Russian?

*J'étudie le russe **depuis** le 1er juillet, **depuis que** je travaille à mi-temps.*
I have been studying Russian **since** 1st July, **since** I've been
working part-time.

NB(1): All these verbs express some kind of **state**, 'continuous action' or 'situation'
(see chapter 4 section 5 on Aspect): *étudier, connaître, travailler, être à la retraite.*

NB(2): If the verb expresses an **event**, the present cannot be used with
depuis + date (e.g. *naître, arriver, se réveiller,* etc.): see 2.4 and 3.2 below.

NB(3): If the verb refers to a period of time which is over, without any
indication of its beginning, use the perfect with *pendant*: see 6 and 7 below.

2.3 *heure*

The word *heure* is ambiguous with *depuis*.

Ex: *Je travaille **depuis deux heures**.*
I have been working **for two hours**.
or:
I have been working **since two o'clock**.

If the context is not sufficient to clarify the meaning or to avoid ambiguity,
an expression equivalent to *depuis* meaning **for** can be used, e.g. *il y a . . . que, cela
fait . . . que, voilà . . . que* (see 3 below).

2.4 *depuis que* + present or perfect?

Compare:

*J'étudie le russe **depuis que je travaille** à mi-temps.*
I've been studying Russian since I've been working part-time.
and:
*J'étudie le russe **depuis que j'ai commencé à travailler** à mi-temps.*
I've been studying Russian since I started working part-time.

In the second case, the stress is on the 'event' of **starting** something, with *commencer à* (perfective aspect), whilst in the first one, it is on the 'continuous action' of working (imperfective aspect). In the second case, the event (i.e. to start something) happened entirely in the past, hence the use of the past tense in French. Thus:

- If the verb refers to a continuous action or a state which is still valid at the time of speaking, the present tense is used.
- If the verb refers to an event which is over and done with at the time of speaking, the perfect is used.
- If the verb does not refer to a single event, but to a repetition of events (iterative aspect), often with appropriate adverb phrases, this makes it comparable to a continuous action or state.

As can be seen from the examples below, the tenses of the verbs on either side of *depuis* do not depend on one another. The tense of each depends upon whether the event is continuing or is completed.

Note that English does not always establish such a difference. Compare:

> *Depuis qu'il vit* (state) *près de chez moi, je le vois tous les jours* (iterative) */ je l'ai vu deux fois* (event).
> Since he's been living near my place, I've seen him every day / I've seen him twice.
>
> and:
>
> *Depuis qu'il s'est installé* (event) *près de chez moi, je le vois tous les jours* (iterative) */ je l'ai vu deux fois* (event).
> Since he moved near me, I've seen him every day / I've seen him twice.

Another example:

> *Depuis qu'il va à l'école* (iterative), *Paul est beaucoup plus heureux* (state).
> Since he's been going to school, Paul has been much happier.

3 Alternatives to *depuis*

il y a . . . que, *cela (ça) fait . . . que* and, to a lesser extent, *voilà . . . que* can all be used as alternatives to *depuis*, with some restrictions.

3.1 Meaning

Consider the following:

> Ex: *Il y a deux heures que je travaille.*
> *Cela fait deux heures que je travaille.*
> *Voilà deux heures que je travaille.*
> I have been working for two hours.

All these expressions can be used instead of *depuis* to indicate a particular length of time. The stress is placed on the **duration** of the action (which is still going on at the time of speaking), as opposed to the **nature** of the action. They are also useful to remove a possible ambiguity with *depuis* + time (see 2.3 above).

> Ex: *Il y a combien de temps que vous étudiez l'espagnol?*
> *Cela fait combien de temps que vous étudiez l'espagnol?*
> *Voilà combien de temps que vous étudiez l'espagnol?*
> > or:
> *Depuis combien de temps étudiez-vous l'espagnol?*
> (informal French: *Vous étudiez l'espagnol depuis combien de temps?*)
> How long have you been studying Spanish?
>
> *Il y a six mois que j'étudie l'espagnol.*
> *Cela fait six mois que j'étudie l'espagnol.*
> *Voilà six mois que j'étudie l'espagnol.*
> > or:
> *J'étudie l'espagnol depuis six mois.*
> I have been studying Spanish for six months.

Note that for both questions and answers, there is only one construction in English.

NB: *cela fait . . . que* and *il y a . . . que* can be used with the future or immediate future whenever the duration of the action or state has not reached its conclusion at the time of speaking. Note that tense markers such as *bientôt* or *demain* can be added to make the utterance more precise.

> Ex: *Cela fera six semaines [demain] que Paul est parti.*
> It will be six weeks [tomorrow] since Paul left.
>
> *Il va y avoir [bientôt] un an que le président a démissionné.*
> It will [soon] be a year since the president's resignation.

3.2 Present or perfect?

As with *depuis*, if the state, continuous action or repeated event is not completed, the present tense is used. However, if dealing with an event (leading to a change), or if the state or continuous action is over, the perfect is used.

– event, repeated:
> Ex: *Cela fait six semaines que j'arrive tous les matins à mon bureau à sept heures.*
> Here, the iterative aspect is provided by appropriate adverb phrases.
> > but:
> **Cela fait six semaines que j'arrive.*
> is not possible.

– state, not completed:
> *Il y a*
> *Cela fait* } *un mois qu'il **habite** chez moi.*
> *Voilà*
> > or:
> *Il **habite** chez moi depuis un mois.*
> He's been living at my place for a month.

– event, leading to a change:

> *Il y a*
> *Cela fait* } *un mois qu'il **est parti**.*
> *Voilà*

or:

> *Il **est parti** depuis un mois.*
> It is a month since he left / He's been gone for a month.

IMPORTANT: if an event happened in the past, was completed in the past, and there is no change, *depuis* **cannot** be used (this is expressed in English by '. . . **ago**').

– event, over:

> Ex: *Il y a*
> *Cela fait* } *un mois que Paul est passé à la télévision.*
> *Voilà*
> Paul was on television a month ago.

but:

> *★Paul est passé à la télévision depuis un mois.*
> is not possible.

il y a . . . que, etc. is thus almost equivalent to *il y a*, when used with a past tense.

> *Il **y a** un mois **que** Paul **est passé** à la télévision.*
> It's been a month since Paul was on television.

or:

> *Paul **est passé** à la télévision **il y a** un mois.*
> Paul was on television a month ago.

NB(1): The latter enables the stress to be put on the **date** when the event took place (rather than on the **duration** between that date and the time of speaking).

NB(2): *il y a* on its own (but not *il y a . . . que*) can only be used to express past events which are completed at the time of speaking. It is therefore **always** used with the perfect tense.

Compare:

> *Il y a cinq minutes qu'il est arrivé.*
> He's been here for five minutes.   almost equivalent:
>   and: difference of emphasis
> *Il est arrivé il y a cinq minutes.*   (see above)
> He arrived five minutes ago.

but:

> *Il y a une heure qu'il mange.*
> He's been eating for an hour.
> (the stress is on the duration)   *il y a* on its own (**ago**)
>   is not possible here:
> *Il mange depuis une heure.*   use *depuis*.
> He's been eating for an hour.
> (the stress is on the action)

Conversely:

> *Il a mangé il y a une heure.*
> He had something to eat an hour ago.
> (the stress is on the time the event took place)
>
> > or:
>
> *Il y a une heure qu'il a mangé.*
> It's an hour since he had something to eat.
> (the stress is on the duration between when the action took place and the time of speaking)
>
> > but:
>
> *★Il a mangé depuis une heure.*

is not possible because 'to have had something to eat' is an event which is over now, at the time of speaking.

4 Use of past tense in main clause

(i)   A French imperfect (state) corresponds to an English past perfect continuous.

(ii) A French compound tense corresponds to an English compound tense:
– a French pluperfect (event) corresponds to an English past perfect.
– a French perfect (event) corresponds to an English perfect.

4.1 Use of the imperfect

(i)   The imperfect is used to express a state, or an event or action begun in the past which was still in progress at the past time referred to. It emphasizes the continuous nature of the past action, event or state.

> Ex: *A cette époque-là, j'**habitais** déjà à Paris depuis un an.*
> At that time, I had already been living in Paris for a year.
>
> *Cela faisait longtemps que je **voulais** aller au Canada.*
> I had been wanting to go to Canada for a long time.
>
> *Il y avait 20 ans que je **connaissais** les Dupont.*
> I had known the Duponts for 20 years.

(ii) The imperfect may also be used to refer to a state or action in the past that was interrupted by another one (also in the past). See chapter 8 Imperfect, section 3.1(ii).

> Ex: *Je **lisais** depuis seulement 5 minutes quand quelqu'un a sonné à la porte.*
> I had only been reading for five minutes when the door bell rang.
>
> *Il y avait un an / Cela faisait un an qu'elle **sortait** avec Patrick quand elle a rencontré Henri.*
> She had been going out with Patrick for a year when she met Henri.

4.2   Use of compound tenses

If the event, action or state in the past is seen to have been completed within the period referred to, a compound tense is used in French and English. If the action is completed, the tense used with *depuis* etc. is the same as the English tense of the main clause.

> Ex: *Elle **a** beaucoup **changé** depuis deux semaines.*
> She has changed a lot in the last two weeks.
>
> *Elle **avait** beaucoup **changé** depuis deux semaines.*
> She had changed a lot in the last two weeks.

5   The negative form and *depuis*

The following can all be used with the negative form:
depuis que . . . /il y a . . . que/cela fait . . . que/voilà . . . que
It is most important to note that the negative form indicates that at the time of speaking, an action has **not** taken place since a particular moment in the past. English has an equivalent expression with **for**, or uses an affirmative form with **since**, but note the difference in tense.

5.1   *ne . . . pas* or *ne . . . plus*?

ne . . . plus is mainly used with the present tense (some people use *ne . . . pas* with the present tense but it is less usual); *plus* stresses whatever used to be the case.

> Ex: *Cela fait des mois qu'on ne les voit pas/plus.*
> It's been months since we last saw them.
>   or:
> *On ne les voit pas/plus depuis des mois.*
> We haven't seen them for months.
>
> *Voilà deux jours que je ne dors pas/plus.*
> It's been two days since I last slept.
>   or:
> *Je ne dors plus/pas depuis deux jours.*
> I haven't slept for two days.

5.2   Present or perfect?

The use of the present implies breaking a habit, while the use of the perfect merely refers to the last time a particular event occurred.

(i)   Present

– The present (*ne . . . pas/plus* + *depuis . . .*) corresponds to the negative form of the English present **perfect continuous** + **for**.

– The present (*ne . . . plus + depuis que . . .*) corresponds to the negative form of the English present **perfect continuous + since**.

> Ex: *Je ne travaille pas **depuis** trois semaines.*
> I have not been working for three weeks.
>
> *Je ne travaille plus **depuis que** j'ai été malade.*
> I have not been working since I have been ill.
>
> *Je ne cours plus **depuis** des mois.*
> I have not been running for months.

(ii)   Perfect

The perfect translates the negative form of the English present **perfect + for** or **since**.

> Ex: *Je ne lui ai pas téléphoné **depuis** une semaine.*
> I have not phoned him for a week.
>
> *Je ne lui ai pas téléphoné **depuis que** nous sommes fâchés.*
> I have not phoned him since we fell out.

Similarly:

> *Il y a/Voilà/Cela fait plus d'un an que je ne l'ai pas vu.*
> It is over a year since I last saw him.
>
> > or:
>
> *Il y a/Voilà/Cela fait plus d'un an que je ne le vois plus.*
> It is over a year since I have seen him.

5.3   The negative form and events

(i)   The negative form of the present followed by *depuis* (*ne . . . pas/plus + depuis*) emphasizes the following points:
– the duration of events
– the length of time during which an action has not occurred.
This is why it is possible to use these verbs with *depuis* (see 3.2 above).

> Ex: *Je **n'ai pas acheté** 'Le Monde' depuis trois mois.*
> I haven't bought *Le Monde* for three months.
> (= last single event)
> > or:
> *Je **n'achète plus** 'Le Monde' depuis trois mois.*
> I haven't been buying *Le Monde* for three months.
> (= breaking a habit)
> > but:
> ★*J'ai acheté 'Le Monde' depuis trois mois.*
> is meaningless. Either say, according to what is meant:
>
> – *J'achète 'Le Monde' depuis trois mois.*
>   *Il y a trois mois que j'achète 'Le Monde'.*
>   *Voilà trois mois que j'achète 'Le Monde'.*
>   I have been buying *Le Monde* for three months.
> > or:
> – *J'ai acheté 'Le Monde' il y a trois mois.*
>   I bought *Le Monde* three months ago.

Similarly:

Je n'ai pas mangé depuis deux jours.
I haven't eaten for two days.

Je n'ai pas dormi depuis trois jours.
I haven't slept for three days.

Paul n'est pas passé à la télévision depuis un mois.
Paul has not been on TV for a month.

In all the above cases, the events or actions are repeated, i.e. they refer to all the missed opportunities of carrying out a certain action. For instance, *Je n'ai pas mangé depuis deux jours* refers to all the mealtimes that have been missed.

(ii) However, there are cases when the negative form turns an action expressed by a stative verb into a non-event, i.e. an event which does not take place. Since there is no repetition, the negative form is not used with *depuis*.

Ex: *Ils sont arrivés depuis trois jours.*
(implies a change)
It's three days since they've arrived.
but:
★*Ils ne sont pas arrivés depuis trois jours.*
is not possible.

être arrivé is a state, but *ne pas être arrivé* is a non-event. This also occurs with *naître, commencer quelque chose*, etc.

6 *depuis* or *pendant*?

(i) Ongoing period of time

As we have seen, *depuis* always **entails the idea of a beginning**, and is used for periods of time up to the present and **beyond**.

Ex: *Nous sommes en vacances **depuis** le mois de juillet / **depuis** deux semaines / **depuis** le 1er avril.*
We've been on holiday **since** July / **for** two weeks / **since** April 1st.

(ii) Finite period of time

pendant means 'during' (which is generally expressed by **for**). It expresses a length of time **without reference to its beginning**. It is used instead of *depuis* if the period of time is **over** (but see NB(2) below). Compare:

*Nous **vivons** aux Etats-Unis **depuis** trois ans.*
(*Nous y vivons encore.*)

We've been living in the United States **for** three years.
(We're still living there.)
> but:

*Nous **avons vécu** aux Etats-Unis **pendant** trois ans.*
(*Nous n'y vivons plus.*)
We lived in the US **for** three years.
(We don't live there any more.)

*Nous **roulons depuis** trois heures.*
We've been driving **for** three hours.
> but:

*Nous **avons roulé pendant** trois heures avant de nous arrêter.*
We drove **for** three hours before stopping.

NB(1): *pendant* may be omitted when the length of time **immediately** follows the verb.
> Ex: *Nous avons vécu trois ans aux Etats-Unis.*
> *Nous avons roulé trois heures avant de nous arrêter.*

Compare:
> *J'ai attendu [pendant] dix minutes à la gare.*
> I have been waiting ten minutes at the station.
>> but:
> *J'ai attendu à la gare pendant dix minutes.*
> (*pendant* is compulsory)
> I have been waiting at the station for ten minutes.

NB(2): *pendant* is used for **actual** periods of time seen in their completion, whether it be in the past, the future or the present.
> Ex: *Il a habité chez nous pendant un an.*
> He lived with us for a year.

> *Je vais faire du tennis pendant une heure et ensuite, j'irai à la piscine.*
> I'm going to play tennis for an hour, then I'll go to the swimming pool.

(iii) *pendant* or *pendant que?*
   − *pendant* is a preposition; *pendant* + **noun**/noun phrase is used to represent the period of time concerned (translated by **for**);
   − *pendant que* is a conjunction; *pendant que* + **subordinate clause** (subject + verb) is used to represent the period of time concerned (translated by **while**).

> Ex: *Je me suis reposée **pendant** une heure.*
> I rested **for** an hour.
>> but:
> *Je me suis reposée **pendant qu'**ils travaillaient.*
> I rested **while** they worked.

7 *pendant* or *pour*?

pour is used instead of *pendant* to express an **intended** length of time, usually in the future. It is used with the following verbs: *être*, *aller*, *venir* and *partir* + intended length of time.

> Ex: *Je **pars** en vacances **pour** deux mois.*
> I'm going on holiday for two months.
>
> *Nous **sommes** à Paris **pour** quelques jours.*
> We are in Paris for a few days.
>
> *Je **suis allée** à Paris **pour** le week-end.*
> I went to Paris for the week-end.

NB: *pour* should not be used with *rester*.

> Ex: *Nous sommes restés trois semaines à l'hôtel.*
> or:
> *Nous sommes restés à l'hôtel pendant trois semaines.*
> We stayed in a hotel for three weeks.

8 *depuis que* or *puisque*?

They are both expressed in English by **since**:

– If **since** means 'ever since', use *depuis que* to indicate the beginning of the action (see above).

– If **since** means 'because', use *puisque* to introduce the reason or explanation (*puisque* is a stronger version of *comme*).

Compare:

> **Since** (= ever since) I have been eating bread at every meal,
> I have put on two kilos.
> ***Depuis que** je mange du pain à tous les repas, j'ai pris deux kilos.*
> and:
> **Since** (= because) you want to lose weight, you'd better not eat so much bread!
> ***Puisque** vous voulez maigrir, vous feriez mieux de manger moins de pain!*

9 *pendant que* or *tandis que*?

(i) *pendant que* means 'while' in the sense of 'during the time (of)'. It is used to express two (or more) simultaneous actions.

> Ex: *Ils jouent **pendant que** je travaille.*
> They play **while** I work.

(ii)   *tandis que* has two meanings:

    – as an equivalent of *pendant que* (see above), it is rarely used.

    – its main meaning is 'while/whilst' in the sense of 'but', indicating an element of **opposition**.

        Ex: *Les chats aiment courir après les souris **tandis que** les chiens, eux, préfèrent courir après les chats . . .*

            Cats like to chase mice, **while** dogs prefer to chase cats . . .

7 Future

1 Introduction

The future is the tense of things to come. It is used in French and in English to express a process situated in the future in relation to the time of speaking.

Since the future is somewhat uncertain, the future tense can also have modal values, expressing uncertainty or probability.

The future has two tenses: the simple future and the future perfect. There is also a way of expressing the 'immediate future'.

2 Formation of the simple future

The radical of the future is generally the infinitive of the verb, whilst the ending is – almost – the present tense of the verb *avoir*:

je .... *ai*	*nous* .... *ons*
tu .... *as*	*vous* .... *ez*
il/elle/on .... *a*	*ils/elles* ..... *ont*

However, there are some irregular radicals.

2.1 Verbs in ER

2.1.1 Regular radical

(i) Most verbs in ER have a regular radical in the future tense.

> Ex: *donner: je **donner**ai*   *nous donnerons*
>   *tu donneras*   *vous donnerez*
>   *il/elle/on donnera*   *ils/elles donneront*

(ii) Verbs in *-rer*: it is a common mistake to forget the 're' of the radical.

> Ex: *préparer*   *je prépare**r**ai*
>   *rencontrer*   *je rencont**r**erai*
>   *considérer*   *je considé**r**erai*

(iii) Verbs in *-ier, -uer, -ouer, -éer*: it is a common mistake to forget the 'e' of the radical.

> Ex: *étudier*   *j'étudi**e**rai*
>   *continuer*   *je continu**e**rai*
>   *nouer*   *je nou**e**rai*
>   *créer*   *je cré**e**rai*

2.1.2 Irregular radical

(i) *aller:* *j'irai*   *nous **irons***
              *tu **iras***   *vous **irez***
     *il/elle/on **ira***   *ils/elles **iront***

(ii) Verbs in *-oyer* and *-uyer* change the '*y*' into '*i*' throughout the conjugation.
             Ex: *nettoyer: je nettoierai*   *nous nettoierons*
                    tu nettoieras   *vous nettoierez*
                   il/elle/on nettoiera   *ils/elles nettoieront*

(iii) Verbs in *-ayer*: the '*y*' can be kept, or changed into an '*i*' (the latter is more modern).
             Ex: *payer: je paierai* or *je payerai* etc.

(iv) *envoyer* is exceptionally irregular:
                    j'enverrai   *nous enverrons*
                    tu enverras   *vous enverrez*
                  il/elle/on enverra   *ils/elles enverront*

(v) Verbs with penultimate '*e*':
     They add a grave accent to that '*e*' throughout the conjugation.
             Ex: *se lever: je me lèverai*   *nous nous lèverons*
                    tu te lèveras   *vous vous lèverez*
                   il/elle/on se lèvera   *ils/elles se lèveront*
     Similarly: *mener, amener, emmener, se promener, peser, laver, semer,* etc.

(vi) Verbs with penultimate '*é*':
     They keep it throughout the conjugation.
             Ex: *régler*   *je réglerai,* etc.
     Similarly: *gérer, céder, espérer, répéter, siéger*

(vii) Verbs in *-eler* or *-eter*:

    – The majority double the '*t*' or '*l*' throughout the conjugation.
             Ex: *appeler*   *j'appellerai,* etc.
                  jeter   *je jetterai,* etc.
     Similarly: *épeler, feuilleter*

    – The exceptions add a grave accent to the mute '*e*':
             Ex: *acheter*   *j'achèterai,* etc.
                  geler   *je gèlerai,* etc.
     Similarly: *haleter, peler, modeler, démanteler*

2.2 Verbs in IR

2.2.1 Regular verbs in IR

Regular verbs in IR have their present participle in *-issant*.

(i)   The radical is the infinitive minus IR.

        Ex: *finir*   *je **finir**ai*, etc.
              obéir   *j'**obéir**ai*, etc.
              haïr   *je **haïr**ai*, etc.

(ii)   Verbs in *-rir*: it is a common mistake to forget the 'ri' of the radical.

        Ex: *périr*   *je **péri**rai*

2.2.2   Irregular verbs in IR

Irregular verbs in IR have their present participle in *-ant*.

(i)   For most, the radical is simply the infinitive minus IR.

        Ex: *sentir*   *je **sentir**ai*, etc.

Similarly: *servir, dormir, bouillir, partir, mentir, sortir, souffrir, ouvrir, couvrir, offrir, fuir*

(ii)   For the others, the correct radical must be learnt for each verb:

    – *venir* and *tenir* (and their derivatives): *je **viendr**ai; je **tiendr**ai*
    – *courir* and *mourir*: *je **courr**ai; je **mourr**ai*
    – *cueillir (accueillir, recueillir)*: *je **cueiller**ai*
    – *acquérir and conquérir*: *j'**acquerr**ai; je **conquerr**ai*

2.3   Verbs in OIR

(i)   *prévoir* and *pourvoir* are regular:

        Ex: *je **prévoir**ai, je **pourvoir**ai*

(ii)   *voir (revoir, entrevoir)* are not:

        Ex: *je **verr**ai*

(iii) *recevoir (apercevoir, concevoir, décevoir, percevoir)*:

        Ex: *je **recevr**ai*

(iv)   *s'asseoir* has two conjugations:

        Ex: *je m'**assiér**ai* or *je m'**assoir**ai*

(v)   Note the radical for each of the following:

        – *vouloir*   *je **voudr**ai*
        – *valoir*   *je **vaudr**ai*
        – *devoir*   *je **devr**ai*
        – *pouvoir*   *je **pourr**ai*
        – *savoir*   *je **saur**ai*
        – *émouvoir*   *j'**émouvr**ai*

        – *falloir*   *il **faudr**a*
        – *pleuvoir*   *il **pleuvr**a*

2.4 Verbs in RE

The radical is the infinitive minus the final '*e*'.
Ex: *vendre*: *je **vend**rai*, etc.
except for *faire* and its derivatives:

*je **fer**ai*	*nous ferons*
tu feras	*vous ferez*
il/elle/on fera	*ils/elles feront*

2.5 *être* and *avoir*

*je **ser**ai*	*nous serons*	*j'**aur**ai*	*nous aurons*
tu seras	*vous serez*	*tu auras*	*vous aurez*
il sera	*ils seront*	*il aura*	*ils auront*

2.6 Negative and interrogative forms

(i) Questions with subject pronoun–verb inversion need a '*t*' in the 3rd person singular to avoid a hiatus.
Ex: *Fera-**t**-il beau demain?*
Will it be fine tomorrow?

*Pourra-**t**-elle venir au concert de l'école?*
Will she be able to attend the school concert?

(ii) The negative form is straightforward:
Ex: *Il **ne** fera **pas** beau demain.*

(iii) Negative interrogative:
Ex: ***Ne** fera-t-il **pas** beau demain?*

3 Uses of the simple future

3.1 Cases of similarity to English usage

The simple future is used in the same way as in English in the following cases:

3.1.1 The future to express an order (imperative future)

The future can be used instead of the imperative, which would be less formal, to express an order, a prohibition or a request.
Ex: *Vous **irez** le voir et vous **vous excuserez**.*
You will go and see him and you will apologize.

*Pour demain, vous **préparerez** le chapitre Dix.*
For tomorrow, you will prepare chapter Ten.

Note that a future in the negative form is actually stronger than an imperative. Compare:

> *Tu n'iras pas au cinéma.*
> You will not go to the cinema.
> (that's an order)
>   and:
> *Ne va pas au cinéma!*
> Don't go to the cinema!
> (could be construed as a request or a plea)

Hence the negative future is used to express a moral obligation, as in the Ten Commandments.

> Ex: *Tu ne tueras point.*
> Thou shalt not kill.

3.1.2 *The future to express probability*

The future can be used to express probability, an objection, a perspective, in other words, some kind of **knowledge** on the part of the speaker.

(i) Probability or a personal hypothesis, generally with *être*.

> Ex: *On sonne à la porte, ce **sera** Jean-Pierre.*
> (= *ce doit être Jean-Pierre*)
> The doorbell is ringing: it must be Jean-Pierre.
>
> *Il est neuf heures: Jean-Pierre **sera** déjà à Londres.*
> (= *Jean-Pierre doit déjà être à Londres*)
> It is nine o'clock: Jean-Pierre must already be in London.

(but not a rumour, a conjecture or allegation, for which the conditional is used – see chapter 13 Conditional, section 3.2.2(vi):

> Ex: *Une bombe a explosé à Belfast: il y aurait des dizaines de blessés.*)

(ii) A possible objection.

> Ex: *Vous **penserez** que ce n'est pas juste.*
> You will think that it is not fair.

(iii) A perspective to be envisaged, a prediction.

> Ex: *Je le connais, il vous en **fera** voir.*
> I know him. He will push you around.
>
> *Ça ne **marchera** pas.*
> It won't work.

3.1.3 *The present instead of the future*

The present can be used instead of a future (see chapter 5 Present, section 3.1(vi)), with appropriate adverbs or adverb phrases.

Ex: *Je quitte Londres demain.*
I am leaving London tomorrow.

Je descends à la prochaine.
I'm getting off at the next stop.

3.1.4   The continuous future

(i)   The continuous future can be expressed by the future of *être* + *en train de* + infinitive, meaning 'to be in the process of' (see chapter 5 Present, section 3.3).

Ex: *Quand vous arriverez, nous **serons en train de** faire nos valises.*
When you arrive, we'll be packing our cases (= in the middle of packing our cases).

Note that it can only be used when the meaning is actually 'to be in the process of doing something' or 'to be in the middle of doing something'. Hence:

(ii)   An English continuous future is more usually rendered as a simple future in French.

Ex: I shall not be leaving before tomorrow.
(or: I shall not leave)
*Je ne **partirai** pas avant demain.*

Will you be seeing Paul tomorrow?
(or: Will you see Paul tomorrow?)
***Verrez**-vous Paul demain?*

3.1.5   The narrative future and the present

The future can be used in conjunction with the present. It then corresponds to a comment from the speaker, who intervenes in the story to 'prophesy' events which will happen after those he/she has just mentioned in the present tense.

Ex: *Les hirondelles **quittent** les régions tempérées pour aller en Afrique où elles **resteront** jusqu'au printemps.*
Swallows are leaving temperate regions to go to Africa where they will stay till Spring.

3.2   Cases of difference from English usage

In the cases that follow, there is no direct correspondence between the French and the English expressions of tense.

3.2.1   The future after conjunctions of time

In French, the future tense is used after the following conjunctions of time: *quand, lorsque, dès que, aussitôt que, pendant que, tandis que, tant que, aussi longtemps que, jusqu'au jour où*, etc. whereas in English, the present is usually used after: 'when', 'as soon as', 'while', 'as long as', etc.

The verb in the main clause is in the future or the imperative.

Ex: **Quand** *vous* **serez** *calmé, je vous* **écouterai**.
When you have calmed down, I will listen to you.

Appelez-*moi* **dès que** *vous le* **pourrez**.
Call me as soon as you can.

NB: Present or future can be used with *quand* followed by *vouloir*.
Ex: *Viens quand tu veux/quand tu voudras.*

3.2.2 'shall' and 'will' to express requests and wishes

In the following cases, 'shall' and 'will' are expressed by *vouloir* in the present tense + infinitive or subjunctive (see also chapter 21 Modals, section 4).

(i) To express an offer
Ex: Will you shut the door?
Voulez-vous fermer la porte?

Shall I help you?
[*Voulez-vous que*] *je vous aide?*

(ii) To express a wish or determination ('will')
Ex: He won't (= isn't willing to) do it.
Il ne veut pas le faire.

I will not be talked to in that tone of voice.
Je ne veux pas qu'on me parle sur ce ton.

3.2.3 The future instead of a past tense

The future can be used in the place of a past tense in a narrative. The reader is thus 'transferred back' to the time when the reported events took place.

In a historical context, the future can be used in conjunction with a past historic or a 'historic present'.

Ex: 'S'inspirant d'un idéal antique, il (Saint-Just) **préconise** une république égalitaire et vertueuse. Il **contribue** à l'élaboration de la Constitution de l'an I, qui ne **sera** jamais appliquée.'

Christian Melchior-Bonnet, *Le grand livre de l'histoire de France*

NB: The future can also be used with a combination of present and past tenses, particularly in 'journalese'!

Ex: 'Après un délibéré de près de deux heures, la cour **rejette** les conclusions de la défense. Le procès **pourrait** commencer, mais il **faut** faire l'appel des quelques cent quatre-vingts personnes qui **déposeront** comme témoins ou comme experts. Volontiers tatillon, le président Pacaud **s'est accordé** le temps nécessaire aux interrogatoires approfondis puisque les derniers témoins **sont** convoqués pour le 21 février.'

Le Monde, 19 January 1991

4 The future perfect

The future perfect is made up of the future of the appropriate auxiliary (*être* or *avoir*), plus the past participle of the verb to be conjugated.

> Ex: *Je serai parti.*
> *Vous aurez mangé.*
> *Ils se seront promenés.*

4.1 The future perfect in independent clauses

The future perfect can be used in independent clauses to express the following:

(i) Completion of an action or event in the future ('will have')

The future tense refers to an event which will be **in progress** at some time in the future, known as the non-accomplished aspect. However, the future perfect refers to an event which is seen as already **completed** at some time in the future, known as the accomplished aspect (see chapter 4 section 5, Aspect).

> Ex: *Tu **auras terminé** cet article ce soir?*
> **Will** you **have finished** this article by tonight?
>
> *Elle arrivera demain. Vous **serez** déjà **parti**.*
> She will arrive tomorrow. You **will** already **be gone**.
>
> *Attendez-moi! J'**aurai fini** dans une minute!*
> Wait for me! I'**ll have finished** in a minute!

(ii) Conjecture, supposition (modal value), i.e. something that is assumed/highly likely to have happened ('must have'). This is used instead of *devoir* (perfect) + infinitive. See chapter 21 Modals.

> Ex: *Il est en retard: il **se sera** encore **trompé** de chemin.*
> or:
> *Il est en retard: il **a dû** encore **se tromper** de chemin.*
> He is late: he **must have taken** the wrong way again.
>
> *Grand-mère n'est pas dans le train. Elle l'**aura manqué**.*
> Grandmother is not on the train. She **must have missed** it.

Note that when the future perfect expresses something that is nearly certain, the perfect can be used instead. This is translated by the present perfect in English.

> Ex: *Ils ne sont pas encore arrivés? Ils **ont manqué** leur train.*
> Haven't they arrived yet? They **have missed** their train.

Compare:

> – *Il n'a pas téléphoné?*
> – *Non, il **a oublié**.*
> (statement of fact)
> – He **has forgotten**.
> and:
> – *Non, il **aura oublié**.*
> (supposition)
> – He **must have forgotten**.

4.2 The future perfect in subordinate clauses

The future perfect can be used in subordinate clauses, to express an action which will be completed prior to another in the future. It can be used with either:
– a conjunction of **time**
    or:
– a conjunction of **cause**.

(i) The future perfect can be used in a subordinate clause of **time**, with a conjunction of time showing anteriority: *quand, lorsque; après que; tant que; aussitôt que, dès que; à peine . . . que.* In English, the present perfect is used.
>   Ex: *Je te prêterai mon livre quand j'aurai fini de le lire.*
>   I will lend you my book when I **have finished** reading it.

>   *Tu verras: dès que tu auras reçu des nouvelles, ça ira mieux.*
>   You'll see: as soon as you **have received** some news, it will be better.

NB: Because *dès que, aussitôt que* and *à peine . . . que* indicate actions that happened just before the main action, the two verbs can also be in the simple future, thus keeping the same tense.
>   Ex: *A peine sera-t-il dans le train qu'il se rendra compte qu'il a oublié son billet!*
>   As soon as he is on the train, he will realize that he has forgotten his ticket!

(ii) The future perfect can be used in a subordinate clause of **cause**. In English the future perfect is used too.
>   Ex: *Vous aurez faim parce que vous n'aurez pas assez mangé.*
>   You will be hungry because you **will** not **have eaten** enough.

>   *Vous ne comprendrez pas parce que vous n'aurez pas fait attention.*
>   You will not understand because you **will** not **have paid** attention.

4.3 The pluperfect of the future

The pluperfect of the future is not commonly used in French. However, some grammarians argue that it can be useful to underline the rapid succession of two events, something which a future perfect tense might not convey as accurately. Compare:
>   *Dès qu'elle aura fini son travail, elle viendra me rejoindre.*
>   and:
>   *Dès qu'elle aura eu fini son travail, elle viendra me rejoindre.*

5 The immediate future

5.1 Formation

(i) The immediate future (*futur immédiat* or *périphrastique*) is formed with the present of the verb *aller* + the infinitive of the verb concerned ('to be going to' + infinitive), which can itself be the verb *aller*.

> Ex: *Nous **allons commencer**.*
> We're going to begin.
>
> *Je **vais aller** faire les courses.*
> I'm going to go shopping.

(ii) The imperfect is the past tense which is always used to express an immediate future in the past.

> Ex: *J'**allais** vous **dire** quelque chose mais on nous a interrompus.*
> I was going to say something to you but we were interrupted.

(iii) For a 'very immediate' future, use *être sur le point de* + infinitive ('to be about to' + infinitive).

> Ex: *Nous **sommes sur le point de commencer**.*
> We're about to begin.

Note that, unlike *aller* + infinitive, *être sur le point de* can be used in all tenses.

> Ex: *Nous **avons été** plusieurs fois **sur le point de commencer** la démonstration mais les retardataires continuaient à arriver.*
> We were about to begin the demonstration several times but latecomers were still arriving.

5.2 Use

The immediate future ('to be' + 'going to' + infinitive) and the simple future ('will/shall' + bare infinitive) are frequently interchangeable in English. However, it is not the case in French. Generally speaking, the immediate future places the process in the continuation of the time of the speaker, whereas the simple future appears more like being cut off from it. Hence:

(i) If the future is linked to the present with an adverb such as *immédiatement*, *maintenant*, *tout de suite*, etc., or an imperative, the immediate future is normally used in French.

> Ex: ***Maintenant**, je **vais lire** ton article.*
> (and not: **Maintenant, je lirai ton article.*)
>
> *Je **vais** le **faire tout de suite**.*
> (and not: **Je le ferai tout de suite.*)
>
> ***Viens**, je **vais** te **montrer**.*
> (and not: **Viens, je te montrerai.*)

113

In English on the other hand, 'shall' and 'will' can be used with 'now', 'at once', 'right away', etc.

> Ex: Now I shall read your article.
> I'll do it right away.
> Come! I'll show you.

(ii) In French, the immediate future is used if the future event (which may be in the distant future) is connected to the present time of the speaker insofar as it may be inevitable, intentional or dependent. In English, either the immediate future or the simple future can be used.

> Ex: *Je vais faire du café.* (intentional)
> I am going to make some coffee/I'll make some coffee.

NB: **Je ferai du café.*
begs the question: When? (see below)

> *Il est 8 heures, je vais me lever.* (dependent)
> (and not: **Il est 8 heures, je me lèverai.*)
> It's 8 o'clock, I'll get up.
> > but:
> *Comme Paul vous l'expliquera, ça n'a jamais été notre intention.*
> As Paul will explain to you, this was never our intention.
> i.e. he will explain it to you only if you ask him: it is neither inevitable nor linked to the present.

If, on the contrary, the intention is that he **should** explain it to you, the immediate future should be used.

> Ex: *Comme Paul va vous l'expliquer . . .*

(iii) When a time or date is given (explicitly or implicitly), the immediate future can be used as an alternative to the simple future.

> Ex: *Demain, je ferai une tarte aux pommes.*
> > or:
> *Demain, je vais faire une tarte aux pommes.*
>
> *Je passerai l'année prochaine au Japon.*
> > or:
> *Je vais passer l'année prochaine au Japon.*
>
> *Un jour ou l'autre, nous mourrans.*
> > or:
> *Un jour ou l'autre, nous allons mourir.*

Note that in this case, the immediate future is particularly used in informal French.

(iv) Beware of the translation of 'if . . . going to' (see chapter 21 Modals, section 4.5).

> Ex: If they're **going to** win the elections, they'd better start campaigning now.
> *S'ils **veulent** gagner les élections, ils feraient mieux de se mettre en campagne dès maintenant.*

Remember that a *si* of condition can **never** be followed by a future (not even an immediate future!) or a conditional. (See chapter 13 Conditional, section 3.2.3.)

8 Imperfect

Rien n'est imparfait sauf le subjonctif

1 Introduction

The imperfect (*imparfait*) puts the process expressed by the verb in the past. Like the present, the imperfect expresses the non-accomplished aspect, hence its other name: *présent du passé*. In the discourse situation, the imperfect expresses the non-accomplished aspect by opposition to the perfect (*passé composé*), which expresses the accomplished aspect. In historical texts, it is opposed in the same way to the past historic (*passé simple*).

The imperfect in French thus expresses continuation or repetition in the past. Hence it is often used to describe situations or habits. However, there are cases where:

– both English and French express continuation or repetition with another past tense (simple past and perfect). This reflects a difference of aspect: the action or situation is seen from the present rather than from the past.

– English can describe situations and habits in the simple past, whilst French uses the imperfect.

The imperfect in French can also be used instead of a perfect or past historic for stylistic effect (narrative imperfect).

Finally, besides these temporal and aspectual values, the imperfect also has modal values.

The imperfect in subordinate clauses is treated in chapters 6 *depuis* and Other Tense Markers and 41 Reported Speech, section 3.10.

2 Formation

The imperfect tense is formed with a radical of the main verb (i.e. the 1st person plural of the present indicative which is invariable) + the appropriate imperfect ending as shown below.
It is by far the easiest tense to conjugate.
The imperfect endings are the same for all verbs:

–ais	–ions
–ais	–iez
–ait	–aient

2.1 Verbs in ER

(i)   The radical is the infinitive minus the ending ER, even for *aller*.

> Ex: *chanter: je **chant**ais*   *nous **chant**ions*
> *tu **chant**ais*   *vous **chant**iez*
> *il/elle/on **chant**ait*   *ils/elles **chant**aient*
>
> *aller: j'**all**ais*   *nous **all**ions, etc.*

(ii) Verbs in *-ier*, *-uer* and *-éer*: note the juxtaposition of vowels with *nous* and *vous*.

> Ex: *étudier*   *j'étudiais*   *nous étud**ii**ons*
> *continuer*   *je continuais*   *nous contin**u**ions*
> *créer*   *je créais*   *nous cré**i**ons*

(iii) Verbs in *-ger* must add an 'e' before 'a' to keep the sound [ʒ].

> Ex: *manger: je mang**e**ais*   *nous mangions*
> *tu mang**e**ais*   *vous mangiez*
> *il/elle/on mang**e**ait*   *ils/elles mang**e**aient*

(iv) Verbs in *-cer* must add a cedilla before 'a' to keep the sound [s].

> Ex: *placer: je plaçais*   *nous placions*
> *tu plaçais*   *vous placiez*
> *il/elle/on plaçait*   *ils/elles plaçaient*

2.2 Verbs in IR

(i)   For regular verbs in IR (they have their present participle in *-issant*), the radical is the present participle minus *-ant*.

> Ex: *finir (finissant): je finissais*   *nous finissions*
> *tu finissais*   *vous finissiez*
> *il/elle/on finissait*   *ils/elles finissaient*
>
> *haïr (haïssant):*   *je haïssais, etc.*
> *obéir (obéissant):*   *j'obéissais, etc.*

(ii) For other verbs in IR, the radical is simply the infinitive minus *-IR*.

> Ex: *servir*   *je **serv**ais, etc.*
> *cueillir*   *je **cueill**ais, etc.*

(iii) *fuir* changes the '*i*' of the infinitive into a '*y*':

> *je **fuy**ais, etc.*

(iv) *fleurir:*

– The literal meaning 'to flower' is regular:
> Ex: *De mon temps, les roses ne fleurissaient qu'en juin!*
> In my days, roses would only blossom in June!

– With the metaphorical meaning 'to prosper', the radical becomes *flor-:*
> Ex: *En ce temps-là, le commerce florissait.*
> In those days, commerce was flourishing.

This is also valid for the present participles:
> *fleurissant/florissant.*

2.3 Verbs in OIR

(i) Most are regular insofar as the radical is the infinitive minus OIR.

   Ex: *devoir*   *je **devais**, etc.*
       recevoir   *je **recevais**, etc.*

(ii) But note the following exceptions:

   – *s'asseoir* has two conjugations:
       *je m'**assey**ais*   *nous nous **assey**ions*
   or: *je m'**assoy**ais*   *nous nous **assoy**ions*

   – *voir* changes the '*i*' of the infinitive into a '*y*':
       *je **voy**ais*   *nous **voy**ions*
   Also: *revoir, prévoir, entrevoir, pourvoir*

2.4 Verbs in RE

(i) The radical is regular: infinitive minus -RE.

   – All the verbs in *-endre* (except ***prendre*** and its derivatives, see (vii) below), *-ondre, -ordre, -erdre, -andre, -ompre, -attre, -ettre, -ivre*.
       Ex: *vendre*   *je **vend**ais*   *nous **vend**ions*
           vivre   *je **viv**ais*   *nous **viv**ions*

   – *inclure, conclure, rire* and *sourire*: note the juxtaposition of vowels with *nous* and *vous*.
       Ex: *rire*   *je riais*   *nous **rii**ons*   *vous **rii**ez*
           inclure *j'incluais*   *nous inc**lui**ons* *vous inc**lui**ez*

However, there are a lot of exceptions, even for very common verbs.

(ii) Verbs which add an 's' to the radical of the infinitive:

   – Certain verbs in *-ire*:
       Ex: *dire*   *je **dis**ais*   *nous **dis**ions*
   Also: *interdire, contredire, médire, prédire, lire, relire, élire; suffire* (but: *maudire: je **maudiss**ais*)

   – Certain verbs in *-aire*:
       Ex: *plaire*   *je **plais**ais*   *nous **plais**ions*
   Also: *(se) taire, faire, défaire, satisfaire*

   – All verbs in *-uire*:
       Ex: *conduire*   *je **conduis**ais*   *nous **conduis**ions*

(iii) Verbs which add a '*v*' to the radical of the infinitive:

   – Certain verbs in *-ire*:
       Ex: *écrire*   *j'**écriv**ais*   *nous **écriv**ions*
   Also: *décrire, inscrire, prescrire, souscrire, transcrire*

(iv) Verbs which turn the '*i*' of the radical into '*y*':

— Certain verbs in *-aire*:
Ex: *distraire*   *je* **distray***ais*   *nous* **distray***ions*
Also: *soustraire*

— *croire*   *je* **croy***ais*   *nous* **croy***ions*

(v)   All verbs in *-aître* or *-oître* drop their circumflex accent and replace the '*t*' by '*ss*':
Ex: *connaître*   *je* **connaiss***ais*   *nous* **connaiss***ions*
croître   *je* **croiss***ais*   *nous* **croiss***ions*

(vi) All verbs in *-aindre*, *-eindre* and *-oindre* turn their '*nd*' into '*gn*':
Ex: *craindre*   *je* **craign***ais*   *nous* **craign***ions*
peindre   *je* **peign***ais*   *nous* **peign***ions*
(NB: same as *peigner*!)
joindre   *je* **joign***ais*   *nous* **joign***ions*

(vii) The following are particularly irregular:

— *prendre*   *je* **pren***ais*   *nous* **pren***ions*
Also: *entreprendre, surprendre, apprendre, comprendre*

— *boire*   *je* **buv***ais*   *nous* **buv***ions*

— *vaincre*   *je* **vainqu***ais*   *nous* **vainqu***ions*

— *résoudre*   *je* **résolv***ais*   *nous* **résolv***ions*
Also: *dissoudre, absoudre*

— *coudre*   *je* **cous***ais*   *nous* **cous***ions*

— *moudre*   *je* **moul***ais*   *nous* **moul***ions*

2.5 *avoir* and *être*

avoir and *être* are regular, except that *être* changes its '*ê*' into '*é*':

*j'***avais**	*nous* **avions**	*j'***étais**	*nous* **étions**
tu **avais**	*vous* **aviez**	*tu* **étais**	*vous* **étiez**
il **avait**	*ils* **avaient**	*il* **était**	*ils* **étaient**

3 Use

The imperfect is often called the 'present in the past'. It generally expresses a continuous action, a state of affairs or a habit in the past, without reference to their beginning or end. It is also frequently used for descriptive purposes. The emphasis is placed on the **duration** or **habitual** occurrence of the action; also, in the case of repeated actions, on viewing the event(s) from the past.

It corresponds roughly in English to the past continuous (e.g. 'He was leaving'), or to the 'habitual past' expressed by **would** (e.g. 'He would get up at 6 every day') or **used to** (e.g. 'He used to go to his country cottage every weekend'). However, English also uses the simple past to express the French imperfect, particularly in descriptions of situations, and with stative verbs such as 'to know'.

3.1 Temporal values of the imperfect

It is important to note that, unlike the past historic or the perfect tenses, the imperfect must be accompanied by an adverb or adverb phrase of time, unless it expresses a habit or a state of affairs.

(i) **Continuous actions**

The non-accomplished aspect of the imperfect goes particularly well with verbs which have an imperfective meaning and express duration.

Ex: *Pendant le dîner, tout le monde **parlait** à la fois.*
During the dinner, everybody was talking at the same time.

*Hier, je **lisais**.*
Yesterday, I was reading.

NB(1): *Hier, j'**étais en train de lire**.*
This turn emphasizes the continuous aspect of the action: see continuous present and future in chapters 5 Present, section 3.3 and 7 Future, section 3.1.4.

NB(2): In all these cases, the actions are seen from the past. The reader or interlocutor is thus 'placed in' the action. However, if the action is seen from the present (often but not necessarily with an indication of the duration of the event), then the perfect is used.

Ex: *Hier, j'**ai lu** pendant une heure.*
Yesterday, I read for an hour.

(ii) **Interrupted actions**

The action in the imperfect can form the 'background' (*toile de fond* or *arrière-plan*) for events expressed in the perfect or past historic.

Ex: *Quand le soir est venu, il **lisait** encore.*
When night came, he was still reading.

*La semaine dernière, le tremblement de terre eut lieu alors que toute la ville **dormait**.*
Last week, the earthquake happened while the whole town was asleep.
(= 'was sleeping')

NB: If a continuous action took place and was completed while another was in progress, the imperfect expresses the action still in progress and the perfect the completed one.

Ex: *Pendant que tu **parlais**, j'**ai préparé** le déjeuner.*
While you were talking, I made lunch.

(iii) **Simultaneous actions**

The imperfect is used for two actions simultaneously in progress in the past.

Ex: *Pendant que je **travaillais**, mes sœurs **jouaient**.*
While I worked, my sisters played.
(or: While I was working, my sisters were playing.)

Note that either the simple or the continuous form can be used in English.

(iv) **Repeated actions**

When the imperfect expresses repeated actions, it can be used with verbs which have either a perfective or an imperfective meaning. Repetition is emphasized with appropriate adverbs or adverb phrases, e.g. *chaque fois que, régulièrement, rarement, souvent, tous les matins, tous les jours,* etc. If the **habitual** nature of the action is emphasized, i.e. seen from the past, the imperfect is also used.

Ex: *Chaque fois qu'ils **posaient** une question, j'**essayais** d'y répondre.*
Each time they asked a question, I would try to answer it.

*S'il **parlait**, c'était pour raconter des histoires invraisemblables.*
Note that here, *si* has an iterative value (= whenever).
Whenever he spoke, it was to tell tall stories.

*Quand je la **voyais**, je lui **disais** bonjour, mais elle ne **répondait** pas.*
Whenever I saw her, I would say hello but she wouldn't answer.

Note that here, *quand, lorsque,* etc. have the value of *à chaque fois que.* They can also introduce a single event, in which case the perfect or past historic are used.

Ex: *Quand je l'**ai vue**, je lui **ai dit** bonjour mais elle n'a pas **répondu**.*
(single event)
When I saw her, I said hello but she did not answer.

*A cette époque-là, il **mangeait** au restaurant tous les soirs.*
In those days, he would eat in restaurants every evening.

NB(1): The perfect tense is used if the emphasis is NOT placed on the habitual nature of the action, i.e. if the events are merely recorded and then recounted from the present. Compare:

*Pendant les vacances, elle lui **téléphonait** souvent.*
During the holidays, she would often ring him.

The emphasis is on '*souvent*': the action is seen from the past.
and:

*Pendant les vacances, elle lui **a téléphoné** souvent.*
During the holidays, she often rang him.

The emphasis is on '*pendant les vacances*': the action is seen from the present.

NB(2): The nature of the frequency markers can help determine whether the emphasis is on habit or whether several occurrences of the same event are recorded. For instance, if the frequency or the repetition of the action is defined by expressions such as *une fois, deux fois, plusieurs fois,* the perfect is generally used in French.

Ex: *Pendant les vacances, je lui **ai téléphoné** deux fois.*
During the holidays, I rang him twice.

NB(3): For single events of course the perfect or past historic is used. Compare:

*Un jour il **prenait** le train, le lendemain sa voiture.*

One day he would take the train, the next day [he would take] his car.

(both actions happened more than once)

and:

*Un jour, il **prit** le train.*

One day he took the train.

(single event)

(v) State of affairs

The imperfect is used to describe something static or a state of affairs in the past, hence it is useful to describe the background onto which the events of a story are projected.

Ex: *Au sommet de la colline **se trouvait** un vieux château d'eau.*

At the top of the hill stood an old water tower.

*La route **descendait** vers le village.*

The road sloped down towards the village.

The imperfect is thus often used to describe a situation which was prevalent at the beginning of a narrative.

Ex: *'Dans ma jeunesse mes parents **habitaient**, comme aujourd'hui encore, Villeneuve-sur-Lot.'*

Paul Guth, *Le naïf amoureux*

(vi) Habitual actions

The imperfect is used to describe habitual or lasting actions which happened in the past and which used to be characteristic of that period.

Ex: *Il y a vingt ans, les Anglais ne **buvaient** pas beaucoup de vin.*

Twenty years ago, the English didn't drink much wine.

*Lorsque j'**écrivais** beaucoup, je **buvais** du café toute la journée.*

When I wrote a lot, I drank coffee all day.

or:

When I used to write a lot, I used to drink coffee all day.

Note that English can use either the simple past or 'would'/'used to' to express habit or repeated action.

Consider the following example:

'Judith did not easily come to parties. She would come after pressure [. . .] to correct what she thought was a defect in her character.'

Iris Murdoch, *Nuns and Soldiers*

*Judith ne **venait** pas volontiers aux soirées. Elle **venait** sous la pression [. . .] pour corriger ce qu'elle **croyait** être un défaut de sa personnalité.*

The first verb expresses a lasting characteristic, the second an habitual action and the third a state of mind.

(vii) **The imperfect with** *avoir* **and** *être*

Since these verbs generally express a state as opposed to an action or event, the imperfect is used in French. In English, a simple past is used. However, the perfect or the past historic can be used with *être* and *avoir* to express an action or event. This is so if they are used in a dynamic, rather than a stative (or descriptive) sense, or if the action or even the state is seen from the present.

> Ex: Because of the rain, the roads were slippery.
> *A cause de la pluie, les routes **étaient** glissantes.*
>
> When I went shopping, there were already a lot of people in the shops.
> *Quand je suis allée faire les courses, il y **avait** déjà beaucoup de monde dans les magasins.*

Compare:

> ***Etiez**-vous chez les Brown pour leur pendaison de crémaillère?*
> (state)
> Were you at the Browns' for their house-warming party?
> > and:
> ***Avez**-vous **été** chez les Brown récemment?*
> (action)
> Have you been to the Browns' recently?
>
> *Il **avait** 20 ans quand la guerre a commencé.*
> (state)
> He was 20 years old when the war broke out.
> > and:
> *Il **a eu** 20 ans le 15 décembre.*
> (event: birthday)
> He was 20 years old on December 15.

Consider the following examples:

> *Avant 1945, les femmes n'**avaient** pas le droit de vote.*
> Before 1945, women didn't have the right to vote.

What is expressed here is a state, prevailing in the period before 1945.

> *Les femmes n'**ont** pas **eu** le droit de vote avant 1945.*
> Women didn't get the right to vote before 1945.

What is expressed here is an event, namely something which happened in 1945. Note that English uses the dynamic verb 'to get'.

(viii) **The imperfect with verbs expressing a state of mind**

Generally, these verbs express actions which are seen in their continuity (e.g. *penser, trouver, songer, aimer, désirer, préférer, détester, espérer, regretter,* and the modals *croire, pouvoir, vouloir*), hence the use of the imperfect. Consider the following examples:

> *Paul ne **savait** pas qui vous **étiez**.*
> Paul didn't know who you **were**.

> *Ce poème représente tout ce que Wilfred Owen **détestait**, c'est-à-dire l'idée qu'une guerre puisse être juste.*
>
> This poem represents everything Wilfred Owen **hated**, that is the idea that a war can be just.

In both cases, we have a 'state of affairs in the past' (see section 3.1(v) above).

However, if the verb expresses an action taking place at a precise moment, or within precise limits, then the perfect or past historic is used. Compare:

> *Je **pensais** justement à vous quand j'ai vu qu'il allait pleuvoir.*
> I was just thinking about you when I saw it was going to rain.
> (= I **was** already **thinking** about you at that time)
>   and:
> *J'**ai pensé** à vous quand j'ai vu qu'il allait pleuvoir.*
> I thought about you when I saw it was going to rain.
> (= the prospect of rain **made me think** of you)

(ix) **Stylistic use of the imperfect: the narrative imperfect**

The imperfect can be used to underline or dramatize an important event, where a perfect or a past historic would normally be expected. This use of the imperfect (sometimes called *imparfait pittoresque* or *imparfait historique*, by analogy with the *présent historique*) 'places' the reader 'in' the action. Since one of the functions of the imperfect tense is to present an action in progress (unlike the perfect or the past historic), it creates a cinematographic effect insofar as the action is 'slowed down' and readers or listeners witness it unfolding before them. Their attention is thus hooked from the beginning as they 'relive' the story.

Note that the imperfect is therefore used to express an event with a perfective verb. However, the exact moment is specified by an adverb or adverb phrase of time, or can be understood by the combined use of verbs in the perfect or past historic in the text.

NB: This construction, which can be found in newspaper articles as well as in historical accounts, should be recognized but not necessarily used by students.

Consider the following example:

> '*Le sept septembre 1303, une poignée de Français dirigés par G. de Nogaret, conseiller du roi Philippe le Bel, **pénétraient** dans la petite ville d'Anagni, proche de Rome, où **résidait** le pape Boniface VIII en cette fin d'été.*'

> Christian Melchior-Bonnet, *Le grand livre de l'histoire de France*

Note that '*pénétraient*' is the only verb in the extract which is expressed in the **narrative** imperfect as it replaces a perfect or a past historic tense; '*résidait*' demonstrates the standard use of the imperfect to describe the background to events (see 3.1(v) above). The systematic use of the imperfect instead of the perfect or the past historic therefore creates a 'levelling' effect on the whole text, as the stative '*résidait*' is placed on the same level as the dynamic '*pénétraient*'.

3.2 Modal values of the imperfect

In most of its modal values, the imperfect is preceded by *si*.

3.2.1 Main clause in the conditional

The imperfect with *si* is used when the main clause is in the conditional (see chapter 13 Conditional, section 3.2.3). The imperfect expresses the potential or unreal nature of the present, i.e. the non-accomplishment of the process.

> Ex: *Si j'étais riche, j'achèterais un château fort en Ecosse.*
> If I were rich, I would buy a castle in Scotland.
>
> *Je viendrais si je le pouvais.*
> I would come if I could.

3.2.2 No main clause

When there is no main clause, the verb in the imperfect preceded by *si* can have different values according to the context:

– a proposal, a suggestion:

> Ex: *Si on prenait un verre?*
> How about [having] a drink?
>
> *Si tu faisais un peu moins de bruit?*
> How about making a little less noise?

– a supposition:

> Ex: *Et s'il ne venait pas?*
> What if he didn't come?

– a wish:

> Ex: *Si seulement c'était les vacances!*
> If only it were the holidays!

NB: To express a regret, the pluperfect should be used (see chapter 11 Other Past Tenses, section 2.2.4).

– expression of politeness:
The imperfect, with or without *si*, is used as a form of politeness, with verbs of request.

> Ex: *Je me demandais si je pouvais vous accompagner.*
> I was wondering if I could come with you.
>
> *Je voulais vous confirmer notre rendez-vous.*
> I wanted to confirm our appointment.

For other ways to ask something politely, see chapter 13 Conditional, section 3.2.2.

3.2.3 The imperfect instead of the conditional perfect

The imperfect is sometimes used instead of the conditional perfect to express more vividly what **might** have happened (value of 'unreal'). The imperfect thus expresses the non-accomplishment of the process.

Ex: *Une minute de plus et je* **manquais** *mon train!*
(= *et j'aurais manqué . . .*)
Another minute and I would have missed my train!

3.3 Immediate future and recent past

(i) **Immediate future**

To express what was just about to happen, *aller* is used in the imperfect + infinitive.

Ex: *Elle* **allait partir** *quand le téléphone a sonné.*
She was about to leave when the telephone rang.

NB: *aller* in the imperfect + infinitive is ambiguous. However:

– the past tense of the immediate future is generally accompanied by an **opposition** or **interruption** marker.

Ex: *J'allais plonger quand le moniteur m'a crié d'arrêter.*
I was going to dive when the instructor shouted to me to stop.

– the verb *aller* in the imperfect tense to express an action which was **usual** is generally accompanied by an adverb or adverb phrase of frequency.

Ex: *J'allais plonger dans la piscine de l'hôtel* **tous les matins**.
I would go and dive in the hotel swimming-pool every morning.

(ii) **Recent past**

To express what had just happened, *venir de* is used in the imperfect + infinitive.

Ex: *Elle* **venait de quitter** *la pièce quand le téléphone a sonné.*
She had just left the room when the telephone rang.

NB: The imperfect is often used instead of a recent past, especially with *arriver, sortir, rentrer, revenir.*

Ex: *Puis il rencontra un journaliste qui* **arrivait** *de New York.*
is more elegant than:
Puis il rencontra un journaliste qui **venait d'arriver** *de New York.*
Then he met a journalist who had just come from New York.

To emphasize the recent past, *juste* can be added after the verb.

Ex: *Puis il rencontra un journaliste qui* **arrivait juste** *de New York.*

The imperfect is particularly useful with *revenir* as *venir de revenir* is simply too repetitive.

Ex: *Il* **revenait** *[juste] du régiment lorsque je fis sa connaissance.*
He was just back from military service when I met him.

9 Perfect

Moins il est simple, plus il faut avec son passé composer

1 Introduction

The perfect tense is generally used to express past actions or events which are completed at the time of speaking but can have a bearing on the present. It often indicates when the action or event took place. There is no emphasis placed on the duration of actions or events (as expressed by the imperfect). However, reference may be made to the duration to indicate the completion of the event. The French perfect (*passé composé*) can be expressed by the present perfect, present perfect continuous or simple past in English.

Like other compound forms, the perfect has values of accomplished aspect and anteriority:
- as accomplished, it is opposed to the present, which is non-accomplished.
  > Ex: *Elle est contente: elle **a** enfin **trouvé** la solution à son problème.*
  > She's happy – she's found a solution to her problem at last.
- as anteriority, the perfect has the same aspectual values as the past historic.
  > Ex: *Sylvain **est parti** pour l'Afrique en 1968.*
  > Sylvain left for Africa in 1968.

The perfect is opposed to the imperfect in the following ways:
- if the perfect is used with its accomplished value, the imperfect represents the non-accomplished.
  > Ex: *Quand il **était** à Las Vegas, Paul **jouait** beaucoup au casino. Maintenant, il **a abandonné** tout ça.*
- if the perfect is used with its temporal value, the same opposition as that between imperfect/past historic is created.
  > Ex: *Marie **lisait** le dernier roman de Marguerite Duras quand Paul et ses amis **sont arrivés**.*

In addition to the role described above, the perfect is also used as a replacement for the past historic in spoken French, and indeed in literature for stylistic purposes (see chapter 10 Past Historic, section 3).

The perfect with *si, depuis*, and the modals is treated in the relevant chapters.

2 Formation

The perfect is made up of the auxiliary **avoir** or **être** in the present indicative plus the past participle of the verb to be conjugated.

There are many irregular past participles, and they should always be learnt at the same time as the infinitive.

2.1 Verbs in ER

(i) The ER of the infinitive is replaced by '-é', even for an otherwise irregular verb like *aller*.

> Ex: *donner* → *donné*
> *manger* → *mangé*
> *aller* → *allé*

Note that *créer* does take a double '*éé*':

> *créer* → *créé* (feminine: *créée*)

(ii) **only** verbs in ER can have their past participles in '-é', with the exception of *naître* → *né*.

(iii) Verbs in *-ier* or *-uer*: it is a common error to forget the '*i*' or '*u*' before the '*é*'.

> Ex: *étudier* → *étudié*
> *habituer* → *habitué*

2.2 Verbs in IR

2.2.1 *Regular verbs in IR*

(i) Regular verbs in IR have their present participle in *-issant*. Their past participles are also regular: the IR of the infinitive is replaced by '-*i*'.

> Ex: *finir (finissant)* → *fini*
> *obéir (obéissant)* → *obéi*
> *réjouir (réjouissant)* → *réjoui*

(ii) *haïr*:
The '*i*' of *haïr* is kept:

> *haïr (haïssant)* → *haï*

(iii) *bénir (bénissant)* has two past participles:
− *béni* (= blessed; glorified)

> Ex: *Le ciel en soit **béni**!*
> *Une union **bénie**.*

− *bénit* (= consecrated things only)

> Ex: *du pain **bénit***
> *de l'eau **bénite***

2.2.2   *Irregular verbs in* IR

(i) Most irregular verbs in IR (they have their present participle in *-ant*) also have their past participle in '*-i*':

$$
\begin{array}{ll}
\text{Ex: } partir~(partant) & \rightarrow~parti \\
servir~(servant) & \rightarrow~servi \\
dormir~(dormant) & \rightarrow~dormi \\
bouillir~(bouillant) & \rightarrow~bouilli \\
cueillir~(cueillant) & \rightarrow~cueilli
\end{array}
$$

NB: *fuir (fuyant)* → *fui*

(ii) *acquérir* and *conquérir* change their radical and take a final '*s*':

$$
\begin{array}{ll}
acquérir & \rightarrow~acquis \\
conquérir & \rightarrow~conquis
\end{array}
$$

(iii) For all other irregular verbs in IR, it is best to learn the correct past participle for each verb. The most frequent ending after '*i*' is '*u*':

Ex: − *venir* → *venu*

and its derivatives, e.g. *parvenir, devenir, (se) souvenir.*

− *tenir* → *tenu*

and its derivatives, e.g. *appartenir, obtenir, contenir.*

− *courir* → *couru*

and its derivatives, e.g. *secourir, parcourir.*

− *vêtir* → *vêtu*

(iv) The following verbs have their past participle in *-ert*: *ouvrir, couvrir, découvrir, offrir, souffrir.*

Ex: *ouvrir* → *ouvert*

(v) Finally, note that *mourir* is particularly irregular:

mourir → **mort**

2.3   Verbs in OIR

(i) All verbs in OIR have their past participle in '*u*' except (*s'*)*asseoir* → *assis*, but attention must be paid to the radicals.

(ii) The following are regular in that the radical is the infinitive minus OIR:

$$
\begin{array}{ll}
valoir & \rightarrow~valu \\
vouloir & \rightarrow~voulu \\
falloir & \rightarrow~fallu \\
voir & \rightarrow~vu \\
prévoir & \rightarrow~prévu \\
pourvoir & \rightarrow~pourvu
\end{array}
$$

(iii) Verbs in *-cevoir* have their past participles in *-çu*:

Ex: *décevoir* → *déçu*

(iv)   The following have a particularly contracted past participle:

savoir   → *su*
pouvoir → *pu*
devoir   → *dû*
pleuvoir → *plu* (NB: same as *plaire*!)
mouvoir → *mu*
émouvoir → *ému*

NB: There is a circumflex accent for the masculine singular past participle of *devoir* (*dû*) so that it is not confused with the partitive *du*, but the feminine is *due*.

2.4   Verbs in RE

– Most past participles end in '-*u*', but in all cases, particular attention should be paid to the radical.

– Note that verbs in -*ire*, -*ivre* and -*aire* are particularly difficult as they are divided into several categories, according to radical and ending.

(i)   The radical is the infinitive minus RE, the ending is in '-*u*'.

– Verbs in -*attre*:
Ex: *battre* → *battu*

– Verbs in -*endre* (except *prendre* and its derivatives, see (iii) below), -*ondre*, -*ordre*, -*erdre*, -*ompre*:
Ex: *vendre* → *vendu*
perdre → *perdu*
rompre → *rompu*

Note that *vaincre* is also 'regular':
vaincre → *vaincu*

(ii)   There is a change of radical in the following:

– Verbs in -*aître*:
Ex: *connaître* → *connu*
Exception: *naître* → *né*

– *vivre* and its derivatives:
Ex: *vivre* → *vécu*
survivre → *survécu*
For *suivre* and derivatives, see (iv).

– Verbs in -*ure*:
conclure → *conclu*
exclure → *exclu*
inclure → *inclus* (fem.: *incluse*)

- The following have an exceptionally contracted past participle:

$$
\begin{aligned}
&\textit{boire} &\rightarrow &\ \textbf{bu}\\
&\textit{croire} &\rightarrow &\ \textbf{cru}\\
&\textit{croître} &\rightarrow &\ \textbf{crû}\ (\textit{croire} \rightarrow \textit{cru}, \text{without a circumflex})\\
&\textit{taire} &\rightarrow &\ \textbf{tu}\ (\text{not to be confused with the } \textit{tué} \text{ of } \textit{tuer})\\
&\textit{plaire} &\rightarrow &\ \textbf{plu}\ (\text{same as } \textit{pleuvoir} \rightarrow \textit{plu})\\
&\textit{lire} &\rightarrow &\ \textbf{lu}\\
&\textit{élire} &\rightarrow &\ \textbf{élu}
\end{aligned}
$$

- Verbs in -*oudre* are particularly irregular:

$$
\begin{aligned}
&\textit{coudre} &\rightarrow &\ \textit{cou}\textbf{su}\\
&\textit{moudre} &\rightarrow &\ \textit{mou}\textbf{lu}\\
&\textit{résoudre} &\rightarrow &\ \textit{ré}\textbf{solu}
\end{aligned}
$$

But: *dissoudre* → *diss**ous*** (fem.: *diss**oute***)
    absoudre → *abs**ous*** (fem.: *abs**oute***)

(iii) The following have their past participles in -*is*:

- *prendre* and its derivatives, e.g. *apprendre, comprendre, surprendre, entreprendre*.
    Ex: *prendre* → *pri**s***

- Verbs in -*ettre*:
    Ex: *mettre* → *mi**s***

(iv) The following have their past participles in -*i*:

$$
\begin{aligned}
&\textit{rire} &\rightarrow &\ \textit{ri}\\
&\textit{sourire} &\rightarrow &\ \textit{sour}\textbf{i}\\[4pt]
&\textit{suffire} &\rightarrow &\ \textit{suff}\textbf{i}\\[4pt]
&\textit{suivre} &\rightarrow &\ \textit{suiv}\textbf{i}\\
&\textit{poursuivre} &\rightarrow &\ \textit{poursuiv}\textbf{i}
\end{aligned}
$$

For *dire, écrire* and their derivatives, see (v).
For *lire* and derivatives, see (ii).

(v) The following have their past participles in -*it*:

- *dire* and its derivatives, e.g. *interdire, maudire*.
    Ex: *dire* → *di**t***

- *écrire* and its derivatives, e.g. *décrire, inscrire, prescrire*.
    Ex: *écrire* → *écri**t***

For *lire* and derivatives, see (ii).
For *rire, suivre*, and their derivatives, see (iv).

(vi) *faire* and its derivatives, e.g. *satisfaire, distraire, soustraire*, have their past participles in -*ait*:
    Ex: *faire* → *fai**t***

For *plaire* and (*se*) *taire*, see (ii).

(vii)   Verbs in *-uire* have their past participles in *-uit*:
             Ex: *conduire* → *cond**uit***

(viii)   Verbs in *-aindre, -eindre* and *-oindre* have their past participles in *-aint, -eint* and
          -oint respectively:
             Ex: *plaindre* → *pl**aint***
                  peindre → *p**eint***
                  joindre → *j**oint***

2.5   *être* and *avoir*

In addition to their roles as auxiliaries, ***être*** and ***avoir*** can also be used as ordinary
verbs. In the perfect tense, they are both conjugated with ***avoir***:

avoir: j'ai eu   *nous avons eu*
        tu as eu   *vous avez eu*
        il/elle/on a eu   *ils/elles ont eu*

être: j'ai été   *nous avons été*
        tu as été   *vous avez été*
        il/elle/on a été   *ils/elles ont été.*

3   Auxiliary and agreement

Past participles may agree with the subject OR the object of the verb, in the
cases detailed below (but see also appendix 1). Note that these rules also affect
the other compound tenses, e.g. pluperfect, past anterior, etc. (see relevant
chapters). Agreement of past participles with pronominal verbs is treated in
chapter 20 Pronominal Verbs, section 3.1.2.

3.1   'ADVENT' verbs

The term 'ADVENT' is one of various mnemonic ways to remember the following
list of verbs which take *être* as their auxiliary:

      A arriver
         partir

      D descendre★
         monter★

      V venir
         (revenir, devenir, parvenir,
         intervenir, survenir, convenir★)
         aller

      E entrer (rentrer★)
         sortir★

N *naître*
  mourir

T *tomber*
  rester, demeurer★
  retourner★
  passer★

These verbs are in principle intransitive (see chapter 2 Syntax, section 2.6), i.e. they cannot take an object. The past participle agrees with the subject.

> Ex: ***Elle*** *est arrivée;* ***ils*** *sont partis.*
> She arrived; they left.

However, some of these verbs (marked with a ★ on the list) can have a transitive meaning, whereupon they are conjugated with ***avoir*** (note the English rendering for each of them). For instance:

— *descendre*:

> ***Elle est*** descen**due** *dans la salle à manger.*
> She went downstairs to the dining room.
>> but:
> ***Elle a*** *descen**du** ses livres.*
> She took her books downstairs.

— *monter*:

> ***Elle est*** *mon**tée** dans sa chambre.*
> She went upstairs to her bedroom.
>> but:
> ***Elle a*** *monté le courrier.*
> She took the mail upstairs.
>> or:
> ***Elle a*** *monté les escaliers.*
> She went up the stairs.

NB: 'escaliers' is considered as a direct object, even though the stairs are not being 'taken' anywhere!

— *rentrer*:

> ***Elle est*** *rentrée chez elle à dix heures du soir.*
> She went back home at ten o'clock at night.
>> but:
> ***Elle a*** *rentré le linge avant la pluie.*
> She took the washing in before it rained.

— *sortir*:

> ***Elle est*** *sortie ce matin.*
> She went out this morning.
>> but:
> ***Elle a*** *sorti le chien.*
> She took the dog out.

— *retourner*:

>*Elle **est** retournée à la maison à 8 heures.*
>She returned home at 8 o'clock.
>>but:
>*Elle **a** retourné le livre pour en voir le prix.*
>She turned the book over in order to see its price.

— *passer*:

>*Elle **est** passée nous voir.*
>She came by to see us.
>>but:
>*Elle **a** passé son parapluie à Françoise.*
>She passed her umbrella to Françoise.
>>and:
>*L'été dernier, **j'ai** passé trois mois à la mer.*
>Last summer, I spent three months by the seaside.

— *convenir*:
  — *convenir à quelqu'un/quelque chose* is conjugated with *avoir*:
>Ex: ***La solution** proposée nous **a** convenu.*
>The proposed solution suited us.

  — *convenir de (faire) quelque chose* is conjugated either with *être* (literary) or *avoir*:
>Ex: ***Nous avons** convenu de notre erreur.*
>We admitted we had made a mistake.

>'*Dans le parc de Saint-Leu, où **les deux jeunes gens étaient** convenus d'aller.*'
>In the Parc of Saint-Leu, where the two young people had agreed to go.
>>Honoré de Balzac — cited in *Le petit Robert*

— *demeurer*:

Compare:

>*Je **suis** demeuré silencieux. (= je suis resté)*
>I remained silent.
>>and:
>*J'**ai** demeuré cinq ans à Paris. (= j'ai habité)*
>I lived in Paris for five years.

3.2   Other verbs

All the other verbs take *avoir* as an auxiliary (but see appendix 1).

3.2.1   *Agreement of past participle*

The past participle agrees with the **direct object** of the verb, but only if this direct object appears **before the verb** in the sentence.

Ex: *Les **pêches** que j'ai achet**ées** n'étaient pas mûres.*
The peaches I bought were not ripe.

*'Il ne **m**'a pas **vue**', a dit Catherine.*
'He didn't see me', Catherine said.

*Quels **vins** avez-vous achet**és**?*
What wines did you buy?

Hence if the direct object appears **after the verb**, there is no agreement.
Ex: *J'ai acheté des **pêches**.*
*Paul a **vu** **Catherine** hier.*
*Nous avons acheté des **vins** de Bourgogne.*

3.2.2   *No agreement of past participle*

The past participle does not agree in the following cases:

(i)   With other complements (indirect objects, adverbs, etc.)
Ex: *la tante à qui j'ai écrit*
the aunt to whom I wrote

l'année où j'ai écrit un livre
the year when I wrote a book

(ii) When the subject is impersonal *il*
Ex: *Quand je pense à la patience qu'il a fallu pour faire cette tapisserie!*
When I think of the patience needed to do this tapestry!

(iii) When verbs such as *marcher, courir, attendre, demeurer, vivre, dormir, durer, régner, coûter, peser* and *valoir* are followed by an expression of time, distance or amount
Ex: *les 100 mètres qu'il a cour**u** en dix secondes*
the 100 metres he ran in ten seconds

*les deux heures que j'ai attend**u**/que ça a dur**é***
the two hours I waited/it lasted
but:
*les risques qu'il a cour**us***
the risks he ran
and:
*C'est Marie que j'ai attend**ue** hier pendant deux heures.*
It was Marie I waited two hours for yesterday.
where *risques* and *Marie* are direct objects.

(iv) When the direct object is the object pronoun *en*, whatever *en* may stand for, or *le*, even when *le* represents a whole clause
Ex: *Des cerises? J'en ai acheté.*
Compare:
les dépenses** que j'avais **prévues**
and:
*Ce sont des dépenses plus élevées que je ne **l**'avais **prévu**.*

(v)   When the verb is followed by an infinitive

– when the object is in fact the object of the infinitive (which is always the case with *faire*)

Ex: *Ma robe était tachée: je l'ai fait nettoyer.*
(= nettoyer ma robe)
My dress was stained; I had it cleaned.
'*l*'' is the direct object of the infinitive '*nettoyer*' (not of '*ai fait*').

Où sont les devoirs que vous auriez dû me donner?
(= me donner les devoirs)
Where is the homework you should have given me?

NB: With *devoir, croire, pouvoir*, the verb *faire* is often elided, if it is already present in the main clause.

Ex: *Vous n'avez pas fait la dissertation que vous auriez dû.*
(= que vous auriez dû faire)

Vous n'avez pas fait les tâches que vous auriez pu.
(= que vous auriez pu faire)

– when the object of the main verb is also that of the infinitive

Ex: *l'histoire que j'ai entendu raconter*
(= J'ai entendu raconter une histoire.)
'*histoire*' is the object of '*ai entendu*' and of '*raconter*'.

Otherwise, there is an agreement.

Ex: *la cantatrice que j'ai entendue chanter*
(= J'ai entendu la cantatrice qui chantait.)
'*cantatrice*' is the object of '*ai entendue*' but the subject of '*chanter*'.

Compare:

les airs que j'ai entendu jouer
(= J'ai entendu les airs.)
the pieces that I heard [being] played
    and:
les violonistes que j'ai entendus jouer
(= J'ai entendu les violonistes qui jouaient.)
the violinists that I heard play

Consider the following example:

*les gens **que** j'ai vus partir*
the people I saw leaving

'*que*' (antecedent: '*les gens*') is the direct object of the conjugated verb '*ai vus*' (and not of the infinitive *partir*).
Indeed, one could say:

J'ai vu les gens (qui partaient).
('*les gens*' is the object of '*ai vu*')
but not (see example above):
★J'ai fait ma robe (qui nettoyait)!
('*ma robe*' is not the object of '*ai fait*').

See also chapter 15 Infinitive, section 3.1.3.

4   Negative and interrogative forms

(i)   In the interrogative form with inversion of verb–subject pronoun, a '*t*' must be added to the third person singular with *avoir* in order to avoid a hiatus.

        Ex: *A-**t**-il terminé son travail?*
             Has he finished his work?

             *A-**t**-elle sorti le chien?*
             Has she taken the dog out?

(ii)   The negative form is straightforward: *ne* and *pas* are placed before and after the auxiliary respectively.

        Ex: *Je **n'**ai **pas** terminé mon travail.*
             I have not finished my work.

             *Nous **ne** sommes **pas** sortis hier.*
             We did not go out yesterday.

(iii)   Interro–negative.

        Ex: ***N'**avez-vous **pas** sorti le chien?*
             Haven't you taken the dog out?

             *Bruno et Catherine **ne** sont-ils **pas** encore arrivés?*
             Haven't Bruno and Catherine arrived yet?

5   Use

The perfect is used in the following cases:

5.1   Action/event completed or state no longer true

The action, event or state took place in the past, either recent or distant (but recent in the mind of the speaker), and is now completed. It is often accompanied by a tense marker.

        Ex: *Je **suis allé** à Paris **il y a dix ans**.*
             I went to Paris ten years ago.

             *J'**ai été** très malade **la semaine dernière**.*
             I was very ill last week.

             *Elle **est arrivée tout à l'heure**.*
             She arrived a moment ago.

5.2   Beginning or end of action, event or state indicated

        Ex: *J'**ai travaillé** à mon article **jusqu'à minuit, puis** je **suis allée** me coucher.*
             I worked on my article until midnight, then I went to bed.

*Il **est resté** dans la maison en flammes **jusqu'au dernier moment**!*
He stayed in the burning house until the last moment.

*__Après avoir écrit__ sa dissertation, Paul **est allé** au bar.*
After writing his essay, Paul went to the bar.

5.3   Time or date of event, action or state indicated

The action, event or state happened at a precise moment in the past, indicated by a time or a date, or an expression indicating when it took place.

Ex: *__Quand__ je **suis entré** dans la salle de bain, j'ai vu une grosse araignée dans la baignoire . . .*
When I went into the bathroom, I saw a large spider in the bath . . .

*Les Accords d'Evian **ont été** signés **en 1962**.*
The Evian Agreements were signed in 1962.

5.4   Sudden action indicated

Note the use of appropriate adverbs: *soudain, tout à coup, immédiatement, tout de suite*, etc.

Ex: *__Soudain__, tout le monde **est parti**.*
Suddenly, everybody left.

*J'ai fait remarquer qu'il était déjà très tard et ils **sont partis tout de suite**.*
I pointed out it was already very late and they left immediately.

5.5   Present state resulting from past action or event

The action or event was accomplished at an undetermined moment in the past and has a bearing on the present though the action or event is no longer in progress.

Ex: *Les enfants **ont** encore **laissé** tous leurs jouets par terre. C'est dangereux.*
The children have left all their toys on the floor again. It's dangerous.

*Son chien **a disparu**. Elle le cherche partout.*
Her dog has disappeared. She is looking for him everywhere.

*Tu **as** encore **mangé** de l'ail!*
You have been eating garlic again!

5.6   Repeated action or event, may happen again

The action or event has been repeated and is likely to be repeated again. It has a bearing on the present.

Ex: *Je vous **ai** déjà **demandé** trois fois de fermer cette porte.*
I have already asked you three times to shut the door.

5.7 Duration of action or state indicated

The action or state happened within a given length of time, which can be explicit (often with *pendant*) or implicit in the sentence.

> Ex: *Je lui **ai parlé** [pendant] quelques instants.*
> I spoke to him/her for a few moments.

> *La guerre **a duré** cent ans.*
> The war lasted a hundred years.

5.8 Actions repeated but not usual

The perfect is used even if the action is regarded as frequent or repeated (but not usual, for which the imperfect is used), with adverb phrases such as *chaque fois que, régulièrement, rarement, souvent, tous les matins, tous les jours*, etc. Compare:

> *J'ai nagé tous les jours pendant les vacances.*

(The stress is on '*pendant les vacances*', on the end of the action in the past: the action is seen from the present.)

> I swam every day during the holidays.
> and:
> *Je **nageais** tous les jours pendant les vacances.*

(The stress is on '*tous les jours*', on the habitual nature of the action: one is put back in the past.)

> I would swim every day during the holidays.

See also 3.1(iv) in chapter 8 Imperfect.

5.9 The perfect replaces the future perfect

When the future perfect expresses something which is factual or near certain (e.g. in a relative clause), the perfect can be used instead.

> Ex: *Vous me montrerez ce que vous **avez choisi**.*
> (or: *Vous me montrerez ce que vous aurez choisi*)
> You will show me what you have chosen.

See also chapter 7 Future, section 4.

10 Past historic

1 Introduction

The past historic (*passé simple*) and the perfect (*passé composé*) both express the accomplished or completed aspect. However, there are some differences (see below).

The past historic also makes the events 'stand out', detaches them from the present more than the perfect does, and both are opposed to the imperfect (*imparfait*), which describes or comments on them.

The past historic is not easy to conjugate as there are many irregular forms to learn.

2 Formation

Each verb has the same radical throughout, but there are three sets of endings.

For verbs in ER, the endings are:

–ai	–âmes
–as	–âtes
–a	–èrent

For all the other verbs there are two sets of endings, subsequently referred to as endings I or U (but see exceptions in 2.2.2(iii) below):

I: –is	–îmes	U: –us	–ûmes
–is	–îtes	–us	–ûtes
–it	–irent	–ut	–urent

2.1 Verbs in ER

(i) The radical is the infinitive of the verb minus ER, the endings are regular, even for *aller*.

Ex: *chanter: je **chant**ai*	*nous **chant**âmes*
*tu **chant**as*	*vous **chant**âtes*
*il/elle/on **chant**a*	*ils/elles **chant**èrent*

*créer: je **cré**ai*	*nous **cré**âmes*
*tu **cré**as*	*vous **cré**âtes*
*il/elle/on **cré**a*	*ils/elles **cré**èrent*

$$
\begin{array}{ll}
aller: j'\textbf{all}ai & nous\ \textbf{all}âmes \\
tu\ \textbf{all}as & vous\ \textbf{all}âtes \\
il/elle/on\ \textbf{all}a & ils/elles\ \textbf{all}èrent
\end{array}
$$

(ii)   Verbs in *-cer* or *-ger*:

In order to keep the sound [s] of '*c*', a cedilla must be added to the '*c*' before '*a*', '*o*', '*u*': this rule affects the whole conjugation except the 3rd person plural.

$$
\begin{array}{lll}
\text{Ex: } placer: je\ \textbf{plaç}ai & nous\ \textbf{plaç}âmes \\
tu\ \textbf{plaç}as & vous\ \textbf{plaç}âtes \\
il/elle/on\ \textbf{plaç}a & ils/elles\ \textbf{plac}èrent
\end{array}
$$

In order to keep the sound [ʒ] of '*g*', an '*e*' must be added after the '*g*' before '*a*', '*o*', '*u*': this rule affects the whole conjugation except the 3rd person plural.

$$
\begin{array}{lll}
\text{Ex: } manger: je\ \textbf{mange}ai & nous\ \textbf{mange}âmes \\
tu\ \textbf{mange}as & vous\ \textbf{mange}âtes \\
il/elle/on\ \textbf{mange}a & ils/elles\ \textbf{mang}èrent.
\end{array}
$$

2.2   Verbs in IR

2.2.1   *Regular verbs in IR*

They have their present participles in *-issant*.

The radical is the infinitive of the verb minus IR, with I endings (see above), hence the singular forms are often identical with those of the present indicative.

$$
\begin{array}{lll}
\text{Ex: } finir: je\ \textbf{fin}is & nous\ \textbf{fin}îmes \\
tu\ \textbf{fin}is & vous\ \textbf{fin}îtes \\
il/elle/on\ \textbf{fin}it & ils/elles\ \textbf{fin}irent
\end{array}
$$

$$
\begin{array}{lll}
obéir: j'\textbf{obé}is & nous\ \textbf{obé}îmes \\
tu\ \textbf{obé}is & vous\ \textbf{obé}îtes \\
il/elle/on\ \textbf{obé}it & ils/elles\ \textbf{obé}irent
\end{array}
$$

NB: *haïr* keeps its '*ï*' throughout the conjugation:

$$
\begin{array}{ll}
je\ haïs & nous\ haïmes \\
tu\ haïs & vous\ haïtes \\
il/elle/on\ haït & ils/elles\ haïrent
\end{array}
$$

2.2.2   *Irregular verbs in IR*

They have their present participles in *-ant*.

The endings can be of the I or U type, except for *venir* and *tenir*, which have their own special endings.

(i)   The radical is the infinitive minus IR, with I endings.

$$
\begin{array}{lll}
\text{Ex: } partir & je\ \textbf{part}is & nous\ \textbf{part}îmes \\
fuir & je\ \textbf{fu}is & nous\ \textbf{fu}îmes \\
ouvrir & j'\textbf{ouvr}is & nous\ \textbf{ouvr}îmes
\end{array}
$$

Similarly: *sentir, servir, dormir, mentir, sortir, bouillir, couvrir, cueillir, offrir, souffrir,* etc.

(ii) The radical is the infinitive minus IR, with U endings.

courir: je **courus** *nous* **courûmes**   *mourir*: je **mourus** *nous* **mourûmes**
          tu **courus** *vous* **courûtes**   *tu* **mourus** *vous* **mourûtes**
          il **courut** *ils* **coururent**   *il* **mourut** *ils* **moururent**

(iii) The following are irregular: note both radicals and endings.

venir: je **vins** *nous* **vînmes**   *tenir*: je **tins** *nous* **tînmes**
          tu **vins** *vous* **vîntes**   *tu* **tins** *vous* **tîntes**
          il **vint** *ils* **vinrent**   *il* **tint** *ils* **tinrent**

Also: *devenir, prévenir, parvenir, (se) souvenir*
         appartenir, maintenir, obtenir, contenir, soutenir, entretenir

2.3 Verbs in OIR

(i) The radical is the infinitive minus OIR.

– with I endings:
   Ex: *voir*: je **vis**   *nous* **vîmes**
              tu **vis**   *vous* **vîtes**
              il/elle/on **vit**   *ils/elles* **virent**
Also: *revoir, entrevoir, prévoir* (but not *pourvoir*: see below).

NB: *s'asseoir* drops the 'e' of the radical of the infinitive.
              je m'**assis**   *nous nous* **assîmes**
              *tu t'***assis**   *vous vous* **assîtes**
              *il/elle/on s'***assit**   *ils/elles s'***assirent**

– with U endings:
   Ex: *pourvoir*: je **pourvus**   *nous* **pourvûmes**
                     tu **pourvus**   *vous* **pourvûtes**
                     il/elle/on **pourvut**   *ils/elles* **pourvurent**
Also: *valoir, vouloir, falloir*

(ii) The following have a 'reduced' radical, all with a U ending.
       Ex: *recevoir*: je **reçus**   *nous* **reçûmes**
Also: *apercevoir, décevoir, concevoir, percevoir*

       savoir   je **sus**   *nous* **sûmes**
       pouvoir   je **pus**   *nous* **pûmes**
       devoir   je **dus**   *nous* **dûmes**

       pleuvoir: il **plut**

2.4 Verbs in RE

2.4.1 *Regular radical, with I endings*

The following verbs are 'regular': the radical is the infinitive minus RE, with I endings.

(i) Verbs in *-endre* (except **prendre** and its derivatives, see 2.4.4(v) below), *-ondre*, *-ordre*, *-erdre*, *-andre*, *-ompre*:
       Ex: *vendre*   je **vendis**   *nous* **vendîmes**

(ii)   Verbs in *-attre*:
> Ex: *battre*   je **batti**s   nous **battî**mes

(iii)   Verbs in *-uivre*:
> Ex: *suivre*   je **suivi**s   nous **suivî**mes

Also: *poursuivre*

NB: *vivre* is irregular (see 2.4.5 below).

2.4.2   *Radical 'nd' becomes 'gn', with ɪ endings*

Verbs in *-aindre, -eindre, -oindre*:
> Ex: *craindre*   je **craigni**s   nous **craignî**mes

2.4.3   *One letter added to the radical*

The following verbs add a letter to the radical of the infinitive.

(i)   Verbs in *-uire* add an '*s*', with ɪ endings:
> Ex: *conduire*   je **conduisi**s   nous **conduisî**mes

NB: For *luire* and *reluire*, the following form has now taken over:
> je **relu**is   nous **reluî**mes

(instead of: *je reluisis   nous reluisîmes*)

(ii)   Some verbs in *-ire* add a '*v*', with ɪ endings:
> Ex: *écrire*   j'**écrivi**s   nous **écrivî**mes

Also: *décrire, inscrire, souscrire, transcrire, prescrire*

2.4.4   *'Reduced' radical*

(i)   Verbs in *-ure* drop a '*u*', with ᴜ endings:
> Ex: *conclure*   je **conclu**s   nous **conclû**mes

(ii)   Some verbs in *-ire* drop an '*i*':

– with ɪ endings:
> Ex: *rire*   je **ri**s   nous **rî**mes
> *dire*   je **di**s   nous **dî**mes

Also: *sourire; médire, contredire, interdire, prédire; suffire*

– with ᴜ endings:
> Ex: *lire*   je **lu**s   nous **lû**mes

Also: *relire, élire*

(iii)   Verbs in *-oire, -aire*: the radical is the infinitive minus *-oire/-aire*

– with ᴜ endings:
> Ex: *croire*   je **cru**s   nous **crû**mes
> *boire*   je **bu**s   nous **bû**mes
> *plaire*   je **plu**s   nous **plû**mes
> *(se) taire*   je me **tu**s   nous nous **tû**mes

– with I endings:

> Ex: *faire*   *je **fis***   *nous **fîmes***

Also: *défaire, refaire, satisfaire*

(iv) Verbs in *-aître* (except *naître*, see 2.4.5 below): the radical is the infinitive minus *-aître*, with U endings.

> Ex: *connaître*   *je **connus** nous **connûmes***

(v) *prendre* and its derivatives: the radical is the infinitive minus *-endre*, with I endings.

> Ex: *prendre*   *je **pris***   *nous **prîmes***

Also: *apprendre, surprendre, comprendre, entreprendre*

(vi) Verbs in *-ettre*: the radical is the infinitive minus *-ettre*, with I endings.

> Ex: *mettre*   *je **mis***   *nous **mîmes***

2.4.5 Irregular radicals

moudre	*je **moulus***	*nous **moulûmes***
coudre	*je **cousis***	*nous **cousîmes***
résoudre	*je **résolus***	*nous **résolûmes***
vivre	*je **vécus***	*nous **vécûmes***
naître	*je **naquis***	*nous **naquîmes***
croître	*je **crûs***	*nous **crûmes***

NB: *croître* takes a '*û*' with all the persons to distinguish it from *croire* (see 2.4.4(iii) above), hence only *nous* and *vous* are common to the two verbs.

Finally, note that there is **no** past historic for the following verbs (see other 'defective' verbs in chapter 4 Introduction to Verbs, section 4.4): *clore, paître, traire, gésir, absoudre, dissoudre*.

2.5 *être* and *avoir*

*je **fus***	*nous **fûmes***	*j'**eus***	*nous **eûmes***
*tu **fus***	*vous **fûtes***	*tu **eus***	*vous **eûtes***
*il **fut***	*ils **furent***	*il **eut***	*ils **eurent***

2.6 Negative and interrogative forms

(i) Negative form
ne and *pas* are placed either side of the verb.

> Ex: *Je **ne** fus **pas** surprise de le voir.*
> I was not surprised to see him.

(ii) Interrogative form
A '*t*' between hyphens is added for the 3rd person singular with verbs in ER (the ending is '*a*').

> Ex: *Avala-**t**-elle le poison?*
> Did she swallow the poison?

(iii)   Interro–negative form
        Ex: ***Ne** crurent-ils **pas** votre version des faits?*
        Didn't they believe your version of events?

3 Use and meaning

3.1   The past historic

The past historic is used to express:

– events

Verbs with a perfective meaning which express a completed, punctual process are
particularly well adapted to the accomplished aspect of the past historic. The
events are situated at a precise moment in the past.
        Ex: *A mon appel, les deux chats **accoururent**.*
        At my call, the two cats ran towards me.

        *Il **naquit** le 20 août 1940.*
        He was born on 20th August 1940.

– duration

With imperfective verbs, the past historic cannot express a punctual process. It
expresses a completed process whose duration may be specified by adverb phrases
of time.
        Ex: *Il **travailla** jusqu'à six heures, puis **se reposa** un peu.*
        He worked until 6, then rested a little.

        *La guerre **dura** cent ans.*
        The war lasted a hundred years.

– repetition

The past historic is used with both perfective and imperfective verbs.
        Ex: *Il ne **mangea** que des pâtes pendant trois jours.*
        He ate only pasta for three days.

        *Pendant les vacances, il **sortit** tous les soirs.*
        During the holidays, he went out every evening.
It is the context which shows that there is repetition.

3.2   The past historic and the perfect

– With the past historic, there is a clear break from the present. The past historic
underlines the limits of the length of the process and reinforces the expression
of the accomplished aspect. It is thus used to give a global view of an event in
the past (though not necessarily remote) and independently of its duration. The
event is presented in its totality and is completely disconnected from the
speaker's time frame.

Consider the following sentences, which could be the start of a story:

> Summer **came** and the sun **shone** on the flowers. Isabelle was
> nearly 16 and was still going to school.

This opening calls for the use of the past historic in French as both verbs, 'came'
and 'shone', express events that are detached from the present. The story then
goes on with the descriptive imperfect, and Isabelle very much present in the
narrator's mind.

> *L'été **arriva** et le soleil **brilla** sur les fleurs. Isabelle avait presque 16 ans et
> allait toujours à l'école.*

– With the perfect, the process is also in the past but the break with the present
is less clear. The perfect is used for events which took place in the past but
have a link with, or repercussion on, the present.

> Ex: *Ils **ont joué** au tennis toute la journée, c'est pourquoi ils sont fatigués.*
> They have been playing tennis all day, which is why they are tired.

In informal French, the perfect is also used in the cases when the past historic
should be used. It thus expresses both the definite and the indefinite past. The
past historic is very often kept for formal speeches, personal accounts of a
biographical nature (where the speaker considers his/her own past as completely
dissociated from the present), radio and TV broadcasts on historical topics and
some newspaper articles, particularly the sports page.

> Ex: *'Si le stade de Reims **perdit** deux finales de Coupe d'Europe des clubs
> champions face au Real de Madrid [. . .], il **remporta** six titres de
> champion de France [. . .] et deux victoires en Coupe de France.'*

> *Le Monde*, 3 January 1991

However, this is not to say that the perfect cannot be found in literature. Indeed,
authors such as Camus and Prévert have made ample use of it.

3.3   The past historic and the imperfect

Like the perfect, the past historic is used in conjunction with the imperfect. The
past historic and imperfect tenses are opposed aspectually:

– The imperfect describes an event in its duration or repetition or as a
background against which other events are taking place. It does not envisage
the temporal limits of the process. It expresses its **duration**, whether it be long
or short.

– The past historic, like the perfect, embraces the whole of a past event, from its
beginning to its end. It views a past event as a **complete entity**, within its
temporal limits, whether they be long or short.

In the past historic, the emphasis is on the actual occurrence of the event itself.
This is why it is so appropriate for the narration of successive events (stories are
recounted in the past historic). It is essential when the chronology of events is
important. However, whilst the past historic (notably its 'perfective' aspect) will
express the successive **events** in a narrative, the imperfect (its 'imperfective'
aspect) expresses the **background** to the narrative. See chapter 8 Imperfect,
section 3.1.

145

Consider the following text:

> '*Il **se déshabilla, se glissa** dans le lit chaud. Au lieu de s'endormir, il **continua** à penser à la jeune morte de la Place Vintimille. Il **entendait**, dehors, Paris s'éveiller petit à petit [. . .]. Les concierges **commençaient** à traîner les poubelles [. . .]. Dans l'escalier **résonnèrent** les pas de la petite bonne du crémier qui **allait** poser les bouteilles de lait devant les portes.*'

> Georges Simenon, *Maigret et la jeune morte*

The use of the past historic for *se déshabiller* and *se glisser* is straightforward, as both verbs refer to events, stated in their chronological order. However, it is interesting to note the use of the past historic for *continuer* and that of the imperfect for *entendre*: '*continua à penser*' thus is part of the chronology of events, while '*entendait*' expresses a state of the narrator, not an event in itself.

English would say: 'He got undressed, and slipped into the warm bed . . . he continued to think of . . . He could hear, outside, . . .' Had the author said: '*il continuait*', the English would have been: 'he was still thinking of . . .' Hence English establishes a similar distinction between '*entendait*' ('could hear') and '*entendit*' ('heard'): the same goes for other verbs of perception. Further down, the imperfect is used for *commencer à traîner*. English would say: '. . . were beginning to drag . . .' Had it been '*commencèrent*', the English would have been: '. . . began to . . .' Then the past historic is used for *résonner*. English would say: '. . . echoed'. The use of the imperfect for *résonner* would be a little more difficult to justify as it would have to be the background noise for all the other events of the morning!

3.4 Connotations

Today the past historic belongs to a specific register. If used injudiciously, it can appear ridiculous or pedantic, like the misused imperfect subjunctive (see chapter 12 Subjunctive, section 3.2). There are two main reasons for this effect:
- the past historic refers to events which are of little or no consequence to the present and it is therefore associated with the third person, the only one that can convey the corresponding sense of detachment.
- the endings of the first person plural (*âmes, îmes, ûmes*) and the second person plural (*âtes, îtes, ûtes*) are very different from the endings of the first and second persons plural in other tenses. It is their unusual sound which makes them seem ridiculous or pathetic in spoken French, particularly if the subject matter is mundane.

> Ex: *Ce jour-là, nous **allâmes** chez le boulanger et nous **achetâmes** une baguette et deux croissants.*
> *Le lendemain, vous **prîtes** votre cabas et **allâtes** au marché.*

Note that it is not really possible to find the equivalent sense of archaic pedantry in English. Maybe an approximate parallel could be found in the English use of 'wouldst', 'shalt', etc.

In the following transcription of a radio programme, a lot of past historics and imperfect subjunctives are used to provide rhyming puns.

Lettre à Fabius

Mon cher Lolo,
Dans la basse-cour France, lorsque nous nous connûmes,
Nous les petits poulets, vous le coq, nous nous plûmes.
Cette part du gâteau, bien qu'un peu émiettée,
Il n'était pas normal que vous en pâtissiez.
Votre ardeur juvénile, jointe à des nerfs d'acier,
Tout de suite le plus clair, ce fut que vous fonciez.
Vous avez pour cela des méthodes nouvelles,
Regard tout en velours, vous jouez d'la prunelle.
La prunelle pour vous, ça vous remet d'attaque,
Tandis que Gaston Defferre, c'est le vieillard maniaque.
(Non . . . c'est le vieil armagnac, pardon, excusez-moi Monsieur le
   Ministre!)
Du manteau du Français moyen vous vous couvrîtes,
Pour faire votre trou, ah, quelle ardeur vous mîtes!
De relever la France vous vous préoccupâtes:
Vous virâtes des singes qu'autrefois vous primâtes.
Dans le Rhône vous vous expliquâtes, dans les Landes vous pérorâtes,
Bref, vous consacrâtes à notre éducation tout le temps que vous . . . eûtes.
Pour la prostitution vous fîtes ce que vous pûtes.
Et, comme Georges Marchais jadis s'était vanté
De vous envoyer paître, avec lui vous paissez.
Sur certains plans, ce fut la pleine réussite,
Mais hélas sur le chômage seulement vous faillîtes.
Malgré les coups de clairon, même dans l'infortune,
Que vous sonnâtes, que vous sonnâtes au clair de lune . . .
Réveiller le Français, quel rêve vous caressiez!
Mais lui restait au lit sans que vous le pussiez.
Dormant sur son pécule, il craignait angoissé,
Que ce petit matelas, vous le lui plumassiez.
L'argent, l'argent, c'est l'os à moelle du Français salarié,
Qui ne craignait rien tant que vous ne le sussiez.
L'Europe chancelante consacra vos mérites,
Le Hollandais s'émiette et le Belge s'effritte . . .
Pour le mouton anglais, fier, vous vous rebêêêllâtes,
Mais pour la pomme de terre alors vous m'épatâtes.
Voilà mon cher Lolo qui mal y pense honni soit,
Car je vous ai parlé, Monsieur, en vrai François.

L'oreille en coin, France-Inter, 10 February 1985

11 Other past tenses

1 Introduction

The pluperfect, past anterior and double compound past are the compound forms of the imperfect, past historic and perfect respectively. They have been put together in this chapter so that their uses can be more easily compared with one another.

2 The pluperfect

The pluperfect (*plus-que-parfait*) is the compound form of the imperfect.

2.1 Formation

The pluperfect is formed with the imperfect of the auxiliary *être* or **avoir** plus the past participle of the verb to be conjugated, and corresponds to the English past perfect 'I had done', or past perfect continuous 'I had been doing'.

> Ex: *Ils avaient mangé.*
> They had eaten / They had been eating.
>
> *J'étais revenue.*
> I had come back.

2.2 Uses

The relation between the pluperfect and the imperfect is the same as that between the perfect and the present insofar as both the pluperfect and the perfect are compound tenses. See also chapters 6 *depuis* and Other Tense Markers, 8 Imperfect, 13 Conditional and 41 Reported Speech.

2.2.1 *The pluperfect to express anteriority*

Like the English past perfect, the pluperfect is used to relate a past event, action or state which took place prior to another event, action or state which happened further back in the past. Hence it is used to express anteriority, in conjunction with the past historic or the perfect. The past action is sometimes merely implied.

Ex: *Catherine arriva en retard; son réveil n'**avait** pas **sonné**.*
      Catherine arrived late: her alarm-clock **had** not **rung**.

*Ils ont parlé de la manifestation à laquelle ils **avaient participé** le matin-même.*
They talked about the demonstration they had joined that morning.

NB: French is sometimes more precise than English in establishing the order of events, and the use of a pluperfect may be necessary where a simple past tense is sufficient in English.
      Ex: *Paul voulait savoir à quelle heure nous **étions partis**.*
      Paul wanted to know at what time we **left**.

2.2.2   *The pluperfect* vs *the past anterior or double compound past*

(i)   In independent clauses

It expresses the accomplished aspect of the imperfect, with dates or adverbs or adverb phrases of time such as *déjà, depuis longtemps*, etc.
      Ex: *Depuis longtemps, il **avait rêvé** de faire le tour du monde.*
      For a long time, he had been dreaming of going round the world.
On the contrary, the past anterior expresses the accomplished aspect of the past historic (see 3.2(i) below) and the double compound past expresses the accomplished aspect of the perfect (see 4.2(i) below).

(ii)   In subordinate clauses of time

The pluperfect is used in clauses introduced by a conjunction of time: *quand, lorsque* (when), *aussitôt que, dès que, à peine . . . que* (as soon as), *après que* (after). It indicates that a usual action or state took place before another usual action or state in the imperfect. The emphasis is on the **habitual nature of the process** rather than on its simple occurrence (for which past anterior and past historic would be used: see 3.2(ii) below, or double compound past and perfect: see 4.2(ii) below).
      Ex: ***Quand** il **avait fini** de lire, il **dormait** un peu.*
      When he had finished reading, he would sleep a little.

2.2.3   *The pluperfect to express a request in a very polite way*

Note that the use of the pluperfect, in conjunction with a conditional present, owes more to an apology than a request.
      Ex: *J'**avais pensé** que peut-être, vous **voudriez** bien me recevoir . . .*
      I had thought you would perhaps agree to see me . . .

Compare with the use of the imperfect for a polite request (see chapter 8 Imperfect, section 3.2).

2.2.4   *The pluperfect after* si *(modal value)*

The pluperfect is used (often in conjunction with the conditional perfect), after *si* in sentences expressing a condition. It is therefore used in a subordinate clause of hypothesis to evoke an event which did not take place (hence its 'unreal' value).

It is used in the sense of 'what could have been if' and not 'what can still be done if'. Therefore, it is used to express a regret, since nothing can be done about it now.

> Ex: *Si je m'étais dépêché, je n'aurais pas manqué mon train!*
> If I had hurried, I wouldn't have missed my train!
>
> *Si j'avais su!*
> If [only] I had known!
>
> *Si seulement vous aviez pu vous parler!*
> If only you had been able to talk to each other!

Compare with *si* + imperfect to express a desire, a wish (see chapter 8 Imperfect, section 3.2.2).

> Ex: *Si seulement vous pouviez vous parler!*
> If only you could talk to each other!

However, the possible consequences **can** be placed in the present or the future as well as the past.

> Ex: *Si elle avait eu le temps, elle serait venue me voir.*
> If she'd had the time, she would have come to see me.
>
> *Si j'avais travaillé plus vite, j'aurais déjà terminé mon livre.*
> If I had worked faster, I would have already finished my book.
>
> *Si j'avais terminé mon manuscrit pour septembre, il pourrait encore paraître en janvier.*
> If I finish my manuscript by September, it could still come out in January.

3 The past anterior

The past anterior (*passé antérieur*) is the compound form of the past historic.

3.1 Formation

The past anterior is formed with the past historic of *être* or *avoir*, followed by the past participle of the verb.

> Ex: *(quand) je fus parti*
> *(quand) j'eus fini*
> *(quand) je me fus reposé*

NB: As the past anterior is mainly used to express anteriority to another action, expressed in the past historic (see below), it is often shown preceded by *quand*.

3.2 Past anterior vs pluperfect

The past anterior is used only in formal **literary** French, in passages where the main narrative tense is the past historic. It is used in place of the pluperfect in the following cases:

(i)   In independent clauses: to express the accomplished aspect of the past historic, often to stress the rapid completion of an action after adverb/adverb phrases such as *bientôt, enfin, vite, en un instant*.

> Ex: *En l'espace d'une seconde, j'**eus compris** ce qui se passait.*
>   In a second/a flash, I had understood what was happening.
>
> *Il **eut** bientôt **fait** le nécessaire.*
> He had soon done the necessary.

(ii)   In subordinate clauses of time: to express the anteriority of one process to another, expressed in the past historic (for the conjunctions of time used, see 2.2.2(ii) above). It indicates that the completion of an action was immediately anterior to another action (in the past historic). Note that there is a close correlation between the two actions, **without any reference to duration or repetition**.

> Ex: *Dès qu'il **eut terminé** son cours, tous les étudiants **applaudirent**.*
>   As soon as he **had finished** his lecture, all the students clapped.
>
> '*Quand Jonas **eut terminé**, sans effort particulier, ses études, il **eut** encore la chance d'entrer dans la maison d'éditions de son père pour y trouver une situation . . .*'
>
> Albert Camus, *L'exil et le royaume*

NB(1): English does not distinguish between past perfect and past anterior. However, note the presence of 'would' in the first example below as opposed to the simple past. Compare:

> *Quand il **avait fini** de lire, il **dormait** un peu.*
> When he had finished reading, he would sleep a little.

The emphasis is on the **habitual** nature of the process.

> and:
> *Quand il **eut fini** de lire, il **dormit** un peu.*
> When he had finished reading, he slept a little.

The emphasis is on the actual **occurrence** of the process.

NB(2): If the action happens almost simultaneously with the action of the past historic, i.e. if the verb expresses a **result** or **causality**, rather than a **process** or a **sequence**, the past historic can be kept. Compare:

> *Aussitôt qu'elle **vit** ses chats, elle les **appela**.*
> As soon as she saw her cats, she called them.
>
> *Dès qu'il **apprit** la nouvelle, il en **informa** ses amis.*
> As soon as he learnt the news, he informed his friends.
>
> and:
> *Quand il **eut rangé** sa chambre, il **alla** au cinéma.*
> When he had tidied his room, he went to the cinema.

In other words, calling the cats was a direct consequence of seeing them; he could not have informed his friends before learning the news, but he could have gone to the cinema before tidying his room.

NB(3): The imperfect can of course appear in a sentence with a past historic and a past anterior.

> Ex: '*Et cette fois-là, comme toujours, à peine l'**eus**-je **ingérée**, que je **sentis** le froid paralyser mon tube intérieur, en même temps que j'**éprouvais** une poussée de fièvre.*'

> Paul Guth, *Le naïf amoureux*

4 The double compound past

The double compound past (*passé surcomposé*) is the compound form of the perfect.

4.1 Formation

Note that each of the compound tenses has a corresponding double compound form:

> – *j'ai fini* → *j'ai eu fini*
> – *j'avais fini* → *j'avais eu fini*
> – *j'eus fini* → *j'eus eu fini*.

However, only the double compound past is still common usage.

It is formed with the perfect of the auxiliary *être* or *avoir* plus the past participle of the verb. It is not used with pronominal verbs, and has no passive form.

4.2 Uses

It is used in a similar way to that of the past anterior (see 3.2 above) but in non–literary French, to express:

(i) In independent clauses: the accomplished aspect of the perfect.
> Ex: *Très vite, il **a eu compris** ce qui se passait.*
> In a flash he had understood what was happening.

(ii) In subordinate clauses of time: anteriority of a process to another, expressed in the perfect. For the conjunctions of time used, see 2.2.2(ii) above).
> Ex: *Quand il **a eu rangé** sa chambre, il **est allé** au cinéma.*
> When he had tidied his room, he went to the cinema.

An alternative to the use of the double compound past would be to use an appropriate conjunction of coordination with two perfects.
> Ex: *Il a rangé sa chambre. Puis/Ensuite, il est allé au cinéma.*
> He tidied his room. Then, he went to the cinema.

NB: If the verb expresses a **result** or **causality**, the perfect is normally kept (see 3.2 NB(2) above).
> Ex: *Dès que nous **avons appris** la nouvelle, nous vous en **avons informé**.*
> As soon as we learnt the news, we informed you.

12 Subjunctive

The subjunctive is a mood which is very frequently used in everyday French. It is a non-temporal mood. Temporality is indicated by the context.

> Ex: *Je veux que tout **soit** prêt pour demain.*
> *J'aurais voulu que tout **soit** prêt hier.*

In common usage, only two tenses are used: present and perfect. In formal usage, the four tenses are used: present, perfect, imperfect and pluperfect (see table in 3.2.2 below).

The subjunctive is mainly used in subordinate clauses (although it also survives in independent clauses and in some fixed expressions). The subordinate clauses concerned are: *que*-clauses (*complétives*), adverbial clauses (*circonstancielles*) and relative clauses. In each case, it is important to know whether the subjunctive OR the indicative should be used.

– In *que*-clauses (introduced by the conjunction *que*), the use of the subjunctive depends on what is expressed by the **verb** or impersonal construction in the main clause.

– In adverbial clauses (introduced by a conjunction other than *que*), the use of the subjunctive depends on the **conjunction** used.

– In relative clauses, a modifier of the antecedent (e.g. definite or indefinite article, type of adjective) may determine the choice between subjunctive and indicative.

Indicative and subjunctive moods are traditionally distinguished in the following way:
– the indicative is used to express processes that are actual or real
– the subjunctive is used to express processes that are virtual or imagined.

Although this distinction is true to a certain extent, there are certain 'grey' areas (e.g. the difference between possibility and probability) and only one mood can be selected! An example of this can be seen in the following sentence:

> *Bien qu'il **fasse** froid, je ne mettrai pas de manteau.*

The cold is very real and is perceived as such by the speaker, yet the subjunctive is compulsory. In other cases – notably in interrogative and negative forms – the choice of mood will depend on the way the speaker perceives the process.

2 Formation

The tenses of the subjunctive are the present, the imperfect, the perfect and the pluperfect.

Because the subjunctive is so frequently introduced by a verb followed by *que*, it is customary to show subjunctive conjugations preceded by *que*.

2.1 Present subjunctive

2.1.1 *Verbs in* ER

(i)   Most verbs in ER only have one radical in the present subjunctive (which is the same as for *nous* in the present indicative). The endings are:

-e	*-ions*
-es	*-iez*
-e	*-ent*

Ex: *donner: que je **donne***   *que nous **donnions***
          *que tu **donnes***   *que vous **donniez***
        *qu'il/elle/on **donne***   *qu'ils/elles **donn**ent*

(ii)   *aller* is irregular: *que j'**aille***   *que nous **all**ions*
                *que tu **ailles***   *que vous **all**iez*
           *qu'il/elle/on **aille***   *qu'ils/elles **aill**ent*

(iii)   The rules regarding verbs with penultimate '*e*' or '*é*' are the same as for the present indicative (see chapter 5 Present, section 2.1).
        Ex: *mener*   *que je **mène***   *que nous menions*

               gérer   *que je **gère***   *que nous **gér**ions*

(iv)   The rules regarding verbs in *-eler* and *-eter* are the same as for the present indicative (see chapter 5 Present, section 2.1).
        Ex: *jeter*   *que je **jette***   *que nous **jet**ions*

            acheter   *que j'**achète***   *que nous **achet**ions*

            appeler   *que j'**appelle***   *que nous **appel**ions*

            geler   *que je **gèle***   *que nous **gel**ions*

(v)   Verbs in *-ier* or *-uer*
Note the juxtaposition of vowels with *nous* and *vous* (and in particular the repetition of '*i*' with verbs in *-ier*).
        Ex: *étudier, oublier: que j'étudie*   *que nous étudiions*
                       que tu étudies   *que vous étudiiez*
                 qu'il/elle/on étudie   *qu'ils/elles étudient*

               continuer: que je continue   *que nous continuions*
                     que tu continues   *que vous continuiez*
                 qu'il/elle/on continue   *qu'ils/elles continuent*

(vi) *créer*

Note the juxtaposition of vowels, particularly with *nous* and *vous*:

que je crée	*que nous créions*
que tu crées	*que vous créiez*
qu'il/elle/on crée	*qu'ils/elles créent*

(vii) Verbs in *–ayer, –oyer, –uyer*

They follow the same rules as for the present indicative (see chapter 5 Present, section 2.1). Note the presence of both '*y*' and '*i*' with *nous* and *vous*.

Ex: *nettoyer:* *que je nettoie*	*que nous nettoyions*
que tu nettoies	*que vous nettoyiez*
qu'il/elle/on nettoie	*qu'ils/elles nettoient*

As in the indicative, *payer* has two conjugations:

que je paie	*que nous payions*
que tu paies	*que vous payiez*
qu'il/elle/on paie	*qu'ils/elles paient*

or:

que je paye	*que nous payions*
que tu payes	*que vous payiez*
qu'il/elle/on paye	*qu'ils/elles payent*

2.1.2 Regular verbs in IR

Regular verbs in IR have their present participle in *–issant*. The radical is the infinitive minus IR, and the endings are:

–isse	*–issions*
–isses	*–issiez*
–isse	*–issent*

(i) *finir*

que je finisse	*que nous finissions*
que tu finisses	*que vous finissiez*
qu'il/elle/on finisse	*qu'ils/elles finissent*

Similarly: *choisir, réussir, frémir, définir, pâlir, rougir, grandir, grossir,* etc.

(ii) *haïr*

Note that *haïr* keeps its diaeresis throughout the conjugation:

que je haïsse	*que nous haïssions*
que tu haïsses	*que vous haïssiez*
qu'il/elle/on haïsse	*qu'ils/elles haïssent*

2.1.3 Irregular verbs in IR

Irregular verbs in IR have their present participle in *–ant*. The endings are the same as for verbs in ER:

–e	*–ions*
–es	*–iez*
–e	*–ent*

Most verbs in IR only have one radical in the present subjunctive, but note exceptions in (ii) below.

(i)   The radical is the infinitive minus IR

Ex: *partir: que je **parte***   *que nous **partions***
         *que tu **partes***   *que vous **partiez***
         *qu'il/elle/on **parte***   *qu'ils/elles **partent***

Similarly: *sentir, mentir, sortir, servir, dormir, courir, bouillir, faillir, défaillir, cueillir, offrir, souffrir, ouvrir, couvrir, revêtir,* etc.

(ii)   The following verbs have two radicals, one for *nous* and *vous*, one for the other persons:

– *venir, tenir,* and their derivatives:

Ex: *venir: que je **vienne***   *que nous **ven**ions*
         *que tu **vienne**s*   *que vous **ven**iez*
         *qu'il/elle/on **vienne***   *qu'ils/elles **vienn**ent*

– *mourir: que je **meur**e*   *que nous **mour**ions*
         *que tu **meur**es*   *que vous mouriez*
         qu'il/elle/on meure   *qu'ils/elles meurent*

– *fuir: que je **fuie***   *que nous **fuy**ions*
         que tu fuies   *que vous fuyiez*
         qu'il/elle/on fuie   *qu'ils/elles fuient*

– *acquérir; conquérir:*

Ex: *acquérir: que j'**acquière***   *que nous **acquér**ions*
         que tu acquières   *que vous acquériez*
         qu'il/elle/on acquière   *qu'ils/elles acquièrent*

2.1.4   *Verbs in* OIR

The endings are those of a regular verb in ER except for *avoir.*

(i)   *s'asseoir* has two conjugations

– with one radical:

         *que je m'**asseye***   *que nous nous **assey**ions*
         que tu t'asseyes   *que vous vous asseyiez*
         qu'il/elle/on s'asseye   *qu'ils/elles s'asseyent*

– with two radicals:

         *que je m'**assoie***   *que nous nous **assoy**ions*
         que tu t'assoies   *que vous vous assoyiez*
         qu'il/elle/on s'assoie   *qu'ils/elles s'assoient*

(ii)   The following verbs have one radical:

– *pouvoir*   *que je **puisse***   *que nous **puissions***

– *savoir*   *que je **sache***   *que nous **sachions***

– the impersonal verb *falloir* is only conjugated with impersonal *il: qu'il **faille***

– the 'weather' verb *pleuvoir* is most of the time conjugated with impersonal *il: qu'il **pleuve***

(iii) The following verbs have two radicals, one for *nous* and *vous*, one for the other persons:

- *vouloir*: *que je **veuille***   *que nous **voul**ions*
  - *que tu veuilles*   *que vous vouliez*
  - *qu'il/elle/on veuille*   *qu'ils/elles veuillent*

- *devoir*   *que je **doive***   *que nous **dev**ions*

- *émouvoir*   *que j'**émeuve***   *que nous **émouv**ions*

- *voir* and its derivatives:
  - *que je **voie***   *que nous **voy**ions*

- *recevoir* and its derivatives:
  - *que je **reçoive***   *que nous **recev**ions*

2.1.5 Verbs in RE

The endings are those of a regular verb in ER, except for *être*.

(i) The following verbs have only one radical, the same as that of the infinitive:

- verbs in *-endre* except *prendre* and its derivatives (see (iii) below).
- verbs in *-ondre*
- verbs in *-ompre*
- verbs in *-erdre*
- verbs in *-ordre*
- verbs in *-attre*
- verbs in *-ettre*
- verbs in *-ivre*
- *rire, sourire, inclure, conclure*
  - Ex: *vendre*: *que je **vende***   *que vous **vend**ions*
    - *que tu vendes*   *que vous vendiez*
    - *qu'il/elle/on vende*   *qu'ils/elles vendent*

NB: *rire, sourire, conclure, inclure*: note the juxtaposition of vowels with *nous* and *vous*.

- Ex: *rire*: *que je rie*   *que nous **rii**ons*
  - *que tu ries*   *que vous **rii**ez*
  - *qu'il/elle/on rie*   *qu'ils/elles rient*

(ii) The following verbs only have one radical, but different from that of the infinitive:

- verbs in *-aindre*, *-eindre* and *-oindre*:
  - Ex: *craindre* (*peindre, joindre*): *que je **craigne***   *que nous **craign**ions*

- verbs in *-aître* and *-oître*:
  - Ex: *connaître*   *que je **connaisse***   *que nous **connaiss**ions*
  - *croître*   *que je **croisse***   *que nous **croiss**ions*

– The following verbs in *-ire* (*écrire* and its derivatives) add a '*v*' to the radical of the infinitive:

      écrire, décrire, inscrire,
      souscrire, transcrire, prescrire
      Ex: *écrire*   *que j'***écriv***e*   *que nous ***écriv***ions*

– The following verbs in *-ire* add an '*s*' to the radical of the infinitive:

      dire, médire, contredire, interdire, prédire,
      lire, relire, élire,
      (se) plaire, (se) taire,
      cuire, luire, nuire,
      instruire, construire, détruire,
      conduire, produire, introduire,
      déduire, réduire, séduire, traduire,
      suffire
      Ex: *dire: que je ***dis***e*   *que nous ***dis***ions*

– *maudire*   *que je ***maudiss***e*   *que nous ***maudiss***ions*

– *faire*   *que je ***fass***e*   *que nous ***fass***ions*

– *clore*   *que je ***clos***e*   *que nous ***clos***ions*

– *résoudre, absoudre, dissoudre:*
      Ex: *résoudre*   *que je ***résolv***e*   *que nous ***résolv***ions*

– *coudre*   *que je ***cous***e*   *que nous ***cous***ions*

– *moudre*   *que je ***moul***e*   *que nous ***moul***ions*

– *vaincre*   *que je ***vainqu***e*   *que nous ***vainqu***ions*

(iii) The following verbs have two radicals, one for *nous* and *vous*, one for the other persons:

– *boire: que je ***boiv***e*   *que nous ***buv***ions*
     que tu boives   *que vous buviez*
    qu'il/elle/on boive   *qu'ils/elles boivent*

– *croire: que je ***croi***e*   *que nous ***croy***ions*
     que tu croies   *que vous croyiez*
    qu'il/elle/on croie   *qu'ils/elles croient*

– *prendre* and its derivatives:
        *que je ***prenn***e*   *que nous ***pren***ions*
        que tu prennes   *que vous preniez*
      qu'il/elle/on prenne   *qu'ils/elles prennent*

2.1.6   *être and* avoir

être: *que je ***sois***   *que nous ***soyons***
     *que tu ***sois***   *que vous ***soyez***
  *qu'il/elle/on ***soit***   *qu'ils/elles ***soient***

avoir: *que j'***aie**   *que nous ***ayons**
      *que tu ***aies**   *que vous ***ayez**
  *qu'il/elle/on ***ait**   *qu'ils/elles ***aient**

2.2   Perfect subjunctive

The perfect subjunctive is made up of the present subjunctive of *être* or *avoir* +
past participle.

    Ex: *prendre: que j'aie pris*   *que nous ayons pris*
           que tu aies pris   *que vous ayez pris*
         qu'il/elle/on ait pris   *qu'ils/elles aient pris*

      venir: que je sois venu(e)   *que nous soyons venu(e)s*
          que tu sois venu(e)   *que vous soyez venu(e/s/es)*
           qu'il/on soit venu   *qu'ils soient venus*
            qu'elle soit venue   *qu'elles soient venues*

    s'asseoir: que je me sois assis(e)   *que nous nous soyons assis(es)*
            que tu te sois assis(e)   *que vous vous soyez assis(e/es)*
            qu'il/on se soit assis   *qu'ils se soient assis*
            qu'elle se soit assise   *qu'elles se soient assises*

2.3   Imperfect and pluperfect subjunctive

(i)   The imperfect is rarely used and conjugations should be checked in a dictionary
or book of conjugations.

Note that the form of the imperfect subjunctive 3rd person singular of certain
irregular verbs is similar to that of the past historic. The only difference is the
circumflex accent before the '*t*'.

    Ex: imperfect subjunctive   past historic

	imperfect subjunctive	past historic
être	*qu'il fût*	*il fut*
avoir	*qu'il eût*	*il eut*
boire	*qu'il bût*	*il but*
venir	*qu'il vînt*	*il vint*
faire	*qu'il fît*	*il fit,* etc.

(ii)   The pluperfect is made up of the imperfect subjunctive of *être* or *avoir* + past
participle.

    être: que je fusse   *que nous fussions*
        que tu fusses   *que vous fussiez*
   qu'il/elle/on fût   *qu'ils/elles fussent*

    avoir: que j'eusse   *que nous eussions*
        que tu eusses   *que vous eussiez*
   qu'il/elle/on eût   *qu'ils/elles eussent*

  Ex: *que j'eusse pris*
     que je fusse venu(e)
     que je me fusse assis(e), etc.

3 Use of past tenses

3.1 Perfect subjunctive

The perfect subjunctive is used when the action of the verb in the subordinate clause happens **before** that of the main clause, hence it expresses the accomplished aspect (the present subjunctive is used when the action of the verb in the subordinate clause happens **simultaneously** with that of the main clause, or **after** it). The tense of the main clause can be present, future, perfect or imperfect indicative, or conditional in either case (see table in 3.2.2 below). Compare:

> *Je veux que vous **lisiez** le premier chapitre pour demain.*
> I want you to read the first chapter for tomorrow.

> *Nous avons insisté pour qu'ils **viennent** la semaine prochaine.*
> We insisted that they should come next week.

> *Tu veux que j'y **réfléchisse**?*
> Would you like me to think about it?

> and:

> *Je doute qu'ils **aient compris** ce que j'ai dit.*
> I doubt they understood what I said.

> *Ils sont étonnés que tu **aies payé** pour tout le monde.*
> They are surprised that you paid for everybody.

> *Il est possible qu'ils **aient racheté** l'affaire.*
> It is possible that they have bought back the company.

It can also express anteriority:

> Ex: *Il est regrettable que vous **soyez arrivé** en retard hier.*
> It is regrettable that you arrived late yesterday.

3.2 Imperfect and pluperfect subjunctive

3.2.1 Uses

The imperfect and pluperfect are considered as literary tenses today, and authors like Proust or Verlaine are favourite sources of quotations.

> Ex: '*Françoise qui ne laissait pas passer le plus léger de ceux [malaises] qu'elle éprouvait, si je souffrais détournait la tête pour que je n'**eusse** pas le plaisir de voir ma souffrance plainte, même remarquée.*'

> Marcel Proust, *Le côté de Guermantes*

The imperfect and pluperfect are almost never used in conversation or everyday writing, particularly as their forms tend to sound very strange and even sometimes ridiculous, particularly in the 1st and 2nd persons (e.g. *que nous nous exprimassions*). The 3rd person singular (which looks like the 3rd person of the past historic) sounds slightly more 'acceptable' (e.g. *qu'il s'exprimât*)! See chapter 10 Past Historic, section 3.4.

The pluperfect can also have a modal value: it can express unreality in the past (= pluperfect conditional).

Ex: *S'il **eût lu** Machiavelle, il **eût fait** meilleure carrière en politique.*
Had he read Machiavelli, he would have been more successful in politics.

There is a difference in the sequence of tenses with a subjunctive in the subordinate clause between formal and informal French. This is illustrated in 3.2.2 below with the sample verbs *choisir* and *venir*.

However, the imperfect is sometimes still used in formal French (e.g. formal radio or television interviews, formal presentations of one's work to an educated audience). The following examples were heard on the radio:
'Mon père aurait voulu que je **fisse** droit.'
'Il avait été question qu'on le **sélectionnât**.'

It is also used as a source of comedy, as demonstrated by the following extract.

Amédée
. . . Oui, j'ai hérité cette grande maison d'une vieille tante il y a plus de trente ans. Il **eût** évidemment **fallu** que j'y **fisse** des travaux, que je la **modernisasse** au fil des années, mais vous savez ce que c'est . . . A force de remettre au lendemain . . .

. . .

Katia
. . . On a du mal à vous comprendre. C'est vrai, vous causez pas comme tout le monde.

Amédée
Je sais que j'abuse un peu de l'imparfait du subjonctif, mais je ne pensais pas être abscons [. . .]. En fait, l'imparfait du subjonctif, c'est un traumatisme de jeunesse.

Katia
Ah bon? Moi, je croyais que c'était un truc de conjugaison.

Amédée
C'en est un. Mais, quand j'étais petit, mon père, qui était instituteur, m'obligeait à faire des phrases avec l'imparfait du subjonctif. A grands coups de règle sur les doigts. Et qu'est-ce qu'il tapait fort, la vache! Il y avait donc intérêt à ce que je **pigeasse** vite pour ne pas finir avec des moignons.

. . .

Katia
C'est quoi votre nom?

Amédée
. . . Amédée . . . Amédée Rousseau. J'**eusse** évidemment **préféré** que mes parents me **prénommassent** Jean-Jacques . . .

Alain Reynaud-Fourton, *Monsieur Amédée*

3.2.2 *Sequence table*

(i) **Simple forms**

	formal	informal
il faut il faudra il a fallu il faudrait	qu'il choisisse qu'il vienne	qu'il choisisse qu'il vienne
il fallut	qu'il choisît qu'il vînt	--- ---
il fallait il avait fallu il aurait fallu	qu'il choisît qu'il vînt	qu'il choisisse qu'il vienne

(ii) **Compound forms**

	formal	informal
il faut il faudra il a fallu il faudrait	qu'il ait choisi qu'il soit venu	qu'il ait choisi qu'il soit venu
il fallut	qu'il eût choisi qu'il fût venu	--- ---
il fallait il avait fallu il aurait fallu	qu'il eût choisi qu'il fût venu	qu'il ait choisi qu'il soit venu

4 The subjunctive vs the indicative

The subjunctive (present and perfect tenses) is mainly used in *que*-clauses. However, it also appears in adverbial clauses and, to a lesser extent, in relative and independent clauses.

4.1 *que*-clauses

que-clauses (*propositions complétives*) entail the use of either subjunctive or indicative. The mood is dependent on the meaning of the **verb** in the main clause, or on the interrogative or negative nature of the whole sentence.

To avoid the onerous listing of all the verbs and expressions that are followed by the subjunctive and the indicative respectively, these verbs and expressions may be considered in the following semantic groups.

(i) The SUBJUNCTIVE is used after verbs and expressions which represent four broad groups:
 – uncertainty
 – opinion
 – wish, order, obligation
 – feeling.

(ii) The INDICATIVE is used after verbs and expressions which represent four broad groups:
- certainty
- judgement
- promise, resolution, decision
- observation, declaration, statement.

4.1.1   Uncertainty vs certainty

(i)   **Uncertainty or impossibility → subjunctive**

Possibility, doubt, uncertainty, improbability and impossibility are mainly expressed by impersonal expressions with *il*:
- *il est douteux / peu probable / improbable / possible / impossible*, etc. *que*
- *il semble, il se peut; il n'est pas possible, il arrive*, etc. *que*

to which the verb *douter* should be added. (Note that *se douter que* and *il **me** semble que* are followed by the indicative. See 4.1.2(ii) below.)

> Ex: *Après ce que vous avez dit, je **doute qu'il vienne**!*
> After what you've said, I doubt [that] he'll come!
>
> *L'inégalité existe encore mais **il semble qu'**elle ne **soit** plus un fléau de notre société.*
> Inequality still exists but it seems it is no longer a scourge of our society.

NB: If *il semble* or *il paraît* are followed by an adjective +*que*, it is that **adjective** which determines the mood.

> Ex: *Il semble **certain** que c'**est** la France qui va gagner.*

(ii) **Certainty or probability → indicative**

Certainty or probability are mainly expressed by impersonal expressions with *il*: *il est probable / certain / vrai / sûr / évident / clair*, etc. *que*, to which the verb *parier* should be added.

> Ex: ***Il est probable que** je **pourrai** assister à cette réunion.*
> I will probably be able to attend that meeting.
>
> *Je **parie que** vous **allez** encore gagner!*
> I bet you're going to win again!

4.1.2   Opinion vs judgement

(i)   **Opinion → subjunctive**

Opinion, moral or intellectual criticism, are expressed by:

- impersonal expressions with *il*:

il est (c'est) heureux / fâcheux / dommage / regrettable / préférable / bon / bien / mal / juste / naturel / utile / logique / douteux / inévitable / normal / indispensable / nécessaire / ironique / fréquent / rare / important / incontestable / essentiel/ curieux / surprenant / étrange / bizarre / extraordinaire, etc. *que*

163

il convient que; il vaut mieux que; il importe que; il suffit que; il est temps que; peu m'importe (t'importe, lui importe, etc.) que; ce n'est pas que

> Ex: **Il est logique qu'il faille** utiliser le subjonctif dans ce cas.
> It is logical that one should use the subjunctive in this case.
>
> *Certains pensent qu'il est peut-être un peu **ironique que** la devise de la France **soit**: 'Liberté, égalité, fraternité'.*
> Some people think that it is perhaps a little ironic that France's motto should be: 'Liberty, equality, fraternity'.
>
> **Ce n'est pas que** je **sois** malade, mais je ne me sens pas très bien quand même . . .
> It's not that I am ill, but I don't feel all that well all the same . . .

– verbs:

nier; regretter, contester; aimer, aimer mieux, préférer; approuver; proposer; comprendre
> Ex: *Je **regrette que** vous le **preniez** si mal.*
> I am sorry you are taking it so badly.

NB: When a verb or expression is followed by an infinitive, it is the **verb in the infinitive** that determines the use of the subjunctive or indicative. Compare:

> *Je **regrette que** vous le **preniez** si mal.*
> and:
> *Je **regrette de voir que** vous **êtes** malade.*
> (see 4.1.4(ii) below)
> I am sorry to see that you are ill.
>
> **Il ne faut pas s'attendre à ce qu'ils viennent** vous voir.
> (see 4.1.3(i) below)
> You should not expect them to come and see you.
> and:
> **Il faut savoir qu'ils ont décidé** de ne pas céder.
> (see (ii) below)
> You should know that they have decided not to give in.

(ii) Judgement → indicative

Judgement can be expressed by:

– verbs:
dire (declaration), *croire, trouver, penser, affirmer, savoir, juger, imaginer, supposer, sentir, se rendre compte, se douter, espérer, prévoir, avoir l'impression, estimer*, etc. *que*
> Ex: *Je **crois qu'il a** tort.*
> I think he is wrong.

NB: *se douter que* means you are almost sure it **is** the case, hence it is followed by the indicative, while *douter que* means you are almost sure it is **not** the case, hence it is followed by the subjunctive.

Ex: *Je **me doute que** tu **sais** ce qui est arrivé.*
I am pretty sure that you know what happened.
> but:

*Je **doute que** tu **saches** ce qui est arrivé.*
I doubt that you know what happened.

− impersonal expressions with *il*:
il me semble que, il paraît que

NB(1): *il paraît que* means 'it is said that', i.e. it is a statement, hence it is followed by the indicative.

Ex: ***Il paraît qu'**il y a eu une grosse tempête sur la Manche hier.*
Apparently, there was a violent storm on the English Channel yesterday.

NB(2): *il me semble que means* 'I think that', hence the indicative, while *il semble que* means 'it looks as if', i.e. there is a high degree of subjectivity, hence the subjunctive.

Ex: ***Il me semble que** vous **avez changé** d'avis.*
It seems to me that you have changed your mind.
> but:

***Il semble que** vous **ayez changé** d'avis.*
It looks as if you have changed your mind.

− *être* + adjective + *que*:
être sûr / certain / convaincu / persuadé, etc. que

Ex: *Je **suis sûre que** Lizzy me **donnera** sa souris . . .*
I am sure Lizzy will give me her mouse . . .

4.1.3 *Wish and obligation* vs *promise and resolution*

Note that wish and obligation imply a 'passive' notion whereas promise and resolution are more 'active'.

(i) **Wish and obligation → subjunctive**

Wish, will, command, necessity, obligation and interdiction are all expressed by the following:

− verbs:
vouloir, vouloir bien, souhaiter, désirer; aimer, avoir envie; demander, suggérer, commander, ordonner, exiger, compter, tenir à; insister pour; dire, écrire (injunctions); *attendre, s'attendre à; permettre, proposer, recommander, consentir à; être décidé à, se décider à, accepter, admettre; autoriser, accorder; s'opposer à, empêcher, refuser, défendre, interdire; veiller à, éviter, etc. que*, but see NB(1)

Ex: *Nous **attendons que** le courrier **soit** distribué.*
We are waiting for the mail to be delivered.

NB(1): When a verb which includes *à* is followed by the subjunctive, *ce que* must be added.

Ex: *Est-ce que vous **tenez** vraiment **à ce que** j'**écrive** ce rapport?*
Do you really insist that I should write that report?

> *Très bien, je **veillerai à ce que** ce **soit** fait.*
> Very well, I will see that it is done.

NB(2): Prohibition is often expressed by a negative: *ne pas admettre/autoriser, ne pas vouloir, ne pas aimer,* etc. *que.*

> Ex: *Je **n'aime pas que** tu **mettes** les verres en cristal dans le lave-vaisselle.*
> I don't like you to put the crystal glasses in the dishwasher.

– impersonal expressions with *il*:
il est nécessaire / obligatoire / essentiel / indispensable que; il faut que; il ne faut pas que; il suffit que; il est temps que; ce n'est pas la peine que (note that *il faut que* is more commonly used than *il est nécessaire que*)

> Ex: ***Il faut que** j'aille à la bibliothèque faire des photocopies.*
> I must go to the library to do some photocopies.
>
> *Puisque je vous verrai dimanche, **ce n'est pas la peine que** vous **envoyiez** mon livre.*
> Since I'll see you on Sunday, don't bother to post my book.

– imperative constructions (expressing a command, a wish, or prohibition)

> Ex: ***Attendez que** j'aie fini!*
> Wait until I have finished!

(ii) Promise and resolution → indicative

Promise, resolution and decision are expressed by the following verbs:
dire, savoir, promettre, décider, annoncer, affirmer, se rendre compte, assurer, déclarer, maintenir etc. *que*

> Ex: *Je **me suis rendu compte que** je m'étais trompé.*
> I realized that I had made a mistake.

Note that *décider* takes the indicative, whilst *être décidé à* and *se décider à*, which merely express a wish, take the subjunctive (see section 4.1.3(i) above).

> Ex: *J'ai **décidé qu'**il **viendra**.*
> I have decided that he will come.
>> but:
> *Je **suis décidé à ce qu'**il **vienne**.*
> I have made up my mind that he should come.

4.1.4 Feeling vs observation

(i) Feeling → subjunctive

Feelings and emotions (surprise, regret, sorrow, happiness, sadness, joy, anger, fear, etc.) can be expressed by:

– verbs:
craindre que [+ *ne*], *avoir peur que* [+ *ne*]; *s'étonner; regretter; se plaindre; détester; aimer, aimer mieux, préférer; désirer, souhaiter, se réjouir; accepter, approuver,* etc. *que*

> Ex: *Les gens ne contrôlent pas leurs chiens et ensuite ils **s'étonnent que** les rues **soient** sales!*
> People do not control their dogs and then they are surprised that the streets are dirty!

> *Il s'est plaint de ce que* vous **soyez** *toujours en retard.*
> He complained that you're always late.

– impersonal expressions with *cela*:
cela m'ennuie (vous ennuie, etc.) / me fâche / m'étonne / me réjouit, etc. *que*

> Ex: **Cela m'étonne que** *tu ne* **puisses** *pas venir avec nous demain.*
> I am surprised that you cannot join us tomorrow.

– *être* or *sembler* + adjective + *que*:
être (sembler) triste / content / heureux / satisfait / désolé / ravi / fier / mécontent / furieux / fâché / en colère / étonné / surpris / déçu / honteux / choqué, etc. *que*

> Ex: *Nous* **sommes** *très* **heureux que** *vous* **ayez pu** *venir.*
> We're very glad you were able to come.

– *avoir* + noun phrase + *que*:
avoir de la chance, avoir horreur / besoin / envie, etc. *que*

> Ex: *Vous* **avez de la chance que** *je vous* **aie attendu!**
> You're lucky I waited for you!

(ii) **Observation → indicative**

Observation and statement can be expressed by a verb: *dire, constater, observer, voir, remarquer, se souvenir, comprendre, admettre* etc. *que*

> Ex: *Je* **dis que** *tu ne* **peux** *pas le faire en une minute.*
> I say that you can't do it in one minute.

> *Tu* **vois** *bien* **que** *c'est faisable en fait!*
> So you see that it is feasible after all!

NB: *dire* can have several meanings (see section 4.1.5 below).

4.1.5 Cases when there is a choice

There is a choice between the subjunctive and the indicative (even in the affirmative form) with the following verbs, depending on whether they express an order (subjunctive) or a declaration (indicative): *dire, comprendre, prétendre, supposer, admettre, être d'avis, expliquer,* etc. *que*

> Ex: *Paul* **a dit que** *Pierre* **aille** *le voir samedi prochain.*
> (order)
> Paul said that Pierre must go and see him next Saturday.

> *Paul* **a dit que** *Pierre* **ira** *le voir samedi prochain.*
> (statement)
> Paul said that Pierre would go and see him next Saturday.

4.1.6 Interrogative and negative forms

In the negative or interrogative forms, *que* is followed either by the indicative or the subjunctive, depending on what is meant: a fact or an opinion on the possible realization of the process (this subtlety is often missing from the English translation). Note that in most cases, it is an opinion that is expressed, hence the subjunctive is the better guess in case of doubt (see also section 4.3 below, on the subjunctive with relative clauses).

(i) **Opinion**

If the negative or the interrogative form implies that an opinion is being expressed rather than a fact, the subjunctive is used with those verbs normally taking the indicative.

Ex: – *penser*:
  Ils pensent que c'est faisable.
  They think it is feasible.
  → *Ils ne pensent pas que ce soit faisable.*
  (The stress is on their opinion)
        but:
  → *Ils ne pensent pas que c'est faisable.*
  (The stress is on the fact that it may be feasible, even though they do not think so.)

  – *se souvenir*:
  Je me souviens qu'elle a mentionné son nouveau mari.
  I remember her mentioning her new husband.
  → *Vous souvenez-vous qu'elle a mentionné son nouveau mari?*
  (The fact is that she did mention him: do you remember it?)

  → *Vous souvenez-vous qu'elle ait mentionné son nouveau mari?*
  (An opinion is sought: she may or may not have mentioned him.)

NB: In conversation, *je ne crois pas que* or *je ne pense pas que* most of the time express an opinion, hence the use of the subjunctive.

(ii) **Fact**

An interrogative or negative form can reinforce the certainty of an event hence the possibility of the indicative with verbs normally followed by a subjunctive.

Ex: – *douter*:
  Je doute qu'il ait fait de son mieux.
  I doubt he did his best.

  Je ne doute pas qu'il a fait de son mieux.
  (= *j'en suis certain*: statement of fact)
        but:
  Je ne doute pas qu'il ait fait de son mieux.
  (= *c'est mon opinion*)

Again, in conversation, the subjunctive tends to take over.

4.2 Adverbial clauses

Adverbial clauses (*propositions circonstancielles*) are subordinate clauses introduced by:
– either a conjunction other than *que*
– or a compound conjunction with or without *que*.
An exception to this rule is the elliptical use of *que* instead of *pour que* (see section 4.2.4(ii) below).

These conjunctions may also be considered in semantic groups. Note that in all cases the 'simple' conjunctions (*où, quand, comment, pourquoi, combien, si, comme,* etc.) always take the indicative:

> Ex: *Il ne m'a pas dit **où** il **allait**.*
> He didn't tell me where he was going.

Most conjunctions, however, are compound. It is the **conjunction** (not the verb) which determines the mood in the subordinate clause.

(i) The **subjunctive** is found after conjunctions expressing posteriority (the action of the subordinate clause takes place after that of the main clause); and when the subordinate clause is the aim/goal of the main clause.

(ii) The **indicative** is found after conjunctions expressing anteriority or simultaneity; addition, exception, comparison, cause, explanation, justification, etc. which are all factual notions; and when the subordinate clause is the consequence/result of the main clause.

(iii) Either the **subjunctive** or the **indicative** are found after condition, supposition, conjecture; concession, opposition, restriction, depending on the conjunction used.

4.2.1 *Anteriority and simultaneity* vs *posteriority*

(i) **Anteriority or simultaneity → indicative**

If the action of the subordinate clause takes place **before** that of the main clause, or **simultaneously** with it, the subordinate clause takes the indicative (as there is a strong element of certainty!). These subordinates are introduced by: *après que, lorsque, dès que, sitôt que, aussitôt que, au moment où, en même temps que, de la même manière que, à peine . . . que, depuis que, une fois que, maintenant que, à présent que, du jour où, pendant que, tandis que, alors que, à chaque fois que, toutes les fois que, cependant que, aussi longtemps que, (au fur et) à mesure que, tant que,* etc.

> Ex: *C'est un proverbe qu'il cite **à chaque fois qu**'il le **peut**.*
> It is a proverb that he quotes whenever he can.
>
> *A **peine** étions-nous arrivés **qu'**il **fallait** déjà repartir.*
> We had hardly arrived when we had to leave.
>
> ***Quand** le chat n'**est** pas là, les souris dansent.*
> When the cat's away, the mice will play.

NB(1): *lorsque* is slightly more formal than *quand.*

NB(2): After *après que,* the indicative should be used (although in informal French the subjunctive is often heard, by analogy with *avant que*).

NB(3): *comme*:
– *comme = puisque*
> Ex: ***Comme** le train **va** arriver avec du retard, j'ai le temps d'aller acheter un journal.*
> **Since** (because) the train is going to arrive late, I have time to go and buy a paper.

comme is always in first position when expressing a cause.

— *comme = alors que, quand*
> Ex: **Comme** *je finissais de dîner, Catherine est arrivée.*
>> or:
>> *Catherine est arrivée **comme** je finissais de dîner.*
>> Catherine arrived **as** I was finishing dinner.

(ii) Posteriority → subjunctive

If the action of the subordinate clause takes place **after** that of the main clause, the element of uncertainty is greater and the subjunctive is used, introduced by: *avant que* [+ ne], *jusqu'à ce que, en attendant que, sans que, sans attendre que, d'ici à ce que, d'ici que* (informal French only), *le temps que.*
> Ex: *Il est parti **sans que** je m'en **aperçoive**.*
> He left without my noticing it.

> *Nous le verrons **avant qu'il ne parte**.*
> We shall see him before he leaves.

NB(1): The English **until** is translated by *jusqu'à (ce que)* except if it means 'before' in a negative sentence, when it is translated by *avant (que)*.
> Ex: I hope you won't be playing outside **until** dark!
> *J'espère que vous n'allez pas jouer dehors **jusqu'à ce qu'il fasse nuit**!*
>> but:
>> We shan't put the house up for sale **until** after Christmas.
>> *Nous ne mettrons pas la maison en vente **avant que** Noël soit **passé**.*

NB(2): *le moment où*. Although the compound conjunctions *jusqu'à ce que, avant que* and *en attendant que* take the subjunctive, *jusqu'au moment où, avant le moment où* and *en attendant le moment où* take the indicative, since we now have simultaneity.
> Ex: *J'ai attendu **jusqu'au moment où** les feux d'artifice **ont commencé**.*
> I waited until the moment when the fireworks started.

4.2.2 Consequence/result vs aim/goal

(i) Consequence, result → indicative

The adverbial clause of consequence expresses a fact which is presented as the consequence or the result of the fact expressed in the main clause. The consequence is fully envisaged with *au point que, à ce point que, à tel point que, tant* (+ verb) *que, tellement* (+ verb(pp)/adj/adv/noun) *que,* [*tant et*] *si bien que, si* (+ adj/adv) *que.*
> Ex: *Ils ont insisté **tant et si bien que** finalement elle **a cédé**.*
> They insisted so much that eventually she gave in.

> *Ils avaient **tellement** mangé **qu'ils n'arrivaient** plus à se lever.*
> They had eaten so much that they could not get up.

> *Il avait plu **au point que** la rivière **avait débordé** de son lit.*
> It had rained so much that the river had burst its banks.

(ii) **Aim, goal → subjunctive**

The aim is something which is either wished for or refused, i.e. the intention is to obtain the result or, on the contrary, a fear is expressed about the result being obtained: *pour que, afin que; de peur que* [+ *ne*], *de crainte que* [+ *ne*].

Ex: *Les voisins ont tiré leurs rideaux **de peur qu**'on ne les **voie** . . .*
The neighbours have pulled their curtains for fear they might be seen . . .

*Je parle lentement **pour que** tout le monde me **comprenne**.*
I speak slowly so that everybody can understand me.

Consider the following example:
'He slipped in quietly but, as usual, not quite so quietly that Mrs Wisbeach failed to hear him.'

George Orwell, *Keep the Aspidistra Flying*

*Il se glissa silencieusement dans la maison, mais comme d'habitude, pas assez silencieusement **pour que** Mrs Wisbeach ne l'**entendît** pas/**manquât** de l'entendre.*

NB(1): *afin que* is stronger than *pour que*.

NB(2): *que* is often used elliptically instead of *pour que*, particularly after a main clause in the imperative.

Ex: *Prenez ce foulard, **que** vous n'**ayez** pas froid.*
Please take this scarf, so that you don't get cold.

Il y a des chances [***pour***] ***que*** *cette politique de détente **puisse** faire avancer les relations entre les pays.*
There is a chance that this policy of *détente* can further relations between the countries.

NB(3): *pour que* can also express a cause.

Ex: ***Pour que** vous **soyez** de si mauvaise humeur, il faut bien qu'il y ait une raison!*
There must be a reason for you to be in such a bad mood!

(When *pour que* expresses a cause, *pour* cannot be omitted.)

4.2.3 *Condition, supposition and conjecture*

The most frequent construction is the subordinate clause introduced by *si*, but *quand* is also used, as well as conjunctive phrases constructed with *que* or *où*. The subordinate clause contains a hypothesis whose possible consequences are in the main clause. Either the indicative or the subjunctive is used, according to the conjunction.

(i) **Indicative**

si, selon que, suivant que, ne . . . que si, seulement si

Ex: *'**Selon que** vous **serez** puissant ou misérable,*
Les jugements de cour vous rendront blanc ou noir.'

La Fontaine, *Les animaux malades de la peste*

*Je n'irai **que si** vous y **allez** aussi.*
I'll only go if you go too.

NB(1): *au cas où, dans le cas où, pour le cas où* are generally followed by the conditional.

Ex: ***Au cas où** vous **seriez** de retour après dix heures, je laisserai la clé sous le pot de fleurs.*
In case you are back after ten o'clock, I'll leave the key under the flower pot.

NB(2): With *quand* (formal French only), as a conjunction of hypothesis (= *même si*), both verbs are in the conditional, present or perfect.

Ex: ***Quand** vous **insisteriez**, je ne cèderais pas.*
Even if you insisted, I would not give in.

***Quand** vous **auriez insisté**, je n'aurais pas cédé.*
Even if you had insisted, I would not have given in.

NB(3): Concerning *si*, see also chapter 13 Conditional, section 3.2.1.

(ii) **Subjunctive**

à [la] condition que, à supposer que, en supposant que, pourvu que (condition); *pourvu que* (wish); *si tant est que, [si . . .] et que . . . , en admettant que, non que, que . . . ou que; soit que . . . soit que, pour peu que, que . . . ou non/pas*

Ex: ***Que** vous **soyez** d'accord **ou pas** n'a pas d'importance.*
Whether you agree or not does not matter.

*Tout ira bien, **pourvu que** vous ne **perdiez** pas votre sang-froid.*
Everything will be all right, provided you do not lose your cool.

***En admettant que** vous **ayez** raison, vous pourriez quand même être un peu plus poli.*
Supposing you are right, you could still be a little more polite.

NB: *à [la] condition que* can be followed by the future. Compare:
*Je vous attends, **à condition que** vous **vous dépêchiez**.*
(= now)
        and:
*Je viendrai à votre dîner, **à la condition que** nous ne **parlerons** pas des prochaines élections.*
(= when it happens)

4.2.4 *Concession, opposition, restriction*

When the result is not what was expected, it is called a concession or a concessive opposition. Either the indicative or the subjunctive is used, according to the conjunction.

(i) **Indicative**

même si, alors que, tandis que, au lieu que, si bien que, si tant est que

Ex: *Les enfants ont joué avec la petite table du salon **si bien que** maintenant elle **est** cassée.*
The children have been playing with the coffee table in the lounge so now it's broken.

(ii) **Subjunctive**

quoique, bien que, malgré que, soit que . . . soit que . . . , à moins que [+ ne], sans que [+ ne], pour peu que, de peur que [+ ne], de crainte que [+ ne], si tant est que, quelque (noun) que, quelque (adj) que, si (adj) que, pour (adj) que, aussi (adj) que, tout (adj) que, [pour] autant que, quel (quelle, quels, quelles) que.

Note that *quelque* (+ adj. + *que*), and *tout* (+ adj. + *que*) here are adverbs: *quelque* remains invariable, but *tout* agrees (see chapter 36 Indefinite Words, sections 5.2 and 5.7). However, *quelque* (+ noun + *que*) is an adjective and therefore agrees.

Ex: **Bien qu'il n'ait** pas beaucoup **travaillé** *en français, il a eu une assez bonne note . . .*
However he had not done much work in French, he got a fairly good mark . . .

*Je suis partie **sans que** personne **ne s'en aperçoive**.*
I left without anybody noticing.

Quelque *intéressants* **que soient** *vos arguments, nous devons remettre cette discussion à plus tard.*
However interesting your arguments [may be], we shall have to adjourn this discussion.

NB(1): Note the verb–subject inversion with a noun subject:
Ex: **Si** *intelligents* **que soient** *ces étudiants, ils se trompent parfois.*
However intelligent these students may be, they are sometimes wrong.
but not with a pronoun subject:
Si *intelligents* **qu'ils soient** . . .
However intelligent they may be . . .

NB(2): *quand* and *quand bien même* are followed by the conditional (*quand* on its own in this sense is used in formal French only):
Ex: **Quand bien même** *il* **pleuvrait,** *il irait à son bureau à pied.*
Even if it rained, he would walk to his office.
(See 4.2.3(i) above.)

4.2.5 *Factual notions*

Addition, exception, comparison, cause, explanation and justification are all factual notions, and thus take the indicative.

(i) **Addition and exception**

outre que, sans compter que, sauf que, excepté que, sinon que, sauf si, excepté si
Ex: *Je vais bien, **sauf que** j'ai un peu mal à la tête.*
I am all right, except that I have a slight headache.

NB: *outre que* normally comes first in the sentence.
Ex: **Outre qu'il reçoit** *déjà plus d'aide que n'importe qui d'autre, il ne cesse de se plaindre.*
Not only does he already get more help than anybody else, but he doesn't stop complaining either.

(ii) **Comparison**

See also chapter 30 Comparatives.

– manner:
comme, de même que, ainsi que, tel que, à mesure que, comme si

Ex: *Je vous l'ai donné **tel que** je l'ai trouvé.*
I gave it to you as I found it.

*Il est parti **comme** il **était venu**.*
He left as he came.

– quantity, quality:
plus . . . que [ne], moins . . . que [ne], aussi . . . que, au point que, mieux que, plutôt que [ne], autant que

Ex: *Vous vous répétez **plutôt que** vous ne **vous expliquez**.*
You are repeating rather than explaining yourself.

*Elle est **plus** âgée **que** vous [ne] le **pensez**.*
She is older than you think.

(iii) **Cause, explanation, justification**

parce que, puisque, comme, étant donné que, attendu que, du fait que, vu que, du moment que, dès lors que, dès l'instant que, maintenant que, d'autant que (formal), d'autant plus que, surtout que (informal), depuis que, sous prétexte que, etc.

Ex: ***Du moment qu'**il n'**insiste** pas pour en savoir plus, je me tais!*
So long as he does not insist on knowing more, I shall keep quiet!

*Il n'est pas venu **sous prétexte qu'**il **avait** une crise de foie.*
He did not come, under the pretext that he had a *crise de foie*.

NB(1): *parce que, puisque, comme, étant donné que*:

– *parce que* entails an explanation (the cause is not yet known):
Ex: *J'ai acheté du pain **parce qu'**il n'y en avait plus!*
I bought bread **because** there was none left!

– *puisque* entails a justification, hence it is often at the beginning of the sentence (the cause is known and given as the reason for what follows):
Ex: ***Puisqu'**il n'y a plus de pain à la maison, il faut que quelqu'un se dévoue pour aller en acheter.*
Since there is no more bread in the house, someone has to volunteer to go and buy some.

– *comme*: if it introduces a new idea in the course of an argument, it comes at the beginning of the sentence (and is very close to *puisque*):
Ex: ***Comme** (**puisque**) vous avez terminé, vous pouvez partir.*
As you have finished, you can leave.

– *étant donné que* implies that a conclusion is about to be drawn and is equally close to *comme* and *puisque* in the same position:
Ex: ***Etant donné que** vous n'avez pas répondu, je suppose que vous n'êtes plus intéressé.*
Since you did not answer, I suppose you are no longer interested.

NB(2): A cause can be stressed with *d'autant plus que, d'autant que* (formal), *surtout que* (informal) or *c'est que* (when the main clause begins with *si*).

Ex: ***Si*** *vous n'y arrivez pas,* ***c'est que*** *vous n'êtes pas organisé.*
If you can't manage, **it is because** you're not well organized.

Je n'y suis pas allé, ***d'autant plus que*** *je n'avais pas été formellement invité!*
I didn't go, **particularly as** I had not been formally invited!

4.2.6 Conjunctions taking either subjunctive or indicative

(i) There is a choice with the following conjunctions, depending on whether an aim/goal or a result/consequence is implied: *de [telle] sorte que, faire en sorte que, de façon [à ce] que, de manière [à ce] que.*

Ex: *Il s'est assis au premier rang* ***de façon à ce que*** *tout le monde le* ***voie***.
(aim: we do not know whether it has been achieved)
He sat in the front row so that everybody could see him.

Il parle lentement ***de sorte que*** *tout le monde le* ***comprenne***.
(aim: the consequence is open to interpretation)
He speaks slowly so that everybody can understand him.
   but:
Il s'exprime ***de telle sorte que*** *tout le monde le* ***comprend***.
(result)
He expresses himself in such a way that everybody understands him.

(ii) *tout . . . que* can be followed by the indicative if the factual nature is underlined:

Ex: ***Tout*** *riche* ***qu'il est***, *il n'arrive pas à entretenir son château.*
Rich though he is, he can't maintain his château.
   but:
Tout *riche* ***qu'il soit***, *il n'en est pas plus heureux pour autant.*
Rich though he may be, he is none the happier for all that.

4.3 Relative clauses

Relative clauses are subordinate clauses introduced by a relative pronoun. See also chapters 2 Syntax, section 3.2.2, and 32 Relative Pronouns.

The subjunctive only appears in the so-called restrictive relative clauses (*relatives restrictives*), when defining a referent which is non-specific, or whose existence is hypothetical or even explicitly denied.

4.3.1 Influence of the verb in the main clause and the nature of the antecedent

(i) The use of the subjunctive is determined partly by the nature of the antecedent of the relative pronoun.

  – If the antecedent is definite (i.e. it does exist and is clearly defined – by a definite article for instance), the mood is indicative. (But see exceptions in 4.3.2 below.)

– If the antecedent is merely envisaged, the mood is subjunctive (e.g. the antecedent is introduced by an indefinite article, or is an indefinite pronoun such as *quelque chose, rien, quelqu'un, personne*).

(ii)   The verbs most frequently used in the main clause for the second type of relative clause are: *chercher, vouloir, demander, désirer, préférer, avoir envie de, avoir besoin de* or *il (me, te, etc.) faut, il s'agit de*, i.e. verbs expressing a wish or an opinion.

Consider the following examples:

– The antecedent is specified by a definite article, hence the use of the indicative.
Ex: *Je préfère **les** jardins dont il ne **faut** pas trop s'occuper.*
I prefer gardens which do not require too much attention.

*Je cherche **la** personne qui m'**a aidé** hier.*
I am looking for the person who helped me out yesterday.

– The same applies to the negative and interrogatives forms.
Ex: *Préférez-vous les jardins dont il ne faut pas trop s'occuper?*
Je ne préfère pas particulièrement les jardins dont il ne faut pas trop s'occuper.

– If the indefinite article is used (or an indefinite pronoun – see above), there is a choice between subjunctive and indicative, depending on whether the antecedent does exist, or is merely envisaged.
Ex: *J'ai besoin d'un apprenti en qui je peux/puisse avoir confiance.*
I need an apprentice I can/could trust.

Ils ont besoin de quelqu'un qui peut/puisse réaliser leurs rêves.
They need someone who can/could realize their dreams.

In informal French however, this distinction tends to disappear and the subjunctive is used most of the time.

NB(1): *qui + être* can be omitted.
Ex: *Je cherche le terrain [qui est] à vendre.*
I am looking for the plot [which is] for sale.

Je cherche un terrain [qui soit] à vendre.
I am looking for a plot [which might be] for sale.

NB(2): With a verb in the main clause other than those listed above, the verb in the relative clause will be indicative, regardless of the nature of the antecedent.
Ex: *Je connais un apprenti qui **sait** faire les portes.*
I know an apprentice who can make doors.

*Je connais l'homme qu'il vous **faut**.*
I know the man you need.

However, a negative or interrogative form could restore the meaning of wish or opinion, in which case the subjunctive would be used.

Ex: *Je ne connais pas d'apprenti qui **sache** faire les portes.*
I don't know any apprentice who can make doors.

*Trouvez-moi un apprenti qui **sache** faire les portes.*
Find me an apprentice who can make doors.

NB(3): In the case of a verb followed by an infinitive, it is the conjugated verb which has to be considered. Compare:

*Je **veux voir** une maison qui me **plaise.***
and:
*Je **vois** une maison qui me **plaît.***

4.3.2 Influence of the antecedent qualifiers

If the antecedent is qualified by *seul, unique, premier* or by a superlative, or is preceded by *il y a peu de, il n'y a pas de*, etc., either the indicative or the subjunctive is used. Compare:

*C'est la première tasse de café que je **bois** ce matin.*
It's my first cup of coffee this morning.
The first cup is one of several – the indicative is used.
and:
*C'est la seule personne qui lui **écrive.***
He/she is the only person who [ever] writes to him/her.
The person is not one of several – the subjunctive is used.

Finally, a superlative followed by a plural (showing dependence on, or belonging to a group) also entails the use of the indicative. Compare:

C'est le plus bel opéra que j'aie [jamais] vu.
It is the finest opera I have ever seen.
and:
C'est le plus beau des opéras que j'ai vus.
It is the finest of all the operas I have seen.

4.3.3 Indefinite relative pronouns

See also chapter 36 Indefinite Words, sections 4.3 and 4.4.

(i) *qui que, quoi que, où que* entail the use of the subjunctive.

Ex: *Je ne laisserai sortir **qui que ce soit.***
I shan't let anybody leave.

***Quoi qu'il fasse**, vous n'êtes jamais content.*
Whatever he does, you are never satisfied.

***Où que** vous **soyez**, appelez-moi.*
Wherever you are, call me.

NB: *où que* + subjunctive should not be confused with *là où* + indicative.

Ex: *Il ira **là où** elle **ira.***
He'll go wherever she goes.

If the place is defined in the mind of the speaker, i.e. **wherever** can be replaced by **where**, use *là où* + indicative. On the contrary, if the place is not defined in the mind of the speaker, i.e. **wherever cannot** be replaced by **where**, use *où que* + subjunctive.

(ii)   *quiconque* is the equivalent of a personal pronoun ('all those who', 'anyone who', 'whoever') and is followed by the indicative.

> Ex: **Quiconque dit** *cela ne* **sait** *pas de quoi il parle.*
> Whoever says this does not know what he is talking about.

4.3.4   *The case of* quel

quel (*quelle, quels, quelles*) *que* followed by *être, pouvoir être* or *devoir être* entails the subjunctive.

> Ex: **Quel que soit** *le projet qu'il entreprenne, il ne le mène jamais à bien.*
> Whatever project he undertakes, he never sees it through.
>
> **Quelle qu'ait pu être** *sa conduite, il faut lui pardonner maintenant.*
> Whatever his/her behaviour may have been, you should forgive him/her now.

4.4   Infinitive clauses

When the subject of the subordinate clause introduced by the conjunction *que* is the same as that of the main clause, and the tense is the same, the infinitive must be used instead of the subjunctive. In the case of adverbial clauses, there is a choice in cases where there is an equivalent preposition (see section 4.4.2 below).

4.4.1   *Infinitive 'object' clause*

In the case of subordinate clauses introduced by *que*, the infinitive must be used with the prepositions *à* or *de* or without a preposition (see also chapter 15 Infinitive).

> Ex: *J'ai besoin* **de manger** *quelque chose.*
> I need to eat something.
>
> *Je tiens* **à partir** *à six heures.*
> I insist on leaving at six o'clock. / I insist I must leave . . .
>
> *Je me rappelle l'* **avoir vu** *hier.*
> I remember seeing him yesterday. / I remember I saw . . .

Consider the following example:

> *Catherine a prêté un pull à Marie. Elle craignait qu'elle ne prenne froid.*

There is no ambiguity in the second sentence: the two *'elle's* **must** refer to two different people.

> Catherine lent a pullover to Marie. She was afraid that Marie might catch cold.
>
> *Marie a emprunté un pull à Catherine. Elle craignait de prendre froid.*

This is the only way to say that it is **Marie** who's afraid to catch cold.

> Marie borrowed a pullover from Catherine. She was afraid of catching cold.

4.4.2 Infinitive adverbial clause

A subordinate clause introduced by a compound conjunction can be replaced by an infinitive clause introduced by the corresponding preposition. The following conjunctions have a corresponding preposition:

Conjunction (+ subjunctive)	Preposition (+ infinitive)
pour que	*pour*
afin que	*afin de*
de peur que [+ *ne*]	*de peur de*
de crainte que [+ *ne*]	*de crainte de*
jusqu'à ce que, en attendant que	*jusqu'à, en attendant de*
de façon que	*de façon à*
de manière que	*de manière à*
en sorte que	*en sorte de*
à moins que [+ *ne*]	*à moins de*
sans que	*sans*
à condition que	*à condition de*
avant que [+ *ne*]	*avant de*
après que	*après*
au point que	*au point de*

> Ex: *Je te verrai **avant que je** [ne] **parte**.*
> > or:
> *Je te verrai **avant de partir**.*
> I shall see you before I leave.

When a conjunction does not have a corresponding preposition (e.g. *bien que, quoique, malgré que*), the conjunction remains with the subjunctive.

> Ex: ***Bien qu*'ils vivent** *dans un petit appartement en ville, ils veulent avoir un Saint-Bernard!*
> Although they live in a small flat in town, they want to have a Saint–Bernard!

4.5 Independent clauses

The subjunctive is used:

– to give an order to a third person or to express a wish or a warning, hence it has an imperative value:

> Ex: *Qu'il attende!*
> Let him wait!

> *Qu'elle fasse un peu attention!*
> Can't she be a little more careful!

– in constructions with *pouvoir* to express a wish:

> Ex: *Puisse-t-elle partir avant qu'il ne soit trop tard!*
> If only she could leave before it is too late!

– in constructions with *être* to express a hypothesis (e.g. in maths textbooks):
> Ex: *Soit un triangle ABC.*
> Let ABC be a triangle.

– in constructions with *vive/vivent*:
> Ex: *Vive la France!*
> Long live France!

– with an exclamative value:
> Ex: *Moi, que je fasse un détour!*
> Me! Do a detour?
> (equivalent to the infinitive: *Moi, faire un détour!*)

– in fixed expressions:
> Ex: *Ainsi soit-il.*
> (religious contexts only)
> Amen.

Compare with: *Qu'il en soit ainsi.*
> So be it.

Other examples:
> *Advienne que pourra.*
> Come what may.
>
> *Coûte que coûte.*
> At all costs.
>
> *Honi soit qui mal y pense.*
> Shame on him who thinks evil of it.
>
> *Soit.* (pronounced [swat])
> (expresses lukewarm agreement)
> Very well then.

5 Translation difficulties

This section concerns mainly translation from English to French.

5.1 Repetition of conjunctions in adverbial clauses

(i) Use of *que*

Whilst conjunctions are not repeated at all in English, *que* is normally used in French to replace the second occurrence of a conjunction, with the same mood. (If emphasis is needed, the same conjunction is repeated.)
> Ex: *Je n'ai pas voulu acheter ce manteau **parce qu**'il **coûtait** très cher et **que** l'hiver **était** presque fini!*
> I didn't want to buy that coat **because** it was very expensive and _ winter was almost over!

Note: With *si* (+ indicative), the subjunctive is used after *que* (see also chapter 13 Conditional, section 3.2.3(iii)).

> Ex: **Si** *vous* **avez** *soif et* **que** *vous* **ayez** *envie d'un jus de fruits, servez-vous!*
> **If** you are thirsty and _ you fancy a fruit juice, please help yourself!

If *si* is repeated for emphasis, the indicative is kept.

> Ex: **Si** *vous* **avez** *soif et* **si** *vous* **avez** *envie d'un jus de fruits* . . .
> **If** you are thirsty and **if** you fancy a fruit juice . . .

(ii) **Alternatives to adverbial clauses**

As is the case with relative pronouns (See chapter 32 Relative Pronouns, section 5), a succession of conjunctions of subordination is considered inelegant. These conjunctions can be replaced by:

— a noun:

> Ex: *Vous pourrez terminer ce travail quand vous aurez plus le temps* **lorsque** **vous serez en vacances.**
> → **pendant vos vacances.**
>
> *Je ne peux pas sortir quand j'en ai envie* **parce que vous vous montrez** *égoïste.*
> → **à cause de votre égoïsme.**

— a juxtaposition (particularly in informal French):

> Ex: *Prends-le puisque tu en as envie et qu'on te le donne!*
> → *Prends-le: tu en as envie et on te le donne!*

— a verb:

> Ex: *Bien que je me sois dépêchée et que j'aie trouvé un taxi tout de suite, j'ai quand même raté mon train.*
> → *J'ai eu beau me dépêcher et trouver un taxi tout de suite* . . .

Note that alternatives are not always possible.

(iii) **Alternatives to *que*-clauses**

An infinitive clause can be used instead of a *que*-clause.

> Ex: *Si intelligent que tu sois, il arrive que tu te trompes et que tu ne comprennes pas tout!*
> → *il t'arrive de te tromper et de ne pas tout comprendre!*

5.2 More than one subjunctive in a sentence

A sentence may contain two or more subjunctives, or a combination of subjunctive and indicative.

Consider the following examples:

> **1** *Il est peu vraisemblable que, si on croit en une égalité inhérente, on* **accepte** *qu'une telle exigence* **puisse être** *jamais satisfaite.*
> It is unlikely that if we believe in an inherent equality, we should accept that such a demand could ever be met.

- '*Il est peu vraisemblable que*' entails the subjunctive ('*accepte*');
- '*Il est peu vraisemblable qu'on accepte*' means '*On ne croit pas vraiment que*', hence also entails the subjunctive ('*puisse être*').

> **2** *Ce qui importe, c'est qu'on **sache** que ses actions **ont** une valeur.*
> What matters is that we should know that his actions are worthwhile.

- '*Ce qui importe, c'est que*' means '*Il est important que*' and entails the subjunctive ('*sache*');
- '*Il est important qu'on sache que*' or '*Il est important de savoir*' means '*On sait que*', hence the indicative ('*ont*').

> **3** *Je voudrais que ce **soit** le cheval qui **a** la crinière tressée qui me **prenne**.*
> I would like the horse with the plaited mane to take me.

- '*Je voudrais que*' (expressing a wish) entails the subjunctive in its object clause ('*soit*');
- '*qui a la crinière tressée*' is a relative clause with an adjectival value: the indicative is required;
- '*qui me prenne*': is envisaged by '*Je voudrais que*', hence the subjunctive.

13 Conditional and the expression of hypothesis

1 Introduction

As a **mood**, the conditional expresses a possible action, depending upon a condition. The present conditional corresponds to the non-accomplished aspect, the perfect conditional corresponds to the accomplished aspect. The conditional is also used as a **tense** in itself, the 'future of the past', without any notion of condition.

It corresponds in English to the conditional formed with **would/should** + verb. However:
- **would/should** have other uses (see chapter 21 Modals, sections 5.6 and 5.8)
- there are cases where a French conditional is not expressed by **would/should** in English (see section 3 below).

2 Formation

There are two tenses, present and past, and two forms of the past: first and second form (or perfect and pluperfect).

2.1 Present conditional

The present conditional is formed with the radical of the future (see chapter 7 Future, section 2) and the endings of the imperfect (see chapter 8 Imperfect, section 2).

Ex: *donner: je **donner**ais*   *nous **donner**ions*
    *tu **donner**ais*   *vous **donner**iez*
    *il/elle/on **donner**ait*   *ils/elles **donner**aient*

    *aller: j'**ir**ais*   *nous **ir**ions*
    *tu **ir**ais*   *vous **ir**iez*
    *il/elle/on **ir**ait*   *ils/elles **ir**aient*

    *voir: je **verr**ais*   *nous **verr**ions*
    *tu **verr**ais*   *vous **verr**iez*
    *il/elle/on **verr**ait*   *ils/elles **verr**aient*

With verbs in *-rer*, it is a common error to forget the '*re*' of the radical.

Ex: *rencontrer:*
    imperfect   *je rencontrais*
    conditional   *je rencontrerais*

2.2 Perfect conditional

The perfect conditional is the compound form of the present conditional. It is formed with the present conditional of *avoir* or *être* + the past participle of the main verb.

Ex: *acheter*   *j'aurais acheté*

     partir   *je serais parti*

     se dépêcher   *je me serais dépêché*

2.3 Pluperfect conditional

The pluperfect conditional is a literary form and, like the pluperfect subjunctive, is formed with the imperfect subjunctive of the auxiliary *être* or *avoir* + the past participle of the main verb.

Ex: *acheter*   *j'eusse acheté*

     partir   *je fusse parti*

     se dépêcher   *je me fusse dépêché*

3 Use

3.1 The present and perfect conditional as a tense: 'future of the past'

The conditional can express the future seen from the past, without any notion of condition.

(i) Present conditional

We have seen that the future expresses a future action in relation to the present (see chapter 7 Future). The present conditional is used to express a future action seen from the past. Compare:

> *Je sais que vous **réussirez**.*
> I know you will succeed.

The future of the present shows that an event is seen as being in progress at some future time.

> and:

> *Je savais que vous **réussiriez**.*
> I knew you would succeed.

The present conditional (future of the past) shows that an event is seen as being in progress at some later time (non-accomplished aspect).

(ii) Perfect conditional

The perfect conditional is used in similar constructions to those in the present conditional. It expresses the future perfect seen from the past. Most importantly, it expresses the **accomplished** aspect, as opposed to the non-accomplished aspect of the present conditional. Compare:

> *Je pense qu'il **aura** bientôt **fini**.*
> I think he will have finished soon.

The future perfect shows that an event is seen as being completed at some future time.

and:

Je pensais qu'il aurait bientôt fini.
I thought he would have finished soon.

The perfect conditional (future perfect of the past) shows that an event is seen as already completed at some later time.

After conjunctions of time (see chapter 7 Future, section 3.2.1), the perfect conditional is used to express an action or state which has to be completed in the past **before** another action or state can take place. English uses the past perfect.

Ex: J'ai promis de lui prêter mon livre quand j'aurais fini de le lire.
I promised I would lend him my book when I had finished reading it.

3.2   The conditional as a mood, expressing hypothesis

Hypothesis can be expressed with the conditional, with or without **si**.

3.2.1   *Hypothesis with* si

(i)   Meaning

– Present conditional

The conditional is thus used in both main and independent clauses. It is used in sentences containing or implying a subordinate clause introduced by *si* which express a condition, hypothesis or conjecture. It describes an action which has not been completed yet and which is considered as either possible in the future or impossible in the present, with the appropriate adverbs or adverb phrases.

Ex: Je viendrais tout de suite si je le pouvais.
(implies 'but I cannot come': impossible in the present)
I would come at once if I could.

Si j'avais des nouvelles de Robert, je vous écrirais.
(implies 'and it may be the case': possible in the future)
If I had any news from Robert, I would write to you.

NB: The rule applies even though there may be another clause embedded in the sentence, and even though the order may be reversed (conditional → *si* + imperfect).

Ex: Le nombre des cancers serait réduit si tous les gens [qui fument plus de soixante cigarettes par jour] se faisaient faire un examen des poumons tous les six mois.
The number of cancers would be reduced if all the people [who smoke more than sixty cigarettes a day] had a lung check-up every six months.

'Si le fils d'analphabète, bardé de diplômes, se retrouvait dans une condition professionnelle équivalente à celle de son père, ce jour-là, le rêve du progrès serait brisé et, avec lui, la cohésion sociale qu'il apportait.'

François de Closets, Le Monde

— Perfect conditional

The perfect conditional describes an action which is imagined as completed. It describes what would have happened had a condition been fulfilled or had a conjecture turned out to be true.

> Ex: *Je **serais venue** tout de suite si je l'avais pu.*
> I would have come at once if I had been able to.
>
> *Si j'avais reçu des nouvelles de Robert, je vous **aurais écrit**.*
> If I'd had any news from Robert, I would have written to you.

(ii) Construction

— When **si** is used, note that there is elision of the 'i' before *il* but not before *elle* or *on*.

> Ex: ***s'il** devait venir.*
>> but:
> ***si** elle devait venir.*
> ***si** on devait venir.*

— IMPORTANT: the conditional is **never** used in the *si*-clause expressing hypothesis. The basic rule is:
si + imperfect → conditional

> Ex: ***Si** j'étais riche, j'**achèterais** un château en Ecosse.*

— The *si*-clause does not necessarily come first. If the *si*-clause comes after the main clause, it has a conditional rather than a hypothetical value. Furthermore, if it is detached from it by a comma, the condition is emphasized. Compare:

> *Si j'avais le temps, je viendrais.* (hypothesis)
> *Je viendrais si j'avais le temps.* (condition)
> *Je viendrais, si j'avais le temps.* (condition, emphasized)

— The *si* can be implicit

The two clauses are juxtaposed and the conditional is used in both clauses.

> Ex: *Il **serait** là, nous le **verrions**.*
> (= ***S'il** était là ...*)
> If he were here, we would see him.
>
> *Il **aurait été** là, nous l'**aurions vu**.*
> (= ***S'il** avait été là ...*)
> Had he been here, we would have seen him.

Note that this turn of phrase is used in informal French only.

— More than one conditional with the same subject.

The English auxiliaries ('would', 'should', etc.) are not normally repeated before each verb with the same subject. It is a common error to ignore this ellipsis when translating into French.

> Ex: If you asked her to help, she **would complain** and **make** a fuss.
> *Si vous lui demandiez d'aider, elle **se plaindrait** et **ferait** toute une histoire.*

(iii)   Hypothesis with *même si* indicating opposition

> Ex: ***Même si*** *vous me le promettiez, je ne vous* ***croirais*** *pas.*
> Even if you promised it to me, I would not believe you.
>
> ***Même si*** *je* ***m'étais dépêché*** *(e), je* ***n'aurais*** *pas* ***pu*** *avoir mon train.*
> Even if I had hurried, I could not have caught my train.

NB: With *quand* as a hypothesis conjunction (= *même si*), both verbs are in the conditional, present or perfect (formal French only).

> Ex: ***Quand*** *vous* ***insisteriez****, je ne* ***cèderais*** *pas.*
> ***Quand*** *vous* ***auriez insisté****, je* ***n'aurais*** *pas* ***cédé****.*

(iv)   Hypothesis with *si* preceded by *comme, sauf* or *excepté*

Note that the conditional is not used in the main clause for:

– comparison, with *comme si*:

> Ex: *Dizzy* ***a dévoré*** *toute une boîte,* ***comme s'il n'avait*** *rien* ***mangé*** *depuis deux jours.*
> Dizzy has scoffed a whole tin, as if he hadn't had anything to eat for two days.

– restriction, with *sauf si, excepté si*:

> Ex: *Ne* ***prenez*** *pas le Munster,* ***sauf si*** *vous* ***aimez*** *vraiment les fromages forts!*
> Don't choose the Munster, unless you really like strong cheeses!

(v)   Iterative value of *si*

si is then equivalent to *à chaque fois que* and the tense, imperfect or present, is the same in the main and the subordinate clause. (See also chapter 8 Imperfect, section 3.1 (iv)).

> Ex: ***Si*** *je la* ***voyais****, je lui* ***disais*** *bonjour mais elle ne* ***répondait*** *pas.*
> Whenever I saw her, I would say hello to her but she wouldn't answer.
>
> *En vacances,* ***s'il fait*** *mauvais, je* ***visite*** *les musées.*
> On holiday, if the weather is bad, I visit museums.

3.2.2   Hypothesis without si

(i)   Expressing a suggestion

The present or perfect conditional can express a suggestion.

> Ex: *A votre place, je* ***travaillerais*** *davantage.*
> In your place (= if I were you), I **would work** more.
>
> *A votre place, j'* ***aurais travaillé*** *davantage.*
> In your place (= had I been you), I **would have worked** more.

Note the importance of '*à votre place*' here, which makes this sentence a suggestion.

(ii)   Expressing a wish

The conditional (present or perfect) can express a wish, or a dream, with the 1st person.

Ex: *Nous **irions** bien faire un tour en ville cet après-midi.*
We **would** quite **like** to go to town this afternoon.

*Nous **serions** bien **allés** faire un tour en ville cet après-midi.*
We **would have** quite **liked** to go to town this afternoon.

NB(1): 'I wish you would (do something)' is translated by *Je voudrais* [*bien*] *que vous* or *J'aimerais* [*bien*] *que vous* + subjunctive (see chapter 12 Subjunctive, section 4.1.3).

Ex: I wish you would hurry up.
*Je **voudrais** bien que vous **vous dépêchiez**.*

We wish you would make a bit of an effort.
*Nous **aimerions** bien que vous **fassiez** un petit effort.*

In informal French, a perfect conditional in the main clause still entails a present subjunctive in the subordinate clause (in formal French, the imperfect subjunctive would be used: see chapter 12 Subjunctive, section 3.2.2).

Ex: *J'aurais bien **voulu** que vous **vous dépêchiez**.*
I wished you had hurried up.

*Nous **aurions** bien **aimé** que vous **fassiez** un petit effort.*
We wished you had made a bit of an effort.

NB(2): 'I wish I could (do something)' is translated by *Je voudrais* [*bien*] [*pouvoir*] or *J'aimerais* [*bien*] [*pouvoir*] + infinitive.

Ex: I wish I could go on holiday too.
J'aimerais [*bien*] [*pouvoir*] *partir en vacances aussi.*

I wished I could have gone on holiday too.
J'aurais [*bien*] *aimé* [*pouvoir*] *partir en vacances aussi.*

(iii)   Expressing an envisaged project

Ex: *Arrivé à destination, il **dormirait** quelques heures, puis **se lèverait**, **prendrait** un bain, **s'habillerait** et **irait** faire un tour.*
Once he'd reached his destination, he would sleep for a few hours, then he'd get up, have a bath, get dressed and go for a walk round.

(iv)   Expressing a polite request

The present or past conditional is used instead of the present indicative, particularly with *vouloir*.

Ex: *Je **voudrais** / j'aurais **voulu** vous parler.*
I would like / would have liked to speak to you.

(v)   Expressing a polite suggestion or reproach with *devoir*

Ex: *Vous **devriez** travailler un peu plus.*
You ought to work a bit more.

*Vous **auriez dû** travailler un peu plus.*
You ought to have worked a bit more.

(vi)   Expressing consequence with the gerund

   Ex: *En mangeant moins, vous **vous porteriez** mieux.*
   By eating less, you would be healthier.
   (= *Si vous mangiez moins, . . .*)

(vii)   Expressing allegations

The conditional is used to express allegations, i.e. events which are presumed to be true but where a doubt exists (e.g. unsubstantiated facts in media reports). It is also used whenever there is a certain degree of reservation about an event or situation.

   Ex: '*La ville de Reims **pourrait** remettre en question son projet de tramway. M. Jean Falala, maire de Reims, **devrait** décider prochainement s'il maintient son accord au projet de tramway décidé en novembre 1990 [. . .]*'

   Le Monde, 22 January 1991

   'The city of Rheims could reconsider its tram project. Mr Jean Falala, mayor of Rheims, should decide shortly whether he is maintaining his agreement to the tram project decided in November 1990 [. . .]'

(Compare with the use of the future for suppositions: see chapter 7 Future, section 3.1.2.)

(viii)   Expressing a contingency with *au cas où*

The conditional is used with *au cas où* to indicate a contingency. The present conditional is used to express a future contingency and the perfect conditional is used to express one in the past. Note that English does not use the conditional after 'in case'.

   Ex: ***Au cas où** vous **voudriez** venir me voir, voici mon adresse.*
   In case you want to come and see me, here's my address.

   *Je lui avais donné des biscuits, **au cas où** elle **aurait eu** faim pendant le voyage.*
   I had given her some biscuits, in case she got hungry during the journey.

3.2.3   Tenses after a hypothetical si

IMPORTANT: A hypothetical *si* is never immediately followed by a future or conditional.

(i)   The conditional or hypothetical *si* is generally followed by the present, the imperfect or the pluperfect, according to the following model:
   − *S'il pleut, je prends un taxi.*
   − *S'il pleuvait, je prendrais un taxi.*
   − *S'il avait plu, j'aurais pris un taxi.*

But see summary below for other tense possibilities.

(ii)   *si* + imperfect [+ . . .] (→ conditional) can be translated by several different structures in English.

> Ex: ***Si j'avais*** *besoin de quelque chose, je vous* ***écrirais.***
> **If** I **needed** anything, I would write to you.
>> but also:
> **If** I **were to need** anything . . .
> **Were** I **to need** anything . . .
> **If** I **should need** anything . . .
> **Should** I **need** anything . . .

(iii)   When two subordinate clauses expressing a hypothesis are coordinated, the second *si* is normally replaced by *que* + subjunctive. However, the second *si* (+ indicative) can be kept for emphasis.

> Ex: ***S'il fait*** *beau* ***et que*** *vous* ***soyez*** *d'accord, nous irons nous promener.*
> **If** the weather is nice and _ you agree, we'll go for a walk.

Compare:

> *Si je ne* ***suis*** *pas trop fatiguée et* ***que*** *les magasins* ***soient*** *encore ouverts, je ferai quelques courses ce soir.*
> **If** I am not too tired and _ the shops are still open, I will do some shopping tonight.
>> and:
> *Si je ne* ***suis*** *pas trop fatiguée et* ***si*** *les magasins* ***sont*** *encore ouverts, je ferai quelques courses ce soir.*
> **If** I am not too tired and **if** the shops are still open, I will do some shopping tonight.

3.3   Summary of tenses used in conditional sentences with *si*

condition/hypothesis	result/consequence
1 *si* + present tense	→ present
	→ imperative
	→ future
	→ future perfect

> Ex: ***Si*** *vous* ***voulez*** *prendre le train de 6 heures, vous* ***devez*** *partir maintenant.*
> ***Si*** *vous* ***voulez*** *prendre le train de 6 heures,* ***partez*** *maintenant.*
> ***Si*** *vous* ***partez*** *maintenant, vous* ***arriverez*** *à 8 heures.*
> ***Si*** *vous* ***partez*** *maintenant, vous* ***serez arrivé*** *pour 8 heures.*

See also iterative *si* in section 3.2.1(v) above.

2 *si* + perfect	→ present
	→ imperative
	→ future
	→ future perfect
	→ imperfect
	→ perfect

Ex: *Si* vous *avez terminé* cet exercice, vous *pouvez* partir.
Si vous *avez terminé*, *partez*!
Si vous n'*avez* pas *compris*, nous *pourrons* en reparler.
Si elle *a réussi* à acheter un billet Apex, elle *aura fait* des économies!
Si on vous *a dit* ça, c'*était* pour vous induire en erreur.
Si vous *avez perdu* votre clé, vous n'*avez* pas *pu* entrer.

3 *si* + imperfect → present conditional
→ perfect conditional

Ex: *Si* j'*avais* le temps, j'*irais* faire les courses avant midi.
*S'*il *était* aussi avare que vous le dites, il n'*aurait* pas *donné* autant
d'argent pour la recherche sur le cancer.

See also iterative *si* in section 3.2.1(v) above.

4 *si* + pluperfect → perfect conditional
→ present conditional

Ex: *Si* vous *aviez été* plus aimable, on vous *aurait servi* plus rapidement.
Si vous *aviez pris* vos précautions, vous n'en *seriez* pas là aujourd'hui.

14 Imperative

1 Introduction

The imperative is a mood. It is used to give orders – to do or not to do something. It is also used to make a suggestion or express a wish. It is therefore generally used in spoken French in the presence of the interlocutor(s) to whom the imperative is directly addressed, i.e. 2nd persons singular and plural (*tu/vous*) and 1st person plural (*nous*). However, the imperative can also appear in written messages or quotations.

> Ex: '*La dictature, c'est **ferme** ta gueule, la démocratie, c'est **cause** toujours.*'
> 'Dictatorship = shut your mouth; democracy = talk all you like.'

The imperative has two 'tenses': the present and the past, and two 'forms': simple and compound. Both relate to the present of its utterance and the future of its realization. The tenses are opposed aspectually, i.e. the present is non-accomplished and the past is accomplished. The present imperative is by far the more commonly used.

The imperative has only three persons (instead of six for the other moods): 2nd person singular (*tu*), 2nd person plural (*vous*, including 'polite' *vous*) and 1st person plural (*nous*). Note that the subjunctive can be used as a substitute for the imperative for the 3rd person (see 4.4 below and chapter 12 Subjunctive, section 4.5).

In written French, imperative sentences normally end with an exclamation mark, a feature shared with exclamative sentences.

2 Present imperative

2.1 Formation

The forms of the imperative are based on those of the present indicative. Hence:

2.1.1 *Verbs in* ER

(i) The forms are the same as those of the present indicative, except that there is no '*s*' with the 2nd person singular.

> Ex: *chanter: chante!*   (present indicative: *tu chantes*)
> *chantons!*
> *chantez!*

> *aller: va!*   (present indicative: *tu vas*)
> *allons!*
> *allez!*

(ii) If the verb is followed by the pronouns *y* or *en*, an '*s*' is added to the verb for phonological reasons (and the two words are hyphenated).

> Ex: *Manges-en!*   Eat some!
> *Vas-y!*   Go (there)!
> *Achètes-en!*   Buy some!
> *Penses-y!*   Think about it!
> *Donnes-en!*   Give some!

If *y* or *en* are followed by an infinitive however, there is no '*s*'.

> Ex: *Va y mettre de l'ordre!*
> *Va en donner à Marie!*

2.1.2   Verbs in IR, OIR and RE

(i) The forms are basically the same as those of the present indicative, but see exceptions below.

> Ex: *finir*   *finis, finissons, finissez*
> *venir*   *viens, venons, venez*
> *recevoir*   *reçois, recevons, recevez*
> *vendre*   *vends, vendons, vendez*

(ii) With *cueillir, couvrir, ouvrir, offrir* and *souffrir*, which are conjugated like regular verbs in ER in the present tense, there is no '*s*' with the 2nd person singular.

> Ex: *ouvrir: ouvre!*
> *ouvrons!*
> *ouvrez!*

(iii) *vouloir* is based on the present subjunctive, though not identical to it. It has two forms: *veuille, veuillez* and *veux, voulez*.
Note that the 1st person plural is almost never used.

– *vouloir* is used:
 – to invite somebody politely to do something, with *veuille, veuillez* (formal usage).
> Ex: *Veuillez vous asseoir.*
> Please take a seat.
 – in letter endings.
> Ex: *Veuillez agréer, Monsieur, l'expression de mes sentiments distingués.*
> Yours faithfully,

– *en vouloir à quelqu'un* means 'to resent someone' and the imperative is always in the negative.
 – formal usage:
> Ex: *Ne m'en veuille pas.*
> *Ne m'en veuillez pas.*
 – informal usage:
> *Ne m'en veux pas.*
> *Ne m'en voulez pas.*

(iv)   *savoir* is also based on the present subjunctive, though not identical to it.
The forms are: *sache, sachons, sachez.*
The meaning depends on the construction.
Compare:
– *savoir* + noun phrase:
      Sachez vos verbes pour la semaine prochaine.
      Learn (and therefore know) your verbs for next week.
      and:
– savoir + *que*-clause:
      Sachez que je ne suis pas un lâche.
      Let me tell you that I am not a coward.

2.1.3 être *and* avoir

(i)   They are based on the present subjunctive in a way similar to *vouloir* and *savoir.*

être	*avoir*
sois	*aie*
soyons	*ayons*
soyez	*ayez*

(ii)   They are mainly used in idioms:
      Ex: *Sois sage! Soyez sages!*
      (to a child: Be good! Behave yourself/yourselves!)

      Sois tranquille! Soyez tranquille(s)!
      Don't worry!

      N'aie pas peur! N'ayez pas peur!
      Don't be afraid!

2.2 Syntax

Particular care should be taken with pronouns and the imperative, particularly as:
– subject pronouns **are not** expressed
– reflexive pronouns **are** expressed
– the order of object pronouns in the affirmative and negative forms differs

2.2.1 *The imperative and object pronouns: affirmative form*

Note the difference in order between the imperative (affirmative form) and the declarative. For a detailed study of object pronouns, see chapter 31 Personal Pronouns, section 2.2.

(i)   *me* and *te* become *moi* and *toi* if they are the only or last pronouns after the imperative.
      Ex: *Donne-le-moi.*   Give it to me.
      Ecoute-moi.   Listen to me.
      but:
      Donne-m'en.   Give me some.

NB: *Donne-moi z'en* is heard but is considered slipshod.

(ii) The pronouns follow the verb and are hyphenated to it.

> Ex: *Donnez-lui des pommes.* → *Donnez-lui-en.*
> Give him some apples. → Give him some.
>
> *Montrez-moi le chemin.* → *Montrez-le-moi.*
> Show me the way. → Show it to me.

(iii) If there are two object pronouns, one direct and the other indirect, the direct object pronoun comes first.

> Ex: *Donnez-**les-nous**.*
> (*donner qch à qn*: '*les*' is the direct object pronoun; '*nous*' is the indirect object pronoun)
> Give them to us.

Compare with the declarative form:

> *Vous **nous les** donnez.*

(iv) With *laisser, faire* or a verb of perception + infinitive

> Ex: *Faites-**moi y** penser.*
> Make sure you remind me.
>
> *Laissez-**les** jouer dans le jardin.*
> Let them play in the garden.
>
> *Ecoutez-**la** chanter.*
> Listen to her singing.

(v) There is no hyphen if the pronoun is the object of the infinitive.

> Ex: *Venez **nous** voir.*
> ('*nous*' is the object of '*voir*')
> Come and see us.
>
> *Va **le** chercher.*
> ('*le*' is the object of '*chercher*')
> Go and fetch him.

2.2.2 The imperative and object pronouns: negative form

(i) *ne* comes before the verb and *pas* comes after, as for simple tenses. There are no hyphens.

> Ex: ***Ne** bois **pas**!*
> Don't drink!

(ii) Object pronouns appear immediately before the verb, in the usual order for a declarative sentence.

> Ex: *Ne **le lui** vend pas!*
> Don't sell it to him/her.
>
> *Ne **lui en** donne pas!*
> Don't give any to him/her!
>
> *Ne **me le** montrez pas!*
> Don't show it to me!

NB: The '*s*' is no longer necessary for ER verbs with this word order (see 2.1.1(ii) above):

> *N'en mange pas!*
>
> *N'y va pas!*

(iii)   With a verb + infinitive

> Ex: *Ne **lui** promettez pas de l'inviter.*
> Don't promise him/her to invite him/her.
>
> *Promettez-**lui** de ne pas l'inviter.*
> Promise him/her not to invite him/her.

(iv)   With *laisser, faire* or a verb of perception + infinitive

> Ex: *Ne **m'y** faites pas penser.*
> Don't remind me!
>
> *Ne **les** laissez pas jouer dans le jardin!*
> Don't let them play in the garden!
>
> *Ne **l'**écoutez pas chanter!*
> Don't listen to her singing!

2.2.3   *The imperative and pronominal verbs*

The important thing to remember is that **only the reflexive pronoun is expressed**.

(i)   In the affirmative form, the reflexive pronoun follows the verb and is hyphenated, becoming: *toi (te), nous, vous.*

> Ex: *se dépêcher: Dépêche-**toi**!*
> *Dépêchons-**nous**!*
> *Dépêchez-**vous**!*
>
> *s'en aller: Va-**t'**en!*
> *Allons-**nous**-en!*
> *Allez-**vous**-en!*
>
> *s'asseoir* has two conjugations:
> *Assieds-toi!*   or: *Assois-toi!*
> *Asseyons-nous!*   *Assoyons-nous!*
> *Asseyez-vous!*   *Assoyez-vous!*

(ii)   In the negative form, the reflexive pronoun follows the *ne*, becoming: *te, nous, vous.*

> Ex: *se dépêcher: Ne **te** dépêche pas!*
> *Ne **nous** dépêchons pas!*
> *Ne **vous** dépêchez pas!*
>
> *s'en aller: Ne **t'**en va pas!*
> *Ne **nous** en allons pas!*
> *Ne **vous** en allez pas!*

(iii)   The *se* of a pronominal verb can **look** like another object pronoun: for a verb to be pronominal, both the imperative and the object pronoun must be of the same person (see object pronouns in 2.2.1).

> Ex: *Tiens-**toi** droit!*
> (*se tenir*)
> Stand/sit up straight!
> > but:
> *Tiens-**moi** fort!*
> (*tenir quelqu'un*)
> Hold me tight!

Compare:

> *Buvons!* Let's drink!
> > and:
> *Buvons-nous?* Are we drinking?

3 Past imperative

The past imperative is formed with the auxiliary *avoir* or *être* in the present subjunctive, plus the past participle of the main verb.

> Ex: *Ayez fini.*
> *Soyez rentré.*

It is used to order or advise someone to carry out an action which will have to be completed at a certain moment in the future. Thus it expresses the accomplished aspect and anteriority in relation to some time in the future. Note that this tense is rarely used.

> Ex: *Aie fini ce devoir avant mon retour.*
> *Soyez rentré pour huit heures.*

In informal French, one would use *tâcher de*, which is the equivalent of 'make sure that you have/are . . .'

> Ex: *Tâchez d'avoir fini ce devoir.*
> Make sure that you have finished this homework.
>
> *Tâche d'être rentré pour huit heures.*
> Make sure you are back by eight o'clock.

4 Use of the imperative

The present imperative is used with the 2nd person but also, to a lesser extent, with the 1st person.

4.1 The present imperative with the 2nd person (singular or plural)

The present imperative is used, as in English, to express:

(i)   An order

Ex: ***Viens** ici!*
Come here!

Allez-vous-en!
Go away!

NB(1): *toi* or *vous*, followed by a comma at the beginning of the sentence, constitute an address to the interlocutor (apostrophe). They can be:
− a way of giving different orders to several people.

Ex: ***Vous, mettez** la table et **vous, allez** chercher le vin.*
You, lay the table and you, go and fetch the wine.

− a way of (rudely) drawing the interlocutor's attention.

Ex: ***Toi, fais**-le! **Vous, faites**-le!*
You do it!

***Toi, fais** attention! **Vous, faites** attention!*
You be careful!

*Eh, **vous, fermez** la porte! Eh, **toi, ferme** la porte!*
Hey you, close the door!

Note that the comma after *toi* or *vous* is crucial. Indeed, *'Vous faites attention'* is a plain statement in the present indicative whilst '★*Toi fais attention*' is the same but with a mistake: '*toi*' instead of '*tu*' (see chapter 31 Personal Pronouns).

NB(2): Alternatively, to 'personalize' an order, French can use the emphatic form *toi-même* or *vous-même(s)*.

Ex: *Fais-le toi-même!*
Faites-le vous-même! } Do it yourself/yourselves!
Faites-le vous-mêmes!

(ii)   A prohibition

Ex: *Ne **bouge** pas! Ne **bougez** pas!*
Don't move!

(iii)   A piece of advice; a request; a suggestion

Ex: ***Fais** attention!*
Be careful!

*Ne **parlez** pas trop vite!*
Don't speak too fast!

(iv)   An instruction

Ex: ***Prenez** la deuxième à gauche.*
Take the second left.

(v)   An invitation

Ex: ***Prenez** place, je vous prie!*
Take a seat, please.

***Assieds-toi** s'il te plaît!*
Please sit down!

(vi)   A wish

           Ex: ***Dors*** *bien!* ***Dormez*** *bien!*

                Sleep well!

(vii)   A prayer

           Ex: '***Pardonnez***-*nous nos offenses . . .*'

                'Forgive us our sins . . .'

(viii)   An apology

           Ex: ***Excusez***-*moi!* / ***Pardonnez***-*moi!*

                Sorry!

(ix)   Irony or indignation

           Ex: *Ne* ***vous gênez*** *pas!*

                Do you mind!

                Allez-y! ***Faites*** *comme chez vous!*

                Go ahead! Feel at home!

                Ne ***poussez*** *pas, enfin!*

                Don't push!

(x)   Exclamations

           Ex: *Ça n'est pas grave,* ***va****!*

                Come on, it's not serious!

                Tiens*, il n'y a personne ici!*

                I say, there's no one here!

Note that both these exclamations belong to informal French.

(xi)   In juxtaposed or coordinated clauses, the imperative can introduce a reasoning. The meaning depends on the context. For instance, it can be used to express a hypothesis or a supposition. In this case, the verb in the clause corresponding to the main clause – if *si* were used – is in the present or future indicative:

           Ex: ***Travaillez*** *bien et vous* ***réussirez*** *à vos examens.*

                (= *Si vous travaillez bien, vous réussirez . . .*)

                Work hard and you will pass your exams.

                Répète *ça et je te* ***tue****.*

                (= *Si tu répètes ça, je te tue.*)

                Say that again and I'll kill you.

(xii)   The imperative can also be used to express politeness with turns of phrase such as:

           Ex: ***Faites-moi le plaisir d'****accepter mon invitation.*

                Ayez la bonté de *me retourner cette lettre.*

See also special uses of *vouloir* in 2.1.2(iii) above.

4.2 Alternatives to the imperative (with the 2nd person)

(i) The future

The future can be used instead of the imperative in order to transform an abrupt order into a more formal request.

> Ex: *Quand il arrivera,* **vous me le direz** [*s'il vous plaît*].
> (instead of: *dites-le moi*)
> When he comes, please let me know.

See also chapter 7 Future, section 3.1.1.

(ii) The infinitive

The infinitive is also used instead of the imperative, particularly in public notices, instructions to use equipment, official forms, cookery recipes, etc. (See also chapter 15 Infinitive, section 3.3.2(iv).)

> Ex: − On a train:
> *Ne pas* **se pencher** *au-dehors.*
> Do not lean out of the window.

> − On the road:
> **Serrer** *à droite.*
> Keep right.

> − In a recipe:
> **Ajouter** *un œuf et bien* **mélanger** *le tout.*
> Add an egg and mix well.

(iii) The subjunctive

The subjunctive is used to address an order to a third party (see 4.4. below).

(iv) An interrogative structure

An interrogative structure with modal verbs such as *vouloir* or *pouvoir* can be used to express an order.

> Ex: **Voulez-vous** *enfin* **cesser** *ce bruit?*
> Will you stop this noise at last?

(v) A subordinate clause, including infinitive clauses

A subordinate clause can be the object of a verb of command.

> Ex: **Je vous ordonne de** *sortir.*
> I am ordering you to leave.

4.3 The present imperative with the 1st person plural

(i) It corresponds in English to 'let us (do something)'. Note that 'let' is not translated as such. Only the verb is conjugated.

> Ex: Let's go!
> **Partons! Allons-***y!*

NB: 'let' can also be the verb 'to let' (= *laisser, permettre*).

    Ex: Let me tell you something.
        Laissez-moi vous dire quelque chose.

        Let us tell you something.
        Laissez-nous vous dire quelque chose.

(ii)   It generally expresses an encouragement, an exhortation or a reflection.

    Ex: ***Dépêchons-nous****! Nous allons manquer le train.*
        Let's hurry! We're going to miss the train!

        Essayons *encore une fois!*
        Let's try once more!

        Allons*, ça ne peut pas être si grave que ça!*
        Come on, it can't be all that bad / as bad as all that!

        Voyons *cela.*
        Let's see.

4.4   Expression of the imperative in the 3rd person

(i)   *que* and the subjunctive can be used to express an order or a request.

    Ex: *Qu'elle vienne me voir cet après-midi!*
        Let her come and see me this afternoon!

(ii)   If the order or request is to be transmitted to a third person, this is expressed in English by 'Tell him/her/them, etc. to do something'. French can use either the subjunctive as described above or *Dis-lui, dis-leur, dites-lui, dites-leur*, etc. *de faire quelque chose.*

    Ex: *Qu'il vienne me voir demain.*
          or:
        Dites-lui de venir me voir demain.
        Tell him to come and see me tomorrow.

        Qu'ils se taisent!
          or:
        Dites-leur de se taire.
        Tell them to be quiet.

4.5   Verbs that cannot be used in the imperative

Some verbs are not normally used in the imperative form, namely verbs which refer to involuntary actions, e.g. *voir* (to see) as opposed to *regarder* (to look at) and *entendre* (to hear) as opposed to *écouter* (to listen to). However, some authors do use these 'involuntary' verbs in the imperative for stylistic reasons. This practice should not be imitated by students.

    Ex: '***Vois*** *sur ces canaux*
        Dormir ces vaisseaux
        Dont l'humeur est vagabonde'

                              Charles Baudelaire, *L'invitation au voyage*

15 Infinitive

1 Introduction

The infinitive is a non-temporal and non-personal mood. It is used in dictionaries to give the lexical meaning of the verb, and is given as a basis for the conjugations. It functions both as a verb and as a noun, hence its designation of 'nominal form of the verb'. The use of the infinitive can be problematic because:

- There is no one-to-one correspondence between an English and a French infinitive, as English often uses a form in '-ing' instead (see also chapter 16 Present Participle, section 3.4).

- There is no one-to-one correspondence between French and English as regards which preposition – if any – to use before the infinitive as a verb.

- There are cases when French can (and sometimes must) use an infinitive clause when English uses a subordinate clause.

- It is a frequent mistake to confuse an infinitive in ER with a past participle in '*é*', as they share the same sound.

NB: In this chapter, examples given concentrate on **noun** subjects and objects of the infinitive. For further details of the position of **pronoun** subjects and objects of the infinitive, see chapter 31 Personal Pronouns, section 2.2.3.

2 Forms

The infinitive has two forms, present and past, which do not have any real temporal value. The present infinitive expresses the non-accomplished aspect, and the past infinitive expresses the accomplished aspect.

2.1 The present infinitive

The present infinitive is the usual form of the infinitive.
    Ex: *partir*; *chanter*

(i) The present infinitive is used to form the recent past with *venir de* and the immediate future with *aller*.

Ex: *Je viens de le **faire**.*
I've just done it.

*Je vais le **faire**.*
I'm going to do it.

See also chapter 5 Present, sections 3.5 and 3.6.

(ii) Note that the pronoun ***se*** still agrees in person and number with the subject, even in the infinitive.

Ex: ***J'**essaie de **me** souvenir!*
I am trying to remember!

*Comment avez-**vous** fait pour **vous** perdre?*
How did you manage to lose your way?

See chapter 20 Pronominal Verbs, section 2.1.

2.2 The past infinitive

The past infinitive is formed with the infinitive of the auxiliary *avoir* or *être* + the past participle of the verb. The past participle follows the same agreement rules as the past participles in compound tenses (see chapter 9 Perfect, section 3).

The past infinitive can express:

– anteriority:

Ex: *Après **avoir fait** les courses, vous passerez prendre les enfants à l'école.*
After doing the shopping, you will pick up the children from school.

– accomplished aspect:

Ex: *Je suis contente d'**avoir terminé** mon travail.*
I am pleased I have finished my work.

NB: Unlike in English with 'after', when *après* is followed by a verb, this verb is always in the past infinitive.

Ex: ***Après nous être reposés**, nous irons nous promener.*
After resting, we'll go for a walk.

*Après **avoir allumé** un cigare, il a ouvert le journal.*
After lighting a cigar, he opened the paper.

2.3 The negative form of the infinitive

Note the position of ***ne*** and ***pas*** before a present infinitive (including the special case of *être* and *avoir*), and before a past infinitive.

2.3.1 The negative form and the present infinitive

With the present infinitive, ***ne pas*** comes before the infinitive, and before the object pronouns (see chapter 31 Personal Pronouns, section 2.2.3).

Note that negating the infinitive is not the same thing as negating the conjugated verb.

> Ex: *Mon chat espère manger du poisson ce soir.*
> My cat is hoping to eat fish tonight.

> → *Mon chat n'espère pas manger de poisson ce soir.*
> My cat isn't hoping to eat fish tonight.

> → *Mon chat espère ne pas manger de poisson ce soir.*
> My cat is hoping he won't eat fish tonight.

NB: With *être* and *avoir*, ne and pas can also be on either side of the auxiliary, although this construction tends to belong to formal French.

> Ex: *Elle a peur de n'être pas prête à temps.*
> or:
> *Elle a peur de ne pas être prête à temps.*
> She's afraid she may not be ready in time.

> *J'espère n'avoir pas à refaire ce travail.*
> or:
> *J'espère ne pas avoir à refaire ce travail.*
> I hope I won't have to re-do this job.

2.3.2 The negative form and the past infinitive

With the past infinitive, *ne pas* comes before the auxiliary, or the two words split on either side of it.

> Ex: *Il croyait ne pas avoir rencontré Paul.*
> or:
> *Il croyait n'avoir pas rencontré Paul.*
> He thought he had not met Paul.

2.4 The passive infinitive

It is the infinitive of the auxiliary *être* + past participle of a direct transitive verb (see also chapter 18 Active and Passive Voices, section 3).

> Ex: *Il espère être élu au premier tour.*
> He is hoping to be elected at the first ballot.

> *Catherine vient d'être convoquée pour une interview.*
> Catherine has just been invited for an interview.

3 Uses

The most common use of the infinitive is as the **direct or indirect object** of a conjugated verb (see 3.1 below). It can also function as:
– a **noun** (see 3.2)
– a **nominal infinitive**, as the subject of a conjugated verb, the subject/complement of *être*, or without a conjugated verb (see 3.3)

– a **modifier of an adjective or noun**, as a noun or adjective complement (see 3.4)
– an **adverb phrase**, with a preposition (see 3.5)

3.1 The infinitive as object of a conjugated verb

This is the most common use of the infinitive. There are three possible constructions:
– main verb + infinitive (direct object)
– main verb + *à* + infinitive (indirect object)
– main verb + *de* + infinitive (indirect object)

In the case of a conjugated verb followed by an infinitive, it is important to know whether there is a preposition in between and what that preposition is!

Ex: *J'ai cru _ mourir.*
*J'ai cherché **à** comprendre.*
*J'ai décidé **de** partir.*

French verbs that are followed by a preposition are in fact the easiest to deal with, as they **must** be followed by an infinitive (except *en* – see chapter 16 Present Participle, section 3.4) whether the English is an infinitive, a form in '-ing' or a main clause + subordinate clause.

Ex: I started eating / I began to eat.
*J'ai commencé **à manger**.*

I remembered [that] I had left the lights on.
*Je me suis souvenu **d'avoir laissé** la lumière allumée.*

However, French verbs that can be immediately followed by an infinitive (i.e. without an intermediary preposition) can – and sometimes must – replace this infinitive with a *que*-clause (see 3.1.3.2(vi) and (vii) below). Finally, some prepositions (e.g. *avant de, après*) have a 'corresponding' conjunction.

– *avant de* (preposition) + infinitive
  or:
avant que (conjunction) [+ *ne*] + subjunctive.

Ex: *Je viendrai vous voir **avant de partir**.*
I'll come and see you before leaving.
  or:
*Je viendrai vous voir **avant que je** [**ne**] **parte**.*
I'll come and see you before I leave.

– *après* (preposition) + past infinitive
  or:
après que (conjunction) + indicative (past tense).

Ex: *Je viendrai vous voir **après avoir fait** mes courses.*
  or:
*Je viendrai vous voir **après que j'ai fait** mes courses.*
I shall come and see you after I have done my shopping.

See also chapter 12 Subjunctive, section 4.4.2.

3.1.1   The infinitive as object of a verb + preposition à

> Ex: *Il a tenu **à** tout **faire** lui-même.*
> He insisted on doing everything himself.
>
> *Elle cherche **à comprendre**.*
> She is trying to understand.
>
> *Les enfants s'amusent **à taquiner** le chien.*
> The children are having fun teasing the dog.
>
> *Nous avons passé le week-end **à nous promener**.*
> We spent the weekend walking.
>
> *Pensez-vous vraiment **à quitter** l'Angleterre pour aller aux Etats-Unis?*
> Are you really thinking of leaving England to go to the United States?

3.1.2   The infinitive as object of a verb or impersonal construction + preposition 'de'

(i)   The infinitive after verbs + ***de***

> Ex: *Ils n'ont pas l'air **de s'intéresser** à ce que je dis.*
> They do not look as if they are interested in what I am saying.
>
> *Ils ont fait semblant **de** ne pas nous **voir**.*
> They pretended not to see us.
>
> *Abstenez-vous **de boire** du vin avec vos antibiotiques.*
> You should refrain from drinking wine with your antibiotics.
>
> *Vous ne vous souvenez pas **d'avoir dit** ça?*
> You don't remember saying that?

NB: Like *se rappeler*, *se souvenir de* is normally followed by a past infinitive.

(ii)   The infinitive after impersonal constructions + ***de***

Most constructions with impersonal *il* are followed by *de* + infinitive. Notable exceptions are *valoir* and *falloir* (see 3.1.3.2(v) below).

Compare the following synonymous expressions:
> *Il s'agit maintenant **de faire** très attention.*
>> but:
> *Il faut maintenant **faire** très attention.*
> We/You should be very careful now.
>
> *Il est préférable **de voyager** seul.*
>> but:
> *Il vaut mieux **voyager** seul.*
> It is better to travel alone.

3.1.3   *The infinitive as direct object*

There are two cases:

– the subject of the main verb and that of the infinitive are the same. This is the most difficult case and requires a little attention.

– the subject of the main verb and that of the infinitive are different.

3.1.3.1   DIFFERENT SUBJECTS

The subject of the main (conjugated) verb and that of the infinitive are different (i.e. the object of the main verb is the subject of the infinitive). The main verb is **always** followed by an infinitive. It is the case with:

(i)   The following **verbs of motion**: *emmener, envoyer, mener.*
   Ex: *Nous **avons emmené** les enfants **faire** un tour sur les manèges.*
   We took the children for a ride on the merry-go-rounds.

   *J'ai **envoyé** Paul **faire** les courses.*
   I sent Paul to do the shopping.

(ii)   **Verbs of perception** (seeing, hearing, feeling), e.g. *apercevoir, voir, regarder, écouter, entendre, sentir.* The word order can either be:
   subject + conjugated verb + **infinitive** + **object**
      or:
   subject + conjugated verb + **object** + **infinitive**

   Ex: *Je **regardais jouer** les enfants.*
         or:
   *Je **regardais** les enfants **jouer**.*
   I was watching the children play.

NB(1): If the subject of the infinitive is very long, it comes after the infinitive.
   Ex: *Je **regardais jouer** les enfants de l'école d'à côté.*
   I was watching the children of the school next door playing.

NB(2): If the infinitive has an explicit direct object, the subject may or may not be expressed.
   Ex: *Ce soir, j'**ai entendu** [quelqu'un] **jouer** un air de Chopin.*
   Tonight, I heard a tune by Chopin being played.

NB(3): If the infinitive has explicit subject and object, the subject comes before the infinitive and the object comes after it.
   Ex: *Nous **écoutons** l'orchestre **jouer** un morceau de Chopin.*
   (and not **Nous écoutons jouer l'orchestre un morceau de Chopin*)
   We are listening to the orchestra playing a tune by Chopin.

(iii)   *laisser*

The factitive (see chapter 4 Introduction to Verbs, section 7.1(v)) *laisser* can have an active or a passive sense.

– active sense:

'to let someone/something do something': *laisser quelqu'un/quelque chose faire quelque chose*. The subject of the infinitive, if expressed, can be either before or after the infinitive.

        Ex: *Je **laisse** les enfants **jouer** dans le jardin.*
             or:
        *Je **laisse jouer** les enfants dans le jardin.*
        I let the children play in the garden.

        *J'ai **laissé** l'eau **déborder**.*
             or:
        *J'ai **laissé déborder** l'eau.*
        I let the water overflow.

– passive sense:

'to let something be done': *laisser faire quelque chose* and 'to let something be done to oneself': *se laisser faire quelque chose (par quelqu'un)*.

        Ex: *J'ai **laissé faire** le pire.*
        I let the worst happen.

        *Il **s'est laissé prendre** au piège.*
        He let himself be trapped.

NB: The past participle *laissé* is **always invariable** in this construction.

Object pronouns with *laisser* are treated in chapter 31 Personal Pronouns, section 2.2.3.3.

(iv)   *faire*

The factitive *faire* can also have an active or a passive sense. Note that, unlike with *laisser*, the subject of the infinitive must appear **after** the infinitive (→ *Je fais venir Pierre* and not *★Je fais Pierre venir; J'ai fait appeler un médecin* and not *★J'ai fait un médecin appeler*).

– active sense:

'to make someone do something': *faire faire quelque chose à quelqu'un*. The subject provokes the action but does not carry it out.

        Ex: ***Faites entrer** le candidat.*
        Ask the applicant to come in.

        *Ils **ont fait attendre** les invités dans un petit salon.*
        They made the guests wait in a small waiting room.

        *Voulez-vous que je **fasse venir** un médecin?*
        Would you like me to call for a doctor?

– passive sense:

'to have something done': *faire faire quelque chose* and 'to have something done for oneself': *se faire faire quelque chose*.

Ex: *Nous **avons fait construire** une maison à la campagne.*
or:
*Nous **nous sommes fait construire** une maison à la campagne.*
We had a house built in the country.

*Elle **s'est fait décolorer** les cheveux.*
She had her hair bleached.

*J'ai **fait appeler** un médecin.*
I had a doctor called.

NB: The past participle *fait* is **always invariable** in this construction.

Note the following other expressions based on *faire*.
− *faire voir* (= *montrer*):
Ex: ***Faites voir** à grand-père vos diapositives sur le Kremlin!*
Please show grandpa your slides of the Kremlin!

− *faire savoir* (= *apprendre à qn, informer qn*):
Ex: *J'ai **fait savoir** à Paul ce qu'il devait faire.*
I told Paul what he had to do.

Object pronouns with *faire* are treated in chapter 31 Personal Pronouns, section 2.2.3.3.

3.1.3.2   SAME SUBJECTS

The subject of the main (conjugated) verb and that of the infinitive are the same. The verb is followed by the infinitive, but see exceptions in sections (v), (vi) and (vii) below.

(i)   The following **verbs of motion**: *aller, courir, descendre, entrer, monter, partir, rentrer, retourner, revenir, sortir, venir,* with or without an adverb of time or place, are always followed by the infinitive.
Ex: *Paul **est descendu** [à la cave] **chercher** une bouteille de vin.*
Paul went down [to the cellar] to fetch a bottle of wine.

***Venez voir** les enfants [la semaine prochaine].*
Come and see the children [next week].

If the purpose is to be stressed, ***pour*** is added.
Ex: *Paul **est descendu** [à la cave] **pour chercher** une bouteille de vin.*
Paul went down [to the cellar] in order to fetch a bottle of wine.

(ii)   The following **verbs of taste or preference**: *aimer, aimer mieux, aimer autant, adorer, détester, préférer, daigner* are always followed by the infinitive.
Ex: *Par-dessus tout, il **aime** ne rien **faire**!*
More than anything else, he likes doing nothing.

(iii) *paraître, sembler, s'avérer, se révéler, être censé, faillir* are always followed by the infinitive.

> Ex: *Il **semble attendre** quelqu'un.*
> He seems to be waiting for someone.
>
> *Je ne **suis** pas **censé savoir** tout ce que vous faites.*
> I am not supposed to know everything you do.
>
> *J'ai **failli glisser** sur cette peau de banane!*
> I nearly slipped on that banana skin!

(iv) **Verbs of will and expectation**: *désirer, souhaiter, vouloir, oser, compter, avoir beau,* etc. are always followed by the infinitive.

> Ex: *Vous **aurez beau faire**, vous ne lui ferez pas changer d'avis.*
> Whatever you do, you won't make him change his mind.
>
> *Je **comptais partir** à cinq heures.*
> I was expecting to leave at five o'clock.

(v) *devoir, pouvoir, falloir, valoir*

– The infinitive is compulsory after the modals *devoir* and *pouvoir*.

> Ex: *Je **dois m'en aller**.*
> I must go.
>
> *Ils **peuvent faire** tout ce que vous voulez.*
> They can do everything you want.

In a longer sentence, it is important not to lose track of verbs following modals: they must be in the infinitive!

> Ex: *La littérature **peut être** une manière de s'évader de la vie réelle et nous **montrer** que tout est possible.*
> Literature can be a means to escape from reality and show us that anything is possible.

– There is a choice between the infinitive and *que* + subjunctive after *il faut* and *il vaut mieux* (see also chapter 19 Impersonal Verbs, sections 3(i) and 6(vi)).

> Ex: *Il **vaut mieux partir** tout de suite.*
> or:
> *Il **vaut mieux que vous partiez** tout de suite.*
> It is best if you leave now.
>
> *Il **faut s'attendre** à des orages pour demain.*
> or:
> *Il **faut que nous nous attendions** à des orages pour demain.*
> We must expect thunderstorms tomorrow.

Note that *que* + subjunctive is more precise and should be used if the context is insufficient to determine the subject. For instance:

> *Il faut partir.*
> can mean:
> *Il faut que je parte / que tu partes / que nous partions / que vous partiez.*

(vi) **Verbs of declaration**: *affirmer, jurer, déclarer, dire, prétendre, reconnaître, nier, confirmer* (+ past infinitive)

– either a **que-clause** or an **infinitive** can be used, although the *que*-clause often makes more sense in the present, while the infinitive is generally considered more elegant.

> *Je dis que j'ai faim!*

sounds better than the vague and somewhat incongruous:

> *Je dis avoir faim!*
> I am saying that I am hungry!

However:

> *Nous avons déclaré être partis à huit heures.*

is more elegant than:

> *Nous avons déclaré que nous étions partis à huit heures.*

– **prétendre** has two meanings: 'to maintain' or 'to pretend' (synonymous with *faire semblant de* + infinitive), and can therefore be ambiguous when seen outside its context. Compare:

> *Il a prétendu s'évanouir = Il a fait semblant de s'évanouir.*
> He pretended to faint.
>
>   and:
>
> *Il prétendait connaître tout le monde.*
> = *Il faisait semblant de connaître tout le monde?*
> = *Il maintenait qu'il connaissait tout le monde?*

– **nier** + infinitive is only acceptable if there is no risk of ambiguity.

> Ex: *Le manifestant a nié avoir mis le feu à une voiture.*
> The demonstrator denied setting a car on fire.

If used with a *que*-clause, *nier* can be followed by the indicative or the subjunctive. Compare:

> *Le manifestant a nié **qu'**il **a** mis le feu à une voiture.*
> (= *il y a pourtant mis le feu*)
>
> *Le manifestant a nié **qu'**il **ait** mis le feu à une voiture.*
> (= *on ne sait pas s'il l'a fait ou non*)

See also chapter 12 Subjunctive.

(vii) **Verbs of thinking**: *savoir, penser, croire, espérer, se rappeler, se figurer, s'imaginer*

– **espérer** means that one expects something may well happen in the **future**, hence the possibility of using a *que*-clause in the future tense as well as the infinitive.

> Ex: I hope I can go to Paris next week.
> *J'espère **pouvoir aller** à Paris la semaine prochaine.*
>   or:
> *J'espère **que je pourrai aller** à Paris la semaine prochaine.*

A past infinitive can also be used:

> Ex: *J'espère **avoir terminé** pour demain.*
> I hope I'll have/to have finished by tomorrow.

Another tense for *espérer* may entail another tense in the *que*-clause.

> Ex: *J'espérais pouvoir y aller.*
>> or:
> *J'espérais que je pourrais y aller.*
> I was hoping to go/I could go there.

(The conditional here is the 'future in the past' – see chapter 13 Conditional, section 3.1.)

NB(1): The present can often be used instead of the future to stress the likelihood of the event (the event taking place is considered as a strong possibility), but this should be avoided in formal French.

> Ex: *J'espère que je peux y aller.*

NB(2): In the two examples above, the use of the modal *pouvoir* reinforces the idea of a possibility. Without *pouvoir*, the present is not possible.

> Ex: *J'espère voir Christine demain.*
>> or:
> *J'espère que je verrai Christine demain.*
> I hope I can see Christine tomorrow.
>> but not:
> **J'espère que je vois Christine demain.*

– *savoir* has two meanings:

  – 'to know (how to)' in the sense of 'having a skill' (see chapter 22 *Savoir* and *Connaître*, section 2(iv)).

  > Ex: I know how to make flaky pastry.
  > *Je sais faire la pâte feuilletée.*

  > I know how to get there/how to do it.
  > *Je sais comment y aller/comment le faire.*

  – 'to know' in the sense of 'to be conscious of'.

  > Ex: I know I eat too much!
  > *Je sais que je mange trop!*

Hence:

> *Je sais que je suis paresseux.*
> I know I am lazy.
>> and, if anything:
> *Je sais être paresseux!*
>> is likely to be interpreted as:
> I know how to be lazy!

– *penser* has two meanings:

  – 'to intend to do something', hence the **future** should be used with a *que*-clause.

  > Ex: I am thinking of leaving at 5 pm.
  > *Je pense partir à cinq heures.*
  >> or:
  > I think I'll leave at 5 pm.
  > *Je pense que je partirai à cinq heures.*

but:
Je pense que je pars à cinq heures.
I think I leave at 5 pm.
(the present does not sound right to express an **intention**!)

– 'to believe' (= *croire*): the present is possible here.
Ex: I think I'm going mad.
*Je **pense**/Je **crois** que je deviens folle.*
or:
*Je **pense**/Je **crois** devenir folle.*

I thought I was going mad.
*J'ai **cru**/Je **croyais** devenir folle.*
or:
*J'ai **cru**/Je **croyais** que je devenais folle.*

Similarly:
Ex: I think I know what's going on.
*Je **crois** que je sais / Je **crois** savoir ce qui se passe.*
*Je **pense** que je sais / Je **pense** savoir ce qui se passe.*

– *se rappeler, s'imaginer, se figurer*:
can be followed either by the infinitive or a *que*-clause, but the infinitive is by far the more commonly used (and the more elegant form).
Ex: *Je **m'imaginais** déjà **être** en vacances.*
or:
Je m'imaginais déjà que j'étais en vacances.
I was already imagining myself on holiday.

NB(1): *se rappeler* is normally followed by the past infinitive:
Ex: *Elle **se rappelle avoir pris** le train de six heures.*
She remembers catching the six o'clock train.
except when reminiscing (narrative present).
Ex: *Je **me rappelle être** chez ma grand-mère, **soigner** les lapins . . .*
I remember being at my grandmother's, looking after the rabbits . . .

NB(2): *se souvenir* is followed by **de**, hence **must** be followed by the infinitive (see section 3.1.2(i) above).

3.1.4 *The infinitive as object of a verb* + de/à *or another preposition*

(i) Some verbs take either **de** or **à** without a change of meaning.
Ex: *La pluie **a commencé de tomber**.*
*La pluie **a commencé à tomber**.*

*La pluie **continue de tomber**.*
*La pluie **continue à tomber**.*

(ii) Verbs of 'beginning' or 'end' are followed by **par**, but note the difference of meaning between *commencer **par*** and *commencer **de**, finir **par*** and *finir **de***.

Ex: *Vous pouvez commencer **par** me **dire** tout ce que vous savez sur cette affaire!*
You can start **by** telling me everything you know about this matter.

*Vous pouvez commencer **à** me **dire** tout ce que vous savez sur cette affaire.*
You can start telling me everything you know about this matter.

*Elle a fini **par** tout **avouer**.*
She eventually confessed everything.

*Elle a fini **de** tout **ranger**.*
She has finished tidying everything.

3.2 The infinitive as a noun

(i) Certain infinitives have become nouns by improper derivation. These are either single infinitives or two hyphenated infinitives. They are generally masculine.

Ex: *un devoir* (assignment), *le rire* (laughter),
le savoir-faire (know-how), *le savoir-vivre* (etiquette).

NB: Not all verbs can become nouns: their existence should be checked in a dictionary.

(ii) The infinitive can be part of a noun.

Certain infinitives make up part of a noun in the following formations:
− noun + *à* + infinitive
− infinitive [+ hyphen] + noun

In the first case, the gender is dictated by that of the noun with which the infinitive is combined; in the latter, it is generally masculine.

Ex: *une salle à manger* (dining-room), *du fil à coudre* (sewing cotton); *un aller-retour* (return ticket); *un être humain* (human being)

3.3 The infinitive as a nominal infinitive

The infinitive can be the subject of a conjugated verb, or the complement of *être*, or appear in an independent clause with no conjugated verb.

3.3.1 *Subject of conjugated verb or complement of* être

The nominal infinitive can be the subject of a conjugated verb or the complement of verb *être*, with the same function as a noun, but **without an article**. The English equivalent is either an infinitive or a form in '-ing'.

(i) The infinitive as subject of a conjugated verb:
Ex: ***Lire** tard le soir peut abîmer vos yeux.*
Reading late at night can damage your eyes.

***Se fâcher** ne sert à rien!*
Getting angry won't help!

(ii)   The infinitive as subject or complement of *être* is often (but not exclusively) used in idioms:

> Ex: ***Attendre*** *serait vain.*
> It would be pointless to wait.
>
> ***Voir*** *c'est* ***croire.***
> Seeing is believing.

Note that *c'est* rather than *est* is used when both subject and object are infinitives in the affirmative form. In the negative form, either *n'est pas* or *ce n'est pas* can be used.

> Ex: *Consentir* ***n'est pas*** *approuver.*
>   or:
> *Consentir,* ***ce n'est pas*** *approuver.*
> Consent is not approval.

(iii) If infinitive and conjugated verb are permuted (e.g. with an impersonal expression) so that the infinitive follows the conjugated verb, ***de*** is required.

> Ex: *Il ne sert à rien* ***de se fâcher.***
> There is no point in getting angry.
>
> *Il serait vain* ***d'attendre.***
> It would be pointless to wait.

3.3.2   The infinitive in an independent clause with no conjugated verb

The infinitive is used without either a subject or a conjugated verb:

(i)   In a rhetorical question, to express deliberation.

> Ex: *Que faire?*
> (= *Que peut-on faire? Que pouvons-nous faire?*)
> What can we/you do?
>
> *Pourquoi la vendre?*
> Why sell it?

(ii)   In an exclamation, to express surprise, admiration, anger, indignation, impatience, etc. It is a comment.

> Ex: *Voir Venise et mourir!*
> See Venice and die!
>
> *Se faire teindre les cheveux en vert! Quelle horreur!*
> Having your hair dyed green! How awful!

(iii) In a declarative clause, to express the infinitive narrative (a literary turn of phrase) preceded by *et de*: it presents the consequence of a previously mentioned fact.

> Ex: '*Avez-vous imaginé ce qui se passerait si, un jour* [. . .] *une descente de police avait lieu dans les locaux de Sky-Rock* [. . .]? ***Et de poser*** *cette question demeurée sans réponse dans le débat* [. . .].'

Libération, 13 April 1994

(iv)   As an equivalent to an imperative

It can be used to give written orders or instructions in an impersonal way, instead of an imperative which can be deemed as too 'personal' (see chapter 14 Imperative, section 4.2(ii)). Note that *il faut/il ne faut pas* is implied.

> Ex: ***Prendre*** *deux comprimés matin et soir.*
> Take two tablets morning and evening.

> ***Servir*** *très frais.*
> Serve very cool.

> '***Boire*** *ou* ***conduire***, *il faut choisir.*'
> 'Drink or drive: make a decision.' (= Don't drink and drive.)

(v)   As an equivalent to a subjunctive

The infinitive in questions and exclamations is very close to the subjunctive, as they both express a virtual process (see chapter 12 Subjunctive, section 4.5).

> Ex: *Moi,* ***faire*** *le premier pas?*
> (= *Moi, que je fasse le premier pas?*)
> Me, take the first step?

3.4   The infinitive as a modifier

The infinitive can modify a noun or adjective with *de* or *à*.

3.4.1   à + infinitive as modifier

The infinitive can modify a noun or adjective with preposition *à*.

(i)   **Modifying a noun**

The infinitive refers to something 'to be done' to or with the noun. Note that unlike in 3.2(ii), the '*à* + infinitive' construction is **not** part of the noun. (However, depending on usage, this difference may become tenuous.)

> Ex: *Il y a un appartement* ***à louer*** *au troisième.*
> There is a flat to rent on the third floor.

> *Voulez-vous quelque chose* ***à boire***?
> Would you like something to drink?

NB: The infinitive, as the equivalent of a relative clause, can also be the object of:
− *le premier, le deuxième*, etc.
− *le dernier, le seul*

> Ex: *Vous n'êtes pas* ***le premier à m'en parler***.
> (= *qui m'en parle*)
> You are not the first one to tell me about it.

> *Il a été* ***le seul à réagir***.
> (= *qui ait réagi*)
> He was the only one to react.

(ii) **Modifying an adjective**

    – The adjective states the ease or difficulty, convenience or inconvenience, of the task to be done (e.g. with adjectives of habit or ability: *habitué, prêt, lent, rapide*).

        Ex: *Je suis prête **à partir**.*
        I am ready to leave.

        *Cette valise est très lourde **à porter**.*
        This suitcase is very heavy to carry.

    – Impersonal constructions with *ce + être* + adjective: *à* is used before the infinitive when the apparent or grammatical subject is *ce*.

        Ex: *Ce n'est pas compliqué **à faire**.*
        *Vous avez passé de bonnes vacances: c'est facile **à voir**.*

See also chapter 35 *C'est/Il est*, section 3.

    – Idioms:

        Ex: *Otto est laid **à faire peur**.*
        Otto is as ugly as sin.

        *C'est triste/ridicule **à pleurer**.*
        It is so sad/ridiculous you could cry.

3.4.2 de + *infinitive as modifier*

The infinitive can modify a noun or adjective with preposition *de*.

(i) **Modifying a noun**

    – With a conjugated verb:

        Ex: *Nous avons la permission **d'entrer**.*
        We have permission to go in.

        *Je n'ai pas le temps **de me reposer**.*
        I don't have time to rest.

    – With an impersonal construction with *il*:

        Ex: *Il est temps **de partir**.*
        It is time to go.

(ii) **Modifying an adjective**

    – The infinitive can modify an affective adjective (expressing the state or mood of a person) after *être*.

        Ex: *Il était sûr **de passer** son permis du premier coup.*
        He was certain he would pass his driving test first time round.

        *Vous êtes libre **de ne rien dire**.*
        You are free not to say anything.

        *Ils ont été forcés **de tout avouer**.*
        They had to confess all.

        *Il est désolé **de vous avoir manqué** hier soir.*
        He is sorry he missed you last night.

– The infinitive in impersonal constructions with *être* + adjective: *de* is used before the infinitive when the infinitive is the real subject of *être* + adjective. The apparent subject is impersonal *il*.

> Ex: ***Il** n'est pas facile **de faire** la mayonnaise.*
> (the infinitive is the real subject
> → *Faire la mayonnaise n'est pas facile*.)

NB: *ce* is often used instead of impersonal *il* in informal French.

> Ex: *Ce n'est pas facile de faire la mayonnaise.*

3.5 The infinitive as an adverb phrase with other prepositions

– To express an aim or a plan with *pour, afin de, à force de*

> Ex: ***Pour faire** un gâteau, il faut de la farine, du beurre et des œufs.*
> To make a cake, you need flour, butter and eggs.
>
> *Je l'ai fait **afin d'aider** Sophie.*
> I did it in order to help Sophie.
>
> ***A force de répéter**, il finira bien par se faire comprendre!*
> By dint of repetition, he will eventually make himself understood!

– To express a cause with *pour*

> Ex: *Il a été arrêté **pour avoir grillé** un feu rouge.*
> He was arrested for going through a red light.

– To express a way or a manner with *sans*

> Ex: ***Sans avoir pris** conscience de la gravité de la situation, il est parti **sans dire** au-revoir.*
> Without having realized the seriousness of the situation, he left without saying good-bye.

– To express comparison or opposition with *au lieu de, à moins de, jusqu'à*

> Ex: *Vous feriez mieux de réviser pour vos examens **au lieu de passer** vos soirées au bar.*
> You should revise for your exams instead of spending your evenings in the bar.
>
> ***A moins de faire** la queue, je ne vois pas comment je vais pouvoir avoir un taxi!*
> Unless I join the queue, I can't see how I can get a taxi!
>
> *Je n'irais pas **jusqu'à dire** qu'il a menti mais . . .*
> I would not go as far as saying he lied but . . .

NB(1): ***avant de*** and ***après***: *avant de* is always followed by a present infinitive whereas *après* is always followed by a past infinitive (see 2.2 above).

> Ex: *On apprend à marcher **avant de [pouvoir] courir**.*
> You learn to walk before you can run.
>
> ***Après s'être demandé** ce qu'il devait faire, il a décidé d'appeler la police.*
> After wondering what to do, he decided to call the police.

NB(2): *en* is always followed by a present participle (see chapter 16 Present Participle, section 3.3). It is a common mistake to confuse the preposition *en* (or *en* as part of the gerund) and the personal pronoun *en* (see chapter 31 Personal Pronouns, section 2.2.2.7). Compare:

> ***En faisant*** *le résumé de ce paragraphe, vous le comprendrez mieux.*
> **By summarizing** this paragraph, you will understand it better.
>> and:
> *Vous devez commencer par lire le premier paragraphe, puis **en faire** le résumé.*
> You should start by reading the first paragraph, then **make** a summary **of it**.

Hence:

> *Vous comprendrez mieux ce paragraphe **en en faisant** le résumé.*
> You will understand this paragraph better **by summarizing it**.

4 Translation difficulties

It remains to examine two areas of possible difficulty:
− multiple subordinate clauses introduced by *que*
− multiple infinitives

(i) Multiple subordinate clauses

In English, it is customary to drop certain relative pronouns and conjunctions. French cannot drop relative pronouns (see chapter 32 Relative Pronouns), but it is possible to replace a *que*-clause with an infinitive construction.

Consider the following example:
> This coat [that] she says [that] she has bought.

The literal translation of which is:
> *Ce manteau **qu'**elle dit **qu'**elle a acheté.*
>> relative pronoun   conjunction

Explanation: *dire* can be followed either by an infinitive or a *que*-clause (see section 3.1.3.2(vi) above), hence:
> *Elle dit qu'elle a acheté un manteau.*
>> or:
> *Elle dit avoir acheté un manteau.*
> She said she bought a coat.

Thus the *que*-clause in the first example can be replaced by an infinitive (in the relevant tense) to lighten the sentence, giving:
> *Ce manteau qu'elle dit avoir acheté.*

(ii) Multiple infinitives

A lot of infinitives are rendered by a form in '-ing' in English. Consider the following examples:
> **1** I remember waking up and hearing them whisper something and laugh.
> *Je me souviens de m'être réveillé et de les avoir entendus chuchoter et rire.*

Explanation:
- 'I' is the subject of both 'remember' and 'waking up/hearing'.
- *se souvenir* is constructed with *de*, hence **must** be followed by an infinitive, whether English is itself an infinitive, a form in '–ing' (as is the case here) or a subordinate clause (see 3.1).
- *se souvenir de* is followed by a past infinitive (see section 3.1.2(i) above); hence:
    *Je **me souviens de m'être réveillé** et **de les avoir entendus** . . .*
- verbs of perception (here *voir*) are followed by the infinitive (see section 3.1.3.1(ii) above), even if they are themselves in the infinitive; hence:
    *. . . de les **avoir entendus chuchoter** et **rire**.*

  2 He started pretending he was limping.
    Il a commencé à faire semblant de boiter.

Explanation:
- 'He' is the subject of 'started', 'pretending' and 'was limping'.
- *commencer* can be followed by *de* or *à* + infinitive (see section 3.1.4(i) above), but since there is another *de* later on in the sentence, it is best to avoid a repetition, hence:
    *Il a commencé **à faire semblant** . . .*
- *faire semblant* is followed by *de* + infinitive (see section 3.1.2(i) above), even if it is itself in the infinitive, hence:
    *. . . **faire semblant de boiter**.*

  3 It's a story that I must be prepared to deny having heard.
    C'est une histoire que je dois être prête à nier avoir entendue.

16 Present participle

1 Introduction

The present participle is one of the non-personal moods of the verb. From a syntactic point of view, it is the adjectival form of the verb. However, like a verb, it can also have a complement and it thus has a dual nature as a verb and an adjective. Similarly the gerund (see 3.3 below) is both a verb and an adverb. Furthermore, the present participle can be used as a noun by improper derivation and it can form participial clauses that function like adverbial clauses.

There is no one-to-one correspondence between French and English regarding forms in -*ant* and forms in '-ing'. For instance a French infinitive often translates an English form in '-ing' (see 3.4 below).

Finally, the presence or absence of *en* is a common source of errors (see 3.2.2.2 below).

2 Formation

(i) Present participle

The present participle is formed by adding the suffix -*ant* to the radical of the first person plural in the present indicative.

Ex: 1st person plural present indicative	present participle
nous achetons	*achetant*
nous mangeons	*mangeant*
nous allons	*allant*
nous finissons	*finissant*
nous partons	*partant*
nous voyons	*voyant*
nous prenons	*prenant*, etc.

Exceptions:

nous sommes	**étant**
nous avons	**ayant**
nous savons	**sachant**

(ii) Compound form

The compound form or perfect participle is made up of the present participle of *être* or *avoir* + the past participle of the verb (see also chapter 17 Past Participle).

Ex: *ayant compris; étant parti; s'étant souvenu*

(iii) Passive form

The passive form is constructed with transitive verbs, with the present participle of *être* + the past participle.

Ex: *Les vacances **étant terminées**, il faut reprendre le travail.*

Note that the past participle agrees according to the rules given in chapter 9 Perfect, section 3.

3 Use

The present participle can be used as a noun, an adjective or a verb (present participle and gerund).

3.1 The present participle as a noun

Some present participles have become nouns in their own right, by improper derivation. They take a determiner and can have feminine and plural forms. Note that the English equivalent is seldom a form in '-ing'.

– animates (mostly humans):

Ex: *un(e) commerçant(e)*	a shopkeeper
un(e) croyant(e)	a believer
un(e) débutant(e)	a beginner
un(e) étudiant(e)	a student
un(e) gagnant(e)	a winner
un(e) perdant(e)	a loser
un(e) manifestant(e)	a demonstrator
un(e) passant(e)	a passer-by
une assistante sociale	a social worker
un fabricant	a manufacturer
un revenant	a ghost

– inanimates:

un calmant	a sedative
un excitant	a stimulant
un fortifiant	a tonic
un remontant	a pick-me-up (drug)
un pliant	a folding stool
un détachant	a stain remover

3.2   Adjective or present participle?

Some present participles have become adjectives, sometimes called 'verbal adjectives'. It is important to distinguish them from genuine present participles because:
– they may be spelt differently
– syntactically, the adjective behaves like any other qualifying adjective, while the present participle behaves like a verb, except that it is invariable
– semantically, the adjective expresses a state, a quality or a way of being, rather than a particular process.

3.2.1   Spelling

The following adjectives, derived from present participles, are spelt differently (the participle is nearer the radical of the conjugation).

Ex: infinitive	present participle	adjective
fatiguer	*fatiguant*	*fatigant*
convaincre	*convainquant*	*convaincant*
négliger	*négligeant*	*négligent*
équivaloir	*équivalant*	*équivalent*

The following are derived from the old form of the present participle:

savoir	*sachant*	*savant*
pouvoir	*pouvant*	*puissant*

Finally, note the following, which are 'regular':

piquer	*piquant*	*piquant*
exiger	*exigeant*	*exigeant*
affliger	*affligeant*	*affligeant*

NB(1): *être, avoir* and *devoir* do not have an adjectival form.

NB(2): Although the meaning of present participles and their corresponding verbal adjectives are most of the time very close, there can be an important difference in some cases.

Ex: *violant*: present participle of *violer* ('to rape').
violent: adjective ('violent').

3.2.2   Syntax and semantics

3.2.2.1   THE ADJECTIVE

Like any other qualifying adjective, the verbal adjective describes a state or a quality. In case of confusion with a possible present participle, it may be desirable to replace the verbal adjective with an ordinary qualifying adjective.

Ex: *J'ai lu un article **intéressant** → **superficiel**.*
*Ses yeux étaient **brillants** d'émotion → **noirs** de colère.*

(i)   The adjective can be attributive or predicative (see chapter 28 Qualifying Adjectives, section 2), and agrees in gender and number with the noun it qualifies (section 5).

Ex: *un article **intéressant***
an interesting article

*de **charmantes** personnes* OR: *des personnes **charmantes***
charming people

*Votre argument n'est pas **convaincant**.*
Your argument isn't convincing.

They are also used in fixed expressions, where they:
– either agree like an adjective:

Ex: *toutes affaires **cessantes**; séance **tenante***
forthwith; right away

– or remain invariable:

*des **soi-disant** médecins*
would-be doctors

(ii) If an adverb qualifies the adjective, the adverb always **precedes** the adjective (compare with 3.2.2.2(iv) below, where the adverb modifying a present participle follows it).

Ex: *un article **très intéressant***
a very interesting article

*des personnes **absolument charmantes***
absolutely charming people

*Votre argument n'est pas **entièrement convaincant**.*
Your argument isn't entirely convincing.

3.2.2.2 THE PRESENT PARTICIPLE

The present participle is invariable and is basically an aspect, showing a process being accomplished. It has no temporal value of its own but derives one from that of the main verb. To avoid any confusion with a possible verbal adjective, it may be desirable to replace the present participle with a conjugated verb.

Ex: *Ce sont des travaux **fatiguant** l'esprit* → *qui **fatiguent** l'esprit.*
These are tasks which exhaust the spirit.

The perfect participle expresses a process that has already been accomplished.

Ex: *N'utilisez pas de récipients **ayant contenu** de l'acide.*
Do not use any containers that have contained acid.

The present participle:

(i) can have a direct object

Ex: *Paul écrivit à Marie, la **suppliant** de bien vouloir venir le voir.*
('*la*' is the direct object of '*suppliant*').
Paul wrote to Marie, begging her to come and see him.

(ii) can have an indirect object

Ex: *Paul écrivit à Marie, lui **demandant** de bien vouloir venir le voir.*
('*lui*' is the indirect object of '*demandant*').
Paul wrote to Marie, asking her to come and see him.

(iii)   can be preceded by the reflexive personal pronoun *se* (*me, te, se, nous, vous, se*)

        Ex: ***Se penchant*** *par la fenêtre, il essaya de voir la locomotive à vapeur.*

        He was leaning out of the window, trying to see the steam engine.

        J'écrivis à Marie, ***me demandant*** *si c'était bien utile.*

        I wrote to Marie, wondering whether it was really useful.

(iv)   can be modified by an adverb or adverb phrase, which **follows** it

        Ex: *Il présenta une argumentation* ***différant complètement*** *de la mienne.*

        He presented an argument which differed completely from mine.

(v)   can be adjacent to the subject

        Ex: *J'ai trouvé un portefeuille* ***contenant*** *dix mille francs.*

        I found a wallet containing ten thousand francs.

NB: The subject of the present participle is the object of the main verb.

(vi)   can be separated from its subject and appear at different places in the sentence, thus changing the emphasis

        Ex: ***Prenant*** *l'enfant par la main, Catherine le conduisit à l'école.*

        Catherine, ***prenant*** *l'enfant par la main, le conduisit à l'école.*

        Catherine conduisit l'enfant à l'école, le ***prenant*** *par la main.*

NB(1): The subject of the present participle is the same as that of the main verb (see below).

NB(2): The second category of present participles are used mainly in written French. In spoken French, a clause introduced by a conjunction of coordination or subordination, or a relative pronoun, is more commonly used (see below).

(vii)   Meaning of the present participle

The present participle is used to express the following:

– the cause, reason for something

        Ex: ***Ayant réussi*** *à réparer la crevaison, ils ont pu repartir.*

        (= *comme ils avaient réussi* . . .)

        Having managed to repair the puncture, they were able to set off again.

        (= since they'd managed . . .)

        Il a accepté leur invitation, ne ***voulant*** *pas les vexer.*

        (= *parce qu'il ne voulait pas* . . .)

        He accepted their invitation, not wanting to offend them.

        (= because he didn't want to . . .)

– an action taking place **immediately before** that of the main verb

        Ex: ***Prenant*** *son manteau, elle est sortie.*

        (= *Elle a pris son manteau et puis elle est sortie.*)

        Taking her coat, she left.

        (= She took her coat and then she left.)

Compare with:

> ***En prenant*** *son manteau, elle s'est pris les pieds dans le tapis.*
> When taking her coat, she caught her foot in the rug.
> (= adverb phrase of manner and/or time)

> ***Prenant*** *l'enfant par la main, elle le conduisit à l'école.*
> (= *Elle prit l'enfant par la main et puis . . .*)
> Taking the child by the hand, she took him to school.
> (= She took the child by the hand and then . . .)

Compare with:

> ***En prenant*** *l'enfant par la main, elle se rendit compte qu'il n'avait pas ses moufles.*
> When she took the child's hand, she realized that he didn't have his mittens.
> (= adverb phrase of time and/or manner)

– an action taking place **immediately after** that of the main verb, which indicates the result of that action

> Ex: *Il est parti,* ***laissant*** *Marie sans nouvelles pendant plusieurs mois.*
> (= *et il a laissé*)
> He left, leaving Marie without news for several months.
> (= and he left)

– an action which is **simultaneous** with that of the main verb (*en train de*). This is only the case when the subject of the participle is the object of the main verb. When the subjects are the same, the gerund should be used (see above). Compare:

> *J'ai vu Paul* ***en allant*** *à la gare.*
> (= *J'ai vu Paul alors que j'allais à la gare.*)
> I saw Paul as **I** was going to the station.
>   and:
> *J'ai vu Paul* ***allant*** *à la gare.*
> (= *J'ai vu Paul qui allait à la gare.*)
> I saw Paul as **he** was going to the station.

However, if '*allant à la gare*' is in apposition, i.e. detached (see chapter 2 Syntax), its subject is the same as that of the main verb.

> Ex: *Allant à la gare, j'ai vu Paul.*
> As I was going to the station, I saw Paul.

Consider the following example:

> *L'homme regardait le chien, quêtant des caresses et des bouts de saucisson.*

This would be understood as if the man was asking to be stroked and given bits of sausage! Removing the comma would make the sentence grammatically well formed but cumbersome. A relative clause (see below) would be the best way to clarify the intended meaning:

> *L'homme regardait le chien* ***qui quêtait*** *des caresses et des bouts de saucisson.*

– to replace a relative clause with *qui*

> Ex: *Des manifestants* **criant** *des slogans anti-fascistes ont défilé sous nos fenêtres.*
> (= *qui criaient . . .*)
> Demonstrators shouting anti-fascist slogans paraded under our windows.

In spoken French, a relative clause is usually preferred as it allows the expression of tenses and moods. This is particularly so if the present participle emphasizes an action, as opposed to being simply a qualifier (as in e.g. *un portefeuille contenant 10.000 francs*).

> Ex: *Il y a de plus en plus de gens* **qui font** *leurs courses le soir.*
> More and more people do their shopping in the evening.
> rather than:
> *Il y a de plus en plus de gens faisant leurs courses le soir.*

However, when a precise tense is to be avoided, the present participle is preferred.

3.3   The gerund: *en* + present participle

(i)   The gerund (*gérondif*) is also a non-personal mood. It is formed with *en* + present participle, and is invariable. Note that *en* is often not considered as a preposition in its own right, but as part of the gerund.

(ii)   The gerund is mainly an aspect. Like the present participle, it shows a process being accomplished. It does not have its own temporal value but derives it from that of the main verb.

> Ex: *Ne lis pas* **en** *mangeant.*
> (simultaneity of the two processes)
>
> **En** *partant à 6 heures, vous serez de retour demain matin.*
> (succession of two processes, equivalent to a hypothetical clause: *Si vous partez à six heures . . .*)

(iii)   The gerund without *en*

en is absent in some fixed expressions.

> Ex: *Chemin faisant . . .*   Along the way . . .
> *faire qch tambour battant*   to do sth briskly

3.3.1   *The gerund as an adverb phrase*

The gerund is used as an adverb phrase, mainly of time. It answers the question *quand?* It is also, to a lesser extent, used as an adverb phrase of manner or cause. It answers the question *comment?* It corresponds in English to the '-ing' form, preceded by 'by', 'on', 'as' or 'while', or some other means of expressing a process of some duration. Hence it can express:

(i)   The time when an event is taking place
        Ex: *En allant à la bibliothèque, j'ai rencontré Antoine.*
        On my way to the library, I met Antoine.

        En arrivant à Londres, j'irai tout de suite chez mes amis.
        When I arrive in London, I shall go straight to my friends' house.

(ii)   The way, the manner or the means of an action
        Ex: *Elle a perdu du poids en faisant de la gym.*
        She lost weight by working out.

        Il s'est endormi en écoutant la radio.
        He fell asleep while listening to the radio.

        C'est en forgeant qu'on devient forgeron. (proverb)
        Practice makes perfect.

        Il est parti en claquant la porte.
        He slammed the door as he left.

3.3.2   The subject of the gerund

The implicit subject of a gerund **must** be the same as that of the main verb.
        Ex: *Il travaille en écoutant la radio.*
        (= *Il travaille et il écoute la radio.*)
        He is working while listening to the radio.

Compare:
        En partant, il avait l'air inquiet.
        As he was leaving, he looked worried.
                and:
        Quand il est parti, elle avait l'air inquiet.
        When he left, she looked worried.

However, this rule does not apply in certain proverbs and sayings.
        Ex: *L'appétit vient en mangeant.*
        (= *L'appétit vient quand on mange.*)
        Appetite comes with eating.

3.3.3   The gerund + tout *or* rien que

(i)   The addition of ***tout*** associates the action of the main verb more closely with that of the gerund. It is used either:

        – to stress simultaneity and contrast two unrelated processes:
        Ex: *Elle arrive à faire ses devoirs tout en écoutant la radio!*
        She manages to do her homework whilst listening to the radio!

Thus one would not say:
        Ex: *?Il écrit tout en faisant bien attention aux accents.*
                but simply:
        Il écrit en faisant bien attention aux accents.
        He pays close attention to accents when he writes.

But the following is quite possible:

> ***Tout en marchant****, il regarde les fleurs.*
> As he is walking, he looks at the flowers.

– to indicate an opposition, a restriction:

> Ex: ***Tout en étant*** *heureuse d'être là-bas loin de tout, elle voulait retourner chez elle.*
> Whilst she was happy to be there away from everything, she wanted to go back home.
>
> ***Tout en réfléchissant****, je m'arrêtai pour m'asseoir sur un banc.*
> Whilst I was thinking, I stopped to sit on a bench.

NB: In the last two cases, '***tout***' is compulsory with '***en***', because of the opposition.

(ii)   The addition of ***rien que*** stresses the fact that a particular action is sufficient to obtain the desired result.

> Ex: [***Rien qu'****]**en appuyant** sur ce levier, vous aurez toute l'eau nécessaire.*
> By [just] pressing on this lever, you will have all the water necessary.

3.4   Translation of English words in '-ing'

A lot of English constructions in '-ing' are not translated by a present participle in French. Here are a few examples:

(i)   **Nouns**

– '-ing' can be added to countable nouns to form mass nouns, meaning the substance of which they are composed.

> Ex: M. Dupont sells **matting** and **tubing**.
> *M. Dupont vend des **revêtements de sol** et de la **tuyauterie**.*

– '-ing' can be added to verbs to form:

→ abstract nouns, expressing an activity or state.

> Ex: I like **painting, fishing, bathing, skiing** and **driving**.
> *J'aime **la peinture, la pêche, la baignade, le ski** et **la conduite automobile**.*
> (or: *J'aime peindre, pêcher, me baigner, skier et conduire.*)

→ concrete nouns, meaning what results from the activity expressed by the verb.

> Ex: I own a few **paintings**, a few **buildings**, and I also have a few **savings**!
> *Je possède quelques **tableaux**, quelques **bâtiments** et j'ai aussi quelques **économies**!*

(ii) **Adjectives**

> Ex: the **working** population
> *la population **active***
>
> Where is the **shopping** centre please?
> *Où se trouve le centre **commercial** s'il vous plaît?*
>
> And what is even more **surprising** . . .
> *Et ce qui est encore plus **surprenant** . . .*

(iii) **Nominal infinitives**

– as a subject:
> Ex: **Painting** is relaxing.
> ***Peindre** est relaxant.*

Note that here, the English could be interpreted as:
> ***Peindre**, c'est **se détendre**.*

– as a subject complement:
> Ex: His favourite pastime is **playing** cards.
> *Son passe-temps favori est de **jouer** aux cartes.*

(iv) **Infinitives**

– with a verb of perception as the conjugated verb, use either an infinitive or a relative clause (see chapter 15 Infinitive, section 3.1.3.1(ii)).
> Ex: I like to see the rabbits **running** in the fields.
> *J'aime <u>voir</u> les lapins **courir** dans les champs.*
> *(= qui courent)*
>
> I heard the neighbour **talking** to the gardener.
> *J'<u>ai entendu</u> la voisine **parler/en train de parler** au jardinier.*
> *(= qui parlait/ qui était en train de parler)*

NB: A present participle may also be used:
> Ex: I saw rabbits **running** in the fields.
> *J'ai vu des lapins **courant** dans les champs.*

– after all prepositions, except *en*
> Ex: **Instead of complaining**, you ought to do something a bit more constructive.
> ***Au lieu de** vous **plaindre**, vous devriez faire quelque chose d'un peu plus constructif.*
>
> This method has proved quite effective **in dealing** with that kind of problem.
> *Cette méthode s'est montrée plutôt efficace **pour traiter** de ce genre de problème.*
>
> Please knock **before entering**.
> *Vous êtes prié de frapper **avant d'entrer**.*
> but:
> Don't read **while eating**!
> *Ne lis pas **en mangeant**!*

– when governed by another verb, with or without a preposition. The object
clause has the same subject as the main clause (see chapter 15 Infinitive).

Ex: I **would prefer going out** tonight.
*Je **préfèrerais _ sortir** ce soir.*

We **avoided falling** into the trap!
*Nous **avons évité <u>de</u> tomber** dans le piège!*

He **busied himself sawing** wood.
*Il **s'occupa <u>à</u> scier** du bois.*

NB: If the subjects are different, the verb is conjugated in the indicative or
subjunctive (see chapter 12 Subjunctive). The verb in the main clause is of the
type: *aimer, détester, haïr, observer, se souvenir,* etc.

Ex: I don't like my cats **catching** mice.
*Je n'aime pas que mes chats **attrapent** des souris.*

(v) **Relative clauses**

Most relative clauses which are subjects are equivalent to a form in '-ing'. Note
that a present participle can sometimes also be used in French (see (iv) above).

Ex: Look at this cat quietly **sleeping**.
*Regarde ce chat **qui dort** tranquillement.*

Tomorrow you will meet a woman **wearing** a fur coat.
(= who will be wearing)
*Demain, vous rencontrerez une femme **qui portera/portant** un manteau de
fourrure.*

(vi) **Conjugated verbs**

The English continuous form (see chapter 4 Introduction to Verbs, section 4.3.2)
is translated by a present, an imperfect, a future (sometimes with *en train de*) or a
perfect.

Ex: – imperfect:
I **was reading** when they arrived.
*Je **lisais** quand ils sont arrivés.*
(or: *J'étais en train de lire quand . . .*)

– perfect:
I **have been walking** all day.
*J'ai **marché** toute la journée.*

– present:
I **am coming** to see you next week.
*Je **viens** vous voir la semaine prochaine.*

– future:
He **will be speaking** at the conference.
*Il **parlera** au colloque.*

– *être en train de* + infinitive:

Present:

Do not disturb her! She **is working**.
*Ne la dérangez pas! Elle **est en train de travailler**.*

Imperfect:

I **was painting** the garage door when the telephone rang.
J'étais en train de peindre la porte du garage quand le téléphone a sonné.

NB: 'to be' can be omitted. Consider the following text:

'How should she present herself to him? [. . .] Just as she was, in her apron, the busy housewife, straight from the kitchen, **cooking** the midday meal? Or as the lady of leisure, **reading** a book?'

L. P. Hartley, *The Hireling*

*Comment devait-elle se présenter à lui? [. . .] Juste comme elle était, en tablier, en ménagère affairée venant tout droit de la cuisine, **en train de préparer** le déjeuner? Ou en femme du monde, **en train de lire** un livre?*

être would then be omitted in the same way.

In the following example, it is the subject which is omitted in English, but not in French:

Yet, **taking** into account recent events, . . .
(= if we/you are taking into account . . .)
*Cependant, si [l']on **tient** compte des événements récents . . .*
      rather than:
★Cependant, tenant compte des événements récents . . .

(vii) Past participles expressing a position

Present participles expressing a position in English are rendered by a past participle in French.

Ex: He was sitting / kneeling / lying / crouching.
Il était assis / agenouillé / couché, allongé / accroupi.

Note the case of 'standing':

Ex: He was standing.
Il était debout.

3.5 Present participle in French but not English

In certain cases, the present participle is not used in English, although it is used in French:

(i) to translate *comme étant*

Ex: They show artists **as** useless.
*Ils montrent les artistes **comme étant** inutiles.*

He recognizes culture **to be** a form of art.
*Il reconnaît la culture **comme étant** une forme d'art.*

(ii) to describe manner of motion

Note that in French, there is no exact equivalent to the English construction 'verb + preposition' to express manner of motion. Instead, the conjugated verb is used to express the movement indicated by the preposition and a gerund to express the manner of motion indicated by the English verb. See chapter 26 Prepositions, section 14.

> Ex: I hopped in.
> *Je suis entré en sautillant/en boitillant.*

4 Absolute participles and participial clauses

(i) An 'absolute participle' has its own subject, i.e. it is not linked to the main verb. Together, they (participle + subject) can replace an adverbial clause, generally of time or cause. This construction, which is always detached, is called a participial clause (*proposition participe*) and is only used in formal French.

> Ex: *Les sirènes **se mettant** à hurler, les gens se précipitèrent vers les abris.*
> (= *Comme les sirènes se mettaient à hurler . . .*)
> As the sirens began to wail, people rushed towards the shelters.
>
> *Le temps **permettant**, nous irons nous promener.*
> (= *Si le temps le permet . . .*)
> Weather permitting, we shall go for a walk.

NB: With a transitive verb, the participial clause can be in the passive voice, in which case the present participle shows a process which has already been accomplished.

> Ex: *Le spectacle **étant interrompu**, il nous fallut quitter les lieux.*
> As the show had been interrupted, we had to leave the premises.

(ii) In administrative jargon, absolute participles are used without a subject. They are equivalent to a preposition.

> Ex: ***S'agissant** du compte-rendu de . . .*
> Concerning the report of . . .
>
> ***Concernant** votre demande du . . .*
> With reference to your request of . . .

(iii) In other cases, a participial clause without its own subject is considered slipshod.

> Ex: **Neigeant de plus en plus fort, ils ne purent repartir.*
> → *La neige tombant de plus en plus fort . . .*
> → *Comme il neigeait de plus en plus fort . . .*

17 Past participle

1 Introduction

The past participle is one of the non-personal moods of the verb.

From a syntactic point of view it is the adjectival form of the verb. However, like a verb, it can have a complement: it has therefore a dual nature as adjective and verb. It can also be used as a noun by improper derivation. Finally, it can form participial clauses that function like adverbial clauses.

The past participle as a verb is used in the construction of all compound tenses. This is its main role. Without an auxiliary, it has no temporal value of its own and is basically an aspect (see below).

NB: It is a frequent mistake to confuse a past participle and an infinitive in ER, as 'é' and 'er' have the same sound.

2 The past participle as a verb

The past participle is used with an auxiliary verb to form compound tenses. The construction of the past participle is based on the infinitive of the verb concerned. For instance:

verb	past participle
acheter	*acheté*
finir	*fini*
offrir	*offert*
voir	*vu*
mettre	*mis*

Details of the formation and agreements of the past participle are given in chapter 9 Perfect, sections 2 and 3.

3 The past participle as a noun

Some past participles have become nouns in their own right, by improper derivation. They take a determiner and can have feminine and plural forms.

Ex: (*mourir*) *un* **mort**   a dead man
            une **morte**   a dead woman
            les **morts**   the dead
            la **mort**   death
    (*conduire*) *un* **permis** *de conduire*   driving licence
    (*produire*) *un* **produit** *de beauté*   cosmetic product
    (*fondre*) *une* **fondue** *savoyarde*   cheese fondue

4   The past participle as an adjective

(i)   A distinction should be made between adjectives based on intransitive and
      transitive verbs.

      – Intransitive verbs: the past participle is normally used only with verbs whose
        auxiliary is *être*. Those participles present the process as accomplished.
              Ex: *Les enfants* **nés** *après la guerre.*
      – Transitive verbs: the past participle has a passive value.
          – with perfective verbs, it presents the process as accomplished.
              Ex: *Une maison récemment* **construite**.
          – with imperfective verbs, it presents the process as non-accomplished.
              Compare:
                    l'effet **recherché**
                    (imperfective; non-accomplished)
                          and:
                    l'effet **obtenu**
                    (perfective; accomplished)

(ii) The past participle as an adjective can be attributive (in an attached or detached
      position) or predicative (see chapter 28 Qualifying Adjectives). It agrees in gender
      and number with the noun it qualifies. It generally describes a quality or a state.
              Ex: *des tomates* **mûries** *au soleil*
                          attributive, attached
              tomatoes ripened in the sun

              Epuisée, *elle se coucha de bonne heure.*
              attributive, detached
              Exhausted, she went to bed early.

              Catherine semble **fatiguée**.
                                predicative
              Catherine looks tired.

      NB: Some past participles have become invariable: they precede the noun and
      practically function as prepositions.
              Ex: **Vu la manière** *dont il s'est comporté* . . .
              Given the way he behaved . . .

              Etant donné la situation . . .
              Given the situation . . .

(iii) Past participles used as adjectives and which describe a **position** (of the body) are rendered by present participles in English.

> Ex: *Nous étions tous **assis** par terre.*
> We were all sitting on the floor.
>
> *Je suis restée **couchée** toute la journée.*
> I stayed in bed (lit.: lying) all day.
>
> *la Tour **Penchée** de Pise*
> the Leaning Tower of Pisa

Compare with the following examples, where the past participle is part of the conjugated verb, expressing an **action**.

> Ex: *Nous nous sommes assis par terre.*
> We sat on the floor.
>
> *Je me suis couchée parce que j'étais fatiguée.*
> I went to bed because I was tired.

5 Absolute participles and participial clauses

(i) The past participle can form participial clauses functioning like adverbial clauses (also called the 'absolute participle'). The absolute participle is used with a noun or pronoun which is **not the subject** of the conjugated verb of the main clause. The absolute participle agrees with this noun or pronoun.

> Ex: ***La nuit venue**, ils sont repartis.*
> As night came, they left.
>
> ***Son projet achevé**, il put quitter la ville.*
> His project completed, he was able to leave the town.
>
> ***Cela dit**, je ne peux rien vous promettre.*
> Having said that, I can't promise you anything.

(ii) When there is co-reference between the past participle and the subject of the main verb, the participle is considered as an adjective in apposition to the subject of the sentence.

> Ex: ***Assis** sur le rebord de la fenêtre, **le chat** regardait les oiseaux.*
> The cat was sitting on the window sill, looking at the birds.

(iii) A participial clause with elision of its subject is considered slipshod.

> Ex: *Les D520 et 200 sont engagés dans les combats de mai et juin 1940.*
> *Toutefois, ***arrivé** à la fin des hostilités, **les usines** toulousaines sont en ruine.*
> → *. . . le pays arrivé à la fin des hostilités . . .*
> → *. . . quand on arrive à la fin des hostilités . . .*

18 Active and passive voices

1 Introduction

The passive voice (*voix passive* or *diathèse*) is defined by opposition to the active voice. Several factors should be borne in mind when using the passive in French:
- the passive is used more in English than in French
- only direct transitive verbs can be passive in French
- there is more than one way of expressing the passive in French
- active and passive are not interchangeable: they are normally deliberately chosen for stylistic and/or semantic reasons

2 The actants

(i) In the active voice, there is a subject, the **agent**, which performs an action (expressed by the verb) on the object, or **patient**. Agent and patient are called the 'actants'.

> Ex: *Le chat mange la souris*.
>   subject/agent   object/patient
> The cat is eating the mouse.

Note that even in the active voice, the meaning of the verb can make the subject semantically passive.

> Ex: *Paul a reçu une lettre*.
>   subject   object
> Paul has received a letter.

> *Catherine souffre de maux de tête*.
> subject   object
> Catherine suffers from headaches.

(ii) Conversely, in the passive, the patient (as the subject) comes before the agent which acts upon it. In this case, the agent is called an **agentive complement** (*complément d'agent*). This is generally introduced by *par*.

> Ex: *La souris est mangée par le chat*.
>   subject/patient   agentive complement
> The mouse is being eaten by the cat.

(iii)   Not all complements preceded by *par* are agentive complements. A genuine agentive complement must become the subject of the verb in the active form.

Ex: − passive:

*Le voleur est arrêté **par la police**.*
agentive complement

− active:

***La police** arrête le voleur.*
subject

but:

*Le voleur est passé **par la fenêtre**.*
adverb phrase of manner

See chapters 2 Syntax and 29 Adverbs for details on adverbs and adverb phrases.

(iv)   To make a passive form possible, the transitive verb must be followed by a **direct object**. Some adverb phrases which are not introduced by a preposition may *look* like a direct object. Compare:

*Les chats mangent **les souris**.*
'*les souris*' is the direct object of '*mangent*'.
→ *Les souris sont mangées par les chats.*

*Les chats mangent **le matin**.*
'*le matin*' is an adverb phrase of time.

(v)   The passive can appear in its own right without an agentive complement.

Ex: *La maison blanche a été achetée [par M. Dupont].*
The white house was bought [by M. Dupont].

3   Construction

(i)   The passive is thus the object of a transformation. It is usually constructed with *être* (see also (iv) below) + the past participle of the **direct transitive verb** of the active sentence. (See chapter 2 Syntax, section 2.6, for details on transitivity.)

Ex: − active:

*Le chat **mange** la souris.*
− passive:
*La souris **est mangée** par le chat.*

(ii)   The tense of the active verb becomes the tense of *être* in the passive. The past participle agrees in gender and number with the subject of *être*.

Ex: − active voice, present:

*Caroline **fait** tous les vêtements de Robert.*
Caroline makes all Robert's clothes.

− passive voice, present:

*Tous les vêtements de Robert **sont faits** par Caroline.*
All Robert's clothes are made by Caroline.

       – active voice, perfect:
*Un de mes amis **a acheté** la maison d'en face.*
One of my friends bought the house across the road.

       – passive voice, perfect:
*La maison d'en face **a été achetée** par un de mes amis.*
The house across the road was bought by one of my friends.

NB: *été* is **invariable**, i.e. it does not agree with anything.

(iii)   The tenses of the passive voice are, e.g. for *aimer*:

Mood	Tense	
Indicative	present	*je suis aimé(e)*
	imperfect	*j'étais aimé(e)*
	past historic	*je fus aimé(e)*
	future	*je serai aimé(e)*
	perfect	*j'ai été aimé(e)*
	pluperfect	*j'avais été aimé(e)*
	past anterior	*j'eus été aimé(e)*
	future anterior	*j'aurai été aimé(e)*
Imperative	present	*sois aimé(e)*
Conditional	present	*je serais aimé(e)*
	past first form (or perfect)	*j'aurais été aimé(e)*
	past second form (or pluperfect)	*j'eusse été aimé(e)*
Subjunctive	present	*que je sois aimé(e)*
	imperfect	*que je fusse aimé(e)*
	perfect	*que j'aie été aimé(e)*
	pluperfect	*que j'eusse été aimé(e)*
Participle	present	*étant aimé(e)*
	past	*(ayant été) aimé(e)*
Infinitive	present	*être aimé(e)*
	past	*avoir été aimé(e)*

NB: The passive infinitive is the infinitive of the auxiliary *être* + past participle of a direct transitive verb.

      Ex: *Il espère **être félicité** pour son succès.*
            He hopes to be congratulated for his success.

It can also be used in conjunction with the immediate future and the recent past. (See chapters 5 Present and 7 Future.)

      Ex: *Nous espérons qu'elle **va être nommée** chef de section.*
            We're hoping that she's going to be appointed Head of Department.

            *Elle **vient d'être nommée** chef de section.*
            She's just been appointed Head of Department.

(iv)   *rester, demeurer, sembler, paraître* and *passer pour* can all be considered as auxiliaries for the passive voice instead of *être*.

> Ex: *Elle **semble aimée** de tous.*
> She seems to be loved by all.
>
> *La voiture **passe pour vendue**.*
> The car is considered as sold.

4   *de* or *par*?

The agentive complement is generally preceded by ***par*** in French (**by** in English). There are cases however when ***de*** is used in French (**by** or **with** in English).

4.1   Influence of the verb

(i)   When a verb is understood in its figurative sense or a weaker form of its literal sense, the agentive complement expresses a state due to a cause or means. The past participle is seen as an adjective. Hence ***de*** is used without a determiner (which corresponds to **with** in English).

> Ex: *Sa veste est doublée **de** soie blanche.*
> His/her jacket is lined **with** white silk.
>
> *Son dernier livre a été couronné **de** succès.*
> His/her latest book was crowned **with** success.

When the verb is used in its literal sense, use ***par*** (with a determiner).

> Ex: *Le prince a été couronné **par** son père.*
> The prince was crowned **by** his father.

(ii)   After verbs of 'feeling' (*aimer, estimer, adorer, détester, respecter*, etc.) or 'thinking' (*croire, connaître, oublier*, etc.), which also often indicate a state rather than an action, the agent can be introduced by ***de*** followed by a determiner.

> Ex: *Ces enfants sont adorés **de** leurs parents.*
> These children are adored **by** their parents.
>
> *Elle est bien connue **du** (= de + le) public.*
> She is well known **by** the public.

(iii)   After verbs such as *accompagner* and *suivre*, the choice depends on the participation of the agent in the action. Compare:

> *Un chasseur est souvent suivi **de** son chien.*
> A hunter is often followed by his dog.
>
> *M. Dupont est toujours accompagné **de** sa femme.*
> M. Dupont is always accompanied by his wife.
>   and:
> *La femme était suivie **par** un chien hargneux.*
> The woman was being followed by a growling dog.

*Le suspect a été accompagné **par** le policier jusqu'à une cellule.*
The suspect was accompanied by the policeman to a cell.

In the last two cases, the action of following or accompanying is seen to be more intentional, i.e. more 'active'.

4.2   Influence of the agentive complement

Note that the agentive complement is not necessarily human. Indeed, if the agentive complement is an idea or an emotion, ***de*** is normally used (without a determiner).

Ex: *L'enfer est pavé **de** bonnes intentions.* (proverb)
(The road to) hell is paved **with** good intentions.

However, ***par*** + determiner can also be used, to create a stronger effect. Compare:

*Alors que Paul traversait le bois, il fut saisi **de** peur.*
As Paul was walking through the woods, he was seized with fear.
and:
*Alors que Paul traversait le bois, il fut saisi **par la** peur.*

par gives 'life' to *peur* and creates a stronger expression.

If the agentive complement is determined, or modified by a noun complement, use ***par***.

Ex: *Alors que Paul traversait le bois, il fut saisi **par la peur de rencontrer un sanglier**.*
As Paul was walking through the woods, he was seized by the fear of meeting a boar.

5   Avoidance of the passive in French

Since the passive is generally more widely used in English than in French, it is important to be aware of the alternatives.

5.1   Agent expressed

If the agent is expressed, the active form can be used.

Ex: All the money was spent by the children.
→ passive:
*Tout l'argent a été dépensé par **les enfants**.*
        agentive complement
→ active:
***Les enfants** ont dépensé tout l'argent.*
agent

5.2 Agent not expressed

(i) If the agent is not expressed, but refers implicitly to a human animate, an active verb can be used in French with *on* as the agent.

Ex: This house was built in 1930.
→ passive:
Cette maison a été construite en 1930.
→ active:
On a construit cette maison en 1930.

The good news was announced.
→ passive:
La bonne nouvelle a été annoncée.
→ active:
On a annoncé la bonne nouvelle.

NB: Care must be exercised when using *on* because it shifts the emphasis from the patient to an undefined agent (see also section 8 below). Compare:
Le gouvernement a été renversé.
and:
On a renversé le gouvernement.
Here, the use of *on* invites you to guess who did it!

Ce médicament doit se prendre avant les repas. (See 5.3 below.)
and:
On doit prendre ce médicament avant les repas.
Who exactly is this mysterious '*On*'?

(See also chapters 31 Personal Pronouns, sections 2.1.2(ii) and 36 Indefinite Words, section 2.2 for the various values and meanings of *on*.)

(ii) A lot of common passive expressions in English with impersonal '**it**' are rendered in the active in French with *on*. Again this occurs when the implied agent is a human being.

Ex: **It** is believed that . . .
On pense que . . .

It was believed that . . .
On a pensé que . . .

It can be seen that . . .
On peut voir que . . .

(iii) If the agent is not expressed but refers to an inanimate (an instrument or a cause), the passive must be kept in French.

Ex: The town was flooded.
La ville a été inondée.
(*On a inondé la ville* suggests that someone flooded the town on purpose: see (i) above.)

The crops were damaged [by frost].
Les récoltes ont été abîmées [par le gel].

5.3   The middle voice (*voix moyenne*)

(i)   When the following three conditions are fulfilled:
   – the subject of the verb (the patient) is inanimate
   – the agentive complement is not expressed
   – the action is one which is commonplace or expected
then the pronominal form of the verb can be used (see also chapter 20
Pronominal Verbs). This is called the pseudo-reflexive or pronominal passive
structure or middle voice.

> Ex: This word is often used.
> *Ce mot **s'emploie** souvent.*
>
> Rent must be paid in advance.
> *Le loyer **se paie** à l'avance.*
>
> In England, peaches are often sold individually.
> *En Angleterre, les pêches **se vendent** souvent à la pièce.*
>
> The differences can already be seen.
> *Les différences **se font** déjà **voir**.*

NB: When translating, care must be exercised with the meaning of the English
expression.

> Ex: It's not done! (to do such a thing in good company)
> *Ça ne se fait pas!*
>   but:
> It's not done yet! (= You haven't done it yet!)
> *Ça n'est pas encore fait!*

It is a common error to confuse:

> Well done! = *Bravo!*
>   and:
> *Bien fait!* = Serves you right!

(ii)   English verbs which have a **passive meaning** are translated into French by a
pronominal verb.

> Ex: These houses sell well. (= are sold . . .)
> *Ces maisons **se vendent** bien.*
>
> This book reads easily. (= is read . . .)
> *Ce livre **se lit** facilement.*
>
> Your slip is showing! (= can be seen)
> *Votre jupon **se voit**!*

NB: The subject of the verb (the patient) must be non-human, otherwise the
verb is understood as an ordinary reflexive verb and not a passive.

> Ex: *Paul se vend au plus offrant.*
> Paul sells himself to the highest bidder.
>   but:
> *Paul Loup Sulitzer se vend bien.*
> (= *Les livres de Paul Loup Sulitzer se vendent bien.*)
> Paul Loup Sulitzer sells well.
> (= Paul Loup Sulitzer's books sell well.)

243

Exceptions, with verbs of perception.

> Ex: *Avec cette cravate, Paul se voit de loin.*
> With this tie, Paul stands out.
>
> *Avec ces haut-parleurs, Paul s'entend de loin.*
> With these loudspeakers, Paul can be heard far away.

(iii) When there is no agentive complement, the passive might be confused with a state. Therefore a distinction should be made between perfective and imperfective verbs:

– when a perfective verb is not followed by an agentive complement, it expresses a state following a completed process (accomplished aspect). The form corresponds to '*être* + adjective'.

> Ex: *La porte est fermée.*

The corresponding active form is the perfect:

> *On a fermé la porte.*

To express the non-accomplished aspect, the pronominal verb should be used. Compare:

> *La porte est fermée.*
> The door is closed. (accomplished)
> > and:
> *La porte se ferme.*
> The door is closing. (non-accomplished)

– with perfective verbs followed by an agentive complement, and with imperfective verbs, the passive expresses a process (non-accomplished) with a corresponding active form.

> *La porte est fermée par le gardien tous les soirs.*
> → *Le gardien ferme la porte tous les soirs.*
>
> *En France, l'algèbre est étudiée dès la sixième.*
> → *En France, on étudie l'algèbre dès la sixième.*

5.4 Use of nouns and adjectives

(i) An abstract noun in French is often used where a passive form describes an event in English.

> Ex: We are waiting for this grammar book to be published.
> *Nous attendons la publication de ce livre de grammaire.*
> (= *Nous attendons que ce livre de grammaire soit publié.*)

(ii) Ambiguity may arise due to the use of the ubiquitous preposition *de*.

> Ex: *la critique de Benveniste*
> → Benveniste has criticized somebody: active
> → Benveniste has been criticized by somebody: passive.

(iii)   Some adjectives in *-ible* or *-able* can be paraphrased by passive constructions.

> Ex: *Certains légumes ne sont pas très digestibles.*
> (= *ne sont pas facilement digérés*)
> Some vegetables are not easily digested.
>
> *un témoignage non-recevable*
> (= *qui ne peut être reçu*)
> inadmissible evidence

6   Verbs which cannot be passive

(i)   French **indirect transitive** verbs

French indirect transitive verbs, i.e. verbs which take an indirect object, cannot be passive (see chapter 2 Syntax, section 2.6.3).

> Ex: All Frédéric's questions were answered by the Chairman.
> *Le Président **a répondu à** toutes les questions de Frédéric.*
>
> Civil rights are enjoyed by people who live in a democracy.
> *Les gens qui vivent en démocratie **jouissent de** droits civils.*

The two sentences above cannot be passive in French. It is important to note here that a transitive direct verb in English (e.g. **to answer sb/sth**; **to enjoy sth**) is not necessarily rendered by a transitive direct verb in French.

Exception: The following verbs, which take an indirect object, **can** be used in the passive form: ***obéir à qn, désobéir à qn, pardonner (qch) à qn.***

> Ex: − active:
> *Ses parents **lui** ont pardonné.*
> indirect object pronoun
> His parents forgave him.
> → passive:
> *Il **a été pardonné** par ses parents.*
> He was forgiven by his parents.
>
> − active:
> *La nouvelle recrue a désobéi **au caporal**.*
> indirect object
> The new recruit disobeyed the corporal.
> → passive:
> *Le caporal **a été désobéi** par la nouvelle recrue.*
> The corporal was disobeyed by the new recruit.

(ii)   Translation of English **bi-transitive** verbs

Particular care must be exercised with English bi-transitive verbs, i.e. verbs which take both direct and indirect objects (e.g. **to give sth to sb** or **to give sb sth**). See also chapter 2 Syntax, section 2.6.6.

Ex: – active:
Antoine gave Sylvain a book (Antoine gave a book to Sylvain).
→ passive:
Sylvain was given a book by Antoine.

The French equivalent is *donner qch à qn*. Hence in French, only the transitive direct part, *donner qch*, can be passive. Thus:

★Sylvain a été donné un livre.
is not possible.

Sylvain a été donné.
means: Sylvain has been given (away as a gift!)

Un livre a été donné à Sylvain par Antoine. (or: *par Antoine à Sylvain*)
is correct, although a little laboured.

Antoine a donné un livre à Sylvain.
is the active form and may be the best solution here.

The same applies to verbs such as **to sell sb sth** (*vendre qch à qn*), **to show sb sth** (*montrer qch à qn*), etc.

Ex: Eric was sold a car.
Une voiture a été vendue à Eric.
or:
On a vendu une voiture à Eric.

(iii) *avoir* **and** *pouvoir*

The passive is impossible with *pouvoir*, and also with *avoir*, except in the familiar expression '*J'ai été eu(e)*' meaning 'I have been had / I have been swindled.'

(iv) *aimer* **and** *posséder*

aimer and *posséder* may become too emphatic when used in the passive, because they take the meaning of 'loved' and 'possessed' respectively, when 'liked' and 'owned' may be required.

Ex: – active: *Paul aime ce costume.*
– passive: *★Ce costume est aimé de Paul.*

– active: *Paul possède cette maison.*
– passive: *★Cette maison est possédée par Paul.*

If the stress is to be kept on the patient, another verb should be used.

Ex: *Ce costume plaît [beaucoup] à Paul.*
Cette maison appartient à Paul.

However, *aimer* can be used in the passive with a human patient, when the meaning 'loved' is required.

Ex: – active: *Paul aime Marie.*
– passive: *Marie est aimée de Paul.*

(v) Verbs which can be passive in one of their meanings only ('measure verbs'), so that they take a genuine direct object (see chapter 2 Syntax, section 2.10)

Ex: − *courir*:

   ★*Cent mètres ont été courus.*

     but:

   Le cent mètres (= la course) a été couru en dix secondes.

  − *peser*:

   ★*Six kilos sont pesés par le chat.*

     but:

   Le chat a été pesé par le vétérinaire.

  − *mesurer*:

   ★*Deux mètres cinquante de haut sont mesurés par ce mur.*

     but:

   Les murs et les sols seront mesurés par le décorateur.

(vi)   Direct transitive verbs used in a metaphorical sense

The passive is also impossible with direct transitive verbs used in a metaphorical sense:

  Ex: *Il a perdu ses parents dans un naufrage.*
    (= *Ses parents sont morts/ont été tués.*)
    His parents were lost in a shipwreck.

    Nicolas a essuyé un échec.
    (= *Nicolas a échoué.*)
    Nicolas has suffered a failure.

    Sophie a pris la porte.
    (= *Sophie est partie.*)
    Sophie has left.

(vii)   The agent is an infinitive

The passive cannot be used when the subject (the agent) is an infinitive. If a passive is needed, the infinitive should be replaced by a suitable noun.

  Ex: − active:

    Travailler *à l'ordinateur me fatigue les yeux.*
    Working at the computer tires my eyes.

    − passive:

    Mes yeux sont fatigués par **le travail** *à l'ordinateur.*
    My eyes are tired by working at the computer.

7   Expressing the passive in other ways

7.1   No expressed agent → impersonal voice with *il*

The impersonal pronoun *il* can be used as the subject of a passive with direct or indirect transitive verbs, if there is no expressed agent. This is similar to *on* + active, although much less common, as it tends to be used in official documents and not so much in conversation.

Ex: 3000 copies of this book have been sold.
(*vendre qch*)
→ passive:
Il a été vendu 3000 exemplaires de ce livre.
or:
3000 exemplaires de ce livre ont été vendus.
→ active:
On a vendu 3000 exemplaires de ce livre.

John is allowed to leave.
(with *permettre à qn de faire qch*)
→ passive:
Il est permis à John de partir.
→ active:
On permet à John de partir.

NB: With *autoriser* (*qn à faire qch*), an ordinary passive is of course possible:
Ex: John is allowed to leave.
→ passive:
John est autorisé à partir.
→ active:
On autorise John à partir.

Other examples:
Such actions will be stopped.
→ passive: *Il sera mis fin à de telles actions.*
→ active: *On mettra fin à de telles actions.*

A vote was taken.
→ passive: *Il a été procédé au vote.*
→ active: *On a procédé au vote.*

Paul's case was discussed at the meeting.
→ passive: *Il a été discuté du cas de Paul à la réunion.*
→ active: *On a discuté du cas de Paul à la réunion.*

7.2 Expressed agent

(i) Use of *se voir* + infinitive

The construction *se voir* + infinitive can be used, but note that it implies a total lack of control over events on the part of the patient.
Ex: *John s'est vu vendre une voiture par Paul.*
John was sold a car by Paul.

Il s'est vu demander par un agent qui il était.
He was asked who he was by a policeman.

(ii) Use of *s'entendre* + infinitive

If the main verb (here the infinitive) expresses what is said, *s'entendre* + infinitive can be used with the same implications as for *se voir* (see above).

Ex: *Elle s'est entendu dire par son collègue qu'elle devait tout recommencer.*
She was told by her colleague that she had to do it all over again.

(iii)   **se faire** or (**se**) **laisser** + infinitive

se faire + infinitive or (*se*) *laisser* + infinitive can also be used, followed by an agentive complement or not.

— **se faire** implies at least some previous action on the part of the patient.
Compare:
Il a été mis à la porte par le professeur.
He was sent out of the room by the teacher.
        and:
Il s'est fait mettre à la porte par le professeur.
(implies it was the consequence of his actions)

On lui a offert un livre.
She was given a book.
        and:
Elle s'est fait offrir un livre.
(implies that she wanted a book and got someone to give it to her)

— The implied action is even stronger with (**se**) **laisser**:
Ex: *Il a laissé vendre sa maison par un agent véreux.*
He let his house be sold by a crooked estate agent.

Il s'est laissé vendre une maison par un agent véreux.
He let a crooked estate agent sell him a house.

8 Stylistic choice: passive or active?

Although they are considered to be semantically equivalent (*Le chat mange la souris* = *La souris est mangée par le chat*), active and passive are not strictly interchangeable. Indeed, the passive enables the speaker:

(i)   To draw attention to the piece of information which seems most important to him/her, by playing on the possibility of changing the **theme** of the sentence (see chapter 2 Syntax, section 2.15). Compare:
Le juge a condamné le voleur à trois ans de prison ferme.
(The theme is '*le juge*' and puts the emphasis on the person who pronounced the sentence.)
        and:
Le voleur a été condamné à trois ans de prison ferme par le juge.
(The theme is '*le voleur*' and puts the emphasis on what happened to the one who carried out the crime.)

Hence if the stress is to be placed on the patient, the passive should be used.
Ex: His money was given back to him.
Son argent lui a été rendu.
(rather than: *On lui a rendu son argent.*)

(ii)   Not to express the identity of the agent of the process, due to the possibility of doing without the agentive complement (see 2(v) above), either:
— through ignorance:
> Ex: *Yves a été attaqué à la sortie du métro.*

— out of tact:
> Ex: *Le dernier article de Charles n'a pas été très bien reçu.*

— or because the agent is obvious to the interlocutor:
> Ex: *Le voleur a été condamné à un mois de prison avec sursis [par le tribunal].*

Note that the passive can be used with an inanimate agent whereas *on* can only be used for a human agent (see 5.2 above).
> Ex: *Les vignes ont été détruites [par la grêle/par des saboteurs].*
> The vines were destroyed [by hail/by saboteurs].

(iii)   To facilitate the link with another sentence.
> Ex: *La souris s'est sauvée et a été poursuivie par Lizzy.*
> rather than:
> *La souris s'est sauvée et Lizzy l'a poursuivie.*

(iv)   To facilitate cases of ellipsis (a turn of phrase favoured in journalism).
> Ex: *Les devoirs, notés trop sévèrement, ont été recorrigés.*
> (Instead of: '*Les devoirs **qui ont été** notés trop sévèrement . . .*)

(v)   To re-establish the preferred order 'animate subject/inanimate complement'.
> Ex: *Patrick a été heurté par un vélomoteur.*
> rather than:
> *Un vélomoteur a heurté Patrick.*

However, the order 'inanimate subject / animate complement' can be selected for stylistic effect.
> Ex: *Le jardin est fait par Marie, et le ménage par Pierre.*
> Marie does the gardening and Pierre does the housework.

(vi)   To recover the preferred order 'short subject / long object' when the active subject is long and the object is short. Compare:
> *Le monsieur qui se plaignait depuis longtemps de la saleté des voisins d'en face a érigé une palissade.*
> The man who had been complaining for a long time about the mess of the neighbours opposite erected a fence.
> and:
> *Une palissade a été érigée par le monsieur qui se plaignait depuis longtemps de la saleté des voisins d'en face.*
> A fence was erected by the man who had been complaining for a long time about the mess of the neighbours opposite.

Conversely, the passive is not likely to be selected if it contravenes the preferred order. For instance a pronominal agentive complement is rare, except if there is a contrast. Compare:
> *?Le repas a été préparé par moi.*
> and:
> *Le repas a été préparé par moi et non par Paul, qui cuisine très mal.*

NB(1): It is always possible to stress something by adding *c'est/ce sont . . . qui/ que . . .* (see cleft constructions in chapter 2 Syntax, section 2.15.4).

> Ex: − active: *Mr Brown m'a appris l'anglais.*
>> → passive: *L'anglais m'a été appris par Mr Brown.*
>> → stress on *l'anglais*, keeping the active:
>>> *C'est l'anglais que Mr Brown m'a appris.*

NB(2): Some passive transformations can radically modify the meaning of the sentence. This is the case for sentences with logical operations (quantifiers, negation).

> Ex: − active:
> *Un seul chat n'a pas mangé le poisson.*
> (= *tous l'ont mangé, sauf un*)
> Only one cat didn't eat the fish.
>
> − passive:
> *Le poisson n'a pas été mangé par un seul chat.*
> (= *aucun ne l'a mangé*)
> The fish was not eaten by a single cat.

19 Impersonal verbs and the impersonal voice

1 Introduction

An **impersonal verb** does not vary in person or number. Its **subject** is the impersonal or non-referential pronoun *il*. It is thus only conjugated in the 3rd person singular of all its tenses. In the compound tenses, the past participle of an impersonal verb is invariable. Note that impersonal constructions are used more frequently in French than in English.

There are several categories of impersonal verbs:
- 'weather'/'meteorological' verbs
- verbs which are exclusively impersonal: *falloir* and *s'agir de*
- *avoir* and *être*, which are extensively used in impersonal constructions (*il y a*; *il est*)
- verbs which are only occasionally impersonal, with a change of meaning

In the **impersonal voice**, certain verbs can be used with impersonal *il* for syntactic reasons (with no change in meaning).

2 Weather verbs

They are normally intransitive, and only used with impersonal *il*, but see exceptions below.

(i) *neiger, grêler, venter*
> Ex: ***Il a neigé*** *toute la nuit.*
> It has been snowing all night.
>
> ***Il a grêlé*** *hier: les récoltes sont dévastées.*
> We had hail yesterday: the crops are totally destroyed.

NB: *il vente* is now rare, except in idioms:
> Ex: *Qu'**il pleuve** ou qu'**il vente***, *demain, je sors!*
> (= *quel que soit le temps*)
> Come rain or shine, I shall go out tomorrow!

(ii) *pleuvoir* (to rain) and *tonner* (to thunder) can also have personal subjects
> Ex: *'Ici **pleuvent les nouvelles** vraies ou fausses.'*
>
> Michelet – cited in *Robert*
> Here rains the news, whether true or false.

'*Une artillerie* plus puissante, celle de la presse, **tonnait** désormais à l'oreille du peuple.'

Michelet – cited in *Robert*

A heavier artillery, that of the press, now thundered in the ears of the people.

NB: *pleuvoir* can be used figuratively.
  Ex: *Il pleut des cordes.*
  It's raining cats and dogs.

(iii) *geler* can have a personal or an impersonal subject
  Ex: *Il gèle* dehors et nous ne sommes qu'en septembre.
  It is freezing outside and it's only September.

  Cette rivière gèle tous les hivers.
  This river freezes every winter.

  Passe-moi ma veste! Je gèle!
  Please pass me my jacket! I am freezing!

(iv) *tomber*
Another very common way to express atmospheric conditions is to use *tomber* (to fall) with impersonal *il*, followed by the relevant NP.
  Ex: *Il tombe* de la neige, de la pluie, des grêlons.
  It is snowing, raining, hailing.

This construction is particularly useful if the subject is qualified, thus avoiding finishing the sentence abruptly with a short verb.
  Ex: *Il tombe* une petite pluie fine.
  It is drizzling.
  (rather than: *Une petite pluie fine tombe.*)

(v) *faire*
Atmospheric conditions can also be expressed with the impersonal pronoun *il* + *faire* + the relevant adjective or noun.
  Ex: *Il fait* beau, chaud, froid, frais, humide, sec, etc.
  It is fine, hot, cold, cool, humid, dry, etc.

  Il fait jour, nuit, sombre, clair, etc.
  It is daylight, night, dark, light, etc.

  Il fait du soleil, du vent, de la brume, du brouillard, etc.
  It is sunny, windy, misty, foggy, etc.
    but:
  Il y a des nuages.
  It is cloudy.
    or:
  Le ciel est nuageux.
  The sky is cloudy.

NB: *il y a* can also be used as an alternative to *il fait* in e.g. *il y a du soleil, du vent, de la brume, du brouillard.*

3 *falloir* and *s'agir de*

falloir and *s'agir de* are exclusively impersonal. The subject is always impersonal *il*.

(i) *falloir*

This verb can be followed by a noun, an infinitive, or *que* + subjunctive.

Ex: − with a noun:
*Pour faire la mayonnaise, **il faut** d'abord **un jaune d'œuf**.*
To make mayonnaise, first you need an egg yolk.

*Il lui **a fallu six minutes** pour aller à la gare.*
It took him six minutes to go to the station.

− with an infinitive:
*Il **a fallu changer** de tactique.*
It became necessary to change tactics.

NB: *il **me faut*** + infinitive is somewhat affected.
Ex: *Il me/te/lui/nous/vous/leur faut partir maintenant.*
It is necessary for me/you/him/her/us/you/them to leave now.
An alternative is *il **faut que*** + personal pronoun + subjunctive instead (see below).

− with *que* + subjunctive:
*Il **faut que** je **parte** maintenant.*
I must go now.

*Il **faudrait que** tu **fasses** un effort.*
You ought to make an effort.

Note the following:
*Vous pouvez venir demain. **Encore faudrait-il** qu'il y ait des trains.*
You can come tomorrow − provided the trains are running.

(ii) *s'agir de*

This verb can be followed by a noun or pronoun, an infinitive or a subjunctive (note that with the subjunctive, *de* is dropped and replaced by *que*).

Ex: − with a noun or pronoun:
De qui s'agit-il *dans cette affaire? C'est **de moi qu'il s'agit**?*
Who is this matter about? Is it about me?

*Vous avez demandé à me voir: **de quoi s'agit-il**?*
You have asked to see me - what is it about?

*Il **s'agit du rapport** que vous m'avez envoyé hier.*
(and not ★*Ce rapport s'agit de . . .*)
It's about the report you sent me yesterday.

- with an infinitive:

il s'agit de + infinitive means *à partir de maintenant*, *il importe de/il faut* and therefore indicates an obligation.

Il s'agit *maintenant* **de faire** *très attention.*
We/You should be very careful now.

Il s'agit de *ne pas* **se tromper!**
We mustn't make a mistake!

- with *que* + subjunctive (no *de*):
Il s'agit que *vous* **vous dépêchiez** *maintenant!*
(informal French)
You lot had better get a move on!

4   *avoir*

il y a functions as a presentative form (see chapter 2 Syntax, section 2.15.3). See also *c'est* and *il est* below.

(i)   *il y a* (there is/there are) normally indicates the existence of something and can refer to **a singular or plural noun**.

Ex: **Il y a un chat** *sur le toit.*
There is a cat on the roof.

Il y a des chats *sur le toit.*
There are cats on the roof.

(ii)   Negative form

Ex: **Il n'y a pas** *de chats ici.*
There aren't any cats here.

(iii)   Interrogative form
Note the positioning of the hyphens:

Ex: **Y a-t-il** *des chats ici?*
or:
Est-ce qu'il y a *des chats ici?*
Are there any cats here?

(iv)   Tenses
il y a can be used in all tenses, e.g. *il y avait* (there was/were), *il y aura* (there will be), *il y a eu* (there was/were/has been/have been), and with *devoir* and *pouvoir*.

Ex: **Il y a eu** *beaucoup de dégâts.*
There was a lot of damage.

Il pouvait y avoir *500 personnes à la manifestation.*
There could have been 500 people at the demonstration.

Il devrait y avoir *une réunion cette après-midi.*
There should be a meeting this afternoon.

(v) *il y a* can also express the time that has elapsed (see also chapter 6 *depuis* and Other Tense Markers).

> Ex: **Il y a deux heures** *que je travaille.*
> I have been working for two hours.
>
> *Cela s'est passé* **il y a trois jours**.
> It happened three days ago.

(vi) The question *Qu'est-ce qu'il y a?* (or *Qu'y a-t-il?*) on its own means 'What is happening?', or 'What is the matter?'.

> Ex: **Qu'est-ce qu'il y a?** *Vous avez l'air triste.*
> What is the matter? You look sad.
>
> **Qu'est-ce qu'il y a?** *J'entends les sirènes des pompiers.*
> What's happening? I can hear a fire engine.

It is a common error to use *Qu'est-ce que c'est?* instead. The latter means 'What is it?' in the sense of 'What sort of object is it?'

> Ex: *Qu'est-ce que c'est? On dirait une montgolfière!*
> What is it? It looks like a hot-air balloon!

See also chapter 39 Interrogative Structures.

(vii) *il n'y a qu'à* introduces a condition, both necessary and sufficient.

> Ex: *Pour que tout le monde soit content, il n'y a qu'à diminuer les impôts!*
> In order to satisfy everyone, all they need to do is to lower taxes!

5 *être*

c'est and **il est** function like presentative forms (see also *il y a* above).

(i) *il est* + noun is equivalent to *il y a* + noun but is used in formal or literary French only.

> Ex: **Il est un pays** *où il fait toujours beau.*
> There is a country where it is always sunny.
>
> **Il est des cas** *où il vaut mieux se taire.*
> There are times when it is better to keep quiet.

(ii) '*Il était une fois . . .*' is the standard way of beginning a fairy tale in French, which corresponds to the English 'Once upon a time . . .'.

> Ex: **Il était une fois** *une princesse qui . . .*
> Once upon a time, there was a princess who . . .

(iii) *il est* is used to express the time (see also chapter 37 Numbers, section 6).

> Ex: *Quelle heure* **est-il?** **Il est** *six heures.*
> What time is it? It is six o'clock.
>
> **Il est** *temps de partir!*
> It is time to go!
>
> **Il était** *trop tard pour attraper le train de 5 heures.*
> It was too late to catch the 5 o'clock train.

(iv)   *il est* is used in the following constructions with an adjective (see also chapter 12
         Subjunctive, section 4.1).

– **il** + **être** + adjective + **de** + infinitive
             Ex: **Il est bon de se reposer** *de temps en temps.*
                 It is good to have a rest from time to time.

                 Il *ne lui* **a** *pas* **été facile de se passer** *de bière!*
                 It was not easy for him/her to go without beer!

– **il** + **être** + adjective + **que** + indicative
             Ex: **Il est probable que** *nous* **irons** *en Grèce cette année.*
                 We shall probably go to Greece this year.

                 Il est vrai qu'il a fait *beaucoup d'efforts récemment.*
                 It is true that he's made a big effort recently.

– **il** + **être** + adjective + **que** + subjunctive
             Ex: **Il était juste que** *vous* **obteniez** *une augmentation.*
                 It was fair that you should get a pay-rise.

                 Il *n'est* pas **rare qu'il pleuve** *en juillet.*
                 It's not rare for it to rain in July.

6 Verbs which are occasionally impersonal

Some personal verbs are used with impersonal *il* in special constructions, but note
the changes of meaning.

(i)   *convenir*

The construction *il convient de* + infinitive is used in formal French like *il faut* +
infinitive when the sense is 'it is appropriate'.
             Ex: **Il convient d'être** *poli, même avec les gens que vous n'aimez pas.*
                 It is advisable to be polite, even with people you do not like.

Note that *convenir* on its own means 'to be suitable', or 'to agree' (with *être* or
avoir: see chapter 9 Perfect, section 3.1).
             Ex: *Demain à dix heures me convient.*
                 Tomorrow at ten o'clock suits me.

                 *Nous sommes convenus/avons convenu de reporter la réunion à la semaine
                 prochaine.*
                 We agreed to postpone the meeting until next week.

(ii)   *sembler*

– *il semble* + adjective + *de* + infinitive is used like *être*
             Ex: **Il semble préférable de les prévenir**.
                 It seems preferable to warn them.

– *il semble que* + subjunctive

Ex: ***Il semble qu'il y ait** beaucoup de monde aujourd'hui.*
It seems there are a lot of people today.

– *il **me** semble que* + indicative

Ex: ***Il me semble que** tu **as maigri**.*
You seem [to me] to have lost weight.

(iii)   **importer**

– *il importe que* + subjunctive

Ex: ***Il importe que** vous ne **soyez** pas en retard.*
It is important that you should not be late.

– *il importe de* + infinitive

Ex: ***Il importe de** ne pas **perdre** de temps.*
It is important not to waste time.

(iv)   **paraître**

– *il paraît que* + indicative

Ex: ***Il paraît que** Catherine **a divorcé**.*
I heard that Catherine has got divorced. / Apparently Catherine has got divorced.

– *il paraît* + adjective + *que* + indicative or subjunctive, depending on the adjective (see chapter 12 Subjunctive, section 4.1)

Ex: ***Il paraît** maintenant **certain que** la droite **va** l'emporter aux prochaines élections.*
It now seems certain that the right will win the next elections.

***Il paraît peu probable que** vous **puissiez** voter si vous n'êtes pas encore inscrit.*
It seems unlikely that you will be able to vote if you have not registered yet.

(v)   **suffire**

– *il suffit que* + subjunctive

Ex: ***Il a suffi que** j'**aie** le dos tourné pour que vous en profitiez.*
I only had to have my back turned for you to take advantage.

– *il suffit de* + infinitive

Ex: *Ça n'est pas difficile à comprendre: **il suffit d'écouter** attentivement.*
It is not difficult to understand – you just have to listen carefully.

(vi)   **valoir**

– *il vaut mieux que* + subjunctive

Ex: ***Il vaudrait mieux que** vous ne **veniez** pas!*
It would be better if you didn't come!

***Il aurait mieux valu que** je **parte** plus tôt.*
It would have been better if I had left earlier.

    − *il vaut mieux* + infinitive

        Ex: ***Il vaut mieux*** *tout* ***faire*** *soi-même.*
        It is better to do everything oneself.

        *C'est à lui de décider s'***il vaut mieux*** tout* ***garder.***
        It's up to him to decide if it's better to keep everything.

    − Note that these two constructions are weaker versions of ***faire mieux de*** +
    infinitive in a **personal** construction.
        Ex: *Vous feriez mieux de ne pas venir.*
        J'aurais mieux fait de partir plus tôt.
        C'est à lui de décider s'il fait mieux de tout garder.

(vii) ***se passer***: *il se passe* + noun

        Ex: ***Il se passe des choses*** *étranges.*
        Strange things are happening.

(viii) ***rester***

    − *il reste* + noun

        Ex: ***Il reste*** *quelques* ***cacahuètes.***
        There are a few peanuts left.

        Il ne ***reste*** *que des* ***cacahuètes.***
        There are only peanuts left.

    − *il reste à* + infinitive

        Ex: ***Il reste à faire*** *les chapitres Deux et Trois.*
        Chapters Two and Three are still to be done.

        Il ne ***reste*** *[plus]* ***qu'à recommencer.***
        All we can do is start again.

(ix) ***arriver***

    − *il arrive que* + subjunctive

        Ex: ***Il arrive qu'***un promeneur* ***se perde*** *dans le maquis* . . .
        Sometimes a rambler gets lost in the bush . . .

    − *il arrive à quelqu'un de* + infinitive

        Ex: ***Il arrive*** *souvent* ***aux promeneurs de se perdre*** *par ici.*
        Ramblers often get lost around here.

        Il leur arrive *souvent* ***de se perdre.***
        They often get lost around here.

    Note that in:
        Il est arrivé un accident.
        An accident has happened.
    arriver is a personal verb used in the impersonal **voice** (see 7 below).

(x) ***se pouvoir***: *il se peut que* + subjunctive

        Ex: ***Il se peut que*** *nous* ***restions*** *quelques jours ici.*
        We might stay here for a few days.

7 Personal verbs in the impersonal voice

The impersonal **voice** (*voix impersonnelle*) is a syntactic construction which can be chosen **instead of** an active or passive voice. It is not to be confused with impersonal **verbs** which cannot be used in any other way. The 'real' or 'semantic' subject of the sentence (see chapter 2 Syntax, section 2.2) follows the verb. However, the verb still agrees with impersonal *il*. The impersonal voice is used in the following cases (see also chapter 18 Active and Passive Voices, section 7.1):

(i)   When a passive form is required and the verb cannot be passive

Only **direct** transitive verbs can be passive. Hence:

Ex: ***Il est rappelé*** *aux étudiants qu'ils ne doivent pas entrer dans la salle d'examen avec des boîtes de bière.*
(*rappeler qch **à qn***)
Students are reminded that they mustn't bring cans of beer into the examination room.

Il est demandé *au public de bien vouloir ne pas fumer.*
(*demander qch **à qn***)
The public is asked to kindly refrain from smoking.

Il *lui **a été permis*** de quitter la salle d'examen avant la fin.*
(*permettre **à qn** de faire qch*)
He/She was allowed to leave the examination room before the end.

(ii)   To emphasize the verb

Impersonal *il* + verb are followed by the 'semantic' subject of the verb, which **must** be indefinite. In order to avoid ambiguity or clumsiness, it is safest to use only verbs which are intransitive in this construction. Note that the past participle is invariable with impersonal *il*.

Ex: *Plusieurs étudiants manquent dans ce groupe.*
→ ***Il manque*** *plusieurs étudiants dans ce groupe.*
Several students are missing from this group.
    but:
Deux personnes ont mangé dans ce restaurant.
Two people ate in that restaurant.
→ ***Il a mangé*** *deux personnes dans ce restaurant.*
He ate two people in that restaurant.

(iii)   To replace pronominal verbs which have a passive meaning (formal French only)

Ex: *Des maisons se sont construites.*
→ ***Il s'est construit*** *des maisons.*
Houses have been built.

Beaucoup de livres se sont vendus à cette exposition.
→ ***Il s'est vendu*** *beaucoup de livres à cette exposition.*
A lot of books were sold at that exhibition.

(iv)   To replace a passive or a construction with *on* + transitive verb (administrative style)

>   Ex: *Deux portefeuilles ont été retrouvés.*
>
>   or:
>
>   *On a retrouvé deux portefeuilles.*
>   → **Il a été retrouvé** *deux portefeuilles.*

20 Pronominal verbs

1 Introduction

Pronominal verbs include three specific features in their conjugation:
- the presence, before the verb, of the pronoun *se* (becoming *me, te, se, nous, vous, se*, according to the subject of the verb)
- the exclusive use, in compound tenses, of the auxiliary *être* whatever the function of *se*
- the fact that they are not used in the double compound tenses

There are two types of pronominal forms:
- a lexical (idiomatic) form
- a constructed form

2 Formation

2.1 *se* and the subject

In the conjugation of a pronominal verb, the pronoun *se* changes according to the person – it always corresponds to the person of the subject.

person subject	reflexive pronoun
je	*me(m')*
tu	*te(t')*
il/elle	*se(s')*
nous	*nous*
vous	*vous*
ils/elles	*se(s')*

Ex: *se promener: je* **me** *promène*   *nous* **nous** *promenons*
               tu **te** *promènes*   *vous* **vous** *promenez*
              il/elle **se** *promène*   *ils/elles* **se** *promènent*

NB: A verb is only pronominal when *se* is the same person as the subject.
      Ex: **Je me** *regarde dans la glace.*
          I am looking at myself in the mirror.
          (*se regarder*: pronominal)

          Il **me** *regarde.*
          He is looking at me.
          (*regarder qn*: not pronominal)

Je le regarde.
I am looking at him.
(*regarder qn*: not pronominal)

2.2   Infinitive and present participle

se changes with the subject, **even** if the verb is in the infinitive or is a present participle (but **not** a past participle: see 4(ix) below).

Ex: *Nous allons nous promener.*
We are going for a walk.

Je leur ai dit de se taire.
I told them to stop talking.

J'ai pris la fuite, me voyant découvert.
I ran away, seeing that I had been discovered.

2.3   Compound tenses

In the compound tenses, all pronominal verbs are conjugated with *être*.

Ex: *se promener*, perfect:

je *me suis* promené(e)	nous *nous sommes* promené(e)s
tu *t'es* promené(e)	vous *vous êtes* promené/ée/és/ées
il *s'est* promené	ils *se sont* promenés
elle *s'est* promenée	elles *se sont* promenées

– the perfect participle is *s'étant* promené
– the past infinitive is *s'être* promené

2.4   Positioning of *se*

The following cases should be examined for both simple and compound tenses and where relevant, for present participles and infinitives. Note that the pronoun *se* is always immediately before the verb (or before the auxiliary in compound tenses), **except** in the case of the affirmative imperative, when it is placed immediately after the verb and hyphenated. This rule only applies if there is no other personal pronoun. See also chapters 14 Imperative and 31 Personal Pronouns.

(i) Negative form

Ex: *Je ne m'ennuie pas!*
I am not bored!

Ils ne se téléphonent jamais.
They never ring one another.

Je leur ai demandé de ne pas se lever tout de suite.
I asked them not to get up straightaway.

(ii)   Interrogative form
        Ex: *Te rappelles-tu?*
           Do you remember?

           Vous êtes-vous décidé?
           Have you come to a decision?

(iii)   Interro-negative form
        Ex: *Ne te rappelles-tu pas?*
           Don't you remember?

           Ne vous êtes-vous pas décidé?
           Haven't you come to a decision?

(iv)   Imperative affirmative
        Ex: *Dépêchons-nous! Dépêchez-vous!*
           Let's hurry! Hurry up!

(v)   Imperative negative
        Ex: *Ne te dépêche pas! Ne vous dépêchez pas!*
           Don't hurry!

(vi)   With other pronouns, see the order in chapter 31 Personal Pronouns.
        Ex: *Je m'en souviens; je m'en suis souvenu.*
           I remember [it]; I remembered [it].

           Vous vous y plaisez? Vous vous y êtes plu?
               or (more formal):
           Vous y plaisez-vous? Vous y êtes-vous plu?
           Do you like it there? Did you like it there?

           Servez-vous en!
           Use it!

3 Categories

There are two main verb categories:
- constructed:
  - reflexive
  - reciprocal
- idiomatic (lexicalized)

Pronominal verbs with a passive meaning, i.e. the middle voice (*voix moyenne*), are treated in chapter 18 Active and Passive Voices, section 5.3.

3.1 Reflexive and reciprocal

When *se* is added to a verb, the meaning remains the same in the pronominal form.

Ex: − *regarder* (to look at sth/sb);
  − *se regarder* is the corresponding pronominal verb. It can be either:
    → reflexive: to look at oneself;
    → reciprocal: to look at one another.
NB: Some pronominal verbs are either only reflexive or only reciprocal.

3.1.1 The verbs

(i) Reflexive verbs

The subject performs the action on him/herself, directly or indirectly.
  Ex: *Je **me** réveille tous les matins à sept heures.*
    (*réveiller qn*: me refers directly to *je*)
    I wake up every morning at 7 o'clock.

  *Il ne **se** rase jamais le dimanche.*
  (*raser qn*: se refers directly to *il*)
  He never shaves on Sundays.

  *Elle **s'**offre des vacances à l'étranger tous les ans.*
  (*offrir qch à qn*: se refers indirectly to *elle*)
  She treats herself to a foreign holiday every year.
See also 3.1.2.2 below.

NB: A lot of English verbs can be used both transitively and intransitively. Note the cases when the English verb is intransitive, or constructed with 'get' + past participle, and corresponds to a reflexive in French. Compare:
  Stop this car! (transitive)
  Arrêtez cette voiture!
    and:
  I am going to stop for a moment. (intransitive)
  *Je vais **m'**arrêter un instant.*

  I washed the glasses. (transitive)
  J'ai lavé les verres.
    and:
  I am going to get washed. (intransitive)
  *Je vais **me** laver.*

  The little girl dressed her doll.
  La petite fille a habillé sa poupée.
    and:
  The little girl got dressed.
  *La petite fille **s'**est habillée.*

  We've lost our keys.
  Nous avons perdu nos clés.
    and:
  We got lost trying to find the short cut.
  *Nous **nous** sommes perdus en essayant de trouver le raccourci.*

(ii) Reciprocal verbs

The action is carried out by at least two elements (animate or inanimate) which act on each other. Since the action is carried out and undergone by each party, the verb is normally plural (except with **on**). Note that *se* can be the direct or indirect object, which is important for agreements (see 3.1.2 below).

> Ex: *Mon chat et celui du voisin **se** battent constamment.*
> My cat and the neighbour's are constantly fighting.
>
> *Ils **se** parlent pendant des heures.*
> They talk to each other for hours.
>
> *Ils **se** sont regardés en silence.*
> They looked at one another in silence.
>
> *On **se** rencontre demain?*
> Shall we meet tomorrow?

(iii) Reflexive or reciprocal meaning?

- If *avec quelqu'un/ quelque chose* is implied, the verb can have a singular subject. Ambiguity with a reflexive meaning is only minimal.

> Ex: *Ton fils s'est encore battu [avec un autre gamin].*
> is likely to be understood as:
> Your son had a fight again.
> rather than:
> Your son beat himself again.
>
> *Je me suis disputée [ce matin avec mon nouveau collègue].*
> I had a row with someone.
> rather than:
> I had a row with myself.

- To stress the reciprocity or to make it clearer in case of ambiguity, *l'un l'autre* (for two people) or *les uns les autres* (for more than two people) can be added to the pronominal verb. If the verb is followed by *à* or *de*, this preposition is placed between *l'un* and *l'autre* or *les uns* and *les autres*.

> Ex: '*Aimez-vous **les uns les autres**.'*
> (*aimer qn*, more than two people)
> 'Love thy neighbour.'
> i.e. Love one another (not: Love yourself!)
>
> *Pourquoi s'accusent-ils **l'un l'autre**?*
> (*accuser qn*, two people)
> Why do they accuse each other?
>
> *Pourquoi s'accusent-ils **les uns les autres**?*
> (*accuser qn*, more than two people)
> Why do they accuse one another?

Note that:

> *Ils se parlent souvent **les uns des autres**.*
> (*parler à qn de qn*, more than two people)
> would be:
> They often talk among themselves about one another.

– Conversely, (*à*) *soi-même*, *moi-même*, etc. can be added to remove any confusion with a possible reciprocal meaning when a reflexive is intended, or simply to stress the reflexive meaning.

> Ex: *Pourquoi **se** parlerait-il **à lui-même**?*
> Why would he be talking to himself?

– It is not always appropriate to add *l'un l'autre* or *les uns les autres* since it places an element of emphasis on the reciprocity. The context is often sufficient to distinguish between the reflexive and the reciprocal meaning. Furthermore, other pronouns may be more suitable.

> Ex: *Les animaux parlent **entre eux**.*
> rather than:
> *?Les animaux se parlent les uns aux autres.*
> Animals talk to each other.

(iv)   *se faire* + infinitive

se can be the complement of the infinitive, but is still placed before *faire*.

> Ex: *Il s'est fait féliciter.*
> He got congratulated.

Other verbs which operate in the same way are *laisser* and verbs of perception: *écouter, entendre, regarder, sentir, voir.*
Note that *se faire, se laisser, se voir* and *s'entendre* can also be used to express the passive (see chapter 18 Active and Passive Voices, section 7.2).

3.1.2   Agreement of past participles

Whether the pronominal verb is reflexive or reciprocal, *se* can be a direct or an indirect object (see 3.1.1 above). This is important for past participle agreement. See also 3.2.2 below.

3.1.2.1   AGREEMENT

The past participle agrees in gender and number with the subject in the following cases ('*se*' is the direct object).

– reflexive:
> Ex: ***Elle s'est** coupée.*
> She cut herself.
> (think of *★Elle a coupé elle-même.*)
>
> ***Elle s'est** pincée pour être sûre de ne pas rêver.*
> She pinched herself to make sure she was not dreaming.

– reciprocal:
> Ex: ***Ils se** sont aimés pendant trois ans.*
> They loved each other for three years.

The past participle does not agree in the following cases:

(i)   When *se* is an indirect object

- reflexive:

> Ex: ***Elle s'est nui_*.**
> (*nuire à qn*)
> She harmed herself.

- reciprocal:

> Ex: ***Elles se** sont promis_ de se revoir.*
> (*promettre à qn*)
> They promised each other to meet again.
>
> ***Ils se** sont écrit_ tous les jours.*
> (*écrire à qn*)
> They wrote to each other every day.

NB: If a **direct** object appears before the verb, the past participle and the object agree in the usual way (see chapter 9 Perfect, section 3.2.1).

> Ex: ***les lettres** qu'ils se sont écrites*
> the letters they wrote to each other

(ii)   When the verb takes a direct object other than *se*

> Ex: *Elle s'est coupé_ **les cheveux**.*
> She cut her hair.
> (**se** is now the **indirect** object;
> think of: *Elle a coupé les cheveux à elle.*)
>
> *Elle s'est pincé_ **le doigt** dans la porte.*
> She trapped her finger in the door.

Compare with 3.1.2.1 above.

3.2   Idiomatic or inherent (lexicalized) pronominal verbs

3.2.1   Categories

There are two categories of idiomatic pronominal verbs.

(i)   Those which, by adding *se* to the verb, acquire a meaning which is linked in some way to that of the original verb. For instance:

attendre (to wait)	→ *s'attendre à* (to expect)
douter (to doubt)	→ *se douter de* (to suspect)
rappeler (to remind)	→ *se rappeler* (to remember)
servir (to serve)	→ *se servir [de]* (to use; to help oneself)
demander (to ask)	→ *se demander* (to wonder, to ask oneself)
taire (to keep sth quiet)	→ *se taire* (to be/remain silent)

(ii)   Those which only exist in the pronominal form. For instance:

s'évanouir	to faint
se fier (à qn/qch)	to trust (sb/sth)
se méfier (de qn/qch)	to mistrust (sb/sth)
se souvenir (de qn/qch)	to remember (sb/sth)
s'adonner à (une tâche)	to devote oneself to (a task)
se désister	to stand down
s'en aller	to go away, to leave
s'évader (de)	to run away, to escape (from)
se méprendre	to be mistaken
se raviser	to change one's mind
se passer de (qch)	to do/go without (sth)
se vanter de	to boast about
s'obstiner à (faire qch)	to persist in (doing sth)
se résigner à (qch)	to resign oneself to (sth)
s'abstenir de (qch, faire qch)	to abstain from (sth, doing sth)
se moquer de (qn/qch)	to make fun of, to laugh at (sb/sth)
se rebeller (contre qn/qch)	to rebel (against sb/sth)
s'habituer à (qch, faire qch)	to get used to (sth, doing sth)
se mettre à (qch, faire qch)	to begin (sth, to do sth)

NB: The **en** of *s'en aller* should in principle appear before the auxiliary (see order of pronouns in chapter 31 Personal Pronouns).
          Ex: *Il s'**en** est allé.*
In informal French however, it is as if *en* formed one word with *aller* rather than standing as a pronoun in its own right.
          *Il s'est **en** allé.*

(iii)   The same pronominal verb can have several constructions, with as many meanings.
          Ex: *se mettre* (to put oneself):
          Mettez-vous là!
          Sit down here! (literally: Put yourself here!)

          *se mettre **à*** (to begin):
          Ils se sont mis à chanter.
          They began to sing.

          se servir (to help oneself):
          Servez-vous!
          Help yourself!

          *se servir **de** qch* (to use sth):
          Tu te sers toujours de mes bigoudis!
          You're always using my curlers!

Note the various translations of *se sentir*:
          Ex: *Je me sens si fatiguée ce matin.*
                    I feel so tired this morning.

Quand il a appris sa promotion, il s'est senti rajeunir!
When he learnt about his promotion, he felt himself growing young again!

Je ne me sens pas le courage de leur annoncer la mauvaise nouvelle.
I do not feel brave enough to tell them the bad news.

Quand nous avons appris la bonne nouvelle, nous ne nous sentions plus de joie!
When we heard the good news, we were beside ourselves with joy!

3.2.2 Agreement

se is part of the verb and cannot be analysed separately. In compound tenses, the past participle agrees with the subject of the verb.

Ex: **Elle s'est rendue** *à Paris en septembre.*
She went to Paris in September.

Note the following exceptions, depending on the meaning of the verb:
- *s'imaginer que* — to imagine that
- *se plaire (à faire qch)* — to enjoy (doing sth)
- *se rendre compte (de qch)* — to realize (sth)
- *se rire (de qn)* — to mock (sb)

With these four verbs, the past participle remains invariable. Compare:

Elles se *sont imaginé_ que nous ne le ferions pas.*
They imagined we would not do it.
          and:
Elle s'était imaginée mariée avec six enfants . . .
She had envisaged herself married with six children . . .

Les enfants se *sont plu_ à embêter ce pauvre chien.*
The children amused themselves teasing this poor dog.
          and:
Elle s'est *beaucoup plue en Tunisie.*
She liked it very much in Tunisia.

Catherine s'est *soudain rendu_ compte de ce qu'elle avait dit.*
Catherine suddenly realized what she had said.

Ils se *sont ri_ de notre frayeur.*
They laughed at our being startled.

4 Translation problems

Pronominal verbs are more frequently used in French than the construction 'verb + oneself' in English. However:

(i)   A pronominal English verb generally corresponds to a French one.

        Ex: He cut **himself**. (reflexive)
             *Il **s'est coupé**.*

             They love **each other**. (reciprocal)
             *Ils **s'aiment**.*

(ii) A pronominal French verb often corresponds to an intransitive verb in English (see 3.1.1(i) above).

        Ex: *Elle **se fatigue** facilement.*
             She **tires** easily.

             *Ils pensent que l'homme **s'est noyé**.*
             They believe that the man **drowned**.

(iii) A pronominal verb in French often corresponds to a verb with a passive meaning in English (see chapter 18 Active and Passive Voices, section 5.3).

        Ex: *Ces manteaux **se vendent** bien.*
             These coats **sell** well.

(iv) The English passive can under certain conditions be translated by the French middle voice with a pronominal verb (see chapter 18 Active and Passive Voices, section 5.3).

        Ex: Metro tickets **can be obtained** at the counter or from the machines.
             *Les tickets de métro **s'obtiennent** au guichet ou dans les machines.*

(v)   The English construction '**get** + past participle/adjective' is often translated by a pronominal verb (see also 3.1.1(i) above).

        Ex: When I saw Lizzy with a frog, **I got angry**.
             *Quand j'ai vu Lizzy avec une grenouille, je **me suis fâchée**.*

             They **are getting married** on Saturday.
             *Ils **se marient** samedi.*

(vi) Pronominal verbs do not indicate a state. For instance, *se lever* indicates the **action** of getting up, while *être levé* indicates a state, which is the result of getting up.

        Ex: *Il **s'est levé** tôt ce matin.*
             He **got up** early this morning.
                 but:
             *Quand je suis arrivé, il **était** déjà **levé**.*
             When I arrived, he **was** already **up**.

(vii) When the subject carries out an action on a part of his/her body, a pronominal verb is used in French rather than a possessive adjective (see also chapter 24 Possessive Adjectives, section 4.5).

        Ex: *Elle **se** lave **les** cheveux tous les jours.*
             She washes **her** hair every day.

(viii) After certain semi-auxiliaries (*faire* and, to a lesser extent, *laisser*), pronominal verbs tend to lose their *se* in the infinitive, particularly in informal French, unless the result is ambiguous.

> Ex: *se taire*:
> *Faites-les **taire**!*
> (not: *Faites-les se taire*)
> Make them stop talking!
>
> *s'asseoir*:
> *Faites-le **asseoir**.*
> Give him a seat.
>
> *s'envoler*:
> *Tu as laissé **envoler** l'oiseau.*
> You let the bird fly away.
>
> *J'ai fait asseoir les enfants.*
> I made the children sit down.
> > but:
> *Je les ai fait **se** sécher devant le radiateur.*
> I made them dry themselves in front of the radiator.
> (*Je les ai fait sécher* = **I dried them**)

Compare:

> *Nous l'avons fait arrêter.*
> We had him arrested.
> > and:
> *Nous l'avons fait s'arrêter.*
> We made him stop.

(ix) Past participles without an auxiliary (used as adjectives) are not preceded by *se*.

> Ex: ***s'agenouiller***:
> *Il y avait dans l'église beaucoup de femmes **agenouillées**.*
> There were a lot of women kneeling in the church.
>
> ***s'évader***:
> *On a recensé plus de trois mille prisonniers **évadés** l'année dernière.*
> Over three thousand prisoner escapes were recorded last year.
>
> ***s'évanouir***:
> *On trouva sur les lieux de l'accident de nombreuses personnes **évanouies**.*
> At the scene of the accident, a lot of people were found unconscious.

21 Modals: *devoir, pouvoir, vouloir*

Vouloir et pouvoir séparent ce qui s'assume de ce qui se vante

1 Introduction

Modalization is the process by which speakers express their attitudes towards what they say to their interlocutors, from necessity or obligation to possibility or permission.

Modal elements are not exclusively verbs. They can also be:
- adverbs (e.g. *probablement, peut-être, sans doute, selon moi, à mon avis, d'après lui, incontestablement, de toute évidence*)
- adjectives (e.g. *possible, probable, éventuel, certain*)
- quotations (in order for the speaker to distance him/herself from the words which the person quoted is using)
- tenses (e.g. some uses of the imperfect)

The basic modal verbs are *devoir* and *pouvoir*, to which *vouloir* can be added; *savoir* and *connaître* can also be considered as modals (these are treated in a separate chapter, 22, owing to the problems which they present for the English-speaker).

Problems occur with these 'modals' (also called 'semi-auxiliaries') because:
- they can take on different meanings depending on the tense or even person used, and on whether the sentence is affirmative or negative
- the same verb in the same tense can have several meanings, determined only by context
- there is no one-to-one correspondence between French modals and the English **would, could, should, ought to**, etc.

This chapter examines the meanings of the three main French modals. This is followed by a brief review of English modals and the way in which they are translated into French.

2 *devoir*

(i)   When *devoir* is followed by a noun, it means *avoir une dette* (**to owe sth to sb**).

Ex: *Vous me devez cinq mille francs.*
       You owe me five thousand francs.

Son professeur l'a beaucoup aidée: elle lui doit tout.
Her teacher has helped her a lot: she owes him/her everything.

(ii)   As a modal or semi-auxiliary, ***devoir*** is followed by an infinitive. It is mainly used to express necessity and obligation. It can also be used to express probability, intention, expectation, logical implication, supposition, suggestion, auto-suggestion, anticipation, reproach and regret.

2.1   Necessity or obligation

Care must be exercised when using the negative form.

(i)   Affirmative form

devoir + infinitive is the equivalent of *il faut que* + subjunctive, and means *être obligé de*. It corresponds in English to **must**, **have to**. Note that the feeling of necessity is stronger with *falloir* than with *devoir* because *falloir* is unambiguous, whereas *devoir* can mean other things (see below). **All the tenses of the indicative** are possible with this meaning. If *il faut que* is used, *faut* reflects the tense.

> Ex: *Je **dois** lui donner une réponse cet après-midi.*
> *Il **faut** que je lui donne une réponse cet après-midi.*
> I **must** give him an answer this afternoon.
>
> *Vous **devrez** me rendre votre devoir demain au plus tard.*
> *Il **faudra** que vous me rendiez votre devoir demain au plus tard.*
> You **will have to** hand in your work to me tomorrow at the latest.
>
> *Nous **avons dû** renvoyer la marchandise défectueuse.*
> *Il **a fallu** que nous renvoyions la marchandise défectueuse.*
> We **had to** send back the faulty goods.
>
> *Quand j'étais à la ferme, je **devais** travailler même le dimanche.*
> *Quand j'étais à la ferme, il **fallait** que je travaille même le dimanche.*
> When I was on the farm, I **had to** work even on Sundays.

The imperfect in the last example indicates something which was **habitual** (see chapter 8 Imperfect, section 3.1(iv)). The imperfect with *devoir* can also denote something which was **intended** (see 2.2 below), but the context should clarify the meaning.

NB(1):   Consider the following example:
> 'He did not want to go home, but he had got to sit down.'
>
> George Orwell, Keep the Aspidistra Flying
> *Il ne voulait pas rentrer chez lui mais il fallait qu'il s'assît.*
> > OR:
> *Il ne voulait pas rentrer chez lui mais il avait besoin de s'asseoir.*
> Hence, here: 'il faut que' = 'avoir besoin de' (see (ii) below).

NB(2):   With an indefinite or impersonal subject, use *il faut que* rather than *cela doit* in the affirmative form.
> Ex: **It has to be** one or the other!
> *Il **faut que** ce soit l'un ou l'autre!*

(ii)   Negative form

The negative of *devoir* is *ne pas devoir, il ne faut pas que*, i.e. to be obliged **not** to do something ('must not'). Note the other negative: *n'avoir pas besoin de, n'avoir pas à* ('not to have to', 'not to be obliged to').

> Ex: *Je **ne dois pas** boire d'alcool avec ce médicament.*
> *Il **ne faut pas** que je boive d'alcool avec ce médicament.*
> I **must not** drink alcohol with this medicine.
>> but:
>
> *Je **n'ai pas besoin de** lui donner de réponse cet après-midi.*
> I **don't have to** give him an answer this afternoon.
> (= there is no need / there is no hurry)
>
> *Je **n'ai pas à** lui donner de réponse.*
> I **don't have to** give him an answer.
> (= nobody is forcing me)
>
> *Cela/Ça **n'a pas besoin** d'être l'un ou l'autre!*
> It does not have to be one or the other!

(iii)   *il faut que* or *on doit*?

It is better to use *il faut que* than *on doit* to translate 'you have to' when the latter is used in a generic sense.

> Ex: You have to be rich to be happy.
>   ('you' = people in general, not **you** in particular)
>   *Il faut être riche pour être heureux.*
>   sounds better than:
>   *On doit être riche pour être heureux.*

A negation of this statement is:

>   You don't have to be rich to be happy.
>   *Il n'est pas besoin d'être riche pour être heureux.*
>   which sounds better than:
>   *On n'a pas besoin d'être riche pour être heureux.*

(iv)   *devoir* and the conditional

– In the affirmative form, *devoir* in the **conditional** denoting obligation is weaker than in the present tense (English uses **should/ought to** instead of **must**).

> Ex: *Ces développements sont dangereux et **devraient** être évités.*
>   These developments are dangerous and **should/ought to** be avoided.

– In the interrogative form, there is a choice: *devoir* in the **conditional** denotes strong obligation while *devoir* in the **imperfect** is much weaker (**should**).

> Ex: **Should** I invite them to dinner, I sometimes wondered, or **should** I suggest a drink at the local pub?
>   ***Devais**-je les inviter à dîner, me demandais-je parfois, ou **devais**-je suggérer*
>   . . .
>
>   or:
>
>   ***Devrais**-je les inviter à dîner, me demandais-je parfois, ou **devrais**-je suggérer* . . .

    – If necessity is meant, use *falloir*, as *devoir* can mean other things (see 2.4 below).

        Ex: I should be leaving.
            (necessity OR anticipation)
            Je devrais partir.
                or:
            Il faudrait que je parte.
                but:
            I would have to be very stupid to do that.
            (necessity)
            Il faudrait que je sois/fusse stupide pour faire cela.
                and not:
            *Je devrais être . . .

(v)   In legal or semi-legal documents (where English uses **shall** + verb), use *devoir* in the **future** + infinitive of verb. Note that in many cases, the present tense can be used without changing the meaning.

        Ex: The landlord shall inform the tenants of any change.
            *Le propriétaire **devra** informer les locataires de tout changement.*
                or:
            *Le propriétaire **doit** informer les locataires de tout changement.*

2.2 Intention or expectation

(i)   Affirmative form

devoir here means *avoir l'intention de (faire qch)* / *être censé (faire qch)*. It corresponds in English to 'to be supposed to do sth'. In the **present** tense, it expresses expectation. In the **imperfect** tense, it suggests that what was intended did not happen; with the first person, that what was intended will not happen.

        Ex: *Je me suis enfin décidé pour les vacances: je **dois** partir pour la Grèce le mois prochain.*
            I have finally made up my mind about my holidays – I'm supposed to be off to Greece next month.
            (= an expectation, which is very close to a future: *je partirai/je vais partir*)

            *Je **devais** partir pour la Grèce le mois prochain.*
            I was supposed to be off to Greece next month.
            (= now it will probably not happen)

            *Vous **deviez** aller à Séville en mai. Y êtes-vous allé finalement?*
            You were supposed to be going to Seville in May. Did you go eventually?
            (the speaker expresses a doubt)

            *Nous **devons** dîner chez les Dupont ce soir.*
            We are supposed to have dinner at the Duponts' tonight.

NB: the context determines whether '*Nous devons*' means 'We must' or 'We are supposed to' (see 2.1).

*Son article sur la réforme constitutionnelle **doit** être publié la semaine prochaine.*
His/her article on the reform of the constitution is to be published next week.

*Son article sur la réforme constitutionnelle **devait** être publié **la semaine prochaine**.*
His/her article on the reform of the constitution was to be published next week.

(ii)   Negative form

Use *ne pas avoir l'intention de* or *n'être pas censé* (present or imperfect).
    Ex: *Nous **ne sommes pas censés** dîner chez les Dupont ce soir.*
         We're not supposed to have dinner at the Duponts' tonight.

2.3   Logical implication or supposition

Here, *devoir* is used with the **present**, **perfect**, **imperfect** or **pluperfect** (English is **must/must have**). See also chapter 7 Future, section 3.1.2.

(i)   Affirmative form
    Ex: *Paul est absent. Il **doit** être malade.*
         Paul is absent. He **must** be ill.

         *Je ne le vois plus: il **a dû** partir.*
         I can't see him – he **must have** left.

         *Le vin **devait** être excellent car ils en ont commandé une deuxième bouteille!*
         The wine **must have** been excellent since they ordered a second bottle!

         *Comme je ne le voyais plus, j'ai supposé qu'il **avait dû** partir.*
         Since I could not see him any more, I assumed he **must have** left.
         NB: French **must** use a pluperfect here.

(ii)   Negative form

– In most cases, the meaning is 'It cannot [possibly] be the case', for which *ne pas **pouvoir*** + infinitive should be used.

– However, if the meaning is 'I don't think that it is the case', then *ne pas **devoir*** should be retained.
    Ex: *Tu viens de manger un énorme sandwich: tu **ne peux pas** avoir encore faim!*
         You've just eaten a huge sandwich – you **can't** possibly still be hungry!

Compare:
         *Le vin **ne pouvait pas** être très bon: ils l'ont à peine touché.*
         The wine couldn't have been very good – they hardly touched it.

and:

*Le vin **ne devait pas** être très bon: ils l'ont à peine touché.*
I don't think the wine was very good – they hardly touched it.

(iii)   Interrogative form

Use *pouvoir* (English uses **can**).
> Ex: ***Peut**-il avoir encore faim?*
> **Can** he possibly still be hungry?

2.4   Suggestion, auto-suggestion OR anticipation

devoir is used in the **conditional present** (in English: **should, ought to**) and expresses a weaker notion of necessity than in a tense of the indicative: see 2.1(i) and (iv) above.

(i)   Advice/suggestion, auto–suggestion
> Ex: *Tu **devrais** aller voir tes parents ce week-end.*
> You **should/ought to** go and see your parents this weekend.

> *Je **devrais** aller chez le médecin.*
> I **should/ought to** go to the doctor's.

> *Il n'est plus le bienvenu: il **devrait** partir maintenant.*
> He has overstayed his welcome: he **should** leave now.

(ii)   Anticipation, prediction
> Ex: *Je **devrais** avoir fini ce chapitre la semaine prochaine.*
> I **should/ought to** have finished this chapter next week.

> *Ils **devraient** être [arrivés] à Paris maintenant.*
> They **should/ought to** be in Paris by now.

2.5   Reproach or regret

devoir can express reproach (2nd or 3rd person) or regret (1st person) with the **conditional perfect** (in English: **should have, ought to have**).

(i)   Reproach
> Ex: *Elle **aurait dû** être plus compréhensive.*
> She should have been more understanding.

> *Vous n'**auriez** pas **dû** venir si tard.*
> You shouldn't have come so late.

(ii)   Regret
> Ex: *J'**aurais dû** faire le premier pas.*
> I should have made the first move.

> *Je n'**aurais** jamais **dû** l'écouter.*
> I should never have listened to him/her.

3 *pouvoir*

As a semi-auxiliary, *pouvoir* is followed by the infinitive. It is mainly used to express ability or possibility, but also to give permission or make a request, or to express a reproach.

3.1 Ability or opportunity

In this sense, *pouvoir* is equivalent to *être capable de, être en état de, avoir la faculté de*.

(i) English uses **can**, 'to be able to' or 'to be capable of'. **All tenses can be used,** but note a slight difference of meaning with the perfect: see (iv).

> Ex: *Je ne **peux** pas le supporter.*
> I can't stand him.
>
> *Elle ne **peut** marcher qu'avec difficulté.*
> She can walk only with difficulty.
>
> *Comme nous avons un grand jardin, les enfants **peuvent** jouer au ballon dehors.*
> As we have a large garden, the children can play ball outside.

(ii) **could** often translates an imperfect OR a conditional (see chapters 8 Imperfect and 13 Conditional). The context should determine which tense is required. Compare:

> When he had been drinking, he **could** (was able to) recite all of Victor Hugo's poems off by heart.
> (when = whenever: situation repeated in the past)
> *Quand il avait bu, il **pouvait** réciter par cœur tous les poèmes de Victor Hugo.*
>> and:
> Things **could** still get worse if we do nothing.
> (consequence of explicit condition expressed by 'if')
> *Les choses **pourraient** encore empirer si on ne fait rien.*
>
> When their parents were out, the neighbours' children **could** watch television until midnight if they wanted to!
> (the context is habitual in the past)
> *Quand leurs parents étaient sortis, les enfants des voisins **pouvaient** regarder la télévision jusqu'à minuit s'ils le voulaient!*
>
> Nobody is looking after them: the neighbours' children **could** watch television until midnight if they wanted to.
> (the context is present and non-habitual)
> *Personne ne les surveille: les enfants des voisins **pourraient** regarder la télévision jusqu'à minuit s'ils le voulaient.*

(iii) Note that 'he could have' + past participle in English, corresponds to *il aurait pu* + infinitive in French (see chapter 13 Conditional).

> Ex: *Tu **aurais pu** les **accompagner** si tu l'avais voulu.*
> You **could have gone** with them if you had wanted to.

(iv) Because the perfect tense refers to things that took place in the past and are seen as completed now, *pouvoir* often means *réussir (à faire qch)* in the perfect.

> Ex: *Heureusement, j'ai pu nager / j'ai réussi à nager jusqu'au rivage.*
> Fortunately I was able/I managed to swim back to the shore.

(v) When **can** means 'to have a skill', use ***savoir*** (see chapter 22 *savoir* and *connaître*, section 2(iv)). Compare:

> Can you swim/drive/cook?
> (= skill)
> ***Savez**-vous nager/conduire/faire la cuisine?*
>> and:
> I can swim to the end of the pier.
> (= ability)
> *Je **peux** nager jusqu'au bout de la jetée.*

(See (iv) above.)

3.2 Mere possibility

(i) Affirmative form

pouvoir can express a mere possibility with the **present**, **imperfect**, **perfect** or **conditional** tenses. Note that English uses:
- **may/might** for a particular possibility (i.e. something which can happen on a particular occasion or to a particular individual)
- **can/could** for a general possibility (i.e. something which can happen on any occasion or to any individual).

In French, *pouvoir* is used, except in cases of ambiguity where it is necessary to choose between *pouvoir* (**can/could**) and *il se peut que* (**may/might**). See below.

> Ex: They have divorced? Alas, these things **can** happen.
> *Ils ont divorcé? Hélas, ce sont des choses qui **peuvent** arriver.*

> My cat's age? He **may** be ten.
> (no ambiguity)
> *L'âge de mon chat? Il **peut** avoir dix ans.*

Ambiguity can arise with the passive:

> Ex: The building **can** be destroyed [by a high wind].
> (= it is possible to destroy the building: general possibility)
> *Le bâtiment **peut** être détruit [en cas de grands vents].*

> The building **may** be destroyed [in tonight's storm].
> (= it is possible that the building could be destroyed: particular possibility)
> ***Il se peut que** le bâtiment soit détruit / Il est possible que le bâtiment soit détruit [durant la tempête de ce soir].*

Compare:

> It **can** be cold in Nice in winter.
> *Il **peut** faire froid à Nice en hiver.*
>> and:
> This **may** be the best solution.
> *Il **se peut que** cela soit la meilleure solution.*

(ii)   Negative form

When the possibility is negated, use *ne pas pouvoir* (**cannot/could not**).
> Ex: *Votre chat **ne peut pas** avoir dix ans! Il a l'air si jeune!*
> Your cat can't be ten years old! He looks so young!

> *Cela **ne peut** [**pas**] être la meilleure solution.*
> This cannot be the best solution.

However, note the difference between:
> He **cannot** be at home.
> (= it is not possible that he is at home: the possibility is negated)
> *Il **ne peut pas** être à la maison.*
> (= *Il n'est pas possible qu'il soit à la maison.*)
>> and:
> He **may not** be at home.
> (= it is possible that he is not at home: here, the possibility is NOT negated)
> *Il **se peut qu'**il ne soit pas à la maison.*
> (= *Il est possible qu'il ne soit pas à la maison.*)

(iii)   Interrogative form

Use *pouvoir* (**can**).
> Ex: *Cela **peut**-il être la meilleure solution?*
> **Can** it be the best solution?

(iv)   *pouvoir* in the **present conditional** can also express ability (see 3.1(ii)), hence it is very close to the notion of general possibility. However, if what is meant is a particular possibility, *il se peut que* + subjunctive should be used. When translating from English, a further difficulty arises from the fact that English often uses **could** as an alternative to **might**. The following simple test can be used: if **could** can be replaced in the sentence by **can**, use *pouvoir* in the conditional, otherwise use *il se peut que* in the appropriate tense + subjunctive.
> Ex: They **could** bar you from the club.
> (= they can, it is in their power)
> *Ils **pourraient** vous interdire l'entrée du club.*
>> but:
> I haven't seen Paul all day. He **could** be working from home.
> *Je n'ai pas vu Paul de la journée. **Il se peut qu'**il travaille à la maison.*

3.3 Giving or being given permission

In this case, *pouvoir* means 'to be allowed to', 'to have permission to'. **All tenses** can be used, but the perfect should be avoided (see 3.1(iv) above). English uses **can** or **may**. Note that French does not distinguish between **can** and the more formal **may**.

> Ex: *Il y a encore des endroits où les femmes ne **peuvent** pas entrer seules.*
> There are still places where women **cannot/may not**/are not allowed to go in by themselves.
>
> *Tu **peux** t'asseoir ici si tu veux.*
> You **may/can** sit here if you wish.

3.4 Requesting permission or action to be carried out

To request permission or to express a polite request (1st person), use *pouvoir* + present indicative or conditional. English uses **can/could** or **may/might**. Note that French does not distinguish between **can** and the more formal **may**, but the conditional is considered more polite than the present indicative.

(i) To request permission

> Ex: ***Puis**-je ouvrir la fenêtre s'il vous plaît?*
> **May/can/could** I open the window please?
>
> ***Pourrais**-je partir un peu plus tôt ce soir?*
> **Could/may** I leave a little earlier tonight?

(ii) To request action

> Ex: ***Pouvez**-vous me déposer à la gare?*
> **Can/could** you drop me off at the station?
>
> ***Pourriez**-vous me déposer à la gare?*
> **Could** you drop me off at the station?
>
> ***Puis**-je vous demander de répéter s'il vous plaît?*
> **May/can** I ask you to repeat that please?
>
> ***Pourrais**-je vous demander de répéter s'il vous plaît?*
> **Could/might** I ask you to repeat that please?

(iii) Negative form

Use *ne pas pouvoir* if the context is unambiguously 'not to have permission'; otherwise, use *ne pas devoir* (**mustn't** or **may not**).

> Ex: *Non, tu **ne peux pas** emprunter mon sèche-cheveux.*
> No, you may not borrow my hair-dryer.
>
> *Vous **ne devez pas** rentrer plus tard que minuit.*
> You mustn't come back later than midnight.

3.5   Reproach

(i)   *pouvoir* can be used to express a reproach (instead of ***devoir*** – see 2.5(i) above) with the **conditional** (present or perfect). English uses **could (have)/might (have)**.

> Ex: *Vous **auriez pu** me le dire! (= vous auriez dû)*
> You could/might have told me!
> (implied: but you didn't)
>
> *Elle **aurait pu** être plus compréhensive! (= elle aurait dû)*
> She could have been more understanding!
> (implied: but she wasn't)

(ii)   The interro-negative form, as in English, reinforces the tone of the reproach. Note that French would use tone of voice here, **not** inversion (see chapter 39 Interrogative Structures, section 2.1.3).

> Ex: *Elle **n'aurait pas pu** me le dire!*
> Couldn't she have told me!
>
> *Vous **n'auriez pas pu** venir plus tôt!*
> Couldn't you have come earlier!

4   *vouloir*

(i)   When followed by a noun (*vouloir qch* or *qn*), *vouloir* simply means 'to want sth or sb'.

> Ex: *Je veux ton dessert!*
> I want your pudding!
>
> *Elle veut la lune!*
> She's asking for the moon!

(ii)   When followed by a *que*-clause (*vouloir que* + subjunctive), *vouloir* means 'to want sth to happen' (see chapter 12 Subjunctive, section 4.1.3(i)).

> Ex: *Je veux que vous soyez prêt à 8 heures précises.*
> I want you to be ready at 8 o'clock precisely.

(iii)   When followed by an infinitive, *vouloir* can have several slightly different meanings depending on the tense and mood, and the use of *bien*. Particular care must be exercised when using a past tense (see below).

4.1   Wishing or wanting

(i)   If *vouloir* means 'wishing or wanting to do sth', **any tense** can be used, but note that the conditional (particularly in the 1st person), is much more polite than the present indicative.

Ex: *Je **veux** partir tout de suite.*
I **want** to leave at once.

*Je **voudrais** partir avant 5 heures.*
I would like to leave before 5 o'clock.

*Le Directeur **veut** vous parler.*
The Manager **wants** to speak to you.

*Il **voulait** venir avec nous.*
He **wanted** to come with us.

Note that 'I **would rather**' is *je préfère/je préfèrerais*.
Ex: I'd rather leave now, if you don't mind.
Je préfère/préfèrerais partir maintenant, si cela ne vous fait rien.

(ii) Use of ***bien*** with conditional

When used with the conditional, *bien* conveys a greater degree of politeness, by increasing the degree of 'wishfulness'.
Ex: *Je **voudrais** [**bien**] partir tout de suite.*
I would [**really**] **like** to leave at once.

*Il **voudrait** [**bien**] venir avec nous.*
He would [**really**] **like** to come with us.

*Il **aurait** [**bien**] **voulu** venir avec nous.*
He **would have** [**really**] **liked** to come with us.

(iii) Use of ***bien*** with other tenses

When used with other tenses, *bien* changes the meaning of *vouloir* to 'to be willing/to be prepared to do sth'.
Ex: *Je **veux bien** partir tout de suite si c'est ce que vous voulez.*
I **am willing** to leave at once if that is what you want.

*Le Directeur **veut bien** vous parler.*
The Manager **is willing** to speak to you.

*Elle **a bien voulu** partir avec eux.*
She **kindly accepted** to leave with them.

*Il **voulait bien** venir avec nous.*
He **was prepared** to come with us.

(iv) Use of the negative form with the perfect and the imperfect

The imperfect reflects a state of mind, whilst the perfect refers to a particular occasion, hence:

Ex: *Elle **ne voulait pas** sortir avec Bruno.*
(state of mind)
She **did not want** to go out with Bruno.
> but:

*Elle **n'a pas voulu** sortir avec Bruno.*
(refusal on a particular occasion)
She **refused** to go out with Bruno.

NB: *bien* should not be used with the negative form with any tense. If emphasis is needed, use *vraiment, absolument,* etc.

Ex: *Je **ne voudrais vraiment pas** partir tout de suite.*
I really would not like to leave right now.

*Je **ne veux absolument pas/vraiment pas** lui parler.*
I really do not want to speak to him/her.

4.2 Polite and formal request or order

(i) *vouloir* is used either in the **present indicative** in a question, or in the **imperative** (see chapter 14 Imperative, section 2.1.2(iii)). English uses **will, would** or an imperative.

Ex: ***Voulez-vous** attendre un instant?*
Will you wait for a moment?

***Voulez-vous** vous taire!*
Be quiet!

***Veuillez** vous asseoir.*
Please take a seat.

(ii) Note that the use of *bien* reinforces the request or order.

Ex: ***Voulez-vous bien** attendre un instant?*
Will you kindly wait for a moment?
> or:
Would you mind waiting a moment?

***Voulez-vous bien** vous taire!*
Do be quiet!

(iii) Note that 'shall I . . . ?' is equivalent to 'do you want me to/would you like me to . . . ?', whereas 'will I . . . ?' is equivalent to 'is it likely that I will . . . ?'
Compare:

Shall I [come and] see you next week?
Voulez-vous que je vienne vous voir la semaine prochaine?
> and:
Will I see you next week?
Vous verrai-je la semaine prochaine?

4.3 Determination

One of the uses of **will/would** + infinitive in the negative form is to express the wish of not wanting something to happen or to be. In this case, *vouloir* is used (and not a future or conditional!). See also chapters 7 Future, 8 Imperfect and 13 Conditional.

> Ex: Please do not insist – he **will not** be disturbed.
> (= He does not want to be disturbed.)
> *N'insistez pas: il **ne veut pas** être dérangé.*
>
> I tried to explain the situation to him but he **would not** listen.
> (= He didn't want to listen.)
> *Je tentai de lui expliquer la situation mais il **ne voulut rien** entendre.*

4.4 Indignant question

> Ex: *Comment voulez-vous y arriver dans ces conditions?*
> (= *Comment voulez-vous que nous y arrivions?*)
> How are we expected to manage in these conditions?
>
> *Que voulez-vous que j'y fasse?*
> What do you want me to do about it?

4.5 Future of present intention

Note that the *si* of condition is never followed by a future or conditional (see chapter 13 Conditional, section 3.2.3). Hence when for instance 'going to' is preceded by 'if', *vouloir* is used – in the present tense.

> Ex: If we **are going to** succeed, we must change our tactics.
> (= If we want to succeed.)
> *Si nous **voulons** réussir, nous devons changer de tactique.*

5 Overview of English modals and their French equivalents

The main English modals are: **can, could, may, might, must/have to, shall, should, ought to, will, would** and **used to**.

5.1 'can'

(i) Ability: *pouvoir*. See section 3.1.
> Ex: I **can** swim to the end of the pier.
> *Je **peux** nager jusqu'au bout de la jetée.*

(ii) Skill: *savoir*. See section 3.1.
> Ex: I **can** swim and dive.
> *Je **sais** nager et plonger.*

(iii) Giving permission: *pouvoir*. See section 3.3.
  Ex: You **can** (**may**) come in.
    *Vous **pouvez** entrer.*

(iv) Asking for permission, request: *pouvoir* (present indicative/conditional). See section 3.4.
  Ex: **Can** (**may**) I open the window?
    ***Puis**-je / **Pourrais**-je ouvrir la fenêtre?*

(v) General possibility: *pouvoir*. See section 3.2.
  Ex: The road **can** be closed, there is a barrier.
    *On **peut** bloquer la route / La route **peut** être bloquée, il y a une barrière.*

  NB: Particular possibility (**may**): *il se peut que* + subjunctive.
    Ex: The road **may** be closed today.
      ***Il se peut que** la route soit bloquée aujourd'hui.*

(vi) Particular impossibility (**cannot**): *ne pas pouvoir*. See section 3.2.
  Ex: This **can't** be true.
    *Cela **ne peut** [**pas**] être vrai.*
    (= Il n'est pas possible que cela soit vrai.)

(vii) Particular possibility, interrogative: *se peut-il que* + subjunctive. See section 3.2.
  Ex: **Can** this really be true?
    ***Se peut**-il vraiment que ce soit vrai?*

(viii) Logical implication or supposition, negative: *ne pas pouvoir*. See section 2.3.
  Ex: There **cannot** be a mistake.
    *Il **ne peut pas** y avoir d'erreur.*

5.2 'could'

(i) Ability: *pouvoir*. See section 3.1.
  Ex: I **could**/was able to swim to the end of the pier.
    *J'ai **pu** nager/J'ai **réussi** à nager jusqu'au bout de la jetée.*

(ii) Skill: *savoir*. See section 3.1.
  Ex: I never **could** play the guitar.
    *Je n'ai jamais **su** jouer de la guitare.*

(iii) Reproach: *pouvoir* (conditional present or perfect). See section 3.5.
  Ex: You **could have** told me.
    *Vous **auriez pu** me le dire.*

    She **could** do it!
    *Elle **pourrait** le faire!*

   (iv)   Giving or being given permission: *pouvoir*. See section 3.3.

           Ex: They **could** go out or stay at home – it was up to them.

                *Ils/Elles **pouvaient** sortir ou rester à la maison, au choix.*

   (v)   Asking permission; request: *pouvoir* (present indicative, conditional). See section 3.4.

           Ex: **Could** I open the windows?

                ***Puis**-je/**Pourrais**-je ouvrir les fenêtres?*

                Could you take me to the station?

                ***Pouvez**-vous/**Pourriez**-vous m'accompagner à la gare?*

  (vi)   General possibility: *pouvoir*. See section 3.2.

           Ex: Things **could** still get worse if we do nothing.

                *Les choses **pourraient** encore empirer si nous ne faisons rien.*

      NB: Particular possibility (= **might**): *il se peut que* + subjunctive.

           Ex: The road **could** (= **might**) be closed today.

                ***Il se pourrait que** la route soit bloquée aujourd'hui.*

5.3 'may'

   (i)   Giving or requesting permission; request (affirmative): *pouvoir*. See section 3.4.

           Ex: You **may/can** borrow my hair-dryer if you like.

                *Tu **peux** emprunter mon sèche-cheveux si tu veux.*

                May/can I open the windows?

                ***Puis**-je ouvrir la fenêtre?*

   (ii)   Refusing permission: *ne pas pouvoir/ne pas devoir*. See section 3.4.

           Ex: You **mustn't/may not** borrow my hair-dryer.

                *Tu **ne peux pas** emprunter mon sèche-cheveux.*

  (iii)   Particular possibility, affirmative: *il se peut que* + subjunctive. See section 3.2.

           Ex: This **may** be true.

                ***Il se peut que** cela soit vrai.*

      NB: General possibility (**can**): *pouvoir*.

   (iv)   The situation or action is negated but not the possibility (**may not**): *il se peut que* + subjunctive negative.

           Ex: He **may never** finish his thesis.

                ***Il se peut qu'il** ne finisse jamais sa thèse.*

   (v)   As a kind of subjunctive auxiliary, e.g. to express a wish. See chapter 12 Subjunctive, section 4.5.

           Ex: **May** she never set foot here again!

                Qu'elle ne remette jamais les pieds ici!

5.4 'might'

(i)   Asking permission; request (rare): *pouvoir*. See sections 3.4 and 3.5.
> Ex: **Might** I smoke in here?
> ***Pourrais**-je fumer ici?*

(ii)   Particular possibility: *il se peut que* + subjunctive. See section 3.2.
> Ex: What he said **might** be true.
> ***Il se peut que** ce qu'il a dit soit vrai.*

5.5 'shall'

For the use of **shall** in the future and immediate future, see chapter 7 Future.

(i)   Polite offer in questions, 1st person: *vouloir* (present). See 4.2(iii) above.
> Ex: **Shall** I come straightaway?
> ***Voulez-vous que je** vienne immédiatement?*

(ii)   Legal and quasi-legal: *devoir* (future). See section 2.1(v).
> Ex: The vendor **shall** maintain the equipment in good repair.
> *Le vendeur **devra** maintenir l'équipement en bon état.*

5.6 'should'

(i)   As a weaker equivalent of **must, should** = **ought to**: *devoir* (conditional present). See sections 2.1(iv) and 2.4.
> Ex: I **should/ought to** go to the doctor's.
> *Je **devrais** aller chez le médecin.*
>
> They **should/ought to** be in Paris by now.
> *Ils **devraient** être à Paris maintenant.*

(ii)   In a question: obligation: *devoir*, conditional (strong), imperfect (weak). See section 2.1(iv).
> Ex: How **should** she present herself to him?
> *Comment **devait**-elle se présenter à lui?*
> > or:
> *Comment **devrait**-elle se présenter à lui?*

(iii)   **should + have**: *devoir* (conditional perfect). See section 2.5.
> Ex: You **should have** been more patient.
> *Vous **auriez dû** être plus patient.*
>
> I **should** never **have** left France.
> *Je n'**aurais** jamais **dû** quitter la France.*

(iv)   After certain impersonal expressions denoting a feeling: expression + *que* + subjunctive. See chapter 12 Subjunctive, sections 4.1.2 and 4.1.4.

Ex: It is strange that you **should** only remember it now.
*Il est étrange que vous ne **vous** en **souveniez** que maintenant.*

I am sorry that he **should** take it so badly.
*Je suis désolée qu'il le **prenne** si mal.*

(v) 1st person: to express a condition with **should** (= **would**) in main clause (conditional). See chapter 13 Conditional, section 3.3.
Ex: I **should/would** go to the doctor's if I were you.
*Si j'étais vous, j'**irais** chez le médecin.*

(vi) 2nd and 3rd persons: to express a condition with **should** in subordinate clause (imperfect).
Ex: If you **should** change your mind, please let us know.
Should you change your mind, please let us know.
*Si vous **changiez** d'avis, prévenez-nous.*

5.7 'will'

For the use of **will** to express the future tense, see chapter 7 Future.
Ex: Will I see you next week?
Vous verrai-je la semaine prochaine?

(i) Polite and formal offers, or requests/orders: *vouloir*. See section 4.2.
Ex: **Will** you have another cup of coffee?
***Voulez**-vous encore une tasse de café?*

Will you [please, kindly, etc.] open the window?
***Voulez**-vous [bien] ouvrir la fenêtre?*

(ii) Determination, mainly in the negative: *ne pas vouloir*. See section 4.3.
Ex: Please do not insist: he **won't** be disturbed.
*N'insistez pas: il **ne veut pas** être dérangé.*

(iii) Prediction.

– specific prediction: *devoir* (conditional). See section 2.4(ii).
Ex: The game **will/must/should** be finished by now.
*Le match **devrait** être terminé maintenant.*

– timeless or habitual prediction (present indicative). See chapter 5 Present, section 3.1.
Ex: Water boils/**will** boil at 100°.
L'eau bout à 100°.

He**'ll** (always) talk for hours if you give him the chance.
*Il **parle** (toujours) pendant des heures si vous le laissez.*

5.8 'would'

(i) To express a wish, with '**would like to**': *vouloir* (conditional). See section 4.1.
Ex: The children **would** [really] **like to** go to Disneyland!
*Les enfants **voudraient** [bien] aller à Disneyland!*

(ii) Polite and formal requests: *vouloir*. See section 4.2.
Ex: **Would** you excuse me?
__Voulez__-vous m'excuser?

(iii) Determination, mainly in the negative: *ne pas vouloir*. See section 4.3.
Ex: I asked him to help me but he **wouldn't**.
*Je lui ai demandé de m'aider mais il **n'a pas voulu**.*

(iv) Habit, action repeated in the past (imperfect). See chapter 8 Imperfect, sections 3.1(iv) and (vi).
Ex: Every morning, he **would** go for a long walk.
(i.e. it was customary)
*Tous les matins, il **faisait** une longue promenade.*

(v) Condition/hypothesis, in main clause (conditional). See chapter 13 Conditional, section 3.2.
Ex: He **would** smoke too much if I didn't stop him.
*Il **fumerait** trop si je ne l'en empêchais pas.*

It **would** be madness to try and do all that.
*Ce **serait** une folie que d'essayer de faire tout cela.*

(vi) Probability: *pouvoir* (conditional). See chapter 13 Conditional, section 3.2.2.
Ex: It's not as strange as you **would** think.
*Ce n'est pas aussi étrange que vous **pourriez** le penser.*

5.9 'must/have to'

(i) Necessity or obligation (**must = have to**). See section 2.1.

– present tense: *devoir* + infinitive, *il faut que* + subjunctive.
Ex: I **must** give him an answer this afternoon.
*Je **dois** lui donner une réponse cet après-midi.*
or:
__Il faut que__ je lui donne une réponse cet après-midi.

– in tenses other than the present, only **have to** is used, but is still either *devoir* or *il faut que*.
Ex: Yesterday, you **had to** be back by 10 o'clock.
*Hier, vous **deviez** être de retour à dix heures.*
or:
*Hier, il **fallait** que vous soyez de retour à 10 heures.*

(ii)   Negative form

     − negative form of **have to**: 'not to have to', 'not to be obliged to' = *n'avoir pas besoin de, n'avoir pas à.*
          Ex: You **don't have to** be back by 10 o'clock.
              *Vous **n'avez pas besoin** (= **n'êtes pas obligé**) d'être de retour avant 10 heures.*

     − negative form of **must**: 'must not': *ne pas devoir, il ne faut pas que.*
          Ex: I **must not** drink alcohol with this medicine.
              *Je **ne dois pas** boire d'alcool avec ce médicament.*
              *Il **ne faut pas que** je boive d'alcool avec ce médicament.*

(iii)   Logical implication or supposition. See section 2.3.
      must = **have to**: *devoir.*
          Ex: There **must/has to** be a mistake.
              *Il **doit** y avoir une erreur.*

NB: The negative form is **cannot**: *ne pas pouvoir.*

5.10   'ought to'

ought to = **should**: *devoir* (conditional present). See sections 2.1(iv) and 2.4.
          Ex: They **ought to/should** be here by now.
              *Ils **devraient** être ici maintenant.*

5.11   'used to'

used to denotes a state or habit that existed in the past but has ceased (= 'formerly' or 'once' + past): imperfect. See chapter 8 Imperfect, section 3.1(vi).
          Ex: He **used to** sing for hours.
              *Il **chantait** pendant des heures.*

22 *savoir* and *connaître*

1 Introduction

The choice between *savoir* and *connaître* can pose problems for the English-speaking learner since both verbs mean 'to know'. In order to solve these problems, it is necessary to take the following into consideration:
- subject and object restrictions
- syntactic restrictions.

It is also important to know how to distinguish between the uses of the perfect (or past historic) and the imperfect according to their meanings.

The basic distinction between the meanings of *savoir* and *connaître* may be presented as follows:
- *savoir* is used to denote knowledge of facts and skills gained through tuition and practice
- *connaître* is used to denote knowledge of facts gained through experience, and knowledge of people through personal acquaintance.

NB: This is only a **general** distinction which does not account for various additions and exceptions which are explained below.

2 *savoir*

Constructions with *savoir* include the following features:
- the subject is always personal
- the object is always non-personal
- *savoir* is followed by a subordinate clause

Therefore *savoir* (and **not** *connaître*) must be used in the following cases:

(i) ***savoir* + *que*-clause**

If there is a subordinate clause introduced by *que*, *savoir* **must** be used.

> Ex: *Je **sais** **qu'il** ne veut pas y aller.*
> I know he does not want to go there.

> *Je ne **savais** pas **que** vous aviez terminé.*
> I did not know you had finished.

293

NB: **ne pas** *savoir* + *que* is impossible in the present tense with *je*.
> Ex: **Je ne sais pas que Paul est ici.*

Indeed, when we say '*je sais*', it implies that what we know is a fact, hence we cannot say at the same time that we do not know it. In English, 'I don't know that he is here' means 'As far as I know, he is not here', which can be translated as:

> *Pour autant que je sache, il n'est pas là.*

The imperfect, however, is possible because the situation can be remedied:
> Ex: *Je ne savais pas que Paul était ici.*
> (→ *maintenant je le sais*)

(ii) **savoir + *si*-clause (indirect question)**

Here, it is the affirmative form which is impossible.
> Ex: **Je sais si Philippe est là.*

Only the negative and interrogative forms are possible.
> Ex: *Je ne **sais** pas **si** Philippe est là.*
> I don't know whether Philippe is here.

> ***Savez**-vous **si** Philippe est là?*
> Do you know whether Philippe is here?

> *Elle ne **savait** pas **si** elle avait gagné quelque chose.*
> She did not know whether she had won anything.

In other words, with *si*, we can only have indetermination.

(iii) **savoir + other indirect questions**

savoir **must** be used in all other indirect questions, i.e. with *quand, comment, pourquoi, où, qui, ce que, quel*, etc. See also chapter 41 Reported Speech, section 3.5.
> Ex: *Je ne **sais** pas **comment** vous faites!*
> I don't know how you manage!

> *Je **sais pourquoi** il n'est pas content.*
> I know why he is displeased.

> *Nous **savons ce qu'**il faut faire.*
> We know what to do.

(iv) **savoir + infinitive**

savoir + infinitive is frequently translated into English by 'can', in the sense of possessing a skill, 'to know how to'. In principle, infinitives are used to express one's aptitude for practical activities. However, if 'can' expresses permission or possibility, *pouvoir* is used (see chapter 21 Modals, section 3). Compare:
> *Je **sais** faire la cuisine, j'ai suivi un cours.*
> I can cook, I went on a course.
> (= I know how to cook.)

and:

*Je **peux** faire la cuisine si vous voulez.*
I can cook if you want me to.
(= I'm offering to do the cooking.)

***Savez**-vous jouer au bridge?*
Can you play bridge?
and:
***Pouvez**-vous jouer au bridge jeudi?*
Can you play bridge on Thursday?

NB(1): I couldn't tell you.
is either:
*Je **ne pourrais** vous le dire.*
or:
*Je **ne saurais** vous le dire.*

NB(2): *Il sait être aimable quand il le veut.*
means:
*Il sait **comment** être aimable.*
hence it does not have the same meaning as:
Il sait nager (which is a skill).

(v) *savoir* + noun + adjective (object complement)

This construction is possible because it is the equivalent to a subordinate introduced by *que*.

Ex: *Je sais cette personne hostile au projet.*
or:
*Je **sais que** cette personne est hostile au projet.*
I know that this person is against the project.

(vi) *savoir* + noun phrase or equivalent

– *savoir* can be followed by a noun phrase if that noun phrase can be replaced by a subordinate introduced by *que*.

Ex: *Je sais votre goût des voyages.*
= *Je sais **que** vous avez le goût des voyages.*

Je sais l'amour que Paul a pour Marie.
= *Je sais **que** Paul aime Marie.*

Je sais un endroit où nous pouvons dîner merveilleusement bien . . .
= *Je sais **qu'**il existe un endroit où . . .*

However, the use of *savoir* here belongs to a formal, even poetic register – *connaître* would normally be expected. Hence we can have either:

*On **connaît l'intérêt** que vous portez à cette affaire.*
or:
*On **sait l'intérêt** que vous portez à cette affaire.*

− Behind a lot of statements with *savoir*, there is an **implied** question.

> Ex: *Je ne sais pas son adresse.*
>> means:
> *Je ne sais pas **quelle** est son adresse.*
>> equivalent to (see 3(i) below):
> *Je ne connais pas son adresse.*

Hence children will say '*Je sais*' meaning, 'Yes, Miss, I know the answer to the question', and not '*Je connais'.
Similarly:

> *Je sais l'heure (= Je sais **quelle** heure il est.)*
> *Je sais le nom de ton frère (= Je sais **quel** est son nom.)*

− In most cases, the use of *savoir* + noun phrase is considered as the result of learning, i.e. *J'ai appris, donc je sais.* This is opposed to the result of an acquaintance which is expressed by *connaître*, i.e. *J'ai rencontré, donc je connais.* (See 3 below.)

The choice of verb therefore depends on the **relation between the subject and the object**. Hence, with *savoir*, the direct object is a noun (generally abstract) or an indefinite pronoun (which does not refer to a person). The knowledge is understood to be complete, categorical and precise because *savoir* is achieved after thinking or reasoning, learning through study or experience, or being told something or knowing something off by heart.

> Ex: *Il **sait** sa leçon/sa récitation/ses tables de multiplication.*

All these nouns refer to something which can be learnt off by heart, with a method. Hence *apprendre un poème* (to learn a poem) is not the same thing as *apprendre une nouvelle* (to hear some news).
Note that we can have:

> *Je sais les mathématiques, donc je suis mathématicien.*
>> and also:
> *Je sais l'anglais, l'allemand*, etc.
>> but not:
> **Je sais la philosophie, la géographie*, etc.

This is perhaps because it is considered that languages and mathematics can be 'mastered' in a way that other topics of investigation cannot!
Other examples (with indefinite pronouns):

> *Je **sais** tout sur les chauves-souris d'Amérique du Sud.*
> I know all about South American bats.

> *Je n'en **sais** rien.*
> I don't know [anything about it].
>> not to be confused with:
> *Je n'y **connais** rien.*
> I am not knowledgeable, I am not competent.

> *Je voudrais en **savoir** plus.*
> I would like to know more [about it].

(vii) **savoir in idioms**

> Ex: *qui vous savez*
> you know who
>
> *Il n'est pas venu, que je sache.*
> He did not come, as far as I know.

3 *connaître*

Constructions with *connaître* include the following features:
– the subject can be personal or non-personal
– the object can be personal or non-personal
– *connaître* can **only** be followed by a noun phrase

Therefore *connaître* (and **not** *savoir*) must be used in the following cases:

(i) **connaître + noun phrase or equivalent**

The verb *connaître* conveys the idea that something already exists which has been encountered or come across.

– The direct object (a noun phrase or pronoun) is generally a person, animal, place, concrete object, or a state of mind or body.

– The knowledge is neither complete nor categorical. It is generally limited to an acquaintance with the subject. Since the person, object or situation has already been seen or met, it is recognizable. Therefore *connaître* conveys the idea of simply knowing something in the sense of being familiar with or having an understanding of it.

> Ex: *Ils **connaissent** bien les Durand.*
> They know the Durands quite well.
>
> *Je **connais** très bien New York et Tokyo.*
> I know New York and Tokyo very well.
>
> *Tu **connais** ce magasin?*
> Do you know this shop?
>
> *Quand il était jeune, il **a connu** la misère.*
> When he was young, he experienced poverty.
>
> *Ce pays **connaît** de grandes difficultés.*
> This country is experiencing great difficulties.

(ii) **connaître in idioms**

– *s'y connaître (en qch)* = to know all there is to know about sth/to be an expert in sth.

> Ex: *La mécanique? Je m'**y connais**.*
> I know my mechanics.

– *Ça me connaît* means the same thing, but in a more familiar register.

Both imply some kind of **competence** or **expertise**, hence we cannot really say:

> *★?L'Angleterre, ça me connaît.*

unless the speaker gives lectures on England, hence it would be a **topic** that he/she knows.

4 *savoir* and *connaître*

When the object is a noun phrase, but the knowledge is either incomplete, uncategorical or imprecise, *connaître* can be used, hence there is often a choice (compare with 2(vi) above). For instance, we can say either:

> *Je **sais** le théorème d'Euclide.*
> (= I know it by heart and am able to use it.)
>> or:
> *Je **connais** le théorème d'Euclide.*
> (= I know of its existence but do not necessarily know how to use it.)

Similarly:

> *Elle **sait/connaît** le latin et le grec.*
> She knows Latin and Greek.

> *Nous **savons/connaissons** la réponse à votre question.*
> We know the answer to your question.

> *Je **sais/connais** la différence entre un chameau et un dromadaire.*
> I know the difference between a camel and a dromedary.

> *Ils **savent/connaissent** la grammaire française.*
> They know French grammar.

> *Savez-vous/**Connaissez**-vous le nom de ce monsieur?*
> Do you know the name of that gentleman?

> *Je **sais/connais** tous leurs arguments.*
> I know all their arguments.

Compare:

> *Je ne veux pas le **savoir**.*
> I don't want to know about it.
>> and:
> *Je ne veux pas le **connaître**.*
> I don't want to meet him.
>> but:
> *Je ne veux pas **connaître** vos excuses.*
> I don't want to know your excuses.

5 Perfect/past historic or imperfect?

savoir and *connaître* take on a special meaning when used in the perfect/past historic.

(i) **savoir**, + a notion of date, means 'to learn', 'to find out'.

    Ex: ***J'ai su** que Paul avait réussi son permis de conduire quand j'ai téléphoné à sa mère!*

    (= j'ai appris, j'ai découvert)

    I learnt that Paul had passed his driving test when I phoned his mother.

        but:

    *Je **savais** que Paul réussirait son permis de conduire du premier coup!*

    I knew that Paul would pass his driving test first time round!

(ii) **connaître**, + a notion of date, means 'to meet for the first time'.

    Ex: ***J'ai connu** Paul en 1968.*

    (= j'ai rencontré Paul pour la première fois)

    I met Paul in 1968.

        but:

    *Je **connaissais** Paul en 1968.*

    I knew Paul in 1968.

3 Determiners and prepositions

23 Articles

1 Introduction

An article precedes a noun. Its role is to introduce the noun in the discourse. The article also indicates the gender (masculine/feminine) and the number (singular/plural) of this noun. Together with possessive and demonstrative adjectives, articles belong to the subclass of determiners which cannot be combined amongst themselves. They can however be combined with some of the indefinite determiners (e.g. **tous les** *chats*; **les autres** *chats*).

There are three kinds of articles: definite, indefinite and partitive. A noun can also appear without a determiner (the 'zero article'). There is no one-to-one correspondence between English and French as regards these four categories, hence a French definite article, for instance, may be a zero article in English.

	singular		plural
	M	F	M and F
definite article	*le* *l'*	*la* *l'*	*les*
indefinite article	*un*	*une*	*des*
partitive article	*du* *de l'*	*de la* *de l'*	*des*

NB: *des* is considered as either the plural of the partitive or of the indefinite article (see section 4.2.2 below).

Cases when the English possessive adjective is rendered by the definite article in French are treated in chapter 24 Possessive Adjectives, section 4.

See also chapters 26 Prepositions, 30 Comparatives, 36 Indefinite Words, 37 Numbers, 38 Negative Structures and 39 Interrogative and Exclamative Structures.

2 The definite article

The definite articles are: *le*, *la*, *l'*, *les* (**the**). They are **specific** determiners of the noun (with possessive and demonstrative adjectives).

2.1 Forms

(i) *le* and *la* become *l'* before a word beginning with a vowel or a mute '*h*'.

Ex: *l'hôtel*; *l'Alsace*; *l'héroïne*
(Thus *l'* does **not** indicate the gender of a noun.)
but:
le hibou; *la Hongrie*; *le héros*

(ii) *le* and *les* contract with prepositions *à* and *de* to form:

à + *le* = *au*	*à* + *les* = *aux*
de + *le* = *du*	*de* + *les* = *des*

Ex: *Nous allons **au** marché.*
*Paul vit **aux** Pays-Bas.*
*Voici la place **du** marché.*
*le niveau de vie **des** Hollandais*

(iii) *à l'* / *de l'* and *à la* / *de la* do not contract.

Ex: *Ils vont **à l'**église tous les dimanches.*
*les victimes **de l'**explosion*
*Nous passons nos vacances **à la** campagne.*
*Voici la place **de la** République.*

NB: It is a common mistake to confuse the definite articles and the direct object pronouns *le* and *les* (see chapter 31 Personal Pronouns, sections 2.2.2.2 and 2.2.2.3). The latter do **not** contract with *à* or *de*, and are followed by a **verb** rather than a noun.

Ex: *Il a promis **de le** faire.*
He has promised to do it.

*Je me suis décidé **à les** acheter.*
I have decided to buy them.

2.2 Uses

When we speak or write, the 'objects of the world' we mention are either:

a) presented as **existing** but not immediately identifiable by one of the interlocutors, or even both, if preceded by:
– an indefinite article: *un, une, des*
– a partitive article: *du, de la, des*
– a numeral adjective: *un, deux, trois . . .*
– an indefinite adjective: *quelques, peu de . . .*

Ex: ***Une** étudiante est venue me voir hier. Elle m'a dit avoir **quelques** problèmes avec les articles définis.*

or:

b) presented as immediately **identifiable** by both speaker and interlocutor if preceded by:
− a definite article: *le, la, les*
− a demonstrative adjective: *ce(t), cette, ces*
− a possessive adjective: *mon, ton, son . . .*

Identification can be achieved either in the **situation**, i.e. the 'surrounding world' and/or our knowledge of it, or in the **linguistic context**. In any given text, there will normally be a mixture of both identification in situation and in context.

2.2.1   *Identification in situation*

The object has not been introduced in the discourse before but can be identified 'in the situation'. Objects which can be identified in the situation include:
− objects which are physically present in the environment shared by speaker and interlocutor, or present in their minds, and
− objects which exist in the cultural knowledge (called 'extra-linguistic knowledge' or 'knowledge of the world') shared by speaker and interlocutor. The knowledge includes: abstract nouns (*l'amour, la beauté*), abstractions of concrete nouns (countable: *le chat*; uncountable: *l'or, le sang*), i.e. taken in their generic sense, complete dates (*le 6 juillet 1983*), 'unique' objects (*le soleil, la lune*) and proper nouns.

In all those cases, there is a presumption of **identification**: the definite article is used because the speaker presumes that the interlocutor can identify the entity referred to. Note however that not all proper nouns are preceded by the definite article: see 2.2.1.5, 2.2.3, 3.2.5 and 4.2.1 below.

2.2.1.1   OBJECTS IDENTIFIED IN THE ENVIRONMENT

Objects can be pointed to by the speaker (**exophora**) or unambiguously identified by the interlocutor in the shared environment (physical or mental).

Ex: *Où sont **les** chats?*
Where are **the** cats?
i.e. the speaker's own or his/her interlocutor's cats.

*Excuse-moi, je suis en retard: **la** voiture ne voulait pas démarrer.*
I'm sorry I'm late: **the** car didn't want to start.
i.e. the car normally used by the speaker.

*Fermez **la** porte!*
Close **the** door!
i.e. the only one to be open in the room where both the speaker and the interlocutor are.

In all the above examples, the referent is identifiable in the discourse **situation** shared by the interlocutors. This is often called the **deictic** use of the definite article. In this particular case, there is generally a definite article in English as well.

2.2.1.2   ABSTRACT NOUNS

Concepts, ideas, are preceded by the definite article.

Ex: *J'ai étudié **la** philosophie pendant cinq ans.*
I studied philosophy for five years.

***La** parole est d'argent mais **le** silence est d'or.* (proverb)
Words are silver but silence is golden.

***Le** communisme est mort.*
Communism is dead.

***L'**union fait **la** force.* (proverb)
Unity means strength.

*Je n'aime pas **le** vert.*
I don't like green.

*de **la** naissance jusqu'à **la** mort*
from birth to death

***L'**art est le moyen d'obtenir **la** vérité ou **la** connaissance.*
Art is the means to obtain truth or knowledge.

Note that English does **not** use the definite article here.

Hence abstract nouns also include names of languages and other subjects of study (note the absence of capital letters in French).

Ex: *Nous étudions **le** français, **les** mathématiques et **l'**histoire.*
We are studying French, maths and history.

NB: When the name of a language follows the verb *parler* without modification, there is generally no article.

Ex: *Il parle anglais; elle parle français et allemand.*

With modification, the article is optional.

Ex: *Il parle seulement [l']anglais.*
Elle parle un peu [le] français et très bien [l']allemand.
Il parle [l']allemand sans accent.

With other verbs, the definite article is kept all the time.

Ex: *J'apprends **le** russe.*
*Je comprends **le** japonais.*
*Le danois ressemble **au** suédois?*

2.2.1.3   ABSTRACTIONS/GENERALIZATIONS OF COUNTABLE NOUNS

(i) **Plural**

Generalization is normally expressed by the plural and envisages the noun as representing a class or species, i.e. **all** the members of a particular category, as opposed to only one member, or some specified members.

Ex: ***Les*** *mouches ont six pattes mais **les** araignées en ont huit.*
Flies have six legs but spiders have eight.

We are not talking about any particular flies or spiders but about all the members of these two groups of insects: this is called the **generic** sense, and the nouns are **generalized**.

Other examples:
*La nuit, tous **les** chats sont gris.* (proverb)
All cats are grey in the dark.

*Il faut avertir **les** gens des dangers du désarmement unilatéral.*
People should be warned against the dangers of unilateral disarmament.

*Les droits **des** (= de **les**) femmes se sont améliorés.*
Women's rights have improved.

Note that in this case, English does **not** use any article.

(ii) **Singular**

If a noun refers to a class name (abstraction), as opposed to an individual representative, it takes a definite article in English and French. This is very close to the idea of generalization, which is why the two categories are often merged in grammar books. Hence we could also say, in a scientific register:
Ex: ***La*** *mouche a six pattes, mais **l'**araignée en a huit.*
The fly has six legs but **the** spider has eight.

Note that **man** is a special case as far as English is concerned, in that it does not take the definite article in its generic sense.
Ex: ***Le*** *chien est le meilleur ami de **l'**homme.*
The dog is _ man's best friend.
The plural, 'men', however, can also be used in a generic sense. Hence:
Ex: *Nous allons parler aujourd'hui de **l'**homme au travail.*
We are going to talk today about _ man at work.
or:
*Nous allons parler aujourd'hui **des** (= de **les**) hommes au travail.*
We are going to talk today about men at work.

Le *travail **du** (= de **le**) grammairien est ingrat.*
The grammarian's work is unrewarding.
Here, *'le travail'* is specific, identified by *'du grammairien'* (see 2.2.2.2 below) whereas *'le grammairien'* is generic.

2.2.1.4 ABSTRACTION/GENERALIZATION OF UNCOUNTABLE NOUNS

Names of substances (in the singular) are also often used in their generic sense. They are identifiable because they belong to an extra-linguistic world that all interlocutors are supposed to know about. Note that there is **no** article in English.

Ex: *Le bois n'est plus guère utilisé pour le chauffage domestique.*
Wood is no longer used all that much for domestic heating.

Le vin est cher en Angleterre.
Wine is expensive in England.

La bière à la pression est meilleure que la bière en bouteilles!
Draught beer is better than bottled beer!

Compare with:
Le teck est un bois très dur.
Teak is a very hard wood.
(See section 3 below.)

Va chercher du bois pour faire du feu!
Go and fetch some wood to make a fire!
(See section 4 below.)

NB: The definite article (singular or plural) to express generalization is used in particular after verbs *aimer, adorer, préférer, détester.*

Ex: − with uncountable nouns:
J'aime bien le thé mais je préfère le café.
I like tea but I prefer coffee.

− with countable nouns:
Mes enfants détestent les légumes mais adorent les fruits.
My children detest vegetables but adore fruit.

2.2.1.5 GEOGRAPHICAL NAMES

(For the gender of geographical names, see chapter 27 Nouns, section 2.)

2.2.1.5.1 **Names of countries, etc.**

The definite article is used before the names of countries, provinces, large islands, continents, mountains, seas, lakes, rivers and famous buildings (but see exceptions below).

Ex: *la France* — France
le Portugal — Portugal
les Etats-Unis — the United States
la Provence — Provence
le Kent — Kent
la Corse — Corsica
l'Europe — Europe
les Alpes — the Alps
la Méditerranée — the Mediterranean Sea
la Seine — the Seine
la Tour Eiffel — the Eiffel Tower

NB: There is no article before e.g. *Israël, Monaco, Andorre, Cuba, Chypre, Malte.*

2.2.1.5.2 *de, à* + **masculine names of countries, etc.**

The article is used with both prepositions.

(i) **With the preposition *de***

Whether it introduces a noun complement, an indirect object or an adverb phrase of place ('from'), the article is used with nouns that are masculine singular (→ ***du***) or masculine plural (→ ***des***).

> Ex: *Ils sont revenus **du** Japon hier.*
> They came back from Japan yesterday.
>
> *J'aime beaucoup le café **du** Brésil.*
> I like Brazilian coffee very much.
>
> *Je ne connais pas très bien l'histoire **des** Pays-Bas.*
> I do not know the history of the Netherlands very well.

Compare:

> *Parlez-moi **du** Mont-Blanc!* (***le** Mont-Blanc*)
> and:
> *Je me souviens **de** Monaco.* (*Monaco*: no article)

(ii) **With the preposition *à***

The same applies: *à* → ***au*** or ***aux***:

> Ex: *Je ne suis jamais allé **au** Portugal.*
> I have never been to Portugal.
>
> *J'ai habité **aux** Etats-Unis pendant dix ans.*
> I lived in the United States for ten years.

Compare:

> *Le Hokkaido appartient **au** Japon.* (***le** Japon*)
> and:
> *Je vais **à** Cuba l'année prochaine.* (*Cuba*: no article)

However, there are exceptions: for instance, *dans* is used for provinces.

> Ex: *Elle est née **dans le** Jura.*
> *J'habite **dans le** Kent.*

2.2.1.5.3 ***de, à* + feminine names of countries, etc. (or any country beginning with a vowel)**

(i) **The article is used:**

– With the preposition ***de*** or ***à*** introducing an indirect object. Compare:
> *Parlez-moi **de la** Bretagne; je pense encore **aux** (= à les) Vosges.*
> Tell me about Brittany; I am still thinking about the Vosges.
> and:
> *Parlez-moi **d'**Israël.* (*Israël*: no article)
> Tell me about Israel.

– With the preposition ***de*** introducing a noun complement whose referent is specific (but see also (ii) below).
> Ex: *le Président **de la** France*
> *la géographie **de l'**Allemagne*
> *le nord **de l'**Iran*

In all the above examples the main referent is the second noun. Hence we consider e.g. Germany, then we choose to talk about its geography (as opposed to its history or economy, etc.).

– With the preposition *à* introducing an indirect object.
> Ex: *L'Anatolie appartient à la Turquie.*
> Anatolia belongs to Turkey.

(ii) **The article is not used:**

– With the preposition *de* introducing a noun complement with an adjectival value (unlike masculine countries).
> Ex: *la Reine d'Angleterre, le trône d'Espagne, la couronne de Suède, l'ambassadeur de Turquie, l'ancien shah d'Iran*
> (i.e. one of a number of queens, thrones, etc.)
> *les vins de Touraine, les herbes de Provence, le café de Colombie*
> (i.e. a sub-class, or category, of wines, herbs, coffees)
> *l'histoire de France*

In all the above examples we consider one concept only. For instance, we consider French history as a discipline – as opposed to geography, chemistry, etc., or the wines of Touraine – as opposed to those of Bordeaux, etc.

– Note that adverb phrases of place, **to** (a place) or **in** (a place), are introduced by *en* on its own; and **from** (a place) by *de* on its own (unlike masculine nouns).
> Ex: *Je suis rentré de Suisse hier.*
> I came back **from** Switzerland yesterday.
>
> *J'aimerais bien habiter en Provence!*
> I would like to live **in** Provence!
> and:
> *Je ne suis jamais allé en Afrique du Sud.*
> I have never been **to** South Africa.

However, there are exceptions. For instance, *dans* (to/in) + article is used for mountains.
> Ex: *Ils sont allés faire du ski de fond dans les Vosges.*
> They went cross-country skiing in the Vosges.

2.2.1.5.4 **Names of towns**

(i) There is no article before names of towns, e.g. *Londres, Paris, Berlin*, unless they are modified. Compare:
> *Tout le monde aime Paris!*
> Everybody loves Paris!
> and:
> *Je parle du (= de le) Londres d'avant-guerre.*
> I am talking about pre-war London.
>
> *Nous avons étudié la Rome antique à l'école.*
> We studied Ancient Rome at school.

(ii)   'to'/'in'/'at' (+ town) = **à**

        Ex: *Je vais **à** Paris tous les mois.*
            I go **to** Paris every month.

        *J'ai rencontré mon mari **à** Londres.*
            I met my husband **in** London.

        *Le prochain match aura lieu **à** Wembley.*
            The next match will take place **at** Wembley.

(iii)   'from' (+ town) = **de**

        Ex: *Je suis revenue **de** Paris hier.*
            I returned **from** Paris yesterday.

(iv)   A definite article is sometimes included in the name of a town.

        Ex: *Le Mans, Le Havre, Le Bourget, La Rochelle,*
            Le Caire (Cairo), *La Mecque* (Mecca),
            La Havane (Havana), *La Haye* (The Hague),
            La Nouvelle-Orléans (New Orleans)
        Ex: ***Le** Caire est la capitale de l'Egypte.*
            Cairo is the capital of Egypt.

In this case, *le* and *les* contract with *à* or *de*:
        Ex: *Tous les ans, je vais aux 24 heures **du** Mans.*
            Every year, I go to the Le Mans 24-hour race.

        *Pour aller à Southampton, je prends le bateau **au** Havre.*
            To go to Southampton, I take the boat at Le Havre.

        *J'ai pris l'avion à l'aéroport **du** Bourget.*
            I took the plane at Le Bourget airport.

2.2.1.5.5   Names of streets

Streets and street numbers are generally preceded by the definite article, unlike in English, except when giving one's address, when it is not compulsory. Compare:

        *J'habite **dans la** rue de l'Université/**au** (= à **le**) 22 rue de l'Université.*
           or:
        J'habite _ rue de l'Université/_ 22 rue de l'Université.
           and:
        *Le Ministère de la Défense se trouve à l'angle de **la** rue de l'Université et **du** (= de **le**) boulevard Saint-Germain.*

        *Le Théâtre Montparnasse se trouve **au** 31 rue de la Gaîté.*

2.2.2   *Identification in context*

The object has already been introduced in the discourse and thus derives its identification from the **linguistic context**. This is the **specific** use of the definite article. Note that English also uses the definite article in these cases.

We have contextual identification in the following cases:

2.2.2.1   OBJECT ALREADY INTRODUCED IN DISCOURSE

Consider the following examples:

> Ex: *Un chat est arrivé chez moi un beau matin. Dans la cuisine, **le** chat s'est assis devant le réfrigérateur.*

> *Je voulais t'apporter un livre et des revues mais j'ai oublié **le** livre.*

In both the above cases, the referent is identifiable because it has already been introduced in the context. This is called the **anaphoric** use of the definite article, and brings the function of the definite article close to that of the pronoun. Indeed we could have:

> *Un chat . . . **Il** s'est assis . . .*

See chapter 31 Personal Pronouns, section 1.2.

2.2.2.2   OBJECT IDENTIFIED BY EXPANSION OF THE NOUN PHRASE

The object is identified in the context **immediately after** being mentioned, by an expansion of the noun phrase (see chapter 2 Syntax, section 2.1).

These expansions of the noun phrase can be:
− a noun complement
− a relative clause
− an apposition
− an adjective
NB: Not all expansions of the NP provide identification (see below).

Consider the following examples:

> **1** ***Le chat** que j'ai recueilli ce matin est en train de boire son lait dans la cuisine.*

'*le chat*' is identified by its expansion, the relative clause '*que j'ai recueilli ce matin*'.

> *Mettez **le livre**, celui en haut à gauche, à côté des autres.*

'*le livre*' is identified by its expansion, the apposition '*celui en haut à gauche*'. Note that outside any other context, '*autres*' must be identified in the situation.

> *Je connais **la sœur** de Céline.*

'*la sœur*' is identified by its expansion, the noun complement '*de Céline*'.

> **2** *Il leur a donné une idée **des** (= de les) sentiments et **des** (= de les) opinions partagés par ses collègues.*
>
> He gave them an idea **of the** feelings and opinions shared by his colleagues.

The definite article may not appear as such if combined with *à* or *de*, but is still grammatically present. Furthermore, since prepositions must be repeated in French (see chapter 26 Prepositions, section 7), then the contracted form of the 'article + preposition' must be used with each term in a coordination or juxtaposition. This is not necessarily the case in English.

> **3** *Le formidable succès de Frédéric Dard (alias San Antonio) n'étonne plus personne aujourd'hui.*

Here, the adjective '*formidable*' is not sufficient to identify the noun phrase '*le succès*' ('*Le formidable succès n'étonne plus personne aujourd'hui*' still leaves one to wonder 'Whose?' or 'Which?'). It is the prepositional phrase (the noun complement) *'de Frédéric Dard'* which is needed to justify the presence of the definite article.

NB: Proper nouns are by definition identified in the situation, but combined with titles, the linguistic context may have a role to play as well.

> **4** *Prenez votre livre à **la** page 32.*
> Open your books at page 32.

> (in a hotel): ***La** chambre 22 est libre.*
> Room 22 is free.

'la page' and *'La chambre'* are identified by their respective number. Note that English does not use any article here.

2.2.3   *Proper names and titles*

(i)   The definite article is used before most **titles**, unlike in English.
> Ex: ***le** Président Mitterrand*
> President Mitterrand

> ***la** Reine Elizabeth II, **le** Prince Charles*
> Queen Elizabeth II, Prince Charles

(Note that English says 'Queen Elizabeth **the Second**', whilst French says '***La** Reine Elizabeth **Deux**'*.)

> *J'aime les cours de grammaire **du** (= de le) professeur Martin.*
> I like Professor Martin's grammar lectures.

> *Vous devriez en parler **au** (= à le) Dr Dupont.*
> You should tell Dr Dupont about it.

In the above examples, *'la reine'*, *'le professeur'*, etc. are identified by the proper nouns that follow.

NB: The title of *Maître (Me)*, reserved for barristers, is used **without** an article.
> Ex: *Maître Seriès a accepté de défendre l'accusé.*
> Mr Seriès has agreed to defend the accused.

(ii)   For **formal forms of address**, the title should be preceded by *Monsieur, Madame*, etc.
> Ex: *Monsieur le Président*
> *Madame la Duchesse; Madame la Directrice*
> *Messieurs les voyageurs; Messieurs les délégués*

NB: In ceremonious forms of address, *Monsieur, Madame*, etc. can also precede **possessive adjective** + noun.
> Ex: *Comment se porte Monsieur votre père?, Madame votre mère?*, etc.

(iii)   The definite article is neither used before a proper noun, nor *Monsieur/Madame/Mademoiselle* followed by the name of the person.
> Ex: *Nous avons écouté le discours de François Mitterrand.*
> *J'en ai parlé à Madame Grinberg.*

Exceptions:

– The noun is qualified.

> Ex: *la brave Madame Dupont*; *le grand Balzac*
> the good Mme Dupont; the great Balzac

> *Je te parle de la Marie de Fernand, pas de celle de Robert.*
> I'm talking about Fernand's Marie, not Robert's.

> *Le Martin que je connais n'est pas si mal élevé!*
> The Martin I know is not so badly behaved!

– In some regional dialects, it is common to add the definite article before proper nouns, particularly first names, even when not qualified.

> Ex: *Comment ça va, la Marie?*
> (addressing the person OR enquiring about the person)
> How's our Marie?

> *Tu as vu le Joseph aujourd'hui?*
> Have you seen our Joseph today?

This practice should not be imitated!

NB: The plural can be used, as in English, but note the absence of the '*s*' in French.

> Ex: *Je connais bien les Dupont.*
> I know **the Dupont<u>s</u>** very well.

– The definite article can form part of a person's name, e.g. *La Rochefoucauld, La Bruyère, La Fontaine, Le Sage*. Here, the definite article does not normally contract with *de* or *à*, but again, there are exceptions!

> Ex: *L'architecture de Le Corbusier* OR *du Corbusier.*
> but:
> *Les peintures du Gréco, du Titien*, etc.

2.2.4   Specification or generalization?

While French uses the definite article both for specification on the one hand, and generalization or abstraction on the other, English does not use any article, or uses what is called the 'zero article' for the second broad category.

In turn, this means that outside any context, the presence of the French definite article may be understood in two different ways. Consider the following example:

> *Les singes mangent des bananes.*

which has two possible translations:

(i) If we are talking about monkeys in general (generic sense), English uses the zero article (see 2.2.1.3(i) above).

> _ Monkeys eat bananas.

(ii) If we are talking about a particular group of monkeys (specific sense), identifiable either in the situation or in the context (see 2.2.1.1 and 2.2.2.1 above), English uses the definite article.

> **The** monkeys are eating bananas.

2.2.5   Definite article after de

The definite article is used after the preposition *de* between two nouns to indicate possession (i.e. the first noun 'belongs' to the second one), attribution/ allocation (i.e. the second noun 'has' the first one), or the presentation of a characteristic (the first noun represents a characteristic of the second one). In most cases, English simply uses 'of '.

On the other hand, there is no article after *de* (see section 6.5 below) when the second noun has the value of a qualifying adjective for the first one. English is likely to have the two nouns in reverse order. Compare:

> *l'identité **de l'**homme*
> (man has an identity)
> the identity of man
>   and:
> *une carte **d'**identité*
> (a type of card)
> an identity card

> *Qu'est-ce que la fonction **de l'**art?*
> (art has a function)
> What is the purpose of art?
>   but:
> *une œuvre **d'**art*
> a work of art

> *le Ministère **du** Commerce*: the Ministry of Trade
> (*Ministère* is allocated to *Commerce*)

> *Les horreurs **de la** guerre*: the horrors of war
> (*horreurs* is a characteristic of war, not a 'type of horror'!)

Names of illnesses can be problematic and should be checked systematically in a dictionary.

> Ex: *une crise **d'**épilepsie*   an epileptic fit
>   *une crise **de** foie*   a bilious attack
>   but:
>   *la cirrhose **du** foie*   cirrhosis of the liver.

One could argue that '*la cirrhose du foie*' is a type of cirrhosis, hence '*de*' only should be used. Fortunately, English comes to the rescue with 'cirrhosis **of the** liver'!

2.2.6   Idioms

Finally, there are a number of common French phrasal verbs that include the definite article. For instance:

> *avoir le temps (de faire qch)*   to have time (to do sth)
> *avoir la vie facile*   to have an easy life
> *avoir mal à la gorge*   to have a sore throat

315

avoir mal à la tête	to have a headache
avoir mal aux dents	to have toothache
avoir mal au dos	to have backache
avoir froid aux pieds	to have cold feet (literal sense)
demander l'aumône	to ask for charity
faire la guerre	to make war
faire l'amour	to make love
faire la paix (avec qn)	to make peace (with sb)
faire le ménage	to do the housework
faire la vaisselle	to wash up
faire la cuisine	to cook
faire les courses	to do the shopping
faire l'expérience de qch	to experience sth
garder le silence	to keep quiet
partir le premier	to go first
prendre la fuite	to run away

3 The indefinite article

There are three indefinite articles:
- **un** and **une**, which correspond to 'a'/'an'
- **des**, which corresponds to 'some', 'any' or the zero article.

Note that *un*, *une*, can also be numeral adjectives.
> Ex: *Il ne reste plus qu'**une** bouteille de vin.*
> There's only **one** bottle of wine left.

See chapter 37 Numbers, section 2.1(iv).

3.1 Forms

(i) **des** becomes **de** or **d'** before a noun preceded by an adjective.
> Ex: *On m'a donné **des** conseils.*
> I was given advice.
>> but:
> *On m'a donné **de** bons conseils.*
> I was given good advice.
>
> *Vous avez là **d'**adorables chatons!*
> You've got some adorable kittens there!

(ii) It is a common mistake to confuse the indefinite article **des** with the contracted form of the preposition *de* + definite article *les*. Compare:
> *Hier, je suis allé voir **des** amis.*
>> and:
> *C'est un ami **des** (= **de les**) voisins.*

*Il me faut **d'***autres chaussures.*
(plural of '*une autre chaussure*': indefinite *des* contracted to *d'* before
an adjective beginning with a vowel):
I need some other shoes.
> but:

*Le talon **des** (= **de les**) autres chaussures me plaisait mieux.*
I liked the heel **on the** other shoes better.

(iii)   When the adjective is part of a noun, ***des*** must be kept. The most common of
those 'compounds' are:

des jeunes gens	young people
des jeunes filles	girls, young ladies
des petits garçons	young boys
des petites filles	young girls
des grands magasins	department stores
des petits pois	peas
des petits pains	rolls
des [petits] gâteaux secs	biscuits
des bons mots	witty remarks
des gros titres	headlines

Of course, it is always possible to imagine a context in which these pairs should
be interpreted literally, in which case the ***de*** rule would apply.
> Ex: *Ce boulanger fait **de** tout petits pains.*
> This baker makes very small loaves.

3.2   Uses

The indefinite article is mainly used to refer to one or more elements in a
category or set of referents which are not specified in any way and have not yet
been identified. In other words, they could be any one of those elements. Hence
there is existence but **indetermination** (as opposed to identification in the case
of the definite article). The speaker does not presume identification on the part of
his/her interlocutor. Note that once they have been introduced, these elements
are identifiable, and can be replaced by a personal pronoun or repeated, preceded
by a definite article or a demonstrative adjective.

3.2.1   *One or more elements in a category*

In the singular, 'a' corresponds to *un* or *une*. In the plural, English usually uses the
zero article, but 'some' or 'any' can often be substituted without a change of
meaning.
> Ex: *Apportez-moi **une** fourchette s'il vous plaît.*
> Please bring me a fork.

> *J'ai acheté **des** légumes et **des** fruits.*
> I bought [some] fruit and vegetables.

*La haine devint si grande que **des** atrocités eurent lieu.*
Hatred became so intense that [some] atrocities took place.

*Y a-t-il **des** boîtes de bière dans le frigidaire?*
Are there [any/some] cans of beer in the fridge?
> but:

*Paul et Catherine ont **des** tempéraments très différents.*
Paul and Catherine have [two] very different temperaments.

3.2.2   Several items (indefinite) or all the items (definite)?

Compare:
> *Donnez-moi **les** pommes qui sont dans le compotier.*
> Give me **the** apples which are in the fruit-bowl.

'*pommes*' is **specified** (identified) with the expansion '*qui sont dans le compotier*', hence the use of the definite article; and:
> *Donnez-moi **des** pommes du compotier.*
> Give me **some** apples from the fruit-bowl.

i.e. **any** apples.

> ***Les** moutons ont quatre pattes.*
> Sheep have four legs.

'*les moutons*' here is generic, i.e. **all** the elements of a category; and:
> *Il y a **des** moutons qui ont trois pattes.*
> There are [some] sheep with three legs.

'*des moutons*' here is unspecified: **several** elements in a category.

Compare:
> *Les enfants d'aujourd'hui ont **des** idéaux différents de ceux de leurs parents.*
> Today's children have different ideals from their parents'.

Like everybody else, children have **some** ideals (from the set of all ideals that exist), which happen to be different from those of their parents; and:
> ***Les** idéaux des (= de les) enfants d'aujourd'hui sont différents de ceux de leurs parents.*
> Today's children's ideals are different from their parents'.

Note that this is grammatically equivalent to:
> **The** ideals of today's children . . .

Here, we have specified (identified) the **ideals** we are talking about: those of **children** (with 'children' to be taken in its generic sense).

Consider the following examples:
> **1** *On voit de plus en plus les femmes dans **des** postes de responsabilité.*
> Women are seen more and more in positions of responsibility.

We are not talking about all the positions of responsibility that exist, but only some of them. However, it would have also been possible here to use the definite article and make '*postes de responsabilité*' generic:
> *On voit de plus en plus les femmes dans **les** postes de responsabilité.*

Similarly:

> *On voit de plus en plus **les** femmes . . .*
> Women are seen more and more . . .

where '*femmes*' is used in its generic sense. We could also have:

> *On voit de plus en plus **de** femmes . . .*
> More and more women are seen . . .

where '*de (des)*' would refer to a subset of all the women who exist.

> **2** *Il suffit de regarder **la** télévision pour voir **des** images **de** gens **de** pays **du** tiers-monde.*
> You only have to watch television to see pictures of people from Third-World countries.

'*la télévision*': generic; '*des images*': a set of images; '*de gens*': of some people; '*de pays*': of some countries; '*du* (= *de le*) *tiers-monde*': '*tiers-monde*' refers to one particular set of countries, it is specific, in fact 'unique'.

3.2.3   Subject complements

Special care must be taken with subject complements. Consider the following examples:

> **(i) *Les** lions sont **des** animaux sauvages.*
> Lions (generic) are wild animals.

(There are other wild animals.)

> ***Les** lions sont **les** rois de la jungle.*
> Lions (generic) are the kings of the jungle.

('*rois*' is specific: 'nobody' else but the lions.)

> **(ii) *Beaucoup de** femmes sont aussi **des** mères.*
> A lot of women are also mothers.

beaucoup de is a quantifier: it does not represent the whole set but only part of it. Hence the complement cannot be generic. It can of course be specific:

> ***Beaucoup de** femmes sont **les** mères d'enfants nés avant terme.*
> A lot of women are the mothers of premature babies.

It is also possible to have a specific set after *beaucoup de* by qualifying that set with an expansion of the noun phrase (see 2.2.2.2 above).

> Ex: *Beaucoup **des** (= de **les**) femmes qui . . .*
> A lot of **the** women who . . .

3.2.4   Whole set in a generic sense with un/une

The indefinite article singular can also be used to refer to the whole set, in a generic sense (the same applies to English).

> Ex: ***Un** chat a besoin d'affection.*
> A cat needs affection.

This is not about some odd cat from the whole set of cats, but an abstraction of a cat **representing the whole set** (see 2.2.1.3 above). Compare with:

> *Un chat traverse la rue.*
> A cat is crossing the street.

Here, it would be very difficult to interpret *un chat* in a generic sense!

This generic use of the indefinite article is also found in proverbs.

Ex: **Un** *repas sans vin est comme un jour sans soleil.*
(refers to all meals, any meal)
A meal without wine is like a day without sunshine.

3.2.5   *Proper nouns*

The indefinite article can also exceptionally be used with proper nouns:

– to refer to somebody one knows or pretends to know nothing about:

Ex: **Un** *Monsieur Dubois cherchait à vous joindre ce matin.*
or even:
Un *certain Monsieur Dubois cherchait à vous joindre ce matin.*
A M. Dubois was trying to contact you this morning.

– to indicate uniqueness:

Ex: *Il n'a pas le talent* **d'un** *Lamartine.*
He hasn't got the talent of a Lamartine.

– when the proper noun is used in a **metonymic** relation (where a single noun is substituted for the whole noun phrase) with an animate or inanimate object:

Ex: *Martin a acheté* **un** *Braque.* (= *un tableau de Braque*)
Il a sculpté **une** *Vénus.* (= *une représentation de Vénus*)

– when the proper noun is used in an **eponymic** relation (where a proper noun is used as a common noun for an animate which shares the same distinctive characteristics):

Ex: *C'est* **un** *Tartuffe* (a hypocrite); **un** *Don Juan* (a seducer).

4   The partitive article

4.1   Forms

The partitive article is formed with **de** + definite article; its plural is **des**:

de + *le* = **du**
de + *la* = **de la**
de + *l'* = **de l'**

NB: The English partitive ('some'/'any') is not always expressed (zero article) whilst its French equivalent always is.

Note that *de* **on its own** can also combine with a possessive, a demonstrative or an indefinite adjective.

Ex: *Je voudrais* **de ton** *dessert* / **de ce** *dessert* / **de chaque** *dessert* / **de tous les** *desserts.*
I would like **some** of your pudding / of this pudding / of each pudding / of all the puddings.

4.2 Uses

The partitive article is used with nouns which refer to an undetermined quantity of an inanimate which cannot normally be counted (i.e. uncountable nouns). This applies whether the noun is concrete (e.g. *de la terre, du beurre*) or abstract (e.g. *du courage, de la patience*).

4.2.1 Singular partitive

The singular partitive article has two very distinct uses. It can refer:

– to a certain quantity of something taken from a whole:
>Ex: *Je mange **du** (= de le) gâteau que tu m'as apporté ce matin.*
>(part of the whole cake brought)
>I am eating some of the cake you brought me this morning.

– or to an indeterminate quantity not necessarily taken from a specified whole:
>Ex: *Je mange **du** gâteau.*
>(any piece of cake)
>I am eating [some] cake.

>*On servit à Obélix **de l'**agneau bouilli avec **de la** sauce à la menthe.*
>Obelix was served boiled lamb with mint sauce.

NB(1): Some nouns can be either countable or uncountable, depending on the context (see chapter 27 Nouns, section 1(vi)).
>Ex: *Hier, j'ai mangé **du poulet**.*
>Yesterday, I ate chicken.
>>but:
>*Ma grand-mère a **six poulets** et deux lapins.*
>My grandmother's got six chickens and two rabbits.

>*Ils ont **du travail** à faire pour demain.*
>They've got some work to do for tomorrow.
>>but:
>*J'ai encore **un travail** à faire avant de partir.*
>I've got another job to do before I go.

NB(2): A proper noun can be in a **metonymic** relation with an object (see 3.2.5 above), in which case partitive articles may be used.
>Ex: *Il joue **du** Chopin (= des œuvres de Chopin).*
>*Ça c'est **du** Chirac tout craché (= tout à fait ce que Chirac pourrait faire/dire, etc.)*
>*J'ai acheté **du** bordeaux, **du** champagne, etc. (= du vin de . . .)*

4.2.2 Plural partitive

Since the partitive article refers to something which is not countable, one could consider that a 'plural partitive' is a contradiction in terms. However, there are a few nouns which are always used in the plural, even though they refer to a quantity.

> Ex: *J'ai acheté **des** rillettes.* (= a kind of pâté)
> I have bought some rillettes.

> *Voulez-vous **des** petits pois, **des** lentilles, **des** haricots, **des** épinards, **des** frites?*
> Would you like some peas, lentils, beans, spinach, chips?

(which refers to a certain quantity of vegetables, rather than to a particular number of items)

Note that 'pasta' is ***des** pâtes* but (narcotic) 'drugs' is ***de la** drogue*.

5 Definite, indefinite or partitive article?

(i) Definite or partitive?

It is often appropriate to use the partitive article with abstract nouns, to refer to 'some' of what the abstract noun represents, and not all of it. If 'some' or 'some kind of' can be added in English without changing the meaning, the partitive article is likely to be used in French. Compare:

> ***La** musique classique* (generic); *j'aime **la** musique classique.*
> Classical music; I love classical music.

> *Elle aime **la** musique de Wagner.* (specific)
> She loves Wagner's music. (i.e. **the** music of Wagner)
> but:
> *J'écoute souvent **de la** musique classique.*
> I often listen to [some] classical music.

> ***L'**argent* (generic) *est la source de tous les maux.*
> Money is the source of all evil.
> but:
> *Il a fait cela pour gagner **de l'**argent.*
> He did that to earn [some] money.
> or:
> ***De l'**argent a été trouvé sur cette table.*
> [Some] Money was found on this table.

> *Ils n'ont aucun respect pour **l'**art.* (generic)
> They have no respect for art.
> but:
> *Est-ce que vous appelez cela **de l'**art?*
> Do you call that (some kind of) 'art'?

(ii) The indefinite article singular is used (and not the partitive) when English uses 'some'/'any' meaning 'a certain', 'a particular'.

Ex: *Il reconnaît **une** utilité dans les représentations des scènes de chasse.*
He recognizes some usefulness in the representations of hunting scenes.

*Le lecteur doit se demander si ce qu'on fait dans ce monde a **une** valeur.*
The reader must ask himself if what one does in this world has any value.

*Ils sont déprimés et recherchent **un** soulagement dans la drogue.*
They are depressed and seek [some] solace in drugs.

(iii)   When the abstract word is qualified by an expansion which is not sufficient for identification, the indefinite article is used in French. Compare:
*Cet artiste a **la** capacité de faire rire les gens.*
This artist has the ability to make people laugh.
    and:
*Cet artiste a **une** grande capacité comique.*
This artist has great comic ability.

*Tout le monde recevrait alors **le** même traitement.*
Everybody would then receive the same treatment.
    and:
*Tout le monde recevrait alors **un** traitement égal en ce qui concerne la santé, l'enseignement. . . .*
Everybody would then receive equal treatment as regards health, education. . . .

*L'alimentation est très importante pour maintenir **la** santé.*
Nutrition is very important to keep healthy.
    and:
*L'alimentation est très importante pour maintenir **une** bonne santé.*
Nutrition is very important to keep in good health.

*C'est un spécialiste de **l'**humour noir.*
He's a specialist in black humour.
    and:
*Durant son discours, il a fait preuve d'**un** humour débridé.*
During his speech, he showed an unrestrained sense of humour.

6 Zero article

The most frequent case of the zero article with common nouns today is that of expressions with the preposition *de*, introducing an undefined referent: see 6.5 below.

The construction 'noun + *à* + noun' is treated in chapter 26 Prepositions, section 8.1.

6.1 Adjective + *de* + noun

Ex: *plein de*	full of
vide de	empty of
dépourvu de	devoid of, lacking in
vêtu de	dressed in, wearing
couvert de	covered in
entouré de	surrounded with
chargé de	loaded with; with responsibility for

(i) If the noun after *de* is not specified (identified), there is no article.

> Ex: *Leurs ancêtres étaient partisans **de** mœurs plus traditionnelles.*
> Their ancestors were in favour of more traditional mores.

> *La carafe est remplie **de** vin.*
> The jug is full of wine.

Note that a lot of these adjectives are the past participles of the verbs listed in 6.2 below used as adjectives.

(ii) If the noun is specified, then *de* is followed by the definite article, which also means that *de* contracts with *le* to become *du*, and with *les* to become *des* (see section 2.1 above). Compare:

> *Il est entouré **de** gens toute la journée.*
> He is surrounded by people all day.
> > and:
> *Il est entouré **des** (= de les) gens qui l'ont soutenu pendant sa campagne.*
> He is surrounded by the people who supported him during his campaign.

'*gens*' is made specific (i.e. identified) by the relative '*qui l'ont soutenu pendant sa campagne*'.

6.2 Verb + *de* + noun

Ex: *accuser qn de qch*	to accuse sb of sth
avoir besoin de	to need
avoir envie de	to feel like
combler de	to overwhelm with
couronner de	to crown with
couvrir de	to cover with
entourer de	to surround with
garnir de	to decorate with, garnish with
manquer de	to be short of
se munir de	to equip oneself with
parler de	to talk about
remplir de	to fill with
servir de	to serve as; to be used as

(i) If the noun after *de* is not specified, there is no article.

> Ex: *Ils ont besoin **de** choses plus élémentaires, comme **d'eau** potable et **de** système sanitaire.*
> They need more basic things, such as clean water and a sewage system.

(ii) If the noun is specified, the definite article is present, as in English (→ *du, de la, de l', des*). Compare:

> *Il a été accusé **de** vol.*
> He was accused of theft.
>> and:
> *Il a été accusé **du** vol **de la voiture de son voisin**.*
> He was accused of the theft of his neighbour's car.
>
> *Il a été accusé **des** (= de les) vols suivants . . .*
> He was accused of the following thefts . . .

NB: If the noun that follows is countable, it can be preceded by the indefinite article, to mean 'a particular . . .'.

> Ex: *Il a été accusé **d'un** vol, **de** vols.*
> He was accused of a theft, of thefts.

(iii) Some verbs cannot take the zero article after *de*, as the noun which follows is almost always defined (generic or specific), hence the compulsory presence of the definite article.

> Ex: *Il se méfie **de la** politique.*
> He mistrusts politics.

6.3 Adverbs of quantity (quantifiers) + *de* + noun

Ex:	
assez de	enough
assez peu de	relatively little/relatively few
autant de	as much/as many
beaucoup de	much/a lot of/many
beaucoup trop de	far too much/far too many
combien de	how much/how many
moins de	less/fewer
pas mal de	a fair amount of
peu de	few/little
un peu de	a little
plus de	more
que de	so much/so many
tant de	so much/so many
trop de	too much/too many

(i) If the noun after *de* is not specified, there is no article.

> Ex: *Les Anglais mangent trop **de** graisse.*
> English people eat too much fat.

*Leur régime ne comprend pas assez **de** fibre.*
Their diet does not include enough fibre.

*Avec un adverbe, la phrase aurait moins **de** brutalité.*
With an adverb, the sentence would be less brutal.

(ii) If the noun is specified, there is a definite article. Compare:
*Il me reste très peu **de** chocolats.*
I have very few chocolates left.
        and:
*Il me reste très peu **des** (= de les) chocolats que vous m'avez offerts.*
I have very few of the chocolates you gave me left.

*Ce pays fabrique beaucoup **d'**armes.*
This country manufactures a lot of arms.
        and:
*Beaucoup **des** (= de les) armes qui ont été exportées l'ont été illégalement.*
A lot of the arms that were exported were done so illegally.

NB: '**many/a lot of us**' (of you, of them)' is *beaucoup **d'entre** nous (d'entre vous, d'entre eux, d'entre elles),* not *★beaucoup de nous.*

(iii) Adverbs of quantity are not followed by *de* when they modify a verb (i.e. they are only followed by *de* when they modify a noun). See also chapter 30 Comparatives.
        Ex: *J'ai acheté **autant de roses** que **d'**œillets.*
I have bought as many roses as carnations.
            but:
*J'aime **autant les** roses que **les** œillets.*
I like roses as much as carnations.

*Il a **beaucoup de travail**.*
He has a lot of work.
            but:
*Il **aime beaucoup le** travail.*
He likes work a lot.

(iv) **bien, la plupart, la majorité**

   – **bien**, which means 'a lot of', is always followed by the partitive or the indefinite plural article.
        Ex: *Ils me donnent **bien du** souci/**bien de la** peine.*
They give me a lot of worry/a lot of sorrow.

*J'ai lu ce livre il y a **bien des** années.*
I read this book many years ago.

   – **la plupart de, la majorité de** are always followed by the definite article.
        Ex: *Dans **la plupart des** (= de + les) cas.*
In most cases.

***La majorité des** (= de + les) gens sont arrivés.*
Most [of the] people have arrived.

   But note: **la plupart d'entre eux** (most of them)

NB(1): *la plupart* is generally used with a noun (and verb) plural.

> Ex: **La plupart des** *étudiants n'avaient pas compris.*
> Most [of the] students had not understood.

Exception: **la plupart du** *temps* (most of the time)

NB(2): *la plus grande partie / la majeure partie* are generally used with a noun (and verb) singular.

> Ex: *En vacances,* **la plus grande partie de la** *journée est passée à ne rien faire.*
> On holiday, most of the day is spent doing nothing.

6.4 Noun indicating a quantity + *de* + noun

Ex:		
	une boîte de	a box of
	un bouquet de	a bunch of
	une bouteille de	a bottle of
	une collection de	a collection of
	une douzaine de	a dozen _
	un grand nombre de	a large number of
	un kilo de	a kilo of
	un litre de	a litre of
	un manque de	a shortage of
	un paquet de	a packet of
	une quantité de	a quantity of
	une tasse de	a cup of
	une tranche de	a slice of
	un verre de	a glass of
	une liste de	a list of
	un groupe de	a group of, etc.

(i) If the noun after *de* is not specified, there is no article.

> Ex: *Je voudrais une douzaine* **d'œufs** *et un litre* **de** *lait.*
> I would like a dozen eggs and a litre of milk.
>
> *Cette entreprise souffre d'un manque* **de** *personnel.*
> This firm suffers from a shortage of personnel.

(ii) If the noun is specified, there is a definite article. Compare:

> *Ils ont publié une collection* **de** *poèmes.*
> They published a collection of poems.
>
> and:
>
> *Ils ont publié une collection* **des** *(= de les) poèmes trouvés dans l'appartement de Watkin.*
> They published a collection of the poems found in Watkin's apartment.
>
> or:
>
> *Ils ont publié la collection* **des** *(= de les) poèmes de Watkin.*
> They published the collection of Watkin's poems.

6.5   noun + 'de + noun' acting as adjective

Ex: *un carnet de notes*	a notebook
une carte d'identité	an identity card
un champ de bataille	a battlefield
une chemise de soie	a silk shirt
un chien de race	a pedigree dog
un collier de perles	a pearl necklace
un congé de maternité	maternity leave
un homme de génie	a man of genius
l'instinct de préservation	instinct for preservation
du jus de viande	meat juices
un livre de cuisine	a cookery book
un livre de philosophie	a philosophy book
une maison de campagne	a country house
les maladies de cœur	heart diseases
une pomme de terre	a potato (literally: an earth apple!)
des produits de beauté	cosmetics
un sac d'école	a schoolbag
une séance de projection	a film show
un terrain de chasse	a hunting-ground
des troncs d'arbres	tree-trunks
des vins de France	wines from France (French wines)

(i)   The article is omitted before a noun which acts as an adjective for a first noun (the referent of the second noun remains undefined).

Ex: *Elle a droit à six semaines de congé **de** maternité.*
She's entitled to six weeks' maternity leave.

*Les émotions ne sont plus des cocktails **d'**hormones incapables d'arrêter le désir de progrès de l'homme.*
Emotions are no longer cocktails of hormones incapable of stopping man's desire for progress.

(ii)   If the second noun is specified, i.e. if *de* indicates possession, attribution, location or the presentation of a characteristic, the definite article is used (see 2.2.2.2 above).

Ex: *C'est le tronc **de l'**arbre que nous avons dû abattre l'année dernière.*
That's the trunk of the tree we had to fell last year.

As this tends to be a major source of errors, it is important to understand the difference. Compare:

*un clocher **d'**église (= un type de clocher)*
a church steeple
        and:
*le clocher **de l'**église (l'église a un clocher / le clocher de cette église en particulier)*
the church's steeple

*une idée **d'**homme*
(= a man's idea; the kind of idea that a man may have)
      and:
*une idée **de** l'homme*
(= an idea of man; an idea of what man may be)

6.6   Set phrases (*locutions*)

(i)   Adverb phrases

Ex: *à genoux*	on one's knees
(marcher) à reculons	(to walk) backwards
à terre, par terre	on the ground
à vive allure	at great speed
à voix basse	in a low voice
de manière imprévue	in an unexpected manner
en lieu sûr	in a safe place
(voyager) par mer	(to travel) by sea
par monts et par vaux	up hill and down dale
(foncer) tête baissée	(to rush) headlong
but:	
la tête baissée	with bowed head

NB: ***par*** on its own is used in French when the indefinite article is used in English in the sense of '**per**'.

Ex: *trois fois par semaine*	three times a week (= per week)
une fois par an	once a year
and:	
dix francs par personne	ten francs a person/per head.

(ii)   Phrasal verbs (*locutions verbales*)

Ex: *avoir cours*	to be in current use
avoir envie (de qch)	to want (sth)
avoir envie (de faire qch)	to feel like (doing sth)
avoir faim/soif	to be hungry/thirsty
avoir froid/chaud	to be cold/warm
avoir peur (de qn/qch)	to be afraid (of sb/sth)
avoir raison/tort	to be right/wrong
donner congé (à qn)	to relieve (sb of his/her duties)
faire bon marché (de qch)	to treat (sth) cheaply
faire face (à qn/qch)	to face (sb/sth)
faire faillite	to go bankrupt
faire envie (à qn)	to make (sb) envious
faire fortune	to make one's fortune; to become rich
faire peur (à qn)	to frighten (sb)
mettre fin (à qch)	to put an end (to sth)
porter plainte (contre qn)	to lodge a complaint (against sb)
prendre froid	to catch cold
prendre racine	to take root
tenir parole	to keep one's word

NB: 'to meet' (for the first time) is either *faire connaissance* or *faire **la** connaissance* **de qn.**

> Ex: *Ils ont fait connaissance la semaine dernière.*
> They met (for the first time) last week.
>> but:
> *Alain a fait **la** connaissance **de** Catherine la semaine dernière.*
> Alain met Catherine (for the first time) last week.

Hence if the noun is in any way modified, a determiner appears.

> Ex: *avoir _ faim*, but *avoir **une** faim de loup*
> *avoir _ peur*, but *avoir **une** peur bleue*
> *mettre _ fin à qch*, but *mettre **une** fin définitive à qch*

(iii)   Other idioms
There is no article in the following idioms:

> *C'est chose facile.*   That's easily done.
> *C'est mauvais signe.*   That's a bad sign.

6.7   Noun subject complements with a qualifying value

The article is not used in the following case:
− after *être, devenir, paraître, sembler*, and
− if the subject complement (see chapter 2 Syntax, section 2.11) has a **qualifying** value, for instance denoting:
  • nationality
  • profession/occupation
  • rank
  • family status, etc.

> Ex: *Catherine est _ grand-mère.*
> Catherine is a grandmother.

See also chapter 35 *C'est/Il est*, section 6.

6.8   Enumerations

The article can be omitted in enumerations when using literary style.

> Ex: '*Adieu veau, vache, cochon, couvée . . .*'

> La Fontaine, *La laitière et le pot au lait*

6.9   Telegraphic style, interjections, headings, etc.

(i)   Telegraphic style, note form

> Ex: *bateau à vendre; apporte documents; faire vaisselle; arrive demain*
> boat for sale; bring documents; do washing–up; arrive tomorrow

(ii)   Press headings

> Ex: *Canicule à Paris; Risques de verglas*
> Heatwave in Paris; Danger of black ice

(iii) Interjections
      Ex: *Horreur! Grands Dieux! Nom d'un chien! Merde!*

(iv) Textbook titles
    They do not normally take an article.
      Ex: *Equations exponentielles; Morphosyntaxe*

Hence one can be added for stronger effect. For instance, on a restaurant menu: *Les poissons*, instead of simply: *poisson* or *poissons*.

(v) Labels, notices
      Ex: *lait entier; sens interdit*
           whole milk; no entry

(vi) Apostrophes
      Ex: *Dizzy, ô miracle de la nature!*

6.10 Proverbs and popular sayings

There is generally no article in generic statements and proverbs.
      Ex: *Chat échaudé craint l'eau froide.*
           Once bitten twice shy.

           Il y a anguille sous roche.
           There's something in the wind.

           Pierre qui roule n'amasse pas mousse.
           A rolling stone gathers no moss.

           Pauvreté n'est pas vice.
           Poverty is not a sin.

           Bien mal acquis ne profite jamais.
           Ill gotten ill spent;
           Ill-gotten gains seldom prosper.

7 Repetition of the article

7.1 Definite article

(i) Unlike in English, the definite article is repeated before a series of nouns which have each their own referent (but see exceptions below).
      Ex: *Il leur a donné une idée **des** (= de les) sentiments et **des** (= de les) opinions partagées par ses collègues.*
           He gave them an idea of **the** feelings and _ opinions shared by his colleagues.

(ii) With pairs of nouns: if the terms are used in their generic sense, either the definite or the zero article can be used.

Ex: *Chats et chiens ne s'entendent guère.*
or:

Les *chats et* **les** *chiens ne s'entendent guère.*
Cats and dogs don't really get on.

(iii)   If the same repeated noun has several referents, distinguished by adjectives, there is a choice of three constructions.

Ex: **le** *gouvernement français,* **le** *gouvernement anglais et* **le** *gouvernement espagnol*
le *gouvernement français,* **l'**anglais *et* **l'**espagnol
les *gouvernements français, anglais et espagnol*

See also chapter 28 Qualifying Adjectives.

7.2   Indefinite and partitive articles

Like the definite article, the indefinite and partitive articles are repeated in a series of nouns which have each their own referent.

Ex: *Sur la table, il y a* **un** *livre,* **un** *stylo et* **un** *crayon.*
On the table there are a book, a pen and a pencil.

J'ai acheté **du** *pain,* **du** *beurre, etc.*
I bought bread, butter, etc.

But omission is equally possible.

Ex: *J'ai acheté _ pain et _ beurre.*

If the referent is unique, the determiner is not repeated.

Ex: **une** *chatte, ou _ femelle du chat*

7.3   All determiners

The article is not repeated in set phrases (*locutions*).

Ex: **des** *allées et venues*	comings and goings
les *us et coutumes*	habits and customs
les *arts et métiers*	arts and crafts
les *ponts et chaussées*	the Department of National Highways/ the school or department of civil engineering
les *frères et sœurs*	brothers and sisters

8   Negative form

In the context of articles, we should distinguish two types of negation:

− absolute:

ne . . . pas; ne . . . point (rare)*; ne . . . plus; ne . . . jamais; ne . . . guère*

– limited:

ne . . . que; ne . . . pas que

Then we should look at *ni . . . ni.*

8.1 Definite article

The definite article does **not** change after the negative form, whether absolute or limited, with *être* or any other verb.

> Ex: *Elle vendra **la** maison.*
> → *Elle **ne** vendra **jamais la** maison.*
> She will never sell the house.
>
> *Il achète **les** journaux du dimanche.*
> → *Il **n'**achète **que les** journaux du dimanche.*
> He only buys the Sunday papers.
>
> *Il est **le** premier arrivé.*
> → *Il **n'**est **pas le** premier arrivé.*
> He is not the first to arrive.

8.2 Indefinite article

(i) **Absolute negation**

– *un, une, des,* become *de (d')* with all verbs except *être* (no change with *être*).

> Ex: *J'ai acheté **des** pommes* → *Je **n'**ai **pas** acheté **de** pommes.*
> *J'ai pris **un** stylo* → *Je **n'**ai **pas** pris **de** stylo.*
>   but:
> *Ce sont **des** pommes* → *Ce **ne** sont **pas des** pommes.*
> *C'était **une** plaisanterie* → *Ce **n'**était **pas une** plaisanterie.*

– *de* remains *de (d')* before an adjective:

> Ex: *J'ai trouvé **de** belles pommes.*
>   and:
> *Je **n'**ai **pas** trouvé **de** belles pommes.*

– *des* becomes *de* even if the adjective is part of the noun (see section 3.1(iii) above).

> Ex: *J'ai mangé **des** petits pois.*
>   but:
> *Je **n'**ai **pas** mangé **de** petits pois.*

NB: Even with an ellipsis of *ne* or *pas*, the rule still applies.

> Ex: *Je **ne** peux vous donner **de** renseignement.*
> *Désolé, **pas de** gâteaux!*

See also chapter 38 Negative Structures, sections 2.1.2 and 2.1.3.
With the omission of *ne* as part of an informal oral register, anything is possible.

> Ex: *J'vais pas te donner du/de vin quand même!*

(ii) **Absolute negation, with emphasis**

The indefinite article is kept. Compare:

*Je **n'ai pas** acheté **de** vêtements.*
I did**n't** buy **any** clothes.
    but:
*Je **n'ai pas** acheté **une** robe mais **un** manteau.*
I did**n't** buy **a** dress but **a** coat.
    and:
*Je **n'ai pas** acheté **une** robe mais **deux**.*
I did **not** buy **one** dress but **two**.

*Je **n'ai pas** acheté **une seule** robe.*
I didn't buy **a single** dress.

Note that in all these examples, **not . . . any** is *ne . . . pas de*, while **not . . . a/one** is *ne . . . pas un/une*.

(iii) **Limited negation**

The indefinite article remains unchanged.

    Ex: *Il reste **une** pomme.*
There is an/one apple left.
    and:
*Il **ne** reste **qu'une** pomme.*
There is only an/one apple left.

*Il **ne** reste **pas qu'une** pomme, il reste aussi **des** poires.*
There isn't just an apple left, there are some pears too.

8.3 Partitive article

(i) **Absolute negation**

du, de la, de l', become ***de*** (***d'***) with all verbs except *être* (no change with *être*, as for the indefinite article), or if what is negated is specified.

    Ex: *Ils ont **du** travail* → *Ils **n'ont pas de** travail.*
They've got work → They haven't got any work.

*Cette fois-ci, il a eu **de la** chance* → *Il **n'a pas** eu **de** chance.*
This time, he was lucky → He was unlucky.
    but:
*C'est **du** café* → *Ce **n'est pas du** café.*
It is coffee → It is not coffee.
    and:
*Je **ne** veux **pas du** café que vous avez rapporté de Turquie.*
('*que vous avez rapporté de Turquie*' specifies what is negated).
I don't want any of the coffee that you've brought back from Turkey.

(ii) **Limited negation**

If the negative form is limited, the partitive article is kept.

> Ex: *Je **n'**ai acheté **que du** vin rouge.*
> I only bought red wine.

8.4 Negation with *ni . . . ni*

ni . . . ni means **neither . . . nor**.

There is an article if *être* is used or if the noun is specified. There is no article in other cases.

8.4.1 ni . . . ni *with article*

(i) If the verb is *être*, the article (definite, indefinite or partitive) is kept.

> Ex: *Ce n'est **ni du** beurre **ni de la** confiture.*
> It is neither butter nor jam.

> *Ceci n'est **ni un** rat **ni une** souris.*
> This is neither a rat nor a mouse.

> *Ce n'est **ni l'**endroit **ni le** moment!*
> It is neither the time nor the place!

(ii) As in English, there is a definite article if the noun is specified. Compare:

> *Elle n'avait **ni** talent **ni** courage.*
> She had neither talent nor courage.
> and:
> *Elle n'avait **ni le** talent **ni le** courage de sa mère.*
> She had neither the talent nor the courage of her mother.

8.4.2 ni . . . ni, *no article*

(i) With other verbs, there is no partitive or indefinite article.

> Ex: *Il ne reste **ni** beurre **ni** confiture.*
> There is no butter or jam left.

> *Il n'y a jamais **ni** bon endroit **ni** bon moment pour vous parler.*
> It is never the right time or place to talk to you.

(ii) The presence or absence of a **definite** article follows English usage.

> Ex: *Je n'ai trouvé **ni** chaussettes **ni** chaussures dans ta valise!*
> I found neither socks nor shoes in your suitcase.
> but:
> *Cette fois-ci, il n'a oublié **ni les** chaussettes **ni les** chaussures.*
> This time, he forgot neither the socks nor the shoes.

(where *'chaussettes'* and *'chaussures'* are identified in the situation or context: see 2.2 above).

24 Possessive adjectives, possession, attribution

1 Introduction

Possessive adjectives, like definite articles and demonstrative adjectives, belong to the class of specific determiners. They determine a noun, in this case the 'thing possessed'. Possessive adjectives can combine with non-specific determiners (**tous** *mes chats*; *mes* **autres** *chats*). The relation of possession establishes the **identification** of the element possessed (see 3.1 below). The possessive adjective agrees in gender and number with the noun that it determines (i.e. the thing possessed) and it agrees in person and number with the possessor(s).

The possessive adjective expresses several types of 'possession':
– literal possession:
>   Ex: *mon appartement, mon argent, ma voiture.*
– family links:
>   Ex: *mon père, ma mère.*
– a relation of friendship:
>   Ex: *mes amis.*
– a relation of affection:
>   Ex: *mon amour, mon Dizzy adoré.*
– abstract possession:
>   Ex: *Mon train est à 5 heures.*
>   *Ne perdez pas votre temps.*
>   *Ils ont passé leurs vacances en Grèce.*

Note that:
– Agreement rules differ between English and French.
– There are a number of cases when English uses a possessive adjective and French uses the definite article (the parts of the body in particular, see 4 below).

2 Agreement

2.1 Possessor and thing possessed

The possessive adjective agrees in person and number with the possessor(s), and in gender and number with the thing possessed. Hence:

my	is either	*mon*	*ma*	or	*mes*	
your (*tu*)	is either	*ton*	*ta*	or	*tes*	
his	is either	*son*	*sa*	or	*ses*	
her	is either	*son*	*sa*	or	*ses*	} IMPORTANT
its	is either	*son*	*sa*	or	*ses*	
our	is either		*notre*	or	*nos*	
your (*vous*)	is either		*votre*	or	*vos*	
their	is either		*leur*	or	*leurs*.	

Ex: *Paul a apporté* **son** *livre et* **ses** *notes de cours.*
Paul has brought **his** book and **his** lecture notes.

Marie a apporté **son** *livre et* **ses** *notes de cours.*
Marie has brought **her** book and **her** lecture notes.

The possessor, Paul (or Marie), is 3rd person singular and determines a choice between *son, sa* or *ses*:
– The first thing possessed, '*livre*', is masculine and singular, hence '*son*'.
– The second thing possessed, '*notes*', is feminine and plural, hence '*ses*'.

NB: In English, the possessive adjective agrees in person with the possessor plus, in the case of I/we, with the number of the possessor(s) and, in the case of he/she, with the gender of the possessor.
Ex: Paul's book: his book.
Paul's lecture notes: his lecture notes.

Mary's book: her book.
Mary's lecture notes: her lecture notes.

Summary:

		ONE thing possessed		SEVERAL things possessed	
		singular		plural	
	persons	M	F	M and F	
ONE	*je*	*mon*	*ma*	*mes*	my
possessor	*tu*	*ton*	*ta*	*tes*	your
	il, elle	*son*	*sa*	*ses*	his/her/its
		M and F		M and F	
SEVERAL	*nous*	*notre*		*nos*	our
possessors	*vous*	*votre*		*vos*	your
	ils, elles	*leur*		*leurs*	their

2.2   *ma, ta, sa / mon, ton, son*

mon, ton, son are used before masculine nouns, and *ma, ta, sa* before feminine ones, but *ma, ta, sa* become *mon, ton, son* respectively before a feminine word (noun or adjective) beginning with a vowel or a mute '*h*'.

Ex: *ma bonne histoire*   but: ***mon** absurde histoire*
  ***ta** fierté*   ***ton** immense fierté*
  ***sa** honte*   ***son** habitude*

Exception: *onze* and *onzième*, where the 'o' is treated as a consonant.
  Ex: *Ça ne marche pas très fort, j'en suis à **ma** onzième cigarette.*
   I am not doing very well, I'm on my eleventh cigarette.

3 Uses

3.1 Identification of the referent

(i) The referent can be present in the **context**.

  Ex: ***Catherine** a pris **son** manteau.*
   Catherine took her coat.
The possessive adjective refers to a 'possessor', here the referent '*Catherine*', previously mentioned in the context. This is known as the **anaphoric** use of the possessive adjective.

Note that the possessive adjective can also appear **before** the referent in the context, in which case we have a **cataphor**.
  Ex: *Avec **sa** chemise à fleurs, **Antoine** faisait très années soixante.*
   With his flowery shirt, Antoine had a very sixties look.

(ii) The referent can be present in the discourse **situation**.

  Ex: *Passe-moi **ton** sac s'il te plaît.*
   Pass me your bag please.
There is nothing in the context to determine the possessor. Here, the referent – the possessor of the bag – is the person addressed by the speaker, and is thus defined by the discourse situation. This is known as the **deictic** use of the possessive adjective.

3.2 The possessive adjective and indefinite pronouns

(i) The possessive adjectives *son, sa, ses* are generally used with the indefinite pronouns *on, chacun, personne* or the indefinite adjective *chaque* + noun.
  Ex: ***On** ne peut pas prévoir **son** avenir.*
   One cannot predict one's future.

  ***On** ne peut pas toujours faire à **sa** guise.*
  You can't always do what you like.

  ***Chaque élève** devra apporter **ses** propres livres.*
  Each pupil will have to bring his/her own books.

  ***Chacun** veut faire prévaloir **son** point de vue.*
  Everybody wants his/her/their own opinion to prevail.

NB: Unlike its English equivalent, *chacun* **cannot** be followed by a plural possessive adjective. However, when *chacun* follows another noun or personal pronoun + verb, the agreement is with that noun or pronoun, i.e. the subject of the verb.

> Ex: ***Christophe et Pierre*** *avaient apporté* **chacun leur** *livre.*
> *Je voudrais que* **vous** *leviez* **chacun votre** *verre.*
> ***Nous*** *sommes retournés* **chacun** *dans* **notre** *chambre.*

(ii) *on + notre/nos* belongs to informal French.

> Ex: *On a oublié* **nos** *affaires.*
> We've forgotten our things.
> ('*nous*' and '*notre*'/'*nos*' should be used in formal French.)

3.3 The possessive adjective and collective nouns

Unlike in English, the possessive adjective remains singular with singular collective nouns (see also chapter 31 Personal Pronouns, section 2.1.2(i)).

> Ex: ***La police*** *a* **ses** *propres méthodes.*
> The police have **their** own methods.

> *Le* ***PS*** *a accentué* **son** *avance.*
> The French Socialist Party have increased **their** lead.

> *Marx pensait que la croyance du* **peuple** *en Dieu l'empêchait de penser, de réfléchir à* **sa** *condition.*
> Marx held that the people's belief in God prevented them from thinking and reflecting about **their** condition.

3.4 Ambiguity of *son/sa/ses*

The possessor of *son*, *sa*, *ses* can be ambiguous.

> Ex: *Pierre est fâché que Marie ait oublié* **son livre.**
> '*son livre*' could be Paul's book or Marie's book.

This ambiguity can be resolved with the addition of *à lui*, *à elle*.

> Ex: *Marie a oublié* **son** *livre* **à elle.**
> Marie forgot **her** book.

> *Marie a oublié* **son** *livre* **à lui.**
> Marie forgot **his** book.

> *C'est* **son** *livre* **à elle** *qui manque.*
> It's **her** book that's missing.

> *C'est* **son** *livre* **à lui** *qui manque.*
> It's **his** book that's missing.

Note that this construction belongs to informal French.

3.5 *son, sa, ses / leur, leurs*

Particular attention should be paid to the difference between *son, sa, ses* and *leur, leurs*.

(i)   If there is only one possessor, use *son*, *sa* or *ses*.

Ex: ***Elle*** *a rencontré **sa** tante au Parc Monceau.*
She met **her** aunt at Parc Monceau.

Ce chien *perd tous **ses** poils.*
This dog is losing all **his** hairs.

(ii)   If there are at least two possessors, use *leur* or *leurs*.

Ex: ***M. et Mme Dupont*** *ont rencontré **leur** nièce au Parc Monceau.*
(two possessors; one thing possessed)
M. and Mme Dupont met **their** niece at Parc Monceau.

Les animaux *abandonnent rarement **leurs** petits.*
(several possessors; several things possessed)
Animals seldom abandon **their** young.

3.6   *leur*: possessive adjective or personal pronoun?

It is a common mistake to confuse the possessive adjective *leur* (plural *leurs*) and the personal pronoun plural indirect object *leur*, which never takes an 's' (see chapter 31 Personal Pronouns, section 2.2.2.4(i)).

Ex: *J'ai pris **leurs** devoirs et je **leur** ai dit qu'ils pouvaient partir.*
I took **their** papers and told **them** they could leave.

3.7   Expression of emphasis

The possessive adjective can be emphasized by the addition of the adjective *propre*, or by the addition of *à* + stressed personal pronoun (*à moi*, *à toi*, *à lui*, *à elle*, etc.).

Ex: *Il me traite comme **sa propre** fille.*
He treats me like his own daughter.

*J'ai **ma** chambre **à moi**.*
I've got my own room.

*Ça, c'est **leur** affaire **à eux**.*
That's their own business.

3.8   Special uses of *mon, ma, mes*

The following uses of *mon, ma, mes* are not the same as in English. They can be:

(i)   A sign of affection

For instance, a father or mother speaking to their son or daughter can address them as *mon fils*, *ma fille* or *mes enfants*. In English, the equivalent will probably be just the name of the child or children.

(ii)   A sign of deference or respect

– For instance, a child can address his father or mother, uncle, etc. as *mon père, ma mère, mon oncle*, etc.

- A Catholic priest is addressed as *Mon Père* ('Father').

- In the army, an inferior will address his superior as: *mon capitaine, mon général*, etc.
    >Ex: *A vos ordres, mon colonel!*
    >Yes, Sir!

- Note that the possessive adjective is already part of the noun in:
    >**ma**dame → **mes**dames
    >**ma**demoiselle → **mes**demoiselles
    >**mon**sieur → **mes**sieurs

3.9 Spelling of possessive adjectives and possessive pronouns

It is a common mistake to confuse the spelling of possessive adjectives and that of possessive pronouns (see chapter 33 Possessive Pronouns, section 2). The possessive adjectives *notre* and *votre* do **not** have a circumflex accent.
>Ex: *Dans **notre** société . . .*
>In our society . . .
>>but:
>*Dans cette société qui est **la nôtre** . . .*
>In this society of ours . . .

This is also reflected in the pronunciation:
>*notre* [nɔtr]
>*nôtre* [notr]

3.10 Repetition of the possessive adjective

(i) The possessive adjective should be repeated before each noun, except when these nouns represent the same thing.
>Ex: *Il accompagna **son** père et **son** grand-père à la gare.*
>He took his father and grandfather to the station.
>>but:
>**mon** *collègue et ami Victor Dupont*
>my friend and colleague Victor Dupont

(Note here the idiomatic order of the nouns in both languages.)

(ii) The possessive adjective is not repeated with a pair of nouns in certain idioms.
>Ex: *Veuillez donner **vos** nom et prénom(s).*
>Please give your full name.
>
>*Fais-le à **tes** risques et périls.*
>Do it at your own risk.

(iii) If two adjectives are used to qualify one noun, the possessive adjective is not repeated.
>Ex: **Ses** *longs et beaux cheveux d'or.*
>Her beautiful long golden hair.

(iv) If the adjectives qualify two different instances of the same noun, the possessive adjective must be repeated.

> Ex: *J'ai publié **mon** meilleur et **mon** pire article dans le même journal.*
> (the best and the worst articles are not the same!)
> I published my best and my worst articles in the same journal.

3.11 'One each'

In English, when there is more than one possessor and each one possesses something, the things possessed are expressed in the plural form. However, in French, the things possessed are generally expressed in the singular (if each possessor has got only **one** of these things). This is the case in particular with certain parts of the body or items of clothing, but also with one's country, one's life, etc.

> Ex: Writers want to leave something of themselves on earth after **their deaths**.
> *Les écrivains veulent laisser un peu d'eux-mêmes sur terre après **leur mort**.*
>
> You could tell by **their faces** that they were happy.
> *On pouvait voir sur **leur visage** qu'ils étaient heureux.*
>
> They talked about problems in **their countries**.
> *Ils ont parlé des problèmes dans **leur pays**.*

However, both singular and plural are tolerated in some cases.

> Ex: *Ils ont ôté leur(s) chapeau(x).*

4 Expression of possession with parts of the body

If the thing possessed is a part of the body, a bodily attribute, an item of clothing or another object close to the body, the possessive adjective is seldom appropriate in French. Note that parts of the body include *la tête*, *les bras*, *les jambes*, etc., as well as someone's *allure*, *mémoire*, *vue*, etc.

4.1 Definite article

(i) The definite article is used when the part of the body is not qualified by an adjective (except *droit* or *gauche*, since all human beings normally have a right and left hand, etc.) in common expressions such as:

*hausser **les** épaules*	to shrug one's shoulders
*baisser **la** tête*	to lower one's head
*ouvrir **les** yeux*	to open one's eyes
*tirer **la** langue*	to stick out one's tongue
*dresser **les** oreilles* (for an animal)	to prick up one's ears
*perdre **la** mémoire*	to lose one's memory
*lever **la** main*	to raise one's hand
*lever **la** main droite*	to raise one's right hand

NB: Note the following:

> *grincer **des** (= de les) dents*   to grind one's teeth
> *sentir **des** (= de les) pieds*   to have smelly feet

> Ex: *Tobby a haussé **les** épaules; alors Moffet lui a tiré **la** langue.*
> Tobby shrugged **his** shoulders so Moffet stuck **her** tongue out at him.

> *Levez **la** main droite et dites 'Je le jure!'*
> Raise **your** right hand and say: 'I swear!'

> *Le chien ouvrit **l'**œil et dressa **l'**oreille.*
> The dog opened **his** eyes and pricked up **his** ears.

> *Elle lui tendit **la** main.*
> She held **her** hand out to him.

For parts of the body qualified by an adjective other than *droit* or *gauche* or by a preposition + noun, see section 4.3 below.

(ii)   The definite article is used to convey a person's appearance or attitude with an adverb phrase of manner:

– including a part of the body:

> Ex: *Elle est arrivée, **la tête** haute.*
> She arrived with her head held high.

> *Elle resta immobile, **les yeux** fixés sur l'écran.*
> She remained still, with her eyes fixed on the screen.

> *Ils m'ont accueilli **les bras** ouverts.*
> They welcomed me with open arms.

> *Ils ne sont pas venus **les mains** vides.*
> They did not come empty-handed.

– including a piece of clothing or another object close to the body:

> Ex: *Il est entré dans le bureau du Directeur **le chapeau** sur **la tête** et **les mains** dans **les poches**.*
> He entered the Headmaster's office with his hat on his head and his hands in his pockets.

Compare:

> *Ils sont entrés, **les chaussures** boueuses et **les vêtements** déchirés.*
> They came in with muddy shoes and torn clothes.
>
> and:
>
> *Ils ont enlevé **leurs chaussures** boueuses et **leurs vêtements** déchirés.*
> (where '*chaussures*' and '*vêtements*' are direct objects, not adverb phrases of manner)
> They took off their muddy shoes and torn clothes.

(iii)   With the preposition *à* to convey a more or less permanent physical characteristic by which the animate may be recognized ('with' in English).

Ex: '*L'homme à l'habit rouge*' (sung by Edith Piaf)
The man with the red coat

le chien à la patte cassée
the dog with the broken leg

4.2 Definite or indefinite article?

(i) When describing a particular physical or mental feature with *avoir*, either the definite or the indefinite article can be used when the feature is qualified by an adjective or adjectival phrase – but only when describing a **permanent** property of this feature. If the property is only **transitory**, the **definite article must** be used.

Ex: *Les cochons ont **la/une** queue en tire-bouchon.*
Pigs have a corkscrew tail.
(= permanent feature)

*Ce chien a **les/des** oreilles pointues.*
This dog has pointed ears.
(= permanent feature)

*Elle a **le/un** nez aquilin.*
She has an aquiline nose.
(= permanent feature)
     but:
*Elle a **le** nez qui coule.*
She has got a runny nose.
(= transitory feature)
     hence:
*Il a **le/un** nez crochu, **les/des** yeux bleus, **les** mains sales.*
('*mains sales*' should be a transitory feature!)
He has a crooked nose, blue eyes, dirty hands.

(ii) However, if the adjective or one of the adjectives come **before** the feature, the indefinite article must be used. Compare:
*Il a **le** nez pointu.*
He's got a pointed nose.
     and:
*Il a **un** grand nez pointu.*
He's got a long pointed nose.

'*J'ai **la** mémoire qui flanche.*'
(popular song)
My memory is going.
     and:
*J'ai **une** bonne mémoire.*
I have got a good memory.

(See also chapter 28 Qualifying Adjectives, section 2.3.4, about the meaning of adjectives according to their position with the nouns they modify.)

(iii)   If the feature is plural, there is actually a difference of meaning between the definite and the indefinite articles (see also chapter 23 Articles).

> Ex: *Elle n'a que trente ans et déjà **des** cheveux blancs.*
> (= some, out of the whole head of hair)
> She's only thirty years old and already has some grey hairs.
> but:
> *Elle n'a que trente ans et déjà **les** cheveux blancs.*
> (= the whole head)
> She's only thirty years old and her hair is already grey.

4.3 Possessive adjective

(i)   If the part of the body is qualified by an adjective other than *droit* or *gauche* or by a noun complement, the possessive adjective must be used. This is because the 'possession' is not universal.

> Ex: *Elle a haussé **ses** lourdes épaules.*
> She shrugged her heavy shoulders.
>
> *Le chien dressa **ses** oreilles pointues.*
> The dog pricked up his pointed ears.
>
> *Elle leva vers lui **ses** yeux de turquoise.*
> She raised her turquoise eyes to him.
> but:
> *Elle a haussé **les** épaules.*
> *Le chien dressa **les** oreilles.*
> *Elle leva **les** yeux vers lui.*

(ii)   Idioms

> Ex: *Il lui a consacré sa vie.*
> He devoted his life to him/her.
>
> *Elle lui a accordé sa main (en mariage).*
> She gave him her hand (in marriage).

4.4 Indirect object pronoun

If the action is something one does **to a part of somebody else's body** (including in a figurative sense), the indirect object pronoun referring to the person affected should be used.

> Ex: *Il **nous** a ouvert **les** yeux sur ce qui se passait.*
> He opened **our** eyes to what was going on.
> rather than:
> *Il a ouvert nos yeux . . .*
>
> *Cela ne **me** facilite pas **la** vie.*
> This does not make **my** life any easier.
>
> *Ils **lui** ont essuyé **le** visage.*
> They wiped **his/her** face.

NB: Stative verbs should not be used with this construction.

> Ex: *Il **lui** écoute **le** cœur.*
> He's listening to his/her heart.
> > but not:
> *★Il lui entend le cœur.*
> He can hear his/her heart.
> (→ *Il entend son cœur.*)

4.5   Reflexive pronoun *se*

(i)   When the action is something one does **to a part of one's own body** (as opposed to something one does **with** a part of one's own body), the reflexive pronoun *se* should be used. This functions as an indirect object, and represents the possessor.

> Ex: *Elle **se** lave **les** cheveux.*
> She washes **her** hair.
> > rather than:
> *?Elle lave ses cheveux.*
>
> *Je **me** suis coupé **le** doigt.*
> I cut **my** finger.
>
> *Le chat **se** gratte **la** tête.*
> The cat is scratching **his** head.
>
> *Je **me** suis tordu **la** cheville.*
> I twisted **my** ankle.

Hence:

> *Elle **se** lave **les** mains.*
> She washes her (own) hands.
> > but:
> *Elle **lui** lave **les** mains.*
> She washes his/her (somebody else's) hands.

(ii)   There is no agreement of the past participle since the direct object comes after the verb (see chapters 9 Perfect, section 3 and 20 Pronominal Verbs, section 3.1.2). Hence:

> She burnt her knee.
> *Elle s'est brûlé le genou.*
> (*se* is an indirect object; *le genou* indicates **what** was burnt and is the direct object)
> > but:
> *Elle s'est brûlée au genou.*
> (*se* is a direct object; *au genou* indicates **where** the burn occurred and is an adverb phrase)

(iii)   With less common expressions, the choice between the use of the indirect pronoun *se*, or the possessive adjective, is largely optional.

Ex: *Je **me** suis abîmé **les** cheveux en les lavant trop souvent.*
or:
*J'ai abîmé **mes** cheveux en les lavant trop souvent.*
I have damaged my hair by washing it too often.

5 Other ways of expressing possession

There are several ways of expressing possession or attribution without using the possessive adjective.

5.1 Definite article + *en*

The definite article + *en* can be used when the possessor is an inanimate (concrete or abstract): *en* indicates the possessor. See also chapter 31 Personal Pronouns, section 2.2.2.7.

Ex: *Il aurait voulu commander le caviar mais la qualité **en** paraissait douteuse.*
or:
*. . . mais **sa** qualité paraissait douteuse.*
He would have liked to order the caviar but its quality seemed dubious.

*Je suis entré dans une agence de voyage pour **en** consulter les brochures sur la Grèce.*
I went into a travel agent's in order to look at their brochures on Greece.

*Ce costume n'est pas mal mais les manches **en** sont trop longues.*
This suit is all right but the sleeves are too long.

*J'ai bien lu votre rapport et j'**en** ai compris toute la signification.*
I read your report carefully and understood all its significance.

NB: If *en* is used, the possessive adjective should not be used as well!
Ex: In order to recognize **its** limits and difficulties in surviving in our culture . . .
★*Pour en reconnaître ses limites et ses difficultés à survivre dans notre culture . . .*
→ *Pour **en** reconnaître **les** limites et **les** difficultés . . .*

5.2 *dont* + definite article

See also chapter 32 Relative Pronouns, section 3.4.2. Again, note that after *dont*, there is no possessive adjective because *dont* already indicates the possessor.
Ex: *C'est une étudiante **dont** je connais **les** parents.*
(= *Je connais les parents de cette étudiante/Je connais ses parents.*)
This is a student whose parents I know.
and not:
★*C'est une étudiante dont je connais ses parents.*

5.3 *être à*

à **must** be retained and followed by a tonic pronoun (*moi, toi, lui, elle, nous, vous, eux, elles*), i.e. not replaced by a clitic pronoun.

Ex: *Ce sac est-il à vous? Non, il n'est pas à moi, il est à Cathy.*
Is this bag yours? No, it is not mine, it is Cathy's.

C'est à lui (ce sac)? Non, c'est à elle.
Is that his? No, it is hers.

C'est à vous (ces livres)? Non, c'est aux étudiants.
Are these yours? No, they belong to the students.

5.4 *appartenir à*

Note that *appartenir à* means 'to be owned by'/'to belong to' and also 'to belong to' in the sense of 'being a member of '.

Ex: *J'appartiens à un club de natation.*
I belong to a swimming club.

Ce club de natation m'appartient.
I own this swimming club / This swimming club belongs to me.

5.5 *de* + determiner + noun (or *de* + proper noun)

(i) This construction corresponds to the English possessive case, formed with an apostrophe. See also chapters 23 Articles, section 6.5(ii) and 26 Prepositions, section 8.2.2.3.

Ex: *la maison **de mon** ami*
my friend's house

*les moustaches **du** chat*
the cat's whiskers

*la petite amie **de** Paul*
Paul's girlfriend

*les livres **de ces** étudiants*
these students' books

NB: If *de* + noun is used, the possessive adjective should not be used as well!

Ex: *★L'art devient sa culture et donc l'identité d'un pays.*
→ *L'art devient **la** culture et donc **l'**identité **d'un** pays.*
Art becomes a country's culture and therefore its identity.

(ii) Note that, as in English, when the first noun expresses a process, there can be an ambiguity.

Ex: *le meurtre **de** Paul* (Paul's murder)
This could refer to the fact that Paul murdered someone, or that someone murdered Paul.

(iii) The demonstrative pronouns *celui-ci*, *celle-ci*, or *ce dernier*, *cette dernière* can be used to avoid repetition of the noun.

> Ex: *Marie et Catherine se sont présentées à un concours: le livre **de cette dernière** a été récompensé.*
> (= *le livre **de Catherine***)
> Marie and Catherine took part in a competition – the latter's book won a prize.

6 Translation problems

(i) The possessive adjective is used in French whereas English uses other constructions in the following idioms:

> Ex: *Grand-mère vient de descendre du train: je vais **aller à sa rencontre**.*
> Grandma's just got off the train – I'll go and meet her.
>
> *Il a **couru à mon secours**.*
> He rushed over to help me.
>
> *Il m'a demandé de vous **dire** cela **de sa part**.*
> He asked me to tell you that from him.
>
> ***sauf votre respect***
> with all due respect (to you)
>
> *Il a dû commencer à **gagner sa vie** dès l'âge de seize ans.*
> He had to start earning a living from the age of sixteen.

(ii) The possessive adjective is used in English but not in French in the following idioms:

> Ex: *Il a changé de tactique / d'avis / de chaussures . . .*
> He changed **his** tactics / **his** mind / **his** shoes . . .

(iii) When faced with a special or rare construction in English, it is a good idea to rephrase it in simpler, equivalent terms.

> Ex: 'Hers was beauty that would have made even a wild goose alight.'
>
> Richard Hughes, *In Hazard*
>
> (= Her beauty was such that . . .)
> *Sa beauté était telle que . . .*

25 Demonstrative adjectives

1 Introduction

Demonstrative adjectives – like possessive adjectives and definite articles – belong to the class of specific determiners. They precede and determine a noun with which they agree in gender and number.

The demonstrative adjective is used to point to an element, its referent. This referent is either identifiable in the situation (**deictic**) or refers to an element in the context (**anaphoric**). See also chapter 23 Articles, sections 2.2.1.1 and 2.2.2.1. Compare:

> *Cet après-midi*, *j'irai me promener.*
> This afternoon, I shall go for a walk.

> *Tu as vu **cette fille**!*
> Look at that girl!

where '*cet après-midi*' and '*cette fille*' are only identifiable in the situation of communication; and:

> *Je retourne à **Paris** pour le week-end. **Cette ville** m'enchante.*
> I'm going back to Paris for the week-end. That city is delightful.

where '*cette ville*' refers to '*Paris*', previously cited in the context.

Unlike English, which uses **this/that/these/those** both as adjectives and as pronouns, French has two sets of demonstratives, which should not be confused.

adjectives:	pronouns:
ce (cet), ce (cet) . . . –ci/là	*celui, celui-ci/là*
cette, cette . . . –ci/là	*celle, celle-ci/là*
ces, ces . . . –ci/là	*ceux, ceux-ci/là*
	celles, celles-ci/là
	ce
	ceci, cela

2 Simple forms and meanings

(i) The simple demonstrative adjective has four forms:
   – two masculine (*ce, cet*)
   – one feminine (*cette*)
   – one plural (*ces*)

(ii)   The demonstrative adjective agrees in gender and number with the noun it modifies.

> Ex: *ce livre*; *cette maison*; *ces étudiants*

(iii)   The second form of the masculine singular, *cet*, is used before a noun (or adjective) beginning with a vowel or a mute '*h*'.

> Ex: *cet exploit*; *cet homme*; *cet extraordinaire plan d'action*

(iv)   Repetition

Unlike in English, the French demonstrative adjective is normally repeated before each of the nouns it refers to, even in a list.

> Ex: *A qui sont **ces** livres et **ces** cahiers?*
> Whose are **these** textbooks and exercise books?
>
> *Regarde **ces** hommes et **ces** femmes, tous sur leur trente et un!*
> Look at **these** men and women, all dressed up to the nines!

(v)   'this' or 'that', 'these' or 'those'

The simple demonstrative adjective in French means either **this** or **that**, **these** or **those**, where the distinction between 'this' and 'that' is not important (but see 3 below).

> Ex: *cet arbre* = 'this tree' or 'that tree'

(vi)   Past or future?

ce soir, *ce matin*, etc. can express recent past or near future according to the **tense** used.

> Ex: *Je **rangerai** tout cela **ce soir**.*
> I shall tidy all that up tonight.
> (*ce soir* = near future)
>
> *J'ai fait les courses **ce matin**.*
> I did the shopping this morning.
> (*ce matin* = recent past)
>
> *J'ai bien **dormi cette nuit**.*
> I slept well last night.
> (*cette nuit* = recent past)
>
> *J'espère que je **vais** bien **dormir cette nuit**.*
> I hope I'll sleep well tonight.
> (*cette nuit* = near future)

(vii)   Stylistic use of the demonstrative adjective

The demonstrative adjective is used instead of a definite article when referring to something just mentioned in the previous sentence. It is an alternative to making the second sentence a relative clause.

Ex: *On peut mettre un ignorant sur le chemin de la connaissance en suivant la méthode de Socrate.* **Cette** *méthode consistait à feindre d'être ignorant . . .*
One can put an ignoramus on the road to knowledge by following Socrates' method. This consisted of pretending to be ignorant . . .
  or:
. . . en suivant la méthode de Socrate, qui consistait à . . .

3 Compound forms and meanings

We have seen that:
− *ce, cet* and *cette* correspond to **this** or **that**
− *ces* corresponds to **these** or **those**

It is only when the idea of **this** or **that** (**these** or **those**) is **emphatic** that a distinction is made in French by the addition of the adverbial elements *-ci* or *-là*, after the noun. Hence:

(i) Distinction of space or time

− the idea of proximity to the speaker is conveyed by the addition of *-ci*;
− the idea of distance from the speaker is conveyed by the addition of *-là*.
  Ex: − space:
C'est par **cette** *route-**ci** que nous sommes venus.*
It is by **this** road that we came.

Ces *fruits-**là** ne sont pas assez mûrs.*
Those fruit aren't ripe enough.

− time:
*Ce soir-**là**, je n'ai pas pu m'endormir.*
That night, I couldn't go to sleep.

En **ce** *temps-**là**, les jeunes ne sortaient pas tous les soirs.*
In **those** days, young people weren't allowed to go out every night.
(*en ce temps-là* = in the past)

Il ne fait pas très beau **ces** *jours-**ci**.*
The weather has not been very good lately.
(*ces jours-ci* = recently, or recently and including today)

Je vais à Paris **ce** *mois-**ci**.*
I'm going to Paris some time **this** month.
(*ce mois-ci* = in the near future)

(ii) Opposition

Consider the following examples:

1 *Nous avons vu que même si parfois les croyances empêchent l'exercice de la réflexion, à d'autres moments, elles en forment les bases et sont*

donc nécessaires à son exercice. Dans **ces cas-là**, *on peut dire que les croyances* . . .
('*dans ces cas-là*' refers to '*à d'autres moments* . . .', as opposed to '*même si parfois* . . .')
We have seen that even if religious belief sometimes inhibits the act of reflection, at other times, it forms its very basis and is therefore necessary. In **those cases**, it can be said that religious belief . . .

2 *En prenant conscience de Dieu et de sa volonté, l'homme renonce à être libre, mais pas nécessairement dans* **ce monde-ci**, *car il sait que ses actes sur la terre seront récompensés après sa mort.*
('*ce monde-ci*' is opposed to the world after death)
By acknowledging God and His will, man renounces his freedom – but not necessarily in **this world** – for he knows that everything that he does on this earth will be rewarded after death.

(iii)   Exophora

When an object is literally pointed at (exophora), *-là* is used:
Ex: *A qui appartient* **ce chat-là**?
Whom does **that** cat belong to?

Donnez-moi **ces** *deux éclairs au chocolat-***là**.
I'll have **those** two chocolate eclairs.

4 Summary

	singular		plural
	M	F	M F
simple	*ce, cet* (this/that)	*cette* (this/that)	*ces* (these/those)
compound	*ce (cet)* . . . *-ci* *ce (cet)* . . . *-là* (this/that)	*cette* . . . *-ci* *cette* . . . *-là* (this/that)	*ces* . . . *-ci* *ces* . . . *-là* (these/those)

353

26 Prepositions

1 Introduction

Prepositions are used to subordinate a word or phrase to that which precedes it. The second element is therefore a complement of the first. The preposition introduces the **prepositional phrase** (*syntagme ou groupe prépositionnel*). Prepositions are invariable.

2 Nature and functions of the prepositional phrase

The prepositional phrase can complement a noun, an adjective or a verb. It can act as an indirect object, a subject complement, an object complement or an adverb. For details, see chapter 2 Syntax.

(i) **First element**

– **noun**

Ex: *le chat **de** la voisine*

The noun phrase '*la voisine*' is part of the prepositional phrase '***de** la voisine*' which in turn is part of the larger noun phrase '*le chat **de** la voisine*'. There is therefore a hierarchical relationship between these various elements: '***de** la voisine*' is the complement of the noun phrase '*le chat*'.

Ex: *le chat **de** la voisine **du** rez-de-chaussée*

The prepositional phrase '***du** (= de + le) rez-de-chaussée*' is the complement of the noun phrase '*la voisine*', etc.

– **adjective**

Ex: *couvert **de** neige*

The prepositional phrase '***de** neige*' is the complement of the adjective '*couvert*', forming with it an adjectival phrase.

– **verb**

The verb complement is usually a prepositional phrase but it can also be a whole clause.

Ex: *Il s'en est pris **au** chat de la voisine.*

The **prepositional phrase** '***au** chat de la voisine*' is the complement of the verb '*s'en est pris*' (*s'en prendre à qn*). This is the case for all indirect objects.

Ex: *Nous avons parlé **de** quand nous étions à l'école ensemble.*

The **clause** '***de** quand nous étions à l'école ensemble*' is the complement of the verb '*avons parlé*' (*parler de qch*).

(ii) **Functions**

Words that can be linked by prepositions are all constituents of an **indirect** construction, i.e.:

– indirect object

> Ex: *J'ai parlé **à** Paul.*
> *Cela ne dépend pas **de** moi.*
> *J'ai participé **au** concours.*

– subject complement

> Ex: *Il passe **pour** intelligent.*
> *Il passe **pour** un imbécile.*

– object complement

> Ex: *On a pris Eric **pour** ton frère!*
> *Catherine a traité Eric **d'**égoïste.*

– adverb phrase

> Ex: *Je ne vois pas **de** près.*
> *Il est parti **pour** longtemps.*

In the following examples:

> *Le chat s'était endormi **sur** le lit.*
> *J'ai rencontré Jean-Pierre **près de** la bibliothèque.*

the prepositional phrase depends directly on the **sentence** and therefore can be displaced:

> → ***Sur** le lit, le chat s'était endormi.*
> → ***Près** de la bibliothèque, j'ai rencontré Jean-Pierre.*

See also chapter 2 Syntax, section 2.13.

3 Prepositions followed by a verb: infinitive or gerund?

After all prepositions except *en*, the verb is in the **infinitive** whereas in English it is usually a form in '-ing'.

(i) **Infinitive**

> Ex: *Vous devriez acheter un guide **avant de visiter** l'exposition.*
> You should buy a guide **before visiting** the exhibition.
>
> *Elle a disparu **sans dire** au revoir.*
> She disappeared **without saying** goodbye.

(ii) **Past infinitive**

The preposition *après* is always followed by a **past infinitive** (i.e. *avoir* or *être* + past participle).

> Ex: ***Après avoir chassé** toute la nuit, Lizzy était fatiguée.*
> **After hunting** all night, Lizzy was tired.

With other prepositions, the choice between present and past infinitives is a question of aspect. See chapter 15 Infinitive, section 2.2.

> Ex: *Il est reparti **sans avoir vu** son grand-père.*
> He left **without having seen** his grandfather.
>
> *Robert a été promu **pour avoir travaillé** si dur.*
> Robert was promoted **for working** so hard.

(iii) **Present participle**

The preposition *en* is always followed by a **present participle** to form a gerund.

> Ex: *J'ai vu Antoine **en allant** à la bibliothèque.*
> I saw Antoine on my way to the library.
> (= as I was going to . . .)

See also chapter 16 Present Participle, section 3.3.

4 Morphology

4.1 Simple prepositions

> Ex: *à, après, avant, avec, chez, contre, dans, de, depuis, derrière, dès, devant, durant, en, entre, envers, excepté, jusque, malgré, outre, par, parmi, pendant, pour, sans, selon, sous, sur, vers, voici, voilà,* etc.

4.2 Compound prepositions (*locutions prépositionnelles*)

Compound prepositions are made up of several words.

– Some do not include a noun:

> Ex: *à moins de, à partir de, au-delà de, au-dessus de, au-dessous de, en dessous de, au-devant de, auprès de, autour de, vis-à-vis de, d'après, d'entre, près de, loin de, hors de, lors de, jusqu'à, quant à, par derrière, par-dessus, par-dessous,* etc.

– Some include a noun without article:

> Ex: *faute de, à cause de, à raison de, à propos de, à titre de, à côté de, à force de, à travers, en travers de, en dépit de, en face de, en haut de, en bas de, à droite de, à gauche de, en faveur de, par rapport à, grâce à,* etc.

– Some include a noun preceded by an article:

> Ex: *le long de, du côté de, au milieu de, au lieu de, au sujet de, au travers de, sur la droite de, sur la gauche de, à l'exception de, à l'aide de, à la faveur de, aux dépens de, à l'insu de, aux alentours de, aux environs de,* etc.

NB(1): Most compound prepositions end in *à* or *de,* but there are a few exceptions: e.g. *d'après, d'entre, à travers, par derrière, par-dessus, par-dessous.*

NB(2): The list of compound prepositions should be considered as an open list. Recent additions include *à concurrence de* and the informal *rapport à.*

5 Meaning

The prepositional phrase as a verb complement corresponds to one of the usual adverb phrases of time, place, manner, aim, cause, means, condition, concession, matter, origin, destination, etc. The prepositional phrase may have different meanings depending on the second element.

Ex: *manger avec qn/avec une fourchette/avec gourmandise.*

However, with the exception of *de* and *à* (see details below), most prepositions have a clearly defined meaning.

Ex: *Le chat est **sur** la table/**sous** la table/**près de** la table.*
The cat is **on** the table/**under** the table/**near** the table.

Difficulties arise in the following cases:

(i)   Some prepositions have a similar meaning in French but are not interchangeable, e.g. *à, dans, en*, which translate **at/in** or **to/into**.

Ex: *Il est **en** prison.* He is **in** prison.
*Il est **dans** une prison modèle.* He is **in** a model prison.
*Il est **à** la prison des Baumettes.* He is **at** the Baumettes prison.

*Il est **à** la maison.* He is **at** home.
*Il est **dans** la maison.* He is **in** the house.
*Il est parti **en** maison de retraite.* He's gone **to** a retirement home.

(ii) *de* and *à* are by far the most common prepositions in French. They are said to be 'abstract' or 'empty' when in fact the problem is that they have a lot of meanings.

Ex: *un verre **de** vin*   a glass of wine
*Je reviens **de** Paris.*   I am back from Paris.
*C'est une lettre **de** Paul.*   It's a letter from Paul.

*un verre **à** vin*   a wineglass
*J'habite **à** Paris.*   I live in Paris.
*Ce livre est **à** Paul.*   This book is Paul's.

– Because of this, and whenever there is a risk of ambiguity or even incomprehension, *de* and *à* tend to be used in compound prepositions (rather than by themselves) or are even replaced by another preposition.

Ex: Tell him this **from** me.
*Dites-lui cela **de ma part**.*
(and not **de moi*)

You can choose **from** a wide variety of books.
*On peut choisir **parmi** une immense étendue de livres.*
(and not **d'une*)

I'll walk with you **to** the gate.
*Je vous raccompagne **jusqu'au** portail.*
(and not **au*)

  – In a number of cases however, it is our extra-linguistic knowledge which comes into play and helps us to clarify the meaning according to the context.
  > Ex: *une culotte **de** cheval:*
  > – riding-breeches **or**
  > – cellullite around the hips and thighs
  > *une culotte **de** daim:*
  > a garment made of buckskin

Consider the following examples:
> *un portrait **de** Picasso*

The context should determine whether it is a portrait **of** or **by** Picasso, whereas:
> *un portrait **de** M. Dupont*

is probably a portrait **of** M. Dupont, particularly if it is known that M. Dupont is not an artist.

When the noun is followed by two complements, the meaning should be made more precise by using two different prepositions. Hence:
> *un portrait **de** M. Dupont **par** Picasso*
> a portrait of M. Dupont by Picasso

Note that it is the **second** preposition which is replaced by a more 'meaningful' one.

(iii) Idiomatic use of prepositions in both languages makes choice unpredictable.
> Ex: *Hier, j'ai regardé un film **à** la télévision.*
> Yesterday, I watched a film **on** television.

> *C'est le plus beau chat **du** monde.*
> He is the most handsome cat **in the** world.

> *Une pièce de trois mètres **sur** cinq.*
> A room measuring three metres **by** five.

> *Essayez d'arriver **à** l'heure / Le train est arrivé **à** l'heure.*
> Try to arrive **on** time / The train arrived **on** time.

(iv) Prepositions that are part of a verb seldom correspond directly between the two languages:
> Ex: *Cela ne **dépend** pas **de** moi!*
> It does not **depend on** me!

> *C'est quelque chose qui **ressemble à** l'égalité.*
> It is something which **looks like** equality.

  – There may be a preposition in French but not in English:
> Ex: *Je me **souviens** très bien **de** ce film.*
> I **remember** _ that film very well.

> *L'art **permet aux** gens de rêver.*
> Art **enables** _ people to dream.

  – There may be a preposition in English but not in French:
> Ex: *Je **cherche** _ un livre.*
> I'm **looking for** a book.

6 Prepositions and other parts of speech

Words which look like prepositions can also be other parts of speech, either by homonymy or by improper derivation: see chapters 1 Parts of Speech, section 11 and 28 Qualifying Adjectives, section 5.2(v). See also prepositions and conjunctions in chapter 12 Subjunctive, section 4.4.2.

6.1 Prepositions and adverbs

Some prepositions can become adverbs when they are not followed by a complement. For instance: *après*, *avant*, *avec* (informal French only), *contre*, *depuis*, *derrière*, *devant*, *par derrière*, *par-dessus*, *par-dessous*. Compare:

*J'ai mis tes sacs **devant** la porte.*
preposition
I've put your bags in front of the door.

and:

*J'ai mis tes sacs **devant**.*
adverb
I've put your bags at the front.

*Il faut partir **avant** la pluie.*
preposition
We should leave before the rain.

and:

*Il fallait y penser **avant**.*
adverb
You should have thought of it before.

*Je ne dors plus **depuis** trois jours.*
preposition
I haven't slept for three days.

and:

*J'ai reçu une lettre l'an dernier et **depuis**, plus rien.*
adverb
I received a letter last year and nothing since.

6.2 Prepositions and past participles

Ex: *y compris*, *vu*, *excepté*, *passé*

Compare:

***Passé** 10 heures, il ne faut plus faire de bruit.*
preposition, invariable
After ten o'clock, you are requested not to make any noise.

and:

*J'ai **passé** une heure à t'attendre.*
past participle
I have spent one hour waiting for you.

NB: *passé* can also be an adjective by improper derivation from the past participle.
Ex: *Il est dix heures **passées**, temps d'aller te coucher!*
It is gone ten o'clock, time for you to go to bed!

6.3   Prepositions and present participles

Ex: ***durant, suivant***

Compare:

Suivant *la manière dont vous vous y prenez . . .*
preposition

Depending on the way you go about it . . .

and:

J'ai marché jusqu'au prochain village, ***suivant*** *le chemin indiqué.*
present participle

I walked to the next village, following the path indicated.

NB: ***suivant*** can also be an adjective by improper derivation from the present participle.

Ex: *La semaine* ***suivante****, je suis revenue.*

The following week, I came back.

7   Repetition and coordination of prepositions

(i)   **Repetition and coordination**

– The preposition is repeated

When two prepositional phrases beginning with the same preposition are coordinated, the preposition is normally repeated in French (particularly *à* and *de* which are 'semantically empty') though not necessarily in English (see also chapter 40 Coordination, section 5.1(iii)).

Ex: *Un homme doit subvenir aux besoins* ***de*** *sa femme et* ***de*** *ses enfants.*
(Note that the possessive adjective is also repeated.)
A man must provide for the needs **of** his wife and _ children.

Une des premières choses qu'on apprend, c'est ***à*** *lire et* ***à*** *écrire.*
(*apprendre* ***à*** *faire qch*)
One of the first things you learn is **to** read and _ write.

C'est une atteinte ***aux*** *attitudes parentales,* ***à la*** *conduite sociale,* ***aux*** *talents, etc.*
It is an assault **on** parental attitudes, _ social behaviour, _ talents, etc.

NB: There are exceptions to the repetition of *à* and *de* in set phrases.

Ex: *à vos risques et périls*
at your own risk

(See also chapter 23 Articles, section 6.6.)

– The preposition is not repeated

With other prepositions, there is no repetition when the second phrase is an extension or explanation of the first (i.e. if it does not express a separate idea), unless emphasis is required. Otherwise, the preposition is repeated.

Ex: *Il est arrivé* ***avec*** *ses chiens* ***et*** *ses chats.*
He came with **his** dogs and _ cats.

> *La directrice aime les tenues correctes: je vais me mettre **en** jupe **et** chemisier.*
> The headmistress likes smart dress – I'll wear a skirt and blouse.
> > but:
> *On se marie **pour le** meilleur **et pour le** pire.*
> People get married **for** better or _ worse.

> *Ils disent que c'est normal **pour les** chats de chasser les souris **et pour les** chiens de chasser les chats.*
> They say it is normal **for** cats to chase mice **and for** dogs to chase cats.

– Repetition of the preposition is optional

When the prepositional phrases express neither opposite nor similar ideas, the repetition of the preposition is a matter of personal choice.

> Ex: *C'est un moyen utilisé **pour** reprendre le pouvoir donné à certains individus **et** [**pour**] le redonner aux autres.*
> It's a way of removing the power vested in certain people and giving it to others.

However, it is much more commonly omitted in English than in French.

(ii) Repetition and compound prepositions with *de*

– One preposition + ***de*** + two or more nouns

When a compound preposition is made up of a preposition + *de*, the first preposition is dropped and only *de* is retained with the second or further noun.

> Ex: *Je me suis assise **près de** Julie **et de** Sophie.*
> I sat near Julie and Sophie.

NB: The same principle works with infinitives.

> Ex: *Ils l'ont fait **afin de** nous corrompre **et de** nous dominer.*
> They did it in order to corrupt and dominate us.

– Two prepositions + ***de*** + single noun

When two such prepositions are used with a single noun, it is the *de* of the first compound which is dropped.

> Ex: *Il y avait des policiers **à l'intérieur** et **à l'extérieur de** la maison.*
> There were policemen inside and outside the house.

8 *de* and *à*

8.1 Preposition *à*

à can be part of a verb, introduce adverb phrases or noun complements or indicate possession.

8.1.1 à *and verbs*

When *à* is part of a verb it can be followed by a noun, pronoun or an infinitive. In this case, *à* is generally an 'empty' preposition.

A verb which is constructed **directly** with a noun, for example, may be constructed **indirectly** with an infinitive, for example, and vice versa.

> Ex: *Nous apprenons **l'anglais**.*
> direct object
>
> *Nous apprenons **à jouer** au badminton.*
> indirect object

(i) Verb + *à* + noun

à is always expressed in French (though not necessarily so in English, particularly in bitransitive verbs: see also chapter 2 Syntax, section 2.6.6).

> Ex: *Elle a envoyé le paquet **à** Céline.*
> (*envoyer qch **à** qn*)
> She sent the parcel to Céline.
>
> or:
> She sent _ Céline the parcel.
>
> *Je joue **au** tennis tous les jeudis après-midi.*
> (*jouer **à** qch*)
> I play _ tennis every Thursday afternoon.

NB: *à* + definite article is used with *jouer* followed by the name of a sport or game (*jouer au tennis, à la belote, au tarot*, etc.), but *de* is used before musical instruments (see 8.2.1(i) below).

(ii) Verb + *à* + pronoun

– Personal pronoun
It is usual to use *à* + tonic pronoun for animates (*moi, toi, lui, elle, nous, vous, eux, elles*) and *y* for inanimates. (But see chapter 31 Personal Pronouns, section 2.2.2.6(i) for a refinement of this rule.)

> Ex: *Je pense souvent à mes enfants.*
> → *Je pense souvent **à eux**.*
>
> *Je pense souvent à mes vacances de l'an passé.*
> → *J'**y** pense souvent.*

– Relative pronoun
> Ex: *C'est quelqu'un **à qui** je pense souvent.*
> (*penser **à** qn*)
> That's someone I often think of.

See chapter 32 Relative Pronouns, section 3.3.

– Indefinite, possessive and demonstrative pronouns
> Ex: *Ce chat n'appartient **à personne**/me fait penser **au mien**/me fait penser **à celui-là***.

(iii) Verb + *à* + infinitive

> Ex: *Nous sommes parvenus **à** nous mettre à l'abri.*
> (*parvenir **à** faire qch*)
> We managed to find shelter.

8.1.2 à, no verb

à can introduce adverb phrases, noun complements (see individual meanings) or indicate possession.

8.1.2.1 *à* AND ADVERB PHRASES

(i) **Adverb phrases of place**

When *à* introduces adverb phrases of place, e.g. *au théâtre, à la piscine, au lit, au bois, à la campagne, au milieu de la pièce, au soleil, à l'ombre*, etc., it can indicate **location** as well as **destination** and **direction** depending on the verb used.

> Ex: *J'aime aller **à la piscine**.*
> *Grand-mère préfère se mettre **à l'ombre**.*

Note the following idioms:

à portée de la main	within reach
à droite	on the right
à gauche	on the left
à un autre niveau	on another level
à bord (d'un bateau)	on board (a ship)
à la télévision	on television
à la ligne 16	on line 16
à l'église	in church
au bureau	at the office
à côté de	next to
but:	
***de** côté*	aside

– *à* and *de*

à is often opposed to *de*, which introduces an origin (see also chapter 37 Numbers, section 8(v)). Note that with *le*, *à* becomes *au*, and with *les*, *à* becomes *aux* (see also chapter 23 Articles, section 2.1).

– with names of towns, there is no article, unless there is already one in the name of the town:

> Ex: *J'ai roulé sans arrêt **de** Lyon **à** Marseille.*
> I drove non-stop from Lyons to Marseilles.
> but:
> *Nous allons **au** Mans; je vis **à La** Rochelle.*
> We are going to Le Mans; I live in La Rochelle.

– with masculine names of countries there is an article, but there are exceptions, particularly with certain islands:

> Ex: *Ils vivent **aux** Etats-Unis.*
> They live in the United States.
>
> *J'ai fait le trajet **du** Maroc **au** Portugal en 8 heures.*
> I travelled from Morocco to Portugal in 8 hours.
>
> *Je vais **au** Japon, **à** Ibiza, **à** Paros.*
> I'm going to Japan, Ibiza, Paros.

– *à* and *en*

With feminine names, use *en* + name of country (see 9.2(i) below).

– *à* and *chez*

In informal French, *à* is sometimes used instead of *chez*, when the place implies 'in' or 'at the house of'. This is considered inappropriate in formal French.

> Ex: *?Je vais au coiffeur* → *Je vais **chez** le coiffeur.*
> or: *Je vais **au** salon de coiffure.*

Hence: *Je vais chez ma tante; chez M. et Mme Dupont.*
By extension: *les ouvriers de chez Renault.*
See 13.3 below.

(ii) **Adverb phrases of time**

à is used to refer to a particular time or period of time. For instance:

au mois de mai	in the month of May
au quinzième siècle	in the fifteenth century
au cours du vingtième siècle	during the twentieth century
à l'époque romantique	in the romantic era
à notre époque	nowadays
à l'ère de la Renaissance	in the Renaissance
à l'âge de pierre	in the Stone Age
(arriver) à l'heure	(to arrive) on time
(arriver) à temps	(to arrive) in time
à cette époque-là	in those days
but:	
en ce temps-là	in those days
au même moment	at the same time (moment)
à ce moment-là	at that moment
but:	
en même temps	at the same time (duration)

> Ex: *Le Réalisme, **à** une époque où* . . .
> Realism, at a time when . . .

Note the following idioms:

à demain	see you tomorrow
à ce soir	see you tonight
à tout à l'heure	see you in a moment
à bientôt	see you soon

– *à* and *de*

à is used to express time, and to refer to the end of a defined period of time. It is often used in conjunction with *de* to mark the beginning of that period.

> Ex: *Je suis parti **à** six heures.*
> I left at 6 o'clock.
>
> *Je serai là **de** 5 heures **à** 6 heures.*
> I shall be there from five to six.

– *à* and *en*

The opposition is one of aspect: *à* expresses that which is punctual, whereas *en* expresses that which has a duration.

> Ex: *à ce moment*/*en ce moment*
> *à 8 heures*/*en août*

(iii) **Adverb phrases of manner or means**

– Idioms

Ex: *goutte à goutte*	drop by drop
à toute vitesse	as quickly as possible/at full speed
parler à voix basse	to keep one's voice down
être à jeun	to have/be on an empty stomach
fait(e)(s) à la main	hand-made
remplir le formulaire à l'encre	to fill in the form in ink
à la hâte	hastily
à grand peine	painstakingly; with great difficulty
à regret	regretfully; with regret
à grands pas	with long strides

– *à* and *en*

– *à* is used for a 'natural' means of transport: *à pied, à cheval, à la nage, à dos de chameau*, etc.

– *en* is used for most vehicles: *en voiture, en autobus, en train, en avion*, etc.
Exception:

> *J'y vais à vélo*   OR   *J'y vais en vélo*.
> I cycle there.

8.1.2.2   *à* AND NOUN COMPLEMENTS

This complement can be a noun with a definite article (to indicate a characteristic), a noun without a determiner, or an infinitive (to indicate the use or purpose of something).

(i) *à* + specified noun indicates a characteristic ('with')

> Ex: '*La fille aux bas nylon*' (sung by Julien Clerc)
> 'The girl with nylon stockings'

> '*L'homme à la moto*' (sung by Edith Piaf)
> 'The man with the motorcycle'

(ii) *à* + unspecified noun or infinitive indicates the use or purpose of something or what the item is 'driven by'.

Ex: *une assiette à dessert*	a dessert plate
une brosse à dents	a toothbrush
un moulin à café	a coffee grinder
une cuillère à café	a coffee spoon

365

un pot à lait	a milk jug
un ver à soie	a silk worm
un bateau à vapeur	a steamboat
un briquet à gaz	a gas lighter
une machine à laver	a washing machine
une planche à repasser	an ironing board
une salle à manger	a dining room

8.1.2.3 *à* AND POSSESSION

à can indicate possession with *être à* and *appartenir à* (see also chapter 24 Possessive Adjectives, sections 5.3 and 5.4).

Ex: *Les livres à gauche sont à Frédéric.*
The books on the left are Frédéric's.

Ce château appartient au comte de Ouchtezouk.
This castle belongs to the Count of Ouchtezouk.

NB: *C'est le livre à Robert* instead of *C'est le livre de Robert* is accepted in informal French. Note also the following set phrases:

de la barbe à papa	candyfloss
un fils à papa	a rich, spoilt teenager

8.1.2.4 *à* IN IDIOMS

Ex: *A moi!/Au secours!/A l'aide!*	Help!
A table!	Dinner is ready! (informal)
A vos/tes souhaits!	Bless you! (when sb sneezes)

au contraire	on the contrary
à condition que	on condition that
à ce sujet	on that subject/note
à mon avis	in my opinion
à votre place	in your place/if I were you
à leur façon	in their [own] way
à un mot près	give or take a word

8.2 Preposition *de*

de can be part of a verb, introduce adverb phrases or noun modifiers, or indicate possession. It can also be used to introduce the agent in the passive voice.

8.2.1 de *and verbs*

de as part of a verb can be followed by a noun, a pronoun or an infinitive (see chapter 2 Syntax, sections 2.6.5, 2.6.6 and 2.8).

A verb which is constructed **directly** with a noun, for example, may be constructed **indirectly** with an infinitive, for example, and vice versa.

Ex: *J'ai fini _ ma dissertation.*
I have finished my essay.

J'ai fini d'écrire ma dissertation.
I have finished writing my essay.

(i) **Verb + *de* + noun**

Ex: *Je ne me souviens plus de son nom.*
(se souvenir de qch)
I cannot remember his/her name.

Note: *se rappeler _ qch.*

NB: *de* + definite article is used with *jouer* followed by the name of a musical instrument (whereas *à* is used for sports and games: see 8.1.1(i) above).
Ex: *jouer du piano, de la flûte, de l'harmonica*, etc.

(ii) **Verb + *de* + pronoun**

– Personal pronoun
It is usual to use *de* + tonic pronoun for animates (*moi, toi, lui, elle, nous, vous, eux, elles*) and *en* for inanimates. (But see chapter 31 Personal Pronouns, section 2.2.2.7(i) for a refinement of this rule).
Ex: *J'ai besoin de Nicolas pour ce travail.*
→ *J'ai besoin de lui pour ce travail.*

J'ai besoin de ce chiffon pour essuyer la table.
→ *J'en ai besoin pour essuyer la table.*

– Relative pronoun
Ex: *le livre dont j'ai besoin*
(avoir besoin de qch)
the book [that] I need

la personne de qui je parle
(parler de qn)
the person I'm talking about

– Indefinite, demonstrative and possessive pronouns
Ex: *Ce chat a besoin de quelqu'un.*
Je parle de celui-ci, du mien.

(iii) **Verb + *de* + infinitive**

Ex: *Le communisme a risqué de déclencher une troisième guerre mondiale.*
(risquer de faire qch)
Communism almost started a third world war.
Note: *risquer _ qch.*

8.2.2 de, no verb

de can introduce adverb phrases, noun complements (see individual meanings) or indicate possession. It can also be used to introduce the agent in the passive voice.

8.2.2.1   *de* AND ADVERB PHRASES

(i)   **Adverb phrases of place**

When introducing adverb phrases of place, *de* can indicate origin or separation. It is often used in conjunction with *à*, which indicates destination. (See section 8.1.2.1(i) above). Note that with *le*, *de* becomes *du*, and with *les*, *de* becomes *des* (see also chapter 23 Articles, section 2.1).

>   Ex: *Il a traversé le village, **de** l'église à la gare.*
>   He crossed the village, from the church to the station.
>
>   ***du** début **à** la fin*
>   from [the] beginning to [the] end

−   with names of towns: no article, unless there is already one in the name of the town.   See also chapter 23 Articles, section 2.2.1.5.4.
>   Ex: *J'ai roulé sans arrêt **de** Lyon/**de** La Rochelle à Marseille.*
>   I drove non-stop from Lyons/La Rochelle to Marseilles.

−   with names of countries: see chapter 23 Articles, sections 2.2.1.5.1, 2.2.1.5.2 and 2.2.1.5.3. As a reminder:
    −   feminine: *de, d'*
    >   Ex: *Je suis rentrée **de** Grèce/**d'**Italie hier soir.*
    >   I came back from Greece/from Italy yesterday evening.
    −   masculine: *du*
    >   Ex: *Nous venons d'arriver **du** Portugal.*
    >   We've just come from Portugal.
    −   plural: *des*
    >   Ex: *Ils viennent **des** Pays-Bas, **des** Antilles.*
    >   They come from the Netherlands, the West Indies.
    −   no article: *de, d'*
    >   Ex: *Je reviens **de** Monaco, **d'**Andorre.*

Note the following idioms:
>   *de tous côtés/**de** toutes parts*: on all sides

(ii)   **Other adverb phrases**

−   time: *de* refers to the beginning of a defined period of time. It is often used in conjunction with *à*, which indicates the end of that period. (See 8.1.2.1(ii) above.)
>   Ex: *de 5 à 7*: from 5 to 7
>   *d'août à septembre*: from August to September

−   cause:
>   Ex: *Je tremble **de** froid.*
>   I am shivering with cold.
>
>   *Nous pleurons **de** joie!*
>   We are weeping for joy!

– manner:

> Ex: *Il écrit **d'**une façon bizarre.*
> He writes in a strange way.
>
> *Il est parti **d'**un pas pressé.*
> He walked off in a hurry.

Also:

de cette façon	in this way
d'une manière différente	in a different way
d'une façon ou d'une autre	in one way or another

8.2.2.2 *de* AND NOUN COMPLEMENTS

Unlike *à* which can be used in conjunction with noun or infinitive complements (see 8.1.2.2 above), the complement after *de* is always a noun. This construction has adjectival qualities. The resulting noun phrase expresses 'a type of something' and the noun complement is **not** preceded by an article. (See also chapter 23 Articles, section 6.5.)

> Ex: *le niveau **de** vie; une carte **d'**identité*
> the standard of living; an identity card

Some express more specifically:

– matter:

> Ex: *une veste **de** cuir*
> a leather jacket

NB: *en* is also used.

> *une bague en or; une table en chêne massif*
> a gold ring; a table in solid oak

– contents:
  Compare the following:

> Ex: *une cuillère **de** soupe*: a spoonful of soup
> *une cuillère **à** soupe*: a soup spoon

8.2.2.3 *de* AND POSSESSION, DEPENDENCE AND ATTRIBUTION

de indicates possession, dependence or attribution with a specified noun complement. (See chapters 24 Possessive Adjectives, section 5.5, and 23 Articles, section 6.5(ii).)

> Ex: *la maison **de mes** parents*
> my parents' house

8.2.2.4 *de* AND AGENT IN PASSIVE VOICE

> Ex: *L'idéal était alors le mariage, suivi **de** la vie au foyer.*
> The ideal then was marriage, followed by life at home.

See chapter 18 Active and Passive Voices, section 4, about the use of *de* versus *par*.

8.3 *de* in idioms

(aimer qn) **de** *tout son cœur*	(to love sb) with all one's heart
(être) rouge **de** *colère*	(to be) purple with rage
(être) bouillant **de** *colère*	(to be) seething with rage
(être) taché **de** *sang*	(to be) stained with blood
(être) amoureux **de** *qn*	(to be) in love with sb
augmenter/baisser **de** *prix*	to go up/down in price
(être) sain **de** *corps et* **d'***esprit*	(to be) sound in body and mind
(connaître qn) **de** *nom,* **de** *vue*	(to know sb) by name, by sight
(être) **de** *garde*	(to be) on duty (soldier, nurse)
être **d'***avis que*	to be of the opinion that

9 Preposition *en*

en can:
- be part of a verb
- introduce adverb phrases or noun complements
- be used to form the gerund
- be a pronoun (see chapter 31 Personal Pronouns, section 2.2.2.7).

9.1 *en* after verbs

- *en* is often used to express a transformation: 'into'.

      Ex: *La grenouille s'est changée* **en** *prince.*
      The frog changed into a prince.

      Il faut couper ce saucisson **en** *tranches très fines.*
      This sausage should be cut into very thin slices.

- *en* is also used in the sense of 'as'.

      Ex: *Il s'était déguisé* **en** *agent de police.*
      He had disguised himself as a policeman.

Note:

      Hélène n'a pas confiance **en** *son médecin.*
      Hélène does not trust her doctor.

9.2 *en* introducing adverb phrases

(i) **Adverb phrases of place**

en is used to express **location** as well as **destination** (see 8.1.2.1(i) above). It is the verb that dictates what is meant.

      Ex: *Je suis* **en** *Normandie / Je vais* **en** *Normandie.*
      I am **in** Normandy / I am going **to** Normandy.

– With names of countries, continents and provinces that are feminine (all ending with '*e*').

> Ex: *en France, **en** Afrique, **en** Lorraine, **en** Ecosse*

(but: *au Mexique*)

– With names of countries (even masculine) beginning with a vowel.

> Ex: *en Israël, **en** Iran, **en** Andorre, **en** Afghanistan, **en** Equateur*

(NB: *Israël* and *Andorre* do not take any article.)

– With names of large islands which are feminine.

> Ex: *en Corse, **en** Sicile, **en** Sardaigne, **en** Crète*

(but see also *à* above: *à Ibiza, à Paros*)

– *en* can be used before a noun without a definite article (see also *dans* below, which requires one).

> Ex: *Ce sont des exercices à faire **en** classe.*
> These are exercises to do **in** class.

Compare with:

> *Il y a 20 élèves **dans la** classe.*
> There are 20 pupils **in the** class.

Note the following idioms:

en pleine poitrine	right in the chest
en pleine mer	on the high seas
en route	on the way

(ii) Adverb phrases of time

en is used with months, seasons and years (see chapter 37 Numbers, sections 4.1(iii), 4.4(iv) and 5.5(ii)).

> Ex: *en mai* (or: *au mois de mai*)   in May
> *en été*   in summer
> (but: *au printemps*   in spring)
> *en 1984*   in 1984
> *en l'an 2001*   in the year 2001
> *en plein hiver*   in the middle of winter

Also:

> *en plein jour*   in broad daylight
> *en même temps*   at the same time

Hence *en* is used to indicate the time needed to accomplish a task.

> Ex: *Elle a écrit son article **en deux semaines**.*
> She wrote her article **in two weeks**.

which should not be confused with:

> *Elle va écrire son article **dans deux semaines**.*
> She will write her article **in two weeks' time**.

(iii) Adverb phrases of manner

en is used to indicate:

– the means of locomotion, when the person is in a vehicle (but see 8.1.2.1(iii) above):

Ex: *en train, en voiture, en bateau, en avion, en autobus, en autocar, en aéroglisseur*, etc.
but: *à pied; à cheval* and *en vélo* or *à vélo.*

NB: For objects being carried, use **par**.
Ex: *envoyer un paquet **par** avion/**par** bateau*
to send a parcel by air/by sea

− dress:
Ex: *être **en** bras de chemise, **en** grande tenue, **en** robe longue*
to be in shirt sleeves, in formal dress, in evening dress
but:
*être **sur** son trente et un*
to be dressed up to the nines

− state (physical or mental), generally after *être*:
Ex: *être **en** pleine floraison*   to be in full bloom
*être **en** colère*   to be angry
*être **en** pleine forme*   to be in top form
*être **en** bonne santé*   to be in good health
*être **en** vacances*   to be on holiday
*L'armée est **en** état d'alerte.*   The army is on alert.
*L'économie est **en** crise.*   The economy is in a crisis.

9.3   *en* and noun complements

en is used to introduce the material of which an object is made and sometimes its colour or shape (*de* is also used: see above).
Ex: *un toit **en** tuiles du pays*   a roof made of local tiles
*peindre les murs **en** blanc*   to paint the walls white
*un escalier **en** colimaçon*   a spiral staircase

Note that *en* is also used in a figurative sense.
Ex: *C'est une occasion **en** or.*
It is a golden opportunity.

But note also the use of *de* in the following proverb:
*La parole est **d'**argent mais le silence est **d'**or.*

The choice between *en* and *de* is largely a question of usage, but today, *en* tends to be more and more universally accepted. Hence one can say either *une chemise de soie* or *une chemise en soie*. However, ?*une bague d'or* instead of *une bague en or* would sound odd.

9.4   *en* and the gerund

en is used with a present participle to form a gerund (see chapter 16 Present Participle, section 3.3). It can thus be the equivalent of an adverb phrase of time, cause or manner, which is generally translated in English by a form in '-ing' preceded by 'by'/'in'/'on'/'while'.

Ex: *Il s'est endormi **en lisant** son livre.*
He fell asleep **while reading** his book.

*On ne convainc pas nécessairement les gens **en répétant** sans arrêt la même chose.*
You do not necessarily convince people **by repeating** the same thing over and over again.

It may also be the equivalent of a hypothetical *si*-clause (see chapters 13 Conditional, section 3.2.2(vi) and 16 Present Participle, section 3.3.(i)).

Ex: ***En** travaillant plus, vous réussiriez.*
(= ***Si** vous travailliez plus, vous réussiriez.*)
If you worked harder, you would succeed.

9.5 *en* in idioms

en is used in a number of phrases (with an adverbial or prepositional value), **generally without determiners**.

Ex: *en moyenne*   on average
en tout cas   anyhow
en vain   in vain

Note:

***en** conséquence*   consequently
but:
***par** conséquent*   consequently

***en** cas de doute*   in case of doubt
but:
***dans** ce cas*   in this case
***au** cas où*   in case

Exceptions:

en l'absence de   in the absence of
en la présence de   in the presence of
en l'air   in the air
en l'an 1990   in the year 1990 (but: *en 1990*)
en l'espace de   in the space of (period of time)
en l'honneur de   in honour of
en la matière   on the subject
en la personne de   in the person of
en un mot   in a word
en ce temps-là   in those days
en ce moment   at this moment/right now

Finally, *en train de* is used to express the continuous present (see chapter 5 Present, section 3.3).

10 Preposition *pour*

pour is not part of any verb.

(i)   *pour* + noun introduces adverb phrases of

– place (destination):
pour is used to indicate the **destination**, when *à* would be ambiguous (see section 5 above).

> Ex: *Le train **pour** Marseille part à 6 heures.*
> The train **to** Marseilles leaves at 6 o'clock.

– time:
pour is used instead of *pendant* or *durant* with the verbs *être, partir, (s'en) aller* or *venir* (but not *rester*).

> Ex: *Je pars **pour** une semaine.*
> I'm leaving **for** a week.

(but: *Je serai absente pendant* or ***pour** une semaine.*)
See also chapter 6 *depuis* and Other Tense Markers.

(ii)   *pour* + infinitive introduces adverb phrases.

Note that when the meaning of 'to' before an infinitive is 'in order to', *pour* should be used (and not, for instance, *de*). Hence *pour* can express:

– an aim ('to', 'in order to'):

> Ex: ***Pour** faire ce gâteau, il vous faut . . .*
> **To** make this cake, you'll need . . .
>
> *J'ai besoin de quelque chose **pour** me calmer les nerfs.*
> I need something **to** steady my nerves.
>
> *Il faut manger **pour** vivre et non vivre **pour** manger.* (proverb)
> One should eat **to** live, not live **to** eat.

NB: If the infinitive is in the negative, *pour* is translated as 'so as not to' or 'in order not to'.

> Ex: *Il ne boit plus de bière, **pour ne pas** prendre trop de poids.*
> He's given up drinking beer, **so as not to/in order not to** put on too much weight.

– a cause (for doing something):

> Ex: *Il s'est fait arrêter par la police **pour** avoir grillé un feu rouge.*
> He got stopped by the police **for** going through a red light.

(iii)   *pour* + infinitive is equivalent to a relative clause.

> Ex: *Il n'y avait personne **pour** dire à Paul que . . .*
> (= *qui pouvait dire à*)
> There was no one **to** tell Paul that . . .

*Je ne suis pas la meilleure personne **pour** répondre à cette question.*
(= *qui puisse répondre à*)
I am not the best person **to** answer that question.

(iv) ***pour*** + infinitive can act like a conjunction of coordination.

- Two actions are linked without any cause–effect relation.
    Ex: *Il part tous les matins à 7 heures **pour** revenir le soir à 6 heures.*
    He leaves every morning at seven **and** comes back in the evening at six.
- The second action is unexpected or unwelcome.
    Ex: *Il est parti à 6 heures **pour** revenir deux minutes plus tard car il avait oublié ses clés.*
    He left at six **only to** come back two minutes later because he had forgotten his keys.

11 Preposition *dans*

dans introduces adverb phrases (of place or time) and is also found in idioms.

11.1 *dans* and adverb phrases of place

dans + specified noun indicates **location** ('in') as well as **destination** or **direction** ('to') depending on the verb used (of the type *être* or *aller*).

(i) ***dans*** or *en*?

As a rule, ***dans*** is used with names of **masculine** provinces, French *départements* and British counties.
    Ex: *Je suis/je vais **dans le** Var, **dans le** Berry, **dans le** Poitou, **dans le** Yorkshire.*

dans is also used with some **feminine** names of provinces, French *départements* and British counties.
    Ex: *Je suis/je vais **dans la** Lozère.*
But note that ***en*** + noun (no article) is often used too (see chapter 23 Articles).
    Ex: *Je suis/je vais **en** Lorraine, **en** Lozère, **en** Cornouailles.*

(ii) ***dans*** or *à*?

- ***dans*** emphasizes the boundaries or limits of the space named, whereas *à* is used for something which is happening in one area as opposed to another.
    Ex: *J'aime me promener **dans** Paris.*
    I like walking in Paris.
        but:
    *Je préfère marcher **à** Paris qu'à Londres.*
    I prefer walking in Paris to walking in London.

- 'to go to school' is *aller à l'école*, but if 'school' is in any way qualified, *dans* is normally used.

    Ex: *Paul et Marie vont tous les deux à l'école mais **dans** des écoles différentes.*
    Paul and Marie both go to school but to different ones.

- *dans* is used for names of towns if there is a qualifier. Hence:

    À *Paris.* In Paris.
    but:
    ***Dans** le Paris d'aujourd'hui.* In the Paris of today.

(iii) 'in'/'out of'

- *dans* is translated as 'in' in the sense of 'inside something'.

    Ex: *Les biscuits sont **dans** la boîte à biscuits!*
    The biscuits are **in** the biscuit jar!

    *J'ai rangé les assiettes **dans** le buffet.*
    I put the plates **in** the sideboard.

    *Je n'aime pas me sentir enfermée **dans** un ascenseur.*
    I don't like feeling trapped **in** a lift.

- *dans* translates 'out of', in the sense of 'from'.

    Ex: *Quelqu'un a bu **dans** cette tasse.*
    Someone has been drinking **out of** this cup.

    *Je t'ai découpé un article **dans** ce magazine.*
    I cut an article **out of** this magazine for you.

    *Prends une serviette **dans** le placard.*
    Take a towel **out of** the cupboard.

(iv) 'in the works of' (but see also ***chez*** below)

    Ex: *Vous trouverez tout cela **dans** Corneille.*
    You will find all that **in** Corneille.

(v) Figurative use of ***dans***

    Ex: *Ils sont **dans** le besoin.*
    They are **in** need.

    ***Dans** le doute, abstiens-toi.* (proverb)
    When **in** doubt, don't.

    *Le mot 'voie' est utilisé ici **dans** un sens figuré.*
    The word *voie* is used here **in** a figurative sense.

11.2 *dans* and adverb phrases of time

(i) *dans* or *il y a*?

dans followed by a period of time means 'after' or 'at the end of' referring to the future (often translated as 'in'). Its converse is *il y a* meaning 'ago' (i.e. referring to the past).

Ex: *Je vous donnerai ma réponse **dans deux jours**.*
    I'll give you my answer **in two days' time**.
            but:
    *Je vous ai donné ma réponse **il y a deux jours**.*
    I gave you my answer **two days ago**.

(ii) ***dans** or **en***?

dans should not be confused with ***en***, which expresses duration.
            Ex: *J'ai écrit cet article **en deux heures**.*
            I wrote this article in two hours.
            (= It took me two hours to write this article.)
See 9.2(ii) above.

Note: ***dans** les années soixante* but ***en** 1960*.

11.3   *dans* in idioms

Note the translation of the following:
            Ex: *J'ai rencontré Michel **dans** le train.*
            I met Michel **on** the train.

            *Je l'ai fait **dans** le but de vous aider.*
            I did it **with** the aim of helping you.

            *Je l'ai fait **dans** l'idée d'en finir avec tout ça.*
            I did it **with** the idea of putting an end to all this.

            *Nous sommes toujours restés **dans** les limites de la légalité.*
            We've always remained **within** the limits of the law.

            *Je serai chez vous **dans** une heure.*
            I'll be at your place **within** the hour.

12   Preposition *par*

par is used:
– to introduce adverb phrases
– to introduce an agent in the passive voice
– to introduce an infinitive
– in idioms

12.1   *par* and adverb phrases

– ***par*** expresses the act of going through a place ('via' or 'by'). In a figurative
  sense, it is used to indicate the manner in which something happens
  ('through').
            Ex: *Vous pouvez sortir **par** la porte de la cuisine: elle n'est pas fermée à clé.*
            You can leave **by** the kitchen door – it is not locked.

*Je suis passé **par** une mauvaise période le mois dernier.*
I went **through** a bad patch last month.

*C'est **par** les Durand qu'elle a obtenu son nouveau travail.*
It is **through** the Durands that she got her new job.

– **par** is used to indicate the means of transport ('by').
>   Ex: *voyager **par le** train*
>   to travel by train

See also **en**.

– **par** is used to indicate cause ('out of'/'through').
>   Ex: **par** *bonté*   out of kindness
>   **par** *insouciance*   through carelessness

– **par** is used to indicate time in a distributive sense (see chapter 37 Numbers, section 8(iii)), e.g. *par mois, par minute, par jour, par an, par personne*, etc.
>   Ex: *Il faut traire les vaches deux fois **par** jour.*
>   Cows should be milked twice a day.

12.2 *par* and agent in passive voice

(See chapter 18 Active and Passive Voices, section 2.)
>   Ex: *Nous sommes submergés **par** la publicité.*
>   We are swamped **by** advertisements.

12.3 *par* + infinitive

The preposition **par** followed by the infinitive is used after verbs of 'beginning' or 'ending'.
>   Ex: *J'ai fini **par** (me mettre à) travailler.*
>   I eventually got down to work.

>   *Il a commencé **par** démonter toutes les étagères.*
>   He began by dismantling all the shelves.

Note that this is not to be confused with:
– **à:**
>   Ex: *Il a commencé **à** démonter les étagères.*
>   He began dismantling the shelves.
>>   or:

– **de:**
>   Ex: *J'ai fini **de** travailler.*
>   I have finished working.

See chapter 4 Introduction to Verbs, section 5(iii).

12.4 *par* in idioms

par is used in set phrases, e.g.:

un par un	one by one
par terre	on the floor/ground
par hasard	by chance
par-ci, par-là	here and there, etc.

Ex: *J'ai laissé tomber le vase de grand-mère **par terre**!*
I dropped grandmother's vase on the floor!

*J'ai vu Eric **par hasard** dans un cinéma hier.*
I chanced upon Eric in a cinema yesterday.

13 Other prepositions

13.1 *vers, envers*

They both translate 'to', 'towards'.

(i) ***vers*** is used to indicate

– a direction (literally or figuratively)
Ex: *Il s'est dirigé **vers** elle.*
He walked towards her.

*Puis elle a tourné son attention **vers** des questions plus importantes.*
Then she turned her attention to more important questions.

– approximate times (see also chapter 37 Numbers, section 6(vii))
Ex: *Je partirai **vers** deux heures.*
I shall leave around two o'clock.

(ii) ***envers*** concerns feelings or attitude

Ex: *Il s'est mal conduit **envers** nous.*
He behaved badly towards us.

13.2 *avant, devant*

Generally speaking, ***avant*** is used for time and ***devant*** for place.
Ex: *Je vous verrai **avant** le début de la réunion.*
I'll see you **before** the meeting starts.

*Il va présenter son projet **devant** le comité.*
He's going to present his project **before** the committee.

Hence when travelling, they can both be used for giving directions.
*Tournez à gauche juste **avant** l'église.*
(= just before the church)

*Tournez à gauche juste **devant** l'église.*
(= just opposite the church)

Note the following idioms:
*Ils étaient de plusieurs siècles **en avance sur leur temps**.*
They were several centuries **before their time**.

*Il **a couru au-devant de** son père.*
He **ran to meet** his father.

See also *avant* and *devant* as adverbs in 6.1 above, and *avant de* vs *avant que* in chapter 12 Subjunctive, section 4.4.2.

13.3 *chez*

chez means 'at or to the house/home/shop, etc. of' and, by extension, 'in the country of' and 'in the work of' or 'in the society of'.

> Ex: *Nous serons **chez** nous samedi prochain.*
> We'll be at home next Saturday.
>
> *Je reviens juste de **chez** le coiffeur.*
> I'm just back from the hairdresser's.
>
> *Il n'y a pas que **chez** nous que le gouvernement a des problèmes avec les agriculteurs!*
> It's not only here (= in our country) that the government has problems with the farmers!
>
> *On retrouve cette tendance **chez** Proust.*
> This tendency is also to be found with Proust.
> > but:
> *On retrouve cette tendance **dans** l'œuvre de Proust.*
> This tendency is also to be found in the work(s) of Proust.
>
> *Ces problèmes se rencontrent **chez** (= parmi) les personnes d'un certain âge.*
> These problems are to be found with elderly people.

Note: *chez le boulanger, chez le boucher, chez le coiffeur,* etc.
but: *à la boulangerie, à la boucherie, au salon de coiffure.*

13.4 *sur, au-dessus de*

They both introduce adverb phrases of place.

(i) *sur* means 'on top of (a surface)' whilst ***au-dessus de*** means 'above' or 'over'.

> Ex: *Les assiettes sont **sur** la table.*
> The plates are on the table.
>
> *Les avions ne devraient pas être autorisés à voler **au-dessus des** (= de les) habitations la nuit.*
> Aircraft should not be allowed to fly over houses at night.

(ii) *sur* also means *au sujet de.*

> Ex: *Ils se sont informés **sur** notre état de santé.*
> They enquired about our state of health.

(iii) Idioms with ***sur***

> Ex: *Je laisserai la clé **sur** la porte.*
> I shall leave the key **in** the door.
>
> *On pouvait voir **sur** leur visage que c'était la fin.*
> You could tell **by** the look on their faces that it was all over.

13.5   *sous, au-dessous de*

(i)   **sous** means 'under'.

> Ex: *Le chat s'est caché **sous** la table.*
> The cat hid under the table.

(ii)   **au-dessous de** means 'beneath', 'below'.

> Ex: ***Au-dessous de** zéro degrés, il fait bien froid . . .*
> Below zero degrees celsius, it is really cold . . .

(iii)   Idioms with **sous**

> Ex: ***Sous** le règne de Henri VIII.*
> **In** the reign of Henry VIII.
>
> *Cela existe **sous** des formes diverses.*
> It exists **in** different forms.
>
> *Cela peut être vu **sous** des angles différents.*
> It can be seen **from** different angles.

13.6   *avec, sans*

(i)   When **avec** and **sans** + noun ('with'/'without') indicate the **manner** in which something is done, there is no article after the preposition.

> Ex: *Il est parti **sans** chapeau.*
> He left without a hat.

With an abstract noun, the expression is thus the equivalent of an adverb of manner:

> Ex: *Relisez ce chapitre **avec** soin   = soigneusement*
> *Ils l'ont traité **sans** pitié   = impitoyablement*
> *Ils ont agi **avec** courage   = courageusement*

Hence *avec* or *sans* + noun are often used in French:

− when no adverb exists (see chapter 29 Adverbs, section 3.3).

> Ex: *Ils l'ont accueilli **avec enthousiasme**.*
> They welcomed him enthusiastically.
>
> *Il a soulevé le poids de 100 kg **sans difficulté**.*
> He lifted the 100 kg weight easily.
>
> *Prendrez-vous un verre? **Avec plaisir!*** (or: *Volontiers!*)
> Will you have a drink? With pleasure!

− or instead of an adverb, with or without a nuance of meaning (see chapter 29 Adverbs, section 3.3).

> Ex: *avec joie; joyeusement*
> *avec soin; soigneusement*

Note: *avec enthousiasme **et** dédication*
> **with** enthusiasm **and** dedication
>
> *sans effort **ni** concentration*
> **without** effort **or** concentration

(ii) **sans** + infinitive:

> Ex: *Il est resté trois jours **sans** manger et **sans** boire.*
> (or: ***sans** manger **ni** boire* – see also coordination with *ni . . . ni* in chapter 40 Coordination, section 6).
> He remained three days without eating or drinking.

NB: Only *en* is followed by a present participle in French.

(iii) In informal French and in some idiomatic expressions, *avec* and *sans* can be used without a complement.

> Ex: *Il va falloir faire **avec**.*
> We'll have to manage with whatever there is.
>
> *Qu'est-ce qu'on boit **avec**?*
> What do we drink with it?
>
> *Son manteau? Il est parti **sans**.*
> His coat? He left without it.

13.7 *à cause de* ('because of') vs *parce que, car*

The compound preposition *à cause de* introduces a **noun** or pronoun. However, *parce que* or *car*, which are conjunctions of coordination, link **clauses**. (See chapter 40 Coordination and Juxtaposition, section 5.2.)

> Ex: *Je n'ai pas voulu faire les courses **à cause de** la pluie.*
> I didn't want to go shopping because of the rain.

NB: You may hear some people in France say:

> ★*à cause qu'il pleuvait . . .*

This should not be copied! Compare with:

> *Je n'ai pas voulu faire les courses **parce qu'**il pleuvait.*
> I didn't want to go shopping because it was raining.

13.8 *à travers/au travers de; en travers de*

(i) *à travers/au travers de* mean 'through', and *en travers de* means 'across' in the sense of 'placed/lying across'. Note that *à travers* is more common than *au travers de* (and is never used with *de*).

> Ex: *Le soleil essayait de percer **à travers** les nuages.*
> The sun was trying to break through the clouds.
> but:
> *Il y avait un arbre **en travers de** la rivière.*
> There was a tree lying across the river.

(ii) All other meanings of **across** are rendered differently in French.

> Ex: How many bridges are there **across** the Seine?
> *Combien y a-t-il de ponts **sur** la Seine?*
>
> The bakery is **across** the square.
> *La boulangerie se trouve **de l'autre côté de** la place.*

14 Translation of verbs of motion and perception

(i) Preposition in English vs verb in French

Verbs of motion and perception can be difficult to translate from one language into the other as the motion expressed by the preposition in English is often translated by a verb in French.

For instance, with English verbs of motion + 'across', *traverser* is likely to be used in French + an adverb phrase or a gerund to express the type of motion involved.

Ex: He **swam across** the river.
*Il **traversa** la rivière **à la nage**.*

The soldiers **crawled across** the field.
*Les soldats **ont traversé** le champ **en rampant**.*

Paul **limped into** the room.
*Paul **est entré dans** la pièce **en boîtant**.*

He **ran out**.
*Il **sortit en courant**.*

He **ran down** the stairs.
*Il **descendit** les escaliers **en courant**.*

They **rushed out** of the room.
*Ils **sont sortis de** la pièce **en courant**.*
      or:
*Ils **se sont précipités hors** de la pièce.*

Note also:

I **looked up** / I **looked down**.
*J'ai **levé les yeux** / J'ai **baissé les yeux**.*

He **sat up** in his chair.
*Il **se redressa** sur sa chaise.*

(ii) Omission of the nature of the movement in French

If the means of locomotion is obvious, it is omitted in French.

Ex: A bird **flew into** the room.
*Un oiseau **entra dans** la pièce *en volant.*
(the most natural way for birds to go about is to fly!)

Catherine **walked into** the room.
*Catherine **entra dans** la pièce *en marchant.*
(the most natural way for people to go about is to walk!)

He jumped into his car and **drove back home**.
*Il sauta dans sa voiture et **retourna chez lui** *en conduisant.*
(once in the car, he obviously drives it!)

I **walked downstairs**.
*Je **descendis** l'escalier *en marchant.*

4 Nouns, pronouns and modifiers

27 Nouns

1 Introduction

Nouns are also called **substantives** (*substantifs*), as traditionally they were said to represent 'substances'. However, they also represent other things such as processes (e.g. *une promenade*) or qualities (e.g. *la beauté*). They have a gender (masculine or feminine) and a number (singular or plural). They are generally preceded by a determiner (but see chapter 23 Articles, section 6 for exceptions). Finally, they can be simple (*un chien*; *une horloge*) or compound (*un porte-drapeau*; *un roman-photo*).

They also have various properties, called **lexical features**.

(i) Common or proper nouns

– Common nouns:
They refer to all the elements of the same category, begin with a lower-case letter and are generally preceded by an article or other determiner.
      Ex: *un enfant, la ville, ma patrie, ce chat*

Note that certain common nouns originate from a proper noun.
      Ex: *une poubelle* a dustbin   (from Eugène Poubelle)
            un tartuffe a hypocrite   (from Molière's *Le Tartuffe*)
See also chapter 23 Articles, sections 3.2.5 and 4.2.1.

– Proper nouns:
They refer to a particular animate (see (ii) below), place or organization and begin with a capital letter.
      Ex: *Antoine, Mme Dupont, Dizzy*
            Paris, la France, le boulevard St-Michel, le Ministère des Finances
(For the presence or absence of determiner, see chapter 23 Articles, sections 2.2.1.5 and 2.2.3.)

(ii) Animate and inanimate nouns

– Animates refer to living beings and can be further subdivided into human and non-human:
  – human:
      Ex: *un berger*
  – non-human:
      Ex: *un mouton*

       – Inanimates refer to everything else, including concrete or abstract nouns
         (see (iii) below).
            Ex: *une bergerie, de la paille*; *l'amour*

(iii)   Concrete and abstract nouns

       – Concrete nouns represent elements that can be touched or felt, seen or
         heard:
            Ex: *une boîte, un chat, un nuage, une chanson*

       – Abstract nouns refer to concepts, actions (events, situations) and qualities
         (beliefs, judgements) and are often related to a verb or adjective with a
         corresponding meaning.
            Ex: *la philosophie, la marche (marcher), le courage (courageux)*

(iv)   Countable and uncountable (mass) nouns

       – Countable nouns refer to elements that can be counted, hence they can be
         used in the singular or plural, with definite or indefinite articles.
            Ex: *une table, des maisons*

       – Uncountable nouns refer to quantities and are normally preceded by the
         partitive article. Thus they are not used with indefinite articles or in the plural.
            Ex: *de l'eau, du sable*

(v)   Collective and individual nouns

       – Collective nouns refer to a group, a collection of items of the same category:
            Ex: *le peuple, la foule, la police, la famille, une troupe, la main-d'œuvre, le linge,*
               la vaisselle

       – Individual nouns:
            Ex: *une personne, un policier, une mère, un soldat, un ouvrier, un drap, une*
               assiette

(vi)   Recategorization

It is almost always possible to recategorize a noun. This has an effect on the use
of determiners. For instance:
– from uncountable to countable (meaning 'a type of'):
        Ex: ***de l'eau*** → ***une/des*** *eau(x) minérale(s)*
– from concrete to abstract:
        Ex: ***De l'argent*** (concrete) *a été trouvé sur cette table.*
           L'argent (abstract) *fait tourner le monde.*
See also chapter 23 Articles.

2 The gender of nouns

Nouns have a gender: masculine or feminine (the neuter gender does not exist in French). Although it is possible to a large extent to determine the gender of a noun by looking at its ending, there are many exceptions. Hence it is always best to learn a new noun with its gender, preferably with *un/une*, as *l'* (before a noun beginning with a vowel or a mute '*h*') does not indicate the gender. The adjective agrees with the noun. Hence in a text where the article is *l'*, the agreement of an adjective can help to determine the gender of a noun.

> Ex: *l'horloge est cassée* (→ '*horloge*' is feminine)
> *l'espoir est permis* (→ '*espoir*' is masculine)

2.1 Masculine and feminine nouns of people

Words which refer to male or female human beings are likely to be masculine or feminine respectively – although not always! (See section 2.1.2(ii) and (iii) below.) As in English, nouns which refer to persons according to their sex tend to be 'irregular' in that the words which represent the male and the female can look very different or follow rules similar to those governing the gender of adjectives.

2.1.1 *Forms*

(i) Irregular noun pairs

Ex:		
un homme	*une femme*	
un mari	*une femme*	
un mâle	*une femelle*	
un monsieur	*une dame*	
un garçon	*une fille*	
un frère	*une sœur*	
un père	*une mère*	
un oncle	*une tante*	
un roi	*une reine*	
un Suisse	*une Suissesse*	
un dieu	*une déesse*	
un héros	*une héroïne*	

NB: The words *mâle* and *femelle* are not the direct equivalent of the English terms 'male' and 'female'. They have an impersonal biological connotation – male/female of the species – and are therefore best avoided unless the context is strictly non-human.

> Ex: *La hase est la femelle du lièvre.*
> A female hare is called a doe.

(ii) Regular noun pairs

However, a lot of nouns which refer to men and women are regular in that they simply change the article if there is already a final '*e*', or they add an '*e*' to the masculine written form.

389

Ex: *un élève*   *une élève*
    un artiste   *une artiste*
    un collègue   *une collègue*
    un locataire   *une locataire*
    un cousin   *une cousine*
    un ami   *une amie*
    un étudiant   *une étudiante*
    un Français   *une Française*
    un mineur   *une mineure*

Exception: *un enfant   une enfant*

(iii)   Nouns in *-teur* have their feminine in *-trice* or *-teuse*

Ex: *un instituteur*   *une institutrice*
    un directeur   *une directrice*
    un acteur   *une actrice*
    un menteur   *une menteuse*
    un chanteur   *une chanteuse*

(iv)   Other nouns in *-eur* have their feminine in *-euse*

Ex: *un coiffeur*   *une coiffeuse*
    un danseur   *une danseuse*
    un vendeur   *une vendeuse*
    un voyageur   *une voyageuse*

(v)   Nouns in *-er* have their feminine in *-ère*

Ex: *un boulanger*   *une boulangère*
    un boucher   *une bouchère*
    un charcutier   *une charcutière*
    un fermier   *une fermière*
    un romancier   *une romancière*

(vi)   Nouns in *-on, -an, -en* have their feminine in *-onne, -anne, -enne*

Ex: *un baron*   *une baronne*
    un paysan   *une paysanne*
    un musicien   *une musicienne*
    un Italien   *une Italienne*

(vii)   Nouns in *-f* have their feminine in *-ve*

Ex: *un Juif*   *une Juive*
    un veuf   *une veuve*

(viii)   Nouns in *-x* have their feminine in *-se*
Ex: *un époux*   *une épouse*

2.1.2 Semantic considerations

(i) Some names of occupation can change their meaning when they go from one gender to the other. This is particularly true for military ranks, but also in politics.

Ex: *le général*	the general
la générale	the general's wife
le colonel	the colonel
la colonelle	the colonel's wife
le gouverneur (de Californie)	the governor (of California)
les gouvernants	the establishment
une gouvernante	a governess

(ii) A lot of nouns of profession only exist in the masculine form, even if they refer to women.

Several attempts at 'feminizing' those terms have taken place, in particular upon the initiative of the Office International de la Langue Française, but in practice, their proposals are much more observed in Canada, Belgium and Switzerland than in France itself. Finally, the *Dictionnaire Féminin–Masculin des professions, des titres et des fonctions*, published in Geneva, offers the following:

- *un président/une présidente*
- *un auteur/une auteure*
- *un ingénieur/une ingénieure*

Note: These are by no means universally accepted!

A lot of names, however, retain their masculine form:

Ex: *un médecin, un professeur, un peintre*

Also: *un témoin, un mannequin*

Ex: **Mme Dupont, l'un des témoins** *de l'accident*

(iii) Some names of professions or occupations only exist in the feminine, even when they refer to men: *une sentinelle, une recrue, une vedette, une star, une sage-femme* (the *Dictionnaire Féminin–Masculin* suggests either *sage-femme* or *sage-homme*).

Also: *une victime, une brute, une connaissance, une dupe, une personne*

Ex: **Mick Jagger, une grande star** *du pop-rock*

2.2 Masculine and feminine nouns of animals

As in English, names of animals (particularly pets and farm animals) are complex as there can be up to three names for each animal: one which refers to the type of animal (generic), then the nouns which refer specifically to the male or the female of the type. For instance:

Ex: *un chat* cat	*un matou* tom	*une chatte* she-cat
un mouton sheep	*un bélier* ram	*une brebis* ewe
un cheval horse	*un étalon* stallion	*une jument* mare
un poulet chicken	*un coq* cock	*une poule* hen
un porc/un cochon pig	*un verrat* boar	*une truie* sow
un bœuf ox	*un taureau* bull	*une vache* cow

There are often only two nouns: one generic and one specific (male or female depending on the animal).

Ex: *un chien* dog	*un chien* dog	*une chienne* bitch
un lion lion	*un lion* lion	*une lionne* lioness
un canard duck	*un canard* drake	*une cane* duck
un lapin rabbit	*un lapin* rabbit	*une lapine* rabbit
un renard fox	*un renard* dog-fox	*une renarde* vixen
un tigre tiger	*un tigre* tiger	*une tigresse* tigress
un loup wolf	*un loup* wolf	*une louve* she-wolf
une chèvre goat	*un bouc* billy-goat	*une chèvre* nanny-goat
une oie goose	*un jars* gander	*une oie* goose

Most of the time however, there is only one name to refer to both the male and the female of the species, at least in common usage:

Ex: *un rat* rat
un moineau sparrow
un saumon salmon
un papillon butterfly
un écureuil squirrel
un hérisson hedgehog

une hirondelle swallow
une truite trout
une guêpe wasp
une souris mouse
une girafe giraffe
une grenouille frog
une taupe mole

2.3 Masculine nouns based on categories (inanimates)

The following are useful to know as they have fewer exceptions than those based on morphology (see 2.4 below).

(i) Names of trees and shrubs

Ex: *le chêne* oak, *le hêtre* beech, *le bouleau* birch
le pommier apple tree, *le poirier* pear tree
le prunier plum tree, *le chèvrefeuille* honeysuckle
Exceptions: *la vigne* vine, *la ronce* bramble
la bruyère heather

(ii) Names of fruit and vegetables not ending in '*e*'

Ex: *un abricot* apricot, *un citron* lemon
un artichaut artichoke, *un chou* cabbage
un haricot bean, *un avocat* avocado

(iii)   Names of metals and minerals

        Ex: *le cuivre* copper, *le laiton* brass, *le fer* iron
        le plomb lead, *l'or* gold, *l'argent* silver
        l'acier steel, *le platine* platinum
        le carbone carbon, *le souffre* sulphur
        le diamant diamond, *le rubis* ruby, *le topaze* topaz
        le saphir sapphire
Exceptions: *la tôle* sheet metal, *la fonte* cast-iron
        une émeraude emerald, *une perle* pearl
        une pierre stone

(iv)   Names of languages

        Ex: *le français, l'anglais, l'allemand, le portugais, le grec*
NB: *le russe, l'arabe*, are both masculine even though they end with an '*e*'.
Note also: *un langage* (a language style) but *une langue* (a formal language/tongue).

(v)   Names of colours

These are obtained by improper derivation from adjectives.
        Ex: *le bleu, le blanc, le rouge, le jaune, le vert, le marron, le violet, le noir*

(vi)   Names of metrical weights and measures, cardinal numbers, fractions, letters of
the alphabet (see also chapter 37 Numbers)
        Ex: *un gramme, un kilogramme*
        un litre, un décilitre
        un mètre, un kilomètre
        un cinq, un six, un sept
        un tiers, un quart, un demi, un neuvième
        un a, un b, un c
Exception: *une moitié*

(vii)   Names of days of the week, months, seasons, points of the compass
        Ex: *un jour, le lundi, le mardi* . . .
        un mois, en février prochain, en avril dernier
        un printemps, un été . . .
        le nord, le sud, l'est, l'ouest
Also: *un an, un siècle*, but *une semaine, une saison*

(viii)   Names of rivers, regions and countries not ending with an '*e*'
        Ex: *le Rhin, le Doubs, le Lot, le Tarn*
        le Béry, le Limousin, le Languedoc, le Roussillon
        le Poitou, le Kent, le Pays de Galles
        le Brésil, le Paraguay, le Portugal, le Danemark
        le Japon, le Canada, le Maroc
But also *le Yorkshire, le Berkshire, le Maine*, etc.

Names of cities are generally considered masculine.
        Ex: *le grand Londres, le vieux Nice, l'éternel Paris*

(ix)   Names of French *départements*

    – Names based on rivers take the gender of the corresponding river or of the first one if there are two.
        Ex: *le Doubs, le Haut-Rhin, le Loir-et-Cher, le Lot-et-Garonne*

    – Names that do not end in '*e*' are masculine, and so are compounds whose first noun does not end in '*e*'.
        Ex: *le Calvados, le Jura, le Pas-de-Calais*
              le Puy-de-Dôme, le Val-de-Marne

2.4   Masculine nouns based on morphology

The following are a few examples for familiarization with masculine nouns.

(i)   Nouns in *-age*

    Ex: *un garage, un langage, un paysage, le courage, le ménage, un voyage*
        un village, le chômage, un étage, le fromage, le pourcentage, le visage
        un nuage, un page (page-boy)

Exceptions: *une image, une plage, une cage, une page* (page)

(ii)   Nouns in *-al*

    Ex: *un journal, un canal, le mal*

(iii)   Nouns in *-asme* or *-isme*

    Ex: *un pléonasme, le sarcasme, le marasme*
        le romantisme, l'alcoolisme, l'héroïsme

(iv)   Nouns with a final consonant

    Ex: *un banc* [bã], *l'estomac* [ɛstɔma]
        du cognac [kɔɲak], *un lac* [lak], *un sac* [sak]
        un but [by], *un toit, un droit*
        un amour, un tour (turn), *le pourtour, un jour*
        un vers [vɛr]
        un outil [uti]
        un bar
        un pied, le bord, le fond, un regard
        un nez [ne], *le riz* [ri], *le gaz* [gɑz]
        un nom, un prénom, un surnom
        un adjectif, l'actif, le passif
        un club [klœb]
        un étang, un poing
        un choix
        un puits, un enduit
        du maïs [mais]
    Exceptions: *une nuit, une fois, une tour* (tower)

(v)   Nouns in *-ème, -ège, -ède*

        Ex: *un problème, un système, un poème, le carême*
            un collège, un cortège, un piège, un siège
            un remède
and the names of fractions:
        Ex: *un dixième, un centième*
Exception: *la crème*

(vi)   Other nouns with an '*e*' preceded by a consonant

        Ex: *un groupe, le rire, un magazine*
            un couvercle, le monde, un remède
            un terme (→ à court terme)
            le manque, le silence
            un ange, un mélange
            un doute (→ sans aucun doute)
            un abîme, un armistice, un astérisque
            un éloge, un équinoxe, un pétale, un obélisque
            l'enthousiasme, le domaine, le peuple
But: *une chemise, une âme, une ferme*

(vii)   Nouns in *-eau*

        Ex: *un bureau, un tableau, un chapeau, un seau, un bateau, un oiseau*
            un marteau, un cadeau, le cerveau, le rideau, le drapeau
Exceptions: *l'eau, la peau*

(viii)   Nouns in *-at* or *-et*

        Ex: *le chocolat, le climat, le combat*
            l'état, le résultat
            un ballet, un paquet, le parquet
            un secret, un objet, un sujet

(ix)   Nouns in *-ail, -eil, -euil* or *-ueil*

Note that the last two are both pronounced [œj].
        Ex: *l'ail, le corail, le détail, le travail, le vitrail*
            un appareil, un conseil, un orteil, un réveil, le soleil
            un écureuil, un fauteuil, un deuil, le seuil
            un accueil, un recueil, un écueil, l'orgueil

(x)   Nouns in *-eur*

  – Machines:
        Ex: *un ordinateur, un moteur, un accélérateur, un radiateur, un tracteur*
            un aspirateur

– Abstract nouns:

> Ex: *l'honneur, le déshonneur, le bonheur, le malheur, le labeur*

Also: *le cœur, l'équateur, le secteur, l'extérieur, l'intérieur*

See also 2.6(iv) for feminine nouns in *-eur*: mainly abstract and referring to qualities, feelings, colours, etc.

(xi) Nouns in *-er* and *–ier*

> Ex: *l'enfer, le cancer, le fer* (note that the ending is pronounced [ɛr])
> *le clocher, le déjeuner, le dîner*
> *un papier, un panier, un cahier, un cendrier, un chantier, un métier*
> *un sentier, un tablier*

Exception: *la cuiller* (pronounced [kɥijɛr]) but note alternative spelling: *la cuillère*

(xii) Nouns in *-ent* or *–ment*

> Ex: *un agent, un appartement, le logement, un département, le gouvernement*
> *un élément, un changement, un bâtiment*

Exceptions: *une dent, une jument*

(xiii) Nouns in *-oir*

> Ex: *un espoir, un soir, un trottoir, un couloir, un miroir, un rasoir*
> *un mouchoir, un tiroir*

(xiv) Present and past participles in their masculine form, obtained by improper derivation. (See also chapters 16 Present Participle, section 3.1 and 17 Past Participle, section 3.)

> Ex: *un compromis, un passé*
> *un calmant, un fortifiant*

(xv) Nouns ending with a vowel other than '*e*'

> Ex: *un piano, un cargo, un bistro, un casino, l'écho, un numéro*
> *un cinéma, un opéra, un visa, un agenda*
> *un trou, un hibou, un chou, un genou, un clou, un bijou*
> *un café, un thé, le blé, le défilé, le marché*
> *un balai, un délai, un essai*
> *un abri, un cri, un parti, un défi, un appui, l'ennui*
> *un emploi, un envoi*

Exceptions:

> *la mafia, la malaria, une villa, la vodka*
> *la samba, la polka*
> *une photo* (short for *photographie*)
> *une auto* (short for *automobile*)
> *l'acné, une clé*
> *une fourmi*

Note the following:
- *la foi* faith
  le foie liver
  '*il était une fois*' 'once upon a time'
- *la merci* mercy
  [*le*] *merci* thank you
- *la loi* the law, which should be observed
  le droit:
    - law, as an object of study
    - the right e.g. to do something

(xvi) Nouns in *-acle*

Ex: *un miracle, un obstacle, un spectacle*
Exception: *la débâcle*

2.5   Feminine nouns based on categories

(i) Names of fruit and vegetables ending in '*e*'

Ex: *une banane, une orange, une pomme, une fraise, une cerise*
une pomme de terre, une laitue, une carotte, une betterave
Exceptions: *un pamplemousse, un concombre*

(ii) Names of rivers, regions, countries, continents ending with an '*e*'

Ex: *la Seine, la Loire, la Garonne, la Moselle, la Tamise*
la Champagne, la Bourgogne, la Provence, la Cornouailles
l'Ecosse, l'Irlande, la Belgique, la Chine, la Norvège
l'Australie, l'Asie, l'Afrique
Exceptions: *le Rhône, le Mexique, le Cambodge*
NB: The rule does not apply to foreign rivers:
le Gange, le Danube

(iii) Names of French *départements*

- Names based on river-names take the gender of the corresponding river, or of the first one if there are two.
  Ex: *la Somme, la Moselle*
  la Meurthe-et-Moselle, la Loire-Atlantique

- Plural names are generally feminine.
  Ex: *les Ardennes, les Landes, les Vosges, les Côtes-du-Rhône*
  Exception: *les Hauts-de-Seine*

- Nouns that end in '*e*' are feminine and for compounds, those whose first part ends in '*e*'
  Ex: *la Lozère, la Manche, la Savoie, la Haute-Savoie*
  Exception: *le Vaucluse*

(iv)   Names of arts, trades, sciences, school subjects

> Ex: *la peinture, la sculpture*
> *l'ébénisterie, la menuiserie*
> *la physique, l'arithmétique, les mathématiques*
> *la philosophie, la psychologie, la géographie, la métallurgie*
> *la chimie, la géométrie, l'histoire*

Exceptions: *le calcul, le dessin, le droit* (law), *le génie*

2.6 Feminine nouns based on morphology

(i)   Nouns ending with an '*e*'

> Ex: *une table, une chaise, une casserole*

But see numerous exceptions in 2.4.

(ii)   Nouns ending with an '*e*', when this '*e*' is preceded by a vowel or a double consonant

> Ex: *la poésie, la pluie, une rue, une roue*
> *une journée, une vallée, l'arrivée*
> *la terre, la guerre, une pierre, une barre*
> *une bouteille, une feuille*
> *la famille, une bataille*
> *une salle, une poubelle*
> *une grenouille, une patrouille*
> *la jeunesse, la politesse*
> *une classe, la graisse*
> *l'angoisse, la paroisse*
> *une gomme, une somme*
> *une serviette, une cigarette*
> *une patte, une botte, une goutte, une lutte*
> *une griffe, une truffe*
> *une antenne, une colonne*
> *une enveloppe, une grappe, la grippe*
> *une anagramme, une épigramme, une femme, une gamme*

Exceptions: *un musée, un lycée, un trophée, un apogée*
> *un astérisque, un obélisque*
> *un génie, un incendie, un parapluie, un sosie*
> *le lierre, le tonnerre, le parterre, le verre*
> *du beurre, un leurre*
> *un intervalle, un violoncelle*
> *le chèvrefeuille, le portefeuille*
> *un carosse, un narcisse, un pamplemousse*
> *un squelette, un dilemme, un gramme, un monogramme*

(iii)   Nouns in *-ance*, *-anse*, *-ence* or *-ense*

> Ex: *la chance, l'enfance, une ambulance, la confiance*
> *la danse, l'anse*
> *la science, la patience, la violence, la prudence, l'essence*
> *la défense, la dépense*

Exceptions: *le silence, le suspense*

(iv)   Nouns in *-eur*

They are mainly abstract and refer to qualities, feelings, etc.

> Ex: *une couleur, la ferveur, la douleur, la fraîcheur*
> *la valeur, la douceur, la chaleur, la peur, la fureur*
> *la longueur, la largeur, la profondeur, la grandeur*

But see exceptions in 2.4(x).
Also: *une fleur, une liqueur, la sueur, la vapeur, la lueur, une erreur*

(v)   Nouns in *-ière*

> Ex: *une prière, une barrière, la bière, la frontière*
> *la lumière, la rivière*

Exceptions: *un cimetière, le derrière*

(vi)   Nouns in *-sion*, *-ssion*, *-tion* or *-xion*

> Ex: *la télévision, une invasion, une décision, une occasion*
> *une mission, la possession*
> *une conversation, une question, une nation, une ration*
> *une portion, une action, la civilisation, une condition*
> *une position, une description*
> *la connexion, la réflexion*

Exception: *le bastion*

(vii)   Past participles, and present participles in their feminine form and used as nouns (improper derivation)

> Ex: *une allée, une venue*
> *une commerçante, une débutante*

See also chapters 16 Present Participle, section 3.1, and 17 Past Participle, section 3.

(viii)   Nouns in *-son*

> Ex: *une chanson, une maison*
> *une raison, une saison, une combinaison*
> *une comparaison, une liaison*

Exceptions: *un son, un poison* poison
un poisson fish

(ix)   Nouns in *-té* or *-tié*

        Ex: *la piété, la santé, l'unité, l'égalité, la bonté, la volonté*
             la nouveauté, la cité, la difficulté, la majorité
             la pitié, l'amitié, la moitié, la responsabilité
    Exceptions: *un été, un comité, un traité, un pâté, un côté*
              un arrêté

(x)   Nouns in *-ure, -ude*

        Ex: *une voiture, une monture, une ceinture*
             la nature, la confiture
             une figure, une doublure, une fourrure
             une injure, une serrure, une mesure
             une attitude, une certitude, une étude, une habitude
    Exceptions: chemical substances
        Ex: *le bromure, le mercure*
    Also: *le murmure*

(xi)   Nouns in *-ace*

        Ex: *l'audace, la glace, la menace, la place, la race, la surface*
    Exception: *le palace*

(xii)   Nouns in *-ade*

        Ex: *l'ambassade, la cascade, la façade, la salade, la promenade*
    Exceptions: *un stade, un grade*

(xiii) Nouns in *-aine, -eine, -oine*

        Ex: *une aubaine, une fontaine, une graine*
             la peine, la veine
             l'avoine, la macédoine
    Also: *une dizaine, une douzaine, une centaine*, etc.
    Exceptions: *un capitaine, un chanoine, un moine* (all referring to animates)

(xiv)   Nouns in *-èche, -èque, -èse, -ève*

        Ex: *une brèche, une flèche*
             une bibliothèque, une discothèque
             l'hypothèse, la thèse, la synthèse
             la grève, la sève
    Exceptions: *un diocèse, un évêque* (animate)

(xv)   Nouns in *-ine* and *-ise*

        Ex: *la colline, la cuisine, la farine*
             la machine, la racine, la ruine
             la chemise, la crise, l'église
             *la marchandise, la surprise, **la** brise*
    Exceptions: *le magazine, le platine*
              ***le** pare-brise*

2.7 Nouns with two genders and the same or related meaning

(i) *amour*:

> Ex: *un amour fou* → *des amours fous* or *des amours folles* (poetic)

(ii) *chose*:

une chose is feminine but the pronoun *quelque chose* is masculine (see chapter 36 Indefinite Words, section 2.1).

> Ex: *Une chose est certaine: c'est quelque chose de compliqué.*
> One thing is certain – it is something complicated.

(iii) *personne*:

une personne is feminine but the pronoun *personne* is masculine (see chapter 36 Indefinite Words, section 3.3).

> Ex: *Deux personnes sont arrivées.*
> Two people have arrived.
>
> *Personne n'est parfait.*
> Nobody is perfect.

(iv) *délice*:

délice singular is masculine but *délices* plural is feminine.

> Ex: *Cette glace à la framboise est un délice.*
> This raspberry ice-cream is delicious.
>
> *Cette glace à la framboise ferait les délices de n'importe quel gourmet!*
> This raspberry ice-cream would delight any gourmet!

(v) *gens*:

Adjectives and participles qualifying *gens* are masculine. However, if *gens* is **preceded** by an adjective with a distinctive form in the feminine, *gens* becomes feminine.

> Ex: *tous les gens; des gens démunis; des gens ennuyeux*
> but:
> *de vieilles gens, de bonnes gens, toutes les vieilles gens*

Hence:

> *Tous les gens étaient arrivés.*
> but:
> *Toutes les vieilles gens étaient arrivées.*

NB: This rule does not apply to *jeunes gens* (to be considered as one word), which remains masculine at all times.

> Ex: *Ces jeunes gens sont bien bruyants!*
> These young people are very noisy!

(vi) *orgue*:

orgue (organ) is masculine but the expression *les grandes orgues* referring to a church organ for instance is always feminine.

> Ex: *Le père de Philippe lui a acheté un orgue portatif.*
> *J'aime écouter les grandes orgues à l'église.*

(vii) *Pâques* is:
   − feminine in greetings:
        Ex: *Joyeuses Pâques!*
           Happy Easter!
   − masculine as a date:
        Ex: *Quand Pâques sera passé . . .*
           When Easter is over . . .

2.8 Nouns with two genders and different meanings

The following is not an exhaustive list.

Ex: *un livre* a book	*une livre* a pound (weight)
	a pound (money)
un manche a handle	*une manche* a sleeve
	La Manche the English Channel
un mode a mood; method, way	*une mode* fashion
un pendule pendulum	*une pendule* clock
le physique appearance	*la physique* physics
un poste post (e.g. military)	*une poste* a post–office
position (employment)	*la poste* postal service
set (e.g. television)	
le rose the colour pink	*la rose* rose (flower)
un vase a vase	*la vase* silt
un voile a veil	*une voile* a sail
le crêpe crepe	*une crêpe* a pancake
un critique a critic (person)	*une critique* criticism; review
le mémoire memorandum	*la mémoire* memory
les mémoires memoirs	
le merci thanks, thank-you	*la merci* mercy
un tour turn; tour; trick	*une tour* tower
un vapeur a steamer	*la vapeur* steam
un page a page-boy	*une page* a page
un poêle a stove	*une poêle* a frying-pan
un moule a mould	*une moule* a mussel

2.9 The gender of compound nouns

Compound nouns can be made up of:

− noun + adjective	*un coffre-fort*
− adjective + noun	*un bas-côté*
− noun + noun	*un wagon-restaurant*
− adjective + adjective	*un sourd-muet*
− noun + preposition + noun	*un dessus-de-lit*
− adverb/prefix + noun	*une contre-offensive*
− preposition + noun	*un en-cas*
− verb + noun	*un tire-bouchon*

In the majority of cases, the gender is that of the noun, or of the first noun if there is more than one. However, exceptions are numerous!

> Ex: *un chou-fleur (un chou)*; *un gratte-ciel (le ciel)*
>> but:
>
> *un rouge-gorge* (*la gorge*, but it is ***un*** *oiseau*)
> *un ouvre-boîte* (***une*** *boîte*, but it is ***quelque chose*** (masculine) *pour ouvrir une boîte*)

Note that the hyphen can eventually disappear.

> Ex: *un portefeuille; un survêtement; un portemanteau*

2.10 The gender of acronyms (*sigles*)

Acronyms generally take the gender of the main noun.

> Ex: *L'ONU (**Organisation** des Nations Unies) a été **humiliée** à Sarajevo.*
> *Les HLM (**Habitations** à Loyer Modéré) sont **réservées** en priorité aux revenus modestes.*

However, in some cases the gender can also be derived from what the acronym represents, for instance *une HLM* is *un immeuble*, hence may also be masculine, as illustrated in this song by Renaud:

> '*Putain qu'**il** est blême, mon **HLM**,*
> *Et la môme du huitième, le hash elle aime.*'

2.11 The gender of foreign words

The tendency is to use what would be the gender of the French equivalent word.

> Ex: ***la*** *Poll-Tax (la taxe)*
> ***le*** *fax (le fac-similé)*
> ***le*** *pressing (le nettoyage à sec)*

2.12 The gender of nouns derived from a brand name

The new noun derives its gender from what it represents.

> Ex: *une Peugeot (une voiture)*
> *un Berliet (un camion)*
> *un Airbus (un avion)*
> *du Banania (du chocolat en poudre)*
> *une Guinness (une bière)*
> *un Kleenex (un mouchoir en papier)*
> *du Scotch (du ruban adhésif)*

Note that in a lot of cases, however, the masculine is the unmarked gender and serves for most new nouns.

3   The plural of nouns

3.1   Plural of simple nouns

The plural of simple nouns is generally formed in the same way as the plural of adjectives, i.e. by adding an 's' to the singular written form.

Ex: *un fil* [fil] → *des fils* [fil]

(i)   Nouns which end in 's', 'x' or 'z' do not add anything in the plural.

Ex: *un fils* [fis]   → *des fils* [fis]
un nez [ne]   → *des nez* [ne]
un gaz [gɑz] → *des gaz* [gɑz]
un os [ɔs]   → *des os* [o]
un as [ɑs]   → *des as* [ɑs]
un bus [bys] → *des bus* [bys]
un mois   → *des mois*
un avis   → *des avis*
un poids   → *des poids*
une voix   → *des voix*

(ii)   Nouns in *-eu, -ieu, -au, -eau* or *-œu* take an 'x'.

Ex: *un cheveu*   → *des cheveux*
un feu   → *des feux*
un jeu   → *des jeux*
un lieu   → *des lieux*
un tuyau   → *des tuyaux*
un noyau   → *des noyaux*
un seau   → *des seaux*
un moineau → *des moineaux*
un chapeau → *des chapeaux*
un préau   → *des préaux*
un vœu   → *des vœux*

Exceptions: *un landau* → *des landaus*
un pneu → *des pneus*
un bleu (the colour blue; a bruise) → *des bleus*

Also: *un bleu de travail* (overalls) → *des bleus de travail*

(iii)   The following nouns in *-ou* take an 'x' (all the others take an 's'): *bijou, caillou, chou, genou, hibou, joujou, pou,* and also the recent word *ripou* (conman/rip-off merchant).

Ex: *de beaux bijoux* but: *de grands trous*

(iv)   Nouns in *-al* become *-aux*.

Ex: *un canal*   → *des canaux*
un signal   → *des signaux*
un cheval   → *des chevaux*
un journal   → *des journaux*

$$un\ animal \rightarrow des\ animaux$$
$$un\ hôpital \rightarrow des\ hôpitaux$$
$$un\ mal \rightarrow des\ maux$$
$$un\ rival \rightarrow des\ rivaux$$
$$un\ tribunal \rightarrow des\ tribunaux$$
$$un\ général \rightarrow des\ généraux$$

Exceptions: *un bal* → *des bals*
un carnaval → *des carnavals*
un festival → *des festivals*
un récital → *des récitals*
un régal → *des régals*
un chacal → *des chacals*

NB: *un val* → *des vals*, except in the expression:'*par monts et par vaux*' (over hill and dale).

un idéal → *des idéals* or *des idéaux*

(v) Nouns in *-ail*

– plural in *-aux*:
Ex: *un travail* → *des travaux*
un vitrail → *des vitraux*
un bail → *des baux*
un émail → *des émaux*
un soupirail → *des soupiraux*

– plural in *-ails*:
Ex: *un détail* → *des détails*
un éventail → *des éventails*
un portail → *des portails*
le rail → *les rails*
un gouvernail → *des gouvernails*
un épouvantail → *des épouvantails*

NB: *l'aïl* → *les aïls* or *les aulx*

le bétail (cattle) is a collective noun which has no plural.

(vi) Note the following irregular plurals:

– *œil, ciel*:
Ex: *un œil* → *des yeux*
le ciel → *les cieux*

NB: *œil* becomes *œils* in compounds.
Ex: *des œils-de-bœuf*

– *aïeul*:
Ex: *un aïeul* → *les aïeuls* (grandparents)
→ *les aïeux* (ancestors)

405

      – *œuf* and *bœuf*:

The plural is regular but note the pronunciation:

        un œuf [œf]   →   *des œufs* [ø]

        un bœuf [bœf] →   *des bœufs* [bø]

(vii)   Generally speaking, words of foreign origin are treated as French words and thus form their plural by adding an '*s*' to the singular.

        Ex: *un album*   → *des albums*

              un référendum → *des référendums*

              un week-end → *des week-ends*

              un barman   → *des barmans*

              un solo   → *des solos*

              un concerto   → *des concertos*

              une pizza   → *des pizzas*

NB: Some French speakers (particularly in the media) may want to appear fashionable and show their knowledge of the foreign language concerned by using the foreign plural.

(viii) Items of clothing which are in effect *une paire de* are singular in French and plural in English.

        Ex: *un short*   shorts

             un collant   tights

             un pantalon   trousers

             un maillot de bain swimming trunks

             un slip   pants

(ix)   Some nouns are only ever used in the plural. They are:

      – nouns with a collective meaning:

        Ex: *des archives*   archives

             les annales   annals

             les échecs   chess

             les dames   draughts

             les décombres   rubble, debris

             les mœurs   mores

             les ténèbres   darkness

             des arrhes   deposit

             les alentours, les environs   surroundings

             les frais   costs

             les honoraires   fees

             les gens   people

NB: If a singular is needed for '*gens*', use '*une personne*' (See also chapter 36 Indefinite Words, section 2.4.)

      – nouns expressing a duration, or ceremonies with several phases:

        Ex: *les vacances*   holidays

             les fiançailles   engagement

             les funérailles, les obsèques funeral

             les représailles   reprisals

             les pourparlers   talks, negotiations

(x) Some nouns have an additional meaning in the plural.
> Ex: *une lettre*   a letter (alphabet)
> a letter (post)
> *les lettres*   letters (literature)
>
> *une lunette*   a telescope, a field-glass
> *des lunettes*   spectacles
>
> *un gage*   a pledge
> *des gages*   wages

(xi) Unlike in English, family names do not take an 's' in the plural.
> Ex: *Les Dupont viennent d'arriver.*
> The Duponts have just arrived.
>
> *Nous allons chez les Dupont.*
> We're going to the Duponts'.

3.2 Plural of compound nouns

Verbs, prepositions or adverbs in a compound noun remain invariable in the plural. Adjectives and nouns take the plural, except if the meaning prohibits it for the noun (e.g. uncountable nouns).

(i) Two countable nouns:
> Ex: *un chou-fleur* → *des choux-fleurs*
> *un chien-loup* → *des chiens-loups*

(ii) Noun (countable) + noun (uncountable):
> Ex: *un timbre-poste* → *des timbres-poste*
> (*poste* = postal system)
> *une pause-café* → *des pauses-café*
> (= *pour prendre le café*)
> *un coup d'œil* → *des coups d'œil*
> (with only one eye!)

(iii) Adjective + countable noun:
> Ex: *un rouge-gorge* → *des rouges-gorges*
> *un grand-père* → *des grands-pères*

Note that *mini* remains invariable:
> Ex: *une mini-jupe* → *des mini-jupes*
> *un mini-ordinateur* → *des mini-ordinateurs*

(iv) Countable noun + adjective:
> Ex: *un coffre-fort* → *des coffres-forts*

(v)   Verb + countable noun:

Ex: *une garde-robe*   → *des garde-robes*
      un garde-fou   → *des garde-fous*
      un couvre-lit   → *des couvre-lits*
      un tire-bouchon   → *des tire-bouchons*
      un ouvre-boîte   → *des ouvre-boîtes*
      un tourne-disque   → *des tourne-disques*
      un pèse-lettre   → *des pèse-lettres*

In some cases, the noun complement is always plural:

Ex: *un porte-avions*
      un cure-dents
      un sèche-cheveux

(vi) Verb + noun (uncountable/abstract/'unique' object):

Ex: *un gratte-ciel*   → *des gratte-ciel*
      un brise-glace   → *des brise-glace*
      un chasse-neige   → *des chasse-neige*
      un garde-boue   → *des garde-boue*
      un chauffe-eau   → *des chauffe-eau*
      un porte-monnaie   → *des porte-monnaie*
      un coupe-papier   → *des coupe-papier*
      un porte-bonheur   → *des porte-bonheur*
      un abat-jour   → *des abat-jour*

NB: '*jour*' here means 'light', not 'day'.

(vii) Adverb + countable noun:

Ex: *une arrière-pensée* → *des arrière-pensées*
      un haut-parleur   → *des haut-parleurs*
      une contre-offensive → *des contre-offensives*

(viii) Adverb + past participle:

Ex: *un nouveau-né* → *des nouveau-nés*
      (*nouveau = nouvellement*)

Exceptions: *un nouveau-venu* → *des nouveaux-venus*
            un nouveau-marié → *des nouveaux-mariés*
            (where '*nouveau*' is treated as an adjective)

(ix) Preposition + countable noun:

Ex: *un en-tête* → *des en-têtes*
                but:
      un sous-main → *des sous-main*

(x)   Verb + adverb:

Ex: *un passe-partout* → *des passe-partout*

(xi)   Noun + preposition + noun:

   – In most cases, only the first noun becomes plural.
   Ex: *un arc-en-ciel*   → *des arcs-en-ciel*
         un chef-d'œuvre   → *des chefs-d'œuvre*
         une langue-de-chat → *des langues-de-chat*

   – Some remain invariable.
   Ex: *un pied-à-terre* → *des pied-à-terre*
         un pot-au-feu   → *des pot-au-feu*
         un tête-à-tête   → *des tête-à-tête*

(xii) Verb (+ conjunction of coordination) + verb:
       they remain invariable.
   Ex: *un va-et-vient*   → *des va-et-vient*
         un laissez-passer → *des laissez-passer*

(xiii) Note the following, where the mark of the plural also appears inside the noun:
         monsieur (M.)   → *messieurs (MM.)*
         madame (Mme)   → *mesdames (Mmes)*
         mademoiselle (Mlle) → *mesdemoiselles (Mlles)*
         un bonhomme   → *des bonshommes*
         un gentilhomme   → *des gentilshommes*

28 Qualifying adjectives

1 Introduction

A qualifying adjective expresses a particular **quality**, a characteristic (essential or accidental) of the 'substance' represented by the noun or pronoun. It agrees in gender and number with the noun or pronoun it refers to. Adjectives form an open class, i.e. new qualifying adjectives can be created (recent examples include *allergisant, antisismique, autocorrecteur, anabolisant*). They can be attributive or predicative, joint or detached, and placed before or after the noun they refer to (see also chapter 2 Syntax) according to the following pattern:

- attributive → joint → before the noun
                      → after the noun
              → detached
- predicative

In a noun phrase, the presence of the adjective is optional. But it can be completed or modified itself (forming an **adjectival phrase**), and this may affect its place in the noun phrase or even in the sentence.

Although it is estimated that around two-thirds of adjectives appear **after** the noun in French, the factors which come into play to affect their position are diverse and their combination complex.

Adjectives other than qualifying adjectives are now classed as 'determiners', alongside articles (see chapter 1 Parts of Speech, section 4). They are:
- demonstrative
- possessive
- numeral
- interrogative
- exclamative
- relative
- indefinite

These adjectives/determiners are treated in the relevant chapters.

2 The adjectival phrase

2.1 Attributive and predicative adjectives

Note that the French for 'attributive' is *épithète* but the French for 'predicative' is *attribut*. This should be borne in mind when using a French grammar book written in French.

(i) **Attributive**

- An adjective placed immediately beside the noun it qualifies is attributive (*épithète*).

- An attributive adjective is an optional constituent of the noun phrase (see chapter 2 Syntax, section 2.1.2(i)).
  Ex: *Un chien [**enragé**] | a mordu le [**gentil**] facteur.*

(ii) **Predicative**

- An adjective separated from the noun it qualifies by the copula *être* (or *devenir, sembler, paraître, rester, passer pour*) is predicative (*attribut*).

- A predicative adjective is thus a constituent of the verb phrase (see chapter 2 Syntax, sections 2.11 and 2.12).
  Ex: *Le chien | est devenu **enragé**.*
  Note that in the verb phrase, the adjective is no longer optional:
  ★Le chien est devenu.

2.2 Attributive adjective: joint or detached

- Joint attributive adjectives are adjacent to the noun they qualify and are placed immediately before or after that noun. It is the positioning, before or after the noun, which causes most problems for the Anglophone learner.

- Detached attributive adjectives are in apposition, i.e. they are not part of the noun phrase, or even the sentence in which they appear.

2.3 Attributive adjective: joint

The joint attributive adjective generally expresses a quality which is durable or closely linked or even inherent to the element qualified. Most attributive adjectives follow the noun in French, while they precede it in English. However, there are numerous exceptions to this rule.
  Ex: *un chat **noir**; de **longs** cheveux **blonds***
  *de **belles** pommes; le secteur **public***

- Qualifying adjectives can themselves be modified or complemented to form adjectival phrases.

- There are two types of adjectives which do not 'qualify' the noun in the same way as ordinary qualifying adjectives. They are:
  - **relational adjectives** (always placed after the noun)
    and:
  - **short common adjectives** (generally placed before the noun)
  However, they still belong to the category of attributive adjectives.

2.3.1 Qualifying adjectives and their complements or modifiers

(i) A qualifying adjective can be completed by a noun, a prepositional phrase, an infinitive, another adjective or a *que*-clause.

411

    – a noun:

        Ex: *Un foulard* **bleu** <u>ciel</u>

    – a prepositional phrase:

        Ex: *un chat* **fier** <u>*de ses prouesses*</u>

              une paysanne **dure** <u>*à la tâche*</u>

              un visage **rouge** <u>*de confusion*</u>

    – a verb in the infinitive:

        Ex: *une recette* **facile** <u>*à faire*</u>

    – another adjective:

        Ex: *un tissu* **vert** <u>*pâle*</u>

    – a *que*-clause:

        Ex: *Je suis* **contente** <u>*qu'il parte*</u>.

(ii)   A qualifying adjective can be modified by an adverb to indicate:

    – the intensity of the quality:

        Ex: *un fauteuil* <u>*très*</u> **confortable**

    See also section 6 below and chapter 29 Adverbs, section 5.1.

    – a certain aspect of the quality:

        Ex: *un endroit* <u>*merveilleusement*</u> **calme**

    See also chapter 29 Adverbs, section 5.1.

(iii)   A qualifying adjective can be subject to comparisons:

        Ex: *un quartier* <u>*plus*</u> **résidentiel** *qu'un autre*

    See chapter 30 Comparatives, sections 2.2 and 3.

2.3.2   *Relational adjectives*

Relational adjectives (sometimes called pseudo-adjectives) are generally interchangeable with noun complements. They establish a relationship between the noun and another nominal element. These adjectives are all formed by derivation from the corresponding noun. Hence they can be paraphrased by a prepositional phrase:

        Ex: *la frontière italienne* (= *de l'Italie*)

              une manifestation étudiante (= *d'étudiants*)

              l'industrie pétrolière (= *du pétrole*)

              la campagne électorale (= *pour les élections*)

    – They cannot normally be intensified or be subject to comparisons (see 2.3.1 above). Indeed, *la frontière italienne* cannot be *moins italienne qu'une autre*, or *la plus italienne* or *très italienne*. However, with a change of emphasis, we can have:

        Ex: *Elle a un chic très parisien.*

              She's got a very Parisian type of elegance.

'*parisien*' here does not mean '*de Paris*' but '*qui rappelle celui que doit avoir toute Parisienne*' or '*au plus haut point conforme à ce qu'on peut attendre d'une Parisienne*'.

– They cannot be coordinated with an ordinary qualifying adjective:

> Ex: *une manifestation étudiante et ordonnée

However, given an adequate context, the same relational adjective can function like an ordinary qualifying adjective with different interpretations.

> Ex: *Elle a un chic parisien.*
> (relational)
> She's got a Parisian-type elegance.
>
> *Son chic est parisien à tout crin.*
> (qualifying = characteristic of a Parisian)
> She's got a quintessentially Parisian type of elegance.

2.3.3 Short adjectives

They are generally placed before the noun. They have lost their qualifying value – this can be verified when looking at their homonyms, placed **after** the noun (see 2.3.4.3 below).

For instance, they can express a positive or negative evaluation:

> Ex: *une sale affaire*; *un sacré menteur*

They can also express the exemplary character of the referent in relation to its class:

> Ex: *un bel homme*; *un net succès*

2.3.4 Place of attributive adjectives

2.3.4.1 AFTER THE NOUN

They generally have a **classifying** value.

The following types of adjectives always follow the noun:

(i) Adjectives which give the noun a distinctive quality (e.g. colour, shape, taste; nationality, religion, philosophy; rank, profession, social class, political group, artistic movement; administrative, technical, geographical or social category), i.e. which place the noun in a category. Note that they include all **relational adjectives**.

> Ex: *un béret basque*
> *du vin mousseux*
> *une tour carrée*
> *des roses rouges*
> *la peinture expressionniste*
> *la politique économique*
> *le réseau électrique*
> *la langue française*

NB: Unlike in English, adjectives of nationality do **not** begin with a capital letter.

413

(ii)   Adjectives derived from a present or past participle (but see exceptions in 2.3.4.4).

> Ex: *une fenêtre fermée*
> *une assiette cassée*
> *un renard apprivoisé*
> *une expression connue*
> *un étudiant fatigué*
> *un travail fatigant*
> *des enfants remuants*
> *l'eau courante*
> *un numéro gagnant*

See also chapters 16 Present Participle, section 3.2, and 17 Past Participle, section 4.

(iii) When those short adjectives which would normally precede the noun (see below) are modified by a complement or a long adverb phrase, they are placed after the noun. Compare:

> *un bon médicament; un très bon médicament*
> and:
> *un médicament très bon pour le foie*

2.3.4.2   BEFORE THE NOUN

Most adjectives placed before the noun are the short adjectives in common use. However, other adjectives can also appear before the noun for emphasis (see 2.3.4.4 below).

In all cases, adjectives which come before the noun qualify the concept, the notion expressed by the noun; they have a **specifying**, **identifying** value. They tend to indicate an inherent or permanent property of the noun which they qualify.

(i)   The most common short adjectives are:

petit, grand, gros, jeune, vieux, joli, beau, vilain, bon, mauvais, excellent, gentil, méchant, long, court, bref, haut, vaste, pauvre

> Ex: *une grande maison*
> *un vieux poêle*
> *une bonne note*
> *de jolies fleurs*
> *un court instant*
> *de hautes montagnes*

NB: The following idioms are exceptions:

− *à voix haute / à haute voix*	aloud
− *à voix basse*	softly
− *à marée haute*	at high tide
− *à marée basse*	at low tide
− *d'un ton bref*	curtly
− *une voyelle brève*	a short vowel

Note also the following:

avoir les cheveux longs	to have long hair
avoir le verbe haut	to have a loud voice
avoir le cœur gros	to have a heavy heart

(ii) In this position, some of these adjectives have lost their semantic content and are used mainly with an affective or pejorative value, a plus or a minus, an addition to the semantic content of the noun.

Ex: *Je voudrais un bon kilo de pommes.*
(= a kilo of apples or slightly over)

Donnez-moi une petite livre de cerises.
(= a pound of cherries or slightly under)

(iii) *court* and *long* do precede the noun except when there is a contrast (explicit or implicit).

Ex: *un court instant, un long moment, une petite fille*
a brief instant, a long while, a little girl
but:
une jupe courte, une jupe longue
a short skirt, a long skirt

des cheveux courts, des cheveux longs
short hair, long hair

(iv) When those adjectives which would normally precede the noun are modified by the following short and common adverbs, they remain before the noun:
très, bien, fort, plus, moins, assez, aussi, si

Ex: *une très belle maison*
un assez long séjour
un bien gentil garçon
une si bonne histoire

(v) As we have seen, classifying adjectives are normally placed after the noun: if placed before the noun, they lose their classifying value (see also section 2.3.4.3 below). Compare:

*Véronique s'est acheté une **robe verte**.*
the adjective brings a piece of information enabling a dress to be selected.
and:

*Ce paysage me rappelle la **verte campagne** de mon enfance.*
the adjective is redundant in relation to the noun (our culture associates 'green' and 'countryside'). Thus its status changes: it has poetic or symbolic values.

(vi) The following pairs of 'adjective + noun' are treated as compound nouns.

Ex: *un jeune homme*	young man
une jeune fille	young woman
une petite fille	little girl
des jeunes gens	young people
des petits pois	peas
des petits pains	bread rolls
un grand magasin	department store
un bon mot	witticism

(recevoir les) sincères condoléances de qn
(to receive) the deepest sympathy from sb

faire la grasse matinée
to have a lie-in

NB: The indefinite plural is **des** (and not *de*) when 'adjective + noun' are considered as one noun (see chapter 23 Articles, section 3.1(iii)).
Ex: **des** *grands magasins*

(vii) When the adjective qualifies a proper noun, it is placed before it.
Ex: *la belle Madame Durand*
la célèbre Sarah Bernhardt
le regretté Picasso . . .
except if the adjective is made into a noun to complement the proper noun (note the presence and place of the definite article).
Ex: *Charles le Chauve*
Pépin le Bref
Ivan le Terrible

2.3.4.3 EITHER BEFORE OR AFTER THE NOUN

(i) **With change of meaning**

The following pairings are in current use:

Ex: *l'histoire ancienne*	*mon ancien travail*
ancient history	my former job
c'est de l'histoire ancienne	*un ancien combattant*
it's water under the bridge	an ex-serviceman
une maison ancienne	*mon ancienne maison*
an old house	my previous house
le beaujolais nouveau	*le nouveau gouvernement*
(a type of Beaujolais)	the new (latest) government
des pommes de terre nouvelles	*une nouvelle robe*
(a type of potato)	a new dress (another one/an additional one or a recent one)
la semaine dernière	*la dernière semaine du mois*
last week	the last week of the month
(= the one before this one)	(= the last in a series of four)
le mois prochain	*la prochaine séance*
next month	the next show (in a series)
(= the one after this one)	
un homme grand	*un grand homme*
a tall man	an important/famous man
(physical description)	

un homme pauvre a poor man (not rich)	*un pauvre homme* a poor man (unfortunate, i.e. who may inspire pity, even if he is rich!)
un homme brave a brave/courageous man	*un brave homme* a good/honest man
un vin cher an expensive wine	*mon cher oncle* my dear uncle
des vêtements propres clean clothes	*mes propres vêtements* my own clothes
des vêtements sales dirty clothes	*une sale affaire* a nasty business
des objets sacrés holy objects	*un sacré menteur* a damn liar
une femme seule a woman by herself/on her own	*une seule femme* only one woman
un repas simple a simple meal	*une simple formalité* a mere formality

Consider the following examples:

1 une histoire drôle **une drôle d'histoire**
a funny story a strange story
(a type of story)

There are very few adjectives that can be followed by *de* before the noun. They are generally adjectives which also exist as nouns.

Ex: *une sotte de femme*
mon imbécile de cousin
son génie de frère

but not: **cette intelligente de femme*

2 une histoire vraie **un vrai conte de fées**
a true story a veritable fairy-tale
(i.e. not fiction)

When *vrai* means 'real', 'genuine', *véritable* is more commonly used.

Ex: *un véritable conte de fées*

3 des idées fausses **un faux problème**
false ideas not a real problem
une fausse alerte
a false alarm
de faux papiers
forged papers

After the noun, *faux* tends to mean 'not genuine' or 'erroneous', while *faux* before the noun tends to mean 'which does not exist'. But note an exception with *faux papiers* which means 'not genuine'. See also the positions and meanings of *différent, divers, certain* and *même* in chapter 36 Indefinite Words, sections 5.1, 5.3 and 6.1.

Note that this list is not exhaustive in the meanings it itemizes (a dictionary should be consulted for extensive definitions). Its purpose is to stress the importance of the place of the adjective to avoid a faux pas!

(ii)   **Without change of meaning**

The non-classifying adjectives (those that imply the **subjectivity** of the speaker – especially affective adjectives) can be placed **before or after** the noun. While this does not change the meaning, it does give emphasis (see below). Those adjectives are generally longer than the noun which they qualify. The most common are: *effrayant, épouvantable, énorme, interminable, inoubliable, adorable, merveilleux, extraordinaire, exceptionnel.*

   Ex: *Elle a écrit quelques romans **interminables**.*
         or:
      *Elle a écrit quelques **interminables** romans.*
      She has written a few rambling novels.

2.3.4.4   CONSTRAINTS AFFECTING PLACE

Positioning of the adjective is restricted in the following cases:

– emphasis: the adjective can be placed before the noun for emphasis, to express for instance an emotional reaction or to make it sound more poetic.
   Ex: *Nous avons passé des vacances **inoubliables**.*
      → *Nous avons passé d'**inoubliables** vacances.*
      We had an unforgettable holiday.

– prosody: an adjective that is longer than the noun is likely to be placed after it.
   Ex: *un steak appétissant*
            is preferable to:
      un appétissant steak
      (unless emphasis is particularly desired!)

Note that it is possible to emphasize an adjective modified by an adverb (*une incroyablement fatigante journée*) but not an adjective completed by a prepositional phrase (**une fatigante à l'extrême journée*).

2.3.4.5   POSITION OF MULTIPLE ADJECTIVES

(i)   If one of the adjectives normally comes before the noun and the other after, they keep their respective positions.
   Ex: *une petite pluie fine*
      un beau chat noir
      de grosses pêches juteuses
      une jolie robe blanche

This also applies to nouns forming one unit with an adjective (see section 2.3.4.2(vi) above).

> Ex: *d'excellents petits pois extra fins*
> *un beau jeune homme triste*

(ii) When the two adjectives come before or after the noun, they keep that place and are linked together by *et*.

> Ex: *un cours passionnant, un cours instructif*
> → *un cours passionnant et instructif*
>
> *une belle fée, une bonne fée*
> → *une belle et bonne fée*

(iii) *petit*:

– When *petit* is juxtaposed with another adjective, it has a mitigated semantic value (see 2.3.4.2(ii) above) and is placed next to the noun.

> Ex: *un vilain petit canard*
> an ugly little duckling
>
> *un joli petit village*
> a pretty little village

– If *petit* is coordinated with the other adjective(s), it recovers its proper semantic value and each of the adjectives has its characterizing or restricting value.

> Ex: *les petites et moyennes entreprises*
> small and medium-sized companies

– If *petit* is placed after the noun, it necessarily has its proper, descriptive value, like any other adjective placed after the noun.

> Ex: *Mr Underhill, personnage petit et laid*
> Mr Underhill, a short, ugly character

(iv) For two adjectives to be linked by *et*, they must present two equal and separable characteristics. Otherwise, if the two adjectives complement each other to give one meaning, or if one adjective qualifies a 'noun + adjective' group, there is no *et*.
Note that English follows the same usage.

> Ex: *Le temps est lourd et orageux.*
> The weather is close and thundery.
>
> *un restaurant bon et abordable*
> a good and affordable restaurant
> > but:
> *les romans français contemporains*
> contemporary French novels
> (French novels which are contemporary)

In other words, the adjective which is further from the noun qualifies the grouping made up by the noun + nearer adjective.

> Ex: *une revue littéraire hebdomadaire*
> a weekly literary review
> '*hebdomadaire*' qualifies '*revue littéraire*'

Note that such groupings are generally limited to two adjectives. However, it is possible to add a third one by placing it before the whole grouping.

> Ex: *une excellente revue littéraire hebdomadaire*
> an excellent weekly literary review

(v) If one of the adjectives is modified, it follows the noun.

> Ex: *une belle et vaste maison*
> but:
> *une belle maison assez vaste*
> *une vaste maison assez belle*

(vi) When one of the adjectives is part of the noun (phrases of the type discussed in (i) above), there is no *et*.

> Ex: *d'excellents petits pois*

Hence:

> *un beau jeune homme*
> a handsome young man
> but:
> *un homme jeune et beau*
> a young and handsome man

2.3.4.6 ADJECTIVE QUALIFYING A COMPLEX NOUN

An adjective qualifying a complex noun (i.e. composed of two nouns linked by *de* or *à*) may be placed either before the first noun or after the second, bearing in mind the rules given above.

> Ex: *un **grand** café au lait*
> a large white coffee
>
> *une **belle** canne à pêche*
> a fine fishing rod
>
> *une canne à pêche **cassée***
> a broken fishing rod
>
> *une carte d'identité **déchirée***
> a torn identity card

2.4 Attributive adjective: detached

– The detached attributive adjective (*adjectif apposé*) is separated from the noun by a pause, often expressed in writing by a punctuation mark such as a comma. Note that the adjective is normally detached when qualifying a pronoun or proper noun.

> Ex: *Elle sortit, **fâchée**.*
> *Nicolas, **troublé**, ne répondit pas.*

– In apposition, the adjective or adjectival phrase does not really belong to the noun phrase, since it is in fact detached from the sentence. (Note that this does not only apply to adjectives: see chapter 2 Syntax, section 2.1.2(iii)). Hence it can be displaced:

> Ex: ***Penché sur son bol de lait***, *Dizzy réfléchissait à la misère du monde.*
>   or:
>   *Dizzy réfléchissait à la misère du monde,* ***penché sur son bol de lait****.*
>   or:
>   *Dizzy,* ***penché sur son bol de lait****, réfléchissait à la misère du monde.*

(see emphasis below)

– Detached adjectives or adjectival phrases often have the value of an adverbial clause, particularly of cause, consequence or time. Note that the use of adjectives in a detached position is more elegant than an adverbial clause, as it avoids the use of conjunctions such as *parce que*, *bien que*, etc.

> Ex: *Catherine,* ***souffrante****, ne pourra pas venir.*
>   (avoids *parce qu'elle est souffrante*)

– The adjective is also detached when it is part of a group with a comparison, degree or comment.

> Ex: *Le petit Pierre,* ***beau comme un ange****, tenait sa maman par la main.*

– The distinction between appositions and other attributive adjectives is the same as that between the restrictive and the non-restrictive interpretations of the adjective:

  – restrictive interpretation:

> Ex: *Les fruits trop mûrs ont été jetés.*

What is referred to here is '*les fruits trop mûrs*', a subset of the referent '*fruits*'.

  – non-restrictive interpretation:

> Ex: *Trop mûrs, les fruits ont été jetés.*
>   (= *tous les fruits, qui étaient tous trop mûrs*)

Here what is referred to is '*fruits*', the whole set of the referent '*fruits*', i.e. the referent is not restricted in its interpretation by the adjectival phrase '*trop mûrs*'.

Compare with:

> *Les courageux combattants ont été décorés.*
> (= *tous les combattants, qui sont tous courageux*)
>   and:
> *Les combattants courageux ont été décorés.*
> (= *seulement ceux des combattants qui ont montré du courage*)

2.5   Predicative adjective

It confers a **characteristic** to the noun. Predicative adjectives can characterize subject or object, with which they agree in gender and number (see also chapter 2 Syntax, sections 2.11 and 2.12).

2.5.1   Subject

With verbs such as *être, sembler, devenir, rester.*
Note that those adjectives can have complements.
> Ex: − prepositional phrase:
> *Yves semble responsable [de l'accident].*
> − infinitive:
> *Je suis contente [de pouvoir me reposer].*
> − *que*-clause:
> *Nous sommes ravis [que vous ayez pu venir].*

2.5.2   Object

With verbs such as *rendre, trouver, nommer.*
> Ex: *Marie a rendu Charles heureux.*
> Marie made Charles happy.

> *Je trouve Philippe facile à vivre.*
> I find Philippe easy to get on with.

3   The gender of the adjective

(i)   Generally an '*e*' is added to the masculine **written** form in order to obtain the feminine.

> Ex: *grand* → *grande*
> *petit* → *petite*
> *joli* → *jolie*
> *exquis* → *exquise*

NB: A diaeresis is needed over the '*e*' of the feminine of adjectives in *-gu* in order to keep the [y] sound of the masculine (but see appendix 1).

> Ex: *aigu* → *aiguë*
> *ambigu* → *ambiguë*

(ii)   When the adjective already ends with an '*e*' in the masculine, there are no changes in the feminine.

> Ex: *large* → *large*
> *vaste* → *vaste*
> *aimable* → *aimable*
> *tranquille* → *tranquille* (pronounced [trãkil])
> *moderne* → *moderne*
> *faible* → *faible*
> *rouge* → *rouge*
> *difficile* → *difficile*
> *utile* → *utile*

(iii)   The following adjectives have two forms in the masculine singular. The second form is used before a noun beginning with a vowel or a mute 'h'. The feminine is formed from this second form.

    Ex: *beau bel* → *belle*
          nouveau nouvel → *nouvelle*
          fou fol → *folle*
          mou mol → *molle*
          vieux vieil → *vieille*

(iv)   The masculine ending -*er* becomes the feminine -*ère*.

    Ex: *premier* → *première*
        dernier → *dernière*
        entier → *entière*
        léger → *légère*
        cher → *chère*
        amer → *amère*

Note that the final 'r' is pronounced in *cher* [ʃɛr] and *amer* [amɛr], but not in *léger* [leʒe].

(v)   The masculine ending -*f* becomes the feminine -*ve*.

    Ex: *naïf* → *naïve*
        bref → *brève*
        actif → *active*
        neuf → *neuve*
        veuf → *veuve*
        juif → *juive*
        vif → *vive*
        sauf → *sauve*

(vi)   The masculine ending -*x* becomes -*se* (but see (x) below).

    Ex: *heureux* → *heureuse*
        malheureux → *malheureuse*
        honteux → *honteuse*
        grincheux → *grincheuse*
        jaloux → *jalouse*
        peureux → *peureuse*
        victorieux → *victorieuse*
        paresseux → *paresseuse*

NB: *victorieuse* is also the feminine of *vainqueur*.

(vii)   The masculine ending -*eur* becomes -*euse*, -*eresse*, -*eure* or -*rice*, depending on the particular adjective.

– the feminine is -*euse*:

    Ex: *trompeur* → *trompeuse*
        menteur → *menteuse*
        flatteur → *flatteuse*
        voleur → *voleuse*

– the feminine is -*eresse*:

> Ex: *enchanteur* → *enchanteresse*
> *vengeur* → *vengeresse*
> *pécheur* → *pécheresse*

NB(1): The feminine of *traître* is *traîtresse*.

NB(2): The -*eresse* ending is considered somewhat cumbersome, and words ending with that suffix should be used sparingly.

– the feminine is -*eure* (those adjectives are derived from Latin comparatives):

> Ex: *antérieur* → *antérieure*
> *postérieur* → *postérieure*
> *inférieur* → *inférieure*
> *supérieur* → *supérieure*
> *intérieur* → *intérieure*
> *extérieur* → *extérieure*
> *majeur* → *majeure*
> *mineur* → *mineure*

– the feminine is -*rice*:

> Ex: *admirateur* → *admiratrice*
> *créateur* → *créatrice*
> *conservateur* → *conservatrice*
> *accusateur* → *accusatrice*
> *destructeur* → *destructrice*
> *indicateur* → *indicatrice*

(viii) Adjectives ending with a consonant preceded by a vowel, which double this consonant before the final '*e*'.

> Ex: *bon*   *bonne*
> *baron*   *baronne*
> *breton*   *bretonne*
> *paysan*   *paysanne*
> *ancien*   *ancienne*
> *quotidien*   *quotidienne*
> *européen*   *européenne*
> *sot*   *sotte*
> *net*   *nette*
> *muet*   *muette*
> *gros*   *grosse*
> *gras*   *grasse*
> *bas*   *basse*
> *las*   *lasse*
> *épais*   *épaisse*
> *bel*   *belle*
> *nul*   *nulle*
> *exceptionnel*   *exceptionnelle*
> *gentil*   *gentille* (pronounced [ʒɑ̃tij])

Note that the nasal endings in -*on*, -*an* and -*ien* in the masculine are denasalized in the feminine.

(ix) Adjectives ending with a consonant preceded by a vowel, which do **not** double the final consonant.

> Ex: *féminin* → *féminine*
> *câlin* → *câline*
> *fin* → *fine*
> *vain* → *vaine*
> *brun* → *brune*
> *persan* → *persane*
> *musulman* → *musulmane*
> *complet* → *complète*
> *discret* → *discrète*
> *concret* → *concrète*
> *inquiet* → *inquiète*
> *secret* → *secrète*
> *complet* → *complète*
> *idiot* → *idiote*
> *mauvais* → *mauvaise*
> *général* → *générale*
> *oral* → *orale*
> *original* → *originale*
> *dur* → *dure*
> *plein* → *pleine*
> *enfantin* → *enfantine*
> *brun* → *brune*

(x) The following adjectives have an 'irregular' feminine form.

> Ex: *blanc* → *blanche*
> *franc* → *franche*
> *sec* → *sèche*
> *doux* → *douce*
> *faux* → *fausse*
> *roux* → *rousse*
> *frais* → *fraîche*
> *tiers* → *tierce*
> *favori* → *favorite*
> *andalou* → *andalouse*
> *rigolo* → *rigolote*
> *coi* → *coite*
> *public* → *publique*
> *turc* → *turque*
> *caduc* → *caduque*
> *grec* → *grecque*
> *long* → *longue*
> *malin* → *maligne*
> *bénin* → *bénigne*

NB: The final '*c*' is pronounced in *sec* [sɛk], *turc* [tyrk], etc. but not in *blanc* [blɑ̃] and *franc* [frɑ̃].

(xi)   Some adjectives are invariable.

chic, rococo, standard, disco, snob, and the following adjectives of colour: *marron, orange (cerise, olive,* etc.), *kaki.*

      Ex: *une robe chic*
            une table de cuisine standard
            une armoire rococo

(xii)   Some adjectives are only used in one gender.

   – masculine only:
      Ex: *un pied bot*   a club-foot
            un nez aquilin
            un hareng saur   a smoked herring

   – feminine only:
      Ex: *bouche bée*   open-mouthed, gaping
            la fièvre scarlatine   scarlet fever
            une œuvre pie   a pious deed
            une femme enceinte a pregnant woman

Hence the embarrassment of journalists having to report the pregnancy of '*le Capitaine Prieur*' (a woman) at the time of the *Rainbow Warrior* crisis of 1988!

(xiii)   *grand*

grand remains invariable in:
      grand-mère, grand-rue, grand-messe; à grand peine

4   The plural of the adjective

(i)   An '*s*' is added to the **written** form of the singular (masculine or feminine) to obtain the plural.
      Ex: *grand*   *grands*
            grande   *grandes*
            vaste   *vastes*

(ii)   When there is already an '*s*' or an '*x*' in the singular (masculine only) there is no change in the plural. The feminine form however, if it ends with an '*e*', adds an '*s*'.
      Ex: *un vieux bateau*   *de vieux bateaux*
               but:
            une vieille barque   *de vieilles barques*

            un gâteau exquis   *des gâteaux exquis*
               but:
            une boisson exquise *des boissons exquises*

(iii) The *-al* ending (masculine) becomes *-aux* in the plural (the feminine ending *-ale* becomes *-ales*).

Ex: *le principal interprète*   *les principaux interprètes*
                    but:
       la principale actrice   *les principales actrices*

The following are exceptions to this rule:

final	*finals*
fatal	*fatals*
glacial	*glacials*
naval	*navals*
natal	*natals*
bancal	*bancals*
idéal	*idéals* or *idéaux*

NB: *banal* → *banals* means 'ordinary'.
       banal → *banaux* means 'communal'.
       Ex: *des propos banals*   trivialities
              des fours banaux   communal ovens

(iv) The *-eau* ending (masculine) becomes *-eaux*.

Ex: *beau*   *beaux*   (but: *belle*   *belles*)
       nouveau   *nouveaux*   (but: *nouvelle*   *nouvelles*)

(v) The *-eu* ending:

Ex: *hébreu* → *hébreux*
                    but:
       bleu → *bleus*

(vi) Adjectives that are invariable for gender are usually also invariable for number.

Ex: *des vêtements chic*
       des uniformes kaki
       des meubles rococo
       des collants marron
       des foulards orange

Note that *écarlate*, *mauve*, *pourpre* and *rose*, which were originally nouns, are now treated as adjectives in their own right and so agree in number with the noun they qualify.

Ex: *des camisoles pourpres*

5 Agreement of the adjective

5.1 The adjective agrees

(i) The adjective normally agrees in gender and number with the noun or pronoun it qualifies.

Ex: *le secteur public*
de bonnes notes
Les temps sont durs.
Elle semble inquiète.

It is a common mistake to 'forget' the agreement of the adjective if the latter is not adjacent to the noun!

Ex: *Non content**s** d'exiger un supplément d'âme et un service amélioré,*
***les consommateurs** réclament aussi des prix bas.*

Adapted from *Le Monde*, 19 December 1996

(ii) In the case of 1st and 2nd person personal pronouns, it is important to indicate the gender in writing (and also the number in the case of *vous*).

Ex: *Je suis très fâché(e).*
Nous sommes satisfait(e)s.
Tu es breton(ne)?
Vous êtes prêt/prête/prêts/prêtes?

5.2 The adjective does not agree

There is no agreement i.e. the adjective stays in the 'masculine singular' in the following cases:

(i) After *ce + être*, whatever *ce* stands for.

Ex: *Je suis allée à **une exposition**. **Ce** n'était pas très **intéressant**.*
I went to an exhibition. It was not very interesting.

(ii) When the adjective is used adverbially (it qualifies a verb) in common expressions, such as:

*coûter/valoir **cher***
*parler **fort/haut/bas***
*voir **clair***
*chanter **juste/faux***
*travailler **dur***
*sentir **bon/mauvais/fort***

See also chapter 29 Adverbs, section 4.

NB: *fort* **before** an adjective means *très* (most, very).

Ex: *Tout cela est fort gênant.*
Elle est fort jolie.

See also section 7(iv) below.

(iii) After the pronouns *quelqu'un, personne, quelque chose, rien + de*:

Compare:

*J'ai rencontré **quelqu'un** d'intéressant.*
*Je n'ai rencontré **personne** d'intéressant.*
and:
*J'ai rencontré **une personne** intéressante.*

See also chapter 36. Indefinite Words, sections 2.1(ii) and 3.3.3.

(iv)   Adjectives of colour which are themselves modified by another adjective (or a noun used as an adjective) do not agree and neither do the modifying adjectives. Compare:

>   *une robe verte; une robe claire*
>   and:
>   *une robe vert clair; une robe vert pomme*
>
>   *des rideaux bleus; des rideaux foncés*
>   and:
>   *des rideaux bleu foncé; des rideaux bleu marine*

(v)   Some adjectives based on participles can act as other parts of speech (e.g. prepositions or adverbs) and thus may be invariable. The most commonly found are: *attendu, vu, y compris, étant donné, passé, excepté, ci-joint, mis à part* (see also chapter 1 Parts of Speech, section 11.1.2). Compare:

>   *Veuillez trouver **ci-joint** toutes les lettres.*
>   adverb
>   Please find enclosed all the letters.
>   and:
>   *Vous trouverez dans la lettre **ci-jointe** tous les renseignements que vous recherchez.*   adjective
>   You will find in the enclosed letter all the information you are looking for.
>
>   *Tout est prêt, **excepté** les décorations florales.*
>   preposition
>   Everything is ready, except for the floral decorations.
>   and:
>   *Tout est prêt, les décorations florales **exceptées**.*
>   adjective
>   Everything is ready, the floral decorations excepted.

5.3   Agreement problems

5.3.1   on

The personal pronoun ***on*** is normally masculine singular. However, it is also used as the equivalent of other personal pronouns (especially *nous, vous* and *ils/elles*) and, in informal French, the adjective (or past participle) agrees with what *on* stands for, even though the verb remains 3rd person singular.

>   Ex: *Catherine et Anne-Marie: '**On** a été surprises de voir ça!'*

This should be avoided in formal French.

5.3.2   More than one noun or pronoun

(i)   If the nouns or pronouns are masculine, the adjective is masculine plural.

>   Ex: *Votre chat et le mien semblent **contents**.*
>   *Ces abricots et ces melons ne sont pas **mûrs**.*

(ii)   If the nouns or pronouns are feminine, the adjective is feminine plural.

>   Ex: *Valérie et Catherine sont **heureuses**.*
>   *Vous avez laissé la porte et la fenêtre **ouvertes**.*

(iii)   If the nouns or pronouns are of different genders:

– The adjective is masculine plural (the masculine 'takes over' even if there are more feminine than masculine nouns or pronouns).

    Ex: *Paul et Marie sont **ravis** de vous rencontrer.*

    *Les carottes, les pommes de terre et les oignons ne sont pas **chers**.*

– Placing a masculine adjective immediately after a feminine noun should be avoided, particularly when the pronunciation of the feminine is different from that of the masculine. For instance:

    des chaussures et des gants blancs

        is preferable to:

    des gants et des chaussures blancs

– However, '*des chaussures et des gants blancs*' is ambiguous as it can mean 'white shoes and gloves' as well as 'shoes and white gloves'. In most cases, the context should be enough to clarify which meaning is intended. Otherwise the adjective should be repeated:

    des chaussures blanches et des gants blancs

– Similar considerations apply if the adjective refers to two nouns linked by ***ou***. Compare:

    Donnez-moi une pêche ou un abricot bien mûrs.

    Give me a very ripe peach or apricot.

        and:

    Donnez-moi une pêche ou un abricot bien mûr.

    Give me a peach or a very ripe apricot.

(iv)   When the two nouns are linked by: *ainsi que, aussi bien que, autant que, comme, de même que* or *plus que*:

– If used, as is generally the case, to make a later addition, the adjective and verb are singular.

    Ex: *Paul a été invité ainsi que Marie.*

– If the two constituents are distinct, the adjective and verb are plural.

    Ex: *Paul ainsi que Marie ont été invités.*

– If a constituent is introduced in an apposition, the adjective and verb are singular.

    Ex: *Marie, ainsi que Catherine, est très jolie.*

(v)   Singular adjectives with plural noun

Two or more adjectives, each in the singular, can modify the same plural noun when each refers to only one instance of the noun.

    Ex: *les langues anglaise et espagnole*

        les quinzième et seizième siècles

        les gouvernements belge et allemand

        les religions chrétienne, musulmane et juive

        les codes civil et pénal

5.3.3   demi, semi, mi, nu

(i)   When *demi* or *nu* precede the noun (the adjective and the noun are hyphenated), there is no agreement:

> Ex: *une demi-page; une demi-douzaine*
> > but:
> *une page et demie; une douzaine et demie*
>
> *être nu-tête, nu-pieds*
> > but:
> *la tête nue, les pieds nus*

(ii)   *semi* and *mi* can only precede the noun (or adjective), hence never agree with it:

> Ex: *des pierres semi-précieuses, les semi-voyelles*

Note the following expressions:
à la mi-août, à mi-hauteur, à mi-distance, un travail à mi-temps, mi-figue mi-raisin
See also chapter 37 Numbers, section 2.4.

5.3.4   *Compound adjectives*

(i)   When two adjectives are hyphenated and used as one compound adjective, both halves agree with the noun qualified.

> Ex: *des oranges aigres-douces*
> bitter-sweet oranges

(ii)   If the first half of the compound is adverbial, only the second half agrees.

> Ex: *des personnes haut-placées*
> highly placed people

See also the plural of compound nouns in chapter 27 Nouns, section 3.2.

NB(1): *tout-puissant* (almighty) agrees as follows:

	masculine:	feminine:
singular:	*tout-puissant*	*toute-puissante*
plural:	*tout-puissants*	*toutes-puissantes*

NB(2): *soi-disant* (so-called) is invariable.

> Ex: *des soi-disant experts*
> so-called experts

5.3.5   *Agreement of the adjective with a collective noun or its complement*

The agreement is made according to the meaning.

> Ex: *un groupe de manifestants vociférant* or *vociférants*
> (either the group is '*vociférant*' or the demonstrators are)
> > but:
> *un groupe de manifestants important*
> (the group is likely to be '*important*', rather than the demonstrators)

Putting the adjective first would remove the ambiguity:
> *un important groupe de manifestants*

5.3.6   *The adjective and* avoir l'air

(i)   The adjective normally agrees with the subject if that subject is an inanimate.

> Ex: *Cette clé a l'air bien rouillée!*
> This key looks a bit rusty!

(ii)   The adjective agrees with either the subject or *air* if that subject is an animate.

> Ex: *Catherine a l'air fatiguée.*
> (= *Elle a l'air d'être fatiguée.*)
> Catherine looks tired.
>
> *Catherine a l'air ennuyé.*
> (= *Elle a un air ennuyé.*)
> Catherine looks worried.

6   Expression of degree

Degree can be expressed with or without comparison. Degree with comparison is treated in chapter 30 Comparatives. Degree without comparison can be expressed as follows:

– weak, with:
adverbs preceding the adjective, such as *faiblement, peu, médiocrement*, or prefixes such as *hypo-, sous-, infra-*:

> Ex: *une rue faiblement éclairée; un chat sous-alimenté*

– medium, with:
adverbs such as *assez, moyennement*:

> Ex: *un élève assez intelligent*

– high, with:
  – adverbs such as *vachement* (familiar register), *très, extrêmement, formidablement*:
> Ex: *un vin formidablement bon*
  – intonation:
> Ex: *Elle est bonne, celle-là!*
  – exclamations:
> Ex: *Suis-je bête!*
> *Ce qu'il est doué!*

(See also chapter 39 Exclamative Structures, section 5.)
  – prefixes such as *hyper-, super-, sur-*:
> Ex: *C'est un élève surdoué.*
  – repetition of the adjective:
> Ex: *Le monde est fou fou fou . . .*
  – some lexicalized complements:
> Ex: *pauvre comme Job*
> *bête à décrocher la lune*

(See also section 7(iv).)

7 Remarks on vocabulary

(i) It is a common mistake to confuse adjectives which are similar (but not identical!).

Compare: *étrange* and *étranger*

> Ex: *Le français est une langue **étrangère**.*
> French is a foreign language.
> and:
> *Le français est une langue **étrange**.*
> French is a strange language.

(ii) Particular care should be exercised with English adjectives that translate into different words in French according to a nuance of meaning.

– *mauvais* (bad) is the opposite of *bon* (good).

> Ex: *Ce devoir est bon/mauvais.*
> This paper is good/bad.

– *mauvais* (wrong) is the opposite of *bon* (right/correct).

> Ex: *C'est la bonne/mauvaise réponse.*
> It's the correct/wrong answer.

> *J'ai pris le bon/mauvais chemin.*
> I took the right/wrong path.

NB: It is a common mistake to confuse *mauvais* (= incorrect, not right) and *faux* (= contrary to the truth, to reality), both translated as 'wrong' in English.

– *nouveau* and *neuf*, both translated as 'new' in English: *nouveau* means (a) 'recent' and (b) 'additional', while *neuf* means 'which has not been used' or 'which has not been used for long'.

> Ex: *Ce sont des chaussures **neuves**.*
> These are new shoes.
> (i.e. nobody has worn them yet)

> *Tu as acheté de **nouvelles** chaussures?*
> Have you bought new shoes?
> (i.e. I have not seen these yet)

> *C'est une maison **neuve**.*
> It's a new house.
> (i.e. it has just been built)

> *On a construit une **nouvelle** maison.*
> Another house has been built.

Hence it is possible to say:

> *J'ai acheté une **nouvelle** voiture d'occasion.*
> I bought another second-hand car.

433

(iii)   Note the following *faux-amis*:

– terrible
terrible has two meanings:
  – frightening, terrifying
      Ex: *Hier, il y a eu une tempête terrible.*
         J'ai fait un cauchemar terrible.

  – extraordinary, great (familiar register)
      Ex: *Ton pantalon, il est terrible!*
         Ce type-là, il est terrible!

– formidable
The French adjective *formidable* seldom means 'formidable'. Most of the time it is
equivalent to *sensationnel* or *super*.
      Ex: *C'est un type formidable.*
         He's a great guy.

         J'ai passé des vacances formidables.
         I had a super holiday.

(iv)   Intensifiers

– très and **extrêmement** are intensifiers: they should not be used with adjectives
which already have a superlative meaning, e.g. *merveilleux, extraordinaire, magnifique,
formidable, délicieux, atroce, terrible.* Use *tout à fait* or *absolument* if you really want to
intensify further, or use a superlative construction.
      Ex: *Nous avons vu des sites **merveilleux**.*
         We saw some wonderful sights.

         *Nous avons vu les sites **les plus merveilleux**.*
         We saw the most wonderful sights.

         *Nous avons vu des sites **tout à fait/absolument merveilleux**.*
         We saw some absolutely marvellous sights.

– bien:
bien is also an intensifier but weaker and, together with **fort**, is only to be used in
an 'affective' way.
      Ex: *Voici un **bien** méchant/un **fort** méchant petit garçon.*
         Here comes a very naughty boy.
            but:
         *Parfois, il devenait **extrêmement** violent et menaçait sa famille.*
         Sometimes he would become most violent and threaten his family.

         *Ce cognac est très bon/**fort** bon.*
         This cognac is very good indeed.
            but:
         *L'œuvre de Karl Marx explique **très** clairement les mécanismes économiques
         de ce type de société.*
         The works of Karl Marx explain very clearly the economic
         mechanisms of this type of society.

(v) Negative adjectives

Adjectives can be made negative with prefixes such as *in-*, *im-*, *ir-*.

Ex: *intelligent* → *inintelligent*
mangeable → *immangeable*
buvable → *imbuvable*
prévoyant → *imprévoyant*
réversible → *irréversible*

Not all adjectives can be made negative in this way. The adverb *peu* can also be used.

Ex: *enviable* → *peu enviable*
pratique → *peu pratique*

See chapter 30 Comparatives, section 5 for 'irregular' adjectives such as *bon* → *mauvais*.

29 Adverbs

1 Introduction

Like nouns, verbs and adjectives, adverbs constitute an **open** class of words. But like conjunctions and prepositions, they are **invariable** (e.g. *Nous sommes sortis ensemble*) but see 4.3 for exceptions.

Adverbs and adverbial expressions (made up of several words) add to the meaning of the word they modify. An adverb or adverbial expression can modify a verb, an adjective, another adverb, a whole clause or a whole sentence.

Adverbs of comparison and degree for adjectives and adverbs are treated in chapter 30 Comparatives.

Negative adverbs are treated in chapter 38 Negative Structures.

Interrogative and exclamative adverbs are treated in chapter 39 Interrogative and Exclamative Structures.

2 Categories

Adverbs/adverb phrases are traditionally classified according to their meanings.

– adverbs of manner:
>   Ex: *bien, mal, ainsi, ensemble, peu à peu, mot à mot, tout à fait*, etc. and all the adverbs in *-ment*

– adverbs of time:
>   Ex: *aujourd'hui, hier, tôt, longtemps, actuellement, maintenant; alors, auparavant, autrefois, avant, précédemment; après, bientôt, demain, ensuite, puis, désormais, enfin; jamais, parfois, quelquefois, souvent, toujours*, etc.

– adverbs of place:
>   Ex: *où, dehors, ici, là, ailleurs, partout, loin, près, proche, [là-]dedans, [là-]dessus, [là-]dessous, devant, derrière, autour*, etc.

Note that *y* and *en* can both be adverbs of place, sometimes even called adverbial pronouns (*pronoms adverbiaux*) but see also chapter 31 Personal Pronouns, sections 2.2.2.6 and 2.2.2.7.

– adverbs of quantity and/or intensity:
>   Ex: *beaucoup, trop, aussi, si, assez, tout, très, autant, tant, plutôt, davantage, combien, plus, moins, peu*, etc.

– adverbs of affirmation, doubt or opinion:

> Ex: *oui, si, naturellement, probablement, peut-être, apparemment, assurément, certainement, certes, sûrement, volontiers, vraiment, vraisemblablement, au moins, du moins, aussi, tout au plus, sans doute, à peine,* etc.

3 Formation

Many adverbs indicate manner and end in *-ment,* but there are numerous exceptions.

3.1 Adverbs of manner in *-ment*

They are normally formed by adding the suffix *-ment*:

(i) to adjectives ending in *-e* (see chapter 28 Qualifying Adjectives, section 3).

> Ex: *simple* → *simplement*
> *sage* → *sagement*
> *utile* → *utilement*

(ii) to the feminine form of adjectives not ending in *-e.*

> Ex: *immédiat, immédiate* → *immédiatement*
> *entier, entière* → *entièrement*
> *discret, discrète* → *discrètement*
> *doux, douce* → *doucement*
> *faux, fausse* → *faussement*
> *soigneux, soigneuse* → *soigneusement*
> *sec, sèche* → *sèchement*
> *public, publique* → *publiquement*
> *naïf, naïve* → *naïvement*

(iii) to the masculine form of adjectives ending in *-ai, -é, -i* or *-u.*

> Ex: *vrai* → *vraiment*
> *résolu* → *résolument*
> *absolu* → *absolument*
> *éperdu* → *éperdument*
> *poli* → *poliment*
> *aisé* → *aisément*
> *hardi* → *hardiment*

NB(1): Some of those adjectives add a circumflex accent on the final vowel.

> Ex: *continu* → *continûment*
> *assidu* → *assidûment*
> *cru* → *crûment*

NB(2): *gai* has two adverbial forms:

> *gai* → *gaîment* or *gaiement*

(iv) The *-e* of the feminine changes into '*é*'.

> Ex: *profond, profonde* → *profondément*
> *précis, précise* → *précisément*
> *commun, commune* → *communément*
> *obscur, obscure* → *obscurément*

(v) For some adjectives whose masculine and feminine forms end in *-e*, the '*e*' changes into '*é*'.

> Ex: *aveugle* → *aveuglément*
> *énorme* → *énormément*
> *immense* → *immensément*
> *intense* → *intensément*

(vi) Adjectives ending in *-ant* turn into adverbs in *-amment* and those in *-ent* into *-emment* (both pronounced [amã]).

> Ex: *savant* → *savamment*
> *constant* → *constamment*
> *brillant* → *brillamment*
> *élégant* → *élégamment*
>
> *prudent* → *prudemment*
> *fréquent* → *fréquemment*
> *violent* → *violemment*
> *récent* → *récemment*
> *patient* → *patiemment*

> Exceptions: *lent, lente* → *lentement*
> *présent, présente* → *présentement*
> *véhément, véhémente* → *véhémentement*

(vii) Note the following 'irregular' adverbs:

> Ex: *gentil* → *gentiment*
> *bref* → *brièvement*
> *impuni* → *impunément*
> *traître* → *traîtreusement*
> *prodigue* → *prodigalement*

(viii) Some adverbs in *-ment* have no corresponding adjectives.

> Ex: − *journellement* (every day/daily)
> nouns: *journée, journal*; the nearest adjective is *journalier*
>
> − *notamment* (in particular/particularly, lit. 'worthy of note')
> verb: *noter*
>
> − *précipitamment*
> verb: *précipiter*; nearest adjective: *précipité*
>
> − *sciemment* (knowingly)
> verb: *savoir*

        – *grièvement* (gravely, seriously)
                nearest adjective: *grave*

Note that *grièvement* only survives today in expressions such as *grièvement blessé* or *grièvement atteint* ('seriously wounded').

(ix)   Some adverbs are exceptionally derived directly from nouns.
        Ex: *nuit* → *nuitamment*
            diable → *diablement*

(x)   The meaning of an adverb in *-ment* often corresponds to only one of the various meanings of the adjective. For instance, *vertement* corresponds only to *vert* meaning 'sharp' as in *de vertes réprimandes* ('sharp rebukes'). Sometimes, the meaning of the adverb in *-ment* is totally different from that of the adjective. For instance, the adjective *incessant* means 'continual', 'which does not stop', whereas the adverb *incessamment* means 'very soon'. When in doubt, a dictionary should be consulted.

3.2 Other adverbs

(i)   Other adverbs are linked to adjectives but do not end in *-ment*.
        Ex: *bon* → *bien*
            meilleur → *mieux*
            mauvais → *mal*
            petit → *peu*
(See also chapter 30 Comparatives, section 5.)

(ii)   Not all adverbs are based on adjectives (see also above 3.1(viii)).

Ex:			
maintenant	now	*ainsi*	thus
tard	late	*loin*	far away
debout	standing	*exprès*	on purpose, deliberately
d'abord	first	*ensuite*	then
ensemble	together	*plutôt*	rather

(iii)   Adverbial expressions made up of several words (*locutions adverbiales*):
        Ex: *à peu près, à propos, à présent, à côté, à moitié, à la longue, à la dérobée, à la bonne franquette, au fur et à mesure, au pied levé, de temps à autre, de nouveau, en général, en même temps, jusqu'ici, par hasard, sans doute, bien sûr, mot à mot, peu à peu, petit à petit, quelque part, sur-le-champ, tout à fait, tout de suite*, etc.

(iv)   Some adverbial expressions can exceptionally 'agree' in gender and number.
        Ex: *Il l'a fait **à mon insu**, **à ton insu***, etc.
        He did it without **my** knowledge, without **your** knowledge, etc.

3.3 Adverbial expressions of manner

(i)   There are some adjectives from which no adverb in *-ment* can be formed. These include: *charmant, concis, clairvoyant, content, crédule, fâché*. The adverbial sense can be conveyed by adding an appropriate expression of manner before the adjective or an appropriate preposition before the corresponding noun.

> Ex: *d'une façon/d'une manière charmante*
> *d'un air fâché, d'un air crédule*
> *avec concision, avec clairvoyance*

NB: *sans pitié* (ruthlessly).

(ii) Even if an adverb in *-ment* does exist, expressions of the type described in (i) can also be used.

> Ex: *Ils se sont défendus courageusement* → *avec courage*
> *Vous avez agi prudemment* → *avec prudence*
> *J'ai essayé vainement* → *en vain*
> *Il m'aime follement* → *à la folie*
> *Vous avez répondu légèrement* → *à la légère*
> *On évite le danger instinctivement* → *d'instinct*
> *Ajoutez la crème graduellement* → *peu à peu*
> *Le vent s'est levé subitement* → *tout à coup*

Also: *d'un ton méchant, d'une façon bizarre, avec joie, avec résolution*, etc.

Note that there can be a slight difference of meaning if an adverb in *-ment* does exist.

> Ex: *Il est entré **discrètement**.*
> He came in **quietly**.
> > but:
> *Je lui ai demandé d'agir **avec discrétion**.*
> I asked him to act **discreetly**.

(iii) These alternative constructions can only be used to modify a **verb** or a **whole clause**.

> Ex: *Il s'exprime **aisément**.*
> or: *Il s'exprime **avec aisance**.*
> or: *Il s'exprime **d'une manière aisée**.*

Otherwise, the adverb in *-ment* must be used.

> Ex: *Une voiture de collection peut être **aisément** vendue.*

(iv) Overuse of adverbs in *-ment* can make a sentence very laboured, particularly if an adverb in *-ment* modifies another adverb in *-ment*. In these cases, it is better to try and replace one of the adverbs by 'preposition + noun' as described above.

> Ex: *Il a réagi **extrêmement rapidement**.*
> → *Il a réagi **avec une extrême rapidité**.*

4 Adjectives used adverbially

Some adjectives – generally short ones – are used adverbially by improper derivation in set expressions. As adverbs, they are invariable (see also chapter 28 Qualifying Adjectives, section 5.2(v)).

4.1 Adjectives used adverbially in fixed verbal expressions (*locutions verbales*)

Ex: *parler fort/haut* — to speak loudly
parler bas — to speak in a low voice
chanter faux — to sing out of tune
chanter juste — to sing in tune
deviner juste — to guess accurately
coûter/valoir/vendre/acheter cher — to cost/sell/buy dear
sentir bon — to smell nice/good
sentir mauvais — to smell bad
sentir fort — to have a strong smell
frapper fort — to hit hard
voir clair/juste — to see clearly
travailler dur/ferme — to work hard
gagner gros — to win a lot
perdre gros — to lose heavily
peser lourd — to be heavy/weigh a lot
aller/marcher droit devant — to go/walk straight ahead
aller/marcher/se tenir droit — to go/walk/stand straight
tenir bon — to hold fast, to stand firm
couper court — to cut short
tourner court — to fail
payer cher — to pay dearly for
rire jaune — to laugh on the other side of one's face

boire sec — to be a 'serious drinker'
manger froid — to eat a cold meal
s'arrêter court/net — to stop short/dead
se casser net — to snap in two
refuser net — to refuse point blank
etc.

Note that the use of adjectives and also nouns as adverbs by improper derivation is particularly common in advertising.

Ex: *Mangez léger!*
Votez utile!
Acheter qualité.

4.2 Adjectives used adverbially by themselves

(i) Some adjectives are also used adverbially by themselves, i.e. the masculine form of the adjective is also the adverb. For instance:

bref — in short
juste — exactly
fort — very, hard, loud, etc.
soudain — suddenly

441

(ii)   When an adjective can be used adverbially but also has a regular adverbial form, the two adverbs are not interchangeable in principle. Compare:

>   *Il boit **sec**.*
>   He's a heavy drinker.
>   and:
>   *Il nous a répondu **sèchement**.*
>   He answered us sharply.

>   *Vous parlez trop **fort**.*
>   You speak too loudly.
>   and:
>   *Les prix ont **fortement** baissé.*
>   Prices have gone down a lot.

>   *Pourquoi parlent-ils tout **bas**?*
>   Why are they speaking in a low voice?
>   and:
>   *Ils ont agi **bassement**.*
>   They have behaved basely.

>   *Il a refusé **net**.*
>   He refused point blank.
>   and:
>   *Il s'est expliqué **nettement**.*
>   He explained himself clearly.

4.3   *grand, bon, tout*

(i)   When used adverbially to modify an adjective, the adjectives ***grand*** and ***bon*** agree in gender and number.

>   Ex: *Vous avez encore laissé la porte grande ouverte.*
>   You've left the door wide open again.

>   *Ils sont arrivés bons derniers.*
>   They were the very last to arrive.

(ii)   For euphonic reasons, the adverb ***tout*** varies before a feminine singular or plural adjective beginning with a consonant or a disjunctive 'h'. (See also chapter 36 Indefinite Words, section 5.7.4.)

>   Ex: *Elle est restée toute seule.*
>   *Elles sont revenues toutes contentes de leurs vacances.*

5   Position of adverbs

Adverbs are placed in different positions according to the part of speech which they modify.

–   Verbs:
     –   simple tenses

Adverbs are normally placed after the verb which they modify.

> Ex: *Elle parle **lentement**.*

– compound tenses

Adverbs are placed between the auxiliary and the past participle

> Ex: *Il s'est **tout de suite** excusé.*

– Adjectives and other adverbs:

Adverbs are placed before the adjective or other adverb which they modify.

> Ex: *un chat **vraiment** intelligent*
> *Il m'a regardé **tout** bêtement.*

Adverbs which modify the whole sentence are placed wherever an apposition is allowed (see section 5.3 below).

However, despite these 'rules' governing the positioning of adverbs in French, it should be noted that the position is often affected by emphasis or sentence rhythm. This is particularly the case with adverbs which modify verbs. The only position which is excluded (unlike in English) is that between the subject and the verb, except in poetry.

> Ex: The car **slowly** came to a stop.
> *★La voiture lentement a fini par s'arrêter.*
> → *La voiture a **lentement** fini par s'arrêter.*
> or:
> → *La voiture a fini **lentement** par s'arrêter.*

The position of adverbs of affirmation or doubt, which can precede the verb and be followed by a complex inversion, is treated in chapter 2 Syntax, section 2.4.

Finally, note that a given adverb cannot always modify a verb, adjective or other adverb indifferently (see below).

5.1 Adverbs modifying adjectives or other adverbs

(i) A short adverb (usually of time, place or intensity) is placed before the adjective or other adverb which it modifies (e.g. *toujours, longtemps, encore, déjà, loin, très, trop, peu, si, assez, plutôt, autant*).

– adjectives:

> Ex: *Elle est **très belle**.*
> She is **very** beautiful.
>
> *Vous êtes **trop aimable**.*
> You're **too** kind.

– adverbs:

> Ex: *Je vais **si bien** maintenant!*
> I am feeling so well now!
>
> *C'est **plutôt loin**.*
> It is rather a long way.

(ii)   Adverbs of manner in *–ment* are almost always placed before the adjective or other adverb, particularly if they have an intensifying value.

> Ex: *Vos résultats sont **complètement faux**.*
> Your results are completely wrong.
>
> *Il est **manifestement énervé**.*
> He is obviously irritated.

5.2   Adverbs modifying verbs

An adverb that modifies a verb can have various positions, but it normally comes **after** the verb it modifies.

5.2.1   *Verbs in a simple tense*

(i)   With adverbs of manner or quantity, as well as *bien, mieux, mal* or *pire*, the adverb follows the verb.

> Ex: *Je **répondrai franchement** à votre question.*
> I shall answer your question frankly.
>
> *Il **mange trop**.*
> He eats too much.

Note that the adverb can be separated from the verb.

> Ex: ***Etudiez** ce chapitre **avec soin**.*

(ii)   With adverbs of time or place:

– The adverbs are usually placed after the verb. For emphasis, certain adverbs (e.g. *hier, demain, aujourd'hui, ici, là*) can be placed before both the subject and the verb and are followed by a comma. In this case, they modify the whole sentence (see 5.3 below).

> Ex: *Je ferai les courses **demain**.*
> ***Demain**, je ferai les courses.*

– *y* and *en* always come before the verb.

> Ex: *nous **en** venons; nous **y** allons*

(except in the imperative affirmative: *sortez-en; allez-y*)
See also chapter 31 Personal Pronouns, sections 2.2.2.6 and 2.2.2.7.

– *toujours, souvent, encore, longtemps, à nouveau* and *déjà* normally come after the verb.

> Ex: *Elle **fait souvent** ses courses au supermarché.*
> She often does her shopping at the supermarket.
>
> *Il me **reste encore** quelques cerises.*
> I've still got a few cherries left.
>
> *Ils **se parlent à nouveau**.*
> They're on speaking terms again.

Note that the notion of 'again' is often expressed by adding the prefix *re-* to the verb in French.

> Ex: *Elle ne les **reverra** jamais.*
> She will never see them again.

– *longtemps, déjà* and *souvent* can be placed before both the subject and the verb when they modify the whole clause (see above). Compare:

> *Quand elle était petite, elle adorait **déjà** les chats.*
> When she was young, she already loved cats.
> > and:
> ***Déjà**, quand elle était petite, elle adorait les chats.*
> Already, when she was young, she adored cats.

5.2.2 Past participles

(i) An adverb which modifies a past participle can come before or after that participle.

> Ex: *Ce sont des arbres **récemment plantés**.*
> > or:
> *Ce sont des arbres **plantés récemment**.*
> They are recently planted trees.

(ii) Short and common adverbs normally precede a past participle.

> Ex: *un travail **bien/mal fait***
> a job well/badly done
>
> *un vœu **déjà exaucé***
> a wish already fulfilled

5.2.3 Present participles

Adverbs are placed after the present participle, except for *y* and *en*, which are always placed before it.

> Ex: *En **relisant bien** le texte, ils trouveront la réponse.*
> By reading the text again carefully, they will find the answer.
> > but:
> *en **y** allant; en **en revenant***
> on the way there; on the way back

Note that the first *en* is part of the gerund: see chapter 16 Present Participle.

5.2.4 Verbs in a compound tense or infinitive

In compound tenses, the adverb often comes between the auxiliary and the past participle except for short and common adverbs of time or place (see (iv) below) and interrogative structures (see (i) below).

(i) Short or common adverbs (of manner or quantity) which modify a verb in a compound tense or an infinitive, are placed:
– before the infinitive
– before the past participle in a past infinitive
– between the auxiliary and the past participle in a compound tense

Ex: *Il a cru **bien faire**.*
He thought he was doing the right thing.

*Il ne faut pas se baigner après avoir **trop mangé**.*
One shouldn't swim after having eaten too much/a heavy meal.

*Vous avez **bien fait** de venir.*
You were right to come.

Note the place of the adverb in an interrogative structure with a complex inversion:

*Paul a-t-il cru **bien faire**?*
*Avez-vous **bien fait** de venir?*

(ii)   If the adverb is long (as a lot of adverbs in *-ment* are) and not so common, or if the adverb has other words depending on it, it is normally placed after the past participle.

Ex: *Ils ont fait leurs calculs **séparément** des miens.*
They did their calculations separately from mine.

*On nous a recommandé de **bien** écouter* (but note:) *et de répondre **immédiatement**.*
We were recommended to listen carefully and to answer immediately.

(iii) Adverbs of manner with an intensifying value can be placed either before or after the participle or infinitive.

Ex: *Nous ne devrions pas **complètement oublier** cette affaire.*
or:
*Nous ne devrions pas **oublier complètement** cette affaire.*
We should not forget about this matter completely.

*Ils nous ont **chaleureusement remerciés**.*
or:
*Ils nous ont **remerciés chaleureusement**.*
They thanked us warmly.

(iv)   Most short and common adverbs of **time** or **place** are placed **after** the past participle or infinitive (e.g. *tôt, tard; aujourd'hui, hier, demain; partout, devant, derrière*).

Ex: *Les enfants veulent se mettre **derrière**.*
The children want to sit at the back.

*Elle est allée **partout**.*
She's been everywhere.

NB(1): The above adverbs (except *tôt* and *tard*) can be placed at the beginning when modifying the whole sentence.

Ex: ***Hier**, j'ai acheté ce livre.*
Yesterday, I bought this book.

***Partout**, on ne voyait que des arbres déracinés.*
Wherever you looked, there were only uprooted trees.

NB(2): *tôt* and *tard* seldom appear at the beginning of a sentence, except when modified or in the idiom *tôt ou tard*.

> Ex: **Bien plus tard**, *nous avons appris la nouvelle*.
> Much later, we learnt the news.
>
> **Tôt ou tard**, *il faudra bien que vous vous décidiez*.
> Sooner or later, you'll have to make up your mind.

(v) However, *toujours*, *déjà* and *souvent* normally precede the infinitive, or the past participle in a compound tense or past infinitive.

> Ex: *Pourquoi faut-il* **toujours courir**?
> Why do we always have to run?
>
> *Je lui ai* **souvent raconté** *cette histoire*.
> I often told him this story.

(vi) There is a choice of position with *encore* and *longtemps*. However, these adverbs are usually placed **before** the infinitive or past participle.

> Ex: *Il a fallu* **encore réfléchir**.
> or:
> *Il a fallu* **réfléchir encore**.
> We had to think more.
>
> *Il a* **longtemps prétendu** *ne pas le savoir*.
> or:
> *Il a* **prétendu longtemps** *ne pas le savoir*.
> For a long time he pretended not to know about it.

(vii) *y* and *en* are **always** placed before the **auxiliary** or infinitive:

> Ex: *J'en suis revenu; il ne faut pas* **y** *aller*.

5.3 Adverbs modifying the whole sentence

(i) **Types**

There are two types of adverbs which modify the whole sentence.

– sentence adverbs (*adverbes de phrase*):

These generally appear at the beginning of a declarative sentence (but not interrogative or imperative ones). They can also appear after the verb in an apposition or at the end of the sentence (see chapter 2 Syntax, section 2.13).

> Ex: **Demain**, *Catherine va essayer de vous répondre*.
> *Catherine va essayer,* **demain**, *de vous répondre*.
> *Catherine va essayer de vous répondre* **demain**.

– sentence connectors (*adverbes de relation*):

These link the sentence in which they appear to an external piece of information (e.g. the discourse situation, including the personal circumstances of the speaker). They appear mainly at the beginning of the sentence, but may also be placed in the middle or at the end.

The most commonly used are: *franchement, sérieusement, honnêtement, notamment, simplement, justement, pourtant, cependant, enfin.*

> Ex: ***Franchement****, vous ne savez pas ce que vous dites.*
> Honestly, you don't know what you're talking about.
>
> ***Enfin****, c'est l'intention qui compte.*
> Still, it's the thought that counts.

(ii) **Sentence adverb or verb complement?**

– Adverbs or adverbial expressions which are not indispensable to convey the meaning of the verb modify the whole sentence. Unlike verb complements, therefore, they can appear in various positions within the sentence. Compare:

> *Emma est allée **à Londres**.*

'*à Londres*' is a verb complement, it cannot be omitted.

> (→ *****Emma est allée*)
>   and:
> *J'ai offert une encyclopédie à David **pour son anniversaire**.*

'*pour son anniversaire*' is a sentence complement: it can be omitted without making the sentence meaningless or badly formed.

> (→ *J'ai offert une encyclopédie à David*)

– Adverbs which modify the sentence as a whole, as opposed to just the verb, are most commonly found at the beginning of the sentence, followed by a comma, to express emphasis. Compare:

> *Les choses se passaient différemment **autrefois**.*
>   and:
> ***Autrefois****, les choses se passaient différemment!*
> (The stress is on '*autrefois*').
>
> ***Tout à coup****, il changea de direction.*
> (sounds more 'natural' than:)
> *Il changea de direction **tout à coup**.*

Note that in the absence of a comma in these two examples (or the absence of a pause in spoken French), the adverb modifies the verb only. In the second example for instance, '*tout à coup*' would mean that it was the change of direction which was sudden or brusque and not the actual decision to change direction itself. This is particularly applicable to adverbs of manner. Indeed, there is no difference between *Hier, je suis allée au cinéma* and *Je suis allée au cinéma hier* apart from that of emphasis.

(iii) **Adverbs linking the meaning of two sentences**

Adverbs which link the meaning of a sentence to the previous one, are most commonly placed at the beginning of that sentence.

> Ex: *La sonnette retentit. **Aussitôt**, il se précipita vers la porte.*
> The doorbell rang. Immediately, he rushed to the door.
>
> *De gros nuages noirs apparurent. **Soudain**, il se mit à pleuvoir.*
> Big black clouds appeared. Suddenly, it started to rain.

(iv)   **Adverbs and cleft constructions**

The adverb can be emphasized in a cleft sentence (see chapter 2 Syntax, section 2.15.4).

> Ex: *Il fallait y penser **hier**.*
> → ***C'est hier qu'**il fallait y penser.*

6 Notes on some adverbs

The following have been selected either because they have several different meanings or because they change their meanings according to their positions in the sentence, and may therefore pose a problem when translating into English.

6.1 *aussi*

(i)   **Meanings**

aussi can mean 'too', 'also', 'as well (as)' or 'in addition'. It can modify a noun, pronoun, adjective or verb. Note the place of *aussi* in the sentence in relation to its meaning.

– modifying a noun/pronoun subject:

> Ex: – *Je suis professeur de français. – Moi **aussi**.*
> – I am a teacher of French. – Me too.
>
> *Nathalie **aussi** a entendu ce qu'il a dit.*
> Nathalie heard what he said too.
>
> *Mon chat attrape des souris, et celui de la voisine **aussi**.*
> My cat catches mice and so does the neighbour's.

– modifying a noun/pronoun object:

> Ex: *Mon chat attrape des souris et **aussi** des oiseaux.*
> My cat catches mice and also birds.

– modifying an adjective:

> Ex: *Dizzy est beau et Lizzy est belle **aussi**.*
> Dizzy is beautiful and Lizzy is [beautiful] too.

– modifying a verb:

Compare:

> *Il ne suffit pas de laver les légumes. Il faut **aussi** les peler/les peler **aussi**.*
> Washing the vegetables is not enough. You must peel them too.
>   and:
> *Les légumes sont sales, **aussi** il faut les peler.*
> The vegetables are dirty so you should peel them.

Note that here, '*aussi*' can be considered as a conjunction of coordination (see also (vi) below and chapter 40 Coordination and Juxtaposition, section 2(ii)).

(ii) **Negative form**

The negative form of *aussi* is **non plus** (neither; not . . . either).

Ex: *Je n'en ai pas besoin **non plus**.*
I don't need it either.

Compare:

– *J'ai tout entendu!*	I heard everything!
– *Moi **aussi**!*	Me too!
– *Pas moi!/Moi pas!*	I didn't!
and:	
– *Je n'ai rien entendu!*	I did not hear anything!
– *Moi **non plus**!*	Neither did I!
– *Moi si!*	I did!

(iii) **Cases of ambiguity**

Consider the following examples:

1 *Je peux **aussi** faire la vaisselle.*

This statement is ambiguous as 'aussi' can be understood to bear on 'je' or 'faire la vaisselle'. Hence, either say:

*Moi **aussi**, je peux faire la vaisselle.*
I too can wash up.

or:

*La vaisselle **aussi**, je peux la faire.*
I can do the washing up as well.

2 *Cela me semble **aussi** ridicule.*

Here, 'aussi' is likely to be understood as a comparative:

This seems to me just as ridiculous.

If what is meant is 'This too seems ridiculous to me', say:

*Cela **aussi** me semble ridicule.*

The comparative meaning can be reinforced with the addition of *tout*:

*Cela me semble **tout aussi** ridicule.*

See also chapter 30 Comparatives, section 2.2.2.

(iv) ***si** and **aussi***

si ('so', 'such') can only qualify an adjective or an adverb. In a negative structure, it is equivalent to *aussi* (see also chapters 30 Comparatives, section 2.2.2(iii), and 36 Indefinite Words, section 6.3.1(ii) NB(2)).

Ex: *Nous avons passé de **si** bonnes vacances.*
We had such a wonderful holiday.

*Ne mange pas **si/aussi** vite, tu vas être malade.*
Don't eat so fast, you'll be ill.

(v) ***si**, **tant**, **tellement***

Whereas *si* is only used with an adjective or an adverb, *tant* is only used with a verb and *tellement* can be used with all three.

See also chapter 36 Indefinite Words, section 6.3.

> Ex: *Nous sommes **si/tellement** heureux!* (+ adjective)
> *Vous travaillez **si/tellement** lentement.* (+ adverb)
> *Il mange **tant/tellement**.* (+ verb)

(vi) ***aussi* at the beginning of a clause**

aussi is placed at the beginning of a clause (followed by a complex inversion in formal French or no inversion in informal French) **only** when it means *en conséquence, c'est pourquoi* (see chapter 40 Coordination and Juxtaposition, section 2(ii)).

> Ex: *Il faisait beau, **aussi** mes amis ont-ils décidé d'aller se promener.*
> The weather was nice, so my friends decided to go for a walk.

6.2 *vite*

vite is an adverb, not an adjective. It is the equivalent of *rapidement* and its corresponding adjective is *rapide*.

> Ex: *Cette voiture est très **rapide**.*
> This car is very fast.
>> but:
> *Cette voiture va très **vite**.*
> This car goes very fast.
>
> *Faites **vite** ce travail.*
>> or:
> *Faites ce travail **rapidement**.*
> Please do this job quickly.

NB: Do not be tempted to imitate some journalists who use *vite* as an adjective for stronger effect.

> Ex: *★la femme la plus vite du monde*
> (meaning the fastest woman racer)

Some also say *★la femme la plus haute du monde* meaning the one who jumps highest . . .

6.3 *beaucoup*

Note the following uses of *beaucoup* vs *bien*.

(i) ***beaucoup*** + adjective is only used with the **comparative** adjective of inferiority or superiority (but not if there is no comparison, or with *meilleur* or *davantage*); ***bien*** can be used in all cases.

> Ex: *Il est **beaucoup/bien plus** calme aujourd'hui.*
> He is much calmer today.
>
> *Il est **beaucoup/bien mieux** qu'avant.*
> He is much better than before.
>> but:
> *★Ce poulet est beaucoup meilleur [que l'autre].*
> → *Ce poulet est **bien meilleur** . . .*
> This chicken is a lot better [than the other one].

451

> ★*Il est beaucoup calme aujourd'hui!*
> → *Il est **bien calme** aujourd'hui!*
> He is very (surprisingly) calm today!

Note that *très* can also be used with adjectives (*il est **très** calme*), though not with comparatives (★*il est très moins calme qu'hier*).

(ii) *bien pire, bien inférieur* and *bien supérieur* are more usual than *beaucoup pire/inférieur/supérieur*, but emphasis can be expressed with ***de beaucoup***.

> Ex: *C'est **de beaucoup** supérieur.* It's superior by far.
> is stronger than:
> *C'est **bien** supérieur.* It's far superior.

(iii) ***beaucoup*** and ***beaucoup de*** can only be qualified by the negative adverb ***pas***. Hence 'very much'/'very many' must never be rendered as ★*très beaucoup*! Emphasis should be expressed in another way.

> Ex: I love cherries **very much**.
> *J'adore les cerises.*
>
> They brought us **very many** presents.
> *Ils nous ont apporté **une grande quantité de** cadeaux.*

(iv) 'so' and 'so many'/'so much'

> – If 'many'/'much' followed by a noun is *beaucoup de*, 'so many'/'so much' is ***tant de***.
> Ex: There are **so many** obstacles.
> *Il y a **tant d'**obstacles.*
> (and not ★*si beaucoup*!)
>
> **So much** joy!
> ***Tant de** joie!*

> – 'so' is *si* only before an adjective or adverb.
> Ex: Dizzy, you're **so beautiful**.
> *Dizzy, tu es **si beau**.*
>
> Paul drives **so slowly**!
> *Paul conduit **si lentement**!*

6.4   *peu [de]* and *un peu [de]*

*peu **de*** and *un peu **de*** modify **nouns**.

(i) *peu [de]* means 'little', 'few', 'not very', 'not many'.

> Ex: ***Peu de** gens sont venus.*
> Few people came.
>
> *Il mange très **peu**.*
> He eats very little.
>
> *Ces gens sont **peu** aimables.*
> These people are not very pleasant.

NB: He does **very little**.
> *Il ne fait **pas grand-chose**.*

(ii) *un peu [de]* means 'a little'.

> Ex: *Il a **un peu** plus de trente ans.*
> He's a little over thirty.
>
> *Pourrais-je avoir encore **un peu de** vin s'il vous plaît?*
> May I have a little more wine please?
>
> *Je suis **un peu** en retard.*
> I am a little late.

Hence compare:

> *Il sait **un peu** d'anglais.*
> He knows a little bit of English.
> and:
> *Il sait (très) **peu** d'anglais.*
> He knows (very) little English.

6.5 *arrière/avant, derrière/devant, dessous/dessus*

(i) *arrière* and *avant* may also be used as invariable adjectives.

> Ex: *les roues **avant/arrière** de la voiture*
> the front/back wheels of the car

(ii) *derrière, devant, dessous* and *dessus* may also be used as invariable adjectives preceded by *de*.

> Ex: *les pattes **de devant/de derrière** d'un chien*
> the front/hind legs of a dog
>
> *le salon **de devant***
> the front drawing-room
>
> *les vêtements **de dessous*** (or: *les sous-vêtements*)
> underwear

(iii) All can be used as nouns (masculine).

> Ex: *[à] **l'arrière** de la voiture*   [at] the back of the car
> *[à] **l'avant** de la voiture*   [at] the front of the car
> ***le devant** de la maison*   the front of the house

(iv) *arrière* and *avant* can be used preceded by *en* to mean 'backwards' and 'forwards'.

> Ex: *se pencher **en arrière***   to lean backwards
> *sauter **en avant***   to leap forwards

6.6 *assez* and *suffisamment*

assez has two meanings:

(i) 'enough' or 'sufficiently' when modifying a verb, adjective, adverb or noun (use *assez de* to modify a noun).

> Ex: *Avez-vous **assez** mangé?*
> Have you had enough to eat?

*La soupe est **assez chaude** maintenant: tu veux bien éteindre le gaz?*
The soup is warm enough now. Will you kindly switch off
the gas?

*Je vais **assez lentement** pour vous?*
Am I going slowly enough for you?

*Je n'ai pas **assez de place**.*
I haven't got enough room.

Therefore, *assez* is generally equivalent to *suffisamment* – albeit more frequently
used. However, *assez* means 'enough', in the sense that 'no more is needed';
whereas *suffisamment* means 'enough', in the sense that 'the minimum required has
been reached'. Hence:

Ex: There should be a balance between too much freedom and **enough**
freedom.
(The stress is on the minimum required, not on whether more
might be acceptable.)
*Il faut un équilibre entre trop de liberté et **suffisamment** de liberté.*

(ii) 'fairly', 'somewhat', 'rather', when qualifying an adjective or an adverb. Therefore
it is close to *plutôt*.

Ex: – *Comment allez-vous? – **Assez bien**, merci.*
– How are you? – Not too bad, thank you.

*Son travail est **assez bon**.*
His/her work is fairly good.

*Je vais **assez lentement** pour ne pas effrayer ma grand-mère.*
I am going slowly enough so as not to frighten my grandmother.

The context should determine which meaning is intended.

6.7 *bien*

See also chapter 30 Comparatives, sections 3.2 and 5.

(i) *bien* can have an adjectival meaning (but remains invariable).

Ex: *Ta chambre est **bien**.*
Your room is nice.

*Ce sont des gens **bien**.*
They are nice people.

(ii) As an adverb, *bien* means the following:

– 'well':

Ex: *Elle cuisine **bien**.*
She's a good cook. (lit.: she cooks well)

*Il écrit **bien**.*
He writes well.

– 'very':

Ex: *C'est **bien** compliqué!*
It's very complicated!

(See also 6.3 above.)

– 'indeed', 'really':

Ex: *C'est **bien** ce que je lui ai dit.*
Indeed, that is what I told him.

*Est-ce **bien** vrai?*
Is it really true?

6.8 *combien, comme, comment*

These adverbs may present difficulties as they can all translate **how** (see also chapter 39 Interrogative and Exclamative Structures, sections 3.5(iii) and (v), and section 5).

(i) ***combien*** means **how** in the sense of 'to what extent':

Ex: *Je sais **combien** il est difficile d'étudier et de travailler en même temps.*
I know **how** difficult it is to study and work at the same time.

See also chapter 41 Reported Speech, section 3.5.

(ii) ***comme*** means:

– **like** in the sense of 'in the same way as'.
Ex: *Faites la queue **comme** tout le monde!*
Join the queue **like** everybody else!

*Il mange **comme** quatre.*
He eats **like** a horse.

– **as . . . as** to express similes.
Ex: *Elle est myope **comme** une taupe.*
She's as blind as a bat.

See also chapter 30 Comparatives, section 2.2.2(iv).

– **as** (= *en tant que*).
Ex: *Patrick va travailler **comme** barman pendant les grandes vacances.*
or:
*Patrick va travailler **en tant que** barman pendant les grandes vacances.*
Patrick is going to work **as a** barman during the summer holidays.

(Note that here, there is **no article** after *comme* or *en tant que*.)

– **how** in the sense of 'to what extent' (see *combien* above).
Ex: *Je sais **comme** il est difficile de travailler quand on est malade.*
I know **how** difficult it is to work when you're ill.

– *comme si* is 'as if', 'as though'.
Ex: *Il s'est enfui **comme s'**il avait vu le diable.*
He ran away **as if** he'd seen the devil.

See also chapter 13 Conditional, section 3.2.1(iv).

*Il s'est tu, **comme** assommé par ce qu'il venait d'entendre.*
He went quiet, **as though** crushed by what he had just heard.

– **how**, in exclamations.
> Ex: ***Comme** vous êtes élégante ce soir!*
> **How** elegant you are tonight!

See chapter 39 Exclamative Structures, section 5.

See also chapter 36 Indefinite Words, section 6.3.1.

(iii) ***comment*** means:

– **how**, in the sense of 'in what way'.
> Ex: ***Comment** allez-vous vous y prendre?*
> **How** are you going to go about it?

> *Je sais **comment** je vais m'y prendre.*
> I know **how** I'm going to go about it.

– the interjection **what!**
> Ex: ***Comment?** Vous n'avez pas encore terminé!*
> **What!** You have not finished yet!

Note that *quoi* is also used in this sense and is slightly 'stronger'.

6.9 *encore*

(i) 'still', to express continuation up to the present time
> Ex: *Travaillez-vous **encore** pour Paul Dupont?*
> Are you **still** working for Paul Dupont?

NB: *encore* is similar to *toujours* here (see 6.10(ii) below).

(ii) 'still', to express reinforcement
> Ex: *Il fait **encore** plus mauvais qu'hier!*
> The weather is **even** worse than yesterday!

NB: *encore* is **not** interchangeable with *toujours* here.
See also chapter 30 Comparatives, section 3.6.

(iii) 'again', to express repetition
> Ex: *Répétez **encore** une fois s'il vous plaît.*
> Please repeat once more/once **again**.

> *Il a **encore** manqué son train.*
> He's missed his train **again**.

(iv) 'more', to express further quantity or addition (see also chapter 30 Comparatives, section 2.3.3(iii))
> Ex: *Prendrez-vous **encore** un peu de potage?*
> Will you have a little **more** soup?

> *J'ai **encore** une déclaration à faire.*
> I have one **more** declaration to make.

(v) Negative form

– With *ne . . . pas*: *pas encore* means 'not . . . yet', 'still not'.
Ex: *Je **ne** pense **pas encore** aux vacances.*
I'm not thinking about holidays yet.

*Le bébé **ne** dort **pas encore**.*
The baby has not fallen asleep yet.

*Je **n'ai pas encore** eu le temps de regarder cet article.*
I haven't had time to look at that article yet.

– The absolute negative form of ***encore*** is ***ne . . . plus*** ('not . . . any more').
Ex: *Le bébé **ne** dort **plus**.*
The baby is not sleeping any more.

*Nous **n'avons plus** d'examens à corriger.*
We don't have any more exam papers to mark.

See also chapter 38 Negative Structures, section 2.2.1(iv).

6.10   *toujours*

(i) Repetition ('always')
Ex: *Ils vont **toujours** à la messe le dimanche.*
They always go to mass on Sunday.

*Nous déjeunons **toujours** à une heure.*
We always have lunch at one o'clock.

(ii) Continuation ('still'): equivalent to *encore* (see above)
Ex: *Quand j'ai regardé par la fenêtre, il pleuvait **toujours**.*
When I looked out of the window, it was still raining.

(iii) Negative form

– In a sentence with the negative adverb ***ne . . . pas***, the meaning of *toujours* depends on its position.
Ex: *Il ne travaille **pas toujours**.*
(= *Il y a des moments où il ne travaille pas.*)
He is not always working.

*Il ne travaille **toujours pas**.*
(= *Il ne travaille pas encore, i.e. il continue à ne pas travailler.*)
He is still not working.

Note that *encore* can also be used here instead of *toujours*, though less usual.

– The absolute negative of ***toujours*** is ***jamais*** ('never') or ***plus*** (pronounced [ply]).
Ex: *Il **ne** travaille **jamais**.*
He never works.

*Il **ne** travaille **plus**.*
He is no longer working.

6.11 *alors, puis, ensuite, donc*

They are all translated by 'then' or 'so' in English, but they each mean different things (apart from **puis** and **ensuite**) and therefore are not interchangeable.

6.11.1 *alors*

(i) *alors* can mean *à ce moment-là, à cette époque-là* ('at that time', 'then').

> Ex: *La France était **alors** en guerre contre l'Allemagne.*
> France was at war with Germany **then**.

(ii) *alors* can mean *dans ce cas, en conséquence* ('so', 'then', 'therefore') in a conclusion. It is generally placed at the beginning of a sentence.

> Ex: *Il s'est excusé. **Alors**, n'en parlons plus.*
> He apologized. **So** let's leave it.

> *Vous n'avez rien mangé de toute la journée? **Alors**, il n'est pas étonnant que vous ayez faim!*
> You haven't eaten all day? **Well then**, it is not surprising that you are hungry!

6.11.2 puis *and* ensuite

(i) **puis** means *après cela* ('then'), and **ensuite** means *après cela, plus tard* ('afterwards', 'after that', 'next').

> Ex: *Il se leva, prit son chapeau **puis** partit.*
> He got up, took his hat and then left.

NB: *puis* is placed before the word which it applies to, whereas *ensuite* is placed either before or after the word it applies to. When placed before it, it is often preceded by *et* or starts a sentence; when placed after it, it is equivalent in meaning to *après*.

> Ex: *Paul parla le premier, **puis** ce fut le tour de Pierre.*
> Paul spoke first, then it was Paul's turn.

> *Il faut d'abord humecter les cheveux et **ensuite** les laver avec un shampooing doux.*
> You should first wet the hair, then wash it with a mild shampoo.

> *D'abord, il a passé l'aspirateur. **Ensuite**, il a commencé à épousseter les meubles.*
> First, he hoovered. Then he started dusting the furniture.

> *Terminez d'abord vos devoirs. Vous pourrez regarder la télévision **ensuite**.*
> Finish your homework first. You can watch television afterwards.

(ii) Other expressions based on *suite*

> – *tout de suite* immediately
> – *par la suite* (= *dans la période qui a suivi ou qui suivra*) later on, subsequently
> – *et ainsi de suite* and so on

6.11.3 alors or puis?

Consider the following example:

'After studies at two of France's elite schools of political science and national administration, Sciences-Po and ENA, he [Edouard Balladur] became political advisor to Georges Pompidou, **then** prime minister, from 1963 to 1968.'

The Economist, 3–9 April 1993

In order to translate 'then', it is necessary to know that it was Pompidou who was prime minister from 1963–68 and not Balladur. Therefore, 'then' is '*alors*' in this case, and not '*puis*'.

*Après avoir fait des études à deux des écoles réservées à l'élite de la France, Sciences-Po et ENA, il [Edouard Balladur] est devenu conseiller politique de Georges Pompidou, **alors** premier ministre, de 1963 à 1968.*

6.11.4 donc

(i) When *donc* means 'therefore', 'so' or 'then' (as in the conclusion of a logical argument), it is close in meaning to *alors* (see 6.11.1(ii)). It comes first in the clause and can be considered as a conjunction of coordination (see chapter 40 Coordination and Juxtaposition, section 2(ii)).

Ex: *Je l'ai vu il y a une minute; **donc**, il ne peut pas être bien loin.*
I saw him a minute ago; therefore, he can't be very far away.

(ii) When *donc* means 'so' or 'then' in a weaker sense, it normally follows the verb.

Ex: *Je l'ai vu il y a deux minutes; il ne peut **donc** pas être bien loin.*
I saw him two minutes ago; so he can't be very far away.

(iii) When the verb has no complement, *donc* comes first in the clause.

Ex: '*Je pense **donc** je suis.*'

René Descartes, *Meditationes de Prima Philosophia*

I think therefore I am.

*Tu manges trop de chocolat, **donc** tu grossis.*
You eat too much chocolate, therefore you put on weight.

6.12 *tard* and *en retard*; *tôt* and *en avance*

(i) *tard* means 'late' in the sense of after the habitual time, after a period of time considered as long or at the end of a period.

Ex: *Ce matin, je me suis levé **tard**.*
This morning, I got up late.

*Je n'aime pas rentrer chez moi **tard** le soir.*
I do not like to come back home late at night.

(ii) The opposite of *tard* is *tôt* ('early') and is equivalent to *de bonne heure*.

Ex: *Ce matin, je me suis levé **tôt**/**de bonne heure**.*
This morning, I got up early.

(iii)   *en retard* means 'late' in the sense of after an appointed time, i.e. 'too late'.

Ex: *Je suis **en retard** comme d'habitude!*
I am late as usual!

*Dépêchons-nous! Nous allons encore arriver **en retard** chez les Dupont!*
Let's hurry! We'll be late at the Duponts' again!

NB: For inanimates, *avoir du retard* is more usual.

Ex: *Le train **avait** une demi-heure **de retard** ce matin.*
The train was half an hour late this morning.

(iv)   The opposite of *en retard* is *en avance*.

Ex: *Je préfère arriver un peu **en avance** au cinéma pour pouvoir choisir ma place.*
I prefer to arrive a little early at the cinema so that I can choose my seat.

NB: For inanimates, *avoir de l'avance* is more usual.

Ex: *Ne vous inquiétez pas. Même si le train **a de l'avance**, il ne partira pas avant l'heure habituelle!*
Don't worry! Even if the train is early, it won't leave before the usual time.

6.13   *dessus, dessous, dedans*

All of these can be used instead of *y* to replace a noun preceded by *sur*, *sous* or *dans* respectively in the following cases:

(i)   to stress the position of an object:

Ex: – *Les livres sont [bien] **sur** le bureau?*
– *Oui, ils sont **dessus**.*
is stronger than:
– *Oui, ils **y** sont.*

(ii)   to contradict a statement:

Ex: – *L'argent est **à côté de** ton sac?*
– *Non, il est **dedans**.*

30 Comparatives and superlatives

1 Introduction

Adjectives, adverbs, nouns and verbs can be compared by the use of the comparative and superlative forms. This chapter examines comparatives, intensifiers and other comparative constructions, the superlative, and the comparative and superlative forms of irregular adjectives and adverbs.

The comparative clauses produced by these constructions must be distinguished from ordinary subordinate clauses since they operate in a different way (see chapter 2 Syntax, section 3.2). A comparison is established between two independent qualities or quantities by the combination of adverbs and conjunctions.

2 The comparative

2.1 Introduction

There are three sorts of comparatives, namely of superiority, inferiority and equality.

(i) Generally, comparisons involve adjectives or adverbs, but they can also involve nouns and verbs.

(ii) The comparison does not necessarily involve two terms of the same type.

> Ex: *Marie est plus bête . . .*   Marie is more stupid . . .
> *que méchante.*   than nasty.
> *que Catherine.*   than Catherine.
> *que l'année dernière.*   than last year.
> *que vous ne le pensez.*   than you think.

(iii) As in English, the second term of the comparison is normally omitted if there is no ambiguity.

> Ex: *Mettez-vous plus vers le milieu!*
> Please stand nearer the middle!

(There is no need to add *que vous ne l'êtes*/'than you are').

(iv) When the second part of a comparative of inequality (superiority or inferiority) is a **clause**, either *ne* or *ne le* can be used before the verb of that clause. However, with the comparative of equality, only *le* may be used.

> Consider the following example:
> *M. Durand est plus riche qu'on ne [le] pense.*
> M. Durand is richer than people think.

– In this type of sentence, the *que*-clause contains a negative implication: people do not think M. Durand is as rich as he really is, hence the presence of ***ne***.

– *le* is also present to refer to the general idea expressed in the main clause. However, the ellipsis of *le* is frequent.

– The **inversion subject–verb** is possible after *que* (only if the subject is a noun phrase).
> Ex: *M. Durand est plus riche que **les gens** ne [le] pensent.*
> or:
> *. . . que ne [le] pensent **les gens**.*
> but:
> *M. Durand est plus riche qu'**on** ne [le] pense.*

– With a comparative of equality, only *le* is needed in the *que*-clause (or nothing if the ellipsis is preferred).
> Ex: *M. Durand est aussi riche qu'on [le] pense.*
> M. Durand is as rich as people think.

(v) Use of *possible* with a comparative of equality.

The use of *possible* links the degree of comparison closely to the subject of the verb. Hence there is no comparison with other items having similar qualities or capacities.
> Ex: *Je vais aussi vite que possible!*
> (rather than: *Je vais aussi vite que je [le] peux.*)
> I am going as fast as I can!

(vi) Unlike in English, there is only one way to express pronouns in a comparison, regardless of register.
> Ex: *Il court plus vite **que moi**!*
> He runs faster **than me/than I/than I do**!

2.2 Comparison of adjectives and adverbs

(i) **Position**

– If the adjective is normally placed **before** the noun, it can come either before or after the noun with a comparative.
> Ex: *Nous avons acheté une grande maison.*
> We bought a big house.
> → *Nous avons acheté **une plus grande maison**.*
> or:
> → *Nous avons acheté **une maison plus grande**.*
> → We bought a bigger house.

– If the adjective normally comes **after** the noun, it can only be placed after the noun with a comparative.

> Ex: *Nous avons acheté **une maison moderne**.*
> We bought a modern house.
> → *Nous avons acheté **une maison plus moderne**.*
> → We bought a more modern house.
>   and not:
> → **Nous avons acheté une plus moderne maison.*

(ii) Repetition

Unlike in English, the comparative must be repeated before each adjective or adverb.

> Ex: *Marie est **moins** belle et **moins** intelligente que Catherine.*
> Marie is **less** beautiful and _ intelligent than Catherine.

> *Je conduis **plus lentement** et **plus prudemment** qu'avant.*
> I drive **more** slowly and _ carefully than before.

(iii) *à or que?*

Adjectives derived from Latin comparatives (*supérieur, inférieur, antérieur, postérieur*) are followed by *à*, with the exception of *meilleur* which is followed by *que* (see section 5.1.1.1). Compare:

> *L'œuvre dramatique de Giraudoux est **antérieure à** celle d'Ionesco.*
> Giraudoux's dramatic works are earlier than those of Ionesco.
>   and:
> *Cette bière-ci est bien **meilleure que** celle-là.*
> This beer is much better than that one.

(iv) *égal*, etc.

Adjectives such as *égal, pareil, perpendiculaire, inférieur, supérieur, excellent*, etc., are not normally used in comparisons since they express a quality which does not in principle include degrees. Hence the common joke:

> '*Tous les gens sont égaux, mais il y en a qui sont plus égaux que les autres!*'
> after George Orwell's:
> 'All animals are equal, but some animals are more equal than others.'

> George Orwell, *Animal Farm*

2.2.1 *Comparative of inferiority*

(i) Basic form

moins + adjective/adverb + *que*: **less . . . than**

> Ex: *C'est **moins** difficile **que** je ne [le] croyais.*
> It's less difficult than I thought.

> *Je lis **moins** vite **que** vous.*
> I read less fast than you.

*Ils nous ont reçus **moins** bien **que** la dernière fois.*
> or:
*Ils nous ont **moins** bien reçus **que** la dernière fois.*
They did not receive us as well as last time.

(ii) **Negative form**

pas moins + adjective/adverb + ***que***
> Ex: *Elle n'est **pas moins** prudente **que** toi.*
> She's no less careful than you are.

> *Ils ne nous ont **pas** reçus **moins** bien **que** la dernière fois.*
> > or:
> *Ils ne nous ont **pas moins** bien reçus **que** la dernière fois.*
> They did not receive us any worse than last time.

(iii) **Second part omitted**

> Ex: *Il fait bien **moins** froid dans ce nouvel appartement [**que** dans l'ancien]!*
> It's a lot less cold in this new flat [than it was in the old one]!

2.2.2 *Comparative of equality*

(i) **Basic form**

aussi + adjective/adverb + ***que***: **as . . . as**
> Ex: *Elle est **aussi** jolie **que** sa mère.*
> She is as pretty as her mother.

> *Nous travaillons **aussi** dur **que** vous.*
> We work as hard as you do.

(ii) **Reinforcement with *tout***

The comparative of equality can be reinforced with the adverb ***tout***.
> Ex: *Il est **tout aussi** timide **que** vous!*
> He's just as shy as you are!

(iii) **Negative form**

pas aussi or ***pas si*** + adjective/adverb + ***que***
> Ex: *Votre chat n'est **pas aussi/si** intelligent **que** vous le dites.*
> Your cat is not as clever as you say.

(iv) **Use of *comme***

Similarity can also be expressed by using the adverb ***comme* (as)**, particularly in similes.
> Ex: *Elle est têtue **comme** une mule!*
> She is as stubborn as a mule!

> *Parlez plus fort, il est sourd **comme** un pot!*
> Speak up, he is as deaf as a post!

> *Ils avaient réussi à faire pousser une tomate grosse **comme** une citrouille.*
> They had managed to grow a tomato as big as a pumpkin.

(v)   **Second part omitted**

>   Ex: *Vous conduisez toujours **aussi** vite [que vous conduisiez autrefois]?*
>   Do you still drive as fast [as you used to drive]?

2.2.3   *Comparative of superiority*

(i)   **Basic form**

plus + adjective/adverb + *que*: **more . . . than**
>   Ex: *Mon nouvel appartement est **plus** pratique **que** l'ancien.*
>   My new apartment is more convenient than the old one.

(ii)   **Negative form**

pas plus + adjective/adverb + *que*
>   Ex: *Mon nouvel appartement n'est **pas plus** grand **que** l'ancien.*
>   My new apartment is no bigger than the previous one.

>   *M. Durand n'est **pas plus** riche **qu'on** [le] pense.*
>   M. Durand is no richer than people think.

NB: No *ne* in the subordinate clause because the main clause is negative.

(iii)   **Use of *davantage* instead of *plus***

davantage comes at the end of the sentence, and corresponds to 'more so' (use with adjectives only). Compare:
>   *Pierre est **plus** courageux **que** Charles.*
>   Pierre is more courageous than Charles.
>   and:
>   *Charles est courageux, mais Pierre l'est **davantage**.*
>   Charles is courageous but Pierre is more so.

>   *Charles est **aussi** travailleur **que** Pierre, sinon **davantage**.*
>   Charles is as hard-working as Pierre, if not more so.

NB: An alternative is to use *encore plus* (see 3.6 below).

(iv)   **Second part omitted**

>   Ex: *Maintenant, nous pourrons nous voir **plus** souvent.*
>   Now we shall be able to see each other more often.

2.3   Comparison of nouns

(i)   **Articles**

Nouns are generally preceded by an article, which is kept in the comparative form.

– *du, de la* or *des* become ***de*** after the comparatives *plus, moins, autant*; *de* must be repeated before the noun which is the **object of the comparison**, if it is also the **object of the verb**.

Ex: *Ils ont plus **d'**argent que **de** bon sens.*
('*bon sens*' is compared with the **object** '*argent*')
They've got more money than sense.
>but:

*Ils ont plus **d'**argent que _ nous.*
('*nous*' is compared with the **subject** '*ils*')
They've got more money than we have.

- Definite articles remain definite articles.
Ex: *J'aime les pommes et les poires.*
→ *J'aime autant **les** pommes que **les** poires.*
→ I like apples as much as pears.

(ii) **Repetition**

As in English, the comparatives are **not** repeated before each noun (but *de* is), except for emphasis. Compare:
*J'ai **autant de** copies à corriger et **de** cours à préparer que vous.*
I've got as many scripts to mark and lectures to prepare as you have.
>and:

*Il possède **plus de** maisons, **plus de** voitures et **plus de** chevaux de course que la Reine d'Angleterre!*
He owns more houses, more cars and more race horses than the Queen of England!

(iii) **Idioms**

Idioms consisting of verb + noun (without a determiner) do not add *de* in the comparative.
Ex: *avoir peur*:
*J'aurai **moins peur** si tu viens avec moi.*
I will be less scared if you come with me.

Note that in this case the comparative of equality is formed with *aussi* (not *autant*).
Ex: *J'ai eu tout **aussi peur** en revoyant 'Dracula' pour la troisième fois!*
I was just as scared when I saw 'Dracula' for the third time!

(iv) *il y a*

Remember that *il y a* is invariable, hence:
Ex: There **is** less noise.
Il y a moins de bruit.
>and:

There **are** fewer people.
Il y a moins de gens.

466

2.3.1 *Comparative of inferiority*

(i) **Basic form**

moins de + noun + *que* [+ *de*]: **less . . . than; fewer . . . than**

Ex: *Il y a **moins de** vent qu'hier.*
It is less windy than yesterday.

*Tu as mis **moins de** couteaux **que de** fourchettes sur la table!*
You've put fewer knives than forks on the table!

(ii) **Numbers**

– **than** followed by a number (including fractions) (**less/fewer than**) is translated by *de*, not *que*.

Ex: This holiday cost us **less than** ten thousand francs.
*Ces vacances nous ont coûté **moins de** dix mille francs.*

Eventually, **fewer than** ten people turned up.
*Finalement, **moins de** dix personnes sont venues.*

Women do two-thirds of the work for **less than** half a man's salary.
*Les femmes font les deux-tiers du travail pour **moins de** la moitié du salaire d'un homme.*

– After a noun preceded by a cardinal number, use *de moins que*.

Ex: *Il a deux ans **de moins que** moi.*
He's two years younger than I am.

Compare:
*J'ai **moins de** 10 francs sur moi.*
I have less than 10 francs on me.
     and:
*J'ai 10 francs **de moins** qu'hier.*
I have 10 francs less than yesterday.

– But if **than** introduces a new clause in which the number (or phrase introduced by the number) is the subject of a verb (expressed or implied), **than** is translated by *que*.

Ex: *Tous ensemble, ils en font **moins qu'**un seul d'entre nous [n'en fait].*
All of them together do **less than** just one of us [does].

(iii) **Negative form**

pas moins de + noun + *que* [+ *de*]

Ex: *Paul n'a **pas moins de** soucis **que** nous.*
Paul has no fewer worries than we have.

(iv) **Second part omitted**

Ex: *Il y a **moins de** vent aujourd'hui [qu'hier].*
It is less windy today [than yesterday].

2.3.2 Comparative of equality

(i) **Basic form**

autant de + noun + *que* [+ *de*]: **as much . . . as; as many . . . as**

> Ex: *Il y a **autant de** bruit dans cette rue **qu'**hier.*
> There is as much noise in this street as yesterday.

(ii) **Use of *même* ('same')**

même + noun + *que* indicates similarity

> Ex: *Elle a le **même** poids **que** toi.*
> She is the same weight as you.
> > is a more elegant alternative to:
> *Elle pèse autant que toi.*
> She weighs as much as you.

(iii) **Negative form**

pas autant de + noun + *que* [+ *de*]

> Ex: *Je n'ai **pas autant de** force **qu'**avant.*
> I do not have as much strength as before.

NB: For the use of ***plus*** instead of *pas*, see chapter 38 Negative Structures, section 2.2.1(iv).

2.3.3 Comparative of superiority

(i) **Basic form**

plus de + noun + *que* [+ *de*]: **more . . . than**

> Ex: *Il y a **plus de** fourchettes **que de** couteaux sur cette table!*
> There are more forks than knives on this table!

> *J'ai mis **plus de** beurre **que** d'habitude dans mon gâteau.*
> I put more butter in my cake than usual.

NB: '*d'habitude*' is one word!

(ii) **Use of *davantage* instead of *plus***

davantage can be used instead of *plus*, in the same position.

> Ex: *Cette fois-ci, j'ai mis **plus de** crème dans la sauce.*
> > or:
> *Cette fois-ci, j'ai mis **davantage de** crème dans la sauce.*
> This time, I've put more cream in the sauce.

> *J'ai beaucoup de travail mais Nicolas dit qu'il en a encore **davantage/** qu'il en a encore **plus.***
> I've got a lot of work but Nicolas says he's got even more.

(iii) **Use of *encore* instead of *plus***

When **more** means 'still more', there is no comparative, so ***encore*** should be used, not *plus*.

Ex: There's **more** wine in the cellar, if you're short.
*Il y a **encore** du vin à la cave, si vous en manquez.*

I've got two or three **more** things to do.
*J'ai **encore** deux ou trois choses à faire.*

(iv) Implied noun

The noun can be implied, in which case there is no **de** (see Comparison of Verbs).

Ex: *Il gagne **plus** [d'argent] **que** moi.*
He earns more [money] than I do.

(v) Numbers

– **than** followed by a number (including fractions) is translated by **de**, not **que** (**more than**).

Ex: I don't want to stay there **more than** an hour.
*Je ne veux pas y rester **plus d'une heure**.*

There is **more than** half of it left.
*Il en reste **plus de** la moitié.*

– After a noun preceded by a cardinal number, use **de plus** [**que**].

Ex: *J'ai trois jours de vacances **de plus que** vous.*
I've got three more days' holiday than you.

*C'est une raison **de plus** pour ne pas y aller.*
That's one more reason not to go.

– But if **than** introduces a new clause in which the number (or phrase introduced by the number) is the subject of a verb (expressed or implied), **than** is translated by **que**.

Ex: *Chacun d'entre eux en fait **plus que** dix autres [n'en font].*
Each of them does **more than** ten others [do].

(vi) Negative form

pas plus de + noun + *que* [+ *de*]
Ex: *Il n'a **pas plus** d'argent **que** moi.*
He's got no more money than I've got.

2.4 Comparison of conjugated verbs

2.4.1 *Comparative of inferiority*

(i) Basic form

– simple tense: verb + ***moins*** + ***que***
– compound tense: auxiliary + past participle + ***moins*** + ***que***
or:
auxiliary + ***moins*** + past participle + ***que***

} **less . . . than**

Ex: *Paul lit **moins que** Pierre.*
Paul reads less than Pierre.

*Ils ont **moins** mangé **que** d'habitude.*
or:
*Ils ont mangé **moins que** d'habitude.*
They ate less than usual.

(ii) **Negative form**

– simple tense: ***ne*** + verb + ***pas moins que***
– compound tense: ***ne*** + auxiliary + ***pas*** + past participle + ***moins que***
or:
ne + auxiliary + ***pas moins*** + past participle + ***que***

Ex: *Je **ne** travaille **pas moins que** vous.*
I do not work any less than you.

*Je **n'ai pas** travaillé **moins que** vous.*
or:
*Je **n'ai pas moins** travaillé **que** vous.*
I did not work any less than you.

2.4.2 *Comparative of equality*

(i) **Basic form**

– simple tense: verb + ***autant*** + ***que***
– compound tense: auxiliary + past participle + ***autant*** + ***que***
or:
auxiliary + ***autant*** + past participle + ***que***

} as much . . . as

Ex: *Je travaille **autant que** vous.*
I work as much as you.

*J'ai **autant** travaillé **que** vous.*
or:
*J'ai travaillé **autant que** vous.*
I've worked as much as you have.

(ii) **Negative form**

Use ***pas autant*** or ***pas tant*** . . . ***que***.

Ex: *Je **ne** travaille **pas autant que** vous.*
I don't work as much as you do.

*Je **n'ai pas** travaillé **autant que** vous.*
or:
*Je **n'ai pas autant** travaillé **que** vous.*
I didn't work as much as you did.

2.4.3 *Comparative of superiority*

(i) **Basic form**

– simple tense: verb + ***plus*** + ***que***
– compound tense: auxiliary + past participle + ***plus*** + ***que***
 or:
 auxiliary + ***plus*** + past participle + ***que***

} **more . . . than**

Ex: *Il en sait **plus qu'**il n'en dit.*
 He knows more than he says.

*J'ai **plus** travaillé **que** vous.*
 or:
*J'ai travaillé **plus que** vous.*
 I worked more than you.

(ii) **Use of *davantage* instead of *plus***

davantage can also replace *plus* (**more**) in the same position.
 Ex: *Il s'intéresse **plus/davantage** à ma sœur **qu'à** moi!*
 He's more interested in my sister than in me!

*Il ne m'en a pas dit **plus/davantage**.*
 He didn't tell me more.

(iii) **Negative form**

Ex: *Elle **ne** travaille **pas plus que** vous.*
 She does not work more than you.

*Je **n'**ai **pas** travaillé **plus que** vous.*
 or:
*Je **n'**ai **pas plus** travaillé **que** vous.*
 I didn't work more than you.

2.5 Comparison of infinitives

If the conjugated verb takes a preposition before a following infinitive, this preposition is repeated after ***que***. Otherwise, add ***de*** (see chapters 15 Infinitive, section 3.1 and 26 Prepositions, section 7).
 Ex: *Il pense plus **à** s'amuser **qu'à** travailler.*
 He thinks more about enjoying himself than working.
 (*penser **à*** + infinitive)

*Nous avons autant besoin **de** manger que **de** dormir.*
 We have as much need for eating as for sleeping.
 (*avoir besoin **de*** + infinitive)

*Je préfère m'en aller que **de** vous écouter.*
 I'd rather go than listen to you.
 (*préférer* + infinitive)

3 Other constructions with the comparative

3.1 The double comparative

The double comparative (*plus . . . plus; moins . . . moins; plus . . . mieux; moins . . . plus*, etc.) is used with verbs. Its construction differs from that used in English.

The French construction is basically:
> **plus** + subject + verb phrase, **plus** + subject + verb phrase
> or:
> **moins** + subject + verb phrase, **plus** + subject + verb phrase, etc.

English has a variety of constructions.

> Ex: **Plus** *le sentiment est profond,* **plus** *la propagande est efficace.*
> The deeper the feeling [is], the more efficient the propaganda [is].
>
> **Moins** *on mange,* **mieux** *on se porte!* (popular saying)
> The less you eat, the healthier you are!
>
> **Plus** *il s'explique,* **moins** *on le comprend.*
> The more he explains himself, the less we understand him.

3.2 Use of intensifiers

(i) **With adjectives and adverbs**

The following intensifiers are all adverbs and can be used in comparisons: *bien, beaucoup, tellement, infiniment* (to translate 'much', 'so much').

– adjective:
> Ex: *Nous sommes* **bien plus** *consciencieux* **qu'eux.**
> We are much more conscientious than they are.
>
> *Il n'est pas* **tellement plus** *petit* **que** *vous.*
> He's not that much shorter than you.

NB: Do not use *si* to translate 'so' in a comparison.
> Ex: He is **so** shy!
> *Il est* **si** *timide!*
> but:
> He's **so much less** shy **than** his sister.
> *Il est* **tellement moins** *timide* **que** *sa sœur.*

See also chapter 36 Indefinite Words, section 6.3.1.

– adverb:
> *Nous sommes* **infiniment plus** *à l'aise avec les Martin* **qu'avec** *les Durand.*
> We are infinitely more at ease with the Martins than with the Durands.

(ii) **With nouns**

The same intensifiers can be used in comparisons: *bien, beaucoup, tellement, infiniment* (to translate 'much', 'so much'), but do not forget the *de*!

> Ex: *J'ai **beaucoup plus de** travail à faire **que** toi.*
> I've got much more work to do than you.
>
> *Nous avons **tellement moins de** problèmes avec le nouveau Chef de Section.*
> We have so much less trouble with the new Head of Department.

3.3 Continuous decrease

(i) With adjectives and adverbs

Use *de moins en moins* + adjective or adverb.

> Ex: *Il est **de moins en moins** hostile.*
> He is getting less and less hostile.

(ii) With verbs

Use verb + *de moins en moins*.

> Ex: *Je dors **de moins en moins**.*
> I am sleeping less and less.

(iii) With nouns

Use *de moins en moins **de*** + noun.

> Ex: *J'ai **de moins en moins de** force.*
> I have less and less strength.

3.4 Continuous increase

(i) With adjectives and adverbs

– Use *de plus en plus* + adjective or adverb.

> Ex: *Il fait **de plus en plus** chaud.*
> It is getting warmer and warmer.

– Alternatively, use *toujours plus*.

> Ex: *Les cigarettes sont **toujours plus** chères!*
> Cigarettes cost more and more!

– Note that English can also use 'increasingly' + adjective: it is still *de plus en plus* in French.

> Ex: The ecology movement is increasingly important.
> *Le mouvement écologique est **de plus en plus** important.*

(ii)   With verbs

– Use verb + *de plus en plus*.
> Ex: *Il boit **de plus en plus**.*
> He drinks more and more.

– Alternatively, use *toujours plus* or *toujours davantage*.
> Ex: *Il boit **toujours plus/toujours davantage**.*
> He drinks more and more.

(iii)   With nouns

Use *de plus en plus **de*** + noun.
> Ex: *Il y a **de plus en plus de** voitures sur les routes!*
> There are more and more cars on the roads!

3.5   Use of *d'autant plus/d'autant moins*

(i)   *d'autant plus . . . que* means **all the more . . . as**, or **particularly as**.

> Ex: *Je suis **d'autant plus** mécontente de les voir **qu'**ils n'ont même pas répondu à mes lettres.*
> I am **all the more** displeased to see them **as** they did not even answer my letters.

> *Je n'ai pas à vous faire d'excuses, **d'autant plus que** vous êtes dans votre tort.*
> I don't have to apologize to you, **particularly since** you are in the wrong.

> *Il travaille **d'autant plus** dur maintenant **qu'**il n'a rien fait de toute l'année!*
> He is working **all the** hard**er** now **as** he hasn't done anything all year.

(ii)   *d'autant moins . . . que* means **all the less . . . as**.

> Ex: *On l'aimait **d'autant moins qu'**il ne faisait rien pour se rendre utile.*
> We liked him **all the less as** he did nothing to make himself useful.

3.6   Use of *encore* + comparative

encore plus [de] (**even more**), *encore moins [de]* (**even less/fewer**), *encore mieux* (**even better**), *encore pire* (**even worse**).

> Ex: *Il y a **encore plus de** cerises sur les arbres cette année **que** l'année dernière.*
> There are **even more** cherries on the trees this year **than** last year.

NB: An alternative is to use *davantage [de] . . . que*.

> *M. Durand a attrapé deux lapins et une perdrix mais M. Dupont a fait **encore mieux**: il a attrapé trois lapins, un lièvre et deux perdrix.*
> M. Durand caught two rabbits and a partridge but M. Dupont did **even better** – he caught three rabbits, a hare and two partridges.

4 The superlative

There are two kinds of superlatives: inferiority and superiority. The superlative is formed by putting *le, la* or *les* before the comparative. Where the superlative applies to an adjective, the possessive determiners *mon, ma, mes*, etc. may also be used.

4.1 The superlative of adjectives

(i) Agreement

The definite article (or possessive adjective) agrees in gender and number with the noun modified by the qualifying adjective. The adjective agrees with the noun in the usual way.

> Ex: **les plus belles fleurs**
> the most beautiful flowers

(ii) Translation of **in, on**

The meaning of **in** or **on** after a superlative, which introduces the element of comparison, is conveyed by **de** (**du, de la, de l'**).

> Ex: Sophie is the most dedicated student **in the** group.
> *Sophie est l'étudiante la plus studieuse **du** groupe.*

> It's the cheapest restaurant **in** London.
> *C'est le restaurant le moins cher **de** Londres.*

> It is the greatest nation **on** earth.
> *C'est la plus grande nation **de la** terre.*

(iii) Position of the adjective

There are two constructions:

− construction A
superiority: *le* (*la, les*) ***plus*** + adj + noun
inferiority: *le* (*la, les*) ***moins*** + adj + noun

− construction B
superiority: *le* (*la, les*) + noun + *le* (*la, les*) ***plus*** + adj.
inferiority: *le* (*la, les*) + noun + *le* (*la, les*) ***moins*** + adj.

If the adjective normally comes **before** the noun, either A or B can be used.

> Ex: *un beau chat*
> → *le plus beau chat*
> or:
> → *le chat le plus beau*

If the adjective comes **after** the noun, only B can be used.

> Ex: *un cas compliqué*
> → *le cas le moins compliqué*
> and not:
> → **le moins compliqué cas*

(iv)   With a possessive adjective

When the adjective is preceded by a possessive adjective, there is no article with construction A but there is an article with construction B.

> Ex: *Je vous présente **mes** plus sincères félicitations.*
> but:
> *Je vous présente **mes** félicitations **les** plus sincères.*
> May I offer you my most sincere congratulations.

(v)   Noun implied

As in English, a noun can be implied.

> Ex: *Ce chat est très beau . . . C'est en fait **le plus beau** [du monde]* /
> *[de tous les chats]*.
> This cat is very beautiful . . . In fact, he is the most beautiful
> [in the world] / [of all cats].

(vi)   With two elements or more

There is no distinction in French between e.g. 'the younger' and 'the youngest', 'the older' and 'the oldest'.

> Ex: *Michel est le plus âgé des deux/Michel est l'aîné.*
> Michel is **the elder**.
>
> *Michel est le plus âgé des trois/Michel est l'aîné.*
> Michel is **the eldest**.

(vii)   Repetition of the superlative

– Unlike in English, the superlative (including article) must be repeated before each adjective, unless both adjectives can be placed before the noun.

> Ex: *Ce sont les roses **les plus** belles et **les plus** parfumées de toutes celles que je fais pousser.*
> These are **the most** beautiful and _ perfumed roses of all those
> I grow.
> > but:
> *Il m'a confié **ses plus** intimes et _ horribles secrets.*
> > or:
> *Il m'a confié **ses** secrets **les plus** intimes et **les plus** horribles.*
> He confided **his most** intimate and _ horrible secrets to me.

(See chapter 28 Qualifying Adjectives, section 2.3.4 regarding the position and meaning of adjectives.)

    – If the same adjective applies to two different nouns, both the superlative and the adjective must be repeated (unlike in English).

        Ex: *Il se vantait toujours d'avoir **la plus belle** maison et **la plus belle** voiture.*
        He would always boast that he had **the finest** house and _ car.

(viii)   Translation of '**one of** (the most/least)'

    Use **un des**, **une des** + construction A or B as appropriate (see (iii) above).

        Ex: *Elle habite dans **une des** rues **les plus** passantes.*
        She lives in **one of the** busi**est** streets.

        *Ce fut **l'une des** périodes **les plus** agréables de sa vie.*
        or:
        *Ce fut **l'une des plus** agréables périodes de sa vie.*
        It was **one of the most** enjoyable times of his life.

(ix)   Other meanings of **most**

    When **most** means 'very', use *très*, *fort*, *extrêmement*, *parfaitement*, *tout à fait*, *tout ce qu'il y a de plus* or *des plus* + adjective. In the construction with *des plus*, the adjective which follows is always plural. Hence:

        He's a **most** intelligent man.
        C'est un homme fort/extrêmement/tout ce qu'il y a de plus intelligent.
        or:
        C'est un homme des plus intelligents.

        He was **most** pleasant to us.
        Il a été fort/extrêmement/parfaitement/tout à fait/tout ce qu'il y a de plus aimable avec nous.
        or:
        Il a été des plus aimables avec nous.

4.2   The superlative of nouns, verbs and adverbs

(i)   **Agreement**

    With nouns, verbs and adverbs, *le* before *plus* or *moins* is invariable.

    – noun: *le plus de/le moins de* + noun

        Ex: *C'est le mercredi que j'ai **le plus** [de choses] à faire.*
        It is on Wednesdays that I have the most to do.

        *C'est Antoine qui a fait **le moins de** fautes dans la dictée.*
        It was Antoine who made the fewest mistakes in the dictation.

    – verb: simple tense: verb + *le plus*/*le moins*
           compound tense: auxiliary + *le plus*/*le moins* + past participle
                              or:
                      auxiliary + past participle + *le plus*/*le moins*
        Ex: *Ce sont eux qui boivent **le plus**.*
        It is they who drink the most.

*Ce sont eux qui ont **le plus** bu.*
or:
*Ce sont eux qui ont bu **le plus**.*
It was they who drank the most.

– adverb: ***le plus/le moins*** + adverb
Ex: *Ceux qui habitaient **le plus** près venaient **le plus** souvent.*
Those who lived nearest came most often.

NB: For adverbial expressions based on nouns, see superlative of nouns above.
Ex: *Il a parlé avec enthousiasme.*
He spoke enthusiastically.

→ *C'est Robert qui a parlé avec **le plus** d'enthousiasme.*
→ It was Robert who spoke the most enthusiastically.

(ii) Repetition of the superlative

– adverbs: as for adjectives, the superlative is repeated with each adverb.
Ex: *C'est Charles qui rit **le plus** fort et **le plus** désagréablement.*
It is Charles who laughs **the most** loudly and _ unpleasantly.

– nouns: the superlative is not repeated (except for emphasis).
Ex: *C'est Lizzy qui attrape **le plus** de souris et **d'**oiseaux.*
It is Lizzy who catches **the most** mice and _ birds.

– verbs: the superlative is not repeated (except for emphasis).
Ex: *C'est Eric qui mange et [qui] boit **le moins**.*
It is Eric who eats and drinks **the least**.

(iii) Alternatives to *le plus de* + noun

le plus de can be replaced by *le plus grand nombre de* or *la plus grande quantité de* (for the rhythm of the sentence).
Ex: *C'est l'usine qui emploie **le plus grand nombre d'**ouvriers de la région.*
This is the factory that employs the highest number of workers in the region.
sounds better than:
. . . le plus d'ouvriers de la région.

*C'est l'usine qui produit **la plus grande quantité de** mercure de la région.*
This is the factory that produces the largest quantity of mercury in the region.
sounds better than:
. . . le plus de mercure de la région.

(iv) Use of *possible*

See the use of *possible* with the comparative in section 2.1(v) above.
Ex: *Ils espèrent **le plus possible** de la vie.*
They expect as much as possible from life.

*Les fraises ne sont pas chères en ce moment: je vais en acheter **le plus possible** pour faire de la confiture.*
Strawberries are cheap at the moment – I am going to buy as many as I can to make jam.

5 Irregular adjectives and adverbs

We are going to look at the following:
- adjectives: *bon, mauvais, petit*
- adverbs: *beaucoup, peu, bien, mal*

Special attention should be given to these adjectives and adverbs, particularly as:

- **better** and **best** translate the comparative and superlative of superiority respectively of both *bon* (→ *meilleur, le meilleur*) and *bien* (→ *mieux, le mieux*): see sections 5.1.1.1, 5.1.2.2, 5.2.1.1, 5.2.2.2.

- **many** is *beaucoup*, but **as many . . . as/as much . . . as** is *autant [de] . . . que* (see section 5.1.2.1).

- *pire* (**worse**) and *le pire* (**the worst**) are the comparative and superlative of superiority of both the adjective *mauvais* and the adverb *mal* respectively (see sections 5.1.1.2, 5.1.2.3, 5.2.1.2, 5.2.2.3).

- the comparative of superiority of *beaucoup* is *plus* and its superlative of superiority is *le plus*. Its opposite is *peu*, the comparative of superiority of which is *moins*, and the superlative of superiority, *le moins*.

- **the least** is *le moindre* (one of the two superlatives of superiority of *petit*) and also *le moins* when applied to another adjective, etc. in superlatives.

5.1 Comparatives

5.1.1 Adjectives

Note that the comparatives of inferiority and equality of the following adjectives are regular.

bon	→ *meilleur*
	aussi bon
	moins bon
mauvais	→ *plus mauvais*, **pire**
	aussi mauvais
	moins mauvais
petit	→ *plus petit*, **moindre**
	aussi petit
	moins petit

Particular attention should be paid to the comparatives of *mauvais*, as there is no exact correspondence in English usage (see section 5.1.1.2).

5.1.1.1 *bon*

(i) The comparative of superiority of *bon* (good) is **meilleur** (**better**): *bon* and *meilleur* agree in gender and number with the nouns they qualify.

> Ex: *Cette bière est bonne.*
> This beer is good.
> → *Cette bière est **meilleure que** l'autre.*
> → This beer is better than the other one.

(ii) The other comparatives are regular: *aussi bon; moins bon.*

5.1.1.2 *mauvais*

(i) The comparative of superiority of *mauvais* (bad) is:

– either **pire** or **plus mauvais** (**worse**), but can also be translated by **moins bon**. The latter is frequently used in French to translate **worse** when there is no emotion involved!

> Ex: *Cet itinéraire est **moins bon que** l'autre.*
> This itinerary is worse than the other.

– **plus mauvais** and **pire** are in turn interchangeable but *plus mauvais* retains the notion of comparison and tends to be used when the meaning is 'deficient', whilst *pire* implies 'very bad'.

> Ex: *Catherine est **pire que** sa sœur.*
> Catherine is worse than her sister (who is already 'bad').
> > but:
> *Catherine est **plus mauvaise** en maths **que** Bruno.*
> Catherine is worse than Bruno at maths.
>
> *La circulation est **pire qu'**hier.*
> The traffic is worse than yesterday (which was already 'bad').

(ii) The other comparatives are regular: *aussi mauvais, moins mauvais.*

5.1.1.3 *petit*

(i) The comparative of superiority of *petit* (small) is:

– **plus petit** when used in a concrete sense (i.e. smaller size).

> Ex: *Marie est **plus petite que** Catherine.*
> Marie is shorter than Catherine.

– **moindre** in an abstract sense (i.e. less important).

> Ex: *Maintenant qu'ils ne se voient plus, leur hostilité est **moindre**.*
> Now that they have stopped seeing each other, their hostility has lessened.

Note that *moindre* is seldom used in informal French, when an alternative such as *moins important* would be preferred.

(ii) The other comparatives are regular: *aussi petit, moins petit.*

5.1.2 Adverbs

beaucoup	→	*plus*, *davantage*	*peu* →	*moins*
		autant		*autant*
		moins		*plus*, *davantage*
bien	→	*mieux*	*mal* →	*plus mal*, *pis*, *pire*
		aussi bien		*aussi mal*
		moins bien		*moins mal*

5.1.2.1 *beaucoup* AND *peu*

Note that *beaucoup* and *peu* are opposites.

(i) Superiority and inferiority

– *beaucoup* (much, many, a lot) has as its comparative ***plus/davantage*** (**more**).

> Ex: *Nous avons beaucoup de temps libre.*
> We get a lot of free time.
>
> → *Nous avons **plus/davantage de** temps libre **que** vous.*
> → We get more free time than you do.

– *peu* (little, few) has as its comparative ***moins*** (**less, fewer**).

> Ex: *Nous avons peu de temps libre.*
> We get little free time.
>
> → *Nous avons **moins de** temps libre **que** vous.*
> → We get less free time than you do.

(ii) Equality: ***autant*** (**as many, as much**)

> Ex: *Nous avons sans doute **autant de** temps libre **que** vous.*
> We probably get as much free time as you do.

5.1.2.2 *bien*

(i) Superiority

The comparative of *bien* (well) is ***mieux*** (**better**).

> Ex: *Le professeur X s'explique bien.*
> Professor X explains himself well.
>
> → *Le professeur X s'explique **mieux que** le professeur Y.*
> → Professor X explains himself better than Professor Y.
>
> → ***Mieux** encore, il distribue des polycopiés.*
> → Better still, he hands out notes.

(ii) The other comparatives are regular: *aussi bien*; *moins bien*

(iii) **as well as**

> Ex: *Ma tondeuse marche **aussi bien que** la tienne!*
> My lawnmower works as well as yours!

Note that 'as well as' can also express:

− simultaneity ('as well as' = 'while')
(See also gerunds in chapter 16 Present Participle, section 3.3.3.)

> Ex: **As well as** being one of the most famous artists in his time, he also played a role in the government of his country.
> *Tout en étant l'un des artistes les plus célèbres de son temps, il joua aussi un rôle dans la politique de son pays.*

− alternatives ('as well as' = 'in addition to')

> Ex: Cats also like fish **as well as** meat!
> *En plus de la viande, les chats aiment aussi le poisson!*
>
> Ducks can swim, **as well as** fly.
> *Les canards savent nager, et ils savent aussi voler.*
>
> The exhibition includes drawings and photos, **as well as** watercolours.
> *L'exposition comprend des dessins et des photos, ainsi que des aquarelles.*

5.1.2.3 *mal*

(i) Superiority

The comparative of *mal* (badly) is **plus mal**, **pire** or **pis** (**worse**).

> Ex: *Ça va mal aujourd'hui!*
> Things are going badly today!
>
> → *Ça va encore **plus mal qu'**hier!*
> → It's going even worse than yesterday!
>
> → **Pire encore**, *Philippe s'est trompé de route!*
> → Worse still, Philippe went the wrong way!

Note that **pis** is only used in fixed expressions, such as:
> *aller de mal en pis* to go from bad to worse
> *tant pis/tant mieux* too bad/good for you

and also: *un pis-aller* a stopgap
> *dire pis que pendre de qn* to speak ill of sb

(ii) The other comparatives are regular: *aussi mal; moins mal.*

5.2 Superlatives

5.2.1 Adjectives

The superlatives of adjectives are the same as the corresponding comparatives, plus the article (*le, la, les*) or possessive adjective. They agree in gender and number with the nouns they qualify. Superlatives of inferiority are regular.

bon	→	*le meilleur*
		le moins bon
mauvais	→	*le plus mauvais* or *le pire*
		le moins mauvais
petit	→	*le plus petit* or *le moindre*
		le moins petit

5.2.1.1   *bon*

(i)   Superiority

The superlative of *bon* is **le meilleur (the best)**.
>   Ex: *Le chien est **le meilleur** ami de l'homme.*
>   The dog is man's best friend.

(ii)   Inferiority: *le moins bon.*

5.2.1.2   *mauvais*

(i)   Superiority

mauvais has two superlatives: **le plus mauvais** and **le pire (the worst)**; *le plus mauvais* tends to mean *le moins bon* (i.e. sth/sb has got to be last), whereas **le pire** means it is definitely extremely bad.
>   Ex: *C'est Marie qui a obtenu **la plus mauvaise** note.*
>   It was Marie who got the worst mark.
>
>   *C'est **le plus mauvais/le pire** restaurant de Londres.*
>   It is the worst restaurant in London.

(ii)   Inferiority: *le moins mauvais.*

5.2.1.3   *petit*

(i)   Superiority

petit has two superlatives: **le plus petit (the smallest)** and **le moindre (the least, the slightest, the smallest)**; *le moindre* applies to things less physical and occurs mainly in fixed expressions.
>   Ex: *C'est **la plus petite** voiture qui ait jamais été construite.*
>   It is the smallest car that was ever built.
>   but:
>   *C'est là **son moindre défaut**.*
>   That is the least of his/her faults.
>
>   *Nous avons tout prévu dans **les moindres détails**.*
>   We have planned everything in the smallest detail.
>
>   *Vous me demandez ce que je vais faire maintenant? Je n'en ai pas **la moindre idée**.*
>   You're asking me what I am going to do next? I haven't the slightest idea.
>
>   *Entre deux maux, il faut choisir **le moindre**.* (proverb)
>   One must choose the lesser of two evils.

(Note that French uses the superlative, whether only two or more items are being compared: see section 4.1(vi) above.)

(ii)   Inferiority: *le moins petit.*

5.2.2 Adverbs

The superlatives of adverbs are the same as the corresponding comparatives, plus *le*.

beaucoup →	*le plus*	*peu* →	*le moins*
	le moins		*le plus*
bien →	*le mieux*	*mal* →	*le plus mal, le pis, le pire*
	le moins bien		*le moins mal*

5.2.2.1   *beaucoup* AND *peu*

Superiority and inferiority:

Ex: *Je travaille beaucoup.*
→ *C'est le soir que je travaille le plus.*
→ It's in the evening that I work most.

Je travaille peu.
→ *C'est le soir que je travaille le moins.*
→ It's in the evening that I work least.

Le soir, j'ai beaucoup de temps.
→ *C'est le soir que j'ai le plus de temps.*
→ It's in the evening that I have the most time.

Le soir, j'ai peu de temps.
→ *C'est le soir que j'ai le moins de temps.*
→ It's in the evening that I have the least time.

5.2.2.2   *bien*

(i)   Superiority

Ex: *C'est le soir que je travaille le mieux.*
It's in the evening that I work best.

Note the following expressions with ***mieux***:

− *faire de son mieux*
Ex: *Ne le bousculez pas, il fait de son mieux!*
Don't rush him, he's doing his best!

− *ce que l'on a/ce qu'il y a de mieux*
Ex: *On nous a servi ce qu'il y avait de mieux.*
We were given the best there was.

− *valoir mieux = être préférable [de]*
Ex: *Il vaut mieux faire tout soi-même.*
or:
Il est préférable de faire tout soi-même.
It is better/best to do everything oneself.

− *au mieux*: at best; *au pire*: at worst
Ex: *Au mieux, il n'obtiendra pas plus de cent voix.*
At best, he won't get more than a hundred votes.

(ii)   Inferiority: *le moins bien.*

5.2.2.3   *mal*

(i)   Superiority

> Ex: **Le pire**, *c'est que j'ai oublié mes lunettes.*
> The worst thing is that I have forgotten my glasses.

(ii)   Inferiority: *le moins mal.*

5.3   Expressions with irregular adjectives or adverbs

(i)   **Adjectives**

In idioms involving *bon/mauvais*, the comparative and superlative operate as described in 5.1 and 5.2 above, but with the **regular inferiority** form. For instance:

— *sentir bon/mauvais*

> *Ce parfum-ci sent* **bon**; *celui-là sent* **meilleur**; *c'est le tien qui sent* **le meilleur**.
> This perfume smells nice; that one smells better; it's yours that smells best.

> *Cet évier sent* **mauvais**; *il sent encore* **plus mauvais** *qu'hier; mais ce sont les égoûts qui sentent* **le plus mauvais**!
> This sink stinks; it stinks even more than yesterday; but it's the sewers that smell worst!

NB: *bon* and *mauvais* are invariable after *sentir* (treated as adverbs).

— *avoir bon caractère/mauvais caractère*

> *Il a* **meilleur** / **plus mauvais** / **moins bon** *caractère que son frère.*
> He's got a better temperament than / worse temperament than / his temperament is not as good as his brother's.

> *C'est Françoise qui a* **le meilleur** *caractère; c'est Catherine qui a* **le plus mauvais** *caractère.*
> It's Françoise who is the best-tempered; it's Catherine who is the worst-tempered.

NB: *bon* and *mauvais* agree with '*caractère*', therefore remain masculine singular.

— *être de bonne humeur/de mauvaise humeur*

> *Je ne suis pas de* **bonne** *humeur aujourd'hui; j'étais de* **meilleure** *humeur hier.*
> I'm not in a good mood today; I was in a better mood yesterday.

> *Robert est de* **mauvaise** *humeur; il était d'encore* **plus mauvaise** *humeur hier.*
> Robert's in a bad mood; he was in an even worse mood yesterday.

NB: *bonne* and *mauvaise* agree with '*humeur*', therefore remain feminine singular.

– *être bon/mauvais en* (academic subject)

> Ex: *Catherine est **bonne** en maths mais elle est **meilleure** en français.*
> Catherine is good at maths but she is better at French.

> *Nicolas est **moins mauvais** en anglais qu'en allemand.*
> Nicolas is not as bad at English as at German.

> *C'est Eric **le plus mauvais** en anglais.*
> Eric is the worst at English.

NB: *bon* and *mauvais* agree with the subject of *être*.

– *bon marché* (note that there is no ★*mauvais marché*!)

> Ex: *J'ai trouvé des chaussures **bon marché** dans les soldes.*
> I found cheap shoes in the sales.

> → *J'ai trouvé des chaussures **meilleur marché**.*
> → I found cheaper shoes.

> → *X est **moins bon marché** que Y.*
> → X is less good value than Y.

> → *On trouve les articles **les meilleur marché** aux Puces.*
> → The cheapest articles can be found at the Flea Market.

NB: '*bon*' agrees with '*marché*' and therefore remains masculine singular.

Exceptions regarding the superiority form:
– *avoir bon cœur*

> Ex: *Frédéric a **plus bon cœur** que son frère.*
> Frédéric's more kind-hearted than his brother.

> *C'est lui qui a **le plus bon cœur** de toute la famille.*
> He's the most kind-hearted of all the family.

Note that in both cases, the '*s*' of *plus* is pronounced: [plys].

– *de bonne heure*
de bonne heure is equivalent to *tôt* and its comparatives are based on *tôt* (do not say ★*de meilleure heure*!).

> Ex: *Hier, je suis partie de chez moi **de bonne heure**.*
> Yesterday, I left home early (lit. 'in good time').

> → *Ce matin, je suis partie de chez moi encore **plus tôt**.*
> → This morning, I left home even earlier.

> → *Il est parti **moins tôt** hier.*
> → He didn't leave as early yesterday.

NB: *de plus bonne heure/de moins bonne heure* can also be used, but are rarer.

(ii)   **Adverbs**

The **regular inferiority** form is also used with adverbs.

– *être bien informé/mal informé*

> Ex: *Nous étions **mieux informés** quand Mme Durand était responsable.*
> We were better informed when Mme Durand was in charge.
>
> *J'estime que nous sommes **moins bien informés** qu'avant.*
> I think that we are worse informed than before.

– *se sentir bien/se sentir mal*

> Ex: *Je me sens **mieux**; je me sens **plus mal**.* (or: ***moins bien***)
> I am feeling better; I am feeling worse. (or: less well)
>
> *C'est là que je me suis sentie **le mieux**; c'est là que je me suis sentie **le plus mal**.*
> It was there that I felt best; it was there that I felt worst.

Exception regarding the superiority form:
– *faire mal à qn*

> Ex: *Ce qui me fait **le plus mal**, c'est que vous ne m'ayez rien dit.*
> What hurts me most is that you didn't tell me anything.

31 Personal pronouns

1 Introduction

Despite their name, personal pronouns do not always stand for persons. Indeed only the 1st and 2nd person pronouns do: they stand for the two persons of the discourse. The 3rd person pronoun can stand for a person outside the discourse situation, or indeed an animal, a thing, a concept, etc. Syntactically, the 3rd person pronoun can replace a noun, an adjective or even a whole clause.

1.1 The 1st and 2nd persons

The 1st and 2nd persons singular are **deictic** personal pronouns (*pronoms personnels déictiques*). They designate:
– who is talking
– who is being talked to
i.e. the actants of the communication: *je* and *tu*. In other words, they designate in turn the speaker and his/her interlocutor.

> Ex: *Paul:* **Je** *sais que* **tu** *n'étais pas chez* **toi** *hier.*
> *Marie:* **Je** *t'assure que* **tu te** *trompes!*

Indeed, *je* and *tu* can only be identified in the discourse situation. They behave like provisional proper nouns which are interchangeable in that the person who says *je* as the speaker will be adressed as *tu* when his/her interlocutor speaks to address him/her.

In a written text, the reader can identify the referent of the pronoun *je* from the context. However, *je* is still not a representative pronoun. In a question, a statement or a monologue, *je* designates its referent directly, i.e. the person who speaks here and now 'before us'.

> Ex: *'Le directeur m'a encore parlé. Mais je ne l'écoutais presque plus. Puis il m'a dit: "***Je*** suppose que vous voulez voir votre mère."'*

Albert Camus, L'étranger

'*je*' cannot be replaced by '*le directeur*'. We have to imagine him saying '*je*'.

Note that *nous* and *vous* are extensions of *je* and *tu*, rather than their 'plural' (see 2.1.2(iii) and (iv) below).

1.2   The 3rd person

The pronouns of the 3rd person are **anaphoric** personal pronouns (*pronoms personnels anaphoriques*). They designate who or what is being talked about.

> Ex: *Regarde!* ***Le chat*** *entre dans la cuisine. Maintenant,* ***il*** *va boire son lait.*

The anaphoric representation of '*le chat*' by '*il*' identifies the referent of '*il*'. These pronouns are essentially **representative** (*pronoms représentatifs*).

Even if that person is physically present, he/she does not participate in the discourse. Since he/she is absent in this way, the 3rd person is known as the '**non-person**', i.e. one which is 'away from the discourse situation'. The referent of a 3rd person pronoun is generally to be found in the linguistic context – whether written or spoken.

However, in dialogue, the 3rd person pronoun can also be identified in the situation.

> Ex: *Marie: 'Tout le monde a terminé sauf* ***elle!***' *(en montrant du doigt Catherine).*

1.3   Tonic and clitic personal pronouns

(i)   Clitic (unstressed or joint) personal pronouns (*pronoms conjoints* or *clitiques*) can be the subjects or objects of the verb. They stand near the verb (hence the term 'joint') and are not emphasized (hence the term 'unstressed').

> Ex: ***Je*** *vais en ville.*
> *Paul* ***le*** *sait.*
> *Nous* ***lui*** *avons téléphoné.*

(ii)   Tonic (stressed or disjoint) personal pronouns (*pronoms disjoints* or *toniques*) can be the subjects or objects of a verb.

– They replace an indirect object, preceded by a preposition, when the clitic pronoun is not possible. Compare:

> *Nous* ***leur*** *parlons souvent.*
> We often talk to them.
>   and:
> *Nous pensons souvent* ***à eux***.
> We often think about them.

– When used for emphasis (hence the term 'stressed'), they are used in conjunction with the clitic pronoun but separated from the verb by a comma in written French or a pause in spoken French (hence the term 'disjoint').

> Ex: *Je* ***te*** *connais,* ***toi!***
> I know what **you**'re like!
>
> *Je te connais,* ***moi!***
> **I** know you!

2   Clitic pronouns

They can be a subject or an object.

2.1   Personal clitic pronoun as subject

2.1.1   Forms

1st person singular	*je* (*j'*)	1st person plural	***nous***
2nd person singular	***tu***	2nd person plural	***vous***
3rd person singular	***il/elle/on***	3rd person plural	***ils/elles***

NB: *je* becomes *j'* before a vowel or a mute '*h*'.
　　Ex: ***j'arrive***; ***j'hésite***

2.1.2   Use

(i)   ***il, elle, ils, elles***

– The 3rd person pronouns can refer to animates or inanimates.
　　Ex: ***Elle*** (***Catherine***) *vient d'arriver.*　　(she)
　　　　Ils (***les chats***) *boivent leur lait.*　　(they)
　　　　Il (***le sac***) *est sur la table.*　　(it)

– *il* replaces a masculine noun and *elle* a feminine noun: *elle* should always be used to replace a feminine noun (even if the noun refers to a male, or a group of males or females).
　　Ex: *Trois* ***personnes*** *viennent d'arriver:* ***elles*** *peuvent attendre.*
　　　　Three people have just arrived – they can wait.

　　　　Où est ***la sentinelle?*** ***Elle*** *vient d'arriver à son poste.*
　　　　Where is the sentry? He's just arrived at his post.

NB: Although it is grammatically correct, it looks and sounds awkward to refer **repetitively** to a man as *elle*, and this practice should be avoided. Hence *la sentinelle* for instance can be referred to later as *l'homme* or *le soldat*, then *il*.

– Collective nouns that are singular are replaced by *il* or *elle* (unlike in English).
　　Ex: *Paul a invité* ***sa famille*** *pour Noël:* ***elle*** *arrive dimanche.*
　　　　Paul has invited his family for Christmas; they're arriving on Sunday.

　　　　Quelqu'un a appelé ***la police.*** ***Elle*** *est arrivée quelques minutes plus tard.*
　　　　Someone called the police. They arrived a few minutes later.

NB: Although it is grammatically correct, it looks and sounds awkward to refer **repetitively** to a group of people as *il* or *elle* singular, and this should be avoided. Hence *la police* for instance can be referred to later on as *les policiers*, then *ils*.

– Impersonal *il* is used with impersonal verbs and other verbs in the impersonal voice. It is possible for *il* **personal** and *il* **impersonal** to appear in the same sentence, but note that *il* impersonal is always singular (see chapter 19 Impersonal Verbs).

>Ex: ***Ils*** *savent qu'**il** leur manque la liberté.*
>personal   impersonal
>They know that they lack freedom.

(ii) ***on***

– *on* is a so-called indefinite personal pronoun. It is only used as a **subject** and its referent is always human (see also chapters 18 Active and Passive Voices, section 5.2 and 36 Indefinite Words, section 2.2).

– *l'* should be added before ***on*** for euphonic reasons (avoiding a hiatus for instance) in formal French.

>Ex: *Si **l'on** se réfère à ce qui précède . . .*
>If you refer to what comes before . . .
>
>*Les plages où **l'on** peut se baigner.*
>The beaches where you can swim.

– *on* can be substituted for the pronouns of all three persons.
  – *je*, i.e. authorial *on* (for modesty/academic detachment):
  >Ex: *Dans cet article, **on** a voulu démontrer que . . .*
  >In this article, we have endeavoured to demonstrate that . . .
  >This article has endeavoured to demonstrate that . . .

  – *tu*, i.e. hypocoristic *on* when adressing young children or babies (animates who are not expected to take part in the discourse):
  >Ex: *Comme **on** est mignon, comme ça, avec son bonnet rose . . .*
  >Oh isn't he sweet – with his pink hat on . . .
  >Oh what a sweetie he is with his pink hat . . .

  – *il/elle*, i.e. *on* avoids designating the subject too precisely, for instance because it is not known:
  >Ex: ***On*** *m'a volé mon portefeuille!*
  >(*on* = *quelqu'un*)
  >Someone's stolen my wallet!
  >I've had my wallet stolen!

  – *nous*, i.e. *on* = *nous, y compris moi-même*:
  >Ex: ***On*** *aurait dû y aller plus tôt.*
  >We should have gone there earlier.
  >
  >*Et si **on** allait prendre un verre?*
  >How about going for a drink?

Note that *on* and *nous* are frequently used in the same sentence.
>Ex: ***Nous, on*** *sait ce qu'**on** a à faire.*

This should be avoided in formal French.

– *vous*, i.e. *on* is either used in a kind of hypocoristic sense (see *tu* above) or to avoid designating the subject directly, because it may be imprudent or disrespectful to do so:

> Ex: *Les élèves au professeur à l'annonce d'une interrogation écrite:* '**On** *ne nous avait pas prévenus!*'
>
> = '**Vous** *ne nous aviez pas prévenus!*'

> The pupils say to the teacher when he/she announces that there is going to be a written test: 'We weren't told about that!/No one told us about that!'
>
> = '**You** didn't tell us anything about that!'

– *ils/elles* (see *il/elle* above):

> Ex: **On** *est en train de refaire la toiture chez les Dupont.*
>
> **They** are redoing the roof at the Duponts'.

NB(1): After *on*, the verb is always in the 3rd person singular. However, past participles, predicative adjectives, possessive adjectives, etc. often agree with the gender and number of what *on* represents. This is frowned upon in formal written French.

> Ex: **Catherine et moi, on** *est parti**es** vers six heures.*
>
> → *Catherine et moi, nous sommes parties . . .*

> **Paul et moi, on** *était bien content**s** de pouvoir vendre* **notre** *maison si vite!*
>
> → *Paul et moi, nous étions bien contents . . .*

NB(2): Since *on* does not have an object form, the pronouns *nous* or *vous* are often used as object representations in informal French in a sentence where *on* is the subject. This practice is not acceptable in formal French.

> Ex: **On** *fait ce qu'**on** peut et ils viennent encore* **vous** *critiquer.*
>
> You do what you can and they still go and criticize you.
>
> → *Vous faites ce que vous pouvez . . .*

> **On** *a essayé de partir sans faire de bruit mais la gardienne* **nous** *a vus et* **nous** *a interpellés.*
>
> We tried to leave without making any noise but the caretaker saw us and called out to us.
>
> → *Nous avons essayé de partir . . .*

(iii) **tu and vous**

– **vous** is the 2nd person plural; it normally represents **tu** + other people.

> Ex: *Lui/elle et toi,*
> *Toi et toi,* } **vous** *partirez demain.*
> *Eux/elles et toi,*

– **vous** can also be second person singular. It is the '*vous de politesse*', which indicates neutrality, distance or formality, while **tu** is the more familiar form. Note that the verb is then 2nd person **plural**, but participles and adjectives are **singular** if the referent of *vous* is.

> Ex: **Vous êtes** *bien gentille de m'aider, Madame Dupont.*

– The use of *tu* vs *vous* is linked mainly to sociological factors (intimacy, lack of formality). Hence *tu* is normally used:
  – within a family between parents and children, uncles and nephews, etc. (but is by no means universal)
  – with friends of all ages
  – among young people
  – from an adult to a child.

However, *tu* is also often used between adults in a belligerent situation (e.g. argument between motorists) and by some people, to express their perceived social superiority over other members of society. In these last two cases, *tu* is considered as an insult. **When in doubt**, and in order not to offend, it is wise to say *vous* and wait to be invited to use *tu*. French adults do it too!

– Adjectives and past participles agree in gender and number with the person(s) referred to by *tu* or *vous*.
  Ex: *Tu es beau/belle; vous êtes parti/e/s/es.*

– generic *tu* or *vous*

Its function is to 'personalize' generic statements, by replacing a generic subject (generally *on*) by a *tu* or *vous*. Hence the interlocutor feels more involved in what is being said (informal French only).
  Ex: *Quand **tu** as mangé un gros plat de choucroute, **tu** te sens un peu lourd . . .*
  When you've eaten a massive plate of sauerkraut, you feel a bit bloated . . .

  *Si on lui demande quelque chose, il **vous** répond toujours qu'il n'a pas le temps.*
  If you ask him for something, he always says that he hasn't got time.

(iv) *je* **and** *nous*

– Normally, *nous* represents *je* + other people.
  Ex: *Toi/vous et moi,*
  Lui/elle et moi, } *nous partirons ensemble.*
  Eux/elles et moi,

– *nous* can also be *je* but only in:
  – the 'royal we' (*nous de majesté*) or emphatic *nous*.
    Ex: *Nous, maire de . . . , déclarons la séance ouverte.*
  – the *nous* of modesty or *nous* of authors.
    Ex: *Nous sommes d'accord ici avec Culioli lorsqu'il dit que . . .*
(See also *on* above.)

– Adjectives and past participles agree in gender and number with the person(s) referred to by *je* or *nous*.
  Ex: *Je ne suis pas grand/grande; nous sommes pressé/e/s/es.*

493

2.1.3 Position

(i) The subject pronoun is generally placed **before** the verb.

Ex: *Je reviens de Paris.*
Vous devez partir à cinq heures.
On sera là sans faute!

(ii) The subject pronoun can be placed **after** the verb (called verb–subject pronoun inversion) or after the auxiliary in compound tenses in the following cases:

– interrogative form

Ex: *Depuis quand apprenez-vous le français?*
Since when have you been learning French?

(See chapter 39 Interrogative Structures.)

NB: For euphonic reasons (to avoid a hiatus), a '*t*' must be inserted between two hyphens in the 3rd person singular after the auxiliary *avoir*.

Ex: *Où a-t-elle mis mes affaires?*

– to refer to direct reported speech, either after the quotation, or between two parts of the quotation

Ex: *'Alors, nous sommes partis,' a-t-il expliqué.*
'So we left,' he explained.

'Nous allons maintenant,' dit-il, 'examiner la situation de plus près.'
'We shall now,' he said, 'examine the situation more closely.'

NB: There is no inversion **before** a quotation.

Ex: *Elle a déclaré: 'J'en ai assez!'*
She declared: 'I have had enough!'

(See also chapter 41 Reported Speech, section 2.2.)

– after certain adverbs of opinion, placed at the beginning of the sentence and modifying the verb (for details, see chapter 2 Syntax, section 2.4).

2.2 Personal pronoun as object (direct or indirect)

2.2.1 Forms

(i) The direct object pronouns are: *me, te, nous, vous, le, la, les, en.*

(ii) The indirect object pronouns are: *me, te, nous, vous, lui, leur, y, en.*

(iii) *me* and *te* become *m'* and *t'* before a vowel or a mute '*h*'.

Ex: *Vous m'honorez; il t'entend.*

(iv) *le* and *la* become *l'* before a vowel or a mute '*h*'.

Ex: *L'Angleterre va vite l'habituer au mauvais temps.*
England will soon make him/her used to bad weather.

2.2.2 *Use*

2.2.2.1 *me, te, nous* AND *vous*

(i)   *me, te, nous* and *vous* can be direct **or** indirect objects.

(ii) *me, te, nous, vous,* object pronouns, must be distinguished from *me, te, se, nous, vous, se,* reflexive pronouns of pronominal verbs (see chapter 20 Pronominal Verbs, section 2.1).

> Ex: *Nous **nous** asseyons.* (pronominal)
> *(s'asseoir)*
> > but:
>
> *Vous **nous** avez bien conseillés.* (direct object)
> *(conseiller qn)*
> > and:
>
> *Il **nous** a envoyé un paquet.* (indirect object)
> *(envoyer qch à qn)*

(iii) Unlike in English, clitic object pronouns are placed **before** the verb – hence it is a common mistake to confuse them with the subject.

> Ex: ***Il** nous **surprend**.*
> He surprises us.
> and not: **Il nous surprenons.*

(iv) Particular care should also be exercised with *nous* and *vous* after a relative pronoun. It is essential to establish whether they are the subject or the object of the verb which follows them.

> Ex: *Où est le livre que **vous lisiez** hier?*
> Where is the book you were reading yesterday?
> ('*vous*' is the subject of '*lisiez*')
> > but:
>
> *J'ai trouvé le livre qui **vous manquait**.*
> I found the book you were missing.
> ('*livre*' is the subject of '*manquait*';
> '*vous*' is the indirect object)
> > and:
>
> *C'est un livre qui **vous plaît**?*
> Is this a book you like?
> ('*livre*' is the subject of '*plaît*';
> '*vous*' is the indirect object)

(v)   **The ethical dative** (*datif éthique*)

In informal French, the 1st and 2nd person pronouns are sometimes used as indirect objects to show the speaker's interest in what he/she is saying or doing and to involve his/her interlocutor.

> Ex: *Tu aurais vu le taudis qu'il **m**'a fait dans le salon!*
> *Je **te** lui ai mis un de ces coups de poing dans le nez!*

2.2.2.2 *le, la, les*

(i) *le* (masculine singular), *la* (feminine singular) and *les* (masculine or feminine plural) are direct object pronouns. They refer to animates or inanimates (**it, him, her, them**) and correspond to the subject pronouns *il/elle, ils/elles*.

(ii) They replace noun phrases beginning with a definite article, a possessive or demonstrative adjective, or a proper noun, a demonstrative or possessive pronoun, i.e. something which is specified.

Ex: – *Qui sont **ces gens**? – Je ne **les** connais pas.*
– Who are **these people**? – I don't know **them**.

*Où est **mon sac**? Je **le** cherche partout!*
Where is **my bag**? I've been looking for **it** everywhere!

(iii) The past participle of a compound tense agrees with the direct objects *la* or *les*, since they are always placed before the verb (see 2.2.3 below).

Ex: *Les abricots? Nous **les** avons cueillis.*
*Les cerises? Nous **les** avons cueillies aussi.*
*Françoise? Je **l'**ai connue en 1968.*

(iv) Unlike definite articles (see chapter 23 Articles, section 2.1), *le* and *les* pronouns do not contract with prepositions *à* and *de*.

Ex: *On nous a demandé **de le** mettre ici.*
We were asked to put it here.

*Il s'est mis **à les** trier par ordre alphabétique.*
He started putting them in alphabetical order.

2.2.2.3 *le*

le does not only replace a masculine noun direct object. As a **neutral** pronoun:

(i) *le* can have a whole clause as antecedent, corresponding to an object clause (**it, so, that**).

Ex: *Il est difficile de faire la mayonnaise, je **le** sais.*
(*le = qu'il est difficile de faire la mayonnaise*)
It is difficult to make mayonnaise, I know **that**.

*Vous a-t-il dit la vérité? Je ne **le** crois pas.*
(*le = qu'il vous a/ait dit la vérité*)
Did he tell you the truth? I don't think **so**.

*Il pense que vous ne viendrez pas. En fait, il **le** sait.*
(*le = que vous ne viendrez pas*)
He thinks you won't come. In fact, he knows **it**.

(ii) *le* can refer to an adverbial clause, in which case it is **not** translated in English.

Ex: *Comme je **l'**ai dit, ça n'est pas mon affaire.*
As I said, that's not my business.

*Tu t'expliqueras plus tard, si tu **le** peux.*
You will explain yourself later, if you can.

*Les lois doivent s'appliquer également à tous, comme **le** réclamaient déjà les philosophes du dix-huitième siècle.*
The law must apply equally to everybody, as the eighteenth-century philosophers were already demanding.

NB: In informal French, *le* is often omitted here.

(iii)   *le* can refer to an independent clause, e.g. in a juxtaposition.

Ex: *Les femmes sont **capables de donner naissance**, les hommes ne **le** sont pas.*
Women can give birth, men cannot.

NB: A different pronoun may be needed to refer to **part** of the clause.

Ex: *Les femmes sont capables **de donner naissance**, les hommes n'**en** sont pas capables.*
Women can give birth, men cannot do that.

(iv)   *le* can replace an adjective subject complement, in which case it is not translated in English.

Ex: *Je suis parfois **paresseux**, mais vous, vous **l'**êtes tout le temps!*
I am lazy sometimes, but you are all the time!

– *Elle est très **jolie**! – Oui, elle **l'**est vraiment.*
– She is very pretty! – Yes, she really is.

*La démocratie est égalitaire parce que . . . mais elle ne **l'**est pas parce que . . .*
Democracy is egalitarian because . . . but is inegalitarian because . . .

NB: Conversely, *le* is not present in French where **it** is present in English.
This happens with an adjective complement + infinitive.

Ex: *Je trouve difficile de me concentrer.*
I find **it** difficult to concentrate.

Il a jugé nécessaire de partir.
He deemed **it** necessary to leave.

(v)   *le* can represent an undetermined noun (i.e. without article) when referring to occupations (see chapter 35 *C'est/Il est*, section 6.1.2): the noun is then treated as an adjective.

Ex: *Ils étaient juges, ils ne **le** sont plus.*
They were judges, they no longer are / they aren't any more.

*Elle était institutrice, elle ne **l'**est plus.*
She was a schoolteacher, she isn't any longer.

(vi)   In some idioms, **le** can refer to a whole story or situation.

> Ex: *Il **l'**a très mal pris.*
> He took it very badly.
>
> *Je vous **le** donne en mille!*
> You'll never guess!

(vii)   **le** is optional in comparative clauses after *plus, moins, mieux*, etc. (See chapter 30 Comparatives, section 2.1(iv).)

> Ex: *Il est plus grand que je ne [**le**] croyais.*
> He is taller than I thought.

2.2.2.4   *lui* AND *leur*

(i)   **lui** and **leur** are indirect object pronouns.

(ii)   They can replace **à** + noun (masculine or feminine).

> Ex: *J'ai parlé **à Françoise**/**à ma sœur**.*
> → *Je **lui** ai parlé.* (I spoke to her.)
> *J'ai parlé **à Alain**/**au fils** de Georges.*
> → *Je **lui** ai parlé.* (I spoke to him.)
> *J'ai parlé **à Charles** et **à Françoise**.*
> → *Je **leur** ai parlé.* (I spoke to them.)

Note that with some verbs, only the **tonic** pronoun can be used. (See also 2.2.2.6 *y* and 3.2.3 tonic pronoun objects below.)

> Ex: *Je pense **à mes chats** → Je pense **à eux**.*
> and not **Je leur pense.*

(iii)   Certain indirect transitive verbs in French are direct transitive verbs in English and vice versa. It is therefore important to refer to the French form of the verb in each case, since verbs do not always translate verbatim into English.

> Ex: They obey **their parents**. (direct object – to obey sb)
> but:
> *Ils obéissent **à leurs parents**.* (indirect object – *obéir à qn*)
> hence: *Ils **leur** obéissent.* They obey them.
>
> I'm looking **for my pen**. (indirect object – to look for sth)
> but:
> *Je cherche **mon stylo**.* (direct object – *chercher qch*)
> hence: *Je **le** cherche.* I am looking for it.

Other examples of non-correspondence between English and French:

– English indirect → French direct:

to wait **for** sb/sth	*attendre qn/qch*
to listen **to** sb/sth	*écouter qn/qch*
to look **at** sb/sth	*regarder qn/qch*

– English direct → French indirect:

to telephone sb	*téléphoner **à** qn*
to resemble sb/sth	*ressembler **à** qn/qch*
to need sb/sth	*avoir besoin **de** qn/qch*

2.2.2.5   MORE THAN ONE CLITIC OBJECT PRONOUN

When a verb is preceded by two clitic object pronouns, the 1st and 2nd person pronouns (*me, te, nous, vous*) can only be understood as **indirect** objects.

Ex: *Elle **me** l'a présenté.*
She introduced him **to me.**

Hence it is impossible to have:

Ex: *★Elle me lui a présenté.*

Instead, the tonic pronouns should be used (see section 3 below).

Ex: *Elle m'a présenté(e) **à lui.***
She introduced me **to him**.

NB: *le, la, les*, which are dedicated direct object pronouns, can always appear with the indirect pronouns *lui* and *leur.*

Ex: *Elle la lui présente.*
She introduces her to him/her.

2.2.2.6   *y*

(i)   ***y* as an indirect object pronoun**

In principle, the indirect object pronoun ***y*** is used to represent inanimates only. It replaces ***à*** + noun or ***à*** + clause (particularly after verbs taking ***à*** + object).

Ex: – *Vous ne jouez pas **aux échecs**, n'est-ce pas?*
– You don't play chess, do you?

– *Si, j'**y** joue tous les mardis.*
– Yes, I play every Tuesday.

NB(1): ***y*** can represent an animate when referring to a quality or abstraction of that animate (see also 3.2.3(vii) below), instead of *à lui, à elle, à eux, à elles*. For instance, someone might say to a friend engaged in bungee jumping or some other dangerous sport:

Ex: *Et ta femme, tu **y** penses?*
(In this case, '*ta femme*' is seen as an abstraction, i.e. the fact that the friend is a married man.)

Compare with:

*Et ta femme, tu penses **à elle**?*
(Here, '*ta femme*' is considered literally, as an individual, which would be somewhat incongruous in this context.)

NB(2): Not all verbs can be followed indifferently by *y* or *à lui*, or indeed *leur.* For instance:

Ex: *parler: Je parle à mes amis.* → *Je leur parle.*
→ *★J'y parle.*
→ *?Je parle à eux.*

Note: – *parler* can be reflexive: *se parler*
– subject and object cannot be co-referential: *Il lui parle* (*il* and *lui* are two different people).

Ex: *penser: Je pense à mes amis.* → *J'y pense.*

→ *Je pense à eux.*

→ **Je leur pense.*

Note: − *penser* cannot be reflexive: *se penser

− subject and object can be co-referential: *Il pense à lui* [*-même*] (*il* and *lui* can be the same person).

(ii) **y and agreements**

Since **y** is an **indirect** object, it does not affect the past participle agreement.

Ex: *J'ai reçu **une lettre** et j'**y** ai **répondu** tout de suite.*

I received a letter and I answered it straightaway.

(iii) **y replacing 'à + clause'**

The verb must have the same construction with a noun/pronoun as it has with a clause.

Ex: *Nous avons pensé **à ce que vous avez dit**.*

We have been thinking about what you said.

(*penser à qn/qch*)

→ *Nous **y** avons pensé.*

We have been thinking about it.

but:

*J'apprends **à jouer aux échecs**.*

I am learning to play chess.

(*apprendre qch*)

→ *J'apprends **à y jouer**.*

I am learning to play it.

(not: **J'y apprends*)

hence:

*J'apprends **à faire la cuisine**.*

I am learning to cook.

→ *J'apprends **à la faire**.*

I am learning it.

and:

*Je commence **à jouer aux échecs**.*

I have started to play chess.

(*commencer qch*)

→ *Je commence **à y jouer**.*

I have started to play it.

(iv) **y as an adverbial pronoun**

y can replace a preposition (*à*, *sur*, *sous*, *dans* but not ***de***) + name of place. It is then an adverbial pronoun (or pronominal adverb) of place.

Ex: *Il va **à Paris** pour Noël.*

→ *Il **y** va pour Noël.*

→ He's going there for Christmas.

> *Elle cultive toutes sortes de légumes **dans son jardin**.*
> → *Elle **y** cultive toutes sortes de légumes.*
> → She grows all kinds of vegetables there.

Note that *là* can also be used to emphasize the location, and does not need an antecedent.

> Ex: *Mets ça **là**!*
> Put it there!

(v) ***y* and redundancy**

When ***y*** replaces an adverb or an object, the adverb or object should not appear as well!

> Ex: *＊On ne peut pas y trouver de solution à cette question.*
> → *On ne peut pas trouver de solution **à cette question**.*
> or:
> → *On ne peut pas **y** trouver de solution.*

In informal French however, it is possible to state both for emphasis, provided a pause is marked between the two (shown in writing by a comma).

> Ex: *On ne peut pas **y** trouver de solution, **à cette question**?*
> *Tu **y** es allé, **à Paris**?*

See dislocated constructions in chapter 2 Syntax, section 2.15.5.

(vi) ***y* with verb *aller***

With the future and the conditional of *aller*, ***y*** is omitted for euphonic reasons (to avoid a hiatus).

> Ex: *− Bruno va-t-il au cours aujourd'hui? − Oui, **il y va**.*
> but:
> *− Bruno ira-t-il au cours demain? − Oui, **il ira**.*

(vii) ***y* in idiomatic expressions**

− *y compris*:
> Ex: *Elle a tout nettoyé, **y compris** le placard à balais!*
> She cleaned everything, including the broom cupboard!

− *se faire à qch*:
> Ex: *Evidemment, il pleut toujours en Angleterre mais on **s'y fait**.*
> Of course it rains all the time in England but you get used to it.

− *s'y prendre (bien/mal)*:
> Ex: *Je **m'y suis mal pris**; il faut que je recommence.*
> I didn't go about it the right way; I've got to start again.

− *y aller de l'honneur de*:
> Ex: *Il **y va de l'honneur de** la France!*
> The honour of France is at stake!

− *n'y voir goutte*:
> Ex: *Il n'y a pas de lumière ici: je **n'y vois goutte**!*
> There is no light here, I can't see a thing!

501

— *s'y connaître en*: to be knowledgeable about a certain field.
> Ex: *Je **m'y connais en** mécanique!*
> I know my mechanics!

NB: For more general things, e.g. academic topics, use *être bon en*.
> Ex: *Je **suis bon en** français, **en** mathématiques*, etc.
> I am good at French, at maths, etc.

The following expressions belong to informal French:
> *Ah, j'y suis! = J'ai compris.*   Oh, I get it!

> *Vous y êtes? = Avez-vous compris?*   Do you get it?
> *= Etes-vous prêt?*   Are you there?

> *Allez-y! = Vous pouvez commencer!*   Go ahead/Go on!

> *Allons-y! = Nous sommes prêts!*   Let's go!
> *(à faire qch)*

2.2.2.7   *en*

(i)   ***en* as a direct or indirect object pronoun**

In principle, the direct or indirect object pronoun ***en*** is used to represent inanimates only.

— Indirect object: it replaces the preposition ***de*** (or ***de*** + determiner) + noun after verbs taking ***de*** + object.
> Ex: — *Vous avez besoin de mon livre? — Oui, j'**en** ai besoin.*
> *(avoir besoin **de** qch)*
> — Do you need my book? — Yes, I need it.

> *New York? J'**en** reviens!*
> *(revenir **d'**un endroit)*
> New York? I'm just back from there!

> *Il aime les fleurs et il sait **en** parler.*
> *(parler **de** qch)*
> He loves flowers and he can talk about them.

NB: ***en*** can also stand for an animate when referring to a quality or abstraction of the animate (see also 3.2.3(vi) below and ***y*** above), instead of *de lui, d'elle, d'eux, d'elles*.
> Ex: *Mon mari? Vous trouvez que j'**en** parle trop?*
('*Mon mari*' is seen here as an abstraction, rather than as an individual.)

— Direct object: it replaces a partitive article (***du, de la, de l'***) + noun (equivalent to **some, any**).
> Ex: *Il me reste **de la crème**.*
> I've got some cream left.
> → *Il m'**en** reste.*
> I've got some left.
> → *Vous **en** voulez?*
> Would you like some?

– Direct object: it replaces the indefinite article plural (*des*) + noun.

> Ex: *Il y a **des gens** qui sont sans-gêne.*
> There are some people who are inconsiderate.
> → *Il y **en** a qui sont sans-gêne.*
> There are some who are inconsiderate.
> → *Vous **en** connaissez?*
> Do you know any?

(ii) ***en* and agreements**

It is important to note that even when ***en*** is a **direct** object pronoun, there is **no** past participle agreement.

> Ex: *J'ai trouvé **de beaux verres anciens**: j'**en** ai **acheté** trois.*
> I found some beautiful old glasses; I bought three.

(iii) ***en* and expressions of quantity**

en is used with expressions of quantity (it is a common mistake to forget it):

– which contain ***de*** (*beaucoup de, assez de, peu de, trop de*, etc.). It replaces '***de*** + noun' only, hence *beaucoup, assez*, etc. are kept.

> Ex: *Il y a **beaucoup de pommes** cette année.*
> → *Il y **en** a **beaucoup**.*
> There are a lot of apples this year.
> → There are a lot [of them].
>
> *Reste-t-il **assez de café** pour demain matin?*
> → ***En** reste-t-il **assez** pour demain matin?*
> Is there enough coffee left for tomorrow morning?
> → Is there enough left for tomorrow morning?

– which do not contain ***de***, e.g. numbers (*un, deux*, etc.) and indefinite determiners indicating a quantity (*plusieurs, aucun*, etc.) in which case, *un, deux, plusieurs*, etc. are kept.

> Ex: *J'ai **une** voiture.* → *J'**en** ai **une**.*
> I've got a car. → I've got one.
>
> *J'ai **plusieurs** chats.* → *J'**en** ai **plusieurs**.*
> I've got several cats. → I've got several [of them].

Note that '*une*' in *J'en ai une*, and '*plusieurs*' in *J'en ai plusieurs* are the **pronoun** forms. Hence:

> Ex: *J'ai lu **quelques** romans de Balzac.* → *J'**en** ai lu **quelques-uns**.*

NB(1): When the quantified noun is accompanied by an adjective, *en* can replace the noun while the adjective is kept; *en* here means 'one' or 'ones'.

> Ex: *J'ai deux chats **noirs**.* → *J'**en** ai deux **noirs**.*
> I've got two black cats. → I've got two black ones.
>
> *Il y a beaucoup de très **beaux** arbres dans ce parc.*
> There are many beautiful trees in this parc.
> → *Il y **en** a beaucoup de très **beaux**.*
> → There are many beautiful ones.

NB(2): If the sentence is negative, *un* disappears. In this case, *en* means 'any'.

Ex: *Avez-vous une cigarette?*

→ *Oui, j'en ai **une**/il m'en reste **une**.*

Yes, I've got one/I've got one left.

but:

→ *Non, je n'en ai pas/il ne m'en reste pas.*

No, I haven't got any/I haven't got any left.

However, if 'not a single one' is meant, **un(e)** is kept, to which **seul(e)** may be added.

Ex: → *Non, il ne m'en reste pas **une** [**seule**].*

No, I haven't got [a single] one left.

(iv) ***en* replacing '*de* + clause'**

en can replace '***de*** + clause' if the verb has the same construction with a noun or pronoun.

Ex: *J'ai besoin **de boire quelque chose**.*

*(avoir besoin **de** qch)*

→ *J'**en** ai besoin.*

I need a drink.

→ I need one.

*Il s'est rendu compte **de ce qu'il avait dit**.*

*(se rendre compte **de** qch)*

→ *Il s'**en** est rendu compte.*

He realized what he had said.

→ He realized it.

but:

J'ai oublié de laisser mes livres sur votre bureau.

(oublier qch)

→ *J'ai oublié [de le faire].*

(not: **J'en ai oublié.*)

I forgot to leave my books on your desk.

→ I forgot [to do it].

(v) ***en* as an adverbial pronoun**

en can replace '***de*** + name of place'. It is thus an adverbial pronoun (or pronominal adverb) of place.

Ex: *Il arrive **de Londres** à l'instant.*

→ *Il **en** arrive à l'instant.*

He's just come from there.

*Je viens **de chez ma tante**.*

→ *J'**en** viens.*

I've just come from there.

Note that **de là** can also be used to emphasize the location, and does not need an antecedent.

Ex: *Ils habitent à trois kilomètres **de là**.*

They live two miles from there.

504

(vi) **en instead of a possessive**

en (together with the definite article) is used instead of a possessive when the possessor is an inanimate.

Ex: *Cet imperméable vous irait bien mais les manches **en** sont trop longues.*
This raincoat would suit you but the sleeves are too long.

*J'aime beaucoup Paris et j'**en** admire les monuments.*
I love Paris very much and I admire the monuments.
See also chapter 24 Possessive Adjectives, section 5.1.

(vii) **en and redundancy**

When *en* replaces an object or an adverb, the object or adverb should not appear as well.

Ex: *★Il y en a une multitude d'exemples.*
→ *Il y a une multitude **d'exemples**.*
or:
→ *Il y **en** a une multitude.*

In informal French however, it is possible to state both for emphasis, provided a pause is marked between the two (shown in writing by a comma).

Ex: *Il y **en** a une multitude, **des exemples**.*
or, better still:
***Des exemples**, il y **en** a une multitude.*
See dislocated structures in chapter 2 Syntax, section 2.15.5.

(viii) **en in idiomatic expressions**

– *s'en aller*:
Ex: *Je **m'en vais**. A demain!*
I'm off. See you tomorrow!

– *en aller de même pour/avec*:
Ex: *Il **en va de même pour** tout ce qui est politique.*
The same goes for anything political.

– *n'en plus pouvoir*:
Ex: *J'ai corrigé des copies jusqu'à deux heures du matin: je **n'en peux plus**.*
I marked work until 2 o'clock in the morning – I am exhausted.

– *en vouloir à qn*:
Ex: *Elle **m'en veut** parce que je n'ai pas pu l'aider hier.*
She resents me because I couldn't help her yesterday.

– *s'en vouloir de*:
Ex: *Je **m'en veux de** ne pas avoir acheté ce manteau quand il était en solde.*
I regret not buying this coat when it was in the sales.

– *s'en prendre à qn*:
Ex: *Il **s'en est pris à** moi parce que j'étais arrivé en retard.*
He got at me because I was late.

– en venir:

> Ex: *Où voulez-vous **en venir**, avec vos histoires?*
> What are you getting at, with your stories?

*– **Où en étais-je?***

> Where was I?
> (= Which point of my work, speech, etc. had I reached?)

Note that, because *en* is part of the verb, both *en* and *de* + object can appear together.

> Ex: *en avoir assez (**de** qch):*
> *J'en ai assez de tous ces bavardages.*
> I am fed up with this constant chatter.

The following belong to informal French:

> ***Ne vous en faites pas!***
> Don't worry!

> *Si vous ne voulez pas venir, **je m'en fiche.***
> If you don't want to come, I don't give a damn.

> ***Il s'en est tiré** avec seulement une côte de cassée.*
> He came out of it with just a broken rib.

2.2.3 Position

The basic sequence of personal pronouns is observed when they appear in conjunction with a single verb in the declarative form. The order is slightly different if the verb is followed by an infinitive. The place of pronouns in an imperative sentence is treated in chapter 14 Imperative, section 2.2. Section 2.3 below contains a summary of the various positions in which personal pronouns are placed in the sentence.

2.2.3.1 SINGLE VERB

(i) Affirmative form

direct or indirect object		direct object		indirect object				
me (m')		*le (l')*		*lui*				
te (t')	BEFORE	*la (l')*	BEFORE		BEFORE	*y*	BEFORE	*en*
nous		*les*		*leur*				
vous								

The most important thing to note here is that while *me, te, nous* and *vous* come **first** whether they are **direct** or **indirect** objects, *lui* and *leur* are placed **after** all other direct objects, and *y* and *en* come last.

Object pronouns appear in that order:

(ii) **Before the verb in a simple tense**

> Ex: *Le colis? Je **vous** l'envoie demain.*
> ('*vous*' is the indirect object; '*l*'' is the direct object)
> The parcel? I am sending it to you tomorrow.

(iii) **Before the auxiliary in a compound tense**

> Ex: *Je **le lui** ai envoyé hier.*
> ('*le*' is the direct object; '*lui*' is the indirect object)
> I sent it to him/her yesterday.

(iv) **Negative and interrogative forms**

The same order is observed in the negative and interrogative forms. Note the position of *ne* and *pas*: *ne* comes before the object pronouns and *pas* after the verb or auxiliary.

> Ex: *Je **ne vous** l'enverrai **pas** demain.*
> I shall not send it to you tomorrow.

> *Je **ne vous** l'ai **pas** envoyé hier.*
> I did not send it to you yesterday.

In an interrogative form with inversion, the object pronouns come first, followed by the inversion verb–subject pronoun.

> Ex: ***Me** l'enverrez-**vous** demain?*
> Will you send it to me tomorrow?

> ***Le lui** avez-**vous** envoyé hier?*
> Did you send it to him/her yesterday?

2.2.3.2 VERB + INFINITIVE

The object pronouns usually appear in the same order as in 2.2.3.1 above but **before** the infinitive of which they are the objects.

(i) **Affirmative form**

> Ex: *Je vais **vous en donner**.*
> I'm going to give you some.

(ii) **Negative and interrogative forms**

The same order is observed.

> Ex: *Elle ne voulait pas **les y envoyer**.*
> She did not want to send them there.

> *Etiez-vous donc si heureux de **le leur vendre**?*
> Were you really as happy as all that to sell it to them?

NB: If the negation bears on the infinitive, *ne pas* comes first followed by the object pronouns and the infinitive.

> Ex: *Nous étions si heureux de **ne pas les voir**!*
> We were so happy not to see them!

2.2.3.3 *laisser, faire* OR VERB OF PERCEPTION + INFINITIVE

When an infinitive depends on *faire* or *laisser* or on a verb of perception, e.g. *entendre, sentir, voir, regarder,* or *envoyer* (see chapter 15 Infinitive, section 3.1.3.1), the personal pronoun object of the conjugated verb (and subject of the infinitive) comes **before** the conjugated verb or before the auxiliary in compound tenses (and not before the infinitive).

(i) **Affirmative form**

> Ex: *Elle **les** laisse **jouer** sur la route.*
> She lets them play in the road.
>
> *Je l'ai vu **courir** vers la gare.*
> I saw him running towards the station.
>
> *Je **lui** ai fait **ranger** sa chambre.*
> I made him/her tidy up his/her room.

(ii) **With two pronouns**

The infinitive has a subject and a direct object. Consider the following example:
> *Elle laisse **ses élèves** écouter **la radio** [pendant la récréation].*
> She lets her pupils listen to the radio [during break].

There are two possibilities:
– the two pronouns are placed before the main verb, and the subject of the infinitive becomes an indirect object.
> *Elle **la leur** laisse écouter.*
> She lets them listen to it.

– the pronouns come before the verb of which they are the object. Hence there is a direct object pronoun before each verb. This is the simplest and most common case.
> *Elle **les** laisse **l'écouter.***
> She lets them listen to it.

Note that the accumulation of pronouns is not particularly elegant. Hence, with only one of the pronouns:
> *Elle **les** laisse écouter **la radio**.*
> or:
> *Elle laisse **ses élèves** **l'écouter**.*

(iii) **Negative and interrogative forms**

The same order is observed.
> Ex: *Elle ne **les** laisse pas **jouer** sur la route.*
> She doesn't let them play on the road.
>
> ***Lui** avez-vous fait **ranger** sa chambre?*
> Did you make him/her tidy up his/her room?
>
> ***La lui** avez-vous fait **ranger**?*
> Did you make him/her tidy it up?

2.3 Summary of order for clitic object pronouns

The word order is from left to right, making appropriate selections from each column as needed.

2.3.1 *Single verb, declarative*

subject	reflexive pronoun	direct/ indirect object	direct object	indirect object	*y*	*en*	(auxiliary) verb	(past participle)
	ne							*pas*
je	*me*	*me*	*le*	*lui*				
tu	*te*	*te*	*la*	*leur*				
il/elle	*se*	*nous*	*les*					
nous	*nous*	*vous*						
vous	*vous*							
ils/elles	*se*							

2.3.2 *Verb + infinitive*

subject	*(ne)*	reflexive pronoun	(auxiliary) verb	*(pas)*	(past participle)	object pronouns (same order as for declarative)	infinitive

2.3.3 laisser/faire *or verb of perception + infinitive*

subject	*(ne)*	reflexive pronoun	object pronouns (same order as declarative)	(auxiliary) *laisser/faire* verb of perception	*(pas)*	(past participle)	infinitive

3 Tonic pronouns

They normally refer to animates only (but see 3.2.3(vi), (vii) and (ix) below, and also *y* and *en* above).

509

3.1   Forms

1st person singular	*moi*
2nd person singular	*toi*
3rd person singular	*lui, elle, soi*
1st person plural	*nous*
2nd person plural	*vous*
3rd person plural	*eux, elles*

(i)   Note that *nous, vous, elle* and *elles* are the same as the clitic pronouns.

(ii)   *soi* or *lui/elle?*

   – *soi,* either on its own or reinforced by *même,* generally refers to an indefinite and singular subject pronoun only, such as *on, chacun, aucun, nul, tout* or impersonal *il.*

   Ex: **On** *n'est jamais aussi bien que chez* **soi.**
   There's no place like home.

   Il *faut avoir confiance en* **soi.**
   One must believe in oneself.

   Chacun *travaille pour* **soi.**
   Everybody works for himself.

   – With a determined subject, **lui, elle, eux** or **elles** are normally used.

   Ex: *Dans cette affaire,* **Michel** *a eu contre* **lui** *tous ses collègues.*
   In this matter, Michel had all his colleagues against him.

   Les gens *rentrent chez* **eux.**
   People are going home.

3.2   Use and position

Tonic pronouns can be a subject, a subject complement or an object. They are normally used with animates only. There is no corresponding form for inanimates, hence the use of tonic pronouns is left to the discretion of the speaker.

   Ex: '. . . *lorsque je suis allongé, je vois* **le ciel** *et je ne vois que* **lui.**'

   Albert Camus, *L'étranger*

3.2.1   Subject

The tonic personal pronoun (*moi, toi, lui, elle, soi, nous, vous, eux, elles*) is used as a subject in the following cases:

(i)   For emphasis (hyphenated to the tonic pronoun and in conjunction with the clitic pronoun or a noun subject)

– with *même*:

moi-même	*nous-mêmes*
toi-même	*vous-même(s)*
lui-même, elle-même, soi-même	*eux-mêmes, elles-mêmes*

Ex: ***J'y vais moi-même.***
I am going there myself.

***Yves** fait tout **lui-même**!*
Yves does everything himself.

NB: Use *soi-même* with *on, chacun, tout, aucun, nul* and impersonal *il*.
Ex: ***Il** faut toujours tout faire **soi-même**.*
You always have to do everything yourself.

– with *seul*:
Ex: ***Moi seule** peux vous aider.*
Only **I** can help you.
Compare with the plain:
***Je** peux vous aider.*
I can help you.

– as 'real'/'semantic' subject with impersonal *il* (e.g. with *ne . . . que*):
Ex: ***Il** n'y eut que **lui** de cet avis.*
Only **he** was of that opinion.
Compare with:
***Il** fut le seul de cet avis.*
He was the only one of that opinion.

– in apposition:
Note that the following belong to informal French (see also dislocated
constructions in chapter 2 Syntax, section 2.15.5).
Ex: *Et **lui** là, qu'est-ce qu'**il** peut faire?*
And him over there, what can he do?

***Vous**, qu'est-ce que cela peut **vous** faire?*
What's it to **you** anyway?

– when the subject pronoun:

(a) is opposed to another subject
Compare:
***Ils** le savaient. **Il** ne le savait pas.*
They knew about it. He didn't know about it.
and:
***Eux** le savaient; **lui** pas.*
They knew about it; **he** didn't.

***Vous, vous** pouvez partir, mais **eux, ils** doivent rester.*
You can go but **they** must stay behind.

or (b) reinforces it

Ex: *Je le sais, **moi**.*
I know about it.

Note that ***moi*** and ***toi*** in apposition **must** be accompanied by the clitic pronoun.

Ex: *Moi, je dis que . . . ; toi, tu dis que . . .*
It is **optional** with ***lui*** and ***eux***.

Ex: *Lui, il dit que . . . ; eux, ils disent que . . .*
or:
Lui dit que . . . ; eux disent que . . .

(ii) When the subject pronoun is linked to one or several other subjects (e.g. with *et*, *ni . . . ni . . .*)

– with other nouns:

Ex: ***Mon frère et moi** viendrons ce soir.*
My brother and I will be coming tonight.

*Ils ne sont guère aimables, **ni lui ni son père**.*
They are not very friendly, neither he nor his father.

– with other pronouns:

Ex: ***Ni lui ni moi** ne nous attendions à cela.*
Neither he nor I were expecting this.

NB: – If 1st, 2nd and 3rd person pronouns appear together, the verb agrees with the 1st person plural (***nous***).
– If 2nd and 3rd persons appear together, the verb agrees with the 2nd person plural (***vous***).
– The addition of the unstressed subject pronouns ***nous*** and ***vous*** is not compulsory.

Ex: *Elle et moi [,nous] travaillons toujours ensemble.*
She and I always work together.

Catherine et toi [,vous] vous êtes parlé, n'est-ce pas?
You and Catherine spoke to each other, didn't you?

(iii) After *comme* and *que* in comparative statements (see chapter 30 Comparatives).

Ex: *Comme **moi**, il passe ses vacances à Paris.*
Like me, he is spending his holiday in Paris.

*Elle est plus intelligente que **lui**.*
She is more intelligent than he is.

(iv) After an expression of quantity + *d'entre*.

Ex: *Les Dupont s'y sont pris à l'avance: **trois d'entre eux** ont pu obtenir des billets.*
The Duponts got there early – three of them managed to get tickets.

(v)   In clauses where there is ellipsis of the verb (e.g. answers).

> Ex: − *Qui est là?* − **Moi!** − **Nous!**
>   − Who's there? − Me! − Us!
>   (but: *Je suis là!*)
>
>   − *C'est vous qui avez dit ça?* − Non, pas **nous**, **eux**!
>   − Was it you who said that? − No, not us, them!

(vi) With the exclamative or interrogative infinitive, with the narrative infinitive and with the absolute participle.

> Ex: **Moi!** *Y aller toute seule!*
>   Me! Go there on my own!
>
>   *Et **lui** de se remettre au travail.*
>   And so he resumed work.
>
>   **Eux** *partis, nous avons pu enfin respirer!*
>   With their departure, we were able to breathe at last!

3.2.2   *Subject complement with* être

The tonic forms *moi, toi, lui, elle, soi, nous, vous, eux, elles* can be used as subject complements after the verb *être* (particularly after the presentative *c'est*).

> Ex: *'L'Etat, c'est **moi**.'* (Louis XIV; de Gaulle)
>
>   *Je lui ai dit: 'C'est **toi** qui devrais faire le discours.'*
>   I told him/her, 'You are the one who should make the speech.'

NB: **c'est** *nous/vous* but **ce sont** *eux/elles.*
See also chapter 35 *C'est/Il est,* section 7.

3.2.3   *Object*

The tonic forms *moi, toi, soi, elle, nous, vous, eux, elles* are used as objects in the following cases (see also chapter 14 Imperative, section 2.2):

(i)   For emphasis, in apposition, generally after the clause which already contains the clitic object pronoun (see dislocated constructions in chapter 2 Syntax, section 2.15.5).

> Ex: *On **l'estime**, **elle**.*
>   **She** is esteemed.
>
>   **Toi**, *je ne veux plus **te** voir.*
>   I don't want to see **you** again.
>
>   *On **m'obéira**, à **moi**.*
>   **I** will be obeyed.

(ii) To clarify a plural pronoun object.

> Ex: *Je **vous** aime, **toi** et **ton frère**.*
>   I love you, you and your brother.

(iii)   When the object pronoun is linked (e.g. with *et* or *ni . . . ni . . .*) to one or
several other objects of the same type (nouns or pronouns).

> Ex: *Il a prié **Catherine et moi** de bien vouloir le suivre.*
> He asked Catherine and me to follow him.
>
> *Nous n'avons vu **ni eux ni leurs parents** sur le quai.*
> We saw neither them nor their parents on the platform.

(iv)   After *que* in the restricted negation *ne . . . que*. Compare:

> *Il **les** a vus.*
> He saw **them**.
>   and:
> *Il **n'**a vu **qu'eux**.*
> He saw only **them**.

(v)   In clauses where there is ellipsis of the subject and of the verb (e.g. answers).

> Ex: *Qui demande-t-on?* **Toi.**
> Who do they want? You.
> (but: *On **te** demande.*)

(vi)   After verbs which take *de*.

– If the antecedent is an animate, use the tonic pronoun. Otherwise, use *en* (but
see exceptions below).

> Ex: *J'ai besoin **de Paul**.*
> → *J'ai besoin **de lui**.*
>   I need him.
>
> *Que pensent-ils **de moi**?*
> What do they think of me?
> (No need for an antecedent here!)

NB: To avoid possible ambiguity, *même* can be added to *lui, elle, eux, elles* and is
hyphenated.

> Ex: ***La sœur de Marie** parle toujours d'elle-même.*
> Marie's sister always talks about **herself** [as opposed to 'about
> Marie'].

– It is possible to use *en* with an animate. Note that *de lui* and *d'elle* underline
the individuality of the animate concerned. On the contrary, *en* sees the
animate more globally. Hence:

> *Mes chats? C'est vrai que je parle souvent **d'eux**.*
> (they are seen as individuals)
>
> *Mes chats? C'est vrai que j'**en** parle souvent.*
> (they are seen as an abstraction)

See also *y* above.

Conversely, *de lui, d'elle* can be used with an inanimate, if the intention is to give
it a 'human' individuality. This device is often used in advertisements.

> Ex: *'Ma 205, j'ai besoin d'elle!'*

(vii)   After verbs which take **à**.

- If the antecedent is an animate, use the tonic pronoun. Otherwise, use *y* (but see exceptions below).

  Ex: ***Vos enfants**, il faut penser **à eux**!*
  What about your children? Think of them!

- *y* can be used with animates in the same way as **en**.

  Ex: *Mes amies, je pense **à elles**.*
  (they are seen individually)

  but:

  *Mes amies, j'**y** pense.*
  (they are seen globally, as an abstraction)

See also 2.2.2.6 (i) above.

Note that some verbs can only be constructed with the clitic pronoun (see *lui/leur* above).

  Ex: *Je parle à Paul* → *Je **lui** parle.*
  Je parle aux enfants → *Je **leur** parle.*

(viii) After verbs of motion + **à** (e.g. *aller à, courir à, venir à*) where **à** is the equivalent of **vers**.

  Ex: *Dès que j'arrive le soir, mes chat courent **à moi/vers moi**.*
  As soon as I get home in the evening, my cats come running up to me.

(ix)   With other prepositions, if the antecedent is animate.

  Ex: *Je pars en vacances avec Paul.*
  → *Je pars en vacances **avec lui**.*
  I'm going on holiday with him.

Note that there is no alternative if the antecedent is inanimate. Hence:

  J'arrive ce week-end avec mes meubles.
  → *?J'arrive avec eux.*

(x)   Two objects: when the direct object of the verb is one of the pronouns **me, te, nous** or **vous** or one of the reflexive pronouns **me, te, se, nous** or **vous**, then **à** + tonic pronoun must be used for the indirect object (and not one of the clitic indirect object pronouns).

  Ex: *Je vais **vous** présenter **aux autres invités**.*
  I am going to introduce you to the other guests.
  → *Je vais **vous** présenter **à eux**.*
         direct object   indirect object
  and not: *★ Je vais vous leur présenter.*

See 2.2.2.5 above.

(xi)   ***moi*** can be added to an imperative construction to indicate the interest taken in the action by the speaker, or to indicate that the interlocutor is asked to take a special interest in the action (informal French only). See also the *datif éthique* in section 2.2.2.1(v) above.

Ex: *Goûtez-**moi** ce vin-là!*
(instead of the plain: *Goûtez ce vin-là!*)
Just you taste that wine!

*Regardez-**moi** ça!*
(instead of the plain: *Regardez ça!*)
Just look at this!

32 Relative pronouns

1 Introduction

(i) A **relative pronoun** is a pronoun which joins a main clause to a subordinate clause called a relative clause. The pronoun represents a noun or pronoun in the main clause or even the whole of the main clause. The noun, pronoun or clause represented by the relative pronoun is called its **antecedent**.

(ii) Relative pronouns in French can be **simple** (e.g. *qui*, *que*) or **compound** (e.g. *lequel*, *auquel*, *duquel*).

(iii) Difficulties can arise between French and English because of the following differences:

- Some relative pronouns can be omitted altogether in English. This is never the case in French.

- There can be a choice of relative pronouns in English when translating from French.

- Conversely, there can also be a choice of relative pronouns in French when translating from English.

- French relative pronouns have to be selected according to their antecedents in a way which is different from English.

- French relative pronouns whose antecedent is an indirect object are determined by the preposition that follows the verb.

- In more complex sentences, the word order can be different in the two languages, in the main clause as well as in the relative clause.

- Some English relative pronouns (e.g. **when, why**) can also have other functions (conjunctions or interrogative adverbs), in which case they may be translated differently into French.

This chapter examines the function of the relative pronoun in the relative clause. See chapter 2 Syntax, section 3.2.2 for an explanation of the function of the relative clause in the sentence. The indefinite relative pronouns *qui que*, *quoi que* and *quiconque* are examined in chapter 36 Indefinite Words, sections 4.3 and 4.4.

2 Brief description

2.1 Simple relative pronouns

- *qui*, *que*, *quoi*, *dont*, *où* are all simple **relative pronouns**.

- *qui*, *que*, *quoi*, *où* can also be **interrogative pronouns** (see chapter 39 Interrogative Structures, sections 3.1 and 3.5(i)).

- *quoi*, which as a relative pronoun is always preceded by a preposition, behaves in a slightly different way.

- *où* is sometimes referred to as a **relative adverb** (see section 3.7 below).

- As relative pronouns, *qui*, *que*, *quoi*, *dont*, *où* can act as subjects, objects (direct or indirect), complements or adverbs.

- Simple relative pronouns are invariable and the verb agreement in the subordinate clause is normally done with the antecedent.

2.2 Compound relative pronouns

- They are formed by combining the definite article (*le*, *la*, *les*) and the interrogative adjective *quel*.

- They can themselves be combined with *de* or *à* to give:

		+ à	+ de
masculine singular	*lequel*	*auquel*	*duquel*
feminine singular	*laquelle*	*à laquelle*	*de laquelle*
masculine plural	*lesquels*	*auxquels*	*desquels*
feminine plural	*lesquelles*	*auxquelles*	*desquelles*

- They can act as subjects, objects (direct or indirect) or complements.

- They agree in gender and number with their antecedents.

3 Grammatical functions

There may be a choice of relative pronoun in French depending on its function in the relative clause (e.g. subject or object: see chapter 2 Syntax). Hence each function shall be considered in turn to determine the most appropriate pronoun to use in each case.

3.1 Subject

There are two possibilities: the simple pronoun *qui* or one of the compound pronouns.

3.1.1   qui

qui is **always the subject** of the relative clause. It **cannot be elided** (i.e. *qui* remains *qui* before a vowel or a mute '*h*'). It can have three types of antecedents.

(i)   A noun or pronoun

Unlike in English, it is used whether the antecedent is an animate or an inanimate.

> Ex: *La personne **qui** vient d'arriver.*
> The person **who/that** has just arrived.
>
> *Le chat **qui** traverse la rue.*
> The cat **which/that** crosses the road.
>
> *Mon livre, celui **qui** est sur la table.*
> My book, the one **which/that** is on the table.

(ii)   The neutral pronoun *ce* (→ *la chose qui*)

ce is often found at the beginning of the sentence.

> Ex: ***Ce qui** m'ennuie, c'est que je n'ai pas reçu de nouvelles.*
> **What** bothers me is that I have not heard anything.

(iii)   A whole clause

ce is added before *qui* and after a comma.

> Ex: *Je n'ai pas encore reçu de nouvelles, **ce qui** m'ennuie.*
> I have not heard anything yet, **which** bothers me.
>
> *Elle admire beaucoup ce garçon, **ce qui** m'étonne.*
> She admires this chap a lot, **which** surprises me.
>
> *On a le droit de voter, **ce qui** nous donne la possibilité de changer le gouvernement.*
> We have the right to vote, **which** gives us the possibility of changing the government.

3.1.2   lequel, laquelle, lesquels, lesquelles

They can only take a noun or pronoun as antecedent, which can be an animate or an inanimate. There is always a comma immediately before this relative pronoun. They are used instead of *qui* in the following two cases:

(i)   When there is a possible ambiguity with the antecedent (note that the relative is always detached)

> Ex: *C'est la sœur de mon **cousin**, **lequel** est professeur de français, qui me l'a expliqué.*
> (= *le cousin, et non la sœur, est professeur de français*)
>
> *C'est la **sœur** de mon cousin, **laquelle** est professeur de français, qui me l'a expliqué.*
> (= *la sœur, et non le cousin, est professeur de français*)

519

NB: This structure belongs to formal French. In informal French, a demonstrative pronoun could be used instead to avoid the ambiguity.

> Ex: *C'est la sœur de mon **cousin**, **celui qui** est professeur de français, qui me l'a expliqué.*
>
> *C'est la **sœur** de mon cousin, **celle qui** est professeur de français, qui me l'a expliqué.*

(ii) To avoid repeating *qui* in the same sentence

> Ex: *J'ai pris un raccourci à travers champs **qui** m'a fait gagner du temps, mais je suis tombée sur un fermier, **lequel** n'était guère aimable.*
>
> *'Je trouve que la liberté de l'esprit consiste dans un "automatisme" particulier **qui** réduit au plus tôt les idées à leur nature d'idées, ne permet pas qu'elles se confondent avec ce qu'elles représentent, les sépare de leurs valeurs affectives et impulsives, **lesquelles** diminuent ou falsifient leurs possibilités de combinaisons.'*
>
> Paul Valéry

See also section 5 Stylistic Considerations, about the accumulation of relative pronouns.

3.2 Direct object

There are two possibilities: the simple pronoun *que* (becoming *qu'* before a vowel or mute '*h*') or a compound pronoun.

3.2.1 que

It can have three types of antecedents.

(i) A noun or pronoun

- As in English, it is used for animates or inanimates.
- Unlike in English, it **cannot be omitted**.

> Ex: *les gens **que** j'ai invités*
> the people **whom/that/_** I have invited
>
> *Les chats? Ce sont les miens **que** vous avez vus.*
> The cats? They're mine **that/_** you saw.
>
> *les livres **que** j'ai rangés sur les étagères*
> the books **which/that/_** I have put on the shelves

NB: *que* can also be complement of *être*. It functions like a direct object.

> Ex: *Je ne suis plus l'homme **que** j'étais.*
> I am not the man **whom/that/_** I used to be.

(ii)   The neutral pronoun *ce* (→ *la chose que*)

ce is often found at the beginning of the sentence.

Ex: **Ce que** *je n'aime pas, c'est le fait qu'il n'a pas écrit.*
What I don't like is the fact that he didn't write.

Ce que *je veux, c'est la paix.*
What I want is peace.

*Je suis **ce que** je suis.*
I am **what** I am.

*Il sait **ce qu'**il fait.*
He knows **what** he's doing.

Also:

*Je perds la mémoire: cela ne fait que cinq minutes qu'il m'a dit la réponse, mais je ne me souviens plus de **ce que** c'était!*
My memory's going – he only told me the answer five minutes ago but I can't remember **what** it was!

(iii) A whole clause

ce is added before *que* and after a comma.

Ex: *Il ne m'a pas écrit, **ce que** je déplore.*
He did not write to me, **which** I deplore.

3.2.2 lequel, laquelle, lesquels, lesquelles

They can be used instead of *que* in similar cases to those described in 3.1.2 to avoid ambiguity or repetition.

Ex: *Ils ont apporté des tas de choses **que** j'ai dû trier, dont des tableaux, **lesquels** personne n'a voulu acheter.*

3.3 Indirect object, introduced by *à*

There are three possibilities: the simple pronouns *qui* or *quoi* preceded by *à*, or one of the compound pronouns.

3.3.1 à qui

Normally, *à qui* can only take human beings as antecedents. However, the antecedent can also be an animal, particularly a pet (considered as human!) or a personified institution (e.g. the government or the republic).

When a relative pronoun is used as a complement of a preposition, the relative pronoun can be omitted in English if the preposition appears after the verb in the subordinate clause. This is not the case in French.

Ex: *La personne **à qui** je parlais est un collègue.*
The person **that** I was talking **to** is a colleague.
The person **to whom** I was talking is a colleague.
The person _ I was talking **to** is a colleague.

*Le gouvernement **à qui** nous avons confié notre destinée nous a bien déçus.*
The government **to whom** we have entrusted our fate has disappointed us deeply.

*Le chat **à qui** j'ai donné un bol de lait ce matin m'a griffée.*
The cat **to whom** I gave a bowl of milk this morning scratched me.

3.3.2 auquel, auxquels, à laquelle, auxquelles

Lequel, etc. can be preceded by *à* to give: ***auquel, auxquels, à laquelle, auxquelles*** and can be used with any antecedent, but *à qui* is more usual for animates.

Ex: *La personne **à laquelle/à qui** je pense n'est pas là.*
The person I'm thinking about isn't here.

*Le chat **auquel/à qui** je parle comprend tout.*
The cat I'm talking to understands everything.

*Où est le livre **auquel** il tient tant?*
Where is the book he cares so much about/about which he cares so much?

3.3.3 à quoi

à quoi can have three types of antecedents.

(i) The neutral pronoun *ce* (→ *la chose à laquelle*)

ce is often found at the beginning of the sentence.

Ex: ***Ce à quoi** ils pensent n'a aucun intérêt pour moi.*
(*penser à qch*)
What they're thinking is of no interest to me.

*Il est arrivé **ce à quoi** je m'attendais.*
(*s'attendre à qch*)
What I expected to happen did happen.

*Je sais **ce à quoi** ressemble une montre!*
(*ressembler à qch*)
I know **what** a watch looks like!

(ii) A whole clause

ce is added before *à quoi* and after a comma.

Ex: *Il a passé son permis de conduire du premier coup, **ce à quoi** il ne s'attendait pas.*
He passed his driving test first time, **which** he wasn't expecting.

(iii) *quelque chose* or *rien*

Ex: *Il n'y a rien **à quoi** je ne sois préparé.*
There is nothing **that/which/_** I am not prepared **for**.
There is nothing **for which** I am not prepared.

*Il y a quelque chose **à quoi** tu n'as pas pensé.*
There is something **that/which/_** you have not thought **of**.
There is something **of which** you have not thought.

*N'y a-t-il rien **à quoi** tu puisses t'occuper?*
Isn't there anything _ you can occupy yourself **with**?

NB(1): In literature, *à quoi* may be found instead of *auquel*, etc., although the antecedent is a noun. This should not be imitated (see also 3.5.3(iv) below).
> Ex: '*C'était <u>une idée</u> **à quoi** je ne pouvais pas me faire.*'

Albert Camus, L'étranger

NB(2): When there is no antecedent (often after *voici, voilà*), **ce** can be added but is not compulsory.
> Ex: *Voilà [**ce**] **à quoi** il passe son temps!*
> (*passer son temps à qch*)
> This is **what** he spends his time on!

3.4   Noun complement or indirect object introduced by *de*

There are three possibilities: **de** + simple pronouns **qui** or **quoi**, the simple pronoun **dont** or one of the compound pronouns.

3.4.1   de qui

de qui can be used for human animates only but is rare. It is used for instance with *tenir **de** qn*.
> Ex: *la grand-mère **de qui** je tiens*
> and not **la grand-mère dont je tiens*
> the grandmother I take after
> > but:
> *la personne **dont** je parle*
> the person I am talking about

See 3.4.2 *dont* below.

For cases when *de qui* **must** be used, see 3.6.

3.4.2   dont

dont is used for any antecedent which is not preceded by a preposition (see 3.6 for other cases).

3.4.2.1   NOUN COMPLEMENT

dont is used as a noun complement whether the antecedent is a human animate (**whose, of whom**), a non-human animate or an inanimate (**whose, of which**). Note that when the 'thing possessed' is a direct object in the relative clause, **whom/which** can be omitted in English and **of** repositioned at the end of the sentence, but it is still **dont** in French!

Ex: *l'homme **dont** je connais le frère*
(= *le frère de l'homme*)
the man _ I know the brother **of**
the man **of whom** I know the brother
the man **whose** brother I know

*le livre **dont** j'ai oublié le titre*
(= *le titre du livre*)
the book _ I have forgotten the title **of**
the book **of which** I have forgotten the title
the book **whose** title I have forgotten

NB(1): If **whose** is used, the direct object is placed immediately after the relative pronoun, giving in English:
direct object (no article) → subject → verb.
In French, the order is always:
subject → verb → direct object (**with** article).

NB(2): If *dont* is used, do not use a possessive adjective as well.
Ex: *Je connais le frère de cet homme.*
= *Je connais son frère.*
→ *l'homme **dont** je connais **le** frère*
and not **l'homme dont je connais son frère*
See also chapter 24 Possessive Adjectives, section 5.2.

3.4.2.2 VERB OR ADJECTIVE + *de*

dont is used for verbs and adjectives followed by *de* (but see also 3.4.1 above). It can have four types of antecedents.

(i) A noun or pronoun

In English, **whom/which/that** can be omitted if the relevant preposition is at the end of the sentence, but is still *dont* in French.
Ex: *la personne **dont** tu parles*
(*parler de qn/qch*)
the person **that**/_ you are talking **about**
the person **about whom** you are talking

*Où est le chat, celui **dont** je m'occupe?*
(*s'occuper de qn/qch*)
Where is the cat, the one **which/that/_** I am looking **after**?

*une voiture **dont** je suis très content*
(*être content de qn/qch*)
a car **which/that/_** I am very pleased **with**
a car **with which** I am very pleased

*la manière **dont** la société est divisée*
and not **la manière dans laquelle . . .*
(*être divisé d'une certaine manière*)
the way **in which** society is divided

NB: If *dont* is used, do not use the personal pronoun corresponding to *de* + noun as well.

> Ex: *Je m'occupe **du** chat.* → *Je m'**en** occupe.*
> *le chat **dont** je m'occupe*
> and not **le chat dont je m'en occupe*

(ii) **quelque chose** or **rien**

> Ex: *Il n'y a <u>rien</u> **dont** je veuille vous parler.*
> There is nothing **which/that/_** I want to talk to you **about**.
> There is nothing **about which** I want to talk to you.
>
> *Il y a <u>quelque chose</u> **dont** je voudrais vous parler.*
> There is something **which/that/_** I want to talk to you **about**.
> There is something **about which** I want to talk to you.

(iii) The neutral pronoun *ce* (→ *la chose dont*)

ce is often found at the beginning of the sentence.

> Ex: ***Ce dont** je voudrais vous parler, c'est de la réunion de cet après-midi.*
> (*parler de qch*)
> **What** I would like to talk to you about is this afternoon's meeting.
>
> *Je leur ai parlé de **ce dont** vous aviez besoin.*
> (*avoir besoin de qch*)
> I spoke to them about **what** you needed.
>
> *C'est exactement **ce dont** ils s'étonnent.*
> (*s'étonner de qch*)
> This is exactly **what** surprises them.

(iv) A whole clause

ce is added before *dont* and after a comma.

> Ex: *Ils ont menti, **ce dont** je me suis tout de suite aperçu.*
> (*s'apercevoir de qch*)
> They lied, **which** I immediately realized.

3.4.3 duquel, desquels, de laquelle, desquelles

lequel, etc. can be preceded by *de* to give: *duquel, desquels, de laquelle, desquelles*.
These pronouns are equivalent to *dont*, but *dont* is more usual.
They can be used with any antecedent, and with verbs which take *de* plus complement (they should be avoided with noun complements).

> Ex: *La personne **de laquelle/dont** je vous ai parlé vient d'arriver.*
> The person **that/whom/_** I told you about has just arrived.
>
> *Les livres **desquels/dont** je me sers sont sur mon bureau.*
> The books **that/which/_** I am using are on my desk.

3.4.4 de quoi

(i) *de quoi* can be used instead of *dont* when the antecedent is the neutral pronoun *ce*. However, *dont* is more usual.

> Ex: *Je n'ai pas eu le temps de faire ce travail. C'est **ce de quoi/ce dont** je voudrais vous parler.*
> I have not had time to do this work. That is **what** I would like to talk to you about.

(ii) *de quoi* is mainly used as a relative pronoun followed by an infinitive. It has no antecedent and means 'something which provides a means of / a reason for doing something'.

> Ex: *Vous avez **de quoi** être fier!*
> You've got a lot/something to be proud about!
>
> *Il n'y a pas **de quoi** se vanter!*
> There is nothing to boast about!
>
> *Donnez-moi **de quoi** écrire.*
> Give me something to write with.
>
> *Nous avons tout juste **de quoi** vivre.*
> We have just about enough to live on.

3.5 Other complements, introduced by prepositions other than *de* or *à*

3.5.1 Preposition + qui

The relevant preposition + *qui* should be used for human animates only.

As with indirect objects (see 3.3.1 above), the relative pronoun can be omitted in English if the preposition comes after the verb in the subordinate clause. This is not the case in French.

> Ex: *la personne **avec qui** je travaille*
> the person **that**/_ I work **with**
> the person **with whom** I work
>
> *les gens **sur qui** je compte*
> the people **that**/_ I am relying **on**
> the people **on whom** I am relying
>
> *Paul est la seule personne **en qui** j'aie confiance.*
> Paul is the only person **that/whom**/_ I trust.

3.5.2 Preposition + lequel/laquelle/lesquels/lesquelles

These pronouns are normally preceded by any preposition except *de* (since it is best to use *dont* with *de*), and with an inanimate antecedent.

> Ex: *le tiroir **dans lequel** j'ai mis les couverts*
> the drawer **in which** I put the knives and forks
>
> *les étagères **sur lesquelles** j'ai mis les livres*
> the shelves **on which** I put the books

NB: When the antecedent expresses place or time, *où* is often used instead of preposition + *lequel*.

Ex: *le tiroir **dans lequel/où** j'ai mis les couverts*

In particular, *de* or *à* indicating a place cannot precede *lequel*: *où* must be used.

Ex: *le banc **où** je me suis assise*

or:

*le banc **sur lequel** je me suis assise*

*le magasin **où** je suis allée*

or:

*le magasin **dans lequel** je suis allée*

and not **le magasin auquel je suis allée*

(See also 3.7 below.)

These pronouns should be avoided with human animates (use *qui* as described in 3.5.1) except in the following two cases:

– if the preposition is *avec*, either pronoun can be used.

Ex: *Ce sont des amis **avec qui/avec lesquels** j'ai passé mes vacances l'année dernière.*
They are friends **with whom** I spent my holidays last year.

– if the preposition is *parmi* (**among**) or *entre* (**between**), then *lequel*, etc. should be used.

Ex: *Je me suis jointe à un groupe d'amis **parmi lesquels** il y avait Paul et Françoise.*
I joined a group of friends **among whom** were Paul and Françoise.

*Il y a quatre enfants **entre lesquels** il faut partager le gâteau.*
There are four children **among whom** the cake should be shared.

3.5.3 Preposition + quoi

quoi can be preceded by a preposition in the following cases:

(i)   After a pause (comma or full stop) to refer to a whole clause

Ex: *Il fit ses valises. **Après quoi**, il partit.*
He packed his case. **After which** he left.

(ii) With the neutral pronoun *ce* or an indefinite pronoun such as *rien* or *quelque chose* as the antecedent

Ex: *L'argent? Mais c'est **ce sans quoi** la civilisation n'est pas possible!*
Money? Now that is **something without which** civilization is not possible!

*On a trouvé **quelque chose sur quoi** baser une nouvelle théorie.*
Something has been found **on which** a new theory can be based.

(iii) Without antecedent (often after *voici, voilà*): *ce* can be added but is not compulsory.

> Ex: *Voilà [ce] **avec quoi** j'écris.*
> This is **what** I write **with**.

(iv) In literature, instead of ***lequel***, etc., when the antecedent is a noun. This should not be imitated.

> Ex: '*Elle . . . trouvait <u>mille sujets</u> **sur quoi** interroger son beau-père.*'

> François Mauriac (cited in *Robert*)

3.6 Complement of complement

When the noun complement is an indirect object or a complement itself, ***dont*** must be replaced by ***de qui*** or ***duquel***, etc. if the antecedent is an animate, and by ***duquel***, etc. if the antecedent is an inanimate. The indirect object (or complement and preposition) are placed between the antecedent and the relative pronoun.

> Ex: *Le vendeur **dont** nous appréciions l'honnêteté a volé la caisse.*
> (*apprécier l'honnêteté **de** qn*)
> The sales assistant **whose** honesty we appreciated stole the till.
> > but:
> *Le vendeur **sur** l'honnêteté **de qui/duquel** nous comptions a volé la caisse.*
> (*compter **sur** l'honnêteté **de** qn*)
> The sales assistant **on whose** honesty we relied stole the till.

> *C'est un acteur **dont** la carrière m'intéresse.*
> (*la carrière **de** l'acteur*)
> He is an actor **whose** career interests me.
> > but:
> *C'est un acteur **à** la carrière **de qui/duquel** je m'intéresse.*
> (*s'intéresser **à** la carrière **de** qn*)
> He is an actor **in whose** career I am interested.

> *C'est la rivière **dont** tous les campeurs rêvent.*
> (*rêver **de** qch*)
> It is the river all campers dream of.
> > but:
> *C'est la rivière **au bord de laquelle** tous les campeurs rêvent de s'installer.*
> (*rêver de s'installer **au bord de** qch*)
> It is the river whose banks all campers dream of.

NB: This construction is to be avoided in informal French: use a conjunction of coordination instead.

> Ex: *Nous comptions sur l'honnêteté de ce vendeur et [cependant] il a volé la caisse.*

3.7 Adverbs

où is used as an adverb of time or place (in direct or indirect construction), hence it is also called a 'relative adverb'.

(i)   *où* is used when the antecedent is an adverb of **time**.

> Ex: *le jour **où** il est venu*
> (and **not** *quand*! See 4.1(i) below)
> the day **when**/**that**/_ he came
>
> *la période **où** nous sommes*
> the period **that**/_ we're in
>
> *Août est le mois **où** la plupart des gens partent en vacances.*
> August is the month **when**/_ most people go on holiday.

NB(1): If the antecedent is a 'direct' adverb of time, i.e. not introduced by a preposition, only *où* is possible.

> Ex: *le jour **où** il est venu*
> (e.g. *venir _ le jour du Mardi-Gras*)

NB(2): If the adverb of time is 'indirect', i.e. introduced by a preposition, there are two possibilities.

> Ex: *l'époque **où** nous vivons*
>   or:
> *l'époque **à laquelle** nous vivons*
> (e.g. *vivre **à** l'époque gallo-romaine*)

NB(3): When the antecedent is introduced by an **indefinite** article, use *que*.

> Ex: *un jour **qu'**il passait par là*
> one day when he was passing by

(ii)   *où* (*d'où*, *par où*, *vers où*) is used when the antecedent is an adverb of **place**.

> Ex: *la ville **où** j'habite*
> the town **where** I live
>
> *la ville **d'où** je viens*
> the town **where**/_ I come **from**
>
> *Partout **où** nous allons, c'est la même chose.*
> Everywhere _ we go, it's the same thing.
>
> *C'est là **où** j'ai perdu mon sac.*
> This is **where** I lost my bag.

In informal French, *là que* can be used instead of *là où*.

> Ex: *C'est là **que** j'ai perdu mon sac.*

NB: If the antecedent is a person, *chez qui* ('at the house of') must be used, and not *où* (see chapter 26 Prepositions, section 13.3).

> Ex: *le boulanger **chez qui** j'achète mes croissants*
> the baker **from whom** I buy my croissants
>   but:
> *la boulangerie **où** j'achète mes croissants*
> the bakery **where** I buy my croissants

4 Translation difficulties

4.1 English relative pronouns and conjunctions

Relative pronouns and conjunctions are not clearly defined in English, hence some difficulties may arise when going from one language to the other, particularly with **when** and **why**.

(i) **when**

when can be an interrogative adverb, a conjunction or a relative pronoun. For instance:
– interrogative adverb:

> **When** are we going to see you?
> **Quand** *allons-nous vous voir?*

– conjunction:

> It was at night, **when** we least expected it, that the fights resumed.
> *Ce fut le soir,* **au moment où** / **quand** / **lorsque** *nous nous y attendions le moins, que les combats reprirent.*

– relative pronoun:

> In Paris, Monday is [the day] **when** most shops are closed.
> *A Paris, lundi est* **le jour où** *la plupart des magasins sont fermés.*
> (and not: **lundi est quand . . .*)
> See also section 3.7(i) above.

> She had been waiting since 10 o'clock in the morning, **when** Alec had told her he would come.
> *Elle attendait depuis 10 heures du matin,* **heure à laquelle** *Alec lui avait dit qu'il viendrait.*

Generally speaking, if **when** is preceded by a word which could be an antecedent, it should be translated into French by a relative pronoun.

(ii) **why**

why can be an interrogative adverb or a relative pronoun. For instance:

– interrogative adverb:

> **Why** did you sell your car?
> **Pourquoi** *avez-vous vendu votre voiture?*

– relative pronoun:

> He told us [the reasons] **why** he had sold his car.
> *Il nous a dit* **les raisons pour lesquelles** *il avait vendu sa voiture.*
> (or: *Il nous a dit pourquoi il avait . . .*
> but not: **Il nous a dit les raisons pourquoi . . .*)

4.2 *tout*

When *tout* precedes a relative pronoun, *ce* is inserted: *tout ce qui, tout ce que, tout ce dont*, etc. (not **tout qui, *tout que . . .*)

>Ex: *Nous avons terminé **tout ce qui** restait dans le réfrigérateur.*
>We've finished off **all that** was left in the refrigerator.

4.3 Subject pronoun in French, object pronoun in English

A subject pronoun in French can become an object pronoun in English and vice versa if the verbs dictate so.

>Ex: *Il n'y a rien ici **qui** me plaise.*
>There is nothing here **which/that/_** I like.

Here, for instance, the subject of 'like' becomes the indirect object of *plaire*.

4.4 English present participles

For cases when a present participle in English should be replaced by a relative pronoun + conjugated verb in French, see chapter 16 Present Participle, sections 3.2.2.2 and 3.4.

5 Stylistic considerations

The accumulation of relative pronouns in a sentence is considered clumsy in modern French. Wherever appropriate, they can be replaced by adjectives or nouns with relevant prepositions.

(i)   A relative clause can be replaced by a noun.

>Ex: *Je vais donner la liste de **ceux qui ont participé** à la conférence.*
>→ *Je vais donner la liste des **participants** à la conférence.*

Consider the following example:

>This is what they think women contribute to society.
>*C'est ce qu'ils pensent que la femme contribue à la société.*
>is not very elegant.
>→ *C'est ce qu'ils pensent de la contribution de la femme à la société.*
>or:
>→ *C'est la conception qu'ils ont de la contribution de la femme à la société.*

(ii) A relative clause can be replaced by an adjective.

>Ex: *Ceci n'a rien à voir avec les cas **qui se sont produits précédemment**.*
>→ *Ceci n'a rien à voir avec les cas **précédents**.*

(iii) A relative clause can be replaced by a possessive adjective + noun.

>Ex: *N'êtes-vous pas ému par **la peine qu'il ressent**?*
>→ *N'êtes-vous pas ému par **sa peine**?*

(iv)   A relative clause can be replaced by a preposition + complement.

> Ex: *Le directeur va s'adresser à tous les étudiants **qui sont en deuxième année***.
>
> → *Le directeur va s'adresser à tous les étudiants **de deuxième année***.

NB: Some authors, Proust, Gautier and Tournier in particular, have used the accumulation of relative pronouns with a skill which nobody is required to imitate!

> Ex: '*Il voyait en chacun d'eux autant de solutions au problème de la captivité **qui** toutes s'apparentaient peu ou prou à sa propre solution − **qu'**il n'aurait pu définir encore clairement certes, mais **dont** il avait la certitude qu'elle était un absolu en marche.*'

Michel Tournier, Le roi des Aulnes

33 Possessive pronouns

1 Introduction

Possessive pronouns are the result of the nominalization of the now archaic tonic possessive adjectives *mien, tien, sien,* etc. with the definite article (hence *le mien, le tien,* etc.). The possessive pronoun thus represents a noun or noun phrase determined by a possessive adjective.

A possessive pronoun does not qualify or determine a noun, but **replaces** a noun. Hence it can be the subject, object, etc. of a sentence (see chapter 2 Syntax, sections 2.2 and 2.8).

> Ex: − *M'avez-vous apporté vos dissertations?*
> − ***La mienne*** *est prête mais Marie a oublié **la sienne**.*
>   _{subject}   _{object}
> − Have you brought me your essays?
> − **Mine** is ready but Marie has forgotten **hers**.

2 Forms and agreement

		one thing owned		several things owned		
	persons	M	F	M	F	
one	*je*	*le mien*	*la mienne*	*les miens*	*les miennes*	mine
owner	*tu*	*le tien*	*la tienne*	*les tiens*	*les tiennes*	yours
	il	*le sien*	*la sienne*	*les siens*	*les siennes*	his
	elle	*le sien*	*la sienne*	*les siens*	*les siennes*	hers
		M	F	M and F		
several	*nous*	*le nôtre*	*la nôtre*	*les nôtres*		ours
owners	*vous*	*le vôtre*	*la vôtre*	*les vôtres*		yours
	ils	*le leur*	*la leur*	*les leurs*		theirs
	elles	*le leur*	*la leur*	*les leurs*		theirs

(i) The possessive pronoun is the result of two substitutions according to the following model:

le livre de David → *son livre*

son livre → **le sien**

Thus the possessive pronoun replaces a possessive adjective + a noun and is composed of two words, the first one being a definite article.

Ex: *J'ai apporté mes livres. Avez-vous apporté **les vôtres?***

(= *vos livres*)

I have brought my books. Have you brought **yours**?

*Ma maison est plus proche du centre commercial que **la leur**.*

(= *leur maison*)

My house is nearer the shopping centre than **theirs**.

*Mes parents et **les siens** se connaissent depuis longtemps.*

(= *ses parents*)

My parents and **his/hers** have known each other for a long time.

(ii) Prepositions + possessive pronouns

Since the first word is the definite article, it contracts with the prepositions *à* and *de* to give e.g. *au mien, au nôtre, du tien, du leur, aux siennes, des leurs*, etc.

Ex: *Occupez-vous de vos affaires, pas **des leurs**.*

(*s'occuper **de** qch*)

Mind your own business, not **theirs**.

*Le garage des voisins est rattaché **au nôtre**.*

(*être rattaché **à** qch*)

The neighbours' garage is linked to **ours**.

(iii) Spelling and pronunciation

There is a circumflex accent on the '*o*' of *nôtre* and *vôtre* and a difference in pronunciation from the possessive adjective.

notre [nɔtr(ə)]   *votre* [vɔtr(ə)]

(le) nôtre [notr(ə)]   *(le) vôtre* [votr(ə)]

(iv) Agreement, anaphora and co-reference

In English, possessive pronouns are invariable with gender, except for the 3rd person singular ('his', 'hers') where the change follows the **gender of the owner**. In French, the possessive pronoun, like the possessive adjective, agrees in person with the owner, and in **gender and number** with the **thing owned**.

Ex: *Ta **robe** est blanche; **la mienne** est rouge.*

Your dress is white; mine is red.

*Sa **chemise** est neuve; **la vôtre** ne l'est pas.*

His/Her shirt is new; yours is not.

Hence there is anaphora but no co-reference. Consider the following examples:
> **Ton chat** est très sympathique mais je préfère quand même **le mien**!

'*le mien*' points anaphorically to '*ton chat*' but it is not the same cat! Hence the gender has to be kept, but the number may differ:
> **Tes chats** sont très sympathiques, mais je préfère **le mien**.

3 Uses

(i) **être** + possessive pronoun

When the verb **être** is immediately followed by a possessive pronoun, the subject should be **ce**, not **il** (see chapter 35 *C'est/Il est*, section 7).
> Ex: *Ce n'est pas votre sac, **c'est le mien**.*
> It is not your bag, it's mine.
>
> *J'ai trouvé ce livre. **Est-ce le vôtre?***
> I found this book. Is it yours?

(ii) **c'est à moi** or **c'est le mien**?

After **être**, an alternative to the possessive pronoun is the preposition **à** + tonic personal pronoun (see chapters 31 Personal Pronouns, section 3.2.2, and 35 *C'est/Il est*, section 7). Note that only the possessive pronoun can be the **subject** of a verb, i.e. *à moi* cannot be the subject but *les miens* can (in English, the possessive pronoun is used in all cases).
> Ex: *Ces livres sont **à moi**; ceux-là à vous.*
> These books are **mine**; those are yours.
> but:
> *Ces livres sont les vôtres; **les miens** sont à la maison.*
> These books are yours; **mine** are at home.

Note that *c'est* remains invariable in *c'est à moi, à toi*, etc., whilst it agrees in number with *le mien*, etc.
> Ex: ***Ce sont** les miens, les miennes . . .*

(iii) **un ami à moi** or **un de mes amis**?

As in English, *c'est **un** ami* ('he's **a** friend') would be understood as 'a friend of the speaker'. However, it is possible to emphasize the 'possession' by adding *à moi* ('of mine') or saying *un de mes* ('one of my'). Hence:
> *C'est un ami à moi / C'est un de mes amis.*
> He's a friend of mine / He's one of my friends.

In the same way:
> *C'est une amie à lui / C'est une de ses amies.*
> She's a friend of his / She's one of his friends.

(iv)   Possessive pronouns with indefinite subject pronouns

With indefinite subject pronouns singular (*on, chacun, personne,* etc.), the 3rd person **singular** possessive pronoun should be used. In English however, a singular subject pronoun and verb can be followed by a plural possessive pronoun.

> Ex: *On nous avait demandé de prendre des parapluies.* **Chacun** *avait apporté* **le sien**.
> We had been asked to take umbrellas with us. **Everybody** had brought **theirs**.
>
> *Il nous faudrait des bottes pour marcher dans cette boue et* **personne** *n'a apporté* **les siennes**!
> We'd need boots to walk through that mud and **nobody** has brought **theirs**!

(v)   Ambiguity of **le sien, la sienne** . . .

In case of ambiguity – such as with the use of the possessive adjective – *à lui, à elle, à eux, à elles* can be added to the possessive pronoun.

> Ex: *Ce n'est pas la voiture de sa femme qu'il a vendue: c'est* **la sienne à lui**.
> It's not his wife's car that he sold – it's his own.

Note that this construction belongs to informal French.

4   Idioms using the possessive pronoun

– *y mettre du sien*: to make an effort; to contribute one's share of work, of energy; to pull one's weight (*du sien* becomes *du mien, du tien,* etc.).
> Ex: *Il faut que tu y mettes* **du tien**.
> You must pull you weight.

– *les siens*: one's parents; one's family.
> Ex: *Il a été renié par* **les siens**.
> He was disowned by his own people.
>
> *Je n'ai pas vu* **les miens** *depuis au moins un an.*
> I have not seen my family for at least a year.

By extension, it can mean 'part of a group' or 'party'.
> Ex: *Serez-vous* **des nôtres** *ce soir pour dîner?*
> Will you be with us tonight for dinner?
>
> '*Il est* **des nôtres**, *il a bu son coup comme les autres!*'
> (popular song)
> He's drunk with us, he's one of us!

– *faire des siennes = faire des caprices / faire des bêtises*.
> Ex: *Le chien a encore fait* **des siennes** *dans la cuisine.*
> The dog has been up to his old tricks again in the kitchen.

*Le vent a encore fait **des siennes** hier soir: il y a trois arbres de déracinés!*
The wind has done it again last night – three trees have been uprooted!

– *faire sien*: to adopt as one's own.
> Ex: *Il a fait **siennes** toutes les opinions de son maître.*
> He has adopted all his master's opinions.

– *à la vôtre!*: [to] your good health! (Said as one raises one's glass.)
Also: *à la tienne!* [to] your good health!
> *à la nôtre!* [to] our good health!

34 Demonstrative pronouns

1 Introduction

Like other pronouns, demonstrative pronouns do not qualify nouns, but replace a noun (or syntactic equivalent), which can be the subject, object, etc. of a verb (see chapters 1 Parts of Speech and 2 Syntax, sections 2.2 and 2.8).

> Ex: *Est-ce que **ça** me va?*
> subject
>
> Does **it** suit me?
>
> *Nous savons tout **cela**.*
> object
>
> We know all **this**.

They can be simple or compound, variable or invariable.

2 Forms

		singular		plural		
		M	F	M	F	neutral
variable pronouns	simple	*celui*	*celle*	*ceux*	*celles*	
variable pronouns	compound	*celui-ci* *celui-là*	*celle-ci* *celle-là*	*ceux-ci* *ceux-là*	*celles-ci* *celles-là*	
invariable pronouns	simple					*ce (c', ç')*
invariable pronouns	compound					*ceci* *cela (ça)*

3 Variable demonstrative pronouns

Variable demonstrative pronouns are *celui, celle, ceux, celles,* to which *-ci* and *-la* can be added for contrast or emphasis.

3.1 Simple forms: *celui, celle, ceux, celles*

They are not usually used by themselves (**Je préfère celles*). They must be determined either by a relative clause, a prepositional complement or a participle.

(i) Agreements, anaphora and co-reference

As with possessive pronouns, there is anaphora but not co-reference.
      Ex: *les livres des étudiants et **ceux** du professeur*
'*ceux*' points anaphorically to '*les livres*' but does not refer to the same books. Hence the gender is kept, but the number may differ (*les livres des étudiants et **celui** du professeur*).

(ii) *tous/toutes*

ceux and **celles** can be preceded by **tous** or **toutes** respectively to mean **all those**.
      Ex: ***Tous ceux** que j'ai comptés peuvent partir maintenant.*
      All those I have counted can go now.

      ***Toutes celles** qui ont acheté un billet peuvent se le faire rembourser au guichet numéro trois.*
      All those who bought a ticket can get a refund at counter number three.

3.1.1 With a relative clause

Demonstrative pronouns can be modified by a relative clause.
      Ex: *Voici les reçus! J'ai retrouvé **celui qui** manquait.*
      Here are the receipts! I have found **the one which** was missing.

      *Je cherche une collègue, **celle dont** je t'ai parlé hier.*
      I am looking for a colleague, **the one** [**that**] I mentioned to you yesterday.

      *Ces articles ne sont pas **ceux auquels** je faisais allusion.*
      These articles are not **the ones** [**which**] I was alluding to.

NB(1): **the one** before a relative pronoun should not be translated by ***l'un***. If anything, ***l'un*** (*d'eux*) translates **one** (of them) as in:
      Ex: *J'ai appelé mes deux chats: **l'un** est venu mais l'autre n'avait sans doute pas faim!*
      I called my two cats. **One** came but the other was probably not hungry!

NB(2): *celui qui/que* . . . , *ceux qui/que* . . . can also be used in a general sense (no antecedent) to introduce **animates**, i.e. **he/she who(m)** . . ., **those who(m)** . . . (see 4.1.1 below to introduce inanimates).

> Ex: ***Ceux qui*** *peuvent vivre sans travailler ont bien de la chance.*
> **Those who** can live without working are very lucky.

> ***Celui qui*** *partira le dernier ce soir est prié de fermer la porte à clé.*
> Will **the one who** leaves last tonight kindly lock the door?

NB(3): *celui, celle*, etc. replaces a noun group, whilst *ce* replaces a whole clause. Compare:

> *On a <u>le droit de voter</u>,* ***celui qui*** *nous donne la possibilité de changer le gouvernement.*
> (*celui* stands for '*le droit de voter*')
> We have the right to vote, the one which enables us to change the government.
> > and:
> *On a <u>le droit de voter</u>,* ***ce qui*** *nous donne la possibilité de changer le gouvernement.*
> (*ce* stands for the whole clause '*On a le droit de voter*')
> We have the right to vote, which gives us the possibility to change the government.

See chapter 32 Relative Pronouns.

3.1.2   *With a prepositional complement*

Demonstrative pronouns can be followed by a complement introduced by the preposition *de* to indicate possession or attribution. In English, this is rendered by either **the one/ones of**, **that/those of** or a possessive case.

> Ex: *Il a choisi <u>le tableau de Picasso</u> plutôt que* ***celui de*** *Magritte.*
> He chose the painting by Picasso rather than **the one by** Magritte.

> *Dans leur étude, ils ont comparé <u>la situation sociale des femmes</u> avec* ***celle des*** *hommes.*
> In their study, they compared the social situation of women with **that of** men.

> *Je préfère <u>votre suggestion</u> à* ***celles de*** *Paul.*
> I prefer your suggestion to Paul's.
> I prefer your suggestion to **those of** Paul.

NB(1): The variable pronoun *ceux* should be distinguished from the invariable, neutral pronoun *ce* (see below). Compare:

> ***Ceux*** *qui gouvernent le monde,* ***ce*** *sont les scientifiques.*
> Those who govern the world are the scientists.
> > or:
> ***Ce*** *sont les scientifiques qui gouvernent le monde.*
> It is the scientists who govern the world.

NB(2): As in English, an adjective can be inserted between *celui*, etc. and the possessor.

> Ex: *Je préfère les vins de Bourgogne à **ceux tant vantés de** Bordeaux.*
> I prefer wines from Burgundy to **the much celebrated ones from** Bordeaux.

3.1.3   *With a participle*

Demonstrative pronouns can be modified by a present or a past participle.

> Ex: *Les fillettes portant le nom d'une fleur étaient nombreuses dans le village; **celles portant** le nom d'une sainte l'étaient moins.*
> Floral names for girls were common in the village; saints' names were less common.

> *J'ai acheté beaucoup de plants de tomates cette année, mais sur **ceux achetés** au supermarché, seulement une demi-douzaine ont donné des fruits.*
> I bought many tomato seedlings this year but of those bought in the supermarket, only half a dozen have borne fruit.

3.2   Compound forms with *ci, là*

(i)   Construction

To distinguish between two demonstrative pronouns, *ci* is added after one and *là* after the other. They are both linked to the pronoun with a hyphen. This compound form replaces a demonstrative adjective + noun.

> Ex: *Je voudrais que vous lisiez ce chapitre-ci et non pas **celui-là**.*
> (= *ce chapitre-là*)
> I would like you to read this chapter, not that one.

> *Ils passent leur temps à faire des mots-croisés comme **ceux-ci**.*
> (= *comme ces mots-croisés-ci*)
> They spend their time doing crosswords like these.

> *Lesquelles sont vos chaussures? **Celles-ci** ou **celles-là**?*
> (= *ces chaussures-ci ou ces chaussures-là?*)
> Which are your shoes? These or those?

(ii)   Agreement, anaphora and co-reference

The compound demonstrative pronoun points anaphorically to an element in the context with **or** without co-reference.

> Ex: *Elle regarda la porte et vit **celle-ci** s'ouvrir.*
> She looked at the door and saw it open.

> *Les steaks sont prêts. Tu veux **celui-ci** ou **celui-là**?*
> The steaks are ready. Would you like this one or that one?

(iii)   Meaning

celui-ci and *celui-là* are used in the same sentence to refer respectively to 'the latter' (i.e. the last mentioned) and 'the former' (i.e. the first mentioned), since *ci* represents the word nearer to the demonstrative pronoun in the sentence, and *là* the word further away.

> Ex: *Courchevel et Kaprun sont deux stations de ski très connues.* **Celle-ci** *se trouve en Autriche et* **celle-là** *en France.*
> Courchevel and Kaprun are two well-known skiing resorts. **The latter** is in Austria and **the former** in France.

NB: An alternative construction is to use the numeral pronouns *la seconde* and *la première*.

(iv) *celui-ci* or *celui-là*?

celui-là, *celle-là*, etc. are frequently used in informal French instead of *celui-ci*, *celle-ci*, etc. when the meaning is clear from the context.

> Ex: *Quelle robe as-tu choisie? Je prends* **celle-là**.
> Which dress have you chosen? I'll take this one.

(v) The demonstrative pronoun can be pejorative.

> Ex: **Celui-là**, *il m'énerve*.   or: *Il m'énerve*, **celui-là**.
> That one's really getting on my nerves.

Note that in both cases, '*celui-là*' is in apposition to '*il*'.
See also dislocated constructions in chapter 2 Syntax, section 2.15.5.

4 Invariable demonstrative pronouns

ce (*c'*, *ç'*), *ceci*, *cela* and *ça* are all neutral and invariable demonstrative pronouns.

4.1 Simple form: *ce*

The demonstrative pronoun *ce* is a neutral pronoun. See also chapters 32 Relative Pronouns, sections 3.1.1(ii), 3.2.1(ii), 3.3.3(i) and 3.4.2.2(iii), and 35 *C'est/Il est*.

4.1.1 ce + *relative pronoun*

– If there is no antecedent, *ce qui*, *ce que*, *ce dont*, *ce à quoi* correspond to 'what' or 'that which'. They introduce an **inanimate** (see 3.1.1NB(2) above regarding demonstrative pronouns introducing animates). Note that, unlike in English, the pronoun is normally repeated before the verb *être* that follows, except with *qui*:

> Ex: **Ce que** *je veux*, **c'est** *qu'on me laisse tranquille*.
> **What** I want is to be left in peace.
>
> **Ce dont** *j'ai besoin*, **c'est de** *vacances*.
> **What** I need is a holiday.
>
> **Ce qui** *est arrivé* **est** *tout à fait inattendu*.
> **What** happened is most unexpected.

– If the antecedent is a whole clause, *ce qui, ce que, ce dont, ce à quoi* correspond to 'which'.

> Ex: *Il n'a rien dit, **ce qui** est dommage.*
> He said nothing, **which** is a shame.
>
> *Il n'a rien dit, **ce que** je déplore.*
> He said nothing, **which** I deplore.

– When ***tout*** precedes a relative pronoun, ***ce*** is inserted: ***tout ce*** *qui*, ***tout ce*** *que*, ***tout ce*** *dont*, etc. (not **tout qui*, **tout que* . . .).

> Ex: *Nous avons terminé **tout ce qui** restait dans le réfrigérateur.*
> We've finished off **all that** was left in the refrigerator.

4.1.2 ce *in idioms*

> Ex: *Je leur ai dit ce que je pensais. **Sur ce**, je suis parti.*
> (informal speech only)
> I told them what I thought. On that note, I left.
>
> *Je vais sortir le chien et **pour ce faire**, il me faut la laisse.*
> I am going to take the dog out and so I need the leash.
>
> *Il se versa à boire et, **ce faisant**, se mit à nous raconter son histoire.*
> He poured himself a drink and, as he was doing this, he started to tell us his story.
>
> *Je lui ai donné une bonne note quand même, **et ce** pour ne pas le décourager.*
> I gave him a good mark all the same, in order not to discourage him.

4.1.3 ce + être

(i) ***ce*** ('it'/'that'/'they') is used as the subject of ***être*** or of ***devoir/pouvoir*** + ***être***. This forms one of the most frequently used presentatives, ***c'est, ce doit être, ce peut être***. (See chapters 2 Syntax, section 2.15.3 and 35 *C'est/Il est*).

(ii) ***c'est*** can be used:

– as a presentative identified in situation (deictic value).

> Ex: *Regarde! **C'est** le défilé!*
> Look! It's the parade!

– or as a presentative identified in context (anaphoric value).

> Ex: *Une de mes passions, **c'est** le tir à l'arc.*
> One of my passions is archery.

(iii) All tenses can be used → *c'était, ce sera*, etc.

(iv) ***c'est*** becomes ***ce sont*** with a plural complement (formal French) or remains *c'est* (informal French).

> Ex: ***C'est/Ce sont*** *les voisins du dessus.*

543

(v) **c'est** can be followed:

– by a noun or noun phrase.

Ex: ***C'est*** *un tableau de Picasso.*
It is a painting by Picasso.

C'était *de véritables bus . . .*
They were proper buses . . .

Regarde! ***C'est*** *mon chat!*
Look! **This is** my cat!

– by a proper noun.

Ex: *Il y a quelqu'un à la porte:* ***ce doit être*** *Paul.*
There's someone at the door – it must be Paul.

– by a pronoun.

Ex: ***Est-ce toi****, Marie?*
Is it you, Marie?

C'est quelqu'un *qu'il connaît qui nous a conseillés.*
It is someone he knows who advised us.

C'est le mien*, pas le vôtre.*
It's mine, not yours.

NB: *c'est nous, **c'est** vous,* but ***ce sont** eux.* See also chapter 35 *C'est/Il est*, section 7.

– by an adjective.

Ex: *Les maths?* ***C'est facile!***
Maths is easy!

C'est joli*, ça!*
This is pretty!

– by an adverb phrase.

Ex: *Leeds?* ***C'est en Angleterre****.*
Leeds? It is in England.

– by a preposition + infinitive.

Ex: *Vous allez vous mettre à travailler?* ***C'est à espérer****.*
(= *Je l'espère.*)
Are you going to work? I hope so. (lit.: It is to be hoped.)

– by a relative clause with no antecedent.

Ex: ***C'est ce que je veux****.*
That's what I want.

4.2   Compound forms

ceci, cela and *ça* are neutral pronouns. They are formed with *ce + ci* or *ce + la* (without an accent). Unlike *celui-ci, celui-là,* etc. which have specific referents, ***ceci*** and ***cela*** (**this, that**) have a less specific sense.

They can refer to something identifiable in the discourse situation (deictic use) or in the context (anaphoric use).

– In the discourse situation:

> Ex: *Qu'est-ce que c'est que **cela/ça?***
> What is this/that?
>
> ***Cela** m'ennuie.*
> This/That bothers me.
>
> *Comment **ça** s'appelle?/Comment **cela** s'appelle-t-il?*
> What is this/that called?
>
> *Donnez-moi **ceci/cela/ça**, s'il vous plaît!*
> Please give me this/that!

– In the context (by anaphor or cataphor):

> Ex: *<u>Je vais travailler un peu</u>, après **cela/ça**, je sortirai.*
> ***Ça** a coûté cher, <u>ta robe</u>?*

Note that *çà* (with a grave accent) is an adverb of place, as in *çà et là* ('here and there'), but the demonstrative pronoun *ça* as in '*Ça va?*' ('How are things?') has no accent.

4.2.1   ceci *or* cela?

(i) As a subject or object, ***ceci*** applies in principle to what is nearer the speaker, and ***cela*** to what is further away. They are used (even with *être*) to contrast two items or for emphasis.

> Ex: ***Ceci** est valable mais **cela** ne l'est pas.*
> This is valid but that is not.
>
> *Donnez-moi **ceci** et **cela**.*
> Give me this and that.

(ii) As an object with only one item, ***ceci*** introduces the words that follow, whereas ***cela*** (or more informally, ***ça***) refers back to something already stated. Compare:

> *Il nous a dit **ceci**: 'Rappelez dans quinze jours.'*
> He told us this, 'Please ring back in two weeks' time.'
>
> *Prenez **ceci** (= ce que je vais vous donner) toutes les quatre heures.*
> Take this (= what I am going to give you) every four hours.
>
> *Ecoutez **ceci** (= ce que je vais dire).*
> Listen to this (= to what I am going to say).

and:

> *'Il ne faut pas vendre la peau de l'ours avant de l'avoir tué.' Dites-lui **cela/ça** de ma part.*
> 'One shouldn't count one's chickens before they are hatched.'
> Tell him that from me.

> *Ne soyez pas en retard: le directeur n'aime pas **cela/ça**.*
> Don't be late. The headmaster doesn't like it.

> *Si vous croyez **cela/ça** (= ce qui vient d'être dit), vous êtes bien crédule.*
> If you believe that (= what has just been said), you're very gullible.

NB(1): In informal French, **cela** tends to take over from *ceci*.

NB(2): **ceci dit**, as an idiom, also refers **back** to something already stated.
>   Ex: *Il faut que je sois à mon bureau à 2 heures. **Ceci dit**, allons déjeuner.*
>   . . . Having said that, let's go to lunch.

NB(3): If what is being referred to is specific, the personal pronouns **le/la/les** are used (see also chapter 31 Personal Pronouns, sections 2.2.2.2 and 2.2.2.3). Compare:
>   *La situation est compliquée, mais nous allons essayer de vous expliquer **cela/ça**.*

('*cela*' refers to the whole clause, to the fact that the situation is complicated.)
>   The situation is complicated, but we are going to try and explain
>   **that** to you.
>   and:
>   *La situation est compliquée mais nous allons essayer de vous l'expliquer.*

('*l*'' refers stricly to '*La situation*'.)
>   The situation is complicated, but we are going to try and explain **it**
>   to you.

4.2.2   cela (ça) *or* ce?

Note also that *cela* and *ça* are not always interchangeable (see section 4.2.4 below).

4.2.2.1   WITH *être*

(i)   As a subject and when there is an object pronoun before *être, ça is used* instead of *ce*.

Ex: ***Ça** lui **est** égal.*	but:	***C'est** égal.*
He/She doesn't care.		It doesn't matter.
***Ça** y **est**!*	but:	***C'est** là.*
That's it! Finished! etc.		It is here/there.

(ii)   With the forms of ***être*** which do not begin with '*e*', with ***devoir/pouvoir* + *être*** or with the negative form, either **cela** (**ça**) or *ce* can be used.
>   Ex: ***Cela/Ça/Ce** sera facile.*
>   It will be easy.
>   but:
>   ***Cela** lui sera facile.*
>   It will be easy for him/her.

>   ***Cela/Ç**'aurait été possible.*
>   It would have been possible.
>   but:
>   ***Cela** m'aurait été possible.*
>   It would have been possible for me.

Cela/Ça/Ce ne sera pas facile.
It won't be easy.
> but:

Cela ne nous sera pas facile.
It won't be easy for us.

NB(1): In the past historic, only *ce* is possible (*ce fut*).

NB(2): With *tout*, only *cela/ça* is possible:
> Ex: *Tout cela/ça* n'est pas très intéressant.
> All that isn't very interesting.

except in relatives:
> Ex: *Tout ce* qui brille n'est pas or.
> All that glisters is not gold.

(See 4.1.1 above.)

4.2.2.2   WITH VERBS OTHER THAN *être*

cela (*ça*) is used as the subject of a verb other than *être* to refer to something non-specific in the context.
> Ex: − *Vous allez mieux?* − *Ça* dépend des jours.
> − Are you feeling better? − It depends on the day.

Dîner à dix heures du soir? Non, **cela** *ne me convient pas.*
Dinner at ten? No, that does not suit me.

Ils savent que nous ne pouvons nous défendre, et **cela** *les encourage.*
They know we can't defend ourselves and that encourages them.

Cela *me peine de vous voir si triste.*
It grieves me to see you so sad.

Qu'est-ce que c'est? **Ça** *sent mauvais.*
What is it? It stinks.

Revenez plus tard, **cela** *vaudra mieux.*
Come back later, it will be best.

Tout **ça** *a bien montré qu'ils avaient raison.*
All this certainly showed that they were right.

Note that in this case, there is no elision before the auxiliary '*a*'.

4.2.3   Other uses of cela/ça

cela/ça is also used as a 'strengthening' particle in what would otherwise be one-word replies.
> Ex: − *J'ai gagné le gros lot!* − **Comment ça?**
> − I won the jackpot! − How come?

> − *J'ai décidé de ne plus prendre la voiture.* − **Pourquoi ça?**
> − I have decided not to use the car any more. − Why's that?

> − *J'ai vu Catherine hier.* − **Où ça?**
> − I saw Catherine yesterday. − Whereabouts?

> – *J'ai vu Catherine.* – **Quand** *ça?*
> – I've seen Catherine. – When was that?

> – *J'ai vu Jean-Christophe.* – **Qui** *ça?*
> – I saw Jean-Christophe. – Who (did you say)?

4.2.4 ça: generic or specific?

ça is normally associated with inanimates but under certain circumstances, it can also be used with animates. For the difference between generic and specific, see chapter 23 Articles, sections 2.2.4 and 3.2.4.

4.2.4.1 WITH ANIMATES

(i) Generic

ça can refer to animates named in the context, but in a generic sense.
> Ex: *Les êtres humains,* **ça** *doit manger pour vivre.*
> Human beings must eat to live.

> *Un chien,* **ça** *ne ronronne pas.*
> Dogs don't purr.

> *Les étudiants d'aujourd'hui,* **ça** *n'est pas très studieux!*
> Today's students are not very studious!

Compare with:
> *Les étudiants de mon groupe ne sont pas très studieux.*
> The students in my group are not very studious.

where *étudiants* is used in a specific (not generic) sense: the use of *ça* here would be very derogatory (see below).

(ii) Specific

– *ça* can be used to refer to an animate named in the context in a specific sense. It is thus used to stress the gap between its referential qualities and the noun attributed to it. Neutralizing gender and number in this way is extremely pejorative as it 'demotes' the referent. Note that there is no English equivalent.
> Ex: *Ce mec,* **ça** *croit tout savoir et* **ça** *ne sait rien!*
> That bloke thinks he knows everything and he knows nothing!

– When the referent is not named in the context, either *ça* or a personal pronoun can be used to refer to an animate. Compare:
> *C'est qui,* **ça?** **Ça,** *c'est mon frère.*
> Who's that?
>   and:
> *C'est qui,* **lui?** **Lui,** *c'est mon frère.*
> Who's he?

> *C'est qui,* **elle?** **Elle,** *c'est ma sœur.*
> Who's she?

4.2.4.2   WITH INANIMATES

(i)   Generic

ça can refer to inanimates named in the context in a generic sense.

> Ex: *Un livre de référence, ça ne s'écrit pas en deux mois!*
> You don't write a reference book in two months!

(ii)   Specific

– *ça* can be used to refer to an inanimate named in the context in a specific sense. It is thus used to stress the gap between its referential qualities and the noun attributed to it. Neutralizing gender and number in this way is pejorative, even for an inanimate.

> Ex: *Vous appelez ça un travail bien fait?*
> You call **that** a job well done?

> *J'ai acheté un appartement, si on peut appeler ça/cela un appartement.*
> I bought a flat, if you can call **it** a flat.

– When the referent is not named in the context, *ça* is used with inanimates.

> Ex: – *C'est quoi, ça? – Ça, c'est mon sac.*
> – What's this? – It's my bag.

5   Translation difficulties

The addition of *de* is needed in the following cases:

(i)   *de* is needed between *ceci/cela* and an adjective followed by a *que*-clause.

> Ex: *Ce livre a ceci d'intéressant qu'il traite de cas particuliers.*
> This book is interesting in that it deals with special cases.
>
> or:
>
> What is interesting about this book is that it deals with special cases.

> *Ce livre, La Disparition, a ceci de particulier qu'il ne contient pas la lettre 'e'.*
> This book, *La Disparition*, is peculiar in that it does not contain the letter 'e'.
>
> or:
>
> This book, *La Disparition*, has the particular feature that it does not contain the letter 'e'.

> *Ce que vous dites a ceci d'irritant que personne ne peut comprendre.*
> What you say is irritating in that nobody can understand.

(ii)   *de* is needed between *celui*, etc. and an infinitive.

> Ex: *Je n'ai qu'un désir, celui de partir en vacances bientôt.*
> I wish for only one thing, that is to go on holiday soon.

> *Elle n'a qu'une envie, celle de vous revoir!*
> She has only one desire, that is to see you again!

35 *c'est/il est*

1 Introduction

The choice between ***c'est*** and ***il est*** has always been problematic for English students of French. Indeed:
- 'it is' can be *il est, elle est* or *c'est*
- 'he is' can be *il est* or *c'est*
- 'she is' can be *elle est* or *c'est*
- 'they are' can be *ce sont, ils sont* or *elles sont*

There are two things to consider before making a choice:
- the referent
- the complement

The referent (what *c'est/il est* refers to) can be placed before or after *c'est/il est*. It can take the following forms:
- animate (human or non–human)
- inanimate (things, ideas, etc.)
- indefinite (demonstrative pronouns *ce/cela/ça*)
- unspecified
- a whole clause

The complement can take the following forms:
- adjective
- preposition + infinitive
- adverb
- noun
- pronoun

It should be noted that this discussion only applies to 3rd person subject **pronouns**, i.e. not noun phrases. Hence:

> *Proust est un écrivain.*

but:

> **Il est un écrivain.*

See section 6 below.

2   Adjective complement on its own

2.1   Animate or inanimate referent

(i)   If – as in the most common case – the adjective refers **specifically** to the referent, *il est* or *elle est* are used according to the gender of the person, animal or thing; *ils sont/elles sont* are used in the plural form.

> Ex: *Catherine? **Elle est** très intelligente.*
> Catherine? **She is** very intelligent.
>
> *J'ai vu votre chat. **Il est** très gros.*
> I saw your cat. **He/It is** very big.
>
> *Voulez-vous du Bordeaux? **Il est** très bon.*
> (The reference is to the quality of this bottle of Bordeaux wine in particular.)
> Would you like some Bordeaux? **It is** very good.

(ii)   If the adjective refers more **generally** to the referent, *c'est* is used (see also 2.2). Compare:

> *Regardez ces enfants: **c'est** formidable!*
> (the implication is: '*ce qui leur arrive/ce qu'ils font*')
> Look at these children – **it's** fantastic!
> 　　　and:
> *Regardez ces enfants: **ils sont** formidables!*
> Look at these children – **they are** fantastic!
>
> *Voulez-vous du Bordeaux? **C'est** très bon pour les malades.*
> (The reference is to a quality attributed to Bordeaux wine in general.)
> Would you like some Bordeaux? **It's** very good for invalids.

2.2   Referent unspecified or *ce/cela/ça*

c'est must be used.

(i)   Unspecified

> Ex: *Attention! **C'est** lourd!*
> Careful! It's heavy.

(ii)   *ce/cela/ça*

> Ex: *Ne touchez pas ça! **C'est** dangereux!*
> Don't touch that! It's dangerous.

> NB: With expressions of time, impersonal *il* is used.
> > Ex: ***Il est** trop tôt/très tard.*
> > It is too early/very late.

2.3 Whole clause referent

There are two possible cases:

(i) If the referent has already been expressed, *c'est* is used, followed by the adjective.

> Ex: *Vous devez comprendre: **c'est** essentiel.*
> You must understand: it is essential.

(Note that the verb in the clause referred to is **conjugated**.)

> *Avoir beaucoup d'argent, **c'est** bien agréable!*
> Having a lot of money is quite pleasant!

(Note that the verb in the clause referred to is in the **infinitive**.)

(ii) If the referent follows the adjective, **il est** (impersonal) is used. It is either followed by adjective + *que* + subjunctive or by preposition + infinitive (see 3.2).

> Ex: **Il est** essentiel **que** vous compreniez.
> It is essential that you should understand.

> **Il est** quand même bien agréable **d'**avoir beaucoup d'argent.
> It is nevertheless quite pleasant to have a lot of money.

Compare:

> − *Paul était là. − Il est venu?* ***C'est** bien.*
> − Paul was here. − Did he come? That's good.
> (*ce* refers to the whole preceding clause '*Il est venu*'.)
>   and:
> *Il est bien qu'il soit venu.*
> It is a good thing that he came.

> *Ils sont venus: **c'est** bien.*
> They came. That's good.

> *Il est bien qu'ils soient venus.*
> It is a good thing that they came.

Note that in informal French, *c'est* is used in all cases.

3 Adjective complement + preposition + infinitive

3.1 Animate referent

(i) Referent already expressed

Always use ***il est/elle est*** (or *ils sont/elles sont*) followed by *à* + infinitive.

> Ex: *Catherine?* ***Elle est** difficile à contenter.*
> Catherine? She is difficult to please.

> *Catherine et Paul?* ***Ils sont** difficiles à contenter.*
> Catherine and Paul? They are difficult to please.

(ii)   Referent follows

Use impersonal *il* (*est*), followed by *de* + infinitive.
Ex: *Il est difficile de contenter Catherine.*
It is difficult to please Catherine.

Il est difficile de contenter Catherine et Paul.
It is difficult to please Catherine and Paul.

3.2   Inanimate referent

(i)   Referent already expressed

– If the adjective **generally** refers to the referent (the most common case for inanimates), use *c'est* followed by *à* + infinitive.
Ex: *La mayonnaise? C'est facile à faire.*
Mayonnaise is easy to make.

Les profiteroles? C'est difficile à réussir.
Profiteroles are difficult to make properly.

– If the adjective refers **specifically** to the referent, use *il est/elle est* (*ils sont/elles sont*).
Ex: *Vous n'aimez pas ma mayonnaise sans huile? Elle est très facile à digérer!*
Don't you like my oil-free mayonnaise? It is very easy to digest!

Comment trouvez-vous mes chapeaux? Ils sont beaux, n'est-ce pas?
What do you think of my hats? They're nice, aren't they?

(ii)   Referent follows

Use impersonal *il* (*est*), followed by *de* + infinitive.
Ex: *Il est facile de faire la mayonnaise.*
It is easy to make mayonnaise.
Note that in this case, the 'real' or 'semantic' subject is the infinitive + noun phrase (→ '*faire la mayonnaise est facile*').

Il est agréable d'avoir beaucoup d'argent.
It is nice to have a lot of money.

Il est difficile de réussir les profiteroles.
It is difficult to make profiteroles properly.

4   Preposition + infinitive complement

The referent is a whole clause.

(i)   If the referent has already been expressed, use *c'est*.
Ex: *Allez-vous vous mettre à travailler? C'est à espérer.*
Are you going to get down to work? I hope so.

553

(ii)   If the referent follows, use impersonal *il* (*est*).

> Ex: ***Il est à espérer*** *que vous allez vous mettre à travailler.*
> It is to be hoped that you are going to get down to work.

5 Adverb phrase as complement

5.1 Animate referent

Il est/elle est or ***ils sont/elles sont*** are used, according to the gender and number of the referent.

> Ex: *Où est votre mère?* ***Elle est*** *à Paris.*
> Where is your mother? She is in Paris.
>
> *Où est le chat?* ***Il est*** *dans le jardin.*
> Where is the cat? He/It is in the garden.
>
> *Où sont les chiens?* ***Ils sont*** *dans le salon.*
> Where are the dogs? They are in the lounge.

5.2 Inanimate referent

(i)   If the referent is a place, ***c'est*** is used.

> Ex: – *Où est Londres?* – ***C'est*** *en Angleterre.*
> – Where's London? – **It's** in England.

(ii)   If the referent is anything else, use *il est/elle est* (*ils sont/elles sont*).

> Ex: – *Où est votre sac?* – ***Il est*** *sur ma chaise.*
> – Where is your bag? – **It is** on my chair.
>
> – *Où est votre montre?* – ***Elle est*** *sur la table.*
> – Where is your watch? – **It is** on the table.
>
> *Je ne comprends pas ces messages: **ils sont** en russe.*
> I do not understand these messages – **they are** in Russian.

NB: If the complement refers more **generally** to the referent, use *c'est* (see above).

> Ex: *Je ne comprends pas **ces messages**. **C'est** en russe.*
> I do not understand these messages. **It's** in Russian.

5.3 *ce, cela, ça* or whole clause referent

c'est is used.

(i)   The referent is *ce/ça/cela*.

> Ex: *Je ne comprends pas cela: **c'est** en chinois.*
> I do not understand this – **it is** in Chinese.

(ii)   The referent is a whole clause.

>   Ex: *Je ne comprends pas ce qui est écrit: c'est en russe.*
>   I do not understand what is written – **it is** in Russian.
>
>   *Je ne comprends rien: c'est en hébreu.*
>   I do not understand anything – **it is** in Hebrew.

6 Noun complement

c'est/ce sont are used most of the time but see exceptions below.

6.1 Animate referent

6.1.1 *Noun introduced by a determiner*

If the complement is a noun introduced by a determiner (article, possessive or demonstrative adjective), use *c'est/ce sont*.

(i)   Article

>   Ex: *Je ne les connais pas beaucoup: ce sont des gens que j'ai rencontrés hier.*
>   I don't know them very well – **they are** people I met yesterday.

(ii)   Possessive adjective

>   Ex: *Anne? C'est ma sœur.*
>   Anne? **She is** my sister.

(iii) Demonstrative adjective

>   Ex: *Mon mari? C'est cet homme là-bas.*
>   My husband? **He is** the man over there.

6.1.2 *Nouns indicating nationality, occupation, etc.*

(i)   Use *il est/elle est* without an article before the noun.

>   Ex: *Il est français; ils sont français.*
>   He is French; they are French.
>
>   *Elle est ingénieur; elles sont ingénieurs.*
>   She's an engineer; they are engineers.
>
>   *Il est grand-père; ils sont grand-pères.*
>   He is a grandfather; they are grandfathers.

(ii)   Use *c'est*, regardless of gender, if the name indicating profession, etc. is preceded by an **indefinite** article.

The difference is that in *Il est professeur*, for instance, the noun has an adjectival function and serves to define the person with a quality, while *C'est un professeur* introduces the idea of an explanation: the referent belongs to a particular group or class. Compare:

Que fait-elle dans la vie? ***Elle est*** *journaliste.*
What does she do for a living? She's a journalist.
                 and:
Elle est très curieuse: ***c'est une*** *journaliste.*
She's very nosey – she's a journalist.

(iii) If the noun is itself qualified, ***c'est*** is normally used, with the indefinite article.
        Ex: ***Ce sont de*** *très* ***bons*** *médecins.*
        They are very good doctors.

        C'est une excellente *artiste.*
        She's an excellent artist.

        C'est une *Française* ***d'Outre-Mer.***
        She is a Frenchwoman from the overseas territories.

However, in some lexicalized expressions, ***il est/elle est*** can be followed by a noun and qualifier, without an article.
        Ex: ***Elle est*** *bonne cuisinière.*
        She's a good cook.

Also: *être mauvais joueur/perdant* to be a bad player/loser
        être bon joueur/perdant to be a good player/loser
        être grand seigneur to behave in a lordly fashion

Finally, some well-known authors have ignored that rule – among others!
        Ex: '*Je lui ai fait remarquer qu'en somme,* ***il était un*** *pensionnaire.*'

                                        Albert Camus, *L'étranger*

6.1.3 Proper nouns

If the complement is a proper noun, use ***c'est/ce sont***.
        Ex: ***C'est Paul*** *que je cherche.*
        It is Paul I am looking for.

        Qui sont ces jeunes gens là-bas? ***Ce sont Paul*** *et* ***Marie.***
        Who are those young people over there? They are Paul and Marie.

6.2 Inanimate referent

Use ***c'est/ce sont***.
        Ex: ***C'est*** *une erreur.*
        It's a mistake.

        Ce n'est *pas ma faute!*
        It's not my fault!

        Ce sont *mes chaussures.*
        They're my shoes.

Except to express the time (see 2.2 above) and in the fixed expression '*Il était une fois*' ('Once upon a time').

> Ex: *Il est cinq heures.*
> It is five o'clock.
>
> *Il est temps de partir.*
> It's time to go.
>
> '*Il était une fois dans l'Ouest . . .*'
> 'Once upon a time in the West . . .'
>>   but:
> *Toutes ces querelles, **c'est** de l'histoire ancienne.*
> All these quarrels are ancient history.
>
> *Ces Lalique?* ***Ce sont** mes verres préférés!*
> These Laliques? They are my favourite glasses!

6.3   *ce, cela, ça*, unspecified referent or whole clause

Use *c'est*.

> Ex: − *ce, cela, ça:*
> *Ça, **c'est** une autre histoire.*
> That's another story.
>
> − unspecified referent:
> *Attention!* ***C'est** une scie électrique!*
> Careful! It's an electric saw!
>
> − whole clause:
> *Vous m'avez apporté du chocolat!* ***C'est** une belle surprise!*
> You've brought me some chocolate? That's a nice surprise!

7   Pronoun complement

c'est is used with a pronoun complement (personal, possessive, demonstrative or indefinite) and whatever the referent may be.

− personal pronoun:

> Ex: *Qui a menti?* ***C'est lui**.*
> Who lied? He did.
>
> ***C'est** à **eux** de décider ce qu'ils vont faire.*
> It is up to them to decide what they are going to do.

− possessive pronoun:

> *Ce ne sont pas vos livres.* ***Ce sont les nôtres**.*
> They're not your books. They're ours.

− demonstrative pronoun:

> *Ce n'est pas mon sac.* ***C'est celui** de Nicole.*
> It's not my bag. It's Nicole's.

− indefinite pronoun:

> ***C'est quelque chose*** *de très important.*
> It is something very important.

> *Je ne le connais pas beaucoup:* ***c'est quelqu'un*** *que j'ai rencontré l'année dernière en vacances.*
> I don't know him very well; he is someone I met last year on holiday.

NB(1):   If the complement is plural, ***ce sont*** is used (*c'est* in informal French).

   Ex: ***Ce sont eux*** (*c'est eux*) *qui ont menti.*
     They are the ones who lied.

     Ce sont elles (*c'est elles*) *qui sont parties les premières.*
     They are the ones who left first.

NB(2):   ***c'est*** (and not *ce sont*) is always used before ***nous*** and ***vous***.

   Ex: − *Qui est là?* − ***C'est nous!***
     − Who's there? − It's us!

     C'est vous *qui devrez y aller.*
     You will have to go.
       or (for lexical emphasis):
     You're the one who'll have to go / It's you who will have to go.

36 Indefinite words: adjectives, pronouns, adverbs

1 Introduction

So-called 'indefinite' words include adjectives (determiners), pronouns and adverbs. Although they belong to different parts of speech, they have been treated together in this chapter because of their similarities, which are often a source of confusion. For instance, *chaque* (adjective)/*chacun* (pronoun) and *tout* (pronoun)/*tout* (adjective).

This chapter is divided into five parts in which indefinite words are grouped together according to their proximity of meanings. This is because it is important to know which word is the most appropriate in a particular context.

The chapter is divided up as follows:
– Words which refer to 'somebody' and 'something'
– Words which refer to 'nobody' and 'nothing'
– The concept of 'anybody' and 'anything'
– Indefinite quantifiers
– Words which stress similarities and differences

2 Somebody and something

quelqu'un, *on*, *un*/*une* and *quelque chose* are all **pronouns**.

2.1 *quelqu'un* and *quelque chose*

(i) These pronouns can be a **subject** or an **object**: *quelqu'un* has a human referent (**someone** or **somebody**) and thus operates like a nominal pronoun while *quelque chose* designates an inanimate referent (**something**).

> Ex: ***Quelque chose** est arrivé!*
> subject
> Something's happened!

> *Vous avez trouvé **quelqu'un** pour vous aider?*
> object
> Have you found somebody to help you?

NB: *Il y a quelqu'un?* Is anybody there?

(ii)   When those pronouns are followed by an adjective, **de** must be inserted between *quelqu'un* or *quelque chose* and the adjective. Hence 'something else' is *quelque chose d'autre*. The adjective remains **invariable**.

> Ex: *Y a-t-il **quelqu'un de** mieux informé?*
> Is there someone better informed?
>
> ***Quelque chose de** grave est arrivé.*
> Something serious has happened.

NB: *Quelque chose est arrivé? Has anything happened?*

(iii) Note the meaning of **quelqu'un** and **quelque chose**, unmodified, in exclamations (as complement of *être* or another copula, or *devoir + être*, etc.).

> Ex: *Cet écrivain, c'est **quelqu'un**!*
> This writer is really somebody!
>
> *Trois millions de francs, ce doit être **quelque chose**!*
> Three million francs, that must be quite something!

2.2 *on*

– **on** is an indefinite personal pronoun, 3rd person singular (see also chapters 31 Personal Pronouns section 2.1.2(ii) and 18 Active and Passive Voices, section 5.2).

– It is always a **subject** and masculine singular (but see exceptions below).

(i)   **on** or **quelqu'un**?

on stands for a person and is the equivalent of **quelqu'un**. However, note that **on** can translate a passive, whereas **quelqu'un** is definitely active. Compare:

> **On** *vient de m'apporter ce paquet.*
> I have just been brought this parcel.
>   and:
> **Quelqu'un** *vient de m'apporter ce paquet.*
> Someone's just brought me this parcel.

(ii)   **on** or **les gens**?

on stands for 'people' as an undefined group:

> Ex: **On** *dit qu'un remaniement ministériel est imminent.*
> They say that a cabinet reshuffle is imminent.
>   but:
> **Les gens** *ne surveillent pas assez leurs chiens dans la rue.*
> People don't control their dogs enough in the street.

'*Les gens*' here are seen as individuals and are the important element of the statement, whereas in the first example, it is the cabinet reshuffle which is the important element, regardless of who exactly said it was going to happen.

(iii) *on*: **human beings in general (one)**

> Ex: **On** *aime bien voir ses amis heureux.*
> One likes to see one's friends happy.
>
> **On** *n'est jamais aussi bien que chez soi.*
> There's no place like home.

Note the use of **soi** with **on**: see chapter 31 Personal Pronouns, section 3.1(ii).

2.3 *un*

un/une can be:
– an indefinite article
– a numeral determiner
– a pronoun (**one**), in conjunction with *en*

This is mainly a representative pronoun (with a plural antecedent). See also chapters 23 Articles, section 8.2(ii), 31 Personal Pronouns, section 2.2.2.7(iii) and 37 Numbers, section 2.1(i).

As a pronoun on its own:

(i) *l'un* is often used instead of *un* when it is followed by *de* (or *des*) + noun or pronoun, for euphonic reasons.

> Ex: **L'un de** *nous devrait faire la vaisselle.*
> **One** of us ought to do the washing-up.
>
> *Je vais demander à **l'un de** ces étudiants de nous aider.*
> I am going to ask **one** of those students to help us.

NB: In informal French, *l'* is omitted.

(ii) *l'un* is often used with *l'autre*:

l'un(e) et l'autre (**both**), *l'un(e) . . . l'autre* (**one . . . the other**);
les un(e)s . . . les autres (**some . . . others**); *l'un(e) ou l'autre* (**one or the other/either**); *ni l'un(e) ni l'autre* (**neither one nor the other**).

> Ex: **L'un ou l'autre** *fera l'affaire.*
> Either will do.

See also *n'importe quel* in section 4.1.2 below.

They can refer to an indeterminate referent. Compare:

> – *Où sont les enfants? –* **Les uns** *sont prêts,* **les autres** *sont encore au lit.*
> – Where are the children? – Some are ready, others are still in bed!
> and:
> *On ne sait jamais qui croire.* **L'un** *dit ceci,* **l'autre** *dit cela . . .*
> You never know who to believe. Someone says this, someone else says that . . .

NB: *l'un l'autre, les uns les autres, l'un à l'autre, les uns aux autres, l'un de l'autre* and *les uns des autres* are also used to clarify the meaning of pronominal verbs if a reciprocal (and not a reflexive) meaning is required. (See chapter 20 Pronominal Verbs, section 3.1.1(iii).)

(iii)   Translation of '**one of**' (a group)

    — As a complement of *être*:
        Ex: He isn't one of the group.
           ★*Ce n'est pas un du groupe.*
           → *Ce n'est pas un membre du groupe.*
               or:
           Il ne fait pas partie du groupe.

           It (the bus) was not one of a regular service.
           ★*Ce n'était pas un d'un service régulier.*
           → *Il ne faisait pas partie d'un service régulier.*

    — As a subject:
        Ex: One meaning of this word is . . .
           L'un des sens de ce mot est . . .
Note that English can say either 'one meaning of this word is' or 'one of the meanings of this word is'. French cannot be ★*un sens de ce mot est.*

    — As an object:
        Ex: He has eaten one of the cakes.
           Il a mangé l'un des gâteaux.

2.4   'People'

Note the distinction in meaning between *peuple, gens, monde, personnes, on* (see above) and *habitants*. All can be **people** in English.

(i)   *peuple*

The individuals who form a nation.
        Ex: *le **peuple** français*
           the French **people**

           *un **peuple** primitif/civilisé*
           a primitive/civilized **people**

(ii)   *habitant(e)s*

People who reside in a given place e.g. in a village, town, country, etc.
        Ex: *les **habitants** de la région parisienne*
           the **people** of the Paris region

(iii)   *gens* (always plural)

An undetermined number of people which can therefore be used with *beaucoup de* or *peu de* but not with *quelques* or *plusieurs, un, deux,* etc. (use *personnes* instead). It is also used for generalization as well as specification.

Ex: *Il avait invité beaucoup de **gens** à sa soirée.*
He had invited a lot of **people** to his party.

*Les **gens** (generic) sont méchants.*
People are uncaring.

*Les **gens** que j'ai vus (specific) peuvent partir maintenant.*
The **people** I've seen can leave now.

Note that *les personnes* would be preferred for the last example.

(iv)   *personne* (always feminine)

A determined number of people which is therefore rarely used with *beaucoup de* or *peu de* (for which *gens* is preferred, see above). It is also used for specification but not for generalization.

Ex: *Trois **personnes** sont venues ce matin.*
Three **people** came this morning.

*Plusieurs **personnes** étaient absentes à la réunion.*
Several **people** were absent from the meeting.

(v)   *monde*

monde is used when 'people' refers to an indefinite group seen as a 'mass' rather than individuals (for which *gens* is preferred). Compare:

*Il n'y a pas grand **monde** dans les magasins juste après Noël.*
and:
Pour beaucoup de gens, 'révolte' est inextricablement lié à 'révolution'.

3   Nobody and nothing

– *aucun(e)*, *nul(le)* and *pas un(e)* are **adjectives** or **pronouns**
– *personne* and *rien* are **pronouns**

3.1   *aucun*

aucun(e) is a negative **adjective** and **pronoun** (**no**, **not . . . any**; **none**) and is used with *ne* only (there is no *pas*).

3.1.1   *Adjective*

(i)   Qualifying the subject (*aucun* + subject + *ne* + verb)
Ex: *Est-il vrai qu'**aucun** citoyen **n'**est exempt de l'impôt sur le revenu?*
Is it true that **no** citizen is exempt from income tax?

(ii)   Used instead of *ne . . . pas de* for emphasis when qualifying objects
(*ne* + verb + *aucun* + object).
Ex: *Je **n'**ai trouvé **aucune** erreur dans ce texte.*
I found **no** errors in this text.

(iii)   *aucun(e)* can also appear without *ne* in elliptic constructions, e.g. answers.

Ex: − *Savez-vous à quelle heure il doit arriver? − **Aucune** idée.*
− Do you know what time he is supposed to arrive? − No idea.

Here, the ellipsis is of the subject and verb (*Je **n'**en ai **aucune** idée*).

3.1.2   Pronoun

aucun(e) can be either a representative or a nominal pronoun. Its antecedent is always plural but the pronoun itself is singular since it expresses a zero quantity of this antecedent. Hence it only agrees in **gender**.

(i)   Subject (*aucun **ne*** + verb)

Ex: *Il y a deux films à la télévision ce soir mais **aucun ne** me tente.*
There are two films on TV tonight but **neither** tempts me.

(ii)   Object (***ne*** + verb + *aucun*)

Ex: − *Avez-vous trouvé des champignons? − Non, je **n'**en ai trouvé **aucun**.*
− Have you found any mushrooms? − No, I have**n't** found **any**.

(iii)   *aucun* can also appear on its own (without *ne*) in elliptic constructions.

Ex: − *As-tu reçu des cadeaux pour ton anniversaire? − Non, **aucun**.*
(= *Je **n'**en ai reçu aucun*.)
− Have you received any presents for your birthday? − No, none.

3.2   nul

− As a negative **adjective**, *nul* is equivalent to *aucun*.
− As a negative **pronoun**, *nul* is equivalent to *personne*.

However, *nul* is rarer than *aucun* or *personne*.

3.2.1   Adjective

(i)   Qualifying the subject

Ex: *Nul homme **n'**en sera exempté.*
No man will be exempted.

(ii)   Qualifying an adverb phrase with *sans* (note that there is no *ne*)

Ex: *Il a parlé sans **nulle** gêne.*
He spoke uninhibitedly.

NB: *aucun* is more widely used.

Ex: *Vous pouvez aller là-bas sans **aucune** crainte.*
You can go there without any fear.

(iii)   Complement of *être*: here, *nul* is **not** interchangeable with *aucun*.

− *nul* is used in legal documents and means 'which has no (legal) value'.

Ex: *Ce document est **nul** et non avenu.*
This document is null and void.

– in other contexts, **nul** is very pejorative and should be used with care.

> Ex: *Ce devoir est **nul**.*
> This paper is rubbish.
>
> *Elle est **nulle** en maths.*
> She is hopeless at maths.

NB: *nulle part* (nowhere) is an adverb which is treated in chapter 38 Negative Structures, section 2.2.1(viii).

3.2.2 Pronoun

It can only be a **subject** and is reserved for literary or administrative usage.

> Ex: *A l'impossible **nul n'**est tenu.*
> No-one is expected to do the impossible.
>
> ***Nul n'**est censé ignorer la loi.*
> Everyone is supposed to know the law.

3.3 *personne, rien*

personne (**nobody, not . . . anybody**), *rien* (**nothing, not . . . anything**) are negative **pronouns**.
– *personne* always refers to a human referent. It can be either representative (with a plural antecedent) or nominal.
– *rien* refers to an inanimate referent.
Note that animals are not catered for by the pair *rien/personne*: use *aucun*.

personne and *rien* can be a **subject** or an **object** and are used with *ne* only (without *pas*).

(i) Subject: '***personne ne . . .***'; '***rien ne . . .***'

> Ex: ***Personne n'**a pensé à prendre les croissants.*
> Nobody's remembered to get the croissants.
>
> *Tout l'ennuie et **rien** de ce que vous dites **ne** l'intéresse.*
> Everything bores him and nothing you say interests him.
>
> ***Rien n'**a été dérangé.*
> Nothing has been disturbed.

Because the *n'* does not affect the pronunciation before a verb beginning with a vowel, it is a common mistake to forget to write it after *rien*.

(ii) Object: '***ne . . . personne***'; '***ne . . . rien***'

> Ex: – *Tu vois Paul? – Non, je **ne** vois **personne**.*
> – Can you see Paul? – No, I can't see anybody.
>
> *Qui **ne** risque **rien n'**a **rien**.* (proverb)
> Nothing ventured, nothing gained.

– As a direct object, ***personne* follows** the past participle or the infinitive (like other negative pronouns). However, ***rien* precedes** them.

> Ex: *Je **n'ai vu personne**/Je **n'ai rien vu***.
> I saw nobody/I saw nothing.

> *Je **ne veux voir personne**/Je **ne veux rien voir***.
> I don't want to see anybody/I don't want to see anything.

See also chapter 15 Infinitive.

– As an indirect object, ***rien* follows** the past participle or infinitive, as does ***personne***.

> Ex: *Il **ne veut s'intéresser à rien***.
> He does not want to take an interest in anything.

> *Elle est partie sans **dire** au-revoir **à personne***.
> She left without saying good-bye to anybody.

(iii)   If ***rien*** or ***personne*** are qualified by an adjective, ***de*** must be inserted before the adjective, which remains invariable (see *quelqu'un* and *quelque chose* above).

> Ex: *Heureusement, rien de grave ne s'est passé*.
> Fortunately, nothing serious happened.

> *Je n'ai rencontré **personne de** très **sympathique** à cette réception*.
> I did not meet anybody particularly friendly at that reception.

(iv)   The negation can be reinforced with ***rien du tout*** (= nothing at all) instead of ***rien***, or ***personne du tout*** (= nobody at all), but the latter is comparatively rare. Note that ***du*** is used, not *de*.

> Ex: *Vous n'avez **rien** fait **du tout***.
> You've done nothing at all.

> – *Il est venu quelqu'un? – **Personne du tout***.
> – Did anybody come? – Nobody at all.

Note that in this example, the ellipsis of the verb entails the disappearance of *ne*.

(v)   ***rien* with *pas***

ne . . . pas can appear with ***rien*** to give an affirmative meaning to the sentence.

> Ex: *Vous **ne** pouvez tout de même **pas** ne **rien** faire!*
> (= *Il est indispensable que vous fassiez quelque chose*.)
> You can't just do nothing!

> *Ce **n'est pas** pour **rien** qu'on l'appelle un génie*.
> (= *Il y a une raison au fait que . . .*)
> They don't call him a genius for nothing.

> *Ce **n'est pas rien**!*
> (= *Ce n'est pas négligeable, c'est quelque chose*.)
> That's quite something!

This last example belongs to the familiar register.

(vi) ***rien/personne*** without ***ne*** or ***pas***

rien can appear without ***ne*** or ***pas*** in the following type of expressions:

> *C'est tout ou **rien**.*
> It's all or nothing.

> *Tout cela se réduit à **rien**.*
> It all boils down to nothing.

> *Tout ce travail pour **rien**!*
> All this work for nothing!

> *Il est parti sans avoir **rien** mangé.*
> He left without having eaten anything.

> *Elle connaît cette histoire mieux que **personne**.*
> She knows this story better than anybody.

Also in answers to questions:

> Ex: − *Qu'est-ce que tu as vu?*
> − ***Rien** d'intéressant.*
> − What have you seen?
> − Nothing of interest.

(vii) It is a common mistake to confuse the **pronoun *personne*** (nobody or anybody) and the **noun *une personne*** (a person).

> Ex: − pronoun:
> ***Personne** n'est venu; je n'ai vu **personne**.*
> Nobody came; I didn't see anybody.

> − noun:
> *Une **personne** est venue; plusieurs **personnes** sont venues.*
> One person came; several people came.

(viii) Idioms with ***rien***

− *comme si de rien n'était = comme si rien ne s'était passé; de la façon la plus naturelle*
> Ex: *Après nous avoir insultés, ils ont repris leur chemin **comme si de rien n'était**.*
> After insulting us, they continued on their way as if nothing had happened.

− *rien que = seulement*
> Ex: *Laisse-moi conduire ta Porsche, **rien qu'**une fois!*
> Let me drive your Porsche, just once!

> ***Rien que** pour aller au centre ville, d'ici il faut déjà une heure!*
> Just to get to the town centre takes you one hour from here.

− *ne servir à rien = être inutile*
> Ex: *Cela **ne sert à rien** de vous dépêcher: vous avez déjà manqué votre train!*
> It's no use hurrying − you have already missed your train.

— en un rien de temps = très rapidement

Ex: *Je peux vous faire une mayonnaise **en un rien de temps**!*

I can make mayonnaise for you in no time!

(ix)   ***rien*** and ***aucun***

As a pronoun, ***rien*** (nothing) does not refer to a named antecedent, whereas ***aucun*** (none, not . . . any) does. Compare:

*Je n'ai **rien** trouvé de plus beau.*

I have found **nothing** more beautiful.

and:

*Je **n'en** ai trouvé **aucun** de plus beau.*

I have found **none** more beautiful.

aucun refers to a named antecedent in a previous sentence, in this case, masculine singular.

3.4   *pas un*

(i)   Like *aucun(e)*, ***pas un(e)*** is both a nominal and a representative **pronoun**. The antecedent is always plural, but the pronoun is singular since it expresses a zero quantity of that antecedent. Hence it only agrees in gender. It can be used as:

— a subject: ***pas un(e) ne*** + verb

or:

— an object: ***ne*** + [***en***] + verb + ***pas un(e)***

NB: ***pas un*** can be accompanied by ***seul*** for emphasis.

— Subject:

Ex: *Cette organisation abrite beaucoup de clochards mais **pas un ne** reste.*

This organization shelters a lot of tramps but none of them stay.

— Object:

Ex: *Les oiseaux ont mangé toutes mes cerises. Il **n'en** reste **pas une** / **pas une** seule.*

The birds have eaten all my cherries. There are none left / There is not a single one left.

See also *en* in chapter 31 Personal Pronouns, section 2.2.2.7.

(ii)   ***pas un*** can be a negative **adjective** which can be used with:

— a subject: ***pas un(e)*** + noun phrase + ***ne*** + verb

or:

— an object: ***ne*** + verb + ***pas un(e)*** + noun phrase

— Subject:

Ex: ***Pas un** seul clochard **n'**est resté.*

Not a single tramp stayed.

– Object:

> Ex: *Il **n'y** a **pas une** seule cerise sur mon arbre cette année.*
> There isn't a single cherry on my tree this year.
>
> *Il **n'y** a **pas une** seule rayure sur mes vieux 33 tours!*
> There's no scratch on my old LPs.

4   Any, anybody and anything

4.1   n'importe

– ***n'importe*** on its own means: 'it does not matter', 'it is not important'.

– ***n'importe quel/quelle/quels/quelles*** ('any') is the **adjective**.

– ***n'importe lequel/laquelle/lesquels/lesquelles*** ('any'), ***n'importe qui*** ('anybody'), ***n'importe quoi*** ('anything') are the **pronouns**.

– ***n'importe où*** ('anywhere'), ***n'importe quand*** ('any time'), ***n'importe comment*** ('anyhow') are the **adverbs**.

4.1.1   Adjective

As an adjective, ***n'importe quel*** (***quelle***, ***quels***, ***quelles***) indicates a free choice between several animates or inanimates.

> Ex: *Prenez **n'importe quel** livre.*
> Take any book.

An alternative in formal French would be:

> *Prenez un livre **quelconque**.*

But note that *quelconque* is ambiguous and should be used with care (see section 4.2).

4.1.2   Pronoun

As a pronoun, ***n'importe lequel*** (***laquelle***, ***lesquels***, ***lesquelles***) can be the **subject** or the **object** of the verb.

(i)   ***n'importe lequel***, etc. are mainly representative pronouns and refer to animates or inanimates. They are used when the choice has been stated and agree in gender and number with the choice.

> Ex: *Choisissez un exercice: faites **n'importe lequel*** (= n'importe quel exercice).
> Choose an exercise – do any of them.
>
> *Je pourrais demander à **n'importe laquelle** de mes amies.*
> I could ask any of my friends.

(ii)   ***n'importe qui*** has an undetermined human referent and operates like a nominal pronoun. It is often translated as 'just anybody' to distinguish it from 'anybody at all'.

> Ex: *Je ne peux pas simplement demander à **n'importe qui** de m'aider.*
> I can't ask just anybody to help me.

569

(iii)   ***n'importe quoi*** has an undetermined inanimate referent.
>   Ex: *Vous pouvez me demander **n'importe quoi**.*
>   You can ask me anything you want.

NB: Care should be taken with the use of ***n'importe quoi*** as a (grammatical) object which is not the result of a request, as it is then interpreted as meaning 'nonsense' and is very derogatory.
>   Ex: *Vous dites **n'importe quoi**.*
>   You're talking nonsense.
>
>   *Il leur a raconté **n'importe quoi**.*
>   He told them fibs.
>
>   *Il fait **n'importe quoi**.*
>   He doesn't know what he's doing.

4.1.3   Adverb

n'importe où*, *n'importe quand*, *n'importe comment

>   Ex: *Venez **n'importe quand**: je serai à la maison toute la journée.*
>   Come any time/whenever you like – I'll be in all day.
>
>   *Ils sont libres. Ils peuvent aller **n'importe où**.*
>   They are free. They can go anywhere [they like].
>
>   *Regardez-moi ces assiettes: elles ont été rangées **n'importe comment**.*
>   Look at these plates: they have been put away any old how.

NB: ***n'importe comment*** suggests that things are not as they should be and is derogatory.

4.2   *quelconque*

quelconque is always an **adjective**. It is generally placed after the noun, which is itself preceded by an article. It means:

(i)   some . . . [or other]
>   Ex: *Il est venu me voir sous un prétexte **quelconque**.*
>   He came to see me on some pretext [or other].

(ii)   common, mediocre, of poor value (particularly as subject complement with *être*, or preceded by *très*)
>   Ex: *Il a écrit un article **très quelconque**.*
>   He wrote a rather pedestrian article.
>
>   *La maison **est quelconque** mais le site est merveilleux.*
>   The house is very ordinary but the location is wonderful.

(iii)   *quelconque* applied to people is very derogatory and should be used with care.
>   Ex: *Ce sont des gens très **quelconques**.*
>   They are uninteresting people.
>   Compare with:
>   *Ce sont des gens très simples.*
>   They are unpretentious people.

4.3   *qui que, quoi que*

(i)   *qui que* and *quoi que* are **indefinite relative pronouns** (i.e. they do not have an antecedent). They can refer either to an animate (*qui . . .*) or an inanimate (*quoi . . .*). They introduce a subordinate clause of concession, hence are always followed by the subjunctive (see also chapter 12 Subjunctive, section 4.3.3).

> Ex: *Qui que vous soyez, vous ne m'impressionnez pas.*
> **Whoever** you may be, you do not impress me.

> *Quoi qu'ils fassent, ils ont peu de chances de réussir.*
> **Whatever** they may do, they have little chance of success.

(ii)   It is a common mistake to confuse the indefinite relative pronoun *quoi que* and the conjunction of subordination *quoique*. Compare:

> *Quoi qu'il dise, personne ne le croit.*
> (= *quelle que soit la chose qu'il dise*)
> **Whatever** he may say, nobody believes him.
> and:
> *Quoiqu'il dise la vérité, personne ne le croit.*
> (= *bien qu'il dise la vérité*)
> **Although** he's telling the truth, nobody believes him.

(iii) *Qui que ce soit* and *quoi que ce soit* (direct or indirect objects) are often used by themselves (i.e. not followed by *que*).
– *qui que ce soit* means 'anyone at all', 'whoever it may be';
– *quoi que ce soit* means 'anything at all', 'whatever it may be'.
As objects, they are used in a negative clause (without *pas*). It is important not to confuse them with *n'importe qui*, *n'importe quoi* (see above). Compare:

> *Je ne veux voir qui que ce soit.*
> I do not want to see anybody at all.
> and:
> *Je ne veux pas voir n'importe qui.*
> I do not want to see just anybody.

> *N'achetez quoi que ce soit dans ce magasin.* (= *ne . . . rien*)
> Do not buy anything in this shop whatsoever.
> and:
> *N'achetez pas n'importe quoi!*
> Do not buy any rubbish!

(iv)   *Qui que ce soit qui* is rare.
Quoi que ce soit qui should be avoided. Use instead an expression based on *quelle que soit la chose qui*.

> Ex: *Quel que soit le problème qui vous tracasse . . .*
> Whatever it is that bothers you . . .

4.4 *quiconque*

quiconque is a **relative pronoun**. It always has an undetermined human referent. It is always singular and almost always masculine. It has two meanings:

(i) **whoever, anyone who, all those who**. It is the subject of the relative clause that it introduces, and the subject or the object of the verb in the other clause.

> Ex: ***Quiconque** dit cela n'a pas bien réfléchi à la question.*
> Whoever says that has not considered the question very carefully.
> (subject of '***dit***' and '***a réfléchi***')
>
> *Je répondrai à **quiconque** posera une question.*
> I shall answer anybody who asks a question.
> (indirect object of '***répondrai***' and subject of '***posera***')

NB(1): A less formal alternative is *toute personne qui*.

> Ex: ***Toute personne qui** dit cela n'a pas bien réfléchi à la question.*
> *Je répondrai à **toute personne qui** posera une question.*

NB(2): ***Qui*** is often used in proverbs in the sense of ***quiconque***.

> Ex: ***Qui** dort dîne.*
> He who sleeps forgets his hunger.
>
> ***Qui** va à la chasse perd sa place.*
> He who leaves his place loses it.
>
> ***Qui** vivra verra.*
> What will be will be.

(ii) **anybody**

> Ex: *Il est impossible à **quiconque** de trouver quoi que ce soit ici!*
> It is impossible for **anybody** to find anything here!
>
> *Je défie **quiconque** de prouver le contraire.*
> I defy **anybody** to prove the contrary.
>
> *Je le sais mieux que **quiconque**.*
> I know it better than **anybody**.

5 Indefinite quantifiers

The following are a selection of indefinite quantifiers: ***certains, quelques, quelques-uns, différents, divers, plusieurs, maint, chaque, chacun, tout***.

5.1 *certain*

- *certain, certaine* are **adjectives**
- *certains, certaines* are adjectives or **pronouns**

5.1.1 Adjective

(i) In the **singular**, *certain(e)* **before** the noun, preceded by *un(e)*, is an indefinite quantifier.

– Referring to a **human**, it indicates someone the speaker does not know much about, and wants to say so.

> Ex: *Il y a un **certain** M. Dupont à la porte!*
> (or simply: *Il y a un M. Dupont à la porte.*)
> There's a certain M. Dupont at the door!

(See also chapter 23 Articles, section 3.2.5.)

– Referring to an **inanimate**, it indicates a quantity which is not necessarily trivial but is undefined.

> Ex: *Je connais l'Angleterre. J'y vis depuis un **certain** temps.*
> I know England. I've been living there for a while.

Thus, it can be used ironically:

> Ex: *Vous avez un **certain** toupet!*
> You've got some nerve!

NB: When it is placed **after** the noun or is subject complement with *être*, it is a simple qualifying adjective which means 'certain' in the sense of 'sure'.

> Ex: *Voilà une preuve **certaine** de sa culpabilité.*
> That's definite proof of his guilt.
>
> *Ça ne va pas marcher, c'est **certain**.*
> It's not going to work, that's for sure.

Hence the standard joke in French about:

> *une dame d'un **certain** âge*
> a middle-aged woman (lit. 'a woman of a certain age')
>   and:
> *une dame d'un âge **certain***
> a woman of a definite age (i.e. a woman who shows her age)

(ii) In the **plural**, *certain(e)s* has the value of *quelques* (some) and can refer to **animates** or **inanimates**.

– It is used without an article.

> Ex: ***Certains** verres ne sont pas à leur place!*
> Some glasses are not in the right place!
>
> ***Certaines** personnes n'ont pas payé.*
> Some people have not paid.

– However, if the noun that follows is specific (see chapter 23 Articles), *de* + definite article is used.

> Ex: ***Certaines des** (= de les) personnes qui sont venues n'avaient pas payé.*
> Some of the people who came had not paid.

– It is often used in conjunction with *d'autres*.

> Ex: ***Certains** commerçants sont aimables, **d'autres** ne le sont pas.*
> Some shopkeepers are pleasant, others are not.

5.1.2 Pronoun

As a pronoun, *certains* is always **plural** and means **some**. It can be nominal (with an undetermined referent) or representative.

> Ex: '***Certains** l'aiment chaud*'
> 'Some Like It Hot' – title of a film.
>
> *La plupart de mes amis font du sport mais **certains** ne font rien!*
> Most of my friends do some sport but some do nothing!

Note that there is an innuendo here as *certains* can be interpreted as 'some who shall remain nameless'.
An alternative would be:

> *. . . . mais **il y en a** [quelques-uns] **qui** ne font rien.*

5.2 *quelques, quelques-uns*

- *quelques* is an **adjective**
- *quelque* can be an **adverb** or an **adjective**
- *quelques-un(e)s* is a **pronoun**

5.2.1 Adjective

(i) ***quelques*** indicates a small number (**some**, **a few**) and ***quelque*** a small quantity (**some**). But see also (ii) below.

> Ex: *J'ai pris **quelques** notes.*
> I took a few notes.
>
> *Je vais passer **quelque** temps en Provence.*
> I'm going to spend some time in Provence.

- As in English, when it means **a few**, it can be preceded by an article or other specific determiner.

> Ex: *Je vous ai apporté **les quelques** cerises qui restaient.*
> I brought you the few cherries which were left.
>
> *Quelqu'un a pris **mes quelques** cerises!*
> Someone's taken the few cherries I had!
>
> *Prenez donc **ces quelques** cerises!*
> Do take these few cherries!

- Note that ***quelques*** cannot be used with uncountable nouns (use *un peu de* or the partitive article). Collective nouns such as *gens* are always plural and cannot be 'divided', hence:

> Ex: There are some people who . . .
> *Il y a **des gens** qui . . .*
>   but:
> There are a few people who . . .
> *Il y a **quelques personnes** qui . . .*

In the same way:

>*les gens, des gens, beaucoup de gens, peu de gens*
>>but:
>*une personne, quelques/plusieurs personnes, 1200 personnes*

See also 2.4.

(ii)   In the singular, *quelque* also means **some kind of**.

>Ex: *Il aura trouvé **quelque** occasion de se faire un peu d'argent.*
>He has probably found some opportunity to make a bit of money.

Note that this usage is rare: in informal French, *un/une* would be used, with or without the addition of *quelconque* (see 4.2 above).

>*Il aura trouvé **une** occasion [**quelconque**] de se faire un peu d'argent.*

5.2.2   Pronoun

quelques-uns, *quelques-unes* (**some/a few**) can be nominal (with an undetermined referent, animate or inanimate) or representative. They can be a subject or an object.

(i)   Subject

>Ex: *La plupart des étudiants ont quitté le campus maintenant, mais **quelques-uns** sont encore là.*
>Most students have left the campus now but a few are still around.

(ii)   Object

>Ex: *J'ai cueilli toutes ces cerises: prenez-<u>en</u> **quelques-unes**!*

(It is a common mistake to forget the **en**: see chapter 31 Personal Pronouns, section 2.2.2.7(iii).)

>I have picked all these cherries, please take some!

>*J'ai revu **quelques-unes** de mes anciennes amies.*
>I saw some of my old friends again.

NB: 'some of us' ('some of you', 'some of them') is *quelques-uns **d'entre** nous / **parmi** nous (vous, eux, elles)*, not **quelques-uns de nous*.

5.2.3   Adverb

(i)   As an adverb, *quelque* means 'nearly' or 'about' but this usage is rare.

>Ex: *L'incendie s'étendait sur **quelque** deux cents mètres.*
>The fire spread over some two hundred metres.

(ii)   *quelque part* refers to an indefinite place.

>Ex: *Le livre que tu cherches est **quelque part** dans ta chambre.*
>The book you're looking for is **somewhere** in your room.

>*Y a-t-il **quelque part**/un endroit où je puisse laisser mon manteau?*
>Is there **anywhere** I can leave my coat?

NB: '**somehow**' is translated in various ways, according to the context.
> Ex: − I can't solve that problem.
> − Well, you'll have to solve it **somehow**.
> − *Je n'arrive pas à résoudre ce problème.*
> − *Eh bien, tu devras le résoudre d'une manière ou d'une autre.*

> **Somehow**, she's managed to find the money to buy the coat.
> *Elle a fini par trouver un moyen d'acheter le manteau.*

5.3 *différents, divers*

These are **adjectives** only. They are used in the **plural** and **precede** the noun.

(i) *différents* is the equivalent of *plusieurs* but stresses the different types rather than the overall quantity. Moreover, unlike *plusieurs*, it can be used with a number.
> Ex: *Nous avons trouvé [trois] **différentes** sortes de champignons.*
> We found [three] different kinds of mushrooms.

(ii) *divers* emphasizes the concept of variety more strongly than *différents*, but it cannot be used with a number.
> Ex: *Nous avons trouvé **diverses** sortes de champignons.*
> We found various types of mushrooms.

NB: If they are placed **after** the noun, they become ordinary qualifying adjectives (see chapter 28 Qualifying Adjectives, section 2.3.4). They can be preceded by an article and used in the singular and in superlatives (*plusieurs* cannot: see below).
> Ex: *J'aime faire une activité **différente** tous les jours.*
> I like to do a different activity every day.

> *Il a parlé sur des sujets **divers**.*
> He spoke on a variety of subjects.

(iii) Note the following idiom:
> *un fait **divers***
> an incident

5.4 *plusieurs*

plusieurs can be an **adjective** or a **pronoun**. It is invariable.

5.4.1 *Adjective*

(i) It indicates an undetermined number, normally more than two and no more than ten. It is always **plural**.
> Ex: *J'ai essayé de vous téléphoner **plusieurs** fois.*
> I tried to ring you several times.

(ii)   There is no article after *plusieurs*, unless the noun is specific (see chapter 23
Articles), in which case *plusieurs* is followed by *de* + specific determiner.

> Ex: ***Plusieurs*** *étudiants ont répondu à l'appel de volontaires.*
> Several students answered the appeal for volunteers.
>> but:
> ***Plusieurs de ses*** *étudiants ont répondu à l'appel de volontaires.*
> Several of his/her students answered the appeal for volunteers.

5.4.2   Pronoun

It is mainly used as a representative pronoun and is always **plural**. It can be either
a subject or an object.

> Ex: − subject:
> *J'ai demandé à mes étudiants de se soumettre à un test psychologique.*
> ***Plusieurs*** *ont accepté.*
> I asked my students [if they would be willing] to undergo a
> psychological test. Several [of them] have accepted.
> − object:
> *Quel magazine voulez-vous? J'*en *ai* ***plusieurs***.
> Which magazine would you like? I've got several.

Note the presence of *en* (see chapter 31 Personal Pronouns, section 2.2.2.7(iii)).

5.5   maint

maint (***maints***, ***mainte***, ***maintes***) is always an **adjective**. It is an old word, mainly
used in the plural and which means a great, undetermined number. It is not used
in informal French, for which ***bon nombre de***, *de* ***nombreux***(***-ses***) would be
preferred.

> Ex: *J'ai essayé* ***maintes fois***/***à maintes reprises*** *mais en vain.*
> I have tried many times, but in vain.
> → *J'ai essayé bon nombre de fois/de nombreuses fois . . .*

5.6   chaque, chacun

− ***chaque*** ('each') is an **adjective**
− ***chacun***(*e*) ('each') is a **pronoun**

5.6.1   Adjective

The adjective ***chaque*** (masculine or feminine) is always **singular** and always
comes before the noun (animate or inanimate) with no other determiner. When
using *chaque* (instead of *tout* − see 5.7.1(ii) below), each particular case is
expressed and implies the general case: *chaque* is used in a **distributive** sense.
(However, with *tout*, it is the totality which is expressed and implies the general
case: *tout* is used in a **collective** sense.)

> Ex: *Il faut s'arrêter à* ***chaque*** *page pour comprendre!*
> You have to stop at each page in order to understand!
>
> ***Chaque*** *candidat aura droit à deux minutes.*
> Each candidate will be allowed two minutes.

5.6.2 Pronoun

As a pronoun, *chacun* is masculine singular and *chacune* is feminine singular. It is used for animates or inanimates considered individually but which belong to a group. They can be nominal (with an undetermined referent) or representative.

Ex: *Tous ses amis sont venus: **chacun** avait apporté un cadeau.*
All his/her friends came – everyone had brought a present.

*J'ai fait attention à **chacune** de vos phrases.*
I paid attention to each of your sentences.

NB: 'each of us' (of you/of them) is *chacun **d'entre** nous (**d'entre** vous/eux/elles)*, and **not** **chacun de nous*.

***Chacun** pour soi, Dieu pour tous!* (proverb, with *chacun* as masculine generic).
Each man for himself and the Devil take the hindmost!

5.7 tout

- *tout, toute, tous, toutes*, are **adjectives**
- *tout, tous, toutes*, are **pronouns**
- *tout (toute, toutes)*, are **adverbs**

5.7.1 Adjective

(i) In the **singular**, *tout, toute* means:

- 'all', 'any' in the sense of 'all instances' (and not 'any' in the sense of 'don't care who or what' when *n'importe quel*, etc. should be used: see section 4.1.2 above). It is used without an article and in a general sense, often in proverbs.
  Ex: ***Toute** vérité n'est pas bonne à dire.*
  Some truths are best left unsaid.

  ***Toute** peine mérite salaire.*
  Any/Every effort deserves reward.

  ***Tout** accusé a droit à l'assistance d'un avocat.*
  Anyone charged has the right to a lawyer.

- 'all' in the sense of 'the totality of'. It is followed by a specific determiner, hence it is sometimes called a pre-determiner (*prédéterminant* or *préarticle*).
  Ex: ***Toute la** famille est arrivée.*
  The whole family has arrived.

  *Les grèves peuvent paralyser **tout un** pays.*
  Strikes can paralyse a whole country.

NB: It is a common mistake to confuse *tout le monde* (= **everybody**) and *le monde entier* (= **the whole world**).

- 'all' in a restrictive sense, i.e. 'that and nothing more', 'in total'. There is no article.
  Ex: *Il ne reçoit que mille francs par mois pour **tout** salaire.*
  He's only getting one thousand francs a month total salary.

– 'quite': it is used with an indefinite article, and only in informal French.

> Ex: *C'est **tout un** travail!*
> That's quite a job!
>
> *Il a fait **toute une** histoire.*
> He made quite a fuss.

Note the following expressions with ***tout/toute***:

> Ex: ***A tout hasard**, je passerai vous voir la semaine prochaine.*
> I'll call on you next week on the off chance.
>
> *Elle ne veut pas se marier. Pas encore **en tout cas**.*
> She doesn't want to get married. Not yet anyhow.
>
> *Un accident peut arriver **à tout moment**.*
> An accident can happen at any time.
>
> ***De toute façon**, il ne viendra pas.*
> In any case, he won't come.

(ii)   In the **plural**, ***tous**, **toutes*** means:

(Note that the '*s*' is not pronounced in the adjective ***tous***: [tu]).

– 'the whole lot'/'all' [of them], 'the totality of', and is followed by a specific determiner.

> Ex: ***Tous mes** amis sont là.*
> All my friends are here.
>
> ***Toutes ces** fleurs sont fanées.*
> All these flowers have wilted.

– 'all instances of' (as opposed to 'any', for which *n'importe quel* should be used – see above).

> Ex: *Les femmes sont supérieures dans **tous les** domaines auxquels on peut penser.*
> Women are superior in **all** the domains you can think of.
> but:
> *Elles sont supérieures dans **n'importe quel** domaine.*
> They are superior in **any** domain.
>
> ***Tous les** chemins mènent à Rome.* (proverb)
> All roads lead to Rome.

– **every**: when 'every' means 'all' as opposed to 'each' (or if there is a choice, i.e. if the emphasis is placed on the concept of 'all'). Particularly with a number, *tous/toutes* should be used instead of *chaque* (see 5.6.1 above).

> Ex: *Il y a une année bissextile **tous les** quatre ans.*
> (rather than *chaque quatre ans*)
> There is a leap year **every** four years.
> but:
> *Il y avait des attroupements à **tous les** coins de rue / à **chaque** coin de rue.*
> There were gatherings on **every** street corner.

579

Consider the following example:

> '. . . the study of English literature, to the exclusion of nearly **every** other language and tradition . . .'

George Steiner, Language and Silence

'. . . *l'étude de la littérature anglaise, à l'exclusion de presque **toutes les** autres langues et traditions . . .*'
'every' does mean 'all' here, rather than 'each'.

Note the following expressions with ***tous/toutes***:

> Ex: *de **tous** côtés* on all sides
> *à **tous** égards* in every respect
> ***toutes** taxes comprises* all taxes included

5.7.2 Pronoun

(i) ***tout***, subject or object

It means **everything** or **anything** and is **invariable**.

> Ex: ***Tout** va bien.*
> Everything is fine.
>
> ***Tout** est permis.*
> Anything is allowed.
>
> ***Tout** ce qui brille n'est pas or.* (proverb)
> All that glisters is not gold.
> (See also chapter 32 Relative Pronouns, section 4.2.)
>
> *Il sait **tout**.*
> He knows everything.
>
> *Prenez **tout**.*
> Take the lot.

(ii) ***tous/toutes***, subject, **plural**

Note that the '*s*' **is** pronounced in the pronoun ***tous***: [tus].

They are normally representative pronouns.

> Ex: *J'avais invité <u>mes amis</u> pour mon anniversaire: **tous** sont venus.*
> I had invited my friends over for my birthday – they all came.

However, *tous* (*toutes*) can also be nominal, with a generic referent.

> Ex: *Elle est estimée de **tous*** (or: *de **tous** et de **toutes***).
> She is respected by all.

When ***tous/toutes*** (**everybody** or **all/all of them**) are subject of the verb, the order is either:

> Ex: ***Tous** étaient là.* **or** *Ils étaient **tous** là.*
> Everybody was here/They were all here.

but the second one is more frequent.

However, there may be an ambiguity with the adverb (see 5.7.4 below). Consider the following example:

> (*Les tomates*) **Toutes** *sont mûres.*
> All of them are ripe.
>
> > or:
>
> *Elles sont* **toutes** *mûres.*
> All of them are ripe. **or** They are very ripe.

The context should dictate the meaning. If the context is insufficient, use the first construction, which is unambiguous.

(iii)   ***tous/toutes***, object, **plural**

Note that the '*s*' **is** pronounced in the pronoun *tous*: [tus]

When ***tous*, *toutes*** are the object of the verb, they are placed:

− after the verb in simple tenses.
> Ex: *Je les inviterai* ***tous***.
> I'll invite them all.

− between the auxiliary and the past participle in compound tenses.
> Ex: *Je les avais* ***tous*** *invités.*
> I had invited them all.

5.7.3   The case of 'both'

both can be: ***les deux***; ***tous/toutes les deux*** or ***à la fois*** ('the three, four, etc. of them' or 'all three, four, etc. of them' is ***tous les trois*, *quatre***, etc. ***d'entre eux***). Note that the '*s*' of *tous* is **not** pronounced: [tu].

(i)   **both**, subject

− 'both'/'both my, your', etc./'both these' + noun plural
→ *les/mes, tes*, etc./*ces deux* + noun
> Ex: **Both** sexes are equal.
> ***Les deux*** *sexes sont égaux.*
>
> **Both these** apples are rotten.
> ***Ces deux*** *pommes sont pourries.*

− personal pronoun + 'both' + verb
→ personal pronoun + verb + *tous/toutes les deux*

The personal pronoun is plural (*ils, elles, nous, vous*).
> Ex: **We both** attended the meeting.
> ***Nous*** *avons assisté* ***tous/toutes les deux*** *à la réunion.*

With *ils* or *elles*, an alternative construction is:

> *tous les deux/toutes les deux* + verb.

Hence:

> **They both** came.
>> is either:
>
> ***Ils** sont venus **tous les deux**/**Elles** sont venues **toutes les deux**.*
>> or:
>
> ***Tous les deux** sont venus/**Toutes les deux** sont venues.*

but the first one is more frequently used.

Note:
– the two of us *nous deux*
– the two of you *vous deux*
– the two of them *eux deux, elles deux*

– 'both' as a pronoun on its own, replacing two nouns: *tous/toutes les deux*.

> Ex: *Marie et Catherine ne s'entendent pas mais **toutes les deux** sont mes amies.*
> Marie and Catherine do not get on but they are **both** my friends.

(ii) **both**, object or complement

à la fois; les deux; tous les deux

– 'both' + noun + 'and' + noun

> Ex: I like **both** meat and fish.
> *J'aime **à la fois** la viande et le poisson.*

– 'both' on its own replacing two nouns, i.e. with ellipsis of the nouns

> Ex: Do you prefer meat or fish? → I like **both**.
>> *J'aime **les deux**.*

– 'both' + noun plural

> Ex: I love **both my** children.
> *J'aime **mes deux** enfants.*

– object pronoun + 'both'

> Ex: I love them **both**.
>> → *Je les aime **tous les deux**.*
>
> I saw them **both** leave.
> *Je les ai vus **tous les deux** partir.*

– 'both' + adjective + 'and' + adjective

> Ex: She is **both** beautiful and intelligent.
> *Elle est **à la fois** belle et intelligente.*

– 'both' on its own replacing two adjectives (i.e. with ellipsis of the adjectives)

> Ex: She is **both** beautiful and intelligent. → She is both.
>> *Elle est **les deux**.*

– 'both' + infinitive + 'and' + infinitive

> Ex: They came **both** to eat and drink.
> *Ils sont venus **à la fois** pour manger et pour boire.*

     – 'both' on its own replacing two infinitives, i.e. with ellipsis of the infinitives

> Ex: They came to do **both**.
>
> *Ils sont venus pour faire **les deux**.*

5.7.4   Adverb

As an adverb, ***tout*** means 'entirely', 'completely' or 'very'. It is invariable except – for euphonic reasons – before an adjective which is feminine singular (***toute***) or plural (***toutes***) and begins with a consonant or a disjunctive '*h*'.

> Ex: *Il est **tout** heureux. Ils sont **tout** fiers.*
> He is very happy. They are very proud.
>
> *Elle était **tout** habillée en blanc.*
> She was all dressed in white.
>
> *Elles se sentent **tout** attendries.*
> They are feeling very sentimental.
>   but:
> *Elle est revenue **toute** hâlée par le soleil.*
> She came back very sun-tanned.
>
> *Elles sont **toutes** contentes de leurs vacances.*

Note the ambiguity of the plural in the last example:

> → They are all pleased with their holiday.
> → They are very pleased with their holiday.

See 5.7.2(ii) above.

6 Similarities and differences

     – *même*
     – *autre*
     – *tel*

6.1   même

     – ***même(s)*** can be an adjective (**same**)
     – *le/la **même**, les **mêmes*** are pronouns (**the same**)
     – ***même*** can be an adverb (**even**)

For the use of *moi-même*, etc., see chapter 31 Personal Pronouns, section 3.2.1(i).

6.1.1   Adjective

(i)   As an adjective, ***même*** (**same**) is usually placed before the noun and is itself preceded by an article. It expresses a similarity between the referent of the noun and another referent.

> Ex: *Nous sommes tous **du** (= de le) **même** avis.*
> We are all of the same opinion.

Les mêmes personnes qui applaudissent aujourd'hui sont celles qui sifflaient hier.

The same people who are applauding today are those who were booing yesterday.

(ii) Hence 'the same + noun + **as**' is: *le (la, les) même(s)* + noun + *que*.
Ex: *Elle a **la même** robe **que** moi.*
She's got the same dress as me.
See also chapter 30 Comparatives.

(iii) In English, 'the same' can be said instead of 'the same thing'. This is not the case in French – *la même <u>chose</u>* must always be said.
Ex: It's always the same!
*C'est toujours **la même chose**!*

The same goes for intelligence.
*C'est **la même chose** avec l'intelligence.*

What are we eating tonight? The same as yesterday?
*Qu'est-ce qu'on mange ce soir? **La même chose** qu'hier?*

NB: Exceptions are found in idioms.
Ex: *C'est du pareil au **même**.*
It's all the same.

*Cela revient au **même**.*
It makes no difference/It all boils down to the same thing.

(iv) *même* after the noun (animate or inanimate) is emphatic.
Ex: *Elle était **la bonté même**.*
She was kindness itself.

*Ses amis **mêmes** ne l'ont pas reconnu.*
Even his friends / His very friends did not recognize him.

6.1.2 Pronoun

(i) As pronouns, *le/la/les même(s)* (**the same/same one**) express similarity. As in English, they are preceded by the definite article. They are generally used as representative pronouns.
Ex: *Quant au nombre de pièces, nous avons **le même**.*
As far as the number of rooms is concerned, we've got the same.

It can also be nominal, with undetermined (animate) referents.
Ex: *Ce sont toujours **les mêmes** qui font tout!*
It is always the same ones who do everything!

(ii) 'the same **as**' is: *le (la, les) même(s) que*.
Ex: *Votre sac est **le même que** le mien.*
Your bag is the same as mine.

See also chapter 30 Comparatives, section 2.3.2.

6.1.3 Adverb

As an adverb, *même* (**even**) is invariable and is placed before the word it modifies.

(i)   *même* can modify an adjective, a verb or a noun/pronoun.

– adjective:
> Ex: *Même fatiguées, elles continuent à travailler.*
> Even tired, they carry on working.

– verb:
> Ex: *Il paraît qu'il a même rencontré le Pape!*
> Apparently, he even met the Pope!

– noun or pronoun:
> Ex: *Même ceux qui n'ont pas assisté au cours doivent me rendre leur travail.*
> Even those who did not attend the lecture must hand their work in to me.
>
> *Faites un petit effort: même un enfant pourrait le faire!*
> Make a bit of an effort – even a child could do it!

(ii)   Translation of **even more**

Note that 'even more' is *encore plus* (not **même plus*).
> Ex: The taxi-driver was **even more** laden than he was.
> *Le chauffeur de taxi était encore plus chargé que lui.*

See also chapter 30 Comparatives, section 3.6.

(iii)   Use of *pas même/même pas*

Either *pas même* or *même pas* (**not even**) can be used in all cases except with a **noun subject**, when only *pas même* can be used. However, the more usual construction for all the other cases is *même pas*, since *pas même* sounds affected except in appositions.
> Ex: *M. Dufour, pas même infirmier, se prenait pour un médecin.*
> M. Dufour, who wasn't even a nurse, considered himself a doctor.

pas même/même pas can modify:

– a noun subject:
> Ex: *Pas même Dominique ne peut le faire rire en ce moment.*
> Not even Dominique can make him laugh at the moment.

– a noun object:
> Ex: *Il ne fait même pas la vaisselle!*
> He does not even do the washing-up!

– a verb:
> Ex: *Il n'a même pas essayé d'esquiver le coup.*
> He did not even try to avoid the blow.

– a predicative adjective (subject complement after *être* or other copula):
> Ex: *Il ne semblait même pas déçu.*
> He did not even look disappointed.

– a noun subject complement (after *être* or other copula):

> Ex: '*Ci-gît Piron qui ne fut rien,*
> **Pas même** *académicien*'

> Piron, cited in Le petit Robert

> Here lies Piron who was a nobody
> He was not even a member of the Academy.

– an adverb phrase:

> Ex: *Je ne voyage plus,* **même pas** *en train.*
> I don't travel any more, not even by train.

6.2 *autre*

As *même* expresses similarity, *autre* expresses difference.

– *autre(s)* is an adjective (**other**)
– *l'autre*, *les autres* are pronouns (**the other, the others**)
– *autre part* is an adverb (**elsewhere**)

6.2.1 Adjective

(i) As an adjective, *autre* comes before the noun.

> Ex: *Nous sommes partis à 8 heures mais les **autres** invités sont restés jusqu'à 10 heures.*
> We left at 8 but the **other** guests stayed until 10 o'clock.

> *Je vais vous donner d'**autres** exemples.*
> I'll give you some **other** examples.

It can appear after the noun if it is modified.

Hence, '... **other** + noun + **than**' is: ... *autre(s)* + noun + *que* or ... noun + *autre(s)* + *que*.

> Ex: *L'homme d'aujourd'hui poursuit d'**autres** chemins **que** ceux déjà tracés par ses ancêtres.*
>> or:
> *L'homme d'aujourd'hui poursuit des chemins **autres** que ceux déjà tracés par ses ancêtres.*
> Today's man follows **other** paths / paths **other than** those already trodden by his ancestors.

(ii) In set expressions, *autre* is used without any other determiner.

> Ex: ***Autres** temps, **autres** mœurs.*
> Other times, other mores.

> *sans **autre** forme de procès*
> without further ado

(iii) When placed after the noun, *autre* without *que* means 'different' and is rare.

> Ex: *C'est un problème tout **autre**.*
> It's a totally different problem.

6.2.2 *Pronoun*

(i) As a pronoun (representative, or nominal with an undetermined referent), *autre* is preceded by an article, a possessive, a demonstrative or an interrogative adjective.

> Ex: *Vous devriez aussi penser aux (= à les) autres.*
> You should think of **others** too.
>
> *Vous pouvez prendre ce stylo. J'en ai un autre.*
> You can have this pen. I've got **another one**.

It is a common mistake to forget the *en* (= of them): see chapter 31 Personal Pronouns, section 2.2.2.7(iii).

> *Vous voulez l'autre livre?* **Quel autre?**
> Do you want the other book? **Which other one?**

(ii) *des* contracts to *d'* before *autres*, even as a pronoun.

> Ex: *Certains sont d'avis que . . . , d'autres pensent que . . .*
> Some think that . . . , others think that . . .

(iii) Note the following common expressions with *autre*:

– *nous autres, vous autres* are used to reinforce *nous* and *vous*, and are only used in informal French.

> Ex: *Vous autres, allez vous asseoir là.*
> You lot, go and sit there.

– *l'un et l'autre* as subject, with the verb in the plural

> Ex: *L'un et l'autre sont arrivés.*
> Both arrived.

See other renderings of 'both' in section 5.7.3 above.

– *l'un l'autre, les uns les autres, l'un à l'autre, les uns aux autres, l'un de l'autre* and *les uns des autres* indicate reciprocity and are used to clarify the meaning of pronominal verbs (see chapter 20 Pronominal Verbs, section 3.1.1(iii)).

> Ex: *Aimez-vous les uns les autres.*
> (*aimer qn*)
> Love one another.
>
> *Ils se sont nui l'un à l'autre.*
> (*nuire à qn*)
> They harmed each other.
>
> *Ils sont différents (les uns des autres).*
> *Elles sont différentes (les unes des autres).*
> (*être différent de qn/qch*)
> They're different (from one another).

See also section 2.3 (ii) above.

– *d'un côté . . . , d'un autre côté . . .* , means 'on the one hand . . .', 'on the other hand . . .', but *d'un autre côté* can be used on its own; *d'autre part* means 'besides'.

NB: Do not say *de l'autre côté, unless the literal sense is meant. Compare:

de l'autre côté de la barrière
on the other side of the fence
    and:
Je n'ai pas tellement envie d'y aller, mais **d'un autre côté** si vous insistez . . .
I don't really feel like going, but on the other hand if you insist . . .

6.2.3   Other pronouns based on autre

(i)   **autre chose** (= something else) is not to be confused with **une autre chose** (= another thing); **autre chose** is used as a pronoun and is syntactically equivalent to **quelque chose**. It is invariable and does not take an article. If followed by an adjective, **de** must be inserted between **autre chose** and the adjective.

Ex: Il y a **quelque chose/autre chose** que je veux savoir.
There is something/something else I want to know.

Y a-t-il **autre chose de** nouveau?
Is there anything else new?

(ii)   **autre** can be combined with the following pronouns [+ **de** + adjective]: **personne d'autre** (nobody else); **rien d'autre** (nothing else); **quelqu'un d'autre** (somebody else); **quelque chose d'autre** (something else). See also 2.1(ii) and 3.3.3 above.

Ex: A part M. Durand, avez-vous vu **quelqu'un d'autre** [d'intéressant]?
Apart from M. Durand, have you seen anybody else [of interest]?

Il n'y a **rien d'autre** [d'urgent] à faire.
There is nothing else [urgent] to do.

(iii) **autrui** (= all the others, as opposed to 'me').
autrui is a nominal pronoun with a human referent, and is invariable. It is rarely a subject. It is found mainly in literature or in set phrases.

Ex: Ne fais pas à **autrui** ce que tu ne voudrais pas qu'on te fît. (proverb)
Do as you would be done by.

6.2.4   Adverb

autre part is the equivalent of **ailleurs** (somewhere else/elsewhere) but less common.

Ex: Va jouer **autre part**!
    or:
Va jouer ailleurs!
Go and play somewhere else!

6.3   tel

- **tel** can be an adjective or a pronoun
- **telle, tels, telles** are adjectives
- **un tel, une telle** are pronouns

6.3.1 *Adjective*

As an adjective, *tel* is used as follows:

(i) To express comparison with *que*, as an alternative to *comme* (**as**)

Ex: *Expliquez-moi les choses **telles qu'**elles se sont passées / comme elles se sont passées.*
Explain things to me **as** they happened.

'How should she present herself to him? [. . .] Just **as** she was, in her apron [. . .]?'
'*Comment devait-elle se présenter à lui? [. . .] **Telle qu'**elle était, en tablier [. . .]?/ Comme elle était, en tablier [. . .]?*'

L. P. Hartley, *The Hireling*

(ii) With a demonstrative meaning (**such**)

– as a predicative adjective after *être* (**such**). Note the unusual word order, similar to English.
Ex: ***Tel** est mon destin.*
Such is my destiny.

'. . .': ***telles** furent ses dernières paroles.*
'. . .': **such** were his/her last words.

– as an attributive adjective, it comes before the noun (as in English) and can express intensity (**such, such a**).
Ex: *Nous avons eu **un tel** problème/**de tels** problèmes.*
We've had such a problem/such problems.

NB: Before abstract nouns, use ***tant de/tellement de*** ('such' means 'so much').
Ex: We have had **such** difficulty.
*Nous avons eu **tant/tellement de** difficulté.*
We had so much difficulty.

– as an attributive adjective, it comes before the noun (as in English) and can express similarity (**such, such a**).
Ex: *Je ne veux plus voir **de telles** fautes.*
I do not want to see **such** mistakes again.

*Que peut-on faire devant **un tel** désastre?*
What can one do when faced with **such a** disaster?

Alternatives are: ***comme ça/comme celui-là/tel que celui-là/de cette sorte/de ce genre*.**
Ex: *Je ne veux plus voir de fautes **de ce genre**.*
*Que peut-on faire devant une catastrophe **comme celle-là**?*

NB(1): If the noun is already qualified, the alternatives shown above should be used instead of plain *tel*. Compare:
*Une politique gouvernementale **telle que celle-là** serait vraiment stupide.*
Such a government policy would be really stupid.
and:
*Une **telle** politique serait vraiment stupide.*

NB(2): If 'such' applies to an adjective, use *si* or *aussi*. Compare:

> . . . *face à une contrainte **si** insupportable.*
> . . . faced with **such an** unbearable constraint.
>> and:
> . . . *face à **une telle** contrainte.*
> . . . faced with **such a** constraint.

Compare:

> **Such a** policy will be rejected.
> *Une **telle** politique sera rejetée.*

> A government policy **such as that** would be stupid.
> *Une politique gouvernementale **telle que celle-là** serait stupide.*

> It is **such a** bad policy.
> *C'est une **si** mauvaise politique.*

(iii) To express consequence with *à tel point que . . ./à un point tel que* (**so much that . . .**)

> Ex: *Il nous a énervés **à un point tel que** nous nous sommes mis en colère.*
> He annoyed us so much that we lost our temper.

(iv) To express a fictitious determination ('some . . . [or other]') which is indifferent to the specific identity of the item referred to. It can therefore be coordinated with itself by the conjunction *ou*.

> Ex: *Je ne me souviens plus: c'était dans **tel ou tel** journal.*
> I cannot remember – it was in some paper or other.

See also *quelconque*, section 4.2.

(v) *tel quel* means 'as it is'.

> Ex: *Laissez les choses **telles quelles**.*
> (= *telles qu'elles sont*)
> Leave things as they are.

> *Ils ont tout laissé **tel quel**.*
> They left everything as it was.

NB: *tel quel* here agrees with *tout*.

(vi) Note the use of *tel* on its own before a noun, usually used in pairs and in proverbs.

> Ex: ***Tel** père, **tel** fils.* (proverb)
> Like father, like son.

6.3.2 *Pronoun*

(i) *tel*

As a nominal pronoun with an undetermined referent, *tel* is used in the singular only in formal and literary French. It is equivalent to *celui*.

Ex: '*Tel est pris qui croyait prendre.*'
(= *C'est celui qui croyait prendre qui est pris.*)

La Fontaine

He, who thought himself the trickster, was tricked.

Tel qui rit vendredi dimanche pleurera. (proverb)
He who laughs on Friday weeps on Sunday.

(ii) **un tel**

- In informal French, **un tel** is more commonly used than **tel**, and is the equivalent of *quelqu'un.* Thus, **un tel . . . un tel. . .** is the equivalent of *quelqu'un . . . quelqu'un d'autre . . .*
  Ex: **Un tel** *vous dit ceci,* **un tel** *vous dit cela . . .*
  Someone tells you this, someone else tells you that . . .

- **Un tel** is also used in order to avoid stating a person's name.
  Ex: *Monsieur* **Un Tel**, *Madame* **Une Telle**
  Mr So-and-So, Mrs So-and-So

  Adressez-vous à **un Tel**.
  Go and ask So-and-So.

37 Numbers

1 Introduction

This chapter deals with numbers, including:
- cardinal and ordinal numbers
- approximate numbers and fractions
- measurements
- dates
- seasons and other periods of time
- time of day
- age
- prices/rates

2 Numbers

In French (as in English), **cardinal** numbers are used with nouns to specify a certain number of items; **ordinal** numbers are used to indicate the rank or position of the item to which the noun refers. There are a few exceptions however, particularly with reference to numbers attached to the names of monarchs and popes, or dates which are conveyed differently in the two languages.

2.1 Cardinal numbers

For list, see appendix 2.

(i) **Determiners or pronouns?**

- Cardinal numbers are generally **determiners** which indicate a quantity or a precise number of items. They can be used by themselves, e.g. *deux chats*, or with the following determiners:
  - the definite article   e.g. *les deux chats*
  - the possessive adjective   e.g. *mes deux chats*
  - the demonstrative adjective e.g. *ces deux chats*
  - the interrogative adjective   e.g. *quels deux chats?*

They cannot be used with the indefinite article or with the indefinite quantifiers (note that *quelque* singular as in e.g. *quelque dix personnes* is an adverb and indicates an approximation: see chapter 36 Indefinite Words).

– Cardinal numbers can also be **pronouns**.
  – Subject. Compare:

  Dix *personnes sont arrivées.*
  determiner

  and:

  Dix *sont arrivées.*
  pronoun

  – Object: as an object, the numeral cardinal pronoun requires the presence of the personal pronoun *en* (see chapter 31 Personal Pronouns, section 2.2.2.7(iii)).
    Ex: *Combien avez-vous de chats? J'**en** ai **deux**.*

Cardinal numbers are generally invariable but see exceptions below.

(ii) **Simple forms**

The following cardinal numbers have a simple form:
un, deux, trois, quatre, cinq, six, sept, huit, neuf, dix, onze, douze, treize, quatorze, quinze, seize, vingt, trente, quarante, cinquante, soixante, cent, mille

(iii) **Compound forms**

These compound forms (two or three words) are made up from those in (ii), either by coordination (with *et*) or juxtaposition (with or without a hyphen).
        Ex: *trente-six; soixante-cinq*
            thirty-six; sixty-five
Exceptions: there is no hyphen in the following numbers (all with *et*):

21	*vingt et un*
31	*trente et un*
41	*quarante et un*
51	*cinquante et un*
61	*soixante et un*
71	*soixante et onze*

But:

81	*quatre-vingt-un*
91	*quatre-vingt-onze*

And again:

101	*cent un*
301	*trois cent un*, etc.

There is no hyphen on either side of *cent* or *mille*.
        Ex: *cinq cent trente-deux*
            five hundred and thirty-two

            deux mille six cent quarante-neuf
            two thousand six hundred and forty-nine

(For *million* and *milliard*, see section (ix) below.)

(iv)   **Invariability**

Cardinal numbers are invariable except for **un**.

- **un** has the feminine form **une** and agrees in gender with the noun which it determines.

> Ex: *Va chercher **une** bouteille de vin.*
> Go and fetch **one** bottle of wine.
>
> *Elle a soufflé ses vingt et **une** bougies hier.*
> She blew out her twenty-**one** candles yesterday.

- Other cardinal numbers are invariable, hence *quatre* for instance never takes an 's'.

> Ex: *les **quatre** points cardinaux*
> the four points of the compass

(v)   *septante/octante/nonante*

The old system of numbers (by twenties instead of tens) has survived in France for figures from 61 to 99. However, *septante* (7̶0), *octante* (80) and *nonante* (90) are used in Belgium, Switzerland (*Suisse romande*), and in some dialects of the south-east of France. Hence:

> 7̶1   *septante et un*
> 7̶2   *septante-deux*, etc.

NB: The horizontal bar across the 7 (7̶) should not be omitted when writing to or in France as it could be confused with a 1.

(vi)   *vingt* **and** *cent*

- *vingt* and *cent* take an *s* in the plural if they are **not** followed by another number.

> Ex: *quatre-vingts* (80):
> *Il y avait au moins quatre-vingt**s** participants à cette conférence.*
>
> *deux cents* (200):
> *L'année dernière, il y en avait deux cent**s**!*
> but:
> *quatre-vingt-huit* (88):
> *J'en suis à la page quatre-vingt-huit.*
>
> *deux cent seize* (216):
> *Vous me devez exactement deux cent seize francs.*

- *vingt* and *cent* also take an 's' when they stand before numeral **nouns** such as million, milliard (= *mille millions*) and billion (= *un million de millions*).

> Ex: *quatre-vingt**s** millions*
> *six cent**s** milliards*

- When *vingt* and *cent* are used to indicate particular pages or chapters of a book, acts or scenes of a play (i.e. they are used in an ordinal sense), they are placed **after** the noun and do not take an 's' even if they are not followed by another number.

> Ex: *Ouvrez votre livre à la page quatre-vingt, à la page deux cent.*
> Open your books at page eighty, at page two hundred.

The same applies to addresses and dates.

> Ex: *J'habite au 200 (deux cent) rue de Lille.*
> I live at 200 rue de Lille.

> *Il est né en dix-neuf cent.*
> He was born in nineteen hundred.

NB(1): 'page number 21' is *page numéro 21* and 'number 200 rue de Lille' is *numéro 200 rue de Lille* (not *nombre*). French also says:

> Ex: *Elle portait le brassard numéro trois.*
> She was wearing the number three armband.

> *Qui est le numéro un mondial de la photo?*
> Who is the world number one in photography?

> *Mon numéro de téléphone a changé.*
> My telephone number has changed.

Hence '**number**' is *numéro* when it implies a classification, or serves as a name, a title for the entity concerned. Conversely, the following 'numbers' are all *nombres*.

> Ex: *Connaît-on le nombre des blessés?*
> Is the number of wounded known?

> *Un grand nombre de jeunes possèdent un téléphone portable.*
> A lot of young people own a mobile phone.

Hence '**number**' is *nombre* when it designates a certain number of items, a group of, or the very concept of number (e.g. *les nombres entiers, cardinaux, ordinaux*).

NB(2): Note the following translations of *à* with the word *page*:

> Ex: *Vous trouverez ce mot à la page 6.*
> You'll find this word **on** page 6.

> *Ouvrez votre livre à la page 34.*
> Turn **to** page 34 / Open your book **at** page 34.

(vii) *cent* **and** *mille*

cent (one hundred) and *mille* (one thousand) are **not** preceded by *un*.

> Ex: 111   *cent onze*
> one/a hundred and eleven

> 1120   *mille cent vingt*
> one thousand, one hundred and twenty

See also section 4.4 on dates below.

(viii) *mille*

− *mille* is invariable.

> Ex: *dix mille personnes*
> ten thousand people

– When 'a thousand and one' means a large indefinite number, it is *mille **et** un(e)* (and not *mille un(e)*).

    Ex: *J'ai **mille et une** choses à faire.*
        I have a thousand and one (= a lot of) things to do.

Also: '*Les **Mille et Une** Nuits*'.
    'The Arabian Nights' (lit.: The Thousand and One Nights).

(ix) *million/milliard*

un million (a million), *un milliard* (a billion, i.e. a thousand million) and *un billion* (a trillion, i.e. a million million), are always masculine. They are **nouns**, and take an '*s*' in the plural (even followed by another number) and *de* if they are followed by another noun.

    Ex: *Tokyo a environ trente million**s** d'habitants.*
        Tokyo has about thirty million inhabitants.

    *Paris **en** a huit million**s** cinq cent mille.*
    Paris has eight million five hundred thousand.

(x) Thousands and decimal point

In French, a **dot** indicates the thousands (particularly when writing numbers above 10,000 with figures), and a **comma** indicates the **decimal point**. In English, it is the reverse.

Ex: *12.860*	*douze mille huit cent soixante*
12,860	twelve thousand eight hundred and sixty
6.450.000	*six millions quatre cent cinquante mille*
6,450,000	six million four hundred and fifty thousand
0,1	*un dixième*, or *zéro virgule un*
0.1	zero point one/nought point one
5,06	*cinq virgule zéro six*
5.06	five point zero six
4,25	*quatre virgule vingt-cinq*
4.25	four point two five

(xi) Pronunciation and spelling

Note the peculiar pronunciation of the following numbers (see also chapter 3 Pronunciation).

– the '*f*' of *neuf* is pronounced '*v*' before *ans* and *heures*.

    Ex: *Il a eu dix-neuf ans le mois dernier.* [diznœvɑ̃]
        He was nineteen years old last month.

    Je partirai à neuf heures. [nœvœr]
    I shall leave at nine o'clock.

    but: *Il a neuf enfants.* [nœfɑ̃fɑ̃]

- *six* and *dix* are pronounced [sis] and [dis] and the final consonant is pronounced in *cinq* [sɛ̃k], *sept* [sɛt] and *huit* ['ɥit]. However, when they are followed by a word beginning with a consonant, the final consonant of these numbers is not pronounced, **except** for the '*x*' of *dix*, which is pronounced [z] in *dix-neuf* [diznœf], and the '*t*' of *sept*, which is **always** pronounced.

    Ex: *six francs* [sifrɑ̃]; *dix moutons* [dimutɔ̃]; *cinq minutes* [sɛ̃minyt]
    huit grammes ['ɥigram]
    but: *sept chats* [sɛtʃa]

NB: This rule seems to be relaxed for *cinq* with certain words, probably because it is not easy to hear in some cases.

    Ex: *cinq livres*, *cinq francs*, are more likely to be heard as [sɛ̃klivr], [sɛ̃kfrɑ̃]

- With a word beginning with a vowel or a mute '*h*', a liaison occurs.

    Ex: *six œufs* [sizø]; *huit heures* ['ɥitœr]; *cinq enfants* [sɛ̃kɑ̃fɑ̃]
    dix ans [dizɑ̃]; *six heures* [sizœr]

- there is no liaison in the following numbers:

    81 *quatre-vingt-un* [katrəvɛ̃œ̃]
    91 *quatre-vingt-onze* [katrəvɛ̃ɔ̃z]
    101 *cent un* [sɑ̃œ̃]
    111 *cent onze* [sɑ̃ɔ̃z]

- *vingt* and *cent*
The '*t*' of *vingt* is pronounced before *et*, and in the numbers 22 to 29, but not in the numbers 81 to 99; the '*t*' of *cent* is not pronounced before *un* and *onze*.

    Ex: *vingt et un* [vɛ̃teœ̃]
    vingt-six [vɛ̃tsis]
    quatre-vingt-un [katrəvɛ̃œ̃]
    quatre-vingt-huit [katrəvɛ̃ɥit]
    cent un [sɑ̃œ̃]
    cent onze [sɑ̃ɔ̃z]

- Except in *dix-huit/dix-huitième* and *vingt-huit/vingt-huitième*, there is no liaison or elision with the disjunctive '*h*' of *huit* and *huitième*, and the vowel '*o*' in *onze* or *onzième*.

    Ex: *les onze jours* [leɔ̃ʒur]
    le huitième homme [ləɥitjɛmɔm]

(xii) **premier and dernier**

Unlike in English, *premier* and *dernier* come **after** the cardinal number. This also applies to *suivant/prochain* and *autre*. Note that *suivant* always comes after the noun it modifies.

    Ex: the **first three** chapters
    *les **trois premiers** chapitres*
        and not:
    *les premiers trois chapitres
    *les **cinq dernières** minutes*; *les **dix prochains** jours*
    the **last five** minutes; the **next ten** days

    *les **cinq autres** semaines*; *les **dix** jours **suivants***
    the **other five** weeks; the **following ten** days

(xiii) **zéro**

zéro is used as a determiner in certain contexts.

> Ex: – school: *zéro faute*
> – commercial: *zéro franc*
> – technical/military: *zéro heure*; *zéro heure trente*

Otherwise, use *aucun* or *pas un* (see chapter 36 Indefinite Words, sections 3.1 and 3.4).

> Ex: *pas une erreur*; *aucune devise*

(xiv) **Numbers for monarchs and popes**

Unlike in English, a **cardinal** number is used for the titles of sovereigns and popes, except for *premier*. There is **no article**, even with *Premier*.

> Ex: *Elizabeth II* reads: *Elizabeth Deux*
> *Louis XIV* reads: *Louis Quatorze*
> *François Ier* reads: *François Premier*
> *Le Pape Jean XXIII* reads: *le Pape Jean Vingt-Trois*
> *Le Pape Jean Paul II* reads: *le Pape Jean Paul Deux*

Exception: the Emperor Charles V (1500–58), emperor of the Holy Roman Empire is *l'Empereur Charles-Quint*.

See also section 4 on dates (*le six mai*, but *le **premier** janvier*).

(xv) **Idioms**

There are idioms in which cardinal numbers are approximate.

> Ex: *Il n'y a pas trente-six possibilités.*
> There aren't all that many choices.

> *J'ai trente-six mille choses à faire.*
> I've got a thousand and one things to do.

(xvi) **Adjectives or nouns?**

Cardinal numbers can become nouns (including *zéro*), by improper derivation.

> Ex: *Il fallait jouer le sept!*
> *Elle habite au 17.*
> *J'ai ajouté un zéro.*

2.2 Ordinal numbers

For list, see appendix 2.

Ordinal numbers indicate order, rank or position (as opposed to an exact number for cardinal numbers). They are based on the **forms** of cardinal numbers.

(i) **Adjective or pronoun?**

A distinction should be made between the adjectives and the pronouns:

– The numeral ordinal **adjectives** behave like real qualifying adjectives. They are **always** used after a specific determiner.

> Ex: *mon second fils*
> *cette première fois*
> *la vingtième page*

They agree in gender and number with the noun they determine, but if they refer to a singular item, they remain singular (see chapter 28 Qualifying Adjectives, section 5.3.2(v)).

> Ex: *les dix-neuvième et vingtième siècles*
> (= *le dix-neuvième siècle et le vingtième siècle*)
> the nineteenth and twentieth centuries

– Numeral ordinal **pronouns** are normally representative except in a generic sense.

> Ex: *Catherine a deux <u>chats</u>. **Le premier** s'appelle Gribouille et **le deuxième** Roudoudou.*
> Catherine's got two cats – the first one's called Gribouille and the second Roudoudou.
>
> ***Les premiers** seront les derniers.*
> The first will be last.

(ii) **The suffix *-ième***

Ordinal numbers are formed by adding the suffix *-ième* to the corresponding cardinal number. The final '*e*' of the cardinal number (if there is one) is dropped.

> Ex: *trois → troisième (3ᵉ/3ᵉᵐᵉ)*
> three → third (3rd)
>
> *quatre → quatrième (4ᵉ/4ᵉᵐᵉ)*
> four → fourth (4th)
>
> *trente-sept → trente-septième (37ᵉ/37ᵉᵐᵉ)*
> thirty-seven → thirty-seventh (37th)
>
> *cent → centième (100ᵉ/100ᵉᵐᵉ)*
> one hundred → one hundredth (100th)
>
> *mille → millième (1000ᵉ/1000ᵉᵐᵉ)*
> one thousand → one thousandth (1000th)

(iii) ***premier* and *second***

Note the following irregularities:

– *un → premier (1ᵉʳ), première (1ʳᵉ)*
one → first (1st)

> Ex: *Antoine est le **premier** de son groupe.*
> Antoine is first in his group.

– the regular *unième* form is used in compound numbers.

> Ex: *vingt et un* → *vingt et unième* (*21ᵉ/21ᵉᵐᵉ*)
> twenty-one → twenty-first (21st)
>
> *trente et un* → *trente et unième* (*31ᵉ/31ᵉᵐᵉ*)
> thirty-one → thirty-first (31st)
>
> *cent un* → *cent unième* (*101ᵉ/101ᵉᵐᵉ*)
> one hundred and one → one hundred and first (101st)

– *deux* → *deuxième* (*2ᵉ/2ᵉᵐᵉ*) or *second(e)* [səgɔ̃(d)]
two → second (2nd)

– only *deuxième* is used in compound numbers.

> Ex: *trente-deux* → *trente-deuxième* (*32ᵉ/32ᵉᵐᵉ*)
> thirty-two → thirty-second (32nd)

Finally, note that *deuxième* can be used outside compound numbers (*le deuxième chat*), whereas *unième* cannot.

(iv) **cinquième and *neuvième***

– *cinq* → *cinquième* (do not forget the '*u*')
five → fifth

– *neuf* → *neuvième* (the '*f*' becomes '*v*')
nine → ninth

(v) **huitième and *onzième***

Note the absence of elision (see section 2.1(xi) above).

> Ex: *Marie est **la o**nzième.* [laɔ̃zjɛm]
> Marie is the eleventh.
>
> *Paul est **le h**uitième.* [ləɥitjɛm]
> Paul is the eighth.

(vi) **Numeral adverbs**

Numeral adverbs are formed regularly from the ordinal adjective.

> Ex: *premier* → *premièrement* (first, firstly)
> *deuxième* → *deuxièmement* (secondly)
> (*secondement* is not as common)
> *troisième* → *troisièmement* (thirdly), etc.

Alternatively, the following expressions can be used:

> Ex: *en premier lieu* (in the first place)
> *en deuxième/second lieu* (in the second place)
> *en troisième lieu* (in the third place), etc.

Or: *d'abord* (first, at first)

Note the adverbial use of ordinals.

> Ex: *Paul a parlé **le premier**.*
> Paul spoke **first**.

2.3 Approximate numbers

2.3.1 *The suffix* -aine

(i) Formation

The suffix *-aine* is added to the cardinal number to form a feminine noun, followed by *de* + noun. Where relevant, the 'e' of the cardinal number is dropped. The 'x' of *dix* becomes 'z'.

huit	→ *une huitaine* (*de*)
dix	→ *une dizaine* (*de*)
douze	→ *une douzaine* (*de*)
quinze	→ *une quinzaine* (*de*)
vingt	→ *une vingtaine* (*de*)
trente	→ *une trentaine* (*de*)
quarante	→ *une quarantaine* (*de*)
cinquante	→ *une cinquantaine* (*de*)
soixante	→ *une soixantaine* (*de*)
cent	→ *une centaine* (*de*), *des centaines* (*de*)

(ii) Meanings

– These numbers indicate an approximation:

Ex: *Je vous verrai dans **une huitaine** (de jours), dans **une quinzaine** (de jours).*
I'll see you in about a week, in a fortnight.

***Une quinzaine** de personnes sont venues.*
About fifteen people came.

*Il y a **une vingtaine** d'années que je ne l'ai pas vu.*
I have not seen him for about twenty years.

– Note the following ways of expressing approximate ages:

*Je dirais qu'elle a **la soixantaine**.*
I would say she is about sixty.

*Elle a atteint **la cinquantaine**.*
She is in her early fifties.

*Il a dépassé **la quarantaine**.*
He's over forty.

*Elle a **une quarantaine** d'années.*
She's about forty.

*Il approche de **la soixantaine**.*
He must be nearly sixty./He's pushing sixty.

*Elle doit avoir **entre cinquante et soixante ans**.*
She must be in her fifties.

Note that the suffix *-aine* is not possible with *soixante-dix*, *quatre-vingts* and *quatre-vingt-dix*. Approximation is expressed with prepositions.

Ex: *Elle a **environ** soixante-dix ans/**vers les** quatre-vingt-dix ans.*

– *douzaine*

Note that like in English, *une douzaine* (a dozen) can also mean 'exactly twelve' as in:

> Ex: *Chez la fleuriste: 'Je voudrais **une douzaine de** roses s'il vous plaît.'*
> At the florist's: 'I would like a dozen roses please.'
> (= twelve)

> *J'ai acheté **une demi-douzaine d'œufs.***
> I bought half a dozen eggs.
> (= six)

2.3.2   millier

mille is an exception: *mille* → **un millier** (*de*), **des milliers** (*de*).

> Ex: *Ces peintures ont survécu **des milliers** d'années après la mort du peintre.*
> These paintings survived thousands of years after the death of the painter.

Note the following expressions:

> thousands of **people**: *des milliers de **gens/personnes***
> but:
> one thousand **people**: *mille **personnes***

(See chapter 36 Indefinite Words, section 2.4.)

2.4   Fractions

(i)   Common fractions

The common fractions are *moitié* (*demi*), *tiers* and *quart*.

$\frac{1}{4}$	*un/le quart*
$2\frac{1}{4}$	*deux un quart* or *deux et quart*
$\frac{1}{3}$	*un/le tiers*
$\frac{1}{2}$	*un demi, une demie; une/la moitié*
$3\frac{1}{2}$	*trois et demi, trois et demie*
$\frac{2}{3}$	*[les] deux tiers*
$\frac{3}{4}$	*[les] trois quarts*

(ii)   Other fractions

The numerator is the cardinal number, the denominator is the ordinal number.

> Ex: $\frac{3}{5}$: *[les] trois cinquièmes*
> three-fifths

> $8\frac{4}{5}$: *huit quatre cinquièmes*
> eight and four-fifths

(iii)   Use of **de**

All fractions except *demi* are followed by **de** before the noun.

> Ex: *J'y suis restée **trois-quarts** d'heure.*
>> I stayed there three-quarters of an hour.
>>> but:
>> *J'y suis restée **une demi**-heure.*
>> I stayed there half an hour.

(iv)   Repetition of the determiner

When the noun is preceded by a definite or indefinite article, or a possessive or demonstrative adjective, the fraction is also preceded by the relevant **definite article** (unlike in English).

> Ex: ***Le*** *quart de* ***la*** *population n'a pas pris part au vote.*
> A quarter of the population did not take part in the elections.

> *Je connais maintenant* ***les*** *neuf dixièmes de* ***mes*** *résultats.*
> I now know nine-tenths of my results.

Compare:

> *Paul a bu* ***les*** *trois-quarts d'**un** litre de lait.*
> Paul drank three quarters of a litre of milk.
>> and:
> *J'y suis restée trois-quarts* ***d'****heure.*

See (iii) above.

(v)   **demi** (adjective) and **moitié** (noun): agreement

demi(e) can be an adjective (see chapter 28 Qualifying Adjectives, section 5.3.3). The corresponding noun is *moitié*.

> Ex: *Avez-vous répondu à toutes les questions?*
> Have you answered all the questions?

> *Non, seulement à* ***la moitié****.*
> No, only **half**.

> *Non, seulement à deux questions* ***et demie****.*
> No, only two-**and-a-half** questions.

> *Non, seulement à* ***la moitié d'une*** *question.*
> No, only **half a** question.

(vi)   **demi** and **moitié**: usage

When 'half a . . .' can also be 'a half- . . .', **demi** can in principle be used.

This is generally the case with standard units of measure, e.g. *un demi-centimètre, une demi-douzaine, une demi-heure, un demi-litre, un demi-kilo,* etc. and also in set compounds such as *un demi-frère, une demi-sœur, des demi-mesures.* Otherwise, *moitié* should be used. Hence:

Ex: half the population of a country
     can only be:
  *la **moitié** de la population d'un pays*

He has spent half his life travelling.
*Il a passé la **moitié** de sa vie à voyager.*
    but:
*Je n'aime pas acheter le vin en **demi**-bouteilles.*
I don't like to buy wine in half-bottles.
    and:
*Il a bu une **demie** bouteille de vin.*
    or:
*Il a bu la **moitié** d'une bouteille de vin.*
He drank half a bottle of wine.

NB: When ***demi*** is placed **before** the noun it qualifies and is linked to it by a hyphen, it is invariable.
    Ex: *une **demi**-douzaine d'œufs*
    half a dozen eggs

(vii)   ***moitié*** and ***demi***: adverbs

They are preceded by the preposition ***à***.

– modifying an adjective or participle:
    Ex: *On l'a retrouvé **à moitié/à demi** mort.*
    He was found half dead.

    *Elle se promenait **à demi/à moitié** nue sous la neige . . .*
    She was walking half-naked in the snow . . .

    *L'optimiste dira qu'une bouteille est **à moitié** pleine, alors que le pessimiste, lui, dira qu'elle est **à moitié** vide.*
    The optimist will say that a bottle is half full whereas the pessimist will say that it is half empty.

    *Laissez la fenêtre **à demi** ouverte s'il vous plaît!*
    Please leave the window half-open!

– modifying a verb:
    Ex: *François remplit toujours les verres **à moitié**.*
    François always half-fills glasses.

    *Elle ouvrit la porte **à demi**.*
    She half-opened the door.

(viii)   ***demi*** as a noun

Note the following instances in which the noun has been dropped and the adjective has become a noun.
    Ex: ***un demi***: a beer (in a French bar: in fact not 'half a litre' but only 'half a half-litre'!)
    un demi: a half-back in football (stands for *un demi-arrière*)

(ix) Other ways of expressing fractions

    – Fractions can be expressed by **sur** ('out of').
        Ex: *Seulement deux étudiants **sur** dix avaient rempli le questionnaire.*
        Only two **out of** ten students had filled in the questionnaire.

        *Le magasin est ouvert vingt-quatre heures **sur** vingt-quatre.*
        The shop is open twenty-four hours a day.

    – Fractions can be expressed as percentages.
        Ex: 25%   *vingt-cinq pour cent*
                 twenty-five per cent

2.5 Other ways to express quantity and rank

Other words may also be used to express quantity and rank.

(i) Qualifying adjectives

    – *simple, double, triple, quadruple, centuple*:

Ex: *un **double** whisky*	a double whisky
*mettre les bouchées **doubles***	to work twice as hard and twice as fast
*mener une **double** vie*	to lead a double life
*une **triple** croche*	a demisemiquaver
*La **Triple** Entente*	The Triple Entente

    – *primaire, secondaire, tertiaire, quaternaire*:
        Ex: *l'ère **tertiaire***   the tertiary era

    – *biennal, triennal*:
        Ex: *une fête **biennale***   a biennial celebration

    – *binaire, ternaire*:
        Ex: *le système **binaire***   the binary system

    – *décimal*:
        Ex: *un nombre **décimal***   a decimal number

(ii) Nouns

    – *un couple, une paire, un duo*:
        Ex: ***une paire** de gants*   a pair of gloves

    – *un quatuor, un quintette*:
        Ex: *un **quatuor** à cordes*   a string quartet

    – *un quatrain, un huitain, un dizain*:
        Ex: ***Un quatrain** est une strophe de quatre vers.*
        A quatrain is a stanza of four lines.

    – *un quinquennat, un septennat*:
        Ex: *En France, on appelle **septennat** le mandat présidentiel de sept ans.*
        In France, the seven-year presidential term of office is called
        septennat.

     – *un quadragénaire, un quinquagénaire*:

         Ex: **Un quinquagénaire** *est une personne qui a atteint 50 ans.*

         A quinquagenarian is a person who has reached 50 years old.

     – *un centenaire, un bicentenaire*:

         Ex: *On a fêté* **le bicentenaire** *de la Révolution française le 14 juillet 1989.*

         The bicentenary of the French Revolution was celebrated on 14 July 1989.

(iii)   Adverbs

     – *premièrement, deuxièmement, troisièmement*, etc.

         or:

     primo, secundo, tertio, etc.

         Ex: **Premièrement**, *vous devez écouter.*

     See also 2.2(vi) above.

     – *bis, ter*:

         Ex: *Il habite au 36* **bis** *rue François-Premier.*

         He lives at 36a rue François-Premier.

3 Common measurements

The following constructions apply to *long, haut, large, profond* and *épais*. Note that *épais* and *profond* do not exist in the first construction. Hence *un mur de cinq mètres* **de long** or **de longueur** but *un mur de cinquante centimètres* **d'épaisseur** (not ⋆*d'épais*). The first two constructions are expected in a measuring context; the last three are more literary.

(i)   **long** (long); **longueur** (length)

         Ex: a wall five metres long / a five-metre long wall:

            – *un mur de cinq mètres de long*

            – *un mur de cinq mètres de longueur*

            – *un mur long de cinq mètres*

            – *un mur d'une longueur de cinq mètres*

         The length of the wall is five metres:

            – *La longueur du mur est de cinq mètres.*

(ii)   **haut** (high); **hauteur** (height)

         Ex: The ceilings are four metres high.

            – *Les plafonds ont quatre mètres de haut.*

            – *Les plafonds ont quatre mètres de hauteur.*

            – *Les plafonds sont hauts de quatre mètres.*

            – *Les plafonds ont une hauteur de quatre mètres.*

         The height of the ceilings is four metres:

            – *La hauteur des plafonds est de quatre mètres.*

(iii)   *large* (wide); *largeur* (width)
>   Ex: The street is ten metres wide.
>   – *La rue a dix mètres de large.*
>   – *La rue a dix mètres de largeur.*
>   – *La rue est large de dix mètres.*
>   – *La rue a une largeur de dix mètres.*
>
>   The width of the street is ten metres:
>   – *La largeur de la rue est de dix mètres.*

(iv)   *profond* (deep); *profondeur* (depth)
>   Ex: At the deep end, the swimming-pool is three metres deep.
>   *Dans le grand bain,*
>   – *la piscine a trois mètres de profondeur.*
>   – *la piscine est profonde de trois mètres.*
>   – *la piscine a une profondeur de trois mètres.*
>
>   The depth of the swimming-pool is three metres:
>   – *La profondeur de la piscine est de trois mètres.*

(v)   *épais* (thick); *épaisseur* (thickness)
>   Ex: The walls of this castle are one-and-a-half metres thick.
>   *Dans ce château,*
>   – *les murs ont un mètre et demi d'épaisseur.*
>   – *les murs sont épais d'un mètre et demi.*
>   – *les murs ont une épaisseur d'un mètre et demi.*
>
>   The thickness of the walls is one-and-a-half metres:
>   – *L'épaisseur des murs est d'un mètre et demi.*

NB: '3 metres **by** 4' is *3 mètres **sur** 4.*

4 The date

Cardinal numbers are used for dates (unlike in English), except that *premier* is used for the first day of the month. A date is preceded by *le*, including before *huit* (as the '*h*' is disjunctive) and before *onze* (whose '*o*' is treated as a consonant).
>   Ex: *le 1er (premier) janvier; le 4 (quatre) août*
>   *le 8 (huit) juin; le 11 (onze) novembre*

4.1 Months

(i)   The months of the year are:

janvier	January	*juillet*	July
février	February	*août*	August
mars	March	*septembre*	September
avril	April	*octobre*	October
mai	May	*novembre*	November
juin	June	*décembre*	December

(ii)   Names of the months have **no capital letter** and are **masculine** (*le mois*).
          Ex: *On a eu **un juillet** plutôt pluvieux.*
          We had a rather wet July.

(iii)   Expressions with names of the month:

     – 'in January' is either ***au** mois de janvier* or ***en** janvier*

     – 'last month' is *le mois dernier*
       'next month' is *le mois prochain*

     – 'the following month' is *le mois suivant*
       'the previous month' is *le mois précédent*

4.2 Days

(i)   The days of the week are:

lundi	Monday
mardi	Tuesday
mercredi	Wednesday
jeudi	Thursday
vendredi	Friday
samedi	Saturday
dimanche	Sunday

(ii)   Names of days have **no capital letter** and are **masculine** (*le jour*).
          Ex: ***le mercredi*** *des Cendres*
          Ash Wednesday

(iii)   If the day is given, the order is normally: day, month, year. There are three ways of writing a date when the day is given.
          Ex: – *le mercredi 14 octobre 1992*
             – *mercredi, le 14 octobre 1992*
             – *mercredi 14 octobre 1992*

(iv)   The definite article is used before the name of the day of the week (singular) when the activity is **habitual**.
          Ex: *A Paris, les magasins sont fermés **le lundi**.*
          In Paris, shops are closed **on Mondays**.

          Le dimanche *est traditionnellement le jour du marché.*
          Sunday is traditionally market day.

(v)   For a **particular** occasion, the article is normally omitted:
          Ex: *Je ferai les courses **jeudi**.*
          I'll go shopping **on Thursday**.

          ***Mardi dernier**, je suis allée au cinéma.*
          Last Tuesday, I went to the cinema.

except if that day is defined in any way:

Ex: *J'irai voir ma tante **le jeudi avant la Toussaint** / **le dernier mardi du mois**.*

I'll go and see my aunt on the Thursday before All Saints' Day / on the last Tuesday of the month.

*Je resterai **du lundi au vendredi**.*
I shall stay from Monday to Friday.

(vi) The definite article is used before most saints' days and religious festivals; the word *fête* is understood even when not expressed, hence the feminine.

Ex: [*à*] *la Toussaint*   [on] All Saints' Day
(= *à la Fête de la Toussaint*)
[*à*] *la Saint-Jean*   [on] Midsummer Day
[*à*] *la Pentecôte*   [at] Whitsun
but note:
[*le*] *Vendredi Saint*   [on] Good Friday
and:
à Noël (more common than *à la Noël*)   at Christmas
à Pâques   at Easter

4.3 Weeks

In France, weeks begin on Monday and last seven days like everywhere else. However, note the following expressions:

(i) ***dans une semaine = dans huit jours = en huit***

Ex: *Je vous re-téléphonerai **dans une semaine** / **dans huit jours**.*
I'll ring you again in a week.

*Je vous re-téléphonerai **vendredi en huit**.*
I'll ring you again a week on Friday.

(ii) ***dans deux semaines = dans quinze jours***

Ex: *Je partirai **dans quinze jours**.*
I shall leave in a fortnight.

4.4 Years

(i) ***mille neuf cent*** or ***dix-neuf cent***?

Between 1000 and 2000, the following two forms are possible (but the second form is more commonly used for dates).

Ex: 1789   *mille sept cent quatre-vingt-neuf*
or:
dix-sept cent quatre-vingt-neuf

(ii) Omission of *mille* and *cent*

When referring to a date, *mille neuf cent* or *dix-neuf cent* are frequently omitted altogether.

> Ex: *la guerre de 14–18*
> (which reads: *la guerre de quatorze-dix-huit*)
> the 1914–18 war
>
> *le débarquement de juin 44*
> (which reads: *le débarquement de juin quarante-quatre*)
> the June 1944 landings
>
> *la guerre de 70*
> (which reads: *la guerre de soixante-dix*)
> the Franco-Prussian War (1870)
>
> *Ils se sont mariés en 36.*
> They got married in 1936.
>
> *les présidentielles de 81*
> the 1981 (French) presidential elections

However, when saying **the year in full**, *cent* is never omitted (as it can be in English).

> Ex: in nineteen fourteen
> *en dix-neuf* **cent** quatorze / *en mille neuf* **cent** quatorze

(iii) ***mille*** or ***mil*?**

For a year AD, *mil* can be used except for 'the year 1000': *l'an mille*.

> Ex: 1992 *mil neuf cent quatre-vingt-douze*
>   or:
>   *mille neuf cent quatre-vingt-douze*

Note that 'BC' is *avant Jésus-Christ* (*av. J-C*) and 'AD' is *après Jésus-Christ* (*ap. J-C*).

In legal documents, where dates are always written in words, the form *mil* is used instead of *mille*.

(iv) ***en*** or ***au*?**

> *en 1992*   in 1992
> *en l'an 2000*   in the year 2000
> *jusqu'en 1996*   until 1996

> Ex: **En** *quelle année vous êtes-vous rencontrés?*
> Which year did you meet?
>
> *Nous nous sommes rencontrés* **en** *1990.*
> We met in 1990.
>   but:
> *Nous sommes* **au** *vingtième siècle.*
> We are in the twentieth century.

(v) Decades

When referring to a particular decade of the twentieth century, the relevant cardinal number is preceded by *les années*.

Ex: *les années soixante*   the sixties

4.5   Common ways of asking and telling the date

– *Quelle est la date aujourd'hui? / Le combien sommes-nous aujourd'hui?*
– *Aujourd'hui, c'est le 8 novembre. / Nous sommes le 8 novembre.*

– *Quel jour sommes-nous aujourd'hui? / Quel jour est-ce aujourd'hui?*
– *Aujourd'hui, nous sommes samedi. / C'est aujourd'hui samedi.*

5   Seasons and other periods of time

5.1   Seasons

The seasons are:

le printemps	spring
l'été	summer
l'automne	autumn
l'hiver	winter

(i) Names of seasons are **masculine** although the word *saison* is feminine.

Ex: **Le** *printemps est* **une** *saison.*
Spring is a season.

(ii) The definite article is generally used before names of seasons.

Ex: *En Angleterre,* **l'**été *n'est guère plus agréable que* **l'**hiver.
In England, summer is not much more pleasant than winter.
NB: **au** *printemps*: in [the] spring
but:
en *été,* **en** *automne,* **en** *hiver*: in [the] summer, in [the] autumn, in [the] winter

5.2   *Jour/journée; an/année; matin/matinée; soir/soirée*

– The words *jour, an, matin* and *soir* are masculine and generally indicate **points** in time.

– The words *journée, année, matinée* and *soirée* are feminine and are generally used for the **duration** of these periods of time.

5.2.1   an/année

(i) **an** usually follows cardinal numbers, whilst **année** follows ordinal numbers, or an indefinite or demonstrative adjective (e.g. *chaque, plusieurs, quelques, cette*).

Ex: *Cela s'est passé il y a **trois ans**.*
It happened three years ago.
> but:
*C'est la **troisième année** que je suis en Angleterre.*
It's my third year in England.

*Je suis déjà allée en Grèce **plusieurs années** de suite.*
I have already been to Greece several years running.

année tends to focus the attention on the passage of time within the period, or the events which occurred during that period of time, while *an* merely refers to a date. Hence:

L'année dernière *a été très bonne pour les vins de Touraine.*
Last year was very good for wines from Touraine.

L'année prochaine, *j'irai en Grèce.*
(stress on the period)
> or:
L'an prochain *j'irai en Grèce.*
(stress on the date)
Next year, I shall go to Greece.

(ii) If the 'year' is modified in any way, *année* should be used.
> Ex: *cinq **ans*** but: *cinq **longues années***

*J'ai vécu à Londres pendant **cinq ans**.*
I have lived in London for five years.
> but:
*J'ai gardé un très bon souvenir de mes **cinq années à Londres**.*
I have a very nice memory of my five years in London.

(iii) 'every year' is either *tous les ans* or *chaque année* (see also chapter 36 Indefinite Words, sections 5.6 and 5.7).
> Ex: *Catherine et Emma vont faire du ski **tous les ans**/**chaque année**.*
Catherine and Emma go skiing every year.

(iv) For 'all year' or 'the whole year', *toute l'année* should be used.
> Ex: *Les agriculteurs se sont plaints du mauvais temps **toute l'année**.*
The farmers complained about the bad weather all year.

5.2.2 jour/journée; matin/matinée; soir/soirée

(i) These can all follow either cardinal or ordinal numbers, and indefinite or demonstrative adjectives. They can all be modified.
> Ex: *trois jours; trois journées; ce matin; plusieurs soirées; un beau jour; une grande soirée*

(ii) With 'each' or 'every', use *chaque jour/matin/soir* or *tous les jours/matins/soirs* (see also chapter 36 Indefinite Words, sections 5.6 and 5.7).
> Ex: *Il doit prendre le bus **tous les matins** pour aller à son bureau.*
He has to catch the bus every morning to go to his office.

(iii)   With 'all' or 'the whole', use *toute la journée/matinée/soirée*.
>   Ex: *J'ai dormi **toute la journée**!*
>   I slept all day!

(iv)   Furthermore, *journée, matinée, soirée* tend to focus the attention on the passage of time within the period, or the events which occurred during that period of time, while *jour, matin, soir* merely refer to a point in time.
>   Ex: *J'ai **rencontré** Alain ce **matin**.*
>   I saw Alain this morning.
>>   but:
>   *Je l'ai **cherché** toute la **matinée**.*
>   I have been looking for him the whole morning.
>
>   *Je vous **verrai** demain **soir**.*
>   I shall see you tomorrow evening.
>>   but:
>   *Nous avons **passé** une excellente **soirée**.*
>   We have had an excellent evening.

NB: ***une matinée*** is also the name given to the cinema or theatre performance of the **afternoon**, and ***une soirée*** is also a party.

(v)   To express a habitual time, use *le matin, l'après-midi, le soir* (in the morning/ afternoon/evening).
>   Ex: ***Le soir**, je vais en boîte.* (familiar)
>   In the evening, I go clubbing.

6   Time of day

(i)   Unlike in English, the word *heure(s)* cannot be omitted in French to indicate the time.

>   Ex: *Il est huit **heures** et demie.*
>   It is half past eight.

However, the word *minute(s)* is omitted as in English.
>   Ex: *Il est huit heures moins cinq.*
>   It is five to eight.

(ii)   Only the fractional adjective, *demi*, is used for time (not *moitié*). Hence:

>   *Nous venons dans **une demi-heure**.*
>   We're coming in half an hour.
>>   and:
>   *Nous venons dans **un quart d'heure/trois-quarts d'heure**.*
>   We're coming in a quarter of an hour/in three-quarters of an hour.

(iii)   Different ways of asking/telling the time

Ex: – *Quelle heure est-il? – [Il est] six heures.*
        – What time is it? – [It is] six o'clock.

        – *Quelle heure avez-vous [à votre montre]? – [J'ai] cinq heures cinq.*
        – What time is it [by your watch]? – [I make it] five past five.

        – *Savez-vous quelle heure il est? – [Il est] sept heures moins le quart.*
        – Do you know what time it is? – [It is] a quarter to seven.

        – *A quelle heure venez-vous demain? – [Je viens] à deux heures et demie.*
        – What time are you coming tomorrow? – [I am coming] at half past two.

        – *A quelle heure les attendez-vous? – Pas avant sept heures et quart* (or *un quart*).
        – What time are you expecting them? – Not before quarter past seven.

(iv)   Other time idioms

Ex: *Je suis **en retard de** dix minutes.*
        I am ten minutes **late**.

        *Le train **a** deux minutes **de retard**.*
        The train is two minutes **late**.

        *Je suis **en avance d'**une demi-heure.*
        I am half an hour **early**.

        *Le train **a** une minute **d'avance**.*
        The train is one minute **early**.

        *Ma montre **avance de** trois minutes.*
        My watch is three minutes **fast**.

        *Ma montre **retarde de** cinq minutes.*
        My watch is five minutes **slow**.

        *7 heures? C'est **tôt**!*
        7 o'clock? That's **early**!

        *10 heures? Trop **tard**!*
        10 o'clock? Too **late**!

        *Le résultat, c'est que le niveau de vie en Russie est **d'**une vingtaine d'années **en retard sur** celui des pays occidentaux.*
        The result is that the standard of living in Russia is about twenty years **behind** that in Western countries.

        *Van Gogh était **en avance sur** son temps.*
        Van Gogh was **ahead of** his time.

614

(v) Times in the morning, afternoon, evening

– *midi* and *minuit*:
midi is the middle of the day and *minuit* is the middle of the night. They are both masculine, hence: *midi et demi, minuit et demi*.

– *du matin, de l'après-midi, du soir*:
[*à*] *une heure **du matin***: [at] one o'clock in the morning
[*à*] *cinq heures **de l'après-midi***: [at] five o'clock in the afternoon
[*à*] *onze heures **du soir***: [at] eleven at night

(vi) Official timetables

For official timetables (e.g. train, bus, plane, etc.) and also radio and television listings, the 24-hour clock is used, starting from midnight (= *zéro heure*).

Ex: *Mon avion décolle à **14 heures 15**.*
My plane takes off at 2.15 p.m.

*les informations de **20 heures***
the 8 o'clock news

(vii) Approximation and precise time

– Approximation:
Ex: *Je les attends **vers/à environ** cinq heures.*
I'm expecting them around five o'clock.

*Je pense partir **sur les/vers** quatre heures.*
I'm thinking of leaving around four o'clock.

*Il doit être **environ** six heures.*
It must be about six.

*Il est **près de** huit heures.*
It is nearly eight.

NB: *vers* and *sur* are not normally used after *être*.

– Precise time:
Ex: *à cinq heures **précises***   at five o'clock sharp
*à cinq heures **juste***   on the stroke of five
*à cinq heures **pile***   at five o'clock on the dot

(viii) Translation of 'time'

fois, heure, période, époque and *temps* are all 'time' in English.

– *fois* represents a time in a series, or an occasion.
Ex: *A chaque **fois** qu'il pleut, Dizzy m'apporte une souris.*
Each **time** it rains, Dizzy brings me a mouse.

*C'est bien la dernière **fois** que je vous crois!*
That is definitely the last **time** I believe you!

615

Note that 'at the same time' can be *à la fois* or *en même temps*. Compare:

> *Ne faites pas deux choses **à la fois**.*
> Don't do two things **at the same time**.
> and:
> *Faites les deux **en même temps**.*
> Do both **at the same time**.

– *heure* is used for the time of day.

> Ex: *A quelle **heure** dîne-t-on ce soir?*
> What **time** are we having dinner tonight?

– *période* is used for a period of time in one's life.

> Ex: *C'était une **période** des plus joyeuses de sa vie.*
> It was a most joyful **time** in his life.

– *époque* is used when 'time' means 'era'.

> Ex: *Cela s'est passé à une **époque** où les gens soutenaient encore la monarchie.*
> It happened at a **time** when people still supported the monarchy.

– *temps*:

(a) means 'the right time'

> Ex: ***Il est temps** de s'y mettre!*
> It is **time** to make a start!

> *Nous sommes arrivés juste à **temps**.*
> We've arrived just in **time**.

(b) represents a period of time

> Ex: *Je n'ai pas beaucoup **le temps** de vous aider.*
> I haven't got much **time** to help you.

> *Avec un peu plus de **temps**, il aurait pu terminer sa thèse.*
> Given a little more **time**, he could have finished his thesis.

> *Le **temps** qu'il regagne le pont en courant, il était trop tard.*
> By the **time** he had run back to the bridge, it was too late.

Note the translation of the following English idiom:

> He spent **a merry three months** as a conductor.
> *Il passa **trois joyeux mois** comme receveur.*

7 Age

(i) Unlike in English, the word *an* cannot be omitted in French to indicate an age.

> Ex: *Quel âge avez-vous?*
> How old are you?

> *J'ai seize **ans** mais Catherine **en** a dix-huit.*
> I am sixteen but Catherine is eighteen.
> (Do not forget the *en*: see chapter 31 Personal Pronouns,
> section 2.2.2.7(iii).)

*A quatre-vingt-dix **ans**, elle faisait encore son jardin.*
At ninety, she was still doing her garden.

*un enfant de cinq **ans***
a child of five / a five-year-old child

*Cet arbre a deux cents **ans**.*
This tree is two hundred years old.

(ii) Approximations

Note the use of *années* instead of *ans* in the first example, and the omission of *ans* altogether in the second example.
> Ex: *C'est une femme d'une quarantaine d'années.*
> She's a woman of about forty.
>
> *Elle peut avoir la quarantaine / On lui donne la quarantaine.*
> She is about forty / She looks about forty.

(See also section 2.3.1(ii) above.)

8 Prices/rates

(i) Prices
> Ex: *Je l'ai payé 60 francs.*
> I paid 60 francs for it.
>
> *Cela m'a coûté 60 francs.*
> That cost me 60 francs.
>
> *Je l'ai vendu/acheté pour 80 francs.*
> I sold/bought it for 80 francs.

(ii) Items, units of length, etc.

The **definite article** is used to indicate the price of a commodity **per item** or **per unit** of length, weight, etc.
> Ex: *L'essence coûte environ six francs **le** litre.*
> Petrol costs about six francs a litre.
>
> *Les poires sont à quinze francs **le** kilo.*
> Pears are 15 francs a kilo.
> > but:
> *Les citrouilles sont à dix francs **pièce**.*
> (rather than *la pièce*)
> Pumpkins are ten francs each.

(iii) Units of time

– *par* is used in a **distributive** sense.
> Ex: *Il gagne 40.000 livres **par mois**.*
> He earns 40,000 pounds a month.

> *Ce colloque a lieu deux fois **par an**.*
> This conference takes place twice a year.

> *Prenez ces pillules trois fois **par jour**.*
> Take these pills three times a day.

> *La pension complète coûte 300 francs **par personne** et **par jour**.*
> Full board costs 300 francs per person per day.

– ***tous les/toutes les*** is used in a **collective** sense.

> Ex: *Je vais à la piscine **tous les deux jours**.*
> I go to the swimming pool every other day.

> *Elle change de coiffure **toutes les trois semaines**.*
> She changes her hair style every three weeks.

(See also the use of *chaque* in chapter 36 Indefinite Words, section 5.6.)

(iv)   Speeds

For speed, the preposition *à* is added after *aller* or *rouler* and ***du*** after *faire*.

> Ex: *Il s'est fait arrêter par la police alors qu'il roulait **à** 160 km à l'heure* (or: *160 km/heure*).
> He was stopped by the police as he was doing 100 mph.
> > but:
> . . . *alors qu'il faisait **du** 160.*

(v)   Distance/location

To locate a point, the preposition *à* is used.

> Ex: ***A** quelle distance sommes-nous du prochain village?*
> How far are we from the next village?

> *Nous en sommes **à** six kilomètres.*
> We are six kilometres away.

> *Combien de kilomètres y a-t-il d'ici **au** prochain village?*
> How many kilometres is it to the next village?

> *Il y a six kilomètres d'ici **au** prochain village.*
> It's six kilometres to the next village.

5 Sentences and text

38 Negative structures

1 Introduction

On a syntactic level, the negative sentence is the negation of the corresponding affirmative sentence. On a semantic level, the negation can relate specifically to the verb, the subject or the object, etc. of the sentence.

Consider the following example:
Le chien a cassé le vase.
→ *Le chien n'a pas cassé le vase.*

The negation relates to:
- the subject:
Ce n'est pas le chien qui a cassé le vase mais le chat.
- the object:
Ce n'est pas le vase que le chien a cassé mais un verre.
- the verb:
Le chien n'a pas cassé le vase mais l'a simplement renversé.

However, there is more to expressing a negative in French than ***ne . . . pas***. **Adverbs** which combine with ***ne*** are considered in this chapter.

- absolute negation:
ne . . . pas, ne . . . point
ne . . . jamais
ne . . . plus
ne . . . guère
ne . . . aucunement/nullement/pas du tout
- restricted negation:
ne . . . que, ne . . . pas que

Negative imperative and interrogative sentences are treated in chapters 14 Imperative and 39 Interrogative and Exclamative Structures. Negative determiners and pronouns are treated in chapter 36 Indefinite Words. The negative conjunction *ni* is treated in chapter 40 Coordination and Juxtaposition.

2 Negative adverbs

2.1 *ne . . . pas*

ne . . . pas turns a sentence containing a conjugated verb, infinitive or participle into the negative. The positioning of *ne . . . pas* in the sentence depends on various factors:
- the mood of the verb (the infinitive is treated differently from conjugated verbs)
- the type of tense (simple/compound)
- the presence of:
    - object pronouns
    - adverbs
    - verb–subject inversion (e.g. in a question).

Also the word order changes in the imperative and with conjugated verbs followed by an infinitive.

When combinations occur, all the rules apply!

All the above are treated in the relevant chapters. See chapters 14 Imperative, section 2.2, 15 Infinitive, section 2.3, 23 Articles, section 8, 31 Personal Pronouns, section 2.2.3 and 39 Interrogative Structures, section 2.1.6.

2.1.1 *ne . . . pas du tout, ne . . . pas . . . du tout*

(i) *du tout* can be added to *ne . . . pas* as a reinforcing element.
> Ex: *Il n'y a **pas du tout** de différence.*
> or:
> *Il n'y a **pas** de différence **du tout**.*
> There is no difference at all.

(ii) *pas du tout* can appear on its own if there is ellipsis of the verb.
> Ex: – *Ça t'étonne?* – ***Pas du tout***.
> – Does that surprise you? – Not at all.

Note that in this sense, *du* remains *du*: do not write **pas de tout*!

2.1.2 *pas only*

When there is ellipsis of the verb, *ne* is omitted and only *pas* is used, for instance in answers to questions.
> Ex: – *Qui reveut des légumes?* – ***Pas** moi!*
> – Who wants more vegetables? – Not me!

> *Vous avez vu ma dictée?* ***Pas** une seule faute!*
> Have you seen my dictation? Not a single mistake!

> – *Voulez-vous de la crème sur votre salade de fruits?*
> – *Oui, mais **pas** trop!*
> – Would you like some cream on your fruit salad?
> – Yes please, but not too much!

*Tu es fatigué? Moi **pas**.*
Are you tired? I'm not.

In formal French, *Moi non* would be used instead here (see 2.1.4 below).

NB(1): The omission of ***ne*** from a full negative sentence may be frequent among native speakers in informal French, but is not acceptable in writing, formal or informal, unless of course intentional, and is frowned upon in formal spoken French (e.g. oral examinations).

NB(2): In fixed expressions belonging to the familiar register, ***ne*** can be omitted.

Ex: ***Pas** vu, **pas** pris.*
(= *Ce qui n'a pas été vu alors qu'on le volait est considéré comme non pris/non volé.*)
What the eye doesn't see, the heart doesn't grieve over.

NB(3): ***pas*** can be used by itself to negate individual words or phrases.

Ex: *C'est un enfant **pas** comme les autres.*
He's not like other children.

*Eric est en vacances **pas** loin de Saint-Tropez.*
Eric's on holiday not far from Saint-Tropez.

2.1.3 ne *only*

pas can be omitted in the following cases which all belong to formal French.

(i) With the following verbs:

Ex: ***savoir*** + infinitive:
*Je suis désolée, je **ne saurais** vous renseigner.*
I am sorry, I am unable to inform you.

cesser de + infinitive:
*Il **n'a cessé de** pleuvoir toute la journée.*
It has not stopped raining all day.

oser + infinitive:
*Elle **n'osait** vous parler / vous le demander.*
She did not dare speak to you / ask you.

pouvoir + infinitive:
*Je **ne peux** vous voir avant la semaine prochaine.*
I cannot see you before next week.

(ii) In the following fixed expressions:

Ex: *qu'à cela ne tienne*   never mind
ne vous en déplaise   whether you like it or not
si je ne me trompe   if I am not mistaken

NB: *si je ne m'abuse* is also used instead of *si je ne me trompe* but is considered a *cliché* (hence should be avoided!).

623

(iii) As a stylistic choice in:
 – hypothetical clauses
> Ex: *N'eût été son aide . . .*
>> (= *S'il n'y avait pas eu son aide . . .*)

 – interrogative/exclamative turns of phrase
> Ex: *Que ne me le disiez-vous?*
>> (= *Pourquoi ne me l'avez-vous pas dit?*)

(iv) Expletive or pleonastic **ne** ('ne' *explétif*)

Where **ne** has not got a negative meaning but is used as 'padding'.

 – In *que*-clauses after verbs such as *craindre, avoir peur, éviter, empêcher, prendre garde* (see also chapter 12 Subjunctive, section 4.1).
> Ex: *Il avait peur que vous **ne** soyez en retard.*
> He was afraid you might be late.

NB: In conjunction with *pouvoir, ne* keeps its negative value.
> Ex: *Il avait peur que vous **ne** puissiez tout terminer à temps.*
> He was afraid you would **not** be able to finish everything on time.

In all other cases, *pas* must be added to restore a negative value. Compare:
> *Je crains qu'il **ne** pleuve ce soir.*
> I fear it **might** rain tonight.
>> and:
> *Je crains qu'il **ne** pleuve **pas** ce soir.*
> I fear it **might not** rain tonight.

 – In subordinate clauses introduced by the conjunctions *de peur que, à moins que, avant que* (see chapter 12 Subjunctive, section 4.2).
> Ex: *Je serai revenu avant que vous **ne** partiez.*
> I'll be back before you leave.

 – In comparative clauses of inequality (see chapter 30 Comparatives, section 2.1).
> Ex: *La grammaire est un sujet plus intéressant que je **ne** l'aurais cru.*
> Grammar is a more interesting subject than I thought.

2.1.4 Use of non

(i) In **formal** French, **non** is often used instead of *ne . . . pas* or *pas*. It can be used in such a way in the following cases:

 – before an adjective or a participle (administrative style)
> Ex: *Une plainte **non** déposée dans les délais requis ne sera pas considérée.*
>> (= *Une plainte qui **n'**a **pas** été déposée . . .*)
> A complaint not lodged within the required time will not be considered.

 – before an adverb
> Ex: *Notre domaine est **non** loin du parc d'attractions.*
>> (= *Notre domaine **n'**est **pas** loin du . . .*)
> Our estate is not far from the fairground.

– after the conjunction *ou*, in opposition to a declaration

Ex: *Qu'il soit d'accord ou **non**, nous devons continuer.*
(= *Qu'il soit d'accord ou **pas** . . .*)
Whether he agrees or not, we must proceed.

*Elu ou **non** aux cantonales, il continuera son combat contre la pollution.*
(= *Elu ou **pas** . . .*)
Whether he is elected in the local elections or not, he will continue his fight against pollution.

– in a short answer with ellipsis of the verb, to express the opposite case

Ex: – *J'ai terminé ma dissertation pour demain. Et toi?*
– *Moi **non**.* (= *Moi **pas**.*)
– I have finished my essay for tomorrow. What about you?
– I haven't.

(ii) ***non*** is also used in structures stressing opposition (often in conjunction with ***mais***).

Ex: *Il faut manger pour vivre et **non** [pas] vivre pour manger.* (proverb)
One should eat to live and not live to eat.

***Non** seulement des arbres centenaires **mais** aussi des bâtiments ont été détruits pendant la dernière tempête.*
Not only century-old trees but also buildings were destroyed during the last storm.

*Il n'est pas très populaire, **non** qu'il soit arrogant, **mais** il en donne l'impression!*
He is not very popular: it's not that he is arrogant, but he gives that impression.

*Prenons l'exemple de Copernic, qui déclarait que c'est la terre qui tourne autour du soleil, et **non** [pas] l'inverse.*
Let's take the example of Copernicus, who declared that the earth revolves around the sun and not the other way round.

(iii) Finally, ***non*** can be used as a prefix before certain nouns or past participles and is hyphenated.

Ex: *Il a été accusé de **non-assistance*** (failure to help) *à personne en danger.*

*La **non-exécution*** (failure to carry out) *d'un contrat peut entraîner des poursuites judiciaires.*

*Aux dernières élections, il y avait une cinquantaine de députés **non-inscrits*** (independent).

*L'accusé a bénéficié d'un **non-lieu**.* (The accused was discharged for lack of evidence.)

*J'ai réservé une place dans un wagon **non-fumeur*** (no-smoking).

*Je n'achète que des jus de fruits **non-sucrés*** (unsweetened).
But: 'unleaded petrol' is *essence sans plomb*.

2.2 Negative adverbs other than *ne . . . pas*

There are two types of negation: absolute and restricted.

2.2.1 *Negative adverbs, absolute negation*

By and large, the rules for *ne . . . pas* also apply to the other negative adverbs but see exceptions below.

(i) *ne . . . point*

ne . . . point is equivalent to *ne . . . pas* but is only used in literature or affected speech and also in some regional dialects.

> Ex: *Je n'aime point qu'on me dérange.*
> I do not like to be disturbed.
>
> *Cela n'est point une raison pour ne pas venir.*
> This is no reason not to come.

Note that *point* can appear without *ne* in proverbs (there is no verb):

> Ex: *Point de roses sans épines.*
> No rose without thorns.

(ii) *ne . . . aucunement/nullement/pas du tout*

These are all emphatic forms of *ne . . . pas*, but *pas du tout* is by far the most commonly used (see 2.1.1 above), while the other two are considered a little affected.

> Ex: *Il n'est pas du tout sûr que ce soit correct.*
> He is not at all sure whether this is correct.
>
> *Vous n'avez nullement répondu à la question.*
> You have not answered the question at all.
>
> *Est-ce votre avis aussi? – Aucunement.*
> Is that your opinion as well? – Not at all / Not in the least.

(iii) *ne . . . jamais*

– *ne . . . jamais* ('never') has a temporal value and is the opposite of *toujours* ('always'), *quelquefois, parfois* ('sometimes'), *souvent* ('often') and *de temps en temps, de temps à autre* ('from time to time', 'every now and then').

> Ex: – *Ecrivez-vous à vos parents de temps en temps? – Non, je ne leur écris jamais.*
> – Do you write to your parents every now and then? – No, I never do.

– When *jamais* appears without *ne*:

– it may mean 'ever'.

> Ex: *Avez-vous jamais vu quelque chose de semblable dans votre vie que trois souris aveugles?*
> Have you ever seen such a thing in your life as three blind mice?

*Si **jamais** vous êtes dans le quartier, venez me voir.*
If you are ever in the neighbourhood, come and see me.

– it may be part of a fixed expression.
> Ex: *C'est maintenant ou **jamais**!*
> It's now or never!
>
> ***Jamais** deux sans trois!*
> Things always happen in threes!

(iv) ***ne . . . plus***

ne . . . plus has a temporal ('no longer') or quantitative ('no more') value.
Note that the '*s*' of *plus* is **not** pronounced: [ply].

– ***ne . . . plus*** is the opposite of ***encore*** ('still') or ***toujours*** (meaning 'still') and, applied to a verb, means 'no longer'/'not . . . any more'/'not . . . any longer'.
> Ex: – *Vous travaillez **encore/toujours** là? – Non, je **n**'y travaille **plus** / je **n**'y travaille **plus** depuis trois mois.*
> – Do you still work there? – No, I don't work there any more / I haven't been working there for three months.
>
> *Je suis **toujours** professeur de français mais je **ne** suis **plus** au même collège.*
> I am still a teacher of French but I am not at the same school any more.
>
> – *Vous mangez **encore** du pain? – Non, depuis que je suis au régime, je **n**'en mange **plus**.*
> – Do you still eat bread? – No, since I've been on a diet, I don't eat it any more.

NB: *encore* can also mean 'more'.
> Ex: – *Voulez-vous **encore** un peu de fromage? – Non merci, je **n**'en veux **plus** / je **n**'ai **plus** faim.*
> – Would you like some more cheese? – No thank you, I do not want any more / I'm full (lit. I'm no longer hungry).

See chapter 30 Comparatives, section 2.3.3(iii).
Compare with:
> *Vous voulez **toujours** du fromage?*
> Do you still want cheese?

– ***ne . . . plus*** applied to a noun (or pronoun) means 'no more of . . .', 'no . . . left'.
> Ex: *Je **n**'ai **plus** de tickets de métro.*
> I have no metro tickets left.
>
> *Il **n**'en reste **plus**.*
> There's none left.

Hence ***n'avoir plus de . . .*** can be translated as 'to run out of . . .'.
> Ex: *Nous **n**'avons **plus** de pain.*
> We've run out of bread.

   – *ne . . . plus* with a verb before or after an infinitive means
   'not . . . any more'.
        Ex: *Vous **ne** devriez **plus** y aller, si cela vous déprime.*
           You should not go there any more, if it depresses you.

NB: *ne . . . plus* is 'no more' and *plus* without *ne* is 'more'. The '*s*' of *plus* is
pronounced when it means 'more': [plys]. Compare:
        *Il **ne** m'en faut **plus**.* [ply]
        I don't need any any more.
           and:
        *Il m'en faut **plus**.* [plys]
        I need more.

   – *du tout* can be added for emphasis.
        Ex: *Il **n'y** en a **plus du tout**.*
           There's none at all left.

        *Je **n'y** pensais **plus du tout**!*
        (= J'avais complètement oublié)
        I had completely forgotten!

(v)   *ne . . . guère*

ne . . . guère expresses a partial exclusion.

   – *ne . . . guère* is the equivalent of *pas beaucoup, pas très, presque pas, peu* and *à
peine*, with various nuances.
        Ex: *Mon mari **n'a guère** le temps de faire le jardin.*
           My husband hasn't really got the time to do the garden.

        *Ça **n'est guère** possible.*
        It's not really possible.

        *Je **ne** vais **guère** au théâtre.*
        I hardly ever go to the theatre.

        *Mon mari **n'a pas beaucoup** le temps de faire le jardin.*
        My husband hasn't got much time to do the garden.

        *Mon mari **n'a presque pas** le temps de faire le jardin.*
        My husband has hardly got the time to do the garden.

   – *pas très* can be used with adjectives (do not use *pas beaucoup*).
        Ex: *Il **ne** fait **guère** chaud aujourd'hui.*
           or:
        *Il **ne** fait **pas très** chaud aujourd'hui.*
        It is not very warm today.

   – *pas très* can also be used with nouns which are not preceded by an article (do
not use *pas très* if there is an article).
        Ex: *Je **n'ai guère** envie de sortir.*
           or:
        *Je **n'ai pas très** envie de sortir.*
           or:
        *Je **n'ai pas beaucoup** envie de sortir.*
        I don't really feel like going out.

– *à peine* and *peu*: although syntactically affirmative (note the absence of *ne*), they are semantically close to a restricted negation.

> Ex: *Mon mari a **peu/à peine** le temps de faire le jardin.*
> My husband has little time to do the garden.

– *à peine* can also mean 'scarcely' in the sense of 'just about' or 'only just'.

> Ex: *La pièce venait **à peine** de commencer quand des manifestants l'ont interrompue.*
> The play had only just begun when demonstrators interrupted it.

(vi) **ne . . . pas encore**

ne . . . pas encore is the opposite of *déjà*.

> Ex: *Tous les invités sont **déjà** là mais Sylvain **n'est pas encore** arrivé.*
> All the guests are **already** here but Sylvain has **not** arrived **yet**.
>
> *Etes-vous **déjà** allé en Amérique du Sud? – Non, **pas encore**.*
> Have you **already** been to South America? – No, **not yet**.

NB: **pas encore** is very close in meaning to **toujours pas** (although **toujours pas** suggests a greater concern) but should not be confused with **pas toujours**. Compare:

> *Je n'ai **toujours pas** reçu de réponse.*
> I have still not had any answer.
>
> and:
>
> *Je n'ai **pas toujours** reçu de réponse.*
> I have not always had an answer.

(vii) **ne . . . pas grand-chose**

– **grand-chose** is constructed with *à* + infinitive (in the case of *avoir à* + transitive direct verb).

> Ex: *Il **n'y** a **pas grand-chose** à faire dans le jardin en hiver.*
> There is nothing much to do in the garden in winter.
>
> *Paul **n'a pas grand-chose** à lire en ce moment.*
> Paul hasn't got much to read at the moment.

– **grand-chose** comes after the past participle in compound tenses.

> Ex: *Ils **n'ont pas** vendu **grand-chose**.*
> They didn't sell much.

– **grand-chose** is placed after the infinitive of which it is the object.

> Ex: *Nous nous sommes promis de **ne pas** faire **grand-chose** cet été!*
> We promised ourselves not to do much this Summer!

– **grand-chose** is constructed with *de* + invariable adjective (see also *quelque chose de, rien de*, etc. in chapter 36 Indefinite Words, sections 2.1(ii) and 3.3.3).

> Ex: *Nous sommes allés au Marché aux Puces mais nous **n'avons pas** vu grand-chose d'original.*
> We went to the Flea Market but didn't see much that was unusual.

– **grand-chose** is used without *ne* if there is ellipsis of the conjugated verb.
Ex: *Qu'est-ce qu'elle dit? – Oh,* **pas grand-chose**.
What is she saying? – Oh, not much.

(viii) **ne . . . nulle part**

ne . . . nulle part is often opposed to *quelque part* or *partout*, and comes after the past participle in compound tenses.
Ex: *Ce livre doit pourtant bien être* **quelque part**, *cependant je* **ne** *le vois* **nulle part**.
This book must be somewhere and yet I cannot see it anywhere.

Ils **ne** *sont partis* **nulle part** *pour les vacances.*
They didn't go anywhere for their holiday.

(ix) **non plus, ne . . . pas . . . non plus**

non plus, ne . . . pas . . . non plus are opposed to **aussi**.

– Use **non plus** to agree with a statement in the negative form (to disagree, use **si**). Compare:
– *Je n'ai pas de stylo – Moi* **non plus**.
– I haven't got a pen – Neither have I.
and:
– *Je n'ai pas de stylo – Moi* **si**.
– I haven't got a pen – I have.

NB: If a negative sentence in French translates into an affirmative sentence in English, **non plus** is rendered as **too**.
Ex: *Zut, je n'ai plus de papier! – Moi* **non plus**!
Drat, I've run out of paper! – Me **too**!

– **non plus** comes after the past participle in compound tenses.
Ex: – *Je n'ai pas reçu de billets gratuits pour le concert. Et vous?*
– *Non, on* **ne** *m'en a* **pas** *envoyé* **non plus**.
– No, I wasn't sent any either.

Nous **n'y** *sommes* **pas** *allés* **non plus**.
We didn't go either.

2.2.2 Negative adverbs, restricted negation

Restricted negation is expressed by **ne . . . que** (**only**).

(i) **Place of** *que*

que immediately precedes the word(s) **to which the restriction applies**.
Ex: *Ils* **n'ont** *protesté auprès des autorités* **que** *lorsqu'il était trop tard.*
They only lodged a complaint with the magistrates when it was too late.

On **ne** *peut entrer* **qu'**après s'être essuyé les pieds.
You can go in only after wiping your feet.

(ii)   **Ambiguity**

As in English, *ne . . . que* is ambiguous as it can be seen:
− either as a global concept: '**that** to the exclusion of anything else'
− or as a restricted concept: '**only** that' (e.g. there can be more, worse, etc.)

In practice, the context determines the meaning. Otherwise, adjectives can be added to clarify the intended meaning. Consider the following examples:

1 *Je **n'**ai **que** de petits problèmes.*
        unambiguously means:
My problems are only small.
(restricted concept)
        whereas:
*Je **n'**ai **que** des problèmes.*
        means:
I have got nothing but problems.
(global concept)

2 *Nous **ne** buvons **que** des vins millésimés.*
   We only drink vintage wines.
        can mean:
− either: we do not drink any other wines
(but we drink other things as well: restricted concept)
− or: we drink nothing else
(i.e. no other drink: global concept)
but the first interpretation is more likely!

3 *Son père **ne** lui a donné **que** de l'argent.*
   All his father ever gave him was money.
        but:
*Son père **ne** lui a donné **que** 30 Francs.*
His father only gave him 30 Francs.

Note that ambiguity can be resolved with *ne . . . pas que* (see section (iii) below).

(iii)   ***ne . . . pas que***

ne . . . pas que is used in the sense of ***ne . . . pas seulement***, where ***ne . . . pas*** is a negative and ***que*** has a restrictive meaning.

        Ex: *Nous **ne** buvons **pas que** des vins millésimés!*
                or:
        *Nous **ne** buvons **pas seulement** des vins millésimés!*
        We drink more than just vintage wines!

        *Son père **ne** lui a **pas** donné **que** de l'argent!*
                or:
        *Son père **ne** lui a **pas** donné **seulement** de l'argent!*
        His father gave him more than just money!

(iv) **seulement = ne . . . que**

Whenever **ne . . . que** is used in its restricted sense, it can be replaced by **seulement**, if needed.
> Ex: *Nous buvons **seulement** des vins millésimés.*

(v) **seulement instead of ne . . . que**

seulement should be used instead of **ne . . . que** in the following cases:

− When the verb is the object of the restriction.
> Ex: *Je n'exige rien. Je demande **seulement**.*
> I'm not demanding anything. I'm only asking.
>
> *C'était **seulement** pour rire.*
> It was only a joke.

NB: In this context, ***c'est tout*** can be used instead of ***seulement***.
> Ex: *Je n'exige rien, je demande, **c'est tout**.*
> I'm not demanding anything, I'm asking, that's all.
>
> *C'était pour rire, **c'est tout**.*
> It was meant as a joke, that's all.

− If there is ellipsis of the verb.
> Ex: − *Combien d'étudiants sont arrivés?* − ***Seulement** six.*
> − How many students have arrived? − Only six.
> − *Qui veut y aller?* − ***Seulement** Paul et Marie.*
> − Who wants to go? − Only Paul and Marie.

− When there is already a ***que*** in the sentence.
> Ex: *Ils veulent **que** leur chat chasse les souris.*
> They want their cat to hunt mice.
>
> → *Ils veulent **seulement que** leur chat chasse les souris.*
> All they want is for their cat to hunt mice.

NB: *Ils veulent que leur chat chasse **seulement** les souris / **ne** chasse **que** les souris.*
They want their cat to hunt only mice.

(vi) **seul instead of seulement**

When the restriction applies to the subject of the verb, there is a choice between **seulement** and the adjective **seul**. When the subject has not got any identifying features, use the adverb **seulement**. Otherwise, use the adjective **seul**. Compare:
> ***Seulement** six étudiants ont assisté au dernier cours du trimestre.*
> Only six students attended the last lecture of the term.
> and:
> ***Seuls** Paul et Marie veulent bien y aller.*
> Only Paul and Marie are willing to go.
>
> ***Seulement** trois tables ont été vendues.*
> and:
> ***Seules** les commodes Louis XVI ont été vendues.*

In both cases, *il n'y a que . . .* + subjunctive would be used in informal French, but beware of the accumulation of [k] sounds!

> Ex: *Il n'y a que Paul et Marie qui veuillent bien y aller.*
> There's only Paul and Marie who are willing to go.

(vii)   **Use of *ne faire que* + infinitive**

ne faire que has two meanings which are determined by the context:

– a restrictive meaning, equivalent to *seulement* (see above). The emphasis is on the restricted nature of the action which is expressed.

> Ex: *Je **ne fais que** passer.*
> I'm only passing through.

> *Il **n'a fait que** répéter ce que ses collègues avaient déjà dit.*
> All he did was repeat what his colleagues had already said.

– an iterative or continuous meaning, equivalent to *ne pas arrêter de, ne pas cesser de, ne rien faire d'autre que.* The emphasis is on the continuity or repetition of the action which is expressed.

> Ex: *Elle **ne fait que** tomber malade.*
> (= *Elle ne cesse de tomber malade.*)
> She's forever falling ill.

> *Ils **n'ont fait que** m'agacer toute la journée.*
> (= *Ils n'ont pas arrêté de m'agacer toute la journée.*)
> They kept irritating me all day.

> *Pendant tout le cours, ils **n'ont fait que** chahuter.*
> (= *Ils n'ont rien fait d'autre que chahuter.*)
> During the whole lecture, all they did was mess about.

3   Multiple negation

As in English, two negatives make a positive.

(i)   **Multiple negations without *pas***

See also chapter 36 Indefinite Words, section 3.3.

> Ex: *Je **n'ai** encore **jamais rien** vu de semblable.*
> I have never seen anything like this yet.

> *Ils **ne** nous disent **jamais rien**.*
> They never tell us anything.

> ***Plus rien ne** la touche.*
> Nothing affects her any more.

> *Il **ne** me reste **plus que** 6 francs.*
> I've only got 6 francs left.

> *Nous **ne** voyons **plus jamais personne**.*
> We never see anybody any more.

(ii) **Multiple negations with *pas***

> Ex: *Il **ne** peut **pas ne pas** le savoir.*
> (= *Il le sait certainement.*)
> He certainly does know about it / He can't be ignorant of it.
>
> *Je **ne** dis **pas** que ce **ne** soit **pas** intéressant.*
> (= *C'est sans doute intéressant.*)
> I am not saying it is not interesting.

(iii) **Common errors**

The accumulation of negative adverbs often appears cumbersome and can be a source of confusion. For instance, the following expression is frequently heard in France (on the radio in particular) and is incorrect in the sense that it is intended to say the reverse of what it actually says:

> *'Vous n'êtes pas sans ignorer que . . .'*
> which literally reads:
> 'You are not without not knowing that . . .'
> and actually means:
> 'You don't know that . . .'
> when what is intended is:
> *'Vous n'êtes pas sans savoir que . . .'*
> which literally reads:
> 'You are not without knowing that . . .'
> and actually means:
> 'You know that . . .'

A simpler alternative is:

> *'Vous savez sans aucun doute que . . .'*
> 'No doubt you know that . . .'

4 Ambiguity

(i) Consider the following example:

> *Le projet n'a pas été adopté à cause du facteur temps.*

This could mean either:

> 1 *On a adopté le projet, mais pour d'autres raisons.*
> The project was approved, but for other reasons.
> or:
> 2 *On n'a pas adopté le projet à cause du facteur temps.*
> The project was not approved because of the time factor.

It is possible to clarify this ambiguity with a different wording (see cleft constructions in chapter 2 Syntax, section 2.15.4).

> Ex: 1 *Ce n'est pas à cause du facteur temps qu'on a adopté le projet.*
> It is not because of the time factor that the project was approved.

or:

2 *C'est à cause du facteur temps qu'on n'a pas adopté le projet.*
It is because of the time factor that the project was not approved.

In context of course, an explanation would normally follow for meaning (1), e.g.
. . . , *mais parce que le personnel requis était immédiatement disponible.*
. . . , but because the required personnel were immediately available.

(ii)   Restriction with *tout*

ne . . . pas + tout, tout le monde, etc. only indicates a **restriction**, and not a total absence of, i.e. the scope of the negation has to be taken into account.

Ex: **Tout n'est pas** *exact dans ce que vous dites.*
(= *Certaines des choses que vous dites ne sont pas exactes.*)
Not everything is correct in what you are saying.

Tout le monde ne *peut* **pas** *faire ce qu'il fait.*
(= *Il y a des gens qui ne peuvent pas le faire.*)
Not everybody can do what he does.

Je **n'ai pas tout** *fait.*
(= *J'en ai fait une partie.*)
I haven't done it all.

(iii)   Total absence

In order to express zero quantity or zero degree, one should use a word with the opposite meaning of *tout, tout le monde,* etc.

Ex: **Rien n'est** *exact dans ce que vous dites.*
Nothing is correct in what you are saying.
           or:
Tout *est* **inexact** *dans ce que vous dites.*
Everything is incorrect in what you are saying.

Personne ne *peut faire ce qu'il fait.*
Nobody can do what he does.

Je **n'ai rien** *fait.*
I haven't done anything.

39 Interrogative and exclamative structures

1 Interrogative form: introduction

The interrogative sentence is opposed to declarative, exclamative and imperative sentences. It is generally a request for information and forms the first part of the couple **question**–answer. One should distinguish between the following:

(i) **Total interrogation** (*interrogation totale ou générale*)

Total interrogation is determined and can relate to the verb, the subject, the object, etc. of the sentence (see also chaper 38 Negative Structures, section 1).
  Consider the following example:
>   *Le chien a cassé le vase.*
>   → ***Est-ce que** le chien a cassé le vase?*

The interrogation relates to:
– the subject:
  Oui/Non[, ce n'est pas le chien mais le chat].
– the object:
  Oui/Non[, pas le vase mais le pot de fleurs].
– the verb:
  Oui/Non[, il ne l'a pas cassé; il l'a seulement renversé].

In any case, there is no new information and the question invites a **yes** or **no** answer.

(ii) **Partial interrogation** (*interrogation partielle ou particulière*)

Partial interrogation is undetermined. It appeals for a piece of information which is not contained within the question itself and which is supplied in the answer. The question can relate to:

– the subject (**identity** of the referent).
>   Ex: ***Qui** vient d'arriver? – Eric.*

– a direct or indirect object and, more specifically:
  – the **nature** of the referent which is the object of the verb.
>   Ex: ***Que** manges-tu? – Un pain au chocolat.*
>   ***A quoi** tu penses? – Aux vacances.*

  – the **identity** of the referent of the object.
>   Ex: ***Quel** livre as-tu acheté? – Celui sur les abeilles.*

- a complement of *être*.

> Ex: **Qui** *est Céline? – C'est une collègue.*
> **Qu'**est-ce que c'est? – C'est une table, un chou, etc.*
> **Quels** *sont ces gens? – Ce sont mes voisins.*

- an adverb: the question relates to a circumstance of the action.

> Ex: **Quand** *prenez-vous vos vacances? – En août.*

Note that the question can be worded in such a way that the choice of answer is limited.

> Ex: **Quand** *prenez-vous vos vacances, en juillet ou en août?*
> **Qui** *est Isabelle, ta sœur ou ta mère?*

(iii) **Direct and indirect interrogation**

One should also distinguish between direct interrogation (which always ends with a question mark) and indirect interrogation, either total or partial.

- Direct interrogation appears in an independent clause.

> Ex: *Vous êtes prêt?*
> *Comment allez-vous?*

- Indirect interrogation is introduced by a verb + conjunction which specify the nature of the interrogation. It is a subordinate clause.

> Ex: *Je **me demande si** Paul a reçu ma lettre.*

Indirect interrogation is treated in chapter 41 Reported Speech, section 3.5.

2 Total interrogation

This concerns questions to which the answer is ***oui***, ***non***, ***si***. There are several ways of asking such questions:

(i) Same order as for a declarative construction and:
- use *est-ce que* at the beginning of the sentence
- use *n'est-ce pas* at the end of the sentence
- use intonation.

(ii) Inversion of subject pronoun and verb (**simple inversion**), or nominal subject + inversion of subject pronoun and verb (**complex inversion**).

2.1 Construction

2.1.1 est-ce que

est-ce que (***est-ce qu'***) is placed at the beginning of the declarative sentence and the word order does not change (note that there is already an inversion in *est-ce que*).

> Ex: declaration: *Le chat est dans la cuisine.*
> question: ***Est-ce que*** *le chat est dans la cuisine?*
> Is the cat in the kitchen?

637

2.1.2 n'est-ce pas

Unlike its English equivalent, this construction is **invariable**. It is placed at the end of the sentence, after a comma.

Ex: declaration: *Philippe est dans la cuisine.*

question: *Philippe est dans la cuisine, **n'est-ce pas**?*

Philippe is in the kitchen, **isn't he**?

2.1.3 *Intonation (question intonative)*

This is the minimal interrogation. The sentence finishes with a rising pitch. This is the most common way of asking a question in informal, spoken French.

Ex: declaration: *Le chat est dans la cuisine.*

question: *Le chat est dans la cuisine?*

2.1.4 *Polite interest and further inquiry*

(i) Polite interest is expressed in English by a simple inversion of relevant pronoun and verb/auxiliary. In French, use something like *Vraiment?*, even in the negative.

Ex: – Paul has just arrived. – Has he?

  – *Paul vient d'arriver. – Vraiment?*

  – I'm not going. – Aren't you?

  – *Je n'y vais pas. – Vraiment?*

(ii) Further enquiry after a statement is expressed in English in a similar way but with a different pronoun. In French, use *Et toi/vous/lui*, etc. and in the negative *Pas toi/vous/lui*, etc.

Ex: I don't understand. Do you?

  Je ne comprends pas. Et vous?

I'm leaving now. Aren't you?

Je m'en vais maintenant. Pas vous?

2.1.5 *Verb–subject inversion*

The subject can be a noun or a pronoun.

2.1.5.1 CLITIC PRONOUN SUBJECT *je*

When the subject is *je*, the inversion 'verb–*je*' (called **simple** inversion) normally takes place only with the following verbs:

– in the present indicative:

être	*suis-je?*
avoir	*ai-je?*
devoir	*dois-je?*
aller	*vais-je?*
pouvoir	**puis**-*je?*
dire	*dis-je?*
faire	*fais-je?*
savoir	*sais-je?*
voir	*(que) vois-je?*

– in the future or the conditional:

être	*serai-je? serais-je?*
devoir	*devrai-je? devrais-je?* etc.

The inversion is particularly commonly used when an infinitive follows *aller*, *pouvoir* and *devoir*.

> Ex: **Dois-je partir** *maintenant?*
> Should I go now?

With other verbs, the inversion with *je* should be avoided.

> Ex: *Je pars à midi.*   →   **✶**Pars-je à midi?*
> →   *Est-ce que je pars à midi?*
> →   *Je pars à midi, n'est-ce pas?*
> →   *Je pars à midi?*

NB: The forms *donné-je, aimé-je, parlé-je, prené-je, voulé-je* are now considered archaic. However, *dussé-je* and *eussé-je* (indicating a supposition) and *puissé-je* (indicating a wish) are still used in formal French.

> Ex: *Je ne le ferai pas,* **dussé-je** *encourir la colère des dieux* . . .
> (= *même si je devais* . . .)
> I will not do it, even if I have to face the wrath of the gods . . .

2.1.5.2   OTHER CLITIC PRONOUN SUBJECTS

tu, il, elle, on, nous, vous, ils, elles

(i)   The verb comes first, followed by the subject pronoun (**simple** inversion). They are hyphenated.

> Ex: *Il est heureux*   →   **Est-il** *heureux?*

(ii)   In the 3rd person singular, a '*t*' must be added between two vowels to avoid a hiatus. Hence no '*t*' is added if the verb already ends with a '*t*', nor is one added if the verb ends with a '*d*', as '*d*' is then pronounced [t].

> Ex: *Il ronronne fort.*   →   *Ronronne-**t**-il fort?*
> *Elle arrive demain.*   →   *Arrive-**t**-elle demain?*
> *On mange tout de suite.* →   *Mange-**t**-on tout de suite?*
> *Il y a du monde.*   →   *Y a-**t**-il du monde?*
>   but:
> *Il prend son sac.*   →   *Pren**d**-il son sac?*
> *Elle voit quelqu'un.*   →   *Voit-elle quelqu'un?*
> *On vend des légumes.*   →   *Ven**d**-on des légumes?*
> *Il peut tout faire.*   →   *Peut-il tout faire?*

2.1.5.3   NOUN (OR NON-PERSONAL PRONOUN) SUBJECT

The verb is inverted with *il, elle, ils* or *elles*, and the noun or pronoun (other than *il, elle* . . .) is kept in the same place. This is called **complex** inversion.

> Ex: *La table est mise.*
> →   **La table est-elle** *mise?*
>
> *Quelqu'un est arrivé.*
> →   **Quelqu'un est-il** *arrivé?*

Note that the complex inversion is used even if the noun is qualified.

> Ex: ***Vos voisins d'à-côté ont–ils*** *encore fait du bruit hier soir?*
> Were your next-door neighbours noisy again last night?

Consider the following sentence:

> 'Or less ambitiously, **is a man** who has spent his last years of school and his university career in the study of English literature to the exclusion of nearly every other language and tradition, **an educated man**?'

George Steiner, Language and Silence

When translating this question, there are two points to bear in mind:

– The style is formal, hence the complex inversion is required.

> '. . . , *un homme qui a passé* . . . ***est–il*** [*un homme*] *instruit?*'

– In English, the auxiliaries 'to be', 'to have' or 'to do' are inverted with the subject ('is a man') and so announce that a question is being posed at the beginning of the interrogative sentence. However in French, since the construction

> noun [+ complements] + verb + subject pronoun

is used, it is not until the end of this long sentence that the question form is made explicit. To counteract this, it is appropriate to add a question marker at the beginning of the interrogative sentence. For instance:

> '. . . , ***peut–on dire qu'****un homme qui a passé* . . . *est/soit* [*un homme*] *instruit?*'

2.1.6   *Interro-negative constructions and answers*

(i)   Constructions with declarative forms

ne and ***pas*** are placed on either side of the verb or the auxiliary in the case of compound tenses.

> Ex: *Nicolas **ne** comprend **pas**?*
> *Vous **n'**avez **pas** dit la vérité, n'est-ce pas?*
> *Est-ce qu'il **n'**est **pas** dans la cuisine?*

(ii)   Constructions with inversions

– ***ne*** is placed before the verb and ***pas*** after the subject pronoun.

> Ex: *Eric **ne** vient-il **pas** demain?*

– With a compound tense, ***ne*** is placed before the auxiliary and ***pas*** after the subject pronoun.

> Ex: *Anne **n'**est-elle **pas** encore arrivée?*

– The order of the object personal pronouns is the same as that in a declarative construction (see chapter 31 Personal Pronouns, section 2.2.3).

> Ex: *Dizzy **n'**a-t-il **pas** attrapé de souris?*
> → ***N'****en a-t-il **pas** attrapé?*

(iii)   Answers

si is used instead of *oui* only in the case of an affirmative answer to a negative question, i.e. when the person who answers contradicts the person who asked the question.

> Ex: *Vous avez compris?* **Oui** (*j'ai compris*).
>   but:
>   *Vous n'avez pas compris?* **Si** (*j'ai compris*).

Hence if you agree, say *non!*

> *Vous n'avez pas compris?* **Non** (*en effet, je n'ai pas compris*).

2.2   Semantics

2.2.1   *Choice of forms*

(i)   Declarative constructions

> Ex: *Est-ce que tu pars à midi?*
>   is a 'genuine' question.
>
> *Tu pars à midi?*
>   means I expect a 'yes', or expresses surprise.
>
> *Tu pars à midi, n'est-ce pas?*
>   is a request for confirmation.

(ii)   Verb–subject inversion

– With the exception of lexicalized constructions (see 4.1 below), questions wih inversion are mainly used in formal writing, but also in formal speeches, e.g. a lecture.

– Hence they often expect more than a yes or no answer. For instance, exam questions expect an argued answer!

(iii)   Interro–negative constructions

As in English, the negative form of the interrogative sentence is not the simple negation of a question. It can assume several values, which depend on the situation, intonation, the use of *est-ce que* or *n'est-ce pas* (see 2(i) above), etc. Hence it is sometimes the equivalent of a rhetorical question (see 4.4 below). For instance:

– It can be a request for confirmation of something that the speaker thinks he/she knows already.

> Ex: *N'étiez-vous pas chez les Dupont hier?*
>   Weren't you at the Duponts' yesterday?
>   This is equivalent to:
>   *Vous étiez chez les Dupont hier, n'est-ce pas?*
>   hence one expects a positive answer.

641

Vous n'avez pas compris, n'est-ce pas?
is a request for confirmation: I fully expect a 'no'.

Vous n'avez pas compris?
expresses surprise.

– It can be a question with an invitation to make a full statement.
  Ex: *Tu n'es pas d'accord avec moi?*
  Don't you agree with me?

2.2.2 *Interrogation not a request for information*

Interrogation is normally a request for information. However, it has other functions which are not interrogative in that either they do not call for an answer, or they call for an action and not a verbal reply. For instance:

– request/order:
  Ex: *Pouvez-vous me passer l'eau s'il vous plaît?*
  Pouvez-vous vous taire un instant?
  Voulez-vous ouvrir la fenêtre s'il vous plaît?
These are all requests, and not questions about capabilities or genuine wishes, hence they can be a source of humour when taken literally! See also chapter 21 Modals.

– suggestion/request for confirmation:
  Ex: *Si on allait prendre un verre?*
See also chapter 8 Imperfect, section 3.2.

– offer:
  Ex: *Voulez-vous encore un peu de viande?*

– threat:
Compare:
  Tu veux une gifle?
   and:
  Tu veux un bonbon?

3 Partial interrogation

These are questions which require specific details in the answers. They begin with interrogative words which are either adverbs, adjectives (determiners) or pronouns (variable or invariable). Note that the interrogative word may not necessarily be the first word in the sentence (see example in 3.4).

After an interrogative word, the sentence may be constructed in one of the following ways:
– declarative form
– *est-ce que* + declarative form
– verb–pronoun inversion (= **simple** inversion)
– noun + verb–pronoun inversion (= **complex** inversion)
– verb–noun inversion (= **simple** inversion)

The particular cases are indicated below.

3.1 Short simple (invariable) interrogative pronouns

The short simple interrogative pronouns are *qui*, *que* and *quoi*. They are the equivalents of the English **who, whom, what**, etc. With the exception of *que*, they can be preceded by a preposition. Like relative pronouns without an antecedent, they are **nominal**.

They are used in formal French with complex inversion. In informal French the long pronouns are used (see 3.2). In very informal French (e.g. conversation between friends), the short pronouns can be followed by the declarative form or simple inversion (see details below).

The question relates to the **nature** or the **identity** of the referent.

3.1.1 *Simple interrogative pronoun* qui

In principle, *qui* is used for human animates only. The question relates to the **identity** of the referent (since we already know the nature: a human animate).

qu'est-ce qui should be used for non-human animates and inanimates (see below). However, this poses a problem for non-human animates, e.g. if there is meowing at the door, it is fairly obvious that it is a cat – the question therefore should relate to the specific **identity** of the cat. '*Qu'est-ce qui miaule à la porte?*' implies that one does not even know that it is a cat, i.e. the **nature** of the agent! (The same problem occurs in English.) In this case, it is perfectly legitimate to use *qui* (or *quel chat*). See below.

Consider the following examples:
> Ex: ***Qui** tombe?*

This is a question relating to the **identity** of the referent, to which the answer may be:
> *M. Dupont / ?Dizzy*

but not:
> **une tuile*

Conversely:
> ***Qu'est-ce qui** tombe?*

The question relates to the **nature** of the referent, to which the answer may be:
> *une tuile / un homme / un chat*

but not:
> **Dizzy / *M. Dupont*

Note that *qui* remains *qui* even before a vowel or mute '*h*'.
> Ex: *Qu'est-ce **qui** est tombé?*

and not:
> **Qu'est-ce qu'est tombé?*

(i) *qui* **as a subject**

There is only one construction.
> Ex: ***Qui** est là?*
> Who's there?

> ***Qui** a tiré la queue du chat?*
> Who's been pulling the cat's tail?

NB(1): Interrogative *qui* is normally treated as masculine singular (see above), except as a complement of *être*.
> Ex: **Qui sont** *ces jeunes gens?*

NB(2): Since interrogative *qui* can be both a subject and an object (unlike relative *qui* which is always a subject), ambiguity may arise. Therefore in the construction '*qui* + simple inversion', it is normally understood that *qui* is the subject. Compare:
> **Qui** *va appeler Paul?* (*qui* = subject)
> Who is going to call Paul?
>   and:
> **Qui** *Paul va appeler?* (*qui* = object)
> Who is Paul going to call?

See also *quel, lequel* and *combien*.

(ii) **qui as an object**

- formal style:
> Ex: **Qui a-t-il** *rencontré?*
> Whom did he meet?
>
> **Qui** *les Dupont* **ont-ils rencontré** *à cette soirée?*
> Whom did the Duponts meet at that party?

- very informal style:
> Ex: **Qui** *il a rencontré?* / *Il a rencontré* **qui?**
> **Qui** *les Dupont ont rencontré à cette soirée?* / *Les Dupont ont rencontré* **qui** *à cette soirée?*

(iii) **qui as an object of a preposition**

- formal style:
> Ex: **A qui** *ce chat appartient-il?* / **A qui** *est ce chat?*
> To whom does this cat belong? / Whose is this cat?
>
> **De qui** *tient-il ses renseignements?*
> From whom does he get his information?

- very informal style:
> Ex: **A qui** *vous pensez?* / *Vous pensez* **à qui?**
> Who are you thinking about?
>
> *Ce chat est* **à qui?**
> Whose cat is that?

3.1.2 *Simple interrogative pronoun* que

que is used for inanimates and, in principle, for non-human animates as well. Note that *que* becomes *qu'* before a vowel or a mute '*h*'.

(i) **que as a subject**

que on its own cannot be used as a subject: use **qu'est-ce qui**

> Ex: **Qu'est-ce qui** *fait ce bruit?*
> What is making that noise?

For non-human animates, see 3.1.1 above.

(ii) **que as an object**

It is always followed by a **simple** inversion.

> Ex: **Que dit** *cet homme?*
> What is this man saying?
> and not:
> ⋆*Que cet homme dit-il?*
> ⋆*Que cet homme dit?*
>
> **Que veulent** *les enfants pour le petit-déjeuner?*
> What do the children want for breakfast?

Note that **que** cannot be used as the object of a preposition: use **quoi** (see below).

3.1.3 *Simple interrogative pronoun* quoi

quoi is also used for inanimates (as well as *que*) in the following cases:

(i) **quoi as an object**

As an object, **quoi** is often used for emphasis when asking for confirmation of what has been said.

> Ex: − *J'ai perdu mon billet de 500 francs! − Tu as perdu* **quoi**?
> − I've lost my 500 franc note! − You've lost what?

The first enquiry would normally still be:

> **Qu'est-ce que** *tu as perdu?* / **Qu'as-tu perdu?**
> What have you lost?

However, in very informal style, **quoi** can also be used as an alternative to *que*. It must appear after the verb.

> Ex: **Que** *fais-tu?*   or: *Tu fais* **quoi?**
>
> **Qu'as-tu mangé** *ce matin?*   or: *Tu as mangé* **quoi** *ce matin?*

(ii) **quoi as an object of a preposition**

− formal style: it is followed by a complex inversion.

> Ex: **De quoi** *vos parents parlent-ils?*
> What are your parents talking about?
>
> *Sur* **quoi** *êtes-vous assis?*
> What are you sitting on?

− informal style: use *est-ce que*.

> Ex: **Sur quoi** *est-ce que vous êtes assis?*

645

    – very informal style: declarative construction or simple inversion.

> Ex: ***Sur quoi*** *vous êtes assis?*
>
> ***De quoi*** *vos parents parlent? /* ***De quoi*** *parlent vos parents?*

3.1.4 Simple interrogative pronouns with je

(i)   When the subject is ***je***, the inversion verb–***je*** can only be used with certain verbs (see 2.1.5.1).

> Ex: ***Qui*** *suis-je?*
> Who am I?
>
> ***Que*** *dois-je répondre?*
> What should I answer?
>
> ***Qu'en*** *sais-je, sinon ce que l'on m'en a dit!*
> What do I know about it, apart from what I was told!

Note that '*Que sais-je?*' is also the name of a collection of popular science paperbacks.

(ii)   For other verbs, ***est-ce que*** should be used, even in formal French.

> Ex: ***Qu'est-ce que*** *j'entends?*
> What do I hear?
>
> ***A qui est-ce que*** *je ressemble?*
> Who do I look like?

(*Qu'entends-je?* or *A qui ressemblé-je?* are considered pedantic.)

(iii)   Very informal French:

> Ex: ***A qui*** *je pense?*
> Who am I thinking of?
>
> ***Qui*** *je vais appeler?*
> Who am I going to call?

3.1.5 Summary

	inanimate	animate
subject	—	***qui***
direct object and complement of *être*	***que, quoi***	***qui***
prepositional complement	***quoi***	***qui***

3.2 Long simple (invariable) interrogative pronouns

These are made up of the 'short' pronouns ***qui*** or ***que*** + ***est-ce qui*** for subjects and ***est-ce que*** for objects. Note that there is only one construction for a non-human subject: ***qu'est-ce qui***. Again, this groups inanimates and non–human animates together (see 3.1.1 above).

Long pronouns are mainly used in informal French. Hence:

(i) a human subject: *qui est-ce qui . . . ?*
> Ex: *Qui est-ce qui a pris mon crayon?*
> Who took my pencil?

(ii) a human direct object: *qui est-ce que . . . ?*
> Ex: *Qui est-ce que vous avez appelé au téléphone?*
> Who did you call?

(iii) an inanimate subject: *qu'est-ce qui . . . ?*
> Ex: *Qu'est-ce qui fait sourire Catherine?*
> What is making Catherine smile?

(iv) an inanimate direct object: *qu'est-ce que . . . ?*
> Ex: *Qu'est-ce que vous voulez que je fasse?*
> What do you want me to do?

(v) a human object of a preposition:
> Ex: *De qui est-ce que vous parlez?*
> Who are you talking about?

(vi) an inanimate object of a preposition:
> Ex: *A quoi est-ce que ça sert, ce machin?*
> What's this thing for?
>
> *De quoi est-ce que c'est fait?*
> What is it made of?

3.3 Interrogative adjectives/determiners

Interrogative adjectives have the same forms as exclamative adjectives (see section 5.2): *quel* corresponds to **which** or **what** and asks a question about the **identity** of the referent. It is placed at the beginning of the question followed by the noun it determines, and agrees in gender and number with that noun: *quel, quelle, quels, quelles*. In formal style, it is followed by the complex inversion, except when '*quel* + noun' is the subject. In informal style, use *est-ce que* and in very informal style, use the declarative form.

(i) **Subject**

Note that there is only one construction for formal and informal styles.
> Ex: *Quel livre a reçu le Prix Goncourt l'année dernière?*
> Which book got the Goncourt Prize last year?
>
> *Quels films ont le plus de succès en ce moment?*
> Which films are the most popular at the moment?

(ii) **Object**

— formal style:

Ex: ***Quelles questions*** *vous a-t-on posées?*
What questions were you asked?

— informal style:

Ex: *Quels livres est-ce que Michel a choisis?*
Which books did Michel choose?

— very informal style:

Ex: *Quelles questions on vous a posées?*

(iii) **Object of a preposition**

— formal style:

Ex: ***De quel livre*** *avez-vous besoin?*
Which book do you need?

Sur quelle chaise *dois-je m'asseoir?*
Which chair should I sit on?

— informal style:

Ex: *De quel livre est-ce que vous avez besoin?*
Sur quelle chaise est-ce que je dois m'asseoir?

— very informal style:

Ex: *De quel livre vous avez besoin?*
Sur quelle chaise je dois m'asseoir?

(iv) **Complement of *être***

quel may be separated from its noun by *être* or a combination of
être + pouvoir/devoir: **quel est**, **quel peut être**, **quel doit être**

— When the subject is a human animate, either *quel* or *qui* can be used
(see 3.1.1 above).

Ex: **Quel est** *cet homme?*   or: **Qui est** *cet homme?*
Who is this man?

— When the subject is an inanimate, only *quel* should be used (but see 3.1.1
about non-human animates).

Ex: **Quelles sont** *vos intentions?*
What are your intentions?

A votre avis, **quelle doit être** *notre réaction?*
In your opinion, what should our reaction be?

3.4 Compound (variable) interrogative pronouns

As a pronoun, ***lequel*** replaces '*quel* + noun' and agrees in gender and number
with this noun. It is used to ask questions about the **identity** of elements already
mentioned in the context. In other words, the speaker does not know
the identity of the object but knows its nature. These are mainly **representative**.

Note that compound interrogative pronouns have the same forms as compound relative pronouns (see chapter 32 Relative Pronouns, section 2.2): *lequel*, *laquelle*, *lesquels*, *lesquelles*.

In formal style, they are followed by the complex inversion except when '*lequel* + noun' is the subject. In informal style, use *est-ce que*, and in very informal style, use the declarative form.

(i)   **Subject**

There is only one construction for formal and informal styles.
Ex: *De ces fleurs, **laquelle est** la plus belle?*
Of these flowers, which is the most beautiful?

***Laquelle** [de ces fleurs] **est** la plus belle?*
Which [of these flowers] is the most beautiful?

(ii)   **Object**

   – Formal style:
Ex: ***Laquelle** de ces deux robes **vais-je** mettre aujourd'hui?*
Which of these two dresses shall I wear today?

***Laquelle** Catherine **va-t-elle** mettre aujourd'hui?*
Which one is Catherine going to wear today?

   – Informal style:
Ex: ***Laquelle** de ces deux robes **est-ce que** je vais mettre aujourd'hui?*

   – Very informal style:
Ex: ***Laquelle** de ces deux robes je vais mettre aujourd'hui?*

(iii)   **Object of a preposition**

   – Formal style:
Ex: ***Desquels** [de ces outils] **Paul a-t-il** besoin pour faire cette réparation?*
Which [of these tools] does Paul need to carry out this repair?

   – Informal style:
Ex: ***Desquels** [de ces outils] **est-ce que** vous avez besoin pour faire cette réparation?*

   – Very informal style:
Ex: ***Desquels** [de ces outils] vous avez besoin pour faire cette réparation?*

3.5   Interrogative adverbs

With an interrogative adverb, the question relates to the **circumstances** of the action. The interrogative adverbs are:

où, quand, comment, pourquoi, combien.

(i) **Adverb of place**

où (*d'où*): where (where from)

où is also a relative pronoun or adverb (see chapter 32 Relative Pronouns, section 3.7). As an interrogative word, its meaning is stricly spatial (not temporal). Compare:

> *Où vas-tu?*
> (*où* is an interrogative adverb)
> **Where** are you going?
>   and:
> *Le jour où je suis arrivé, . . .*
> (*où* is a relative pronoun)
> The day **when** I arrived . . .
>
> *D'où venez-vous?*
> **Where** do you come **from**? / **Where** are you **from**?

(ii) **Adverb of time**

quand (*depuis quand, jusqu'à quand*): when (since when, until when)

> Ex: *Jusqu'à quand allez-vous rester?*
> How long are you going to stay?

The answer can be an adverb or an adverbial clause.
> Ex: − *Quand viendras-tu me voir?*
>   − *Dimanche prochain / Quand j'en aurai le temps.*

(iii) **Adverb of manner**

comment: how

comment is used to ask a question about:
− the means by which something is achieved (alternative constructions include: *de quelle manière/façon*).
> Ex: *Comment avez-vous trouvé mon adresse?*
> How did you find my address?

− the quality of the object.
> Ex: *Comment trouves-tu cette robe?*
> What do you think of this dress?

This ambiguity can be a source of humour, for instance:
> *Au restaurant*
> *Serveur: Comment avez-vous trouvé votre bifteck?*
> *Client: Oh par hasard, sous un bout de feuille de salade.*
> Waiter: How did you find your steak?
> Customer: Oh by chance, under a piece of lettuce.

650

NB: 'how' + adjective or adverb ('how big', 'how fast', 'how often', etc.) is never
comment grand . . . Another construction should be used, for example:

> Ex: How fast is your car?
>
> *Quelle vitesse votre voiture peut-elle atteindre?*
>
> or:
>
> *A quelle vitesse peut aller votre voiture?*

(iv) **Adverb of cause**

pourquoi: why

pourquoi is different from *pour quoi* (two words) in that it asks questions about the
cause (*pour quelle raison / pour quel motif*) and not the aim. Compare:

> **Pourquoi** *ne m'avez-vous pas prévenu?*
>
> Why didn't you warn me?
>
> and:
>
> *C'est* **pour quoi** *faire tout ce papier?*
>
> What is all this paper for?

Answers begin either with a prepositional phrase (*à cause de* . . .) or a subordinate
clause (*parce que* . . .).

(v) **Adverb of quantity**

combien (*de*): how much/how many

combien enables one to ask a question about the number of elements or the
quantity.

> Ex: **Combien d'enfants** *avez-vous?*
>
> How many children have you got?
>
> **Combien d'invités** *sont arrivés?*
>
> How many guests have arrived?
>
> **Combien de** *beurre vous faut-il pour ce gâteau?*
>
> How much butter do you need for this cake?
>
> **Combien** *gagnez-vous par an?*
>
> How much do you earn per year?

When the elements or quantity in an object position are referred to
anaphorically, the pronoun *en* should be inserted, to replace *de* + noun phrase.

> Ex: **Combien en** *avez-vous?*
>
> How many/much do you have?
>
> **Combien** *vous* **en** *faut-il?*
>
> How many/much do you need?

Note that for dates, it is usual to say '*On est le combien?*' or '*Tu es arrivé le combien?*'.
See also chapter 37 Numbers, section 4.5.

3.5.1 Complex inversion or use of est-ce que?

With interrogative adverbs, either the verb–pronoun inversion (including *ce, on* and impersonal *il*) or complex inversion should be used in formal French (but see exceptions in 3.5.2); *est-ce que* + declarative order is used in informal French. In very informal French (e.g. conversation with friends), the declarative form can be used, with the interrogative adverb first or even last.

(i) Formal French

> Ex: **Combien** *de livres* **Jacques Dupont a-t-il publiés?**
> How many books has Jacques Dupont published?
>
> *A votre avis,* **pourquoi y a-t-il eu** *tant d'abstentions lors des dernières élections présidentielles?*
> In your opinion, why were there so many abstentions in the last presidential elections?

(ii) Informal French

> Ex: **Combien est-ce que** *vous avez payé ce fauteuil?*
> How much did you pay for this armchair?
>
> **Où est-ce que** *les enfants veulent aller en vacances?*
> Where do the children want to go on holiday?

(iii) Very informal French

> Ex: **Combien** *vous avez d'enfants?*
> How many children have you got?

NB: *combien de* can be followed by the object.

> Ex: **Combien** *d'enfants vous avez?* / *Vous avez* **combien** *d'enfants?*
>
> **Comment** *vous voulez payer?* / *Vous voulez payer* **comment?**
> How do you want to pay?
>
> **Où** *j'ai mis mon parapluie?*
> Where did I put my umbrella?
>
> **Quand** *vous partez?* / *Vous partez* **quand?**
> When are you leaving?

3.5.2 Complex or simple inversion?

(i) *où*

With a verb in a simple tense and nothing after the verb, the inversion is done directly between verb and noun (simple inversion), even in formal French. Compare:

> **Où est** *Monsieur le Ministre?*
> (*★Où Monsieur le Ministre est-il?*)
> Where is the Minister?

Où va l'argent du contribuable?
(*Où l'argent du contribuable va-t-il?)
Where does the taxpayer's money go?
    and:
Où M. le Ministre a-t-il été reçu?
Où M. le Ministre est-il en ce moment?

(ii)   **comment, combien** and **quand**

Either type of inversion can be used.
    Ex: **Combien vaut** *ce tableau?*
        How much is this painting worth?

        Comment va *votre tante?*
        How is your aunt?

        Quand part *le train?*
        When is the train leaving?
           or:
        Combien *ce tableau* **vaut-il?**
        Comment *votre tante* **va-t-elle?**
        Quand *le train* **part-il?**

(iii)   **pourquoi**

Only the complex inversion can be used.
    Ex: **Pourquoi** *ma montre* **s'est-elle arrêtée?**
        Why has my watch stopped?

3.5.3   Compulsory inversion

In principle, **est-ce que** can be used with all interrogative adverbs, except if the result is not satisfactory to the ear (e.g. the rhythm of the question is awkward, or the same sound is repeated at the end of the sentence). Compare:
    Quand est-ce que le train part?
        and:
    ?Comment est-ce que votre tante va?
    ?Où est-ce que mon parapluie est?
    ?Combien est-ce que ce tableau vaut?

3.5.4   Use of declarative construction

In conversation between friends, for instance, it is common to put the interrogative adverb first or even last with a declarative form, except if the result is not satisfactory to the ear (see above).
    Ex: **Quand** *tu pars? Tu pars* **quand?**
        Où *vous allez? Vous allez* **où?**
        Pourquoi *tu fais ça? Tu fais ça* **pourquoi?**

Compare:

> *Ce tableau vaut **combien?***
> and:
> *★Combien ce tableau vaut?*

> *Votre tante va **comment?***
> and:
> *★Comment votre tante va?*

> ***Où** j'ai mis mon parapluie?*
> sounds better than:
> *?J'ai mis mon parapluie où?*

NB(1): With *où*, this choice is only possible with pronouns; with nouns, *où* must come last.

> Ex: *Il est où? / Où il est?*
> *Paul est où? / Où il est, Paul?*
> but not:
> *★Où Paul est?*

NB(2): The declarative structure should not be used with *quand*, as *quand* might then be understood as the conjunction.

> Ex: *★Quand le train part?*

3.5.5 *Interrogative adverbs with subject* je

(i)   When the subject is *je*, the inversion verb–*je* should only be used with certain verbs (see 2.1.5.1 above).

> Ex: ***Combien** vous **dois-je?***
> How much do I owe you?

> ***Où vais-je** aller?*
> Where am I going to go?

> ***Pourquoi fais-je** cela?*
> Why am I doing this?

(ii) With longer verbs, use ***est-ce que***, even in formal French.

> Ex: ***Pourquoi est-ce que** je m'inquiète tant?*
> Why do I worry so much?

(iii) In informal French, use ***est-ce que*** or a declarative form with the short verbs listed, and a declarative form with other verbs.

> Ex: ***Combien est-ce que** je vous dois?*
> or:
> ***Combien** je vous **dois?***
> How much do I owe you?

4 Special cases

4.1 Lexicalized constructions

A number of lexicalized constructions are now considered to be equivalent to rhetorical questions (see 4.4 below) or even exclamative constructions.

(i) With verb–subject pronoun inversion

Ex: *Que sais-je?*
Que veux-tu que je te dise?
Que voulez-vous?
Qu'en pensez-vous?
Comment allez-vous?
Comment se fait-il que . . . ?
Comment voulez-vous que je le sache?

(ii) With a declarative construction

Ex: *Comment ça va?*
Comment ça se fait?
Comment ça s'explique?
Comment ça s'est passé?

The following appear either with an inversion or in the declarative form.
Quel jour sommes-nous?/nous sommes?
Quelle heure est-il?/il est?

(iii) In elliptical constructions with an infinitive

Ex: **Que** *choisir?*
Que *faire? /* **Quoi** *faire?*
Qui *croire?*
Où *aller?*
Lequel *prendre?*
Comment *dire?*
Comment *se débrouiller?*

(iv) With no verb at all

e.g. with *quoi:*

– *être* is implied

Ex: **Quoi** *de neuf?*   What's new?
Quoi *de plus facile?*   What could be easier?

– interjections

quoi can also be used on its own as an interjection or with an adverb to express, for instance:

– surprise

Ex: ***Quoi?*** *Vous êtes encore là?*
What? You're still here!

– exasperation

Ex: ***Quoi*** *encore?*
What now?

Quoi? *Rien n'est encore prêt!*
What? Nothing's ready yet!

Tu viens, oui ou ***quoi?***
Are you coming or what?

NB: ***Quoi?*** on its own, meaning 'What (did you say)?', is not polite. *Comment?* should be used, or better still, *Pardon?*.

4.2 Use of *qu'est-ce qu'il y a?* vs *qu'est-ce que c'est?*

Compare:

Qu'est-ce qu'il y a?
(= 'What is it?' in the sense of 'What's the matter?')
and:
Qu'est-ce que c'est?
(= 'What is it?' in the sense of 'What sort of object is it?')

To ask for a definition of something, use ***qu'est-ce que*** or ***qu'est-ce que c'est que***.

Ex: ***Qu'est-ce qu'un*** *pronom interrogatif?*
Qu'est-ce que c'est qu'un *pronom interrogatif?*
What is an interrogative pronoun?

Qu'est-ce que c'est que *ça?*
What's that?   or: What on earth is that?

Note:

Que se passe-t-il?   and: *Qu'y a-t-il?*
What's happening?   What's the matter?

4.3 Ambiguities

Consider the following example:
– subject:

Combien de fourmis les abeilles ont mangé?
How many ants have the bees eaten?

– object:

Combien de fourmis ont mangé les abeilles?
How many ants have eaten the bees?

Here, the ambiguity is due to the verb *manger* which has an animate subject and an edible object in both cases.

The same goes for the following example:
- subject:

> *Quels Français lisent les Anglais?*
> Which French people read English authors?

- object:

> *Quels Français les Anglais lisent?*
> Which French authors do English people read? / are read by
> English people?

See also 3.1.1(i)NB(2) above and 5.2 NB(2) below.

4.4 Rhetorical questions

They assume the form – but not the function – of a question. An answer is not required since whoever asks a rhetorical question does so with the intention of answering it him/herself immediately afterwards, or the answer is already known by all. They are therefore used for stylistic effect. For example, a speaker may use a rhetorical question to divert the listener's attention onto another topic, or to seek approbation at a strategic point in a speech. Rhetorical questions often include a comparison, a negation or even an infinitive.

> Ex: *La démocratie n'est-elle pas encore le meilleur des systèmes?*
> *Que faire dans un cas pareil?*

5 Exclamative form

Syntactically, the exclamative sentence shares some of its constructions with those of the interrogative and the declarative sentences. It ends with an exclamation mark, a feature shared with the imperative sentence.

Indeed, as in English, simple declarative sentences can in fact be made exclamative by raising the intonation and stressing the last word or, in writing, by the simple addition of an exclamation mark.
- declarative:

> Ex: *Catherine vient la semaine prochaine.*
> Catherine's coming next week.

- exclamative:

> *Catherine vient la semaine prochaine!*
> Catherine's coming next week!

Exclamative adjectives, pronouns and adverbs, and adverbs of intensity, can all be used to relate to the verb or the noun in an exclamation.

5.1 Emphasis on the verb

The emphasis can be placed on the verb or '*être* + adjective', or an adverb modifying a verb. The exclamative words are:

> ***comme***
> ***que*** (***ce que, qu'est-ce que***)
> ***si*** (***tant, tellement***)

or the inversion verb–subject pronoun can be used.

Ex: *Comme il est mignon!*
Que c'est triste Venise!
Que vas-tu penser là!
Ce que vous m'ennuyez avec vos histoires!
Qu'est-ce que tu vas t'imaginer!
Qu'est-ce qu'il a fait froid!
Dizzy est si beau!
Je l'aime tant!
Il est d'une [telle] élégance!
Suis-je bête!

NB(1): *comme, que, si* and the inversion verb–subject pronoun belong to formal French, while *ce que* and *qu'est-ce que* belong to informal French.

NB(2): Note the position of the adjective in French:
Comme il est mignon!
How cute he is!

Que c'est beau!
How beautiful it is!

5.2 Emphasis on the noun

The emphasis can be placed on the noun, with a qualifying or a quantifying value. There is often no conjugated verb. The exclamative words are:
quel
lequel
ce
voici, voilà (see presentatives in chapter 2 Syntax, section 2.15.3)
combien de
que de
tant de, tellement de
qu'est-ce que . . . [*comme*] . . .

Ex: *Quels imbéciles!*
Quel dommage que vous n'ayez pas pu venir!
Quel ne fut pas son étonnement!
Je n'ai qu'un chat, mais lequel!
Ah! Ces chats!
Voilà ce que c'est que de faire l'imbécile!
Combien de fois ne vous ai-je pas répété qu'il fallait faire attention!
Que d'eau! Que d'eau!
Tant de bruit pour rien!
Qu'est-ce qu'il y avait comme monde!

NB(1): Unlike in English, the exclamative adjective *quel* is **never** followed by the article *un* or *une*. The only thing that differentiates it in the written form from an interrogative adjective is the exclamation mark. Hence:
Ex: **Quel** *scandale!*   but: **Quel** *scandale?*
What a scandal!   What scandal?

In conversation, use the correct intonation as you would in English to differentiate between:

> Ex: What a scandal! (stress on 'scandal')
>> and:
> What scandal? (stress on 'what')

NB(2): When the exclamation bears on the object, the object comes first. Compare:

– subject:

> **Quel** *imbécile a fait cela!*
> (*Un imbécile a fait cela.*)
> What idiot did this!

– object:

> **Quelle** *chance vous avez!*
> (*Vous avez de la chance.*)
> How lucky you are!

NB(3): With a complement of *être*, the inversion subject–*être* is optional and is dictated by sentence rhythm. Compare:

> *Quel fantastique comédien il est!*
>> and:
> *Quel fantastique comédien était Coluche!*

NB(4): Note the place of the personal pronouns with presentatives (tonic with *c'est*, clitic with *voici/voilà*).

> Ex: *C'est moi! / C'est toi! / C'est eux!* etc.
> It's me! / It's you! / It's them! etc.
>
> *Me voici! / Te voici! / Les voici!* etc.
> Here I am! / Here you are! / Here they are! etc.

40 Coordination and juxtaposition

1 Introduction

Coordination is the linking of two or more similar items by a conjunction. Coordinating words thus introduce a new element and put it in relation to an element already in place in the phrase or clause. Coordinating words are invariable.

Juxtaposition is the linking of two or more similar items by a comma. The explicit link can be replaced by intonation, hence juxtaposition is mainly a feature of spoken French.

The items may be words, phrases, clauses or sentences.

2 Conjunctions of coordination

Coordination establishes a non-hierarchical relation between the elements it links. Coordinated elements must have the same **nature** (e.g. verb, noun) and the same grammatical **function** (e.g. subject, object). However, ellipsis of part of a clause allows the coordination of, for instance, a noun phrase and a whole clause.

> Ex: *Un café **mais** je ne veux pas de liqueur!*
> (= *J'accepterais un café mais . . .*)

See also 5 below.

(i)   The main conjunctions of coordination are:

mais, ou, et, donc, or, ni, car

and one of the mnemonic phrases to remember them is:
Mais où est donc Ornicar?

They can only appear between the two elements to be coordinated and cannot be combined with one another, apart from *donc*, which can be combined with *et*, *ni* or *or*.

> Ex: *Mon réveil n'a pas sonné **et donc** je suis arrivé en retard à mon rendez-vous.*
> My alarm-clock did not ring **and therefore** I arrived late for my appointment.

Note that *donc* can also be an adverb (see chapter 29 Adverbs, section 6.11.4). In the following example, we have a juxtaposition and *donc* appears as an adverb in the second clause.

> Ex: *Mon réveil n'a pas sonné, je suis **donc** arrivé en retard à mon rendez-vous.*
>
> My alarm–clock did not ring, **so** I arrived late for my appointment.

The same applies to *puis, en effet, alors, ainsi, ensuite, par conséquent, aussi, par contre,* etc. (see below). These are also called '**link adverbs**' (**adverbes de liaison**). Those adverbs can be used together with conjunctions of coordination, but always appear **after**, except with *donc*.

> Ex: *et alors, **mais** ensuite,* etc.
>
> but:
>
> *ainsi **donc***

(ii) Other conjunctions of coordination

These include: *d'ailleurs, ainsi, ainsi que, alors, aussi, aussi bien que, avec, cependant, c'est-à-dire, comme, dans ces conditions, en conséquence, par conséquent, au contraire, par contre, au demeurant, effectivement, en effet, enfin, ensuite, par exemple, de même que, non moins que, néanmoins, ou bien, c'est pourquoi, pourtant, puis, du reste, en revanche, à savoir, non seulement . . . mais encore, sinon, soit, soit . . . ou, soit . . . soit, tantôt . . . . tantôt, toutefois,* etc.

Thus they can be adverb homographs (e.g. *ainsi*), prepositional phrases (e.g. *par exemple*) and even clauses (e.g. *c'est pourquoi*) and are sometimes referred to as 'coordinating adverbs' or 'coordinating phrases' rather than conjunctions of coordination.

NB: An adverb which does not appear between the two elements to be coordinated remains an adverb. This is important as the meaning can be very different.

> Ex: *Mon réveil n'a pas sonné, **aussi** je suis arrivé en retard à mon rendez-vous.*
>
> ('*aussi*' is a conjunction of coordination)
>
> My alarm clock didn't ring and **so** I was late for my appointment.

> *Je suis arrivé en retard à mon rendez-vous **aussi**.*
>
> (or: '*moi aussi*')
>
> I was late for my appointment **too**.

This second category of conjunctions of coordination can be combined with one another or with the first category.

> Ex: *mais par contre*
>
> *comme d'ailleurs*

Note that conjunctions of the type *tantôt . . . tantôt . . .* are also called **disjunctive conjunctions** (*conjonctions disjonctives*): see 3.3 below.

3 Coordination of words and phrases

Coordinators which function between words and phrases are: *mais, ou, et, ni, ou . . . ou, soit . . . soit, soit . . . ou, tantôt . . . tantôt, ainsi que* and *comme* (but only when meaning *et*), and coordinating adverbs of time which indicate a succession of events (e.g. *puis, ensuite, alors*).

– noun phrases:

    Ex: *Cédric, **comme** son frère jumeau, n'est pas très grand.*
           Cédric, like his twin brother, is not very tall.

– adjectives:

    Ex: *Je veux un café noir **et** fort . . .*
           I would like a strong black coffee . . .
           (For the positioning of adjectives, see chapter 28 Qualifying
           Adjectives, section 2.3.4.)

NB: Since attributive adjectives are equivalent to a relative clause when qualifying a noun, it is possible to coordinate such an adjective and a relative clause (see chapter 2 Syntax, section 2.1.3).

    Ex: *J'ai passé des vacances <u>formidables</u> **mais** <u>qui n'ont pas été sans</u>*
           <u>*mésaventures*</u>.
           I had a wonderful holiday but it was not trouble-free.

– verbs:

    Ex: *Il a changé de costume **puis** est sorti.*
           He changed his suit then went out.

– adverbs:

    Ex: *Elle conduit vite **et** bien.*
           She drives well and fast.

3.1 Coordination with *et* ('and')

The most frequently used conjunction of coordination in French is ***et***. It coordinates two or more elements.

(i)   In a list, ***et*** is normally only used between the last two items.

        Ex: *Ils ont apporté du vin, des chocolats **et** des fleurs.*
             They brought wine, chocolates and flowers.

(ii)   But it can be repeated for emphasis or stylistic effect.

        Ex: *Ils ont apporté **et** du vin **et** des chocolats **et** des fleurs.*
             They brought wine and chocolates and flowers.

(iii)   It can be omitted altogether, again for stylistic effect (see section 7 Juxtaposition).

(iv)   A zeugma (*zeugme*) is a special case of syllepsis. It is a coordination which produces an unexpected pairing of terms, often with ellipsis of the verb.

        Ex: *L'air était <u>plein</u> d'encens et les prés _ de verdure.*

                                      Victor Hugo, cited in *Robert*

Such an ellipsis is often used as a source of humour.

> Ex: *Robert fait <u>la vaisselle</u> **et** _ <u>pitié</u>.*
> *Il s'est mis <u>à genoux</u> **et** _ <u>le doigt dans l'œil</u>.*
> *Comme il le répète <u>à l'envi</u> **et** _ <u>à tous les auditeurs</u>* . . .
> (heard on the radio)

3.2 Coordination with *ou* ('or')

ou is normally only used between two items to express an **alternative**, which can be inclusive or exclusive. With more than two items, it is normally only used between the last two, like *et*.

3.2.1 ou *and subjects*

When several singular **subjects** are coordinated by *ou*, either singular or plural **agreement** is possible, according to whether the alternatives are inclusive or exclusive, although the plural is more frequent.

> Ex: *Marie **ou** Paul sera là.*
> or:
> *Marie **ou** Paul seront là.*

Since the 3rd persons singular and plural are identical in English in this case, a certain ambiguity prevails. This can be alleviated by adding other words.

> Ex: *Marie ou Paul sera là.*
> → **Either** Marie **or** Paul will be there.
>
> *Marie ou Paul seront là.*
> → Marie or Paul or both of them will be there.

3.2.2 ou *and objects*

(i) *ou* is used between the last two items.

> Ex: *Comme dessert, il y a de la tarte aux fraises, de la glace **ou** des fruits.*
> For dessert, there is strawberry tart, ice-cream or fruit.

(ii) *ou* can be repeated for emphasis, and is then the equivalent of *soit . . . soit.*

> Ex: *Comme dessert, vous pouvez prendre **ou** de la glace **ou** des fruits.*
> or:
> *Comme dessert, vous pouvez prendre **soit** de la glace, **soit** des fruits.*
> For dessert, you can have either ice-cream or fruit.

(iii) *ou* can be further emphasized by the addition of ***bien***.

> Ex: *Comme dessert, vous pouvez prendre de la glace **ou bien** des fruits.*
> For dessert, you can have ice-cream or else fruit.

(iv) *ou* can also introduce an explanation, in an apposition without a determiner (meaning 'alternatively').

> Ex: *Leur chat siamois, **ou** birman (je ne sais plus!), a gagné de nombreux prix.*
> Their Siamese, or Burmese cat (I'm not sure!), has won many prizes.

3.3 Coordination with *soit . . . soit, soit . . . ou, ou . . . ou, tantôt . . . tantôt*

(i)   When several **subjects** are coordinated by these conjunctions, the verb is normally singular.

> Ex: *C'est **soit** Marie **soit** Paul qui **viendra** vous chercher à la gare.*
> It will be either Marie or Paul who will pick you up at the station.
>
> *On n'avait jamais la paix: c'était **tantôt** l'un **tantôt** l'autre qui **jouait** de la clarinette . . .*
> We never had any peace – either one or the other would be playing the clarinet . . .

(ii)   When several **objects** or **complements** are coordinated by these conjunctions, they must be repeated before each alternative, unlike in English.

> Ex: *Pour les vacances, nous irons **soit** au Maroc, **soit** en Tunisie, **soit** en Grèce.*
> For our summer holiday, we'll be going to **either** Morocco, Tunisia **or** Greece.

(See 3.2.2 above.)

4   Coordination of main and subordinate clauses

(i)   Coordinators can link two relative clauses.

> Ex: *Je cherche une maison **qui** soit assez grande **mais dont** le jardin soit facile à entretenir.*
> I am looking for a house which is fairly big but with a garden which is easy to look after.

(ii)   Coordination of main clauses + a *que*-clause

When two coordinated main clauses are followed by a *que*-clause, they should both entail **either** the indicative **or** the subjunctive. Compare:

> *J'espère **et** je pense qu'il viendra.*
> (= *J'espère qu'il **viendra** et je pense qu'il **viendra**.*)
> I hope and think he will come.
>   and:
> *★Je souhaite et j'espère qu'il viendra.*
> (= *Je souhaite qu'il **vienne** et j'espère qu'il **viendra**.*)
> I wish and hope he will come.
> One solution would be, to avoid repeating *venir*:
> *Je souhaite qu'il vienne **et** j'espère qu'il **le fera**.*

(iii)   Coordination of adverbial clauses

> Ex: *Vous sortirez **quand** vous aurez terminé **et s'**il ne pleut pas.*
> You may leave when you have finished and if it is not raining.

NB(1): Two coordinated adverbial clauses can be introduced by the **same** conjunction:
– with no emphasis: the second one is *que* (+ same mood)

> Ex: ***Comme*** *il pleuvait **et que** je n'avais pas de parapluie* . . .
> As it was raining and I did not have an umbrella . . .
>
> *Vous partirez **quand** vous aurez fini **et que** je serai satisfaite que le travail est bon.*
> You will leave when you've finished and I'm satisfied that your work is all right.

– with emphasis: the second one is repeated (+ same mood)

> Ex: ***Puisque*** *vous êtes en retard **et puisque** ce n'est pas la première fois* . . .
> Since you are late and since it's not the first time . . .

NB(2): If the conjunction is *si*:
– with no emphasis: the second one is *que* (+ **subjunctive**)

> Ex: ***Si*** *vous <u>passez</u> chez moi **et que** je ne <u>sois</u> pas là* . . .

– with emphasis: the second *si* is repeated (+ same mood, i.e. indicative)

> Ex: ***Si*** *vous <u>voyez</u> de la lumière et **s'il** n'<u>est</u> pas trop tard* . . .

See also chapters 12 Subjunctive, section 5.1(i) and 13 Conditional, section 3.2.3(iii).

5 Coordination of independent clauses and sentences

> Ex: *Je suis arrivée en retard; **c'est pourquoi** je vous ai manqué.*
> I arrived late, that's why I missed you.
>
> ***Soit*** *vous partez tout de suite, **soit** vous restez jusqu'à la fin.*
> Either you leave straightaway, or you stay until the end.
>
> *Il pleuvait, **alors** je ne suis pas sortie.*
> It was raining so I didn't go out.
>
> *Il arrive en voiture, **donc** il ne devrait pas mettre trop de temps.*
> He's coming by car, therefore he shouldn't take too long.

5.1 Coordination with *et* and *mais*

(i) **Ellipsis of the subject**

As in English, when coordinated clauses have the same subject, that subject is not repeated, except for emphasis.

> Ex: ***Elle a pris*** *son manteau **et a quitté** la pièce.*
> She took her coat and left the room.

665

(ii) **Ellipsis of the verb**

The verb can be elided when it is common to the two coordinated segments.
Compare:

> *Dizzy chasse les souris et Lizzy les oiseaux.*
> Dizzy catches mice and Lizzy, birds.
> > or:
> *Dizzy chasse les souris et Lizzy aussi.*
> Dizzy catches mice and Lizzy does too.
> > but:
> *Il a quarante ans mais n'est toujours pas marié.*
> He is forty but still [is] not married.

(iii) **Coordination of verbs**

In French, unlike in English, a direct transitive verb cannot be coordinated with
an indirect one. Nor can two indirect transitive verbs followed by a different
preposition be coordinated (nor two adjectives or adverbs which introduce their
complements with different prepositions). One way round this problem is to
replace one of the complements with its pronominal representation. Compare:

> Paul has played and won the lottery.
> *Paul a joué et gagné au loto.*

Both verbs are transitive indirect with preposition *à*.

> > and:
> I rely on and trust Paul.
> **Je compte sur et me fie à Paul.*
> → *Je compte sur Paul et me fie à lui.*

Both verbs are followed by a different preposition.

> According to but independently of your request, . . .
> **Conformément à mais indépendamment de votre demande . . .*
> → *Conformément à votre demande mais indépendamment d'elle . . .*
> (or: . . . *indépendamment de celle-ci/de cette dernière . . .*)

> Perhaps Marie's attitude had turned him away from her and towards
> the gentle Catherine.
> * . . . *l'avait détourné d'elle et vers la douce Catherine.*
> → . . . *l'avait détourné d'elle et poussé vers la douce Catherine.*

'to turn away from', 'to turn towards', are completely different verbs in French.

(iv) **Punctuation**

When two coordinated clauses do not have the same subject, or they express
contrasting ideas, there is a comma in French (as well as in English).

> Ex: *Enlevez une vertèbre, et les deux morceaux de cette tortueuse fantaisie se*
> *rejoindront sans peine.*

> Charles Baudelaire, *Petits poèmes en prose*

5.2 Coordination with *car* and *or*

(i) *car* and *or* are **only** used to link independent clauses or sentences (not words or phrases). They are also normally only used in formal French, to expound arguments.

(ii) *car*

car is used to give the reason or the cause of what is expressed in the previous clause:

> Ex: *'Politique et liberté de l'esprit s'excluent, car politique, c'est idoles.'*
>
> Paul Valéry
>
> Politics and freedom are mutually exclusive, for politics is idolatry.
>
> *J'ai dû prendre un taxi car j'étais déjà très en retard.*
> I had to take a cab as I was already very late.

NB: In less formal French, *parce que* would be used, or even a simple colon.

> Ex: *J'ai dû prendre un taxi parce que j'étais déjà très en retard.*
> or:
> *J'ai dû prendre un taxi: j'étais déjà très en retard.*

(See chapter 2 Syntax, section 3.2(iii).)

However, with a negative main clause, *parce que* presents an ambiguity not shared by *car*.

> Ex: *Catherine n'a pas chanté parce que Nicole était là.*
> can mean either:
> *Catherine n'a pas chanté à cause de la présence de Nicole.*
> (the negation bears on *chanter*)
> or:
> *Ce n'est pas parce que Nicole était là que Catherine n' a pas chanté.*
> (the whole utterance becomes negated)

On the contrary:

> *Catherine n'a pas chanté car Nicole était là.*

only has the first meaning, which brings *car* nearer to *puisque*.

(iii) *or*

or introduces a new element in an argument or a story and is always found at the beginning of a sentence. There is no precise equivalent in English, hence many translations are possible. It belongs to formal French.

> Ex: *Le premier prix était un voyage au Japon. Or elle n'avait jamais visité l'Orient . . .*
> The first prize was a trip to Japan. Now she had never been to the Far East . . .
>
> *Ceci n'aurait pas manqué de provoquer des jalousies. Or nous ne désirions nullement nous brouiller avec eux.*
>
> *Collins/Robert French Dictionary*
>
> This would unfailingly have led to jealousy. Yet we had not the slightest wish to quarrel with them.

6 Coordination with *ni*

6.1 *ni* and nouns or pronouns

ni is the opposite of *et, ou, ou bien, soit*, and applies to:
– the subject(s): *ni . . . ni . . . ne*
– the object(s): *ne . . . ni . . . ni* or *ne . . . pas de . . . ni de*
The last two are synonymous, but *ne . . . ni . . . ni* is more commonly used.

(i) **Subject**

The verb is plural except when one of the subjects excludes the other. Compare:
> *Ni vous ni moi ne sommes en mesure de les aider.*
> Neither you nor I are in a position to help them.
> (The converse would be *Vous et moi sommes . . .*)
> and:
> *Ni Paul ni toi ne sera élu au Conseil Municipal.*
> Neither Paul nor you will be elected to the local council.
> (The converse would be *Paul ou toi sera . . .*)

(ii) **Object**

> Ex: *J'ai oublié mon sac: je n'ai ni argent ni papiers.*
> or:
> *J'ai oublié mon sac: je n'ai pas d'argent ni de papiers.*
> I have forgotten my handbag – I've not got any money or ID.

> *Je ne veux pas boire de thé ni de café.*
> or:
> *Je ne veux boire ni thé ni café.*
> I don't want to drink either tea or coffee.

NB(1): *ni* and articles are treated in detail in chapter 23 Articles, section 8.4.

NB(2): *ni l'un ni l'autre* can be used to avoid repeating the nouns.
> Ex: *Paul et Marie étaient tous les deux invités mais ils ne sont venus ni l'un ni l'autre / ni l'un ni l'autre ne sont venus.*
> Paul and Marie were both invited but neither came.

NB(3): *ni* and prepositions:
– It is a common mistake to confuse the partitive *de* with the preposition *de* attached to a verb: prepositions are kept after *ni*.
> Ex: *J'ai besoin de pain et de fromage.*
> (*avoir besoin de qch*)
> *Je n'ai besoin ni de pain ni de fromage.*
> I need neither bread nor cheese.

> *Elle s'occupe de sa tante et de sa grand-mère.*
> (*s'occuper de qn*)
> *Elle ne s'occupe ni de sa tante ni de sa grand-mère.*
> She does not look after her aunt or her grandmother.

– Whether they are part of a verb or free-standing, prepositions are repeated after each *ni*.

Ex: *Je ne vois pas mon manteau: il **n'**est **ni** sur la chaise **ni sur** le lit . . .*
I can't see my coat – it is not on the chair or the bed . . .

Note the following idioms with **sans** and **ni** with nouns:

sans *foi* **ni** *loi*: godless and lawless
sans *tambour* **ni** *trompette*: without a fanfare

NB(4): When the *ne . . . ni . . . ni* construction is used, *plus* or *jamais* can be inserted.

Ex: *Il **n'**a **jamais** connu **ni** son père **ni** sa mère.*
He never knew either his father or his mother.

6.2   *ni* and clauses

(i)   *ni* and verbs

When a series of **verbs** is negated, *ne . . . pas* (or just *ne* if there is no object) is used in the first clause, and *ni ne* in subsequent clauses.

Ex: *Ce chat est bizarre: il **ne** mange **pas** de viande **ni ne** boit de lait.*
This cat is strange – he neither eats meat nor drinks milk.

*Marie **ne** boit, **ni ne** fume, **ni ne** se drogue.*
Marie neither drinks, nor smokes, nor takes drugs.

Note that with *ni*, the same tense in each clause is not necessary.

Ex: *Je **ne** lui <u>ai</u> **pas** <u>pardonné</u> **ni ne** lui <u>pardonnerai</u> jamais.*
I haven't forgiven him and never will.

(ii)   *ni* and *que*-clauses

ne . . . pas que (or *ne . . . ni que*) is used in the first clause, and *ni que* in the second.

Ex: *Elle **ne** veut **pas** qu'on lui écrive **ni** qu'on lui téléphone.*
or:
*Elle **ne** veut **ni** qu'on lui écrive **ni** qu'on lui téléphone.*
She does not want anybody to [either] ring her or write to her.
(Note that in the second case, *ni* is repeated for emphasis.)

(iii)   *ni* and infinitives

For the use of infinitives after conjugated verbs, see chapter 15 Infinitive. Prepositions (if any) are repeated. Compare:

*Il **n'**aime **ni** nager **ni** skier.*
(*aimer faire qch*)
He likes neither swimming nor skiing / He does not like swimming or skiing.
and:
*Il **ne** songe **ni** à s'excuser **ni** à partir.*
(*songer à faire qch*)
He is not thinking of apologizing or leaving.

7 Juxtaposition

(i) Juxtaposed clauses are separated by a comma or a semi-colon. They may imply either a coordination or a subordination. The meaning of this implicit coordination or subordination rests on context, situation, temporal or modal marks, etc. See also chapter 2 Syntax, section 3.2(iii).

(ii) For **implicit** coordination with *et*, the juxtaposition can be kept in the English translation.

> Ex: *Un chien aboie, un coq chante, un chat miaule.*
> A dog barks, a cock crows, a cat meows.

(iii) In English, unlike in French, subordination, or coordination expressing a link other than addition, are normally explicit, and must therefore be expressed by a suitable conjunction.

> Ex: *Tu aimes ce vin, moi, je le trouve quelconque.*
> (= an implicit relation of opposition: **mais, alors que, tandis que**)
> You like that wine **but** I find it indifferent.
>
> *J'avais froid, j'ai mis un gilet.*
> (= an implicit relation of cause to consequence: **donc, de sorte que, si bien que**)
> I was cold **so** I put a cardigan on.
>
> *Je n'ai rien mangé, il ne restait rien dans le frigo.*
> (= an implicit relation of consequence to cause: **car, puisque, parce que**)
> I didn't have anything to eat **as** there was nothing left in the fridge.

(iv) Expression of **hypothesis**

> – *avoir beau* forces a juxtaposition, since *avoir beau faire qch* is not sufficient by itself.
> > Ex: *Il a beau essayer, il ne les convaincra pas.*
> > Try as he may, he will not convince them.
>
> – *pouvoir* can also be used, with or without the adverb *toujours.*
> > Ex: *Il peut [toujours] essayer, il ne les convaincra pas.*
> > He can always try, he will not convince them.
>
> – Use of **two conditionals** (informal French only)
> > Ex: *Il essaierait, il ne les convaincrait pas.*
> > Even if he tried, he would not convince them.

(v) When juxtaposed clauses have the same subject, that subject may or may not be repeated, but the repetition is more usual in informal French.

> Ex: *Ils boivent, [ils] fument, [ils] discutent.*
> They drink, [they] smoke, [they] talk.

8 Translation difficulties

(i)   *en effet* vs *en fait*

en effet usually introduces a logical follow-up to what has just been said, whereas *en fait* introduces an opposite or contrasting idea (to what has just been said).

Ex: – *Je ne vous ai pas vu chez les Dupont hier. Vous étiez malade?*
   – ***En effet** j'avais la migraine.*
   – I didn't see you at the Duponts' yesterday. Were you ill?
   – Yes, I had a migraine actually.

*On pourrait croire que c'est de l'or. **En fait** ce n'est que du cuivre.*
You could think it's gold. In fact, it is only copper.

(ii)   **Translation of 'and'**

When **and** comes between two verbs in English and means 'in order to', the goal must be expressed in French by an infinitive.

Ex: Please **go and fetch** grandmother at the station.
   ***Va chercher** grand-mère à la gare.*

Can you **come and help me** lay the table?
*Peux-tu **venir m'aider** à mettre la table?*

(iii) **Translation of *et***

et is sometimes translated by 'and then' in English when 'and' would sound insufficient.

Ex: *Il a claqué la porte de sa voiture **et** s'est aperçu qu'il avait laissé ses clés à l'intérieur.*
   He slammed the door of his car **and then** realized he had left his keys inside.

NB: For the rules governing the repetition of the preposition in a coordination, see chapter 26 Prepositions, section 7.

41 Reported speech

1 Introduction

There are three distinct ways to report the words and thoughts of other speakers, according to the relationship between the **reporting** and the **reported** speech (*discours rapportant* or *citant* and *discours rapporté* or *cité*):
- direct reported speech (DRS) (*discours rapporté direct*): reporting and reported speeches are independent
- indirect reported speech (IRS) (*discours rapporté indirect*): the reported speech is subordinate to the reporting speech
- free indirect reported speech (FIRS) (*discours rapporté indirect libre*): this is used mainly in written texts, particularly literary narration, and includes properties of both direct and indirect speech

2 Direct reported speech

Reporting and reported speeches are independent. There are two 'voices': that of the original **speaker** and that of the speaker who reports the utterance, the **reporter**.

2.1 Typographical characteristics

DRS is characterized in written French by the use of:
- quotation marks (*guillemets*)
- dashes (*tirets*) for dialogues, which are placed at the beginning of a new line for each speaker in turn
- italic text (particularly in newspapers)

In spoken French, it is the linguistic context and/or the intonation which marks the separation between reporting and reported speech.

2.2 Introductory verbs

DRS is introduced in the **reporting clause** (*proposition incise*) by a verb of saying or thinking (*dire, s'écrier, affirmer, ajouter, déclarer, expliquer, prétendre, soutenir, répondre, murmurer, crier, chanter, ricaner, maugréer, nier, penser, croire, juger, comprendre*, etc.), which can be placed:

– before the DRS and followed by a colon

  Ex: *François a annoncé: 'Je vais épouser Catherine.'*

– after the DRS and preceded by a comma

  Ex: *'Je vais épouser Catherine', a annoncé François.*

– in the middle of the DRS, between two commas

  Ex: *'Je vais', a annoncé François, 'épouser Catherine.'*

NB(1): In the last two cases, the reporting clause is a **simple inversion** of verb and subject (see chapter 2 Syntax, section 2.4(ii)).

NB(2): In dialogue sequences, the reporting clause is often absent.

  Ex: – *Qui est là?*

    – *C'est le plombier!*

The verbs which introduce DRS are not necessarily the same as those which introduce indirect reported speech (see below). Furthermore, the linguistic context may be sufficient to show that there is DRS.

  Ex: *Paul entra en trombe dans la maison: 'On m'a volé mon portefeuille!'*

Frédéric Dard (alias San-Antonio), among other authors, is very fond of 'unorthodox' ways of introducing DRS.

  Ex: *'– Je pense que, malgré tout, votre vénéré maître aura quelque agrément à nous recevoir, **effronté-je**. (coining a new verb!)*

    – *[. . .]*

    – *Bigre, **souris-je**, les choses ne traînent pas, chez vous, mon seigneur!'*

           San-Antonio, *Ça ne s'invente pas!*

2.3 Kinds of sentence

DRS can be a declaration, an exclamation, an order or a question (i.e. the four modalities of the sentence). It can also be an interjection, an incomplete sentence, a sentence in a foreign language or even an ungrammatical sentence, and may contain 'affective' words, such as *bon*, *hein*, *ah* (unlike IRS: see 3.7 below).

  Ex: *Paul a déclaré:*   *'Ah! Ce qu'on s'emmerde ici!'*

         'I'm leaving.'

         'Moi vouloir toi.'

2.4 DRS and the original utterance

DRS is supposed to be faithful to the original utterance. However, there are various factors relating to the reporter's subjectivity which inhibit this. These include the choice of a particular fragment from the utterance, the context in which it is reported and – in the case of spoken French – the reporter's intonation. Using reporter subjectivity to wilfully distort the original utterance is particularly apparent in the media.

On the other hand, quotations can be reported faithfully to respect the words of another speaker for specific reasons. These include the intention to mark a distance or dissociate oneself from the original utterance (see also 2.5 below).

2.5 Other roles of quotation marks and italics

In addition to reporting speech, quotation marks or italics can be used to introduce a neologism, a foreign word, a technical term, another linguistic register, a metaphor, etc. However, they are generally used to create distance between the reporter and the words of the original speaker. In this case, the reporter assumes a primary role in that he/she does not disappear behind his/her capacity as reporter.

A reporter may seek to dissociate him/herself from elements such as clichés, the discourse of a particular social group or political tendency, or that of a particular profession or field of study.

> Ex: *Nicole Notat a déclaré qu'elle ne participerait pas à cette journée d'action, car la CFDT ne voulait pas s'associer à une 'démarche de politisation syndicale'.*
>
> *Libération*, 14 December 1994
>
> Nicole Notat stated that she would not take part in this day of strike action since the CFDT did not wish to associate itself with 'politicized union tactics'.

The reporter can thus offer a particular image of him/herself to the reader by adopting or rejecting certain speeches.

In spoken French, a comment clause can be added, such as *'et je cite'*, or *'ouvrez les guillemets . . . fermez les guillemets'*.

See also chapter 3 Punctuation, section 12.

3 Indirect reported speech

With IRS, both reporting and reported clauses are **integrated** in the narration. There is therefore only one 'voice' – that of the narrator.

3.1 Syntactic characteristics

IRS is introduced by a verb of communication (e.g. *dire*) and:
– the conjunction *que*
– or the interrogative adjective/pronoun/adverb *si*, *quand*, *où*, *qui*, *lequel*, etc. in the case of indirect interrogative sentences
– or the preposition *de* in the case of infinitive clauses

3.2 Introductory verbs

Most introductory verbs are the same for DRS and IRS but some can only be used in DRS. Compare:

> Ex: *'Non, c'était jeudi,' se reprit Nicolas.*
>   and:
> *Nicolas se reprit que c'était jeudi.*

3.3   Conjunctions

Unlike in English, the conjunction *que* must be repeated with each subordinate clause in French.

> Ex: *Catherine dit **que** lundi nous irons en ville et **qu'elle** nous emmènera au restaurant.*
> Catherine says **that** we'll go to town on Monday and _ she'll take us to a restaurant.

3.4   Imperative sentences

In IRS, the imperative becomes an infinitive clause introduced by *de*.

> Ex: *Je lui ai dit: **'Prends** ton manteau!'*
> → *Je lui ai dit **de prendre** son manteau.*
> I said to him/her, 'Get your coat!'
> → I told him/her to get his/her coat.

The imperative can also become a subjunctive introduced by *que*.

> Ex: *Je lui ai dit **qu'il/elle prenne** son manteau.*
> I told him/her to get his/her coat.

3.5   Interrogative sentences

The **indirect interrogative** form is characterized by the inclusion of the question in an introductory clause with a verb of request or any other verb which introduces a question, e.g. *demander, se demander, interroger, s'informer, ignorer, dire, savoir, regarder, voir, comprendre, indiquer, sentir, deviner*, etc.

There is no rising intonation in spoken French and no question mark in written French.

The indirect interrogation has all the characteristics of indirect speech with regard to persons (personal pronouns, possessive adjectives and pronouns), adverbs of time and space (see 3.9 below) and the rules regarding the sequence of tenses. The only difference is the use of subordinating words.

There are two types of interrogative sentences (see also chapter 39 Interrogative Structures, sections 2 and 3).

3.5.1   Total interrogation

(For questions which require *oui*, *non* or *si* as an answer.)

The indirect question is introduced by the conjunction **si**.

> Ex: *Elle me demande: 'As-tu terminé le livre?'*
> → *Elle me demande **si** j'ai terminé le livre.*
> She's asking me whether I have finished the book.

3.5.2 Partial interrogation

(For questions which require specific information as an answer.)

(i) The indirect question can begin with an interrogative adverb: **combien**, **comment**, **où**, **pourquoi** or **quand** as in a direct question (see chapter 39 Interrogative Structures, section 3.5).

> Ex: *Il m'a demandé: 'Comment vous y prenez-vous?'*
> He asked me, 'How are you going about it?'
> → *Il m'a demandé **comment** je m'y prenais.*
> → He asked me how I was going about it.

Note that the interrogative form with inversion is lost. However, the 'stylistic' inversion (nouns only, **not** pronouns) is still possible.

> Ex: *Elle se demande quand Alain viendra.*
> or:
> *Elle se demande quand viendra Alain.*

(ii) The indirect question can begin with the interrogative adjective **quel** or the interrogative pronoun **lequel** as in a direct question (see chapter 39 Interrogative Structures, sections 3.3 and 3.4).

> Ex: *Le sommelier a demandé: 'Quels vins avez-vous choisis et lequel désirez-vous en premier?'*
> The wine waiter asked, 'Which wines have you chosen and which one would you like first?'
> → *Le sommelier a demandé **quels** vins nous avions choisis et **lequel** nous désirions en premier.*
> → The wine waiter asked which wines we had chosen and which one we'd like first.

Note that the inversion is compulsory if the interrogative word is *quel* as the complement of *être*.

> Ex: *Je me demande quel est son nom.*

(iii) The indirect question can begin with an invariable interrogative pronoun. In indirect speech, the invariable interrogative pronouns of the direct speech (see chapter 39 Interrogative Structures, sections 3.1 and 3.2) change according to the following pattern:

direct speech   indirect speech

For human animates:
qui; qui est-ce qui   → *qui* (subject)
qui; qui est-ce que   → *qui* (direct object)
preposition + *qui* / + *qui est-ce qui* → preposition + *qui* (object of a preposition)

For inanimates (note that non-human animates still present a problem – see chapter 39 Interrogative Structures, section 3.1.1):
qu'est-ce qui   → *ce qui* (subject)
que; qu'est-ce que   → *ce que* (direct object)
preposition + *quoi* / + *quoi est-ce que* → preposition + *quoi* (object of a preposition)

Ex: *Il a demandé: 'Qui veut venir avec moi?'*
      → *Il a demandé **qui** voulait venir avec lui.*
      <small>(human animate – subject)</small>

He asked, 'Who wants to come with me?'
      → He asked who wanted to go with him.

J'ai demandé à Catherine: 'Qui connais-tu ici et à qui as-tu parlé?'
      → *J'ai demandé à Catherine **qui** elle connaissait là et **à qui** elle avait parlé.*
      <small>(human animate – direct object; human animate – object of a preposition)</small>

I asked Catherine, 'Who do you know here and who have you spoken to?'
      → I asked Catherine who she knew there and who she had spoken to.

Je lui ai demandé: 'Qu'est-ce qui fait tout ce bruit?'
      → *Je lui ai demandé **ce qui** faisait tout ce bruit.*
      <small>(inanimate – subject)</small>

I asked him/her, 'What's making all that noise?'
      → I asked him/her what was making all that noise.

On leur a demandé: 'Que prenez-vous comme dessert?'
          or: *'Qu'est-ce que vous prenez comme dessert?'*
      → *On leur a demandé **ce qu'**ils prenaient comme dessert.*
      <small>(inanimate – direct object)</small>

They were asked, 'What would you like for pudding?'
      → They were asked what they would like for pudding.

J'ai demandé: 'Sur quoi Catherine base-t-elle ses décisions?'
      → *J'ai demandé **sur quoi** Catherine basait ses décisions.*
      <small>(inanimate – object of a preposition)</small>

I asked, 'What does Catherine base her decisions on?'
      → I asked what Catherine based her decisions on.

Also: ***ce dont*** and ***ce à quoi***:
      Ex: *Dites-lui **ce dont** vous avez besoin.*
            Tell him what you need.

            *Je lui ai expliqué **ce à quoi** vous faisiez allusion.*
            I explained to him what you were alluding to.

3.6   IRS and the original utterance

In DRS, the original and reported texts are supposed to be linguistically identical. This is not the case in IRS where there is a certain degree of **interpretation** of the original utterance.

– The original and reported speeches are no longer syntactically identical. This is because the reported speech becomes the object of the verb in the original speech. This implies that everything is seen from the angle of the **reporter** of the IRS, and not from that of the original speaker.

677

Ex: *Paul a dit que tu viendrais le voir ici demain.*
tu, *ici* and *demain* can only be understood in relation to the speaker who says '*Paul . . . demain*'.

– The reporter can use certain verbs to introduce IRS which also contain information which influences the way in which the interlocutor will interpret the reported speech. He/she may for instance:
  – imply the falsity of the statement (e.g. *prétendre*)
  – emphasize the chronology of events (e.g. *répondre, conclure*)
  – give details about how the statement was spoken (e.g. *crier, chuchoter*)
Other verbs in these categories include *révéler, déclarer, ajouter, suggérer, demander, insister, expliquer, remarquer, penser, croire, se figurer, admettre, répéter*, etc. Only *dire* could be considered as 'neutral'.

3.7 From DRS to IRS

The transposition of DRS into IRS is not systematic. For instance, incomplete or incorrect sentences, exclamations and sentences in a foreign language, etc. (see above) cannot be transposed into IRS.

Ex: **Il a déclaré que ah, comme c'était beau.*
*Paul a demandé where the cat was.

Furthermore, the modality of a sentence in DRS cannot necessarily be transposed into IRS. Since IRS is only an object of the verb in the reporting clause, its modality is that of the sentence in which it appears. Therefore, an indirect interrogation is only interrogative in its **meaning** – it is not an interrogative modality itself. Compare:

Paul a demandé à Marie: 'M'aimes-tu?'

There are two independent modalities here:
– declarative (*Paul a demandé à Marie*)
– interrogative (*M'aimes-tu?*)
      and:

Paul a demandé à Marie si elle l'aimait.

There is only one modality here:
– declarative (*Paul a demandé à Marie si elle l'aimait.*)

An example of interrogative modality in IRS would be:

Paul a-t-il demandé à Marie si elle l'aimait?

The question mark punctuates the question in the introductory clause '*Paul a-t-il demandé à Marie*' and not to the indirect interrogation '*si elle l'aimait*'.

3.8 IRS and personal pronouns

Personal pronouns, possessive adjectives and possessive pronouns change according to the following patterns:
– *je/tu* = neither the speaker nor the interlocutor

Ex: **Paul** *a dit à Marie:* **'Je** *t'aime.'*
→ *Paul a dit à Marie qu'***il** *l'aimait.*

Je **lui** *dirai:* **'Tu** *as fait du bon travail.'*
→ *Je lui dirai qu'***il** *a fait du bon travail.*

– *je/tu* = speaker

    Ex: ***J'ai dit à Marie: 'Je** t'aime.'*

        → *J'ai dit à Marie que **je** l'aimais.*

        *Il **me** dit: '**Vous** avez bien fait de venir me voir tout de suite.'*

        → *Il me dit que **j'ai** bien fait de venir le voir tout de suite.*

– *je/tu* = interlocutor

    Ex: *Paul **t'a** dit: 'Je **t'aime**.'*

        → *Paul t'a dit qu'il **t'aimait**.*

The interpretation of the IRS may therefore be ambiguous. Moreover, it may be problematic to transfer IRS back into DRS if it is interpreted out of context. This is particularly the case with the 3rd person.

    Ex: *Il lui a dit qu'il lui avait menti.*

        He said to him/her that he'd lied to him/her.

→ *Il lui a dit:*	He said to him/her:
'Je vous ai menti.'	'I lied to you.'
'Vous m'avez menti.'	'You lied to me.'
'Je lui ai menti.'	'I lied to him/her.'
'Il m'a menti.'	'He lied to me.'
'Vous lui avez menti.'	'You lied to him/her.'
'Il vous a menti.'	'He lied to you.'
'Je vous avais menti.'	'I'd lied to you.'
'Vous m'aviez menti.'	'You'd lied to me.'
etc.	

3.9 IRS and deictics

Deictics are words which can only be interpreted by reference to the situation in which an utterance takes place (e.g. *ici/là*, *aujourd'hui/demain*, etc.)

    Consider the following examples:

– If the situations of the speakers of the reporting and reported speeches are identical (or virtually identical), the deictics are not changed.

    Ex: – Speaker 1: *Paul sera <u>ici dans un mois</u>.*

        – Speaker 2: *Qu'est-ce qu'il a dit?*

        – Speaker 3: *Il a dit que Paul sera/serait <u>ici dans un mois</u>.*

– If the situations of the speakers of the reporting and reported speeches are different, the deictics are changed for adverbs in relation to the reporter (e.g. *ici* and *dans un mois* need new adverbs in relation to the speaker).

    Ex: – Speaker 2: *Qu'est-ce qu'il a dit? (quand tu l'as vu)*

        – Speaker 3: *Il a dit que Paul serait <u>à Paris le 14 juillet</u>.*

Note that both the location and the chronology implied in the original speech are made explicit through the linguistic context.

The following are examples of chronological deictics and their transposition into non-deictic adverbs of time:

hier	→	*la veille*
demain	→	*le lendemain*
ce matin	→	*ce matin-là*
ce soir	→	*ce soir-là*
cette semaine	→	*cette semaine-là*
cette année	→	*cette année-là*
la semaine prochaine	→	*la semaine suivante*
la semaine dernière/passée	→	*la semaine précédente.*

Note that complete dates (e.g. *le 14 juillet 1789*) are valid in all contexts.

3.10 IRS and the sequence of tenses (*concordance des temps*)

The tenses in the main and subordinate clauses show the dependency of the IRS. Hence:

- If the verb in the main clause is in the **present**, then the verb in the object clause is present, past or future, depending on when the process happened in relation to that of the main clause.
    Ex: *Paul prétend que Marie a menti.*
The process '*a menti*' is anterior to that of '*prétend*'.

- If the verb in the main clause is in the **past**, then the verb in the object clause is pluperfect, imperfect or conditional (i.e. a form in -*ait*) depending on when the process happened in relation to that of the main clause.
    Ex: *Paul a prétendu (prétendit, prétendait) que Marie avait menti/mentait/mentirait.*

Tenses in IRS can therefore present ambiguities. For instance, when the tense of the object clause in IRS is in the imperfect, it is difficult to deduce whether it was in the present or imperfect in the original speech.
    Ex: *Paul a dit que Marie mentait.*
        → *Paul a dit: 'Marie ment.'*
                or:
        → *Paul a dit: 'Marie mentait.'*

Note that if the IRS has a generic value or represents a 'general truth', the present tense is kept since the meaning of the IRS does not depend on the situation of the original speech.
    Ex: *Le prof de sciences nous **a dit** que l'eau **bout** à 100°.*

If the verb of the IRS expresses a process in the future (or present or past) which is still in the future (or present or past) at the time of speaking, the future is possible (as well as the form in -*ait*).
    Ex: *Patrick a dit qu'il sera/serait ici dans une semaine.*
        Patrick a dit qu'il prendra/prendrait le train de six heures.
        Patrick a dit qu'il vend/vendait sa voiture aujourd'hui.
        Patrick a annoncé qu'il a pris/avait pris sa retraite hier.

Finally, the subjunctive does not change since it depends on the same verb in the two clauses.

> Ex: *J'ai dit: 'Il est temps qu'ils **s'en aillent.'***
> → *J'ai dit qu'il était temps qu'ils **s'en aillent**.*

In literary French, the imperfect subjunctive would be used (see chapter 12 Subjunctive, section 3.2.2).

> Ex: *Il pensa: 'Il est grand temps qu'elle **vienne** enfin me voir.'*
> *Il pensa qu'il était grand temps qu'elle **vînt** enfin le voir.*

3.11 Conclusion

IRS enables the speaker to contract (and also, but less frequently, to expand) the original utterance. The speaker thus can express his/her own ideas and prejudices. This is particularly obvious if one compares the way in which two politically opposed newspapers report the words of the same politician!

4 Free indirect reported speech

FIRS is mainly used in written language and particularly in literary narration. It combines features of both DRS and IRS. FIRS is opposed to DRS and IRS insofar as it cannot be recognized out of context, hence there are numerous cases of ambiguity. Indeed, a particular fragment can be **interpreted** as FIRS even though it does not assume a specific grammatical form. It is the whole linguistic context which enables one to identify the use of FIRS.

4.1 Characteristics

FIRS is characterized by:
- the absence of verbs of communication
- the absence of conjunctions of subordination introducing an object clause
- the absence of quotation marks

The transposition of personal pronouns and tenses is the same as for IRS, that of deictics of time and place can pertain to either DRS or IRS: *ici, maintenant, aujourd'hui,* or *là, la veille, le lendemain,* etc.

Compare the following sentences:
- DRS:

> *Paul a protesté: 'J'étais dans mon bureau hier. Comment avez-vous pu me voir au tabac? Prouvez-le!'*
> Paul protested, 'I was in my office yesterday. How could you have seen me at the tobacconist's? Prove it!'

- IRS:

> *Paul a protesté en disant qu'il était dans son bureau la veille. Il se demandait comment on avait pu le voir au tabac. Il voulait qu'on le lui prouve.*

Paul protested by saying that he was at his office the day before. He wondered how he could have been seen at the tobacconist's. He wanted someone to prove it.

– FIRS:

Paul a protesté. Il était dans son bureau hier. Comment avait-on pu le voir au tabac? Qu'on le lui prouve!
Paul protested. He was at his office yesterday. How could he have been seen at the tobacconist's? Let someone prove it!

4.2 Kinds of sentence

Sentences in FIRS are independent clauses, hence they can contain familiar expressions, foreign words, etc. and also 'affective' words showing the subjectivity of the speaker.

Ex: *Paul en avait assez. Ah oui, alors, il en avait plus que marre.*

Note that FIRS is also possible in spoken French.

Ex: *Il commence à m'énerver: je suis toujours en retard, je ne fais pas mon travail, et patati, et patata . . .*

Unlike IRS, FIRS can keep the modality of the original speech, whether it is interrogative, exclamative or imperative (with the use of the subjunctive of order).

Ex: *Paul se tourna vers Marie. Avait-elle froid? Qu'on lui passe un manteau.*

4.3 FIRS and the original utterance

As there is no introductory verb, there is always an element of doubt as to who is the real speaker. Consider the following example:

Paul soupira. Il commençait à en avoir assez de Marie. Elle le critiquait tout le temps. Sa vie était devenue impossible.

Is Paul saying to himself: '*Je commence à en avoir assez de Marie. Elle me critique tout le temps. Ma vie est devenue impossible*', or are these the words of the narrator who comments on Paul's troubles?

Appendix 1: *Les rectifications de l'orthographe* (1990)

A document entitled *Les rectifications de l'orthographe*, drafted by the Conseil Supérieur de la Langue Française, was published in the *Journal Officiel* on 6 December 1990.

The Conseil were asked to work on five main points. Their recommendations are as follows:

– Hyphens: some compound nouns will no longer be hyphenated but will form one word.

> Ex: *porte-monnaie* → *portemonnaie* (on the model of *portefeuille*)

– Plural of compound nouns: those of the type *pèse-lettre* will follow in the plural the rule applied to simple words.

> Ex: *des pèse-lettres*

– The circumflex accent will no longer be compulsory on any letters '*i*' and '*u*', except in verb endings (e.g. *qu'il fût*) and in a few other words (e.g. *mûr*), where it distinguishes the meaning of the word.

– The past participle will be invariable in the case of *laisser* followed by an infinitive.

> Ex: *Elle s'est laissé mourir.*

– Anomalies:
  – borrowed words will follow the rules applying to French words concerning accentuation and plural.

> Ex: *un imprésario, des imprésarios*

  – 'assorted' series: spellings will be made more consistent.

> Ex: *douceâtre* → *douçâtre* (on the model of *blanchâtre*)
> *boursoufler* → *boursouffler* (on the model of *souffler*)
> *chariot* → *charriot* (on the model of *charrette*).

The document is organized along the following plan:

> Analyses
> > Hyphens
> > Number markers
> > Diaereses and accents
> > > diaereses
> > > grave or acute accent on '*e*'
> > > circumflex accent

Verbs in *-eler, -eter*
Past participles of pronominal verbs
Borrowed words
Anomalies
Rules
Special spellings, standardized or modified
Recommendations to lexicographers and creators of neologisms

Summary of the rules

OLD SPELLING	NEW SPELLING
vingt-trois, cent trois	*vingt-trois, cent-trois*
un cure-dents	*un cure-dent*
des cure-ongles	*des cure-ongles*
un cache-flamme(s)	*un cache-flamme*
des cache-flamme(s)	*des cache-flammes*
je céderai, j'allégerais	*je cèderai, j'allègerais*
puissé-je, aimé-je	*puissè-je, aimè-je*
il plaît, il se tait	*il plait, il se tait*
la route, la voûte	*la route, la voute*
il ruisselle, amoncèle	*il ruissèle, amoncèle*
elle s'est laissée aller	*elle s'est laissé aller*
elle s'est laissé appeler	*elle s'est laissé appeler*
des jazzmen, des lieder	*des jazzmans, des lieds*

Note: THE DOCUMENT IS CONTROVERSIAL AND MANY WRITERS IGNORE IT.

Appendix 2: cardinal and ordinal numbers

1 Cardinal numbers

The cardinal numbers are:

0	zéro		
1	un, une	11	onze
2	deux	12	douze
3	trois	13	treize
4	quatre	14	quatorze
5	cinq	15	quinze
6	six	16	seize
7	sept	17	dix-sept
8	huit	18	dix-huit
9	neuf	19	dix-neuf
10	dix	20	vingt

21	vingt et un(e)	31	trente et un(e)
22	vingt-deux	32	trente-deux
29	vingt-neuf	39	trente-neuf
30	trente		

40	quarante
50	cinquante
60	soixante

70	soixante-dix	80	quatre-vingts
71	soixante et onze	81	quatre-vingt-un(e)
72	soixante-douze	82	quatre-vingt-deux
79	soixante-dix-neuf	89	quatre-vingt-neuf

90	quatre-vingt-dix
91	quatre-vingt-onze

100	cent
101	cent un(e)
102	cent deux
160	cent soixante
170	cent soixante-dix

200	deux cents
201	deux cent un
236	deux cent trente-six

1000	mille
1001	mille un(e)
1600	mille six cents or seize cents
2000	deux mille

10.000	dix mille
1.000.000	un million
1.000.300	un million trois cents
2.800.000	deux millions huit cent mille
500.000.000	cinq cents millions
1.000.000.000	un milliard
6.000.000.000	six milliards

2 Ordinal numbers

The ordinal numbers are:

1er	premier, 1ère première	11^e	onzième
2^e	deuxième/second(e)	12^e	douzième
3^e	troisième	13^e	treizième
4^e	quatrième	14^e	quatorzième
5^e	cinquième	15^e	quinzième
6^e	sixième	16^e	seizième
7^e	septième	17^e	dix-septième
8^e	huitième	18^e	dix-huitième
9^e	neuvième	19^e	dix-neuvième
10^e	dixième	20^e	vingtième

21^e	vingt et unième	31^e	trente et unième
22^e	vingt-deuxième	32^e	trente-deuxième
29^e	vingt-neuvième	39^e	trente-neuvième

30^e	trentième
40^e	quarantième
50^e	cinquantième
60^e	soixantième

70^e	soixante-dixième	80^e	quatre-vingtième
71^e	soixante et onzième	81^e	quatre-vingt-unième
72^e	soixante-douzième	82^e	quatre-vingt-deuxième
79^e	soixante-dix-neuvième	89^e	quatre-vingt-neuvième

90^e	quatre-vingt-dixième
91^e	quatre-vingt-onzième

100^e	centième
101^e	cent unième
102^e	cent deuxième
200^e	deux centième
224^e	deux cent vingt-quatrième

1000ᵉ millième
1001ᵉ mille unième
1400ᵉ mille quatre centième or quatorze centième

10000ᵉ dix millième

Bibliography

Abeillé A., Godard D., eds., 'Nouveaux raisonnements syntaxiques', *Langages*, no. 122, Larousse, Paris, 1996

Achard P., 'Entre deixis et anaphore: le renvoi du contexte en situation', in *La Deixis, Colloque en Sorbonne* (8–9 June 1990), Morel M.-A. and Danon-Boileau L., eds., Collection Linguistique Nouvelle, Presses Universitaires de France, Paris, 1992

Adamczewski H., *Le français déchiffré*, Armand Colin, Paris, 1991

Arrivé M., Gadet F., Galmiche F., *La grammaire d'aujourd'hui*, Flammarion, Paris, 1986

Austin J. L., *How to Do Things with Words*, Oxford University Press, 1962

Benveniste E., *Problèmes de linguistique générale 1*, Gallimard, Paris, 1966
   Problèmes de linguistique générale 2, Gallimard, Paris, 1974

Berretti, J., 'DE, souverain du français', *Faits de Langues*, no. 7, Ophrys, Paris, 1996

Berthoud A.-C., 'Deixis, thématisation et détermination', in *La Deixis, Colloque en Sorbonne* (8–9 June 1990), Morel M.-A. and Danon-Boileau L., eds., Collection Linguistique Nouvelle, Presses Universitaires de France, Paris, 1992
   'Indéfinis et thématisation', *Faits de Langues*, no. 4, Presses Universitaires de France, Paris, 1994

Blanche-Benveniste C., *Recherches en vue d'une théorie de la grammaire française, essai d'application à la syntaxe des pronoms*, Librairie Honoré Champion, Paris, 1975

Bourdin P., 'La concordance des temps, aux confins de l'accord?', *Faits de Langues*, no. 8, Ophrys, Paris, 1996

Byrne L. S. R., Churchill E. L., *A Comprehensive French Grammar*, third edition revised by G. Price, Blackwell, Oxford, 1986

Carlier A., ' "Les gosses, ça se lève tôt le matin": l'interprétation générique du syntagme nominal disloqué au moyen de ce ou ça', *Journal of French Language Studies*, vol. 6, no. 2, Cambridge University Press, 1996

Carruthers J., ' "The passé surcomposé régional": towards a definition in contemporary spoken French', *Journal of French Language Studies*, vol. 4, no. 2, Cambridge University Press, 1994

Cornish F., ' "Antecedentless" anaphors: deixis, anaphor or what? Some evidence from English and French', *Journal of Linguistics*, vol. 32, no. 1, Cambridge University Press, 1996

Danon-Boileau L., 'Dénombrement, pluriel, singulier', *Faits de Langues*, no. 2, Presses Universitaires de France, Paris, 1993

De Carvalho P., 'Deixis et grammaire', in *La Deixis, Colloque en Sorbonne* (8–9 June 1990), Morel M.-A. and Danon-Boileau L., eds., Collection Linguistique Nouvelle, Presses Universitaires de France, Paris, 1992

Delaveau A., Kerleroux F., *Problèmes et exercices de syntaxe française*, Armand Colin Linguistique, Paris, 1985

Dubos U., 'Deixis, temporalité et le concept de "situation" ', in *La Deixis, Colloque en Sorbonne* (8–9 June 1990), Morel M.-A. and Danon-Boileau L., eds., Collection Linguistique Nouvelle, Presses Universitaires de France, Paris, 1992

El Kaladi A., 'Le genre des indéfinis en anglais: pour une approche énonciative', *Modèles Linguistiques*, vol. 15, no. 2, 1994

Eluerd R., *Langue et littérature: grammaire, communication, techniques littéraires*, Nathan, Paris, 1992

Ferrar H., *A French Reference Grammar*, second edition, Oxford University Press, 1967

Fornel M. de, 'Pluralisation de la personne et variation pronominale', *Faits de Langues*, no. 3, Presses Universitaires de France, Paris, 1994

Fuchs C., *Les ambiguïtés du français*, Collection L'Essentiel Français, Ophrys, Paris, 1996

Genette G., *Figures III*, Seuil, Paris, 1972

Grésillon A., Lebrave J. L., eds., *La langue au ras du texte*, Presses Universitaires de Lille, 1984

Grevisse M., *Le bon usage*, twelfth edition revised by A. Goosse, Duculot, Paris-Gembloux, 1986

Guilbaud D., 'Quelques aspects du lexique "européen" dans la presse française', *Cahiers de Lexicologie*, 55, 1994-II

Herslund M., 'Partitivité et possession inaliénable', *Faits de Langues*, no. 7, Ophrys, Paris, 1996

Hilgert J.-M., 'Quelconque: un exemple d'indéfinition par degrés définis', *Cahiers de Lexicologie*, 52, 1993-I

Hybertie C., *La conséquence en français*, Collection L'Essentiel Français, Ophrys, Paris, 1996

Ibrahim A. H., ed., 'Les supports', *Langages*, no. 121, Larousse, Paris, 1996

Joly A., 'Eléments pour une théorie générale de la personne', *Faits de Langues*, no. 3, Presses Universitaires de France, Paris, 1994

Jones M. A., *Foundations of French Syntax*, Cambridge University Press, 1996

Judge A., Healey F. G., *A Reference Grammar of Modern French*, E. Arnold, London, 1983

Khaznadar E., 'Pour une première: la dénomination de la femme dans l'actualité: dichotomie, affixation et alternance', *Cahiers de Lexicologie*, 53, 1993

Kleiber G., 'Anaphore-deixis: deux approches concurrentes', in *La Deixis*, *Colloque en Sorbonne* (8–9 June 1990), Morel M.-A. and Danon-Boileau L., eds., Collection Linguistique Nouvelle, Presses Universitaires de France, Paris, 1992

Kupferman L., 'La construction passive en "se faire"', *Journal of French Language Studies*, vol. 5, no. 1, Cambridge University Press, 1995

Lancri A., 'Remarques sur l'opposition singulier/pluriel en français et en anglais', *Faits de Langue*, no. 2, Presses Universitaires de France, Paris, 1993

Le Goffic P., *Grammaire de la phrase française*, Hachette Education, Paris, 1993
    'La double incomplétude de l'imparfait', *Modèles Linguistiques*, vol. 16, no. 1, 1995

Le Quesler N., 'Tout, chaque, quelque et certain: conditions d'équivalence entre indéfinis', *Faits de Langues*, no. 4, Presses Universitaires de France, Paris, 1994

Maingueneau D., *Eléments de linguistique pour le texte littéraire*, third edition, Dunod, Paris, 1993
    Enonciation en linguistique française, Hachette, Paris, 1994
    Syntaxe du français, Hachette Supérieur, Paris, 1994

Mazodier C., 'Différence dans le mode d'appréhension de la classe en français et en anglais', *Faits de Langues*, no. 2, Presses Universitaires de France, Paris, 1993

Mejri S., 'Séquences figées et expression de l'intensité', *Cahiers de Lexicologie*, 55, 1994

Morel M.-A., *La concession en français*, Collection L'Essentiel Français, Ophrys, Paris, 1996

Nymansson K., 'Analyse grammaticale des formes en -ing', *Cahiers de Lexicologie*, 68, 1996

Perret M., *Enonciation en grammaire du texte*, Nathan, Paris, 1994

Péry-Woodley M.-P., 'French and English passives in the construction of text', *Journal of French Language Studies*, vol. 1, no. 1, Cambridge University Press, 1991

Pinchon J., *Morphosyntaxe du français*, Hachette Université, Paris, 1986

Quirk R., Greenbaum S., Leech G., Svartik J., *A Grammar of Contemporary English*, Longman, 1972

689

Rotgé W., 'Temps et modalité: enquête sur le futur en anglais', *Modèles Linguistiques*, vol. 16, no. 1, 1995

Rousseau A., 'La deixis: un problème de logique et de philosophie du langage', in *La Deixis, Colloque en Sorbonne* (8–9 June 1990), Morel M.-A. and Danon-Boileau L., eds., Collection Linguistique Nouvelle, Presses Universitaires de France, Paris, 1992

Ruwet N., *Théorie syntaxique et syntaxe du français*, Seuil, Paris, 1972

Swart H. de, 'Indéfini et généricité', *Faits de Langues*, no. 4, Presses Universitaires de France, Paris, 1994

Tesnière L., *Eléments de syntaxe structurale*, Klincksieck, Paris, 1982

Tolédano V., 'Traitement lexicographique des sigles', *Cahiers de Lexicologie*, 67, 1995

Vet C., 'Structures discursives et interprétation du discours', *Modèles Linguistiques*, vol. 16, no. 2, 1995

Wagner R. L., Pinchon J., *Grammaire du français classique et moderne*, Hachette Supérieur, Paris, 1991

Waugh L. R., Bahloul M., 'La différence entre le futur simple et le futur périphrastique dans le discours journalistique', *Modèles Linguistiques*, vol. 18, no. 1, 1996

Wilmet M., 'L'aspect en français: essai de synthèse', *Journal of French Language Studies*, vol. 1, no. 2, Cambridge University Press, 1991

'L'articulation mode–temps–aspect dans le système verbal français', *Modèles Linguistiques*, vol. 16, no. 1, 1995

Weinrich H., *Grammaire textuelle du français*, Didier/Hatier, Paris, 1989

Yaguello M., *En écoutant parler la langue*, Seuil, Paris, 1991

Alice au pays du langage, Seuil, Paris, 1981

Zribi-Hertz A., 'De la deixis à l'anaphore: quelques jalons', in *La Deixis, Colloque en Sorbonne* (8–9 June 1990), Morel M.-A. and Danon-Boileau L., eds., Collection Linguistique Nouvelle, Presses Universitaires de France, Paris, 1992

Index